NEW YORK REVIEW BOOKS
CLASSICS

THE COLLECTED ESSAYS OF ELIZABETH HARDWICK

ELIZABETH HARDWICK (1916–2007) was born in Lexington, Kentucky, and educated at the University of Kentucky and Columbia University. A recipient of a Gold Medal from the American Academy of Arts and Letters, she is the author of three novels, a biography of Herman Melville, and four collections of essays. She was a co-founder and advisory editor of *The New York Review of Books* and contributed more than one hundred reviews, articles, reflections, and letters to the magazine.

DARRYL PINCKNEY selected *The New York Stories of Elizabeth Hardwick* (2010). He is the author of two novels, *High Cotton* (1992) and *Black Deutschland* (2016), and of two works of nonfiction, *Out There: Mavericks of Black Literature* (1992) and *Blackballed: The Black Vote and US Democracy* (2014). He also worked for Robert Wilson on his productions of *The Forest, Orlando, Time Rocker, The Old Woman, Letter to a Man*, and *Garrincha: A Street Opera*.

THE COLLECTED ESSAYS OF ELIZABETH HARDWICK

Selected and with an introduction by

DARRYL PINCKNEY

NEW YORK REVIEW BOOKS

New York

THIS IS A NEW YORK REVIEW BOOK
PUBLISHED BY THE NEW YORK REVIEW OF BOOKS
435 Hudson Street, New York, NY 10014
www.nyrb.com

Library of Congress Cataloging-in-Publication Data
Names: Hardwick, Elizabeth, author. | Pinckney, Darryl, 1953– editor.
Title: The collected essays of Elizabeth Hardwick / by Elizabeth Hardwick ; edited
  and with an introduction by Darryl Pinckney.
Description: New York : New York Review Books, [2017] | Series: New York
  Review Books classics
Identifiers: LCCN 2017014041 (print) | LCCN 2017014050 (ebook) | ISBN
  9781681371559 (epub) | ISBN 9781681371542 (paperback)
Subjects: | BISAC: LITERARY COLLECTIONS / Essays. | LITERARY
  COLLECTIONS / American / General.
Classification: LCC PS3515.A5672 (ebook) | LCC PS3515.A5672 A6 2017 (print) |
  DDC 814/.52—dc23
LC record available at https://lccn.loc.gov/2017014041

ISBN 978-1-68137-154-2
Available as an electronic book; ISBN 978-1-68137-155-9

Printed in the United States of America on acid-free paper.
10 9 8 7 6 5 4 3 2 1

CONTENTS

Introduction · ix

Memoirs, Conversations, and Diaries · 3

Anderson, Millay, and Crane in Their Letters · 16

The Subjection of Women · 25

George Eliot's Husband · 38

The Neglected Novels of Christina Stead · 44

America and Dylan Thomas · 51

The Decline of Book Reviewing · 59

Boston · 69

William James: An American Hero · 81

Living in Italy: Reflections on Bernard Berenson · 95

Mary McCarthy · 104

Loveless Love: Graham Greene · 110

The Insulted and Injured: Books About Poverty · 118

Grub Street: New York · 125

Frost in His Letters · 130

Ring Lardner · 137

Grub Street: Washington · 141

Selma, Alabama: The Charms of Goodness · 145

After Watts · 150

The Apotheosis of Martin Luther King · 156

Chicago · 165

Reflections on Fiction · 174

Dead Souls: Ernest Hemingway · 189

In Maine · 195

Militant Nudes · 206

Sue and Arabella · 216

Sad Brazil · 226

Sense of the Present · 239

Simone Weil · 250

Domestic Manners · 258

Wives and Mistresses · 274

Unknown Faulkner · 294

Nabokov: Master Class · 299

English Visitors in America · 306

Bartleby in Manhattan · 323

Katherine Anne Porter · 335

Sons of the City's Pavements: Delmore Schwartz · 344

The Magical Prose of Poets: Elizabeth Bishop · 350

The Teller and the Tape: Norman Mailer · 357

The Genius of Margaret Fuller · 367

Gertrude Stein · 392

The Fictions of America · 404

Mrs. Wharton in New York · 418

On Washington Square · 440

Wind from the Prairie · 453

Mary McCarthy in New York · 471

Edmund Wilson · 481

Paradise Lost: Philip Roth · 494

In the Wasteland: Joan Didion · 507

Tru Confessions: Truman Capote · 517

Locations: The Landscapes of Fiction · 531

Melville in Love · 539

The Torrents of Wolfe: Thomas Wolfe · 555

The Foster Father: Henry James · 574

Funny as a Crutch: Nathanael West · 592

Sources · 607

INTRODUCTION

COME AGAIN, Professor Hardwick said, doing that seesaw dance with her shoulders, as if to say, get a load of him. I'd no idea what she was talking about. She nodded toward the blue-and-magenta paperback on top of my notebook: it was by a distinguished, elderly member of the Columbia faculty. If I was reading that for a class, then I should drop that class right away. Who, she wondered, apart from the professor himself, would make students read him on the Romantics. Not much of interest there, she finished.

The exchange happened faster than it has taken me to recall it, from her getting settled in her seat, to me, the apple-polisher, claiming first chair and opening another notebook. She'd laughed at the class for our thinking we would want to take notes. Most of us persisted. She taught by quotation and aside, citation and remark, stone down the well and echo. Most of her lessons were for later. She would peer over the book and exhale, trusting to Fortuna that somebody sitting around the table might get it eventually.

Perhaps Professor Hardwick wanted to drift off, through the window and away, but she couldn't. Literature meant too much to her and was the only kind of writing she wanted to teach, not that it could be taught. She hoped we'd learn to ask questions of ourselves as we wrote. How can you sustain this tone? Then enough was enough, on to the next person and her or his fifteen minutes of lip-parting attention. I'm afraid I don't find that terribly interesting as an approach, she'd say. Your weekly offering was not much commented upon; she much preferred to be interested in what she was reading. Boredom was not listlessness, it was a nervous strain, while to be occupied with something like a great book could be wonderfully, sometimes painfully, liberating.

Pedagogy—a word she would make fun of, starting from the dash. In the essays of Elizabeth Hardwick that dash is often a warning—beware of sting.

We, her fascinated and silent creative writing class at Barnard College in 1973, knew who she was. Needful facts, as she would say: Elizabeth Hardwick, born in Lexington, Kentucky, in 1916, left graduate school at Columbia University because she wanted to write. I don't remember if she told the class that or not. Her first novel, *The Ghostly Lover*, was published in 1945. The first thing I ever read by her was the opening chapter of *Sleepless Nights*, the novel she was writing then under the title *The Cost of Living*. That stunning first chapter was published in *The New York Review of Books* while I was in her class. She told me later—it has been one of the honors of my life to have studied with her and to have benefited from her generous conversations about literature down through many years—that Stuart Hampshire wrote her at the time to say that the chapter was so amazing he couldn't imagine how she'd be able to go on from there. As a beginning, it was an impossible act to follow. She said she found out that he was right and she ended up breaking up the chapter and redistributing it throughout the novel.

I was about to say that because I'd read her fiction first I always thought of her as more than a critic. But I can hear how blistering she'd be about that phrase—more than a critic. For her, literary criticism had to be up there with its subjects; real literature should elicit criticism worthy of the achievement in question. We got that from her straight off. The kind of modern literary criticism she was talking about—Virginia Woolf, D. H. Lawrence, Edmund Wilson, William Empson, Randall Jarrell, R. P. Blackmur, John Berryman, F. W. Dupee, Mary McCarthy—was as stimulating as the work it was exploring. Then, too, she wanted us to take seriously the essay as a form. The American essay—Thoreau, Emerson, Twain, Henry Adams—was an important part of American history. Professor Hardwick had a fearsome reputation on campus. She wasn't regular faculty; she was that lowly thing, the adjunct, a very New York position in a city full of writers who supplemented their income or saved themselves by the odd teaching job. She did not undertake her duties lightly. She stood for something.

The New York Review of Books, for starters, and that was intimidating enough, once I learned what it was. From the very beginning, I understood that Elizabeth Hardwick was what used to be called a writer's writer.

We would all be better off in law school, because writing wasn't a profession exactly, and certainly not much of a life. She discovered that I thought Grub Street was a novel by Dickens. She made fun of your choices, what you were wasting your time on, but she never made you feel odd for not having heard of something. It was just what you didn't know yet. Samuel Johnson and Alexander Pope were experiences to look forward to, as she once had, up from the University of Kentucky, refusing to be buried alive in graduate school at Columbia University. Moreover, the more you read, the more discriminating you became about what you read. She lived to read. Her passions were instructive.

Of Hardwick's published work, a slender volume of short stories, *The New York Stories of Elizabeth Hardwick*, took a lifetime to accrue, and her three novels, *The Ghostly Lover*, *The Simple Truth*, and *Sleepless Nights*, are separated by years. We think of the essay as a constant in Hardwick's writing life. She published her first review in *Partisan Review* in 1945. In the late 1940s, Hardwick, then in her early thirties, was already doing the "Fiction Chronicle" for *Partisan Review*, writing, for example, about Kay Boyle, Elizabeth Bowen, Theodore Dreiser, William Faulkner, and the dreadful Anaïs Nin. Philip Rahv, together with William Phillips, had revived the journal in 1937 as the organ of the anti-Stalinist left, and in the postwar years, *Partisan Review*, that ring of bullies she called it, was central to the New York intellectual scene, anticommunist, dissident.

What she remembered as the cutting reviews of her youth were long ago. Attacks on inflated reputations were moral battles for young writers just starting out. She said often that it is much harder to write about what you like than it is to write about what you don't like. One of the things she admired about Susan Sontag, she said much later, was that her essays were mostly appreciations, enthusiastic introductions to an American audience of the avant-garde European culture she cared about. It was a pleasure to discover a forgotten writer—one who was worth it. Sometimes a campaign on someone's behalf doesn't work. Hardwick didn't think she'd done anything for Christina Stead—as yet. But one day her view of Stead might be more widely shared. She was amused by Gore Vidal's attempts to revive Frederic Prokosch's fortunes. When Dawn Powell's novels were coming back into print, Hardwick said that she knew that Powell had had a hard life and it was very much like a man for Edmund Wilson to have lost interest in her because she was not pretty, but even so she did not want to write about her enough to do so. Sympathy for an intention was not going to make a book any better than it really was, and the danger of writing from a preconceived position was the harm having to be false does to a writer. No constituency was worth the sacrifice, she cautioned, in those days of feminist and black-nationalist pressure.

Elizabeth Hardwick wrote about what engaged her. Over the years, I would hear her say that she'd had to tell an editor she didn't want to write about a certain book or author because she found she didn't have anything interesting to say after all. It pleased her that John Updike reviewed books, so few novelists of his stature did. She paid attention to what went on in her world, that of serious literature, in English and in translation, and matters of cultural and social interest, an all-hands-on-deck kind of service. She was reasonably aware of audience, of just who was picking up what at the newsstand. But it didn't matter if she was writing for glossy publications with her eye on the word count, for a venerable quarterly with a thick spine, or for a newspaper book-review section not looking for controversy. Every assignment got Hardwick at full sail, all mind and style. Nothing is casual, she said. You are always up against the limits of yourself.

Hardwick published four original volumes of essays in her lifetime. The majority of the essays gathered in *A View of My Own: Essays on Literature and Society* (1962) first appeared in *Partisan Review.* Several of them are, as she would say, of considerable length, and in them she is reading letters, diaries, memoirs, newspapers, novels, poetry, sociology, psychology; she is going to plays and looking back on cities where she has lived. The title perhaps asserts the value of her opinions, of their being hers—when *A View of My Own* was published she had been married for more than a dozen years to Robert Lowell. She'd been one of the few women writers associated with *Partisan Review*, and she was the only other one to join Mary McCarthy and Hannah Arendt as women writers who had their own identities at the magazine and weren't known as literary wives.

In 1959, in an article that appeared in *Harper's*, "The Decline of Book Reviewing," Hardwick attacked what she described as the unaccountable sluggishness of book-review sections. There "had been room for decline . . . and the opportunity has been taken." Sunday mornings with the book reviews is "a dismal experience." She was just getting started. "The flat praise and the faint dissension, the minimal style and the light little article, the absence of involvement, passion, character, eccentricity—the lack, at last, of the literary tone itself—have made *The New York Times* into a provincial literary journal." The drama of the book world was being slowly, painlessly killed, she went on; she deplored the lack of strong editorial direction in such publications.

> The communication of the delight and importance of books, ideas, culture itself, is the very least one would expect from a journal devoted to reviewing of old and new works. Beyond that beginning, the interest of the mind of the individual reviewer is everything. Book reviewing is a form of writing.

In Martin Scorsese's and David Tedeschi's documentary about *The New York Review of Books*, *The 50 Year Argument* (2014), Robert Silvers reads from Hardwick's article on book reviewing. He'd been the young editor, just back from *The Paris Review* and his houseboat on the Seine, who urged her to write the article. In the film, he tells the Town Hall audience commemorating *The Review*'s fiftieth anniversary that Elizabeth Hardwick's words were on his mind when, in 1963, Hardwick, Lowell, Jason Epstein (editorial director of Random House), and his wife, Barbara Epstein, founded *The New York Review of Books*. They asked Silvers to be co-editor, along with Barbara Epstein. Rea Hederman took over from Whitney Ellsworth as the publisher in 1984. For Hardwick, *The New York Review* was freedom. Whenever she chose, what she wrote could now have the most honorable of destinations.

"The drama of real life will not let down the prose writer," she observes in "Grub Street: New York," her first published essay in *The New York Review*.

The New York Review of Books distinguished itself for its unaccommodating reflections by some of our best writers on the catastrophe of the Vietnam War. Hardwick liked Poe's phrase "the intense inane." In her own pieces for "The Paper," as the founders called it, during the turbulent 1960s, she thinks about Selma, Watts, and goes to the march of the striking garbage collectors for whom Dr. King had come to Memphis, Tennessee, when he was killed. She considers the coarse power of popular works about the sexual revolution. Her candor is a pleasure, her judgments unexpected. She once said that Lowell was made uneasy by the thought of what she might contribute to *The New York Review*. After her essay on Robert Frost appeared, Lowell complained to her, only half jokingly, that she was just going to attack all his friends.

In this period, Hardwick went to the theater a great deal. (Lowell's adaptations for the stage were written in the 1960s.) Lincoln Center for the Performing Arts opened down the street from where she and Lowell and their daughter, Harriet, lived—the Epsteins and their two children were only a few doors away—and maybe she could escape her family obligations long enough to immerse herself in a fleeting experience, in imagining others. She has a way in her theater reviews of sounding as though she has just come in, still talking about what she has seen. Moreover, she is coming through the door and analyzing real people as she takes off her coat. Nora, Hedda, their problems. Hardwick's detractors used to say that in her criticism she didn't make enough distinction between fictional characters and the real world. While she was curious about different traditions in the arts, realism on stage, on the page, spoke to her with the most force. She writes somewhere that characters can make structure. But perhaps it is because in realist drama and fiction much depends on a character's motives. It is through the conscious or not conscious enough depiction or projection of what is driving the work that the writer's meaning can be discovered. Hardwick had a thing about people, whether imagined or real, and what made them tick, what their stories were. To have insights, or true insight, about human nature and human histories was the essence of her critical spirit.

An avid reader of old and new works, Hardwick never stopped thinking about the state of fiction. Then, starting in 1970, with an essay on Zelda Fitzgerald, came a series of essays on women writers, taking in treasured amateurs, Dorothy Wordsworth, Jane Carlyle, as well as the geniuses, the Brontës, Sylvia Plath, Virginia Woolf. The essays accumulated quickly, for her, and became the volume *Seduction and Betrayal: Women and Literature* (1974). The era provided occasions, new biographies of culturally important women, for instance, and there was a marked increase in interest in women writers past and present. The second wave of feminism made an immediate difference in American literature. Then, too, Hardwick's way of seeming to understand their lives from the inside perhaps came from knowing something herself about woman's fate. Lowell split up with her in 1970 and they were divorced in 1972. The following year, he published *The Dolphin*, in which he tells through his poetry his version of the end of their marriage and his move to another country in order to be with another woman.

Hardwick would draw on her work in *The New York Review of Books* to fill out two additional books of essays: *Bartleby in Manhattan and Other Essays* (1983), in which the malicious, handsome Frost comes to life again, and *Sight-Readings: American Fictions* (1998), which was somewhat revised for its paperback edition the following year as *American Fictions*.

I thought to look again at Melville's story, "Bartleby the Scrivener," because it carried the subtitle: "A Story of Wall Street."

There did not appear to be much of Wall Street in this troubling composition of 1853 about a peculiar "copyist" who is hired by a "snug" little legal firm in the Wall Street district. No, nothing of the daunting, hungry "Manhattanism" of Whitman: "O an intense life, full to repletion and varied! / The life of the theatre, bar-room, huge hotel, for me!" Nothing of railroad schemes, cornering the gold market, or of that tense exclusion to be brought about by mistakes and follies in the private life which were to be the drama of "old New York" in Edith Wharton's novels. Bartleby seemed to me to be not its subtitle, but most of all an example of the superior uses of dialogue in fiction, here a strange, bone-thin dialogue that nevertheless serves to reveal a profoundly moving tragedy.

The essays of *Sight-Readings*, or *American Fictions*, like those of *Seduction and Betrayal*, have a unity just in being what they are about: the American experience, the assumptions of national character, even the influence of the landscape or the mythic landscape. For Hardwick, the poetry and novels of America hold the nation's history.

What mattered most in the end was a writer's language. She adored Dickens for the wildness of his language, Conrad for his independence of usage, Henry James for his eccentricity, his stunning excess, and William James for being such a nice guy about it all. Hardwick did not write about everything that interested her. Sometimes she didn't feel equal to the task, given what the work deserved or what had been said about it already. You always wish she'd said more about her subject—so did she, she once laughed, but she couldn't. The helpless compression of her fiction can be felt in the essays. The economy expresses her temperament. She won't tell you what you already know. Part of the freedom of *The New York Review* was that she didn't have to spell everything out. Its readers were sophisticated, or wanted to be.

That conciseness, not wanting to waste anyone's time or mar her style with lumber, not only meant that it took a long time for the essays to add up but that she did not conceive of book-length nonfiction projects. Spinning things out, beating things to death, going on and on just to get from cover to cover—that is what academics did, and whatever they did was not to be done. (Historians had no place to be other than the university.) Never mind that many of the writers she respected also taught. To have come of age at *Partisan Review* maybe accounted for her lack of interest in the New Criticism of the McCarthy era and its concentration on the text at the expense of the social or historical context. She was similarly indifferent to deconstruction and its influence on academic criticism in the late 1970s and throughout the 1980s. What she held against academic criticism was that most of it was so badly written. She blamed the computer for finishing a lot of books that ought not to have been.

And then she did commit to a book-length project, a critical biography of Herman Melville for the Penguin short biography series. She said somewhere that Faulkner was the greatest American writer, but in spite of his unevenness she maybe loved "the extraordinary American genius" of Melville more. *Herman Melville*, her incredibly moving study, was published in 2000. It was to be Hardwick's last major creative effort. An unkind review from someone who, she said, clearly had never read *Moby-Dick* made her resigned, diffident about bringing out anything else.

Her late essays in *The New York Review* showed her fascination with sensational murder cases of the 1990s. She was looking for a way to write about murder in literature and murder in real life, the difference being that in literature you can study motive. She kept fewer notes on the subject as time went by. She never liked publishing a book anyway, she said. The vulnerability, she did not need to say. To publish in *The New York Review* meant that she was protected; but it also spurred her on to do her best because of the essays that she knew were going to surround her, the company she was going to keep.

Elizabeth Hardwick's nonfiction—imaginative prose, she called it—spans six decades and includes book reviews, theater reviews, thoughts on opera, travel writing, literary criticism, social essays, memoir. *The Collected Essays of Elizabeth Hardwick* is like the first Collected Works of most poets—its existence invites a revised Collected, because it has not been possible, here, to publish everything. Her *Herman Melville* isn't excerpted, but a late essay on Melville in love goes some way to make up for it. *Seduction and Betrayal* has been left out in its entirety, available, as it is, from New York Review Books, with an introduction by Joan Didion. *Seduction and Betrayal* includes her essays on Ibsen's heroines, and a section of her theater reviews would really miss them, so there are no theater reviews reprinted here.

The remaining omissions are arbitrary, such as occasional pieces, her glossy journalism. Also not here are letters to editors, statements of support for causes, her introductions to books that are still in print. And eulogies. I seem to be writing mostly eulogies these days, she said.

The last piece Elizabeth Hardwick published in *The New York Review of Books* was in 2006, on the death of her dearest friend, Barbara Epstein. Hardwick died the next year.

Most of the essays collected here are of her literary subjects, her excited contemplations of writers on their paths. She approaches their work through their lives, or looks from a work to the life. Hart Crane's letters tell her that maybe he didn't jump overboard, maybe he was having a happy life as a lover of men and of the grape. Three volumes of George Eliot's letters reveal the drama of a woman of melancholy genius at the mercy of her intelligence. Hardwick paid attention to the domestic, to the intimacy—and limitations—of letters and diaries. In her masterful essay "Memoirs, Conversations, and Diaries," she explores what Boswell and the Goncourt brothers mean in their literary cultures. But as interested as Hardwick was in diaries and letters, she was always troubled by biography, a genre that feeds on letters and diaries as raw material. A biography of Hemingway that she is reading is just plain "bad news"—for Hemingway. Her compassion for Dylan Thomas suggests that she may have seen him in the desperate condition of his last years, and Delmore Schwartz, too. She knew Katherine Anne Porter and had been around Frost enough to remember his aura. She wrote about Edmund Wilson and Norman Mailer and their biographies, or the mess Capote made of memoir. It is clear in her essay on Elizabeth Bishop's prose that she knew her, but also that she found the work striking long before she met Bishop, reading her in *Partisan Review* down at the University of Kentucky in 1938.

Hardwick looks at the riddle of Graham Greene's novels about sin and heresy or ponders the fates of the two women in Hardy's *Jude the Obscure*. She follows Byron's and Pasternak's mistresses and sad Countess Tolstoy into their afterlives. She wrote about Auden, Huxley, and Isherwood in America; the literary gifts and accumulation of losses that Nabokov brought with him to America; and the last days of Dylan Thomas in New York City. But as time went by the individual writers whose work she addressed tended to be American.

Melville, Henry James, and Edith Wharton were foundational as novelists of certain kinds of American experience that still have resonance. Carl Sandburg, Ring Lardner, Sinclair Lewis, Nathanael West, and Thomas Wolfe are in themselves American tales. Margaret Fuller, Gertrude Stein—who anticipated Philip Glass, Hardwick says—and Djuna Barnes are women writers, rebels, but also Americans abroad. Joan Didion expresses the restlessness of the America Hardwick felt around her. Yet in the provocative essays included here on the writer's life or the changes in American fiction and its possibilities over the years, her reading is wide, international.

In her published essay collections, Hardwick organized her selections around general themes. However, the essays here are presented chronologically, so that the social essays from the 1960s and 1970s—on the riot in Watts, the protests in Selma, the march in Memphis, the trauma of the Democratic National Convention in Chicago, or the legacy of the 1960s—join with her memories of Boston, Florence, Maine, and, yes, Brazil, to describe her own cultural context. She is reading Lévi-Strauss in Brazil in 1974, understanding how the "great, green density" of the country "makes the soul yearn to create a gray, smooth highway."

When you open the doors, so to speak, to one of her essays, you can sense there on the threshold that this is going to be interesting. She always makes you add to your reading list. In line after line, she is saying things you had not thought of, or telling you something that it is stirring to be told. Her love of literature has in it a profound humility. There is nothing cruel in her intelligence. Her wit and charm are unerring, unfailing. You didn't know the skeptical mind could be so graceful. Her concentration is complete. Elizabeth Hardwick can surprise you. You didn't know you would need to stop right there and go think about what she has just said. You re-emerge, you look up, and you'd no idea her beauty of expression had taken you so far away. Or you didn't expect such exhilaration just from reading about reading. It isn't only what she is saying, it's how she is saying it. Her prose style is unmistakable and like no other.

This volume would not have been possible without the dedication of Susan Barba to seeing Hardwick's work into print.

—DARRYL PINCKNEY

THE COLLECTED ESSAYS
OF ELIZABETH HARDWICK

MEMOIRS, CONVERSATIONS, AND DIARIES

ALAIN, the philosopher and writer, arrives first, Valéry two or three minutes later. "*Les deux illustres*," meeting for the first time, introduced by Henri Mondor, sit down and begin to order luncheon. Valéry, refusing the duck in favor of the meat, remarks, "Without meat, you would have with you only *M. Néant*." Alain professes himself able to eat anything, adds that because of his teaching at the Normale he drinks very little, except sometimes milk. Valéry also likes milk, he explains, but goes to excess only with coffee. And then Alain, unable to restrain himself another moment: "*Avez-vous travaillé, ce matin, Orphée?*" (Italics mine.) Yes, Valéry works in the morning and at eleven o'clock his work for the day is finished.

A note by Clive Bell in the *Symposium* collected in honor of T. S. Eliot's sixtieth birthday: "Between Virginia [Woolf] and myself somehow the poet became a sort of 'family joke': it is not easy to say why." In the same collection, an essay by Desmond Hawkins: "I recall an afternoon tea in the early 1930s. I am the only guest and my host is a 'distinguished literary figure.'... I affect to despise the great man, *of course....*" (Italics mine.)

The night boat from Calais chugs along confidently, taking us, in the *hommage* as in the cuisine, from the French soufflé to the English cold veal.

We hardly know how to approach these "minutes" of the luncheons between literary men in France, those "Mardis" of Mallarmé's, those evenings at Magny's restaurant in the Goncourt *Journals* where Saint-Beuve and Gautier with a mysterious and almost painful genius still

3

exist on the page, neither life exactly nor fiction, but like one of those dreams in which dead friends, with their old crumpled smiles and grunts, their *themes*, meet you turning a corner.

About Valéry, Mallarmé, or Gide you may pluck the same berry from a dozen different vines. An occasion is not recorded by a singular guest of some peculiar stenographic energy, an observant dilettante with no other literary occupation to fill his time; no, breaking up at midnight, *everyone* goes home, not to rest, but to his *journal intime*, his bulging diary. If he is Gide he will ponder himself upon the occasion, if he is another he will "write up" Gide. Abundant comparisons are thus left for posterity: you may read Roger Martin du Gard's "Notes on André Gide"—opening line in 1913, *At last I have met André Gide!*— or Gide's musings in *his* journal on the meetings with Martin du Gard.

The information above on the first meeting of Alain and Valéry is taken from a current copy of the recently revived *La Nouvelle NRF*. At the beginning, M. Mondor informs us that this same event, this "déjeuner chez Lapérouse," was committed to print by Alain himself and appeared in the *old* NRF in 1939. M. Mondor, robust meeter and recorder, has also written on the first meeting of Valéry and Claudel and even the great "*premier entretien*" of Mallarmé and Valéry. His document on the latter begins with the information gleaned from the Alain conference: "Paul Valéry, almost every day, after eleven o'clock in the morning liked to rest from his work." It is by repetition and excess that a national eccentricity is recognized.

This overloaded pantry of memory and dialogue has a genuine literary and historical fascination—and delights of an unnameable sort: the pleasure of frayed picture albums, where no surprise is expected, and still one's heart skips a beat as he looks yet another time at the old faces, the eyes squinting in the sunlight. In France no hint of moderation nags this appetite. Not a word is lost in the afternoon dreaminess, not an accent of Mallarmé's swirls off to oblivion with the pipe smoke in that apartment on the rue de Rome, not even a silence is drowned in the punch, which, you may read in countless sources, is brought in quietly at ten o'clock by Mme. Mallarmé and her daughter. Dining almost anywhere, they have hardly unfolded the table napkins before Valéry is saying, "To read, to write are equally odious to me." Like

Napoleon's hat, these remarks have a national, historical life of their own; a schoolboy would know them any place. But this man who hates to read and to write does not then, as an American might expect, speak of women or sports, but of his feelings of dizziness and fatigue after the first performance of Jarry's *Ubu Roi*! If women are mentioned at all, it is hardly what we mean when we say "they talked about women." Instead Valéry remembers Heine's witticism: "All women who write have one eye on the page and another on some person, with the exception of the Countess of Hahn who has only one eye."

In France not only literary people but the civic powers display a ready courtesy and appreciation of artistic citizens which to their English and American partners must appear almost idolatrous. Our artists *openly* wish such recognition only when they are in a sick mood of persecution or drunkenly blowing their own horns in a way they will regret the next morning. Wandering about Paris, foreigners of a literary mind think, "The Avenue Victor Hugo, that you might expect . . . but the *rue Apollinaire*, and so soon!" Regretfully we remember those Washington Square ladies who tried in vain to get a corner named after Henry James.

It is very difficult for the English and Americans to compose a respectable *hommage*, to spend a lifetime or even a few prime years on private memoirs, even comfortably to keep a journal, a diary. For these activities the French have a nearly manic facility and energy, but when we grind away at this industry it is as if we were trying to make perfume out of tobacco juice. Every sort of bruising stumble lies in wait; you observe one law of social morality only to break another. No matter where one turns the ground of possibility weakens and the writer sinks into an indiscretion at the best, nearly a crime at the worst. Reverence, which the French display without stint, seeing it a privilege, a mark of grace, to serve, to draw near, to be a witness, seems to us to impugn honesty and self-respect. If we cannot do this for the Virgin, the Saints, without an exotic act of the will, how shall we be expected to do it for a mere author of secular dramas? Art is a profession, not a shrine. And even if one does not hesitate to make a fool of himself, there are others to consider. By immoderate praise, rash compliments, one may seriously offend the modesty and reasonable expectations of the great person, who will be thrown into embarrassment by the suspicion of flattery. The fear of toadying is an overwhelming obstacle to the production of an *hommage*.

Nevertheless, we do have a great English classic in this vein; one can say it outdoes the French, that when all the memories of Gide and Valéry are at last gathered together—if an end to that enterprise can be imagined—even then they will be mere fragments by the side of Boswell's *Johnson*. Yet it is remarkable about this work of genius that, though it is known and loved to a fabulous degree, the spectacle of its coming into being has always struck a great many right-thinking readers as repellent. Even a schoolgirl must shrink with disgust from that loathsome young man, Boswell, "buttering up" Dr. Johnson, hanging about his coattails like an insurance salesman after a policy, opening up topics and then with a diseased lack of pride rushing home to write down the answers, as though he wished somehow himself to partake of Johnson's magnificence, to insinuate his own disturbing image on the screen of history. Dr. Johnson is treasured, but odium attaches to his giddy memorialist. Grateful as readers have always been for the book, they cannot imagine themselves stooping to this peculiar method of composition. Until fairly recently Boswell seemed both repugnant and insignificant—everyone knows Dr. Johnson thought his friend missed his chance for immortality by not having been alive when "The Dunciad" was written. And one would have thought the amazing longevity of the Boswell family's shame about this member would have been modified by the undying popularity of his great work. Still they seemed to think: that fourth bout of gonorrhea fully recorded elsewhere by this dog—that is our kinsman! This other thing brings credit only to Dr. Johnson who, unfortunately, is not even a connection of the Boswell family.

Boswell is a stray—he arrived without antecedents and departed without descendants. Anyone who wishes to see the strain we feel before the blank page of veneration may examine the previously mentioned *Symposium* in honor of Eliot's sixtieth birthday. This collection is one long stutter, not about Eliot's greatness, but before the unique and almost revolutionary act of proclaiming this greatness in anything except an "objective" critical essay. From the first a profound inexperience is displayed in the very organization of the project; the editors have been so bold as to reveal the difference between the abstract request and the difficult response. The preface promises a *personal* book, *private* impressions, actual meetings and so on, but what we have is a group of essays which might, with a few exceptions, appear any time. The only rarity of the work is geographical: the comments by people who have not even met Eliot come not only from England and Europe, but from Bengal, Ceylon, and Greece. Perhaps there is another peculiarity—two of the essays are not primarily about Eliot, but about Pound and Irving Babbitt. No one would wish to see this sort of thing increased and multiplied. It is very clearly "against the grain." The fear of toadying is so great nearly everyone celebrates Eliot's birthday as he would celebrate his own, quietly, secretly, hardly mentioning it for fear someone would think he wanted something.

Recently, when Edmund Wilson's "critical memoir" on Edna Millay appeared one heard some literary people expressing a giggly embarrassment. Watch out, there's something *personal* here! We may breathlessly read this document, but we feel obliged in our critical souls to discount it. After all, Wilson seems to have had an "attachment" for his subject and literature is a court where personal knowledge keeps you off the jury.

In the diary, the private journal, one is relieved of the problem of seeming to debase himself in an undemocratic way before his equals or superiors, but another and more crushing burden of conscience cramps the fingers. This is the fear of outrageous vanity, of presuming to offer simply *one's own ideas* and moods, speaking in one's natural voice, which may appear—any number of transgressive adjectives are exact: boastful, presumptive, narcissistic, indulgent. There is no doubt that the diarist is the most egotistical of beings; he quite before our eyes ceases to take himself with that grain of salt which alone makes clever people bearable. Even the most gifted of men must in his own circle be "just like everyone else," not standing upon his accomplishments, but putting them aside like an old smoking jacket worn in private. The unhesitating self-regard of Gide's *Journals* would involve us in so much pain, so great an effort to strike the right note between merely rattling away on "trivialities" and recording "serious" feelings that it will hardly seem worth the while to most exceptional writers. Amateurs, like Pepys, not really writers at all, have the advantage. Our most interesting American and English journals are usually short essays or narratives on various themes, composed with the care, craft, and solemnity of any other public performance; too much of the free, flowing "I" is bad taste. (On this question of the modesty we value so highly, I have heard an extremely intelligent Englishman say that E. M. Forster's relative lack of productivity was due to his not wanting to "lord it over" some of his old and dear friends by constantly and successfully appearing before the public as a novelist. Already, with Forster's reputation, things were bad enough!) In the private journal, that inscrutable scribbler, Boswell, again comes to mind. He cared terribly about literature and was at great pains to polish his style, but fortunately Boswell never got the idea. He wrote as an amateur, giving off accounts of himself so vivid and outrageous one would believe them written by an enemy, if it were not clear at every turn that they are composed with adoration: Boswell's own matchless enthusiasm for his adventures and thoughts. There are enough hints to show how tedious Boswell would have been as a self-conscious English man of letters, in good command of himself and his reputation, thoughtful of the decencies, of pride, of moderation. In spite of his efforts to achieve these qualities, Boswell hadn't the vaguest notion what they were about. There is something nearly insane in his spontaneity.

The *hommage* and an individual's account of his own nature and life are interesting, but they have hardly any of that sinful appeal of those conversations, moments in the lives of famous or infamous persons, taken down and arranged by another. The purpose of the *hommage* is to praise, the usual practice of the diarist is to look inward; but the memoir is concerned with the external, meant to reveal, to pin down others. Unless one has met a number of famous people or endured an historic moment, he cannot in the fullest sense even write his memoirs—"Memoirs of a Nobody," the title signifies an irony. The art of presenting, analyzing, recording living persons is, with us, protected and isolated by countless moral spears and spikes. The very fact that one is in a position to observe for posterity is all the more reason why he should decently refuse to do so. The motives behind this form of historical writing are felt to be unwholesome.

Drummond's *Conversations with Ben Jonson* are a very queer moment in our literature. Still, surpassingly strange as these conversations are, they are extremely "English." They are brief—one doesn't go too far in laboring to preserve even what such a man as Ben Jonson said; people will think you have nothing else to do. Their "manliness" and "objectivity" are great; nothing feminine or gushingly interested like Boswell is involved because Drummond and Jonson did not even like each other! Drummond thought Jonson "a great lover and praiser of himself, a contemner and scorner of others," and was not disqualified as a disinterested recorder by even so much as a high opinion of Jonson's literary work since he believed this man "excelleth only in a translation." Jonson, as a guest, could not proceed without hesitation to name what he thought of Drummond and so confined himself to the mild grumble that his host's verses "smelled too much of the Schools." It is not hard to imagine what Jonson truly thought of Drummond when we read what he had to say these evenings about absent contemporaries: Donne, for not keeping the accent, deserved hanging; Daniel was jealous of him [Jonson]; Drayton feared him; Beaumont "loved too much himself and his own verses"; Raleigh employed the best wits in England to write his history; Sir Philip Sidney had pimples; of his own wife, well, "five years he had not bedded with her." Even if we did not know Jonson to be a great and lovable genius, a profound and generous critic elsewhere, we could say at least that his remarks have a quality dear to us, *honesty*. Jonson is aware, with his violent outspokenness, of a kind of need to remind the listener of this trait; he says, "of all the styles he loved most to be named honest." Having thus enlisted our certainty that he is no flatterer, he then, complex being, falls into a terrible error: he says that of his honesty he "hath one hundred letters so naming him." After this we are immediately led back to a bit of sympathy for the irritated Drummond. A gentleman must right things in such unmanageable cases. These conversations are altogether weird.

The nearest thing in English to the Goncourts is De Quincey—his extraordinary impressions of the Lake Poets, which can hardly be excelled for style, brilliance of observation, skill in narration, and for overwhelming psychological wisdom. However, they are not much like the Goncourts because of their unique tenderness and their striking innocence of worldliness. Grasmere is one thing, Paris another; in Paris you dine with Gautier at the Princess Mathilde's, here you walk twenty miles in the rain with Dorothy and William Wordsworth. The lonely hills nourish eccentricity, not scandal. Noble and loving as they are, De Quincey's impressions provoked resentment in Wordsworth, Southey, and those of Coleridge's relatives living at the time of publication. They do indeed have their tragic moments: that horrible lodging in London where Coleridge lay in the pain and confusion of laudanum, wretchedly facing his series of lectures at the Royal Institute. They do not lack comedy, either. De Quincey adored Wordsworth, still, "useful as they proved themselves, the Wordsworthian legs were certainly not orna-mental." And then this distinguished poet also had a remarkable narrowness and droop about the shoulders which caused Dorothy, walking behind him, to exclaim, "Is it possible—can that be William? How very mean he looks!" Southey may have felt his calm, regular habit of life, his immense energy, his library of beautifully bound books were a bit too faithfully described by De Quincey; the description suggests an overgrowth of secondary literary powers which crowd out the more messy ones of the first magnitude. Nevertheless the genius of everyone, and most of all of De Quincey himself, is brilliantly served by these essays. We would not for anything be without that picture of Wordsworth cutting the pages of one of Southey's lovely books with a greasy butter knife.

In De Quincey and Boswell's *Johnson* there is hardly a hint of "sex"—the subjects are all extremely eccentric in their lack of concen-tration on this instinct. Our own age is even more prudish in this respect; conversational and fictional freedom has increased, but in memoirs and portraits the license has been nearly revoked so that one gets round-about psychoanalytical hints based upon facts which are not revealed. It would be very difficult for us to write, without somehow turning it into an ambiguity or a joke, "At last I have met André Gide," but we can hardly imagine the malice of writing, "I have met Gide, but he was distracted by the sight of a beautiful young boy on the beach..." An interesting scene of this sort occurs in Roger Martin du Gard. He says that he showed his diary to Gide and Gide was fascinated by it. Spender's friendly and very circumspect portraits of living people were by some considered "scandalous." An author would probably be outlawed for *keeping in his mind*, to say nothing of his journal, the following quotation from Flaubert found in the Goncourt work:

> When I was young my vanity was such that if I found myself in a brothel with friends, I would choose the ugliest girl and would insist upon lying with her before them all without taking the cigar out of my mouth. It was no fun at all for me; I did it for the gallery.

The peculiar sanctity that surrounds our image of Flaubert, the unequaled purity of the man and his art, are not altered by this naked bit of anecdote.

Frank Harris, who clearly modeled his volumes on the Goncourts', is, one gathers, either in oblivion or, when remembered, in disrepute. This ineffable being has certain qualifications as a "portraitist," but they are nearly all erased by his incurable English, or American, moralizing. Harris is extremely sensitive to an "opportunity"; at a meeting he approaches the celebrity with the dignified and plausible expectancy of a relative at a promising deathbed. He does not pretend to be disinterested, or himself a mere nothing; but he can say in all honesty that he *cares*. And this is true: he is passionately interested in famous people. His "coverage" is wide and international; his narration of anecdote and description of character are entertaining, even if he does like to frill the edges with "winebearers at the banquet of life," and to add all sorts of conversational pockets which seem designed merely to repeat his own name. "Do you see that, Frank?" or "I will tell you a story, Frank." Harris's great trouble is that he never misses a chance to point out a "flaw" in his subject's discourse. One gets not only Shaw's very interesting claim for his own dramatic Caesar over Shakespeare's, but Harris's long-winded defense of Shakespeare against Shaw. Harris wants you to know he will not hesitate to seek out the great *and* will not allow the greatest of them to get by with "nonsense." Without indicating his refusal to agree or to practice an amiable silence, perhaps he could not have justified his exorbitant pursuit. This is very nearly fatal both for the drama and the humor of his portraits. Here is a bit of nightmare dialogue from the Goncourts, the kind of entry that gives a frightening life to their record:

> Taine: "...In the town of Angers, they keep such a close watch on women there is no breath of scandal about a single one of them."
> Saint-Victor: "Angers? But they are all pederasts...."

Harris would almost certainly have followed this mad moment with: "Permit me, but I have made a special trip to Angers and both of you are stupidly wrong."

Should anyone in English wish to rival the Goncourts? Far from laboring to add more to this kind of "history," perhaps we should find the enjoyment of the Goncourt classic a guilty passion. Henry James was deeply shocked by the appearance of this work. It seemed to him an appalling occupation, every instance of it, from the brothers' account of their contemporaries to Edmond's notes on the death of Jules. Their carrying on the journal is "a very interesting and remarkable fact," but "it has almost a vulgarly usual air in comparison with the circumstance that one of them has judged best to give the document to the light." James cannot abide these "demoralized investigators," he is horrified by their picture of a grumpy and petty Saint-Beuve and points out with a cry that the thirty volumes of Saint-Beuve's *Causeries du lundi* "contain a sufficiently substantial answer to their account of the figure he cut when they dined with him as his invited guests or as fellow-members of a brilliant club." James is not only solicitous for the artists, but for the Goncourts' maid whose bitter adventures are related, and for certain women of the world: "If Madame de Païva was good enough to dine, or anything else, with, she was good enough either to speak of without brutality or to speak of not at all." And the Princess Mathilde: "He stays in her house for days, for weeks together, and then portrays for our entertainment her person, her clothes, her gestures ... relating anecdotes at her expense ... the racy expressions that passed her own lips." James has, from my reading of the charming entries on the Princess Mathilde, a really cloistered notion of "racy expressions," but his objections are not trifling. They are painfully serious and worthy, as one must recognize even when he has just closed his copy of the *Journals* and pronounced them a delight. All of the people are now dead and those who do not survive by their art or historical significance are dead completely, except as they live on for the occasional Goncourt fan or in other documents of the period. Some lively creatures would, no doubt, choose immortality on any terms rather than face the utter oblivion of their names. Yet we do not know this for a certainty; the question cannot even be truly put to the sufferer, since the permanence of a portrait, vicious or pleasing, cannot be known for a long time. A shrewd person might even say: If the book is a masterpiece. I don't mind being atrociously present, because even mediocrities or cads, brilliantly drawn, have a kind of grandeur—but if it is second-rate, leave me out!

In England and America where the temptation to the direct use of actual personages is so buried in hesitation, where so much seems to forbid, the practice may be attended by malice and deliberate distortion; some goddess of revenge and brutality may in fact hold the hand of the muse of history. Nevertheless, writers and readers alike have a rich interest in the living personality, an interest which does not blush even before the squalid or ludicrous revelation. If we do not practice the memoir or diary with unfaltering confidence, we have the *roman à clef* and satires like Pope's. These forms are allowed to be far more brutal than mere reportage; in the latter a certain body of fact must be observed; accuracy is all. In the novel or satire, every effort is made to identify without actually naming the fleshly reality, but once the identity is clear no restraints at all are put upon the free exercise of a malicious imagination. The author can pick and choose as he likes, exaggerate, invent; indeed he is obliged to swell here and shrink there from the necessity of creating a "character," which cannot have the exact fullness and queerness of life, but must be "exposed" more neatly, according to the demands of art. This method is less useful for "history," but it is brilliantly effective in inflicting an injury upon the living. The poor victim cannot say he has been falsely reported, since it is his very soul which is being examined; grimy motives and degrading weaknesses he has never expressed are gaily attributed to him by the satirist. Almost anyone, in his lifetime, would prefer the "pinning down" of the Goncourts to the crucifixion of "The Dunciad."

Yet even with contemporary silence the sensitive celebrity cannot keep posterity in hand. In a highly industrialized society "research" is an honorable calling. Politeness and decency have left us nothing of Emily Dickinson's swoons or suspicious flutters, still ladies and gentlemen coming later can hypothecate depths of perverse commitment about which one can at best only be an agnostic—like the after life these hypotheses cannot be proved true or false from on-the-spot accounts. The scholar can do anything he likes with Walt Whitman, or rest Herman Melville on a bed of Oedipal nails that would puncture the sleep of the most thick-skinned artist. Posterity, dipping into *Harper's Bazaar, The New York Times* "Interviews" and so on, will find a mute and inglorious Faulkner, a kittenish Marianne Moore, a sober Dylan Thomas—perhaps there will not even be a word, but only a picture memorializing an Allen Tate of granite solemnity and dignity, a mutely beautiful Katherine Anne Porter, a schoolmaster with a beard named Randall Jarrell. From our serious periodicals it will be learned that our literary men, and also those of the past, had no life at all: they lived and died as a metaphor. But living people, even thousands upon thousands of students, know our writers, and know them first-hand, to be fantastically interesting and—who would dispute it?—often *fantastic*. Our squeamishness and glorification of privacy may be paid for by a blank. Even a bureaucrat or a play producer might, if he gave thought to it, hesitate to enter history by way of those "profiles" and cover-stories which have become an unyielding bore of joshing flattery, whose only purpose may be to keep literary lawyers busy and neighborly researchers employed in the piling up of a benign lump of fact.

It was clear that something new was needed—nobody is *that* dull, the harried editor heard in his dreams. This something was found, a new, a fearful and quite unprecedented growth, a pioneer and monstrous crossbreeding of indifference and total recall: *The New Yorker* "article" on Hemingway. Before this it seemed never to have occurred to us that brute sound, as it were, might be a novelty, that "pieces" may after all simply be made with words, any words, if they have been truly uttered by a person of some celebrity. One would have expected these offerings to be signed with tiny initials, indicating a stenographer, or better by a few steel tracings of a machine not yet on the market, but showing in its simplicity and efficiency every possibility of easy mass production. In France a person would be guillotined for such an invention, and the very idea of this article was an invention, perhaps in the dawn of time related to the interview or the conversation, but in itself bearing no more relation to those than a cough to a song recital. By comparison, Aubrey's duchesses who "died of the pox" seem sweetly remembered.

Gorky's reminiscences of Tolstoy—a masterpiece. If anyone today were capable of composing this exalted work about a living genius, he would become so befuddled, so bent and harassed with accusation, so fearful of putting in and leaving out, it would be sensible economy to leave off altogether and return to "creative" work. What to do with himself in the reminiscence? Shall he admit his own existence or is that an unpardonable self-assertion? And isn't it putting it on a bit to pretend to "know" the marvelous being when there are so many others who have known him longer and "better."

To these moral and aesthetic questions there is no answer. Meanwhile there is always, instead, *publicity*—so easy to swallow, so difficult to remember a moment later.

1953

ANDERSON, MILLAY, AND CRANE
IN THEIR LETTERS

MANY PEOPLE believe letters the most personal and revealing form of communication. In them we expect to find the charmer at his nap, slumped, open-mouthed, profoundly himself without thought for appearances. Yet, this is not quite true. Letters are above all useful as a means of expressing the ideal self; and no other method of communication is quite so good for this purpose. In conversation, those uneasy eyes upon you, those lips ready with an emendation before you have begun to speak, are a powerful deterrent to unreality, even to hope. In art it is not often possible to make direct use of your dreams of tomorrow and your excuses for yesterday.

In letters we can reform without practice, beg without humiliation, snip and shape embarrassing experiences to the measure of our own desires—this is a benevolent form. The ideal self expressed in letters is not a crudely sugary affair except in dreary personalities; in any case the ideal is very much a part of the character, having its twenty-four hours a day to get through, and being no less unique in its combinations than one's fingerprints.

In the letters of artists and public figures we may not find literary charm, but we do invariably get a good notion of how the person saw himself over the years. This vision does not always strike us as "acute"; we are often tempted to put some poor fellow wise on the subject of his own character, to explain that we are a lot more impressed by his dying on the gallows than by his last "God bless you" to his wife. It is difficult to think of a man except as the sum of his remarkable deeds, a statue surrounded by selected objects and symbols. Private letters are disturbing to this belief. What they most often show is that people do not live their biographies.

*

In the last year or so the correspondence of quite a number of our writers has been published—Pound, Sinclair Lewis, Hart Crane, Gertrude Stein, Sherwood Anderson, Edna Millay—and we have had memoirs on Willa Cather and others. The twenties, which only a few years ago felt so near, are gradually slipping back into that vault called American Literature, where the valuables are kept. The publication of letters is a compliment which suggests the writer is worth a kind of scrutiny not granted every author. As these writers begin to take on that faraway, mysterious, "historical" glaze, publications about them are of considerable importance; a certain ice of opinion, fact and fancy is already spreading over their images. And we cannot assume that eventually all letters, every scrap of interesting material will be published; what is more likely is that the selections, the biography, as we have them now will stand for a time.

It is, then, interesting that the first volume (who knows if there will be another?) of Sinclair Lewis's letters should be entirely given over to communications he wrote and *received* from his publishers. Indeed, this correspondence is rather good fun, dealing as it does with the finagling, financing and advertising which, though uncommonly exposed to this extent, are in some way a part of literary history, as the billboard is a sort of cousin to the performance. We see Lewis composing a fan letter to be sent by his publishers to all the best writers of his day on the subject of that remarkable book *Main Street;* and wondering if perhaps something special isn't needed for the elegant eye and heart of Edith Wharton. This was all a part of the game, but we may doubt Lewis, much as he liked to appear in print, would have been delighted by this whole volume of business testimony.

Sherwood Anderson's letters are unhappily selected for quite the opposite reason. They are often bleak and dull to read because they are chosen upon a principle of reckless high-mindedness, a remorseless tracking of Anderson the writer, the artist, the thinker, at the expense of biography. It is felt that Anderson the advertising man, Anderson before forty, was, though alive, a mute statistic; and even after he has been allowed existence at forty only his literary life is permitted. But with Anderson, "the man" is overwhelmingly important. He appears to have been splintered, repressed, uncertain in an exceptional way; in a very real sense his literary equipment began and ended with this painful state of being. Though he could sometimes grow mannered and arty, he is not particularly vivid if you isolate him as "an artist." It is as *a case* that he is unfailingly interesting, this peculiar rising and waning star, this man who brought to literature almost nothing except his own lacerated feelings. This latter circumstance, and not his Flaubertian dedication, is what makes us think of him sometimes as a typical American writer. With certain other authors an undeviating, purely literary selection would produce not only the most interesting but the truest portrait of the man: Ezra Pound's life seems to have been, almost literally, an *open book*.

Yet, even if one were to admit the validity of excluding all letters written before Anderson became an author, it seems a bit lofty to omit nearly everything that happened to him during the period of authorship. During these years Anderson divorced three wives and married a fourth; a much-married man without love letters gives us a jolt. There is no letter to Anderson's daughter, only two to his son Bob, who worked with him on the newspaper enterprise; a few more to his son, John, get under the wire because John too is an "artist," a painter, and letters relating to that calling are summoned. This selection makes Anderson seem distinctly hard and unreal; wives are divorced in a footnote or abandoned like unpromising manuscripts, grown children when addressed at all are usually given a lecture on art—and the author himself is as naked as can be, stripped to a man who is writing another book. Anderson's strange, restless soul, remarkable beyond all else for painful, shrinking feelings, is uneasy with his literary friends, Waldo Frank, Van Wyck Brooks, Paul Rosenfeld. Struggling to tell them what he is all about he is sometimes like a tenor with the stage all to himself: "I have been to Nebraska, where the big engines are tearing the hills to pieces; over the low hills runs the promise of corn. You wait, dear Brother! I shall bring God home to the sweaty men in the corn rows." Or again he is not so much complex as hidden and diffuse, singing in a voice not always recognizable from one day to the next. He is a man of the Middle West he tells us, close to the people, and yet all sorts of angels seem to be whispering in his ear, correcting his accent.

Edna Millay's letters—after reading them you hesitate to know what you thought you knew about this poet. Can this be that sensational young woman of legend who burnt the candle, built the house on sand, kissed so many lips? More than once you find yourself thinking of quite another enduring American type, Jo in *Little Women*, the resourceful, sensitive, devoted girl, bobbing her hair, not to be a flapper, but to pay for Father's illness. These letters are very charming, although not in the sense one would care much to read them if they were not by Edna Millay, or at least by *someone*, for they haven't that sort of power which can be enjoyed apart from a beforehand interest in the writer. They show, for one thing, an intense, unmixed family devotion; not merely an affection for spruced-up memories of colorful relations, long dead ancestors from a region one no longer visits, not earnestness and the urgings of duty, but an immense love for the present, living, impinging kin. This world of nicknames, old jokes, little gifts flying through the mails is startlingly passionate. With friends too there is very often the same extraordinarily intimate style, the same devotion, fidelity, acceptance—and all the while we know Edna Millay was becoming more remote from everyone, enduring very early "a sort of nervous breakdown which interferes a bit with my keeping my promises," and later in hospitals with "an all but life-size nervous breakdown" and at last horribly alone in the country, cold, without even a telephone, dying miserably after a sleepless night. How is it possible with all this fraternal, familial feeling that the frantic, orphaned creature of the later years came into being? And how is it possible to begin with that this jolly, loving daughter and sister was in her most famous period in such violent revolt? Edna Millay seems to have had a wretched life, much more so than those persons whose earliest days were marked by a blighting, ambiguous relation to their families and later somewhat toward everyone. There is not anywhere a sadder story than this—the aching existence of this woman who loved and was loved by her family and friends, who, flaming youth and all, married only once and then, to all appearances, wisely. Even Emily Dickinson appears on happier ground in her upstairs bedroom.

It seems likely that Edna Millay's fame and success came too early; the racking strain of keeping up to this is suggested everywhere. And more important: I think Edmund Wilson in his fascinating and moving work on her undervalues the spectacular pain of the sort of success she had. She was a woman famous for her fascinating, unconventional personality, and for rather conventional poems. She was not in the deepest sense "famous" or much cared for by many of the really good poets of her own time. Hart Crane's opinion, written to a friend much stricken with Miss Millay, is interesting: "She really has genius in a limited sense, and is much better than Sara Teasdale, Marguerite Wilkinson, Lady Speyer, etc., to mention a few drops in the bucket of feminine lushness that forms a kind of milky way in the poetic firmament of the time (likewise all times);—indeed I think she is every bit as good as Elizabeth Browning...I can only say I do not greatly care for Mme. Browning....With her equipment Edna Millay is bound to succeed to the appreciative applause of a fairly large audience. And for you, who I rather suppose have not gone into this branch of literature with as much enthusiasm as myself, she is a creditable heroine."

This was not an easy situation for Edna Millay to live with. You cannot give, as she did, your whole life to writing without caring horribly, even to the point of despair. And so in 1949 we find that she is planning a satire against T. S. Eliot. In this work she says there is to be, "nothing coarse, obscene, as there sometimes is in the work of Auden and Pound, and nothing so silly as the childish horsing around of Eliot, when he is trying to be funny. He has no sense of humor, and so he is not yet a true Englishman. There is, I think, in these poems of mine against Eliot nothing which could be considered abusive; they are merely murderous."

This is appalling. Edna Millay was not a stupid or even an excessively vain person. She knew, in spite of this wild cry, that the literary approval of Pound was to be valued more highly than that of Frank Crowninshield. (Critics are often wrong, but writers are hardly ever wrong, hide and deny it as they will, in knowing whose opinion really counts.) Her words are not those of a poet secure in her powers, and they are especially harsh for this writer, who was forever generous and warmhearted toward other poets, including nearly all of her feminine rivals. This hopeless, killing bitterness about her own place, as I believe the projected satire reveals, is the end of a whole life which one can at least imagine to have been thrown off its natural, impressive track by a series of seemingly fortunate fatalities. Perhaps she was not meant to go to Greenwich Village at all and certainly not to become famous in her youth. She was sensible, moral, steadfast, a kind of prodigy—among her circle hardly anyone except Edmund Wilson and John Peale Bishop even rose to the second-rate. Not nearly enough was asked of her and she had no time to prepare herself in solitude—until it was too late. It is a tribute, a terrible one, to her possibilities and hopes that she was unable to enjoy the comforts of a strong, public position and split in two. Very few critics can find in Edna Millay's poetry the power and greatness Wilson finds. Still there is something humanly delightful and pleasing in Wilson's obstinacy, like the great Ruskin putting Kate Greenaway among the finest living artists—as he did.

One cannot read even a few of Hart Crane's letters without feeling the editor, Brom Weber, has made a tremendous contribution. (Of course the "contribution" is Crane's, but he could not have presented his own correspondence.) Fishing about in contemporary literature, Weber has dredged up a masterpiece, for these letters are marvelous, wonderful simply to read, important in what they add to our notion of Crane, and in an unruly, inadvertent fashion quite profound for the picture they give of America itself, and in particular the literary scene from 1916 to 1932, from Hart Crane at seventeen until his death at thirty-three. It is easy with this volume to be reminded of Keats's letters, and if Crane's are not quite so extraordinary as that the same must be said for most of English prose.

Poor Crane—a genius from Cleveland—with his little pair of parents, or his pair of little parents, so squeezing in their anxiety and egotism, so screeching in their divorce, the mother rather beached and given to a humble mysticism, the father, dazed and busy, a business success but not really. Crane's parents are curdling and outrageous by their very multiplicity in America, their typicality; they are as real and to be expected, this young couple, as Cleveland itself. Vast numbers of people under middle age now have parents like this and are these persons' only child. Hart Crane was merely a bit in the vanguard by getting there somewhat early. And the son himself, a poet, homosexual, drunkard, a suicide. One had not imagined much could be added to this macabre, but neat, biography. However, what the letters amazingly suggest is the disturbing possibility that Crane had a happy life.

Naturally, he was often much annoyed by his parents, but there is no doubt he was always much fascinated by them. He wrote this middling pair an extremely generous number of lively and often lengthy letters—a source of amazement when we consider Crane's bumming about, drinking, and the dizzy life he had made for himself away from home. In the end he was returning from Mexico, not to New York, but to Chagrin Falls, Ohio, planning fantastically to "be of some help" to his stepmother in the shrunken state of solid assets which became known at his father's death.

Contrary to the guilt feelings usually surmised, Crane seems to have "enjoyed"—no other word occurs to me—his homosexuality, taking about this the most healthy attitude possible under the circumstances. There is not the slightest suggestion in the letters that he worried about his inclinations or was trying to reform; if anything troubles him on this score it is continence, the lack of opportunity. For what it may be worth, we remark that his suicide came at a time when he was involved, and more than a little lukewarmly, with a woman. "You know you're welcome—more than that, my dear, to make this your future headquarters. I miss you *mucho, mucho, mucho*! But I don't think that either of us ought to urge the other into anything but the most spontaneous and mutually liberal arrangements."

Crane also "enjoyed" alcohol—his letters are heathenish in their failure to express intentions to liberate himself from this pleasure. He could, however, be remorseful over his drunken actions and there is no doubt he tried his friends' charity extravagantly. As the Russian proverb about drinking has it, "A man on foot is a poor companion for a man on horseback." Yet Crane somehow never seems to feel he is galloping to destruction. In this he is very different from Fitzgerald, who had in the midst of chaos the rather cross-eyed power of gazing upon his deterioration as if he were not living it but somehow observing his soul and body as one would watch a drop of water slowly drying up in the sun. Crane, on the other hand, expresses over and over the greatest delight in alcohol; he sees himself as a true lover of the grape rather than a snuffling slave of the bottle and, though the results may be the same, the attitude alters the experience along the way. It is one thing to die in ecstasy and another to pass away, moaning, "I knew this stuff would get me in the end." (This is not suggested as the literal deathbed mood of either of these authors, but as a fundamental difference of attitude toward their "difficulties.")

Crane's letters are vivid in every respect—responsive, humorous, beautifully written, fresh—everything and more. The sheer power of mind they reveal is dazzling; his comments upon his reading, his contemporaries, his own work, even the landscape, are always interesting and usually brilliant. It is impossible to think of him, after this, as a natural who knows not what he doeth. What is so appealing about his mind is the utter absence of cant, artiness, and fear—all those things Sherwood Anderson seemed to think were the "copy" a literary man was obliged to wring out of his skin. Even when Crane is wounded in his vanity—self-justifying and "true to human nature" as he will be in his explanation of lapses—there is always something solid and shrewd in the way he goes about reclaiming himself. One can see in him certainly a "neurotic need for affection" but there is also astonishing independence and balance. His melancholy is as short as his enjoyment of things is long. Very near the end, before he jumped into the sea, if he *did* jump, he is writing about the glorious Mexican Easter and the wonderful singers in the cafés ("has the old Hawaiian gurgling backed off the map") and detailing his incredibly funny difficulties with a drunken servant, Daniel. "I took the opportunity to talk to him about sobriety—meanwhile pouring him glass after glass of Tenampe...."

Reading these letters it is hard to remember the withered and anesthetized tragedy we thought Crane had become. Yet you cannot easily account for the amount of joy in them and the joy you receive from getting close again to Crane's life. Perhaps it is his magical freedom from true *disgust* that makes you think this "doomed" poet was, after all, under the protection of a charm.

1953

THE SUBJECTION OF WOMEN

VASSAL, slave, inferior, other, thing, victim, dependent, parasite, prisoner—oh, bitter, raped, child-swollen flesh doomed to immanence! Sisyphean goddess of the dust pile! Demeter, Xantippe, Ninon de Lenclos, Marie Bashkirtsev, and "a friend of mine..." From cave to café, boudoir to microscope, from the knitting needles to the short story: they are all here in a potency of pages, a foreshortened and exaggerated, a mysterious and too clear relief, an eloquent lament and governessy scolding, a poem and a doctoral thesis. I suppose there is bound to be a little laughter in the wings at the mere thought of this madly sensible and brilliantly obscure tome on women by Simone de Beauvoir, *The Second Sex*.

Still the more one sinks into this very long book, turning page after page, the more clearly it seems to lack a subject with reasonable limitations and concreteness, a subject on which offered illustrations may wear some air of finality and conviction. The theme of the work is that women are not simply "women," but are, like men, in the fullest sense human beings. Yet one cannot easily write the history of people! This point may appear trivial; nevertheless, to take on this glorious and fantastic book is not like reading at all—from the first to the last sentence one has the sensation of playing some breathlessly exciting and finally exhausting game. You gasp and strain and remember; you point out and deny and agree, trying always to find some way of taking hold, of confining, defining, and understanding. What is so unbearably whirling is that the author too goes through this effort to include nearly every woman and attitude that has ever existed. There is no difference of opinion, unless it be based upon a fact of which she may be ignorant, she has not thought of also. She makes her own points and all one's objections too, often in the same sentence. The effort required for this work must have been killing. No discredit to the donkey-load undertaking is meant when one imagines Simone de Beauvoir at the end may have felt like George Eliot when she said she began *Romola* as a young woman and finished it an old one. (This touching remark did not refer to the time spent in composition, but to the wrinkling weight of the task.)

I quote a sentence about the *promises* the Soviet Union made to women: "... pregnancy leaves were to be paid for by the State, which would assume charge of the children, signifying not that they would be *taken away* from their parents, but that they would not be *abandoned* to them." There is majesty here and the consolations of philosophy, perhaps also, in this instance, a bit of willful obfuscation; but that kind of strangeness occurs endlessly, showing, for purposes of argument at least, an oversensitivity to difficulties. A devastating dialogue goes on at this author's desk. After she has written, "the State, which would assume charge of the children," there is a comma pause. In that briefest of grammatical rests, voices assault her intelligence saying, "But suppose people don't want their children taken away by the State?" If all these disputing voices are admitted, one on top of the other, you are soon lost in incoherence and fantasy. Another instance: "It is understandable, in this perspective, that women take exception to masculine logic. Not only is it inapplicable to her experience, but in his hands, as she knows, masculine reasoning becomes an underhanded form of force." A few pages on: "One can bank on her credulity. Woman takes an attitude of respect and faith toward the masculine universe ..."

I take up the bewildering inclusiveness of this book, because there is hardly a thing I would want to say contrary to her thesis that Simone de Beauvoir has not said herself, including the fact, mentioned in the preface, that problems peculiar to women are not particularly pressing at the moment and that, by and large, "we have won." These acknowledgments would seem of tremendous importance, but they are a mere batting of the eye in this eternity of "oppression."

In spite of all positions being taken simultaneously, there is an unmistakable *drift* to the book. Like woman's life, *The Second Sex* is extremely repetitious and some things are repeated more often than others, although nearly every idea is repeated more than once. One is justified, then, in assuming what is repeated most often is most profoundly felt. The diction alone is startling and stabs the heart with its vigor in finding phrases of abjection and debasement. It is as though one had lived forever in that intense, shady, wretched world of *Wozzeck*, where the humor draws tears, the gaiety is fearful and children skip rope neither knowing nor caring their mother has been murdered. "Conjugal slavery, annihilation, servant, devaluation, tyranny, passive, forbidden, doomed, abused, trapped, prey, domineer, helpless, imprisoned," and so on. This immediately suggests a masochistic view of life, reinforced by the fact that for the male quite an opposite vocabulary has dug into this mind like a tick: "free, busy, active, proud, arrogant, master, existent, liberty, adventure, daring, strength, courage …"

Things being as they are, it is only fair to say that Simone de Beauvoir, in spite of her absorbing turn of phrase, miraculously does *not* give to me, at least, the impression of being a masochist, a Lesbian, a termagant, or a man-hater, and that this book is not "the self-pitying cry of one who resents being born a woman," as one American housewife-reviewer said. There is a nervous, fluent, rare aliveness on every page and the writer's more "earnest" qualities, her discipline, learning and doggedness, amount not only to themselves, that is, qualities which certainly help one to write long books, but to a kind of "charm" that ought to impress the most contented woman. This book is an accomplishment; on the other hand, if one is expecting something truly splendid and unique like *The Origins of Totalitarianism* by Hannah Arendt, to mention another woman, he will be disappointed.

The Second Sex begins with biological material showing that in nature there are not always two sexes and reproduction may take place asexually. I have noticed in the past that many books strongly presenting feminine claims begin in this manner, as if under a compulsion to veil the whole idea of sexual differentiation with a buzzing, watery mist of insect habits and unicellular forms of life. This is dramaturgy, meant to put one, after a heavy meal, in a receptive frame of mind. It is the dissonant, ambiguous music as the curtain rises on the all too familiar scene of the man at the hunt and the woman at the steaming pot; the scene looks clear enough, but the music suggests things may not be as they appear. That woman may not have to carry those screaming brats in her womb, after all, but will, if you don't watch out, simply "divide"! And the man: it is possible in the atomic age that a pin prick may fertilize the egg and then where will he be? This material is followed by curiosities from anthropology: some primitive societies thought the woman did it all alone and the man was no more important than a dish of herbs or a draft of beet juice.

These biological and anthropological matters are of enormous fascination, but often, and a bit in this present work too, a false and dramatic use is made of them: they carry a weight of mystification and intensity quite unjustified when the subject is the modern woman. They would seem to want to throw doubt upon what is not yet doubtful: the bisexual nature of human reproduction. We are relieved when the dividing amoebas and budding sponges swim out of view.

The claim of *The Second Sex* is that what we call the feminine character is an illusion and so is feminine "psychology," both in its loose meaning and in the psychoanalytical view. None of these female traits is "given"—the qualities and incapacities women have shown rather consistently in human history are simply the result of their "situation." This situation is largely the work of men, the male sex which has sought its own convenience with undeviating purpose throughout history. The female situation does not derive, at least not sufficiently to explain it, from women's natural physical and psychological difference, but has much of its origin in economics. When man developed the idea of private property, woman's destiny was "sealed." At this time women were cut off from the more adventurous activities of war, forays, explorations, to stay at home to *protect* and *maintain* what men had achieved by their far-reaching pursuits. The woman was reduced to a state of *immanence:* stagnation, the doing of repetitive tasks, concerned with the given, with maintaining, keeping, mere functioning. Man, however, is a free being, an *existent* who makes choices, decisions, has projects which are not confined to securing the present but point to the unknown future; he dares, fails, wanders, grabs, insists. By means of his activities he *transcends* his mere animal nature. What a man gives, the woman accepts; she decides nothing, changes nothing; she polishes, mends, cleans what he has invented and shaped. The man risks life, the woman merely produces it as an unavoidable function. "That is why superiority has been accorded in humanity not to the sex that brings forth but that which kills." The man imagines, discovers religions; the women worship. He has changed the earth; she arises each morning to an expectation of stove, nursing, scrubbing which has remained nearly as fixed as the course of our planets. Women continue in immanence not out of desire, but from "complicity." Having been robbed of economic independence, experience, substance, she clings unhappily because she has not been "allowed" to prepare for a different life.

Naturally, it is clear many women do not fit this theory and those who may be said to do so would not describe it in the words of Simone de Beauvoir. These persons' claims are admitted quite fully throughout the book, but always with the suggestion that the women who seem to be "existents" really aren't and those who insist they find fulfillment in the inferior role are guilty of "bad faith."

That is as it may be, but what, one asks at the beginning, about the man who, almost without exception in this work, is a creature of the greatest imagination, love of liberty, devotion to projects; ambitious, potent and disciplined, he scorns a life of mere "love," refuses to imprison himself in another's being, but looks toward the world, seeks to transcend himself, change the course of history. This is an exaggeration of course. For every Ophelia one remembers not only Cleopatra but poor Swann, unable, for all his taste and enthusiasm, to write his book on Vermeer, drowning his talent in the pursuit of pure pleasure which can only be given by the "other," Odette; for every excited Medea who gave up herself, her place, to follow the fickle man you remember not only Joan of Arc but that being of perfect, blowsy immanence, the Duke of Windsor, who abandoned the glories of a complex project for the sweet, repetitive, futureless domesticity of ocean liners and resorts. And Sartre has written a whole book on Baudelaire, a fascinating and immensely belligerent one, that claims Baudelaire resented responsibility for his own destiny, refused his possibilities of transcendence, would not make decisions, define himself, but flowed along on a tepid river of dependence, futility, refusal—like women, fond of scents and costumes, nostalgic, procrastinating, wishful.

It would seem then that men, even some "heroic" ones, often allow themselves to be what women are forced to be. But, of course, with the greatest will in the world a man cannot allow himself to be that most extremely doomed and chained being—the mother who must bear and raise children and whose figure naturally hangs over such a work as *The Second Sex* like Spanish moss. Simone de Beauvoir's opinion of the division of labor established in the Garden of Eden, if not as some believe earlier, is very striking:

> ... giving birth and suckling are not *activities*, they are natural functions; no projects are involved; and that is why woman found in them no reason for a lofty affirmation of her existence—she submitted passively to her biologic fate. The domestic cares of maternity imprisoned her in repetition and immanence; they were repeated from day to day in an identical form, which was perpetuated almost without change from century to century; they produced nothing new.

But what difference does it make that childbearing is not an activity, nor perhaps an instinct; it is a necessity.

The Second Sex is so briskly Utopian it fills one with a kind of shame and sadness, like coming upon old manifestoes and committee programs in the attic. It is bursting with an almost melancholy desire for women to take their possibilities *seriously*, to reject the given, the easy, the traditional. I do not, as most reviewers seem to, think the picture offered here of a woman's life is entirely false—a lifetime of chores is bad luck. But housework, child rearing, cleaning, keeping, nourishing, looking after—these must be done by someone, or worse by millions of someones day in and day out. In the home at least it would seem "custom" has not been so much capricious as observant in finding that women are fairly well adapted to this necessary routine. And they must keep at it whether they like it or not.

George Orwell says somewhere that reformers hate to admit nobody will do the tedious, dirty work of the world except under "some form of coercion." Mopping, ironing, peeling, feeding—it is not absurd to call this unvarying routine *slavery*, Simone de Beauvoir's word. But its necessity does not vanish by listing the tropical proliferation of open and concealed forms of coercion that may be necessary to make women do it. Bachelors are notoriously finicky, we have all observed. The dust pile is revoltingly real.

Most men, also, are doomed to work of brutalizing monotony. Hardly any intellectuals are willing to undertake a bit of this dreadful work their fellow beings must do, no matter what salary, what working conditions, what degree of "socialist dignity" might be attached to it. If artists could save a man from a lifetime of digging coal by digging it themselves one hour a week, most would refuse. Some would commit suicide. "It's not the time, it's the anticipation! It ruins the whole week! I can't even read, much less write!"

Childbearing and housekeeping may be repetitive and even intellectually stunting. Yet nothing so fills one with despair as those products of misplaced transcendent hope, those millions of stupid books, lunatic pamphlets, absurd editorials, dead canvases, and popular songs which have clogged up the sewers and ashcans of the modern world, representing more wretched labor, dreaming, madness, vanity, and waste of effort than one can bear to think of. There is an annihilating nothingness in these undertakings by comparison with which the production of one stupid, lazy, lying child is an event of some importance. Activity, transcendence, project—this is an optimistic, exhilarating vocabulary. Yet Sartre had to disown the horde of "existents" who fell to like farm hands at the table, but were not themselves able to produce so much as a carrot.

Are women "the equal" of men? This is an embarrassing subject.

Women are certainly physically inferior to men and if this were not the case the whole history of the world would be different. No comradely socialist legislation on woman's behalf could accomplish a millionth of what a bit more muscle tissue, gratuitously offered by nature, might do for this "second" being.

On the average she is shorter than the male and lighter, her skeleton is more delicate...muscular strength is much less in women...she has less respiratory capacity, the lungs and trachea being smaller...The specific gravity of the blood is lower...and there is less hemoglobin; women are therefore less robust and more disposed to anemia than are males. Their pulse is more rapid, the vascular system less stable...Instability is strikingly characteristic of woman's organization in general...In comparison with her the male seems infinitely favored.

There is a kind of poetry in this description which might move a flighty person to tears. But it goes on:

These biological considerations are extremely important...But I deny that they establish for her a fixed and inevitable destiny. They are insufficient for setting up a hierarchy of the sexes... they do not condemn her to remain in a subordinate role forever.

Why doesn't this "condemn her to remain in a subordinate role forever"? In my view this poor endowment would seem to be all the answer one needs to why women don't sail the seven seas, build bridges, conquer foreign lands, lay international cables and trudge up Mount Everest. But forgetting these daring activities, a woman's physical inferiority to a man is a limiting reality every moment of her life. Because of it women are "doomed" to situations that promise reasonable safety against the more hazardous possibilities of nature which they are too weak and easily fatigued to endure and against the stronger man. Any woman who has ever had her wrist twisted by a man recognizes a fact of nature as humbling as a cyclone to a frail tree branch. How can *anything* be more important than this? The prodigious ramifications could occupy one for an eternity. For instance:

At eighteen T. E. Lawrence took a long bicycle tour through France by himself; no young girl would be allowed to engage in any escapade, still less to adventure on foot in a half-desert and dangerous country, as Lawrence did a year later.

Simone de Beauvoir's use of "allow" is inaccurate; she stresses "permission" where so often it is really "capacity" that is involved. For a woman a solitary bicycle tour of France would be dangerous, but not impossible; Lawrence's adventure in Arabia would be suicidal and so a woman is nearly unimaginable as the author of *The Seven Pillars of Wisdom*. First of all the Arabs would rape this unfortunate female soldier or, if they had some religious or practical reason for resisting temptation, they would certainly have to leave her behind on the march, like yesterday's garbage, as the inevitable fatigue arrived. To say that physical weakness doesn't, in a tremendous number of activities, "condemn her to a subordinate role" is a mere assertion, not very convincing to the unmuscled, light breathing, nervously unstable, blushing feminine reality.

Arabian warfare is indeed an extreme situation. But what about solitary walks through the town after midnight? It is true that a woman's freedom to enjoy this simple pleasure would be greatly increased if men had no aggressive sexual feelings toward her. Like a stray dog, also weaker than men, she might roam the world at will, arousing no more notice than a few pats on the head or an irritable kick now and then. Whether such a change is possible in the interest of the weaker sex is very doubtful.

There is the notion in *The Second Sex*, and in other radical books on the subject, that if it were not for the tyranny of custom, women's sexual life would be characterized by the same aggressiveness, greed, and command as that of the male. This is by no means certain: so much seems to lead right back where we've always been. Society must, it seems, inhibit to some extent the sexuality of all human beings. It has succeeded in restraining men much less than women. Brothels, which have existed from the earliest times, are to say the least a rarity for the use of women. And yet women will patronize opium dens and are frequently alcoholic, activities wildly destructive to their home life, beauty, manners, and status and far more painful and time-consuming than having children. Apparently a lot of women are dying for dope and cocktails; nearly all are somewhat thrifty, cautious, and a little lazy about hunting sex. Is it necessarily an error that many people think licentious women are incapable of experiencing the slightest degree of sexual pleasure and are driven to their behavior by an encyclopedic curiosity to know if such a thing exists? A wreck of a man, tracking down girls in his Chevrolet, at least can do *that*! Prostitutes are famously cold; pimps, who must also suffer professional boredom, are not automatically felt to be impotent. Homosexual women, who have rebelled against their "conditioning" in the most crucial way, do not appear to "cruise" with that truly astonishing, ageless zest of male homosexuals. A pair seems to find each other sufficient. Drunken women who pick up a strange man look less interested in a sexual partner than in a companion for a drink the next morning. There is a staggering amount of evidence that points to the idea that women set a price of one kind or another on sexual intercourse; they are so often not in the mood.

This is not to say women aren't interested in sex *at all*. They clearly want a lot of it, but in the end the men of the world seem to want still more. It is only the quantity, the capacity in that sense, in which the sexes appear to differ. Women, in the language of sociology books, "fight very hard" to get the amount of sexual satisfaction they want— and even harder to keep men from forcing a superabundance their way. It is difficult to see how anyone can be sure that it is only man's voracious appetite for conquest which has created, as its contrary, this reluctant, passive being who has to be wooed, raped, bribed, begged, threatened, married, supported. Perhaps she really has to be. After she has been conquered she has to "pay" the man to restrain his appetite, which he is so likely to reveal at cocktail parties, and in his pitifully longing glance at the secretary—she pays with ironed shirts, free meals, the pleasant living room, a son.

And what about the arts—those womanish activities which are, in our day, mostly "done at home." For those who desire this form of transcendence, the other liberating activities of mankind, the office, the factory, the world of commerce, public affairs, are horrible pits where the extraordinary man is basely and casually slain.

Women have excelled in the performance arts: acting, dancing, and singing—for some reason Simone de Beauvoir treats these accomplishments as if they were usually an extension of prostitution. Women have contributed very little to the art of painting and they are clearly weak in the gift for musical composition. (Still whole nations seem without this latter gift, which may be inherited. Perhaps even nations inherit it, the male members at least. Like baldness, women may transmit the gift of musical composition but they seldom ever suffer from it.)

Literature is the art in which women have had the greatest success. But a woman needs only to think of this activity to feel her bones rattling with violent distress. Who is to say that *Remembrance of Things Past* is "better" than the marvelous *Emma*? *War and Peace* better than *Middlemarch*? *Moby-Dick* superior to *La Princesse de Clèves*? But everybody says so! It is only the whimsical, cantankerous, the eccentric critic, or those who refuse the occasion for such distinctions, who would say that any literary work by a woman, marvelous as these may be, is on a level with the very greatest accomplishments of men. Of course the *best* literature by women is superior to *most* of the work done by men and anyone who values literature at all will approach all excellence with equal enthusiasm.

The Second Sex is not whimsical about women's writing, but here again perhaps too much is made of the position in which women have been "trapped" and not enough of how "natural" and inevitable their literary limitations are. Nevertheless, the remarks on artistic women are among the most brilliant in this book. Narcissism and feelings of inferiority are, according to Simone de Beauvoir, the demons of literary women. Women want to please, "but the writer of originality, unless dead, is always shocking, scandalous; novelty disturbs and repels." Flattered to be in the world of art at all, the woman is "on her best behavior; she is afraid to disarrange, to investigate, to explode..." Women are timid and fall back on "ancient houses, sheepfolds, kitchen gardens, picturesque old folks, roguish children..." and even the best are conservative. "There are women who are mad and there are women of sound method; none has that madness in her method that we call genius."

If women's writing seems somewhat limited, I don't think it is only due to these psychological failings. Women have much less experience of life than a man, as everyone knows. But in the end are they suited to the kind of experiences men have? *Ulysses* is not just a work of genius, it is Dublin pubs, gross depravity, obscenity, brawls. Stendhal as a soldier in Napoleon's army, Tolstoy on his Cossack campaigns, Dostoevsky before the firing squad, Proust's obviously first-hand knowledge of vice, Conrad and Melville as sailors, Michelangelo's tortures on the scaffolding in the Sistine chapel, Ben Jonson's drinking bouts, dueling, his ear burnt by the authorities because of a political indiscretion in a play—these horrors and the capacity to endure them are *experience*. Experience is something more than going to law school or having the nerve to say honestly what you think in a drawing room filled with men; it is the privilege as well to endure brutality, physical torture, unimaginable sordidness, and even the privilege *to want*, like Boswell, to grab a miserable tart under Westminster Bridge. Syphilis and epilepsy—even these seem to be tragic afflictions a male writer can endure more easily than a woman. I should imagine a woman would be more depleted by epilepsy than Dostoevsky seems to have been, more ravaged by syphilis than Flaubert, more weakened by deprivation than Villon. Women live longer, safer lives than men and a man may, if he wishes, choose that life; it is hard to believe a woman could choose, like Rimbaud, to sleep in the streets of Paris at seventeen.

If you remove the physical and sexual experiences many men have made literature out of, you have carved away a great hunk of masterpieces. There is a lot left: James, Balzac, Dickens; the material in these books, perhaps not always in Balzac, is a part of women's lives too or might be "worked up"—legal practices and prison conditions in Dickens, commerce in Balzac, etc.

But the special *vigor* of James, Balzac, Dickens, or Racine, the queer, remaining strength to produce masterpiece after masterpiece—that is belittling! The careers of women of prodigious productivity, like George Sand, are marked by a great amount of failure and waste, indicating that though time was spent at the desk perhaps the supreme effort was not regularly made. Who can help but feel that *some* of James's vigor is sturdily rooted in his masculine flesh and that this repeatedly successful creativity is less likely with the "weaker sex" even in the socialist millennium. It is not suggested that muscles write books, but there is a certain sense in which, talent and experience being equal, they may be considered a bit of an advantage. In the end, it is in the matter of experience that women's disadvantage is catastrophic. It is very difficult to know how this may be extraordinarily altered.

Coquettes, mothers, prostitutes, and "minor" writers—one sees these faces, defiant or resigned, still standing at the Last Judgment. They are all a little sad, like the Chinese lyric:

> Why do I heave deep sighs?
> It is natural, a matter of course, all
> creatures have their laws.

1953

GEORGE ELIOT'S HUSBAND

SHE WAS melancholy, headachey, with a slow, disciplined, hard-won, aching genius that bore down upon her with a wondrous and exhausting force, like a great love affair in middle age. Because she was driven, worn-out, dedicated, George Eliot needed unusual care and constant encouragement; indeed she could not even begin her great career until the great person appeared to help her. Strange that it should always be said of this woman of bold strength that she "was not fitted to stand alone." She waited for help, standing in the wings, ailing, thinking and feeling—speechless. She was homely, even ugly, and perhaps that accounted for some of her thoroughness and quiet determination; she was afraid of failure and rebuff. She suffered. Who can doubt that she was profoundly passionate and romantic? You cannot read her books or study her personal history, search for her character and temperament, without feeling her passionate nature immediately. It was agony not to be able to *appeal* in a simple, feminine way. Her countenance quite spontaneously brought to mind—the horse. Virginia Woolf speaks of George Eliot's "expression of serious and sullen and almost equine power" and Henry James felt himself nearly in love with the "great, horse-faced, blue-stocking." If she did not appeal, she *impressed* overwhelmingly. Her genius, her splendid power of mind, yes, but there is something powerfully affecting about her too, the fact that it was this particular woman who had the genius and the mind. When she died Lord Acton said, "It seems to me as if the sun had gone out. You cannot imagine how much I loved her."

Nothing was easy. It was always unremitting effort, "raising herself with groans and struggles." Sometimes it seems that she is at the mercy of her intelligence; she is not an argumentative woman and likes peace and affection about her. Still she had to learn German, was compelled by an inner demon to suffer through a decision about going to church with her father; she must read Spinoza, must make up her mind about difficult matters. In an almost helpless way she cared about philosophy, politics, moral issues as other women care about clothes while often wishing they needn't. Again Virginia Woolf: "the culture, the philosophy, the fame and the influence were all built upon a very humble foundation—she was the grand-daughter of a carpenter." A great deal of the drama of this bewitching life can be found in Professor Gordon Haight's edition of the first three volumes of George Eliot's *Letters*. Haight's massive scholarship, his long and brilliant work could hardly be surpassed.

George Eliot's fame was immense; her books sold well and she made money; she was a distinguished public figure; her image and spirit were ennobling without being cold or for the few. She was solid and reassuring, of a dignity as large and splendidly detailed as her solid, deep, dignified novels. It is easy to think of Queen Victoria and some people who cherish George Eliot seem to want us to think of the old, puffy-cheeked Queen. This novelist's history has always contained an instructive moral possibility. She is seen as the supreme cultural fact demonstrating the value of sober living, earnestness, and the brisk attention to matters at hand of a reliable man with a family business. Serene, brilliant, responsible: there she stands in her paradoxically plain grandeur. As one grows older this industrious, slowly developing soul becomes dear for a secret reason—for having published her first story at the age of thirty-eight.

Still, too much is made of the respectability of a great lover. Her most daring act, the most violent assertion of self, was not the "marriage" with Lewes, but her marriage eighteen months after Lewes's death to Mr. Cross, "one many years her junior and totally unknown and obscure." Cross was probably a mistake; in all his public appearances he is firmly on the dull side. (It is astounding to learn in Haight that this man lived on until 1924—a strange old coot for the Jazz Age.) George Eliot was obviously strongly impulsive, but then many of the Victorians were troubled in spirit and indulgent in habits. Even the familiar Dickens had his love problems, Tennyson drank, and Wordsworth had an illegitimate child. George Eliot was certainly not Queen Victoria. She was pre-eminently an artist, with all the irregularity of temperament and determination to do as she pleased common among such personalities. She and her husband, Lewes not Cross, are inconceivable as anything except what they were, two writers, brilliant and utterly literary. They led the literary life from morning to midnight, working, reading, correcting proofs, traveling, entertaining, receiving and writing letters, planning literary projects, worrying, doubting their powers, experiencing a delicious hypochondria. The Brownings, the Webbs, the Garnetts, the Carlyles, Leonard and Virginia Woolf, Middleton Murry and Katherine Mansfield—the literary couple is a peculiar English domestic manufacture, useful no doubt in a country with difficult winters. Before the bright fire at tea-time, we can see these high-strung men and women clinging together, their inky fingers touching. No "partnership" was more fantastic than that of George Eliot and George Henry Lewes. They were heroic, slightly grotesque— nearly the last thing one can imagine is that these two creatures would become a public institution. Edmund Gosse describes the great pair driving home in a victoria. "The man, prematurely ageing, was hirsute, rugged, satyr-like, gazing vivaciously to left and right; this was George Henry Lewes. His companion was a large, thickset sybil, dreamy and immobile, whose massive features, somewhat grim when seen in profile, were incongruously bordered by a hat, always in the height of the Paris fashion, which in those days commonly included an immense ostrich feather; this was George Eliot. The contrast between the solemnity of the face and the frivolity of the headgear had something pathetic and provincial about it."

Her husband: George Henry Lewes. He was witty, lively, theatrical, industrious, a very conspicuous figure in London intellectual life. Lewes sometimes went about lecturing, liked to produce and act in his own plays, and was successful as an important editor. As a literary man he displayed the same animation and variety for which he was known in the drawing rooms of his friends. To give but the slimmest idea of his production one can mention farces by the titles of *Give a Dog a Bad Name* and *The Cozy Corner*, a novel called *Rose, Blanche and Violet*, a large undertaking like the *Biographical History of Philosophy*, separate lives of Robespierre and Goethe, books on the drama, innumerable articles on literature and philosophy—this husband knew all about the pains of a life of composition. Leslie Stephen speaks of Lewes as "one of the most brilliant of the literary celebrities of the time."

Lewes was not exactly the person a match-maker would seize upon as a suitable husband for George Eliot. There is a marked strain of recklessness and indiscretion in his charm; he was, as a temperament, extremely informal—Jane Carlyle called him "the Ape" and found him "the most amusing little fellow in the world." Lewes was not a handsome man, indeed he was "the ugliest man in London," according to Douglas Jerrold. George Eliot herself was somewhat put off by his unimportant appearance and had prejudice in that direction to overcome before she could entirely accept him. The impression he made was an odd one, well enough perhaps for literary circles but not up to snuff for conventional social life. "He had long hair and his dress was an unlovely compromise between morning and evening costume, combining the less pleasing points of both." Some idea of the relaxed standards of Lewes's circle when he was living with his first wife may be found in the following anecdote from Jane Carlyle: "It is Julia Paulet who has taken his [Lewes's] soul captive!! he raves about her 'dark, luxurious eyes' and 'smooth, firm flesh'—! his wife asked 'how did he know? had he been feeling it?'"

Lewes's first wife, Agnes, was beautiful, intelligent, and free-spirited in a literal and alarming way. To her children by Lewes she added two by Thornton Hunt, the son of Leigh Hunt. Lewes endured this fantastic intrusion for some time with a remarkable lack of rancor. Even after his "elopement" with George Eliot good relations were kept up on all sides. Henry James in his first visit to them found George Eliot in a state of great anxiety because one of Lewes's sons had been injured in an accident. She herself paid Agnes's allowance after Lewes died. The attitudes of everyone indicate a generous, unconventional spirit of the sort we are accustomed to find among artists and writers but would not demand of the "respectable" and especially not where matters of such overwhelming emotional charge are concerned. Still it was all very irregular and strange. Looking back at Lewes's pacific behavior, his endurance of suffering and humiliation, we can see a sort of prefiguration of the unusual position in which he later found himself. He was bright and sympathetic and yet there is an infinite longing in his lavish, humble love. As a husband Lewes discovered his wife's genius, or rather he "uncovered" it as one may, peeling off the surface inch by inch, uncover a splendid painting beneath. All this he did with excitement and delight, as if it were his own greatness he had come upon. The most haunting fact ever recorded about this odd man is from Charlotte Brontë: "the aspect of Lewes's face almost moves me to tears; it is so wonderfully like Emily's. . . ." Perhaps what Charlotte Brontë saw in "the Ape" was his wild and tender uniqueness, his inexplicable nature.

Suppose George Eliot had not become a famous novelist: what then would have happened to this marriage in which it was Lewes's role to guide, encourage, protect the most celebrated woman in England? Probably it would have been the same, although on a less grand and public stage; instead of the novelist, Lewes would have protected the diffident translator and essayist, soothed the tired editor. There is no doubt he was profoundly respectful of his chosen lady; he understood everything pained and precious in her nature, saw that striking union of dutifulness and imagination. They had, after all, been introduced by Herbert Spencer.

This grand alliance did not fail to irritate many people. A rival novelist, Eliza Linton, was furious about it. She thought their airs were impossible, their solemn importance not to be endured. Mrs. Linton had met George Eliot before the latter was famous and she says about her: "I will candidly confess my short-sighted prejudices with respect to this to-be-celebrated person. She was known to be learned, industrious, thoughtful, noteworthy; but she was not yet the Great Genius of her age, nor a philosopher bracketed with Plato and Kant, nor was her personality held to be superior to the law of the land. . . . She was essentially underbred and provincial. . . ."

Poor Mrs. Linton had reason to complain. She was not only a rival novelist but, you might say, a rival divorcée. "There were people who worshipped those two, who cut me because I separated from Linton. . . ." Envy and outrage make Mrs. Linton slyly fascinating. (One needn't fear corruption because of the impossibility of anyone succeeding in making George Eliot look foolish and small.) And sometimes Mrs. Linton sums it up perfectly. She writes, "...she had the devotion of a man whose love had in it that element of adoration and self-suppression which is dearest of all to a woman like George Eliot, at once jealous and dependent, demanding exclusive devotion and needing incessant care—but ready to give all she had in return." Also it is Mrs. Linton who has left us George Eliot gravely announcing, "I should not think of allowing George to stay away a night from me."

Leslie Stephen thinks George Eliot's powers were diminished by Lewes's efforts to shield her from criticism, to keep her in a cozy nest of approval and encouragement. But Stephen's opinion is based upon his belief that her later novels are inferior to the earlier ones. Stephen didn't much like *Middlemarch*, nor did Edmund Gosse—both preferred the early work. It is hard to feel either of these men had anything more than *respect* for George Eliot. They were formidable, learned figures, great personages themselves. Something in the Warwickshire novelist fails to attract them. They seem put off by the grandness of her reputation—it makes them uneasy, even somewhat jealous. Gosse says "we are sheep that look up to George Eliot and are not fed by her ponderous moral aphorisms and didactic ethical influence." It is Gosse's opinion that *Middlemarch* is "mechanical," it is "unimaginative satire" and "genius misapplied."

Astonishing that the truest lovers of this "ponderous" and "ethical" writer are the baroque aesthetes Proust and Henry James. And always the strange lover, Lewes, like someone from Dostoevsky taking over duties at the Priory, their house. Before his connection with George Eliot, Lewes had been mad about Jane Austen.

1955

THE NEGLECTED NOVELS OF CHRISTINA STEAD

IT IS ANNOYING to be asked to discover a book that is neither old
nor new. When it must be admitted that the work lacks, on the one
hand, the assurance of age and, on the other, a current and pressing
fame, our resistance grows and our boredom swells. We feel certain we
don't want to read a book no one else is reading or has read. The work
being offered to us appears cold and flat, like a dish passed around for
a tardy second helping. It is gratifying to our dignity to be able to turn
down the offer.

There are many roads to neglect—simple neglect itself, early and
late, is far from being the only way. Very often we find that a writer has
produced a number of books that were, on publication, well and even
enthusiastically received and yet somehow the years passed and the
reputation, the fame, the consideration did not quite take hold. The
public mind, friendly enough at first, turned out to have been but
briefly attracted; the literary mind was, at the moment, fixed upon
other points with the helplessness and passion we have all experienced,
the realization that our delight is kept in its course by some radar of
history or fashion. That there is a good deal of luck, accident, "timing"
and sheer chaos in these matters hardly anyone would deny. People
used to say they wanted to be either rich or poor, anything but shabby-
genteel, and in the same way a state of extremity is perhaps to be sought
in the arts. Attacks upon great work have very nearly the same weight
as praise—*bon chat, bon rat*. It is a painful but honorable destiny to be
laughed at, scorned as a madman, slandered as immoral or irrespon-
sible or dangerous. Even refusal, being entirely ignored, has in its own
way a certain cold and bony beauty.

The notion of a large or small masterpiece lying about unnoticed—

a Vermeer in the hayloft—has always stirred men's hearts. To be attacked or to be ignored offer at the least certain surprising possibilities for the future; the work may be dramatically discovered or excitingly defended, reclaimed. The common and lowly fate of most books is shabby gentility. They are more or less accepted, amiably received—nearly everyone is kind about effort and genial in the face of a completed task—and then they are set aside, misplaced, quietly and firmly left out, *utterly forgotten*, as the bleak phrase has it. This is the dust.

The dust seems to have settled rather quickly upon the works of Christina Stead. Her name means nothing to most people. The title of one of her novels, *House of All Nations*, occasionally causes an eye to shine with cordiality and it may be noted that good things have been heard about this book even if it is not possible to remember precisely what they are. Is it perhaps a three-decker affair by a Northern European once mentioned for the Nobel Prize? The title of her great novel, *The Man Who Loved Children*, doesn't sound reassuring either; the title is in fact, one could remark, not good enough for the book, suggesting as it does a satisfaction with commonplace ironies. (But no title could give a preview of this unusual novel.)

At the present time none of Christina Stead's work is in print. Her name never appears on a critic's or journalist's list of novelists, she is not a "well-known woman writer"; she has written about finance, about Salzburg, Washington, Australia and yet neither place nor subject seem to call her image to the critical eye. Upon inquiring about her from her last American publisher, the information came forth with a *tomba oscura* note: all they had was a *poste restante*, Lausanne, Switzerland, 1947. The facts of her biography seem to be that she is Australian, has lived all over Europe, and lived in America for some time and may still do so. She is, as they say, not in the picture, not right now at least, and therefore one cannot learn much about her past or her future. Yet when *The Man Who Loved Children* appeared in 1940, Rebecca West said on the front page of *The New York Times Book Review* that Christina Stead was "one of the few people really original we have produced since the First World War." Statements of that kind are not a rarity in the public press: the novelty of this one is that it is true. The dust, grimly, meanly collecting, has fallen upon a work of sheer astonishment and success.

The Man Who Loved Children has not been completely buried—it has a small and loyal band of friends. Yet that quaint locution is misleading, because it makes the book sound like a fine but frail old lady living in retirement and occasionally appearing for tea with the selected few. *The Man Who Loved Children* is not a small, perfect, witty book, but a large, sprawling, vigorous work marked by a novelistic, storytelling abundance, the wonderful richness of character and texture the critics are always irritably demanding. It is all this, all story and character and truth and directness, and yet it has been composed in a style of remarkable uniqueness and strength, of truly radical power and authenticity. This book is a genuine novel in the traditional meaning of the term; it is a story of life, faithfully plotted, clearly told, largely peopled with real souls, genuine problems; it is realistically set, its intention and drive are openly and fully revealed; it is also a work of absolute originality.

There has never been anyone in American literature like the great, talkative, tearful, pompous, womanish father, Samuel Clemens Pollit. Sam is a bureaucrat of the office and the home; he has one of those greedy and restless minds that takes in and chews up everything in sight, like a disposal unit attached to the sink. He expresses himself vividly and tirelessly; his conversation is a rich mash of slogans, baby talk, snatches of old songs, remembered bits of information and nonsense. His very glands secrete his own special cant, his own mixture of self-loving exuberance, sensuality, windy idealism, nature lore, and public service. Pollit works as a naturalist in Washington, D.C., in the employment of the government. Perhaps one could not seriously describe *The Man Who Loved Children* as a political novel, but in its vastly suggestive way it has something to do with Washington and with politics. It is not easy to imagine Sam Pollit in any other situation except the one he has here. His free-wheeling, fantastic talents, his active but moderately proportioned ambitions, his dignity and his moralizing fit like a glove his government-post life; a bureaucracy can use his blandly conniving and optimistic nature and assure him a well-settled if not remarkable career. Although he has some specialized knowledge, he is roundly and exhaustively general, like an encyclopedia. His wife sees him as a sort of force who has come into his career, his marriage, his self-satisfaction by the back door. He is "a mere jog-trot, subaltern bureaucrat, dragged into the service in the lowest grades without a degree, from mere practical experience in the Maryland Conservation Commission, and who owed his jealousy-creating career to her father's influence in the lobbies of the capital."

Sam Pollit's overwhelming cantish vitality is probably not a political thing in itself, but it comes from the lush underside, the slushy, rich bottom soil of the political terrain. His every sentence is a speech to his public, his family is a sort of political party to be used, fulsomely praised, and grotesquely subjected to uplifting sermons. He is literally swollen with idealistic feelings and self-love, with democratic statement and profound self-seeking. He is as fertile of lofty sentiments as he is of children. His little ones clamor about him, blushing and laughing, like an office force, working away, pretending to be playing all the while. Here is an example of Pollit's fatherly method of expressing himself to his brood:

> "This Sunday-Funday has come a long way... it's been coming to us, all day yesterday, all night from the mid-Pacific, from Peking, the Himalayas, from the fishing grounds of the old Leni Lenapes and the deeps of the drowned Susquehanna, over the pond pine ragged in the peat and the lily swamps of Anacostia, by scaffolded marbles and time-bloodied weatherboard, north-east, northwest, Washington Circle, Truxton Circle, Sheridan Circle to Rock Creek and the blunt shoulders of our Georgetown. And what does he find there this morning as every morning, in the midst of the slope, but Tohoga House, the little shanty of Gulliver Sam's Lilliputian Pollitry—Gulliver Sam, Mrs. Gulliver Henny, Lagubrious Louisa, whose head is bloody but unbowed, Ernest the calculator, Little Womey... Saul and Sam the boy-twins and Thomas-snowshoe-eye, all sun-tropes that he came galloping to see."

Henny Pollit, the sour mother of Sam's children, is a disappointed daughter of a good and prosperous Maryland family. She is always in debt, always lazy, untidy, hysterical. Although created upon the familiar lines of the disappointed and disagreeable wife, Henny seems completely without antecedents of the literary sort. She is grand and terrifying and inexplicably likeable as she mutters to herself, plays patience, swills tea all day, and screams at the children. As a mother, Henny seems to experience only the most rudimentary maternal feelings; she is as verbose as her detested husband; she is sloppy, mysterious, shabby, a convincing character made up of fantastic odds and ends, leathery grins, stained fingers, squalid lies and brutal hopes. Where Sam presents his family the fruits of his endless moralizing, his flow of nonsense, proverb and hypocrisy, Henny gives them day in and day out the hatred and insult of her heart, the chagrin, anger, poverty, ugliness, and rudeness of the world as she knows it. When she goes downtown she returns with tales of an adventure in a street car and "a dirty shrimp of a man with a fishy expression who purposely leaned over me and pressed my bust..." or outrageous descriptions of people

to whom she would give the go-by, or the cold shoulder, or a distant bow...or a polite good-day, or a black look, or a look black as thunder, and there were silly old roosters...filthy old pawers, and YMCA sick chickens...and all these wonderful creatures, who swarmed in the streets, stores, and restaurants of Washington, ogling, leering, pulling, pushing, stinking, over-scented, screaming and boasting, turning pale at the black look from Henny, ducking and diving, dodging and returning, were the only creatures that Henny ever saw.

Henny's fights with her husband are epics of insult, suffering, and sordid vitality. But there is no way of scoring a point on Sam because he is made of words and will not bleed. After a nightmare family collision he goes right on with his imitations of various accents, his horrible but somehow admirable begetting of children, his exploitation and yet honest enjoyment of these children, his reminiscences. No matter what has happened he sleeps comfortably, his bedside table littered with "pamphlets from the Carnegie Peace Foundation, scientific journals, and folders from humanitarian leagues."

The Man Who Loved Children is sordid and bitter. In it Henny commits suicide, one of the little boys shows his feeling about life by hanging himself in effigy, the stepdaughter, Louie, is worked like a horse by the entire household, Aunt Bonnie is exploited and maltreated in the same fashion. The father's oily vanity and ghastly pawings, the mother's lies and shabby dreams: such is actual material of this novel. The grim unfolding of the drama is, nevertheless, done in such a magical, abundant, inventive manner that the reading is a pleasure from beginning to end. The dialogue is realistic and plausible and at the same time humorous, original, and exciting in a way that is hardly inferior to Joyce. Sometimes the language is more nearly that of England than of America: people "post parcels," drink tea morning, noon, and night, have "elevenses," etc. Still the reader does not find these English turns objectionable—they seem merely another example of the author's incredible gift for amusing and vivid and interesting language. The real triumph of the book is Pollit. He is modern, sentimental, cruel, and as sturdy as a weed. There is no possibility of destroying him. After every disaster, he shoots back up, ready with his weedy, choking sentiments. In the end he is preparing to go on the radio with his "Uncle Sam Hour" and it is inconceivable that the adventure should fail. On the other hand, it will be the tough flowering of all Pollit's coarse reality.

The Man Who Loved Children is Christina Stead's masterpiece, but all of her work is of an unusual power. *House of All Nations* is an excellent, interesting novel, large in scale, intelligent, and splendidly detailed. In a novel like *The Salzburg Tales* one can literally say there is talent to burn, and the talent *is* burned in it. These beautifully composed tales are told by people of all sorts and nationalities who are in Salzburg to see the annual presentation of Hofmannsthal's *Everyman*. It cannot be called a complete success and yet it would have taken anyone else a lifetime to produce such a strangely gifted failure. *The Salzburg Tales* is long, stately, impressive, and unreadable. Her last novels, *For Love Alone* and *Letty Fox*, are also unusual and considerable works. It would be nearly impossible to start out with this author's prodigious talent for fiction and end up without writing something of its own peculiar force and distinction.

In the vast commerce of fame and reputation certain authors are pushed to the front of the counter like so much impatient, seasonal merchandise. It is idle to complain about this and in trying to put Christina Stead's work back on the market one need not insist that she replace anyone, even though there are some highly qualified candidates for retirement. A reminder of her existence should be advertisement enough, especially in the case of such a "genuine article."

1955

AMERICA AND DYLAN THOMAS

HE DIED, grotesquely like Valentino, with mysterious, weeping women at his bedside. His last months, his final agonies, his utterly woeful end were a sordid and spectacular drama of broken hearts, angry wives, irritable doctors, frantic bystanders, rumors and misunderstandings, neglect and murderous permissiveness. The people near him visited indignities upon themselves, upon him, upon others. There seems to have been a certain amount of competition at the bedside, assertions of obscure priority. The honors were more and more vague, confused by the ghastly, suffering needs of this broken host and by his final impersonality. No one seems to have felt his wife and children had any divine rights but that they, too, had each day to earn their place on the open market in the appalling contest of Thomas's last years. Could it have happened quite this way in England? Were his last years there quite as frenzied and unhealthy as his journeys to America? He was one of ours, in a way, and he came back here to die with a terrible and fabulous rightness. (Not ours, of course, in his talents, his work, his joys, but ours in his sufferings, his longings, his demands.) "Severe alcoholic insult to the brain," the doctors said.

Dylan Thomas was loved and respected abroad, but he was literally *adored* in America. Adored, too, with a queer note of fantasy, with a baffled extravagance that went beyond his superb accomplishments as a poet, his wit, amazing and delightful at all times, his immense abilities on the public platform. He was first-rate: one need not be ashamed to serve him or to pursue him. He was also, and perhaps this was more important to some of his admirers, doomed, damned, whatever you will, undeniably suffering and living in the extremest reaches of experience. As Eliot observed about Byron: after the theatricalism, the posing, the scandals, you had to come back to the fact that Byron was, nevertheless, genuinely disreputable. And so it was with Thomas. Behind his drinking, his bad behavior, his infidelities, his outrageousness, there was always his real doom. His condition was clearly critical. It couldn't go on much longer.

There was a certain element of drama in Thomas's readings that had nothing to do with his extraordinary powers. His story preceded him wherever he went; the perverse publicity somehow reached every town before he did and so the drama of his visit started before he arrived. Would he, first of all, really make it? (Awful if he didn't, with the tickets sold, hall hired, cocktail canapés made in advance.) Would he arrive only to break down on the stage? Would some dismaying scene take place at the faculty party? Would he be offensive, violent, obscene? These were alarming and yet exciting possibilities. Here, at last, was a poet in the grand, romantic style, a wild and inspired spirit not built for comfortable ways. He could be allowed anything. They would give him more drinks when he was dying of drink; they would let him spit in the eternal eye of the eternal head of the department, pinch the eternal faculty wife, insult the dull, the ambitious, the rich, tell obscene stories, use four-letter words. It did not make any difference. Thomas was acknowledged, unconsciously perhaps, to be beyond judgment, to be already living a tragic biography, nearing some certain fatality.

And he could make all the passes he chose, have all the love affairs, since the unspoken admission always was that he was doomed, profoundly ill, living as a character in a book, and his true love, beyond all others at this time, was alcohol. Yet so powerful and beguiling was his image—the image of a self-destroying, dying young poet of genius—that he aroused the most sacrificial longings in women. He had lost his looks, he was disorganized to a degree beyond belief, he had a wife and children in genuine need, and yet young ladies *felt* they had fallen in love with him. They fought over him; they nursed him while he retched and suffered and had delirium; they stayed up all night with him and yet went to their jobs the next morning. One girl bought cowboy suits for his children. Enormous mental, moral and physical adjustments were necessary to those who would be the companions of this restless, frantic man. The girls were up to it—it was not a hardship, but a privilege.

Apparently no one felt envious of Thomas or bitter about the attention he received. Even here he was an interesting exception. The explanation for the generosity lay first of all in the beauty and importance of his verse: this circumstance was the plain ground from which the elaborate and peculiar flowering of Thomas's American experience sprang. The madness of the infatuated is, after all, just an exaggeration of the reasonable assent of the discriminating. And so Thomas's personal greatness began it all, and the urgency of his drinking, his uncontrollable destructiveness seemed to add what was needed beyond his talents. He was both a success and a failure in a way we find particularly appealing. What he represented in the vividness of his success and failure was real and of irresistible power to certain art-conscious Americans. He had everything and "threw it all away." In him sophisticated schoolteachers, bright young girls, restless wives, bohemians, patrons and patronesses, found a poet they could love. He was not conservative, not snobbish, not middle-class, not alarmingly intellectual; he was a wild genius who needed caring for. And he was in a pattern we can recognize all too easily—the charming young man of great gifts, willfully going down to ruin. He was Hart Crane, Poe, F. Scott Fitzgerald, the stuff of which history is made, and also, unexpectedly, something of a great actor; indeed he was actually a great actor in a time when the literary style runs to the scholarly and the clerical. He satisfied a longing for the extreme. He was incorrigible and you never knew what he might do. He was fantastically picturesque. His Anglo-Welsh accent delighted everyone who heard it. Every college girl had her Dylan Thomas anecdote and it was usually scandalous, since he had a pronounced gift for that. His fees were exceeded only by the Sitwells, *tous les deux*, and by Eliot. His drinking had made him, at least superficially, as available as a man running for office. Everyone knew him, heard him, drank with him, nursed him. He was both immoderately available and, in the deepest sense, utterly unavailable too. His extraordinary gregariousness was a sign of his extremity. He knew everyone in the world, but for a long time he had perhaps been unable to know anyone. Oddly enough, at the end Thomas was more "fashionable" than he had ever been in his happier days. Even excess, carried off with so great a degree of authenticity and compulsiveness, has a kind of *chic*.

John Malcolm Brinnin's book, *Dylan Thomas in America*, has been praised by some critics, but many others have felt a good deal of moral annoyance about the work. They have found Brinnin a false friend, and they have decided his material might better have gone unpublished. Yet, it seems unfair to accuse Brinnin of treachery or of commercial exploitation of his friendship with Thomas—the most astonishing aspect of his record is just the wild and limitless nature of his devotion to his subject. It has, at times, almost the character of an hallucination.

"The sharpest scrutiny is the condition of enduring fame," Froude said as he set out to tell all he knew about Carlyle. This is the dominion of history and scholarship. But Brinnin's book does not seem to be a product of the historical impulse as we usually think of it. His journal is truly an obsessive document and is most unusual for that reason. It is not easy to think of anything else quite like it, anything one might justly compare it with. His commitment to his subject is of such an overwhelming degree that he cannot leave out anything. He treats Dylan Thomas as a great force of nature and would no more omit an infidelity or a hang-over than a weatherman would suppress the news of an ugly storm. In certain respects, the book is not a piece of composition at all, but is rather the living moment with its repetitions, its naïveté, its peculiar acceptance of and compulsive attachment to every detail of Thomas's sad existence. It is as flat and true as a calendar. As a record, it is oddly open and marked by a helpless, uncomfortable fascination on Brinnin's part. For him Thomas was an addiction. Having once taken on the friendship, Brinnin was trapped, spell-bound, enlisted in a peculiar mission. Here are sentences from the early pages of the journal which tell of Thomas's first American visit:

> He slept, breathing heavily, as I fingered through some English magazines he had brought with him, and watched the early lights

of Manhattan come on through the sleet. As I contemplated Dylan's deep sleep, I tried first to comprehend and then to accept the quality (it was too early to know the dimensions) of my assignment...no one term would serve to define a relationship which had overwhelmed my expectations and already forced upon me a personal concern that was constantly puzzled, increasingly solicitous and, I knew well by now, impossible to escape.

Although Brinnin was the business agent for Thomas's American performances, his presence is due, not to business concerns, but to the notion of a mysterious and compelling destiny, a fatigued and yet somehow compulsory attendance. The "too late now to turn back" theme is heard again and again. "I knew that, above all now, I wanted to take care of him....Just as certainly, I knew that I wanted to get rid of him, to save myself from having to be party to his self-devouring miseries and to forestall any further waiting upon his inevitable collapses." Reading such passages, you are reminded of the fatal commitments in Poe's work, of those nightmares of the irresistible and irrational involvement. Even Thomas's first visit was anticipated by Brinnin as a gloomy necessity; he approached the arrival with a painful and helpless alarm, and yet with a feeling of the inevitable. The commitment was of a quality impossible to analyze. It went beyond any joy that might or might not be found in Thomas's company, beyond mutual interests and personal affinity. It was so deep and so compelling that despair was its natural mood. Because of the fabulous difficulty of Thomas's character, this mood of despair seems more appropriate than the carousing, robust tone some others fall into when they talk of Thomas. In Brinnin's book it is always, in feeling at least, the dead, anguished middle of a drunken night. The despair, the wonder and the helplessness start the book and lead up to the grim, apoplectic end. There is no pretense that it was fun. It was maddening, exhausting, but there it was. And after Thomas died there was no release from the strain because the book had to be written, fulfilled with the same dogged, tired fascination the author felt in the case of the actual events. The self-effacement of the style seems a carry-over from the manner one adopts when he sits, sober, exhausted and anxious, with a drunken friend whose outbursts and ravings one is afraid of. The lists of guests at a party, the lecture dates, the financial details—the reader takes these in nervously, flatly, with the sense of a strange duty being honored. The girls, the quarrels, the summers and winters, the retchings, the humiliations, the heights and the depths—they are all presented in the same gray, aching tone. The writing of the book seems to have been the same sort of hallucinated task as the planning of the lecture tours. There is a unique concentration upon the elemental, upon how much Thomas slept, how much he could be made to eat, upon the momentary predicaments. Of character analysis or literary analysis, there is very little. This is the terrifying breath of life, but of a life without words. "He was ill and downcast again in the morning...." "We broke our trip to Connecticut by a stop in Sturbridge, to drink ale before the wood-burning fireplace of an old inn, and arrived at the University just in time to spend an informal hour with the fourteen students of my graduate seminar." To spend *an hour* with the *fourteen* students! One does not know what to make of the inclusion of so much fact and figure. Thomas's conversation, so rare and beautiful, is not captured at all. The record is of another kind. It is certainly bemused and depressed and yet it is outlandishly successful as a picture of the prosaic circumstances of some months in a dramatic life.

Near the end: "There he ate an enormous dinner—a dinner which, in the course of events, was to be his last full meal." Dylan Thomas died in St. Vincent's Hospital in New York City. His death was miserable and before he passed into the final coma he had delirium tremens, horrors, agonies, desire for death, and nearly every physical and mental pain one can imagine. Brinnin does not try to render the great denouement, but again it is, in an odd and indefinable fashion, rendered by the dazed and peculiarly accurate and endless detail. "His face was wan and expressionless, his eyes half-opening for moments at a time, his body inert." The actual death: "Dylan was pale and blue, his eyes no longer blindly searching but calm, shut, and ineffably at peace. When I took his feet in my hand all warmth was gone...." The final line of the record does fly upward in intention, but it is more clumsy, more earthbound than all of the repetitive detail of all the thousands of preceding lines and it does not even seem true. "Now, as always, where Dylan was, there were no tears at all."

Could it have happened quite this way in England? It is an unhappy circumstance for us that Thomas should have died here, far from his family, far from the scenes he had lived in and written about. The maniacal permissiveness and submissiveness of American friends might, for all we know, have actually shortened Thomas's life, although he was ill and driven in England too. But there was a certain amount of poison in our good will. In the acceptance of his tragic condition there was a good deal of indifference and self-deception. The puzzling contentiousness of his friends and the ugly competition for his favors remain coldly in our minds. According to Brinnin, Thomas made these frantic flights to America because of his "conviction that his creative powers were failing, that his great work was finished." He feared he was "without the creative resources to maintain and expand his position." The financial benefit was destroyed by the familiar condition of our economic life: he spent every penny he made just as soon as he had it in his hands. His wife and his mother wanted him to stay at home *in order* to earn a living for his family. Furthermore Caitlin Thomas felt he had been "spoiled" in America, that he came here for "flattery, idleness and infidelity." Perhaps one shouldn't read too much between the lines, but it is hard not to get the idea that Thomas's American friends, with a cynical show of piety, treated these accusations and feelings as outrageous. They, sinking sensuously into their own suspicious pity, flattered and allowed and encouraged right to the brink of the grave.

In England we have Brinnin's own observation that the deference shown to Thomas was of a quieter, less unreal and unbalancing sort. It might almost have passed for a lack of interest. In a London pub with Thomas, Brinnin was impressed that the poet was, for once, "not the object of everyone's attention." Here in America the approbation was extreme, the notice sometimes hysterical, the pace killing. The cost of these trips was "disproportionate to the rewards." The trip before the last one was felt to be "too exhausting to contemplate," and still it was not only contemplated, it was arranged, it happened, and was followed by an unbelievable another, the last of the three. In these tours Thomas seems like nothing so much as a man in the films, addressing the audience cheerfully, but with a gun in his back. It was a ghastly affair, preserved faithfully and grimly by Brinnin. There is an element in this story of ritual and fantasy, a phantasmagoria of pain and splendor, of talent and untimely death. And there is something else: the sober and dreary fact of the decline of our literary life, its thinness and fatigue. From this Thomas was, to many, a brief reprieve.

1956

THE DECLINE OF BOOK REVIEWING

THERE used to be the notion that Keats was killed by a bad review, that in despair and hopelessness he turned his back to the wall and gave up the struggle against tuberculosis. Later evidence has shown that Keats took his hostile reviews with a considerably more manly calm than we were taught in school, and yet the image of the young, rare talent cut down by venomous reviewers remains firmly fixed in the public mind.

The reviewer and critic are still thought of as persons of dangerous acerbity, fickle demons, cruel to youth and blind to new work, bent upon turning the literate public away from freshness and importance out of jealousy, mean conservatism, or whatever. Poor Keats were he living today might suffer a literary death, but it would not be from attack; instead he might choke on what Emerson called a "mush of concession." In America, now, oblivion, literary failure, obscurity, neglect—all the great moments of artistic tragedy and misunderstand-ing—still occur, but the natural conditions for the occurrence are in a curious state of camouflage, like those decorating ideas in which wood is painted to look like paper and paper to look like wood. A genius may indeed go to his grave unread, but he will hardly have gone to it unpraised. Sweet, bland commendations fall everywhere upon the scene; a universal, if somewhat lobotomized, accommodation reigns. A book is born into a puddle of treacle; the brine of hostile criticism is only a memory. Everyone is found to have "filled a need," and is to be "thanked" for something and to be excused for "minor faults in an otherwise excellent work." "A thoroughly mature artist" appears many times a week and often daily; many are the bringers of those "messages the Free World will ignore at its peril."

The condition of popular reviewing has become so listless, the effect of its agreeable judgments so enervating to the general reading public that the sly publishers of *Lolita* have tried to stimulate sales by quoting *bad* reviews along with, to be sure, the usual, repetitive good ones. (Orville Prescott: *"Lolita* is undeniably news in the world of books. Unfortunately it is bad news." And Gilbert Highet: "I am sorry that *Lolita* was ever published. I am sorry it was ever written.")

It is not merely the praise of everything in sight—a special problem in itself—that vexes and confounds those who look closely at the literary scene, but there is also the unaccountable sluggishness of *The New York Times* and *Herald Tribune* Sunday book-review sections. The value and importance of individual books are dizzily inflated, in keeping with the American mood at the moment, but the book-review sections as a cultural enterprise are, like a pocket of unemployment, in a state of baneful depression insofar as liveliness and interest are concerned. One had not thought they could go downward, since they have always been modest, rather conventional journals. Still, there had been room for a decline in the last few years and the opportunity has been taken. A Sunday morning with the book reviews is often a dismal experience. It is best to be in a state of distracted tolerance when one takes up, particularly, *The Herald Tribune Book Review.* This publication is not just somewhat mediocre; it has also a strange, perplexing inadequacy as it dimly comes forth week after week.

For the world of books, for readers and writers, the torpor of *The New York Times Book Review* is more affecting. There come to mind all those high-school English teachers, those faithful librarians and booksellers, those trusting suburbanites, those bright young men and women in the provinces, all those who believe in the judgment of the *Times* and who need its direction. The worst result of its decline is that it acts as a sort of hidden dissuader, gently, blandly, respectfully denying whatever vivacious interest there might be in books or in literary matters generally. The flat praise and the faint dissension, the minimal style and the light little article, the absence of involvement, passion, character, eccentricity—the lack, at last, of the literary tone itself—have made *The New York Times* into a provincial literary journal, longer and thicker, but not much different in the end from all those small-town Sunday "Book Pages." (*The New Yorker, Harper's, The Atlantic,* the news and opinion weeklies, the literary magazines all devote a good deal of space and thought to the reviewing of books. The often awkward and the always variable results should not go unremarked. However, in these magazines the reviews are only a part of the claim upon the reader's attention, and the peculiar disappointments of the manner in which books are sometimes treated cannot be understood without a close study of each magazine as a whole.)

"COVERAGE" THAT KILLS

It is with dismay that one decides the malaise of the popular reviewing publications—the *Times* and *Tribune* and the *Saturday Review*—is not always to be laid at the door of commerce. It had been simple and reassuring to believe the pressure of book publishers and booksellers accounted for the hospitable reception of trashy novels, commonplace "think" books, and so on. The publishers needed favorable reviews to use for the display of their product, as an Easter basket needs shredded green paper under the eggs. No one thought the pressure was simple and direct; it was imagined to be subtle, practical, basic, that is, having to do with the fact that the advertisements of the publishing business keep the book-review sections going financially. This explanation has, naturally, had an exaggerated acceptance.

The truth is, one imagines, that the publishers—seeing their best and their least products received with a uniform equanimity—must be aware that the drama of the book world is being slowly, painlessly killed. Everything is somehow alike, whether it be a routine work of history by a respectable academic, a group of platitudes from the Pentagon, a volume of verse, a work of radical ideas, a work of conservative ideas. Simple "coverage" seems to have won out over the drama of opinion; "readability," a cozy little word, has taken the place of the old-fashioned requirement of a good, clear prose style, which is something else. All differences of excellence, of position, of form are blurred by the slumberous acceptance. The blur erases good and bad alike, the conventional and the odd, so that it finally appears that the author like the reviewer really does not have a position. The reviewer's grace falls upon the rich and the poor alike; a work which is going to be a best seller, in which the publishers have sunk their fortune, is commended only at greater length than the book from which the publishers hardly expect to break even. In this fashion there is a sort of democratic euphoria that may do the light book a service but will hardly meet the needs of a serious work. When a book is rebuked, the rebuke is usually nothing more than a quick little jab with the needle, administered in the midst of therapeutic compliments. "—— is sometimes self-consciously arch," said one review. "But it contains enough of ——'s famous wit and style to make American publication worthwhile...."

The editors of the reviewing publications no longer seem to be engaged in literature. Books pile up, out they go, and in comes the review. Many distinguished minds give their names to various long and short articles in the *Times, Tribune,* and *Saturday Review.* The wares offered by the better writers are apt, frequently, to be something less than their best. Having awakened to so many gloomy Sundays, they accept their assignments in a co-operative spirit and return a "readable" piece, nothing much, of course. (Alice James wrote in her diary that her brother, Henry, was asked to write for the popular press and assured he could do anything he pleased "so long as there's nothing literary in it.")

The retention of certain disgruntled, repetitive commentators is alone enough to dispute notions of crude commercialism on the part of the reviewing publications. A businesslike editor, a "growing" organization—such as we are always reading about in the press—would have assessed the protests, if any, and put these fumbling minds out to pasture. For instance, what could be more tiresome than J. Donald Adams's attacks on poor Lionel Trilling for trying to be interesting on Robert Frost? Only another attack on Adams, perhaps—who is, like the pressure of commerce, hardly the real trouble with the *Times.* Adams is like one of those public monuments only a stranger or someone who has been away for a while takes notice of. What is truly dismaying about the *Times* and *Tribune* is the quality of the editing.

Recently a small magazine called *The Fifties* published an interview with the editor-in-chief of *The New York Times Book Review,* Mr. Francis Brown. Mr. Brown appears in this exchange as a man with considerable editorial experience in general and very little "feel" for the particular work to which he has been appointed, that is editor of the powerfully important weekly *Book Review.* He, sadly, nowhere in the interview shows a vivid interest or even a sophistication about literary matters, the world of books and writers—the very least necessary for his position. His approach is modest, naïve, and curiously spiritless. In college, he tells us in the interview, he majored in history and subsequently became general editor of *Current History.* Later he went to *Time,* where he had "nothing to do with books," and at last he was chosen to "take a crack at the *Book Review.*" The interviewer, hinting at some of the defects of the *Book Review,* wondered if there wasn't too much reliance on specialists, a too frequent practice of giving a book to a reviewer who had written a book like it, or about the same country or the same period. Mr. Brown felt that "a field was a field." When asked to compare our *Times Book Review* with *The Times Literary Supplement* in London, Brown opined, "They have a narrow audience and we have a wide one. I think in fiction they are doing the worst of any reputable publication."

This is an astonishing opinion to anyone who has followed the reviews in the London *Times* and the other English reviewing papers, such as the Sunday *Times* and *The Observer.* These papers consistently set a standard intrinsically so much higher than ours that detailed comparison is almost impossible. It is not simply what may turn up in an individual review; it is profoundly a matter of the tone, the seriousness, the independence of mind and temperament. Richard Blackmur in a recent article tells of a conversation with the editor of *The Times Literary Supplement* who felt that the trouble with the American book reviews was just this lack of a strong, independent editorial direction and who ventured that very few publishers would withdraw their advertising because of the disappearance of the bland product being put out at the moment. A description of *The Times Literary Supplement,* the London publication, by Dwight Macdonald finds that the English paper "seems to be edited and read by people who know who they are and what interests them. That the vast majority of their fellow citizens do not share their interest in the development of English prose, the bibliography of Byelorussia, André Gide's treatment of his wife, the precise relation of folksong and plainsong, and 'the large blot' in a letter of Dr. Johnson's which has given much trouble to several of his editors... this seems not in any way to trouble them."

REVIEWING AS WRITING

Invariably right opinion is not the only judge of a critic's powers, although a taste that goes wrong frequently is only allowed to the greatest minds! In any case, it all depends upon who is right and who is wrong. The communication of the delight and importance of books, ideas, culture itself, is the very least one would expect from a journal devoted to reviewing of new and old works. Beyond that beginning, the interest of the mind of the individual reviewer is everything. Book reviewing is a form of writing. We don't pick up the Sunday *Times* to find out what Mr. Smith thinks of, for instance. *Dr. Zhivago.* (It would very likely be *Mrs.* Smith in the *Herald Tribune.)* As the saying goes, what do you have when you find out what Mr. Smith thinks of *Dr. Zhivago*? It *does* matter what an unusual mind, capable of presenting fresh ideas in a vivid and original and interesting manner, thinks of books as they appear. For sheer information, a somewhat expanded publisher's list would do just as well as a good many of the reviews that appear weekly.

In a study of book reviewing done at Wayne University, we find that our old faithful, the eternally "favorable review," holds his own with all the stamina we have learned to expect. Fifty-one percent of the reviews summarized in *Book Review Digest* in 1956 were favorable. A much more interesting figure is that 44.8 percent were *non-committal*! The bare meaning of "review" would strongly incline most people to the production of an opinion of some sort and so the reluctance of the non-committal reviewers to perform is a fact of great perplexity. The unfavorable reviews number 4.7 percent.

ONE SUNDAY

A Sunday some months ago in *The Herald Tribune*. The following are excerpts from five reviews of current novels, reviews that sadly call to mind a teen-age theme.

(1) "The real value of the novel lies in its awareness of character, the essential personality, and the subtle effect of time."

(2) "Occasionally some of the workings of the story seem contrived, but this is only a first impression, for foremost of all is the recreation of an atmosphere which is so strong that it dictates a destiny."

(3) "Miss —— writes well, telling the story with a matter-of-factness and vividness that help to carry the strangeness of her central theme. For a reader who relishes a touch of the macabre, it is an intriguing exploration of the imagination."

(4) "——, however, is an interesting and swiftly moving book; more complicated than most of its kind, and with subtler shading to its characters. It makes good reading."

(5) "It is also, within the framework —— has set for himself, a warm, continuously interesting story of what can happen to a group of ordinary people in a perilous situation, a situation, incidentally, at least as likely as the one Nevil Shute postulates in 'On the Beach.'"

("The one Nevil Shute postulates in 'On the Beach'"—the assurance of this phrase would give many a reader a pause, reminding us, as it does, that there are all kinds of examples of what is called "obscurity of reference.")

About the *Saturday Review,* one feels more and more that it is not happy in its job. It is moody, like an actress looking for the right role in order to hit the big time. "Of Literature" has been dropped from the title, an excision the miscellaneous contents of the magazine soundly justifies. The search for feature ideas is as energetic as that of any national magazine; the editors are frantically trying to keep up with the times. With the huge increase in phonograph-record sales, the music departments have absorbed more and more space in the journal. Travel, in all its manifestations, has become an important concern—travel books, travel advice, guides to nearly as many events as *Cue* tries to handle. Even this is not enough. There are Racing Car issues and *SR* Goes to the Kitchen. Extraordinary promotion ideas occur to the staff, such as the *Saturday Review* Annual Advertising Award. Lines from an article on this topic read:

> Because *Saturday Review* is continually concerned with the communications pattern in the United States, it has observed with deep interest the progressive development of advertising as a medium of idea communication, a much more subtle skill even than the communication of news.

The cover may "feature" a photograph of Joanne Woodward and recently in an issue that featured Max Eastman's written ideas on Hemingway, not Eastman, but Hemingway, wearing a turtle-neck sweater, gazed from the cover in a "photo-portrait." The book reviews, the long and the short articles, in *Saturday Review* are neither better nor worse than those of the *Times*; they are marked by the same lack of strenuous effort. They obviously have their audience in mind—one, it is believed, that will take only so much.

EDITORS' WISHES

Literary journalism reaches, in the case of a good many writers, such levels of vitality and importance and delight that the excuse of the fleeting moment, the pressure of time, the needs of a large public cannot be accepted, as the editors would have us do. Orville Prescott of the daily *Times*—is he to be accounted a casualty of speed? Is what is wanting in this critic simply time to write, a month rather than a few days? Time would no doubt produce a longer Orville Prescott review, but that it would produce a more constant inspiration is open to doubt. Richard Rovere mentioned somewhere recently the fact that he could find, today, great fascination in reading some casual article done by Edmund Wilson in 1924 for *Vanity Fair* or *The New Republic*. The longer essays Wilson has done in recent years on whatever topic engages his mind are literary works one could hardly expect regularly or even rarely in the *Times, Tribune,* or *Saturday Review.* Still, his earlier reviews are the sort of high possibility an editor would, or so one imagines, have in mind. Nothing matters more than the kind of thing the editor would like if he could have his wish. Editorial wishes always partly come true. Does the editor of the *Times Book Review* really yearn for a superb writer like V. S. Pritchett, who *does* write almost weekly short pieces in *The New Statesman* with a week after week brilliance that astonishes everyone? Pritchett is just as good on "The James Dean Myth" or Ring Lardner as he is on the Russian novel. Is this the kind of thing our journals hope for, or is it a light little piece by, say, Elizabeth Janeway on "Caught between books"? It is typical of the editorial mind of the *Times* that it most frequently assigns Pritchett to write a casual, light London letter, work of insignificant journalism, which makes little use of his unique talents for writing book reviews.

In the end it is publicity that sells books and book reviews are only, at their most, the great toe of the giant. For some recurrent best sellers like Frances Parkinson Keyes and Frank Yerby the readers would no more ask for a good review before giving their approval and their money than a parent would insist upon public acceptance before giving his new baby a kiss. The book publishing and selling business is a very complicated one. Think of those publishers in businesslike pursuit of the erotic novel who would, we can be sure, have turned down *Lolita* as not the right kind of sex. It is easy enough, once the commercial success of a book is an established fact, to work out a convincing reason for the public's enthusiasm. But, before the fact has happened, the business is mysterious, chancy, unpredictable.

For instance, it has been estimated that the reviews in *Time* magazine have the largest number of readers, possibly nearly five million each week, and it has also been suggested that many publishers feel that the reviews in *Time* do not affect the sales of a book one way or another! In the face of this mystery, some publishers have concluded that *Time* readers, having learned *Time*'s opinion of a book, feel that they have somehow already read the book, or if not quite that, if not read, at least taken it in, *experienced* it as a "fact of our time." They feel no more need to buy the thing itself than to go to Washington for a firsthand look at the latest works of the Republican Administration.

In a world like that of books where all is angular and unmanageable, there hardly seems to be any true need for these busy hands working to shape it all into a small, fat ball of weekly butter. The adaptable reviewer, the placid, superficial commentator might reasonably survive in local newspapers. But, for the great metropolitan publications, the unusual, the difficult, the lengthy, the intransigent, and above all, the *interesting*, should expect to find their audience.

1959

BOSTON

WITH BOSTON and its mysteriously enduring reputation, "the re-verberation is longer than the thunderclap," as Emerson observed about the tenacious fame of certain artists. Boston—wrinkled, spindly-legged, depleted of nearly all her spiritual and cutaneous oils, provincial, self-esteeming—has gone on spending and spending her inflated bills of pure reputation, decade after decade. Now, one supposes it is all over at last. The old jokes embarrass, the anecdotes are so many thrice-squeezed lemons, and no new fruit hangs on the boughs. All the American regions are breaking up, ground down to a standard American corn meal. And why not Boston, which would have been the most difficult to maintain? There has never been anything quite like Boston as a creation of the American imagination, or perhaps one should say as a creation of the American scene. Some of the legend was once real, surely. Our utilitarian, fluid landscape has produced a handful of regional conceptions, popular images, brief and naked: the conservative Vermonter, the boastful Texan, the honeyed Southerner. "Graciousness is ours," brays a coarsened South; and the sheiks of Texas cruise around their desert.

The Boston image is more complex. The city is felt to have, in the end, a pure and special nature, absurd no doubt but somehow valuable. Empiricism will not carry one far; faith and *being*, sheer being above all, are needed. To be it, old Boston, real Boston, very Boston, and—one shrinks before the claim—proper Boston; there lies knowledge. An author can hardly fail to turn a penny or two on this magical subject. Everyone will consent to be informed on it, to be slyly entertained by it. *Actual* Boston is governed largely by people of Irish descent and more and more, recently, by men of Italian descent. Not long ago, the old Yankee, Sentor Saltonstall, remarked wistfully that there were still a good many Anglo-Saxons in Massachusetts, his own family among them. Extinction is foreshadowed in the defense.

Plainness and pretension restlessly feuding and combining; wealth and respectability and firmness of character ending in the production of a number of diverting individual tics or, at the best, instances of high culture—something of that sort is the legendary Boston soul or so one supposes without full confidence because the old citizens of Boston vehemently hold to the notion that the city and their character are ineffable, unknowable. When asked for an opinion on the admirable novel, *Boston Adventure*, or even the light social history, *The Proper Bostonian*, the answer invariably comes, "Not Boston." The descriptive intelligence, the speculative mind, the fresh or even the merely open eye are felt to discover nothing but errors here, be they errors of praise or censure. Still, wrong-headedness flourishes, the subject fascinates, and the Athenaeum's list of written productions on this topic is nearly endless.

The best book on Boston is Henry James's novel, *The Bostonians*. By the bald and bold use of the place name, the unity of situation and person is dramatized. But poor James, of course, was roundly and importantly informed by everyone, including his brother William, that this too was "not Boston." Stricken, he pushed aside a superb creation, and left the impregnable, unfathomable Boston to its mysteries. James's attitude toward the city's intellectual consequence and social charm is one of absolute impiety. A view of the Charles River reveals, "...an horizon indented at empty intervals with wooden spires, the masts of lonely boats, the chimneys of dirty 'works,' over a brackish expanse of anomalous character, which is too big for a river and too small for a bay." A certain house has "a peculiar look of being both new and faded—a kind of modern fatigue—like certain articles of commerce which are sold at a reduction as shopworn." However, there is little natural landscape in James's novel. The picture is, rather, of the psychological Boston of the 1870s, a confused scene, slightly mad with neurotic repressions, provincialism, and earnestness without intellectual seriousness.

James's view of Boston is not the usual one, although his irony and dissatisfaction are shared by Henry Adams, who says that "a simpler manner of life and thought could hardly exist, short of cave-dwelling," and by Santayana who spoke of Boston as a "moral and intellectual nursery, always busy applying first principles to trifles." The great majority of the writings on Boston are in another spirit altogether—they are frankly unctuous, for the town has always attracted men of quiet and timid and tasteful opinion, men interested in old families and things, in the charms of times recently past, collectors of anecdotes about those Boston worthies hardly anyone can still clearly identify, men who spoke and preached and whose fame deteriorated quickly. Rufus Choate, Dr. Channing, Edward Everett Hale, Phillips Brooks, and Theodore Parker: names that remain in one's mind, without producing an image or a fact, as the marks are left on the wall after the picture has been removed. William Dean Howells held a more usual view than Henry James or Adams or Santayana. Indeed Howells's original enthusiasm for garden and edifice, person and setting, is more than a little *exalté.* The first sight of the Chapel at Mount Auburn Cemetery moved him more than the "Acropolis, Westminster Abbey, and Santa Croce in one." The massive gray stones of "the Public Library and the Athenaeum are hardly eclipsed by the Vatican and the Pitti." And so on.

The importance of Boston was intellectual and as its intellectual donations to the country have diminished, so it has declined from its lofty symbolic meaning, to become a more lowly image, a sort of farce of conservative exclusiveness and snobbish humor. Marquand's George Apley is a figure of the decline—fussy, sentimental, farcically mannered, archaic. He cannot be imagined as an Abolitionist, an author, a speaker; he is merely a "character." The old Boston had something of the spirit of Bloomsbury: it was clannish, worldly, and intellectually alive. About the historian, Prescott, Van Wyck Brooks could say, "... for at least ten years, Prescott had been hard at work, harder, perhaps, than any Boston merchant."

History, indeed, with its long, leisurely, gentlemanly labors, the books arriving by post, the cards to be kept and filed, the sections to be copied, the documents to be checked, is the ideal pursuit for the New England mind. All the Adamses spent a good deal of their lives on one kind of history or another. The eccentricity, studiousness, and study-window slow pace of life of the historical gentleman lay every-where about the Boston scene. For money, society, fashion, extravagance, one went to New York. But now, the descendants of the old, intellectual aristocracy live in the respectable suburbs and lead the healthy, restless, outdoor life that atrophies the sedentary nerves of culture. The blue-stocking, the eccentric, the intransigent bring a blush of uncertainty and embarrassment to the healthy young couple's cheek.

Boston today can still provide a fairly stimulating atmosphere for the banker, the broker, for doctors and lawyers. "Open end" investments prosper, the fish come in at the dock, the wool market continues, and workers are employed in the shoe factories in the nearby towns. For the engineer, the physicist, the industrial designer, for all the highly trained specialists of the electronic age, Boston and its area are of seemingly unlimited promise. Sleek, well-designed factories and research centers pop up everywhere; the companies plead, in the Sunday papers, for more chemists, more engineers, and humbly relate the executive benefits of salary and pension and advancement they are prepared to offer.

But otherwise, for the artist, the architect, the composer, the writer, the philosopher, the historian, for those humane pursuits for which the town was once noted and even for the delights of entertainment, for dancing, acting, cooking, Boston is a bewildering place. There is, first of all, the question of Boston or New York. (The question is not new; indeed it was answered in the last decades of the last century in favor of New York as the cultural center of America.) It is, in our day, only a private and personal question: where or which of the two East-ern cities should one try to live and work in? It is a one-sided problem. For the New Yorker, San Francisco or Florida, perhaps—Boston, never. In Boston, New York tantalizes; one of the advantages of Boston is said, wistfully, to be its nearness to New York. It is a bad sign when a man, who has come to Boston or Cambridge, Massachusetts, from another place begins to show an undivided acceptance of his new town. Smugness is the great vice of the two places. Between puffy self-satis-faction and the fatiguing wonder if one wouldn't be happier, more productive, more appreciated in New York, a thoughtful man makes his choice.

Boston is not a small New York, as they say a child is not a small adult but is, rather, a specially organized small creature with its small-creature's temperature, balance, and distribution of fat. In Boston there is an utter absence of that wild electric beauty of New York, of the marvelous excited rush of people in taxicabs at twilight, of the great Avenues and Streets, the restaurants, theaters, bars, hotels, delicatessens, shops. In Boston the night comes down with an incredibly heavy, small-town finality. The cows come home; the chickens go to roost; the meadow is dark. Nearly every Bostonian is in his own house or in someone else's house, dining at the home board, enjoying domestic and social privacy. The "nice little dinner party"—for this the Bostonian would sell his soul. In the evenings, the old "accommodators" dart about the city, carrying their black uniforms and white aprons in a paper bag. They are on call to go anywhere, to cook and serve dinners. Many of these women are former cooks and maids, now living on Social Security retirement pensions, supplemented by the fees for these evening "accommodations" to the community. Their style and the bland respectability of their cuisine keep up the social tone of the town. They are like those old slaves who stuck to their places and, even in the greatest deprivation, graciously went on toting things to the Massa'.

There is a curious flimsiness and indifference in the commercial life of Boston. The restaurants are, charitably, to be called mediocre; the famous sea food is only palatable when raw. Otherwise it usually has to endure the deep-fry method that makes everything taste like the breaded pork chops of the Middle West, which in turn taste like the fried sole of Boston. Here, French restaurants quickly become tearoomy, as if some sort of rapid naturalization had taken place. There is not a single attractive eating place on the water front. An old downtown restaurant of considerable celebrity, Locke-Ober, has been expanded, let out, and "costumed" by one of the American restaurant decorators whose productions have a ready-make look, as if the designs had been chosen from a catalog. But for the purest eccentricity, there is the "famous" restaurant, Durgin-Park, which is run like a boardinghouse in a mining town. And so it goes. Downtown Boston at night is a dreary jungle of honky-tonks for sailors, dreary department store windows, Loew's movie houses, hillbilly bands, strippers, parking lots, undistinguished new buildings. Mid-town Boston—small, expensive shops, the inevitable Elizabeth Arden and Helena Rubinstein "salons," Brooks Brothers—is deserted at night, except for people going in and out of the Ritz-Carlton Hotel, the only public place in Boston that could be called "smart." The merchandise in the Newbury Street shops is designed in a high fashion, elaborate, furred, and sequined, but it is never seen anywhere. Perhaps it is for out-of-town use, like a traveling man's mistress.

Just as there is no smart life, so there is no Soho, no Greenwich Village. Recently a man was murdered in a parking lot in the Chinatown area. His address was given as the South End, a lower-class section, and he was said to be a "free-spender," making enough money as a summer bartender on Cape Cod to lead a free-wheeling life the rest of the year. One paper referred to the unfortunate man as a "member of the Beacon Hill Bohemia set." This designation is of considerable interest because there is no "Bohemia" in Boston, neither upper nor lower; the detergent of bourgeois Boston cleans everything, effortlessly, completely. If there were a Bohemia, its members *would* live on Beacon Hill, the most beautiful part of Boston and, like the older parts of most cities, fundamentally classless, providing space for the rich in the noble mansions and for the people with little money in the run-down alleys. For both of these groups the walled gardens of Beacon Hill, the mews, the coach houses, the river views, the cobblestone streets are a necessity and the yellow brick structures of the Fenway are poison. *Espresso* bars have sprung up, or rather dug down in basements, but no summer of bohemianism is ushered into town. This reluctance is due to the Boston legend and its endurance as a lost ideal, a romantic quest.

Something transcendental is always expected in Boston. There is, one imagines, behind the drapery on Mount Vernon Street a person of democratic curiosity and originality of expression, someone alas—and this is the tiresome Boston note—*wellborn*. It is likely to be, even in imagination, a *she*, since women now and not the men provide the links with the old traditions. Of her, then, one expects a certain unprofessionalism, but it is not expected that she will be superficial; she is profoundly conventional in manner of life but capable of radical insights. To live in Boston means to seek some connection with this famous local excellence, the regional type and special creation of the city.

An angry disappointment attends the romantic soul bent upon this quest. When the archaeological diggings do turn up an authentic specimen it will be someone old, nearly gone, "whom you should have known when she was young"—and could hear. The younger Bostonians seem in revolt against the old excellence, with its indulgent, unfettered development of the self. Revolt, however, is too active a word for a passive failure to perpetuate the ideal high-mindedness and intellectual effort. With the fashionable young women of Boston, one might just as well be on Long Island. In the nervous, shy, earnest women there is a lingering hint of the peculiar local development. Terrible *faux pas* are constantly being made by this reasonable, honorable person, followed by blushes and more false steps and explanations and the final blinking, retreating blush.

Among the men, the equivalent of the blushing, blurting, sensitive, and often "fine" woman, is a person who exists everywhere perhaps but nowhere else with such elaboration of type, such purity of example. This is the wellborn failure, the amateur not by choice but from some fatal reticence of temperament. They are often descendants of intellectual Boston, odd-ball grandsons, charming and sensitive, puzzlingly complicated, living on a "small income." These unhappy men carry on their conscience the weight of unpublished novels, half-finished paintings, impossible historical projects, old-fashioned poems, unproduced plays. Their inevitable "small income" is a sort of dynastic flaw, like haemophilia. Much money seems often to impose obligations of energetic management; from great fortunes the living cells receive the hints of the possibilities of genuine power, enough even to make some enormously rich Americans endure the humiliations and fatigues of political office. Only the most decadent and spoiled think of living in idleness on millions; but this notion does occur to the man afflicted with ten thousand a year. He will commit himself with a dreamy courage to whatever traces of talent he may have and live to see himself punished by the New England conscience which demands accomplishments, duties performed, responsibilities noted, and energies sensibly used. The dying will accuses and the result is a queer kind of Boston incoherence. It is literally impossible much of the time to tell what some of the most attractive men in Boston are talking about. Half-uttered witticisms, grave and fascinating obfuscations, points incredibly qualified, hesitations infinitely refined—one staggers about, charmed and confused by the twilight.

But this person, with his longings, connects with the old possibilities and, in spite of his practical failure, keeps alive the memory of the best days. He may have a brother who has retained the mercantile robustness of nature and easy capacity for action and yet has lost all belief in anything except money and class, who may practice private charities, but entertains profoundly trivial national and world views. A Roosevelt, Harriman, or Stevenson are impossible to imagine as members of the Boston aristocracy; here the vein of self-satisfaction and public indifference cuts too deeply.

Harvard (across the river in Cambridge) and Boston are two ends of one mustache. Harvard is now so large and international it has altogether avoided the whimsical stagnation of Boston. But the two places need each other, as we knowingly say of a mismatched couple. Without the faculty, the visitors, the events that Harvard brings to the life here, Boston would be intolerable to anyone except genealogists, antique dealers, and those who find repletion in a closed local society.

Unfortunately, Harvard, like Boston, has "tradition," and in America this always carries with it the risk of a special staleness of attitude, and of pride, incredibly and comically swollen like the traits of hypocrisy, selfishness, or lust in the old dramas. At Harvard some of the vices of "society" exist, of Boston society that is—arrogance and the blinding dazzle of being, *being at Harvard*. The moral and social temptations of Harvard's unique position in American academic life are great and the pathos is seen in those young faculty members who are presently at Harvard but whose appointments are not permanent and so they may be thrown down, banished from the beatific condition. The young teachers in this position live in a dazed state of love and hatred, pride and fear; their faces have a look of desperate yearning, for they would rather serve in heaven than reign in hell. For those who are not banished, for the American at least, since the many distinguished foreigners at

Harvard need not endure these piercing and fascinating complications, something of Boston seems to seep into their characters. They may come from anywhere in America and yet to be at Harvard unites them with the transcendental, legendary Boston, with New England in flower. They begin to revere the old worthies, the houses, the paths trod by so many before, and they feel a throb of romantic sympathy for the directly-gazing portraits on the walls, for the old graves and old names in the Mount Auburn Cemetery. All of this has charm and may even have a degree of social and intellectual value—and then again it may not. Devious parochialisms, irrelevant snobberies, a bemused exaggeration of one's own productions, pimple the soul of a man upholding tradition in a forest of relaxation, such as most of America is thought to be. Henry James's observation in his book on Hawthorne bears on this:

> ... it is only in a country where newness and change and brevity of tenure are the common substance of life, that the fact of one's ancestors having lived for a hundred and seventy years in a single spot would become an element of one's morality. It is only an imaginative American that would feel urged to keep reverting to this circumstance, to keep analysing and cunningly considering it.

If the old things of Boston are too heavy and plushy, the new either hasn't been born or is appallingly shabby and poor. As early as Thanksgiving, Christmas decorations unequaled for cheap ugliness go up in the Public Garden and on the Boston Common. Year after year, the city fathers bring out crèches and camels and Mother and Child so badly made and of such tasteless colors they verge on blasphemy, or would seem to do so if it were not for the further degradation of secular little men blowing horns and the canes of peppermint hanging on the lamps. The shock of the first sight is the most interesting; later the critical senses are stilled as year after year the same bits are brought forth and gradually one realizes that the whole thing is a sort of permanent exhibition.

Recently the dying downtown shopping section of Boston was to be graced with flowers, an idea perhaps in imitation of the charming potted geraniums and tulips along Fifth Avenue in New York. Commercial Boston produced a really amazing display: old, gray square bins, in which were stuck a few bits of yellowing, dying evergreen. It had the look of exhausted greenery thrown out in the garbage and soon the dustbins were full of other bits of junk and discard—people had not realized or recognized the decorative hope and saw only the rubbishy result.

The municipal, civic backwardness of Boston does not seem to bother its more fortunate residents. For them and for the observer, Boston's beauty is serene and private, an enclosed, intense personal life, rich with domestic variation, interesting stuffs and things, showing the hearthside vitality of a Dutch genre painting. Of an evening the spirits quicken, not to public entertainment, but instead to the sights behind the draperies, the glimpses of drawing rooms on Louisburg Square, paneled walls and French chandeliers on Commonwealth Avenue, bookshelves and flower-filled bays on Beacon Street. Boston is a winter city. Every apartment has a fireplace. In the town houses, old persons climb steps without complaint, four or five floors of them, cope with the maintenance of roof and gutter and survive the impractical kitchen and resign themselves to the useless parlors. This is life; the house, the dinner party, the charming gardens, one's high ceilings, fine windows, lacy grillings, magnolia trees, inside shutters, glassed-in studios on the top of what were once stables, outlook on the "river side." Setting is serious. When it is not serious, when a splendid old private house passes into less dedicated hands, an almost exuberant swiftness of deterioration can be noticed. A rooming house, although privately owned, is no longer in the purest sense a private house and soon it partakes of some of the feckless, ugly, municipal neglect. The contrasts are startling. One of two houses of almost identical exterior design will have shining windows, a bright brass door knocker, and its twin will show a "*Rooms*" sign peering out of dingy glass, curtained by those lengths of flowered plastic used in the shower bath. Garbage lies about in the alleys behind the rooming houses, discarded furniture blocks old garden gateways. The vulnerability of Boston's way of life, the meanness of most things that fall outside the needs of the upper classes, are shown with a bleak and terrible fullness in the rooming houses on Beacon Street. And even some of the best houses show a spirit of mere "maintenance," which, while useful for the individual with money, leads to civic dullness, architectural torpor, and stagnation. In the Back Bay area, a voluntary, casual association of property owners exists for the purpose of trying to keep the alleys clean, the streets lighted beyond their present medieval darkness, and to pursue other worthy items of neighborhood value. And yet this same group will "protest" against the attractive Café Florian on Newbury Street (smell of coffee too strong!) and against the brilliantly exciting Boston Arts Festival held in the beautiful Public Garden for two weeks in June. The idea that Boston might be a vivacious, convenient place to live in is not uppermost in these residents' thoughts. Trying to buy groceries in the best section of the Back Bay region is an interesting study in commercial apathy.

A great many of the young Bostonians leave town, often taking off with a sullen demand for a freer, more energetic air. And yet many of them return later, if not to the city itself, to the beautiful sea towns and old villages around it. For the city itself, who will live in it after the present human landmarks are gone? No doubt, some of the young people there at the moment will persevere, and as a reward for their fidelity and endurance will themselves later become monuments, old types interesting to students of what our colleges call American Civilization. Boston is defective, out-of-date, vain, and lazy, but if you're not in a hurry it has a deep, secret appeal. Or, more accurately, those who like it may make of its appeal a secret. The weight of the Boston legend, the tedium of its largely fraudulent posture of traditionalism, the disillusionment of the Boston present as a cultural force make quick minds hesitate to embrace a region too deeply compromised. They are on their guard against falling for it, but meanwhile they can enjoy its very defects, its backwardness, its slowness, its position as one of the large, possible cities on the Eastern seacoast, its private, residential charm. They speak of going to New York and yet another season finds them holding back, positively enjoying the Boston life. . . .

. . . Outside it is winter, dark. The curtains are drawn, the wood is on the fire, the table has been checked, and in the stillness one waits for the guests who come stamping in out of the snow. There are lectures in Cambridge, excellent concerts in Symphony Hall, bad plays being tried out for the hungry sheep of Boston before going to the hungry sheep of New York. Arnold Toynbee or T. S. Eliot or Robert Frost or Robert Oppenheimer or Barbara Ward is in town again. The cars are double-parked so thickly along the narrow streets that a moving vehicle can scarcely maneuver; the pedestrians stumble over the cobbles; in the back alleys a cat cries and the rats, enormously fat, run in front of the car lights creeping into the parking spots. Inside it is cosy, Victorian, and gossipy. Someone else has *not* been kept on at Harvard. The old Irish "accommodator" puffs up stairs she had never seen before a few hours previously and announces that dinner is ready. A Swedish journalist is just getting off the train at the Back Bay Station. He has been exhausted by cocktails, reality, life, taxis, telephones, bad connections in New York and Chicago, pulverized by a "good time." Sighing, he alights, seeking old Boston, a culture that hasn't been alive for a long time . . . and rest.

1959

WILLIAM JAMES

An American Hero

THE JAMESES were, as Henry phrases it, almost "hotel children." They were packed and unpacked, settled and unsettled, like a band of high livers fleeing creditors—except, of course, they were seeking not fleeing. The children knew a life of sudden change, unexpected challenge, residential insecurity and educational heresy that would nowadays be thought negligent and promising to delinquency. They went from Albany to New York, from America to Europe, from New York to Boston, back and forth, without thought of continuity, without regional roots. Their father was seeking a higher continuity for his children: the old man's restlessness was cosmic and just a bit comic, with his gentle, sweet and outrageous purity of mind and spirit. Yet Henry James says that he would not have exchanged his life at "our hotel" for that of "any small person more privately bred."

It was, no doubt, the very purity of the elder Henry James that gave the family its special nature. The Jameses had tremendous natural gifts for friendship; they were talented, popular, respected always and everywhere; they were courteous and eccentric. The father was passionately devoted to his family; he adored being at home and he *was* at home, where he could make out on his considerable inheritance and be privately employed as a writer and thinker. He loved, he doted, he was completely unself-conscious and completely original. Yet the James family was shot through, too, like a piece of Irish tweed, with neurasthenia. Some of it was useful, as perhaps Henry's failure to marry was useful to his prodigious career as a creative writer; some of it was deadly, like Robertson's drinking and Alice's long, baffling invalidism which finally became cancer, providing, as William's letters interestingly reveal, a sort of relief to them all—the relief of an incapacity identified at last.

They were a gregarious family, too. Henry's dinings-out were not more plentiful than William's appearances, lecture dates, travels; Alice had her "circle." The elder Henry James knew everyone in the intellectual world. When William was born, Emerson was taken up to the nursery to bestow a nonsectarian blessing; Thackeray, popping out of the James library, asked, in the way of visitors spying a child of a friend, to see young Henry's "extraordinary jacket."

The James family life, their interior and material circumstances, their common experience have a sort of lost beauty. Their existence is a successful enterprise not easily matched. It is less difficult to understand the painful—Gosse's bleakly evangelical family, Mill's exorbitantly demanding father, or Virginia Woolf's father, Leslie Stephen, who seems to have been nervously exhausting to his daughter—than the special inheritance of the unusually loving. The memorably bitter Victorian family scenes, rich in their merciless peculiarity, are more dramatic and more quickly recoverable than the life Henry and Mary James gave to their children. Henry James writes of his father that "it was a luxury... to have all the benefit of his intellectual and spiritual, his religious, his philosophic and his social passion, without ever feeling the pressure of it to our direct irritation and discomfort." Compare this with Charles Francis Adams, in his *Autobiography*, and the *list* of his father's mistakes which he, the son, had never been able "sufficiently to deplore." Adams deplores, and sufficiently too, his father's lack of interest in exercise or sport, he deplores the fact that he wasn't sent to a boarding school, he deplores his parents' failure to think of definite amusements for their children; he ends by announcing, "I do not hesitate to say these mistakes of childhood have gravely prejudiced my entire life."

The Jameses are very much of the nineteenth century in the abundance of their natures, their eccentricity, the long, odd, impractical labors of the father and the steady Victorian application of at least two of the sons. And yet this family group is American, too, and of an unusually contemporary accent: the life at home is relaxed, the education "progressive," the parents, permissive. The elder Henry James was a man of religion, enthusiastically so, but his family did not go to church on a Sunday. They had private means and yet they were utterly unlike "society" people. They might go from New York to Newport to London and back with great, leisurely, upper-class frequency, but they must have done so with a good deal of simplicity and restless shabbiness—they were after all intellectual and magically indifferent to bourgeois considerations. Their style as a family was manly, bookish, absent-minded and odd, rather than correct or tasteful or elegant. They were high-minded but "bred in horror of conscious propriety." Henry certainly later struck many observers as snobbish and outlandishly refined, but at the same time there is his literally mysterious energy and grinding ambition, his devilish application like that of an obsessed prospector during the gold rush. There is a long, flowing cadence in the family tone and an elaborate, fluent expressiveness. Even when Alice and Robertson write, they have an opulent, easy command of style that seems to be a family trait. William sometimes needs to put aside this legacy, as if he felt the Jamesian manner too unpragmatic for this work; but his highest moments are drawn from it rather than from his more robust, lecturing, condensed style.

They were not the "Great James family" until the revival of interest in the novels and personality of Henry James, a revival of the last few decades. Of course, William was immensely celebrated and important, but the half-ironical interest in the elder James, the publication of Alice James's *Journal* in 1934, forty-two years after her death, seem hardly possible without the interest in Henry James. In the effort to understand the novelist, the greatness of the family as a whole somehow took shape. Even the father's Swedenborgianism has been exhaustively examined as a clue to the novelist son. The family mystery, the beasts in the jungle, the "vastations," the obscure hurts have come to have an almost mythical and allegorical meaning. The James family stands now with the Adams family as the loftiest of our native productions.

The life of William James, the eldest child, was filled with energy and accomplishment, but it was not visited by scores of dramatic happenings or by those fateful, tragic events that make some lives seem to go from year to year, from decade to decade, as if they were providing material for a lively biography to be written long after. Actually, an extraordinary biography *was* written: Henry James's *A Small Boy and Others* and *Notes of a Son and Brother*, undertaken as a memorial after William died. Nevertheless, in these surpassingly fascinating works it is always noted that William, the original protagonist, keeps vanishing from the center stage. John Jay Chapman, a friend of William's, says, "And yet it is hard to state what it was in him that gave him either his charm or his power, what it was penetrated and influenced us, what it is that we lack and feel the need of, now that he has so unexpectedly and incredibly died." Ralph Barton Perry in *The Life and Thought of William James* gathered together, with extraordinary industry and power of organization, all the James material in order to write a personal and intellectual biography. Perry uses James's letters, many for the first time, his diaries, his philosophical and psychological writings—everything known about him—and even then James does not quite come through as a character. An equable, successful man is not the ideal subject for portraiture, perhaps, but in the case of William James there is something more: a certain unwillingness to take form, a nature remaining open to suggestion and revision, a temperament of the greatest friendliness and yet finally elusive because of his distaste for dogmatism.

He was born in 1842 and died in 1910. He married and had four children who lived to adulthood and another who died in infancy. "William, perhaps, did not take quite so enthusiastically to parenthood as his own father," says Margaret Knight in her introduction to a Penguin selection of James's writings. *No one* was quite so at ease paternally as the elder Henry James, and yet William's endurance in this respect is notable when compared with that of the usual father. He began, caught up in those repetitions that persist throughout the generations, to cart his children abroad, back and forth, sending them to this school and that, and although there are a good many groans and alarms, the burden didn't seem to waste his energies or thin out his intellectual interests. When he was abroad, he missed the good, old plain America, and when he was at home, he soon got enough of the plainness and wanted the beauty of Europe once more. His family, his writing, his teaching, his lecturing, his traveling—those are about all you have to build with, biographical twigs and straw of a very commonplace kind. But no one was less commonplace than William James; his mind and sensibility were of the greatest charm, vigor and originality. He was not in the least bland or academic as the list of the pleasant little wrinkles of his nature would seem to indicate. He is usually thought to be the most significant thinker America has produced, and everyone who knew him liked him, and since his death everyone has liked him, too, because our history has not left a single man, except perhaps Jefferson, with so much wisdom and so much sheer delight, such tolerance of the embarrassments of mankind, such a high degree of personal attractiveness and spiritual generosity.

Santayana's superb description of James in *Character and Opinion in the United States* says, "He showed an almost physical horror of club sentiment and of the stifling atmosphere of all officialdom." And of course we admire him more and more for that. We commend him with our most intense feelings for not becoming a mere "professor"; we note that he did not seem interested in playing the gentleman and that he lived in Boston and Cambridge without its ever occurring to him that this meant some sort of special residential gift from the gods. Santayana adds that James was a "sort of Irishman among the Brahmins, and seemed hardly imposing enough for a great man." And for that we thank him, for his escape from dryness and thinness. He is truly a hero: courteous, reasonable, liberal, witty, expressive, a first-rate writer, a profoundly original expression of the American spirit as a thinker, inconceivable in any other country, and yet at home in other countries and cultures as few of us have been.

But James had, as we say now, "his problems." Ralph Barton Perry speaks of the "morbid traits" and the very phrase has an old-fashioned sound of something gangrenous, liverish, perforated with disease. James's "morbidity" is of a reassuring mildness and would not be remarkable at all in the dark lives of some other philosophers. In James, like a speck on the bright, polished surface of a New York State apple, it has considerable fascination, and everyone who writes about the man considers the "depression." It began in his youth, around 1867, and hung on for five or six years. James felt discouraged about the future, he experienced a kind of hopelessness and did not believe that time and change would alter the painful present—sentiments typical of the fixed convictions of a man suffering from a depressive attack. At this time he wrote of his sufferings, "*Pain*, however intense, is light and life, compared to a condition where hibernation would be the ideal of conduct, and where your 'conscience,' in the form of an aspiration towards recovery, rebukes every tendency towards motion, excitement or life as a culpable excess. The deadness of spirit thereby produced 'must be felt to be appreciated.'"

He had somatic symptoms, also—the most striking was the "dorsal insanity," as he named it, the same obscure back pains which had "long made Harry so interesting." He tells a correspondent, "on account of my back I will write but one sheet." The back, for which he went from spa to spa, is an interesting instance of a sort of family affliction in which suggestion seems to play a large part. After James's recovery, the back that had been so much cared for and bathed and warmed and rested was not heard from again. His other symptoms were insomnia, weakness, digestive disorders, and eyestrain—the latter the only one usually considered to have had a physical basis.

During the two years in Germany William James felt quite lonely, homesick, and much thrown back upon himself. He wrote his beautifully expressive early letters to his friends and family, letters of considerable length and great energy of feeling and observation. He speaks, in suitably stoical, manly terms of his own illness, but he also speaks of other people, shows a much truer interest in the world about him than one would expect from a man in a deep depression. His suffering is genuine, but it does not override the claims of the impersonal. A common-sense melody sings through the saddest part of the story, although some of this may be bravado or pride. It is hard to know how to estimate the depth of this early collapse.

There is no doubt that occupational uncertainty was the cause of James's low spirits. It is the usual thing of a young man in medicine or law who does not want to be in medicine or law. (Those innumerable poets who found themselves enrolled for the clergy!) Listlessness came on like a weakening fever as the absence of genuine interest became more and more obvious. "It is totally impossible for me to study now in any way, and I have at last succeeded in *genuinely* giving up the attempt to." James puts every obstacle in the way of the successful practice of medicine; there are even moral objections and he does not fail to notice the toadying young medical students must go in for with their professors, the kind of anxious flattery and unctuous activity necessary to advance professional interests. James did not want to be a doctor and yet it would have been difficult for a young man in his twenties to decide that he was going to be a "psychologist" or a "philosopher." One became a philosopher as a culmination, as one became wise or great or full of special insight. In youth it was different, and even the novelist, Henry James, somehow incredibly found himself briefly enrolled at the Harvard Law School.

Moderate and finally benign the depression proved to be, but James *did* have it and other similar emotional disturbances, nightmarish times, and sensations approaching a state of hallucination. His special awareness of merging states of mind, of the blurred flow of consciousness, the involuntary, subconscious mental life was probably sired by the odd helplessness he experienced during his youthful struggles. The case of "The Sick Soul" in *The Varieties of Religious Experience*, an extraordinarily vivid piece of composition, has been widely called upon to give testimony to James's profound experience of the darkest corners of horror. In this dreadful vignette, attributed in the book to a Frenchman but later acknowledged by James to have come from his own experience, he tells of sitting alone in a "state of philosophic pessimism," and of then going suddenly into his dark dressing room and finding his mind involuntarily assaulted by the memory of a poor epileptic he had seen in an asylum. The remembered person was a "black-haired youth with greenish skin, entirely idiotic.... He sat there like a sort of sculptured Egyptian cat or Peruvian mummy, moving nothing but his black eyes and looking absolutely non-human. This image and my fear entered into a species of combination with each other. *That shape am I*, I felt, potentially. Nothing that I possess can defend me from that fate, if the hour for it should strike for me as it struck for him." This classical experience of abysmal fear, of the dreaded double, of the annihilation of the self is written with a touch of Poe and even of Henry James. The "pit of insecurity" remained long afterward, and James said the whole thing "made me sympathetic with the morbid feelings of others."

James was thirty-six years old when he married, forty-eight years old when his first important work, *The Principles of Psychology*, was completed. For all his energy and genius, there was a sort of hanging back about him, a failure of decision beginning from those first early days of anxiety about his career. He seems to have been capable of any amount of activity, but his ambition was not of the greediest sort. Inspiration and verve made it fairly easy for him to accomplish what he wished, but it was probably procrastination, in all its joy and sorrow, that made him such a great writer on the quirks of human nature. He was a sort of poet of "habit" and "will" and never able to bring himself under their pure, efficient control. A recurring hesitation to commit himself was at the very heart of his philosophical and personal nature. Santayana believed James would have been uncomfortable in the face of any decided question. "He would still have hoped that something might turn up on the other side, and that just as the scientific hangman was about to dispatch the poor convicted prisoner, an unexpected witness would ride up in hot haste, and prove him innocent." This everlasting question mark is part of James's appeal for the contemporary mind. He dreaded Germanic system-making, he feared losing touch with the personal, the subjective, the feelings of real human beings more than he feared being logically or systematically faulty. Everyone complained of the looseness of his thought. Chapman: "His mind is never quite in focus." Ralph Barton Perry speaks of James's "temperamental repugnance to the processes of exact thought." And everyone realized that it was the same openness that saved James from pedantry and egotism.

Religion: sometimes an embarrassment to James's reasonable admirers. His nuts and cranks, his mediums and table-tappers, his faith healers and receivers of communications from the dead—all are greeted by James with the purest, melting latitudinarianism, a nearly disreputable amiability, a broadness of tolerance and fascination like that of a priest at a jam session. James's pragmatism, his pluralism, his radical empiricism have been the subject of a large amount of study and comment. Reworking the sod from whence so many crops have come in their season seems profitless for the enjoyment of James's letters, letters that are nearly always personal, informal, nontechnical, and rather different in this way from, for instance, Santayana's recently published correspondence in which philosophy keeps cropping up everywhere. Religion, on the other hand, was a sort of addiction for James, and all of his personality is caught up in it, his unique ambivalence, his longing, as Oliver Wendell Holmes says, "for a chasm from which might appear a phenomenon without phenomenal antecedents."

Whenever someone near to him died, James could not restrain a longing for the comforts of immortality. To Charles Eliot Norton, when he was very ill in 1908, James wrote, "I am as convinced as I can be of anything that this experience of ours is only a part of the experience that is, and with which it has something to do; but *what* or *where* the other parts are, I cannot guess. It only enables one to say 'behind the veil, behind the veil!'..." When his sister Alice's death was obviously near, an extraordinary letter to her said, "When that which is *you* passes out of the body, I am sure that there will be an explosion of liberated force and life till then eclipsed and kept down. I can hardly imagine *your* transition without a great oscillation of both 'worlds' as they regain their new equilibrium after the change! Everyone will feel the shock, but you yourself will be more surprised than anybody else." A memorial address for his old friend, Francis Boott, ends, "Good-by, then, old friend. We shall nevermore meet the upright figure, the blue eye, the hearty laugh, upon these Cambridge streets. But in that wider world of being of which this little Cambridge world of ours forms so infinitesimal a part, we may be sure that all our spirits and their missions here will continue in some way to be represented, and that ancient human loves will never lose their own."

Immortality was a great temptation and so, also, was the tranquility James had observed to be at least sometimes a result of religious belief. "The transition from tenseness, self-responsibility, and worry, to equanimity, receptivity, and peace...This abandonment of self-responsibility seems to be the fundamental act in specifically religious as distinguished from moral practice." James had at hand any amount of sympathy for the believer, along with the most sophisticated knowledge of the way in which the religious experience could be treated as a neurotic symptom by the nonbeliever. At the beginning of *The Varieties* he writes, "A more fully developed example of the same kind of reasoning is the fashion, quite common nowadays among certain writers, of criticizing religious emotions by showing a connection between them and the sexual life. . . . Medical materialism finishes up Saint Paul by calling his vision on the road to Damascus a discharging lesion of the occipital cortex, he being an epileptic."

Some of the enchantment of *The Varieties* comes from its being a kind of race with James running on both teams—here he is the cleverest skeptic and there the wildest man in a state of religious enthusiasm. He can call St. Theresa a "shrew," and say that the "bustle" of her style proves it, and yet he can appreciate the appeal the Roman Catholic Church will often have for people of an intellectual and artistic nature. And beyond conventional religion, beyond God and immortality and belief, there is the "subliminal door," that hospitable opening through which he admits his living items of "psychical research." True his passion was instructive, scholarly and perhaps psychological in many cases, but that does not explain the stirring appeal for him in the very vulgarity of the cults, the dinginess of the séances. The Boston medium Mrs. Piper sometimes bored him; even his colleague Myers, a much more devoted psychical researcher, called this lady, "that insipid Prophetess, that tiresome channel of communication between the human and the divine." But in the end, James finally said about Mrs. Piper: "In the trances of this medium, I cannot resist the conviction that knowledge appears which she has never gained by the ordinary waking use of her eyes and ears and wits." Even as late as 1893 James had eighteen sessions with a "mind-curer" and found his sleep wonderfully restored. He says, by way of testimonial to her remarkable powers, "I would like to get this woman into a lunatic asylum for two months, and have every case of chronic delusional insanity in the house tried by her."

In 1884, the American chapter of the Society for Psychical Research was founded. James became a member and was still a member at the time of his death. Working in psychic research was not just a bit of occasional dashing about to séances and mind readings. The whole movement was filled with bickering intensity, with all the nervous, absorbing factional struggles "minority" beliefs and practices usually develop. An endless amount of work went into this research: the communications from beyond tended to be lengthy. In 1908, James wrote Flournoy, "I have just read Miss Johnson's report on the S.P.R. Proceedings, and a good bit of the proofs of Piddington's on cross-correspondence between Mrs. Piper, Mrs. Verrall, and Mrs. Holland, which is to appear in the next number. You will be much interested, if you can gather the philosophical energy to go through with such an amount of tiresome detail. It seems to me that these reports open a new chapter in the history of automatism; and Piddington's and Johnson's ability is of the highest order." On his defense of faith healers when they were being attacked as charlatans by the medical profession, James wrote a friend, "If you think I *enjoy* this sort of thing you are mistaken."

James's son, Henry, the first editor of his letters, believed that it was only in the interest of pure research that his father gave so much time to these psychic manifestations and "not because he was in the least impressed by the lucubrations of the kind of mind" that provided such material. Ralph Barton Perry attributes the time spent to James's psychological interest in unusual cases and also to his natural liberal tendency to prefer the lowly—spiritualism, faith healing, and the like—rather than the orthodox and accepted. The picturesqueness, the dishonesty even, seems to have given James the sort of delight that amounted almost to credulity. He would be fatigued and morally discouraged with such people as the Neapolitan medium, Eusapia Palladino, about whom he said, "Everyone agrees that she cheats in the most barefaced manner whenever she gets an opportunity," and yet he concludes optimistically that "her credit has steadily risen." He reports that in England the two daughters of a clergyman named Creery whose feats of thought-transference had much impressed certain strict investigators were later found to be signaling each other. There were many disheartening moments and infidelities. James and his fellow researcher, Hodgson, went on a trip and spent "the most hideously inept psychical night, in Charleston, over a much-praised female medium who fraudulently played on the guitar. A plague take all white-livered, anaemic, flaccid, weak-voiced Yankee frauds! Give me a full-blooded red-lipped villain like dear old D.—when shall I look upon her like again?" In the letters of a few weeks previously he had described the medium, dear old D., as a "type for Alexander Dumas, obese, wicked, jolly, intellectual, with no end of go and animal spirits...that woman is one with whom one would fall wildly in love, if in love at all—she is such a fat, *fat* old villain." You do not find the delight, the hospitality, the enjoyment in the other psychic researchers—only credulity and reports and statistics on "controls," those spirits who give off conversation and information to the strange vessels capable of hearing them. One control accused the psychologist Stanley Hall of having murdered his wife.

James seems to have enjoyed all this as another learned man might enjoy burlesque, but at the same time he took it with a great deal of seriousness. His yea is followed by his nay, as is usual with him, and yet he hoped that these manifestations would be scientifically validated, that the endless, wearisome, fantastic proceedings of the Society for Psychical Research would be an important contribution to knowledge. In all this James is a sort of Californian; he loves the new and unhistorical and cannot resist the shadiest of claims. He, himself, and most of the people who write piously about him felt that he died without saying all he might have said, without finishing his system, without in some grand conclusion becoming the great philosophical thinker that he was, or at least without in the end truly and thoroughly writing his final thoughts on the universe and life. Perhaps there is a sense in which this may have been the case, but perhaps it is only the usual scholarly appetite for the weighty and lengthy. William James without his gaiety, his spooks, his nuts and frauds, his credulity and his incongruous longings for something more than life, even though he was committed to testing every belief *by* life, would not be the captivating and splendid spirit he is. It is usual to remember his wit, his courtesy, his geniality, his liberalism, but in the end his image is indefinable and one does not know how to name the quality that shines in every bit of his writing, in all we know about him, in the character and spirit we believe him to have been. Perhaps it is his responsiveness, his unexpected sympathies, even his gullibility. Or his goodness. Whatever it may have been, we feel it as something simple many others might have and yet hardly anyone seems to possess. A certain flatness and repetitiveness appear in people's attempts to define him, for he is odd but not dark, rich not in peculiarities but rather peculiar in the abundance of his endowment with the qualities and dispositions we admire in all men.

About his letters the same ideas come to mind—were we better, more gifted, more abounding in our feelings we might have written them ourselves. James's correspondence is spontaneous and casual. Letters are not necessarily of that order; every sort of letter, the formal, the affected, the merest scribble or a showpiece composed with all the deliberation of a sonnet, all these have been at some time written wonderfully by someone. Yet a special regard is given to the impulsive, free letter because such unrevised and personal moments have an authenticity utterly innocent of posthumous longings. They are the nearest things we have to the lost conversations of memorable persons. James's letters are felicitous, easy, genuine as talk, hurriedly written, each for its own occasion, and yet very much written, with all the sense of form and beauty and the natural power to interest that come from a man with a pure gift for the art of letter writing. They are intimate and personal; they have a romantic fullness of emotion; they are the productions of a social creature, a man of the world, at least in the sense of complicated obligations and a conscientious regard for friendships. They have a poetical sweetness; they delight and charm, and they are deeply affecting, even somewhat sad, as they reveal year by year a life and sensibility of great force and great virtue.

It certainly did not occur to William James at the beginning of his career that he was going to be an important writer, that this, rather than painting, was the art he was going to master. Indeed, after his first review he said, "I feel that a living is hardly worth being gained at this price." He spoke of "sweating fearfully for three days, erasing, tearing my hair, copying, recopying, etc." It was often hard for him to settle down to philosophical and professional writing; yet once started, his marvelous clarity, humor, and his superb prose style carried him along rapidly enough. Letter writing, on the other hand, was a pure pleasure, a duty and an indulgence at the same time. His desire, in letters to friends, was to give happiness—compare this with D. H. Lawrence who seemed when he felt the desire to communicate with his friends to want, at best, to instruct, and, at the worst, to chastise.

James's affections appear to be without limits. "Darling Belle-Mère," he addresses his mother-in-law and signs off with "oceans of love from your affectionate son." His colleagues are greeted with "Glorious old Palmer" and "Beloved Royce." James is, as his letters show, quite susceptible to women; he is their correspondent on suitable occasions with great and convincing gallantry. He has such pleasure in his friends that the reader of his letters longs to know the recipients—a condition far from being the usual one with great letter writers. (Madame de Sévigné's daughter is one of the last persons we would want to recall from the shades.) Grace Norton, Fannie Morse, Thomas Ward, Henry Bowditch, and Mrs. Whitman seem persons of the most pleasing dimensions as we meet them in James's correspondence. His attitude toward them all is benevolent, loving, loyal, and completely without pompousness or self-importance. James was almost *curiously* modest. People crowded to his lectures, he was truly a public figure, and an international celebrity, too, but there is never anything of rigidity or conceit in his character. He hardly seemed to believe he had done anything unusual. His tenderness, too, was of the most luxuriant variety and stayed with him forever. John Jay Chapman thought he always liked everything and everyone too well.

1960

LIVING IN ITALY

Reflections on Bernard Berenson

IN THE rather meek, official narration of the life of Mrs. Jack Gardner, I came across an arresting photograph of Bernard Berenson as a young man, a student at Harvard. Here among the illustrations relating to the subject of the biography (Mr. and Mrs. Gardner with Mr. and Mrs. Zorn in Venice; the Gothic Room at the Gardner Museum, etc.), among the details of ancestry, the accounts of endless journeys and evening parties, of purchases and decisions, courageous endurance and interesting self-indulgence, the passionate, young face of Berenson gazed out serenely, a dreaming animal caught in the dense jungle growth of a rich, lively woman's caprice and accomplishment. This early photograph is a profile, as fine and pleasing as a young girl's; the hair, worn long, curls lightly, falling into layers of waves; there is a perfect, young man's nose, a pure, musing, brown-lashed eye, fortunate long, strong bones of chin and jaw. The collar of the young man's jacket is braided with silk and he looks like an Italian prodigy of the violin, romantically, ideally seen, finely designed, a gifted soul, already suitable to court circles.

We spent the winter of 1950 in Florence and used to go out to see Berenson, as so many had gone before and would go afterward. This unusual man was marvelously vivacious and, in more than one respect, actually inspiring; and yet I would always leave him, somewhat troubled, ungratefully adding and subtracting, unable to come to a decision about him or his life. He was not what I had expected, but I despaired of having an original, fresh or even an honest opinion about him. He was too old, had been viewed and consulted far too much; you had a belated feeling you were seeing the matinée of a play that had been running for eight decades. And even the guests staying at his house approached him with caution, fearing to be taken in by an ancient "tourist attraction." Sometimes one of Berenson's guests would take the night off and come to our apartment in Florence where we would drink too much or talk too much and the guest would return to his host, much too late, defiantly clanging the bell to have the gates of the villa opened. When I thought about Berenson, his young profile of sixty-five years before would come back to my memory, mistily mixing the lost image with the reality of his famous, white-haired, aged elegance, his spare and poetical look, his assurance and his suppressed turbulence. His turbulence and disorderly emotions were not suppressed, I believed, for psychic hygiene so much as for reasons of practicality. In Berenson's beauty there was the refinement, the discipline, the masculinity of a little jockey and some of that profession's mixture of a fiercely driving temperament with the capacity for enjoying a judicious repose. He understood that the proud, small person, believing in art and comfort, must have singular powers and unrelenting watchfulness. Indulgence feminizes; perfection and beauty, without restraint, provoke the unconscious, fatten and soften the will.

At the real beginning of his adult life, Berenson made the profound decision, accepted the necessity for dislocation, and decided to live abroad, in Italy. The fact that Italy was his profession, his art, does not remove the fact of his exile from interest. Ruskin and others pursued the art of Italy without expatriation. It was not a wandering, exiled scholar that Berenson became; he became a sort of foreign prince, a character in a fairy tale with all his properties and drama neatly laid out around him, symbolically ordered. And, indeed, who would dream of severing Berenson and Italy? Where can he be imagined? In Boston? On Fifth Avenue or established on Long Island? He united himself with his residence in the way a nobleman is united with his title and yet, like the nobleman again, it was not altogether convincing as the final existential truth of his life. The depth of the sense of alienation in one so consciously and conscientiously placed is a part of the peculiar affliction and, in another sense, one of the privileges of the voluntary exile.

After the war, Italy came into a multitudinous rediscovery and the old exiles who had been shut off from sight and correspondence for a few years came forth too, as old women with their market baskets appear after a siege. With Berenson, postwar prosperity meant an unexpected sweetening of his public image. His possessions, his worldliness, his aestheticism seemed in a frightened, inflationary world, at the least harmless and, at the best, admirably eternal and shrewd. In the Depression decade before the war, his villa, *I Tatti*, with its splendid library, its pictures—its Sassetta and Domenico Veneziano—might have been thought exorbitantly self-centered. In 1950, the first thing I thought about it was that it was not luxuriously beautiful, at least not as such places are abroad. It was not a *paradiso* for an interesting idler, but simply a passable Italian villa, serviceable, comfortable, rather staid, with a good many brownish sofas and draperies. True, it had its garden, its dramatic cypresses and pieces of suitable sculpture, indeed everything graceful and practical that might be expected; still it was most memorable for its solidity, the somewhat Northern substantiality, the thickness of stuffs and things, the reminders of the comfortable Beacon Street standards of Berenson's youth. And the house seemed to ask that the occupants and guests conduct themselves in a discreet and plausible manner, keeping the spirit of reasonable calm and well-polished utility. Politeness, adaptability, the habits of social efficiency were strongly stated if not rigidly demanded; they were the firmness upon which a unique personal history rested. A steady pace, familiar and satisfying, reigned benevolently.

There was no Mediterranean slackness about Berenson, no languor or sunstroke or tropical vegetation. On the receptive, hospitable Italian soil, he built an orderly, conscience-driven life. Heaters glowed in the library; curtains were drawn and brown lamps turned on at dusk. At the fireside you might have been listening to the conversations of a character in Thomas Mann, one of those highly individual scholars in *Doctor Faustus*, with their passionate convictions, their quirks of taste. In the working household there was a noticeable number of non-Italians: a Scotch chauffeur and steady, fair-faced people gave the air of a punctual and neat reliability. Berenson was an intellectual first and, secondly, a person leading a rich and elaborate social life. No doubt, particularly when he was older, some of his habits and needs were suggested by the successful customs of the comfortable, non-intellectual world. He lived with the silky regularity and pleasurable concentration of energies that are at once opulent and sacrificial—the prudence of the sensual. He knew the grace of the steady rounds, the ritual and faithful observance of a kind of liturgical year with its feasts and fastings, its seasonal pilgrimages to Rome and Venice, the stately moves from the winter at Settignano to the summer in the vale of Vallombrosa. He had his morning privacy for work and his afternoon walks. This constancy, rich people seem to think, keeps the bones oiled, provides activity and change without encouraging the hazards or assaults of the unexpected, the wayfarer's disappointments, the explorer's disillusions. Beautiful things, sweet experiences may, like the sudden fluttering of a butterfly on the window pane, appear without warning, but organization, foresight and routine will prevent sleepless nights and throbbing temples. (In his *Sketch for a Self-Portrait*, Berenson cites the fact of heavy drinking in America as one of his reasons for leaving.) No matter, Berenson himself was still the host to all the sufferings of an unusual, gifted nature. There is, it seems, always a hole in the wall where the cold wind can enter.

In Italy, looking about, we remembered Dylan Thomas saying after some complaint of ours about America, "You needn't live in that bloody country, America! You could go somewhere else, you know." The possibility of escape never entirely deserts the greedy dreams of the "self-employed." It flares up and dies down, like malaria; it is a disease arrested, not cured; a question without an answer. The thought that one might himself settle far, far away gives a kind of engrossing sub-plot to one's travels. And the Americans who have made the choice, those colonies with their stoves turned high in the winter, provide the occasional, rushing visitor, resting at the end of the day in his hotel room, with insolent or jealous thoughts.

A man may exile himself for isolation—Santayana in his convent in Rome—for the freedom of solitude, the purity of the release from useless obligations and conventions; or he may exile himself, from America at least, for the freedom of hospitality, the enlargement of possibilities. You may be a hermit or an innkeeper. Berenson's nature destined him to be an innkeeper. Whether he loved humanity or not, he had an enormous appetite for meeting it, being visited by it, for serving it lunch and tea. He seemed helpless before the appeal of a new person, a soul who carried either an accidental or earned distinction. No one was easier to see than Berenson. He could not be called a snob, although his appetite embraced the merely social and the merely rich. When we mailed a letter of introduction to him, he accepted it as a bizarre formality because, of course, he who saw everyone was willing and happy to see yet another. One was never tempted to think it was ennui or triviality that produced this state of addiction; the absorbing inclination seemed to be a simple fear of missing someone, almost as if these countless visitors and travelers had a secret the exile pitifully wished to discover. The expatriate sometimes suffers painfully from the dread of losing touch with the world he has left but towards which he looks back with longings and significant emotions, with guilt and resentment, with all the tart ambivalence of the injured lover. It is, after all, the fickle, abandoned country for which the exile writes his books, for which his possessions are ultimately designated; money and citizenship, nieces and nephews, language and memory—the very skin of life—remain in their old place.

As the years pass, the feelings of loss and uncertainty appear to grow stronger not weaker for those who live abroad. The traveler from home is important, the visitor, the acquaintance passing through bring knowledge, prejudices, fashions that cannot be acquired from the newspapers. A feeling of guilt persists about the very beauty of life abroad, the greater ease, and above all the parasitism of the exile's condition. The dream-like timelessness of Italy is a captivity into which uneasiness creeps. Americans who removed themselves to England were usually seeking manners, civilization, congenial spirits; in Italy the senses were enchanted, brought under the spell of the great sun, the heartbreaking landscape, the sweetness of peasant faces, toiling and enduring, the lemon tree against the wall. It appears that an American cannot become an Italian—property, marriage to the aristocracy, nothing seems to insure assimilation. And the answer must be that Americans want to live in Italy but do not wish to become Italians. Many once wished to become Englishmen and succeeded; foreigners from every land have become Frenchmen of a sort. The Italian exile, with his nostalgic, feudal temperament, is also a person with a wound, not so very different in his feelings from those beachcombers and divorcées in the Caribbean, all who seek to soothe their hurt spirits with the sun, with flowering winters, with white houses opened to the new air and entangled with old vines. Everywhere in Italy, among the American colony, one's envy is cut short time and time again by a sudden feeling of sadness in the air, as of something still alive with the joys of an Italian day and yet somehow faintly withered, languishing. Unhappiness, disappointment support the exile in his choice. Even the endlessly productive Santayana revealed at times his wounds from America and Harvard. Of his career at Harvard he wrote dryly, that it had been "slow and insecure, made in an atmosphere of mingled favour and distrust." He pretended not to care. He made very little use of Italy; it was a refuge in which he wrote his books, tirelessly.

Was Berenson shady, crooked? Did he make his fortune with the help of false as well as genuine attributions? Whatever the truth, certainly large numbers of his critics and his admirers accepted the charge of profitable dishonesties back in his past. By choosing to use his knowledge for the sale of works of art he brought himself under the suspicion of financial immorality. The "attribution" of venality clung to this famous humanist. Old scandal, dubious gains, lingering doubts, gave a drama and tension to his life; but his work, his books were authentic and he was, himself, a pure creation—that everyone agreed. Berenson lamented that his fame as an art expert "degenerated into a widespread belief that if only I could be approached in the right way I could order this or that American millionaire to pay thousands upon thousands and hundreds of thousands for any daub that I was bribed by the seller to attribute to a great master. Proposals of this nature...became a burden; and in the end I was compelled in self-defence to refuse to see people unless I was sure that they brought no 'great masters' with them. Needless to say that every person I would not receive, every owner whose picture I would not ascribe to Raphael or Michelangelo or Giorgione, Titian or Tintoretto...turned into an enemy."

Berenson's success, the money he made as a young man, aroused superstitious twitchings among people everywhere, even those who delighted in him as a friend, and certainly among his colleagues. Hadn't life turned out to be too easy for this poor Jewish fine arts scholar from Boston? Was knowledge, honestly used, ever quite so profitable, especially knowledge of art? He had, it was felt, sold himself to the devil by demanding life on his own terms, by asking more than other scholars, by becoming a *padrone* instead of a simple professor. Italian critics were far from hospitable to his ideas and great feuds raged. They did not give over their art to a foreigner without a fight, without accusations and sneers.

Some of the uneasiness felt by the world will inevitably be felt by the man himself. Stubbornness of attitude became a defense for a whole life. A hardening and narrowing, repetition of positions taken long ago, obstinate rejections disguised pain and fear of obsolescence. In Italy, the tremendousness of the past reinforces the spirit in its old assumptions; nothing new seems to be required. It was part of Berenson's idyllic removal that he couldn't like much of the art of his own time. The gods will not grant every gift. He set himself against violence, fragmentation, improvisation, primitivism. He couldn't accept Picasso, Stravinsky, T. S. Eliot, Kafka. He was apprehensive about these productions, irked by the broken forms. He liked Homer, Goethe, and Proust, but Faulkner disposed him to fretfulness. He looked upon so many contemporary things with painful distaste and something like hurt feelings. He seemed to see his own essence threatened with devastation. For him, the agile will, the effort to maintain security and preserve courage had been everything. Hesitation, nihilism, abstraction appalled this pulsing ego that had sought to define in his work and personal existence a compact, ennobling, classical example. It was odd that in the lighter arts, in living personalities, he was extremely in-the-know, open to feeling, to humor, to affection, to wild originality.

Pride and conscience urged Berenson to the gritting work of writing. His style was clear and sensible, but literally brought forth in sorrow because he hadn't the luck of ready eloquence, except in conversation. Santayana's contented industry puzzled him. "He loved writing! Preferred it to reading and talking. Imagine such a man!" Still, write Berenson did, and some of the vices and temptations of the literary character were his as much as if he had been living in New York, producing regularly for the art publications. He gave hints of jealousy and of thinking himself undervalued. He was inclined at times to composition on topics that did not deeply engage him, but which he felt necessary to undertake because of wishing to keep in step with subtle changes in taste and emphasis. I once heard another art critic cry out in pain, "That wicked B. B.! He would never have thought of writing a book on Caravaggio if he hadn't known I was doing one!" Berenson noted with chagrin the fee Sir Kenneth Clark was reported to be receiving for his lectures on the nude in the National Gallery in Washington. (The older critic had lived a longer life than most are granted well before the age of plushy lectures, easy endowments, fabulous stipends.) His disappointments were only reality, his firm sense of things as they were in life. A deeper truth of his nature was caught in odd moments—I remember seeing him, ancient, regal, stepping along nimbly, like a little gnome king, on the arm of the dancer, Katherine Dunham.

The great age Berenson achieved did not strike one as an accident, a stroke of fine heredity or luck; longevity was an achievement, the same as his books, bought with a good deal of anguish and hard work. His nature, with its prudence, its routine, its rich mixture of work and pleasure, seemed to have been designed for long use. We happened to be paying a call on him in Rome, where he was installed for his yearly state visit like Queen Victoria on her business-like holidays, when the news came that Croce had died. "I should have gone first! The dear man was younger than I!" Berenson said with feeling. Everyone smiled. It was not only that Berenson had lived so long but his wanting to go on living still longer that annoyed certain people. Age was another of his slightly disreputable luxuries.

When he died, at ninety-four, he left, besides his books and the pleasure he had given, a peculiar monument. He left his villa, his library, to Harvard, the home of his lost youth, so that gifted young Americans, interested in art and history, might look out on the Tuscan landscape and be saved from barbarism and provinciality. Berenson seemed to want to leave his daily existence to America, bequeath his setting, his chosen life. Like all his gifts to the world, this too was received with misgivings and hesitation. Did he have enough money to make such a gift? Before she could be accepted the gift must have a dowry, money for her own upkeep, as if she were a bride. "We will all starve! For Harvard!" they used to say in his household. The arrangements were made and the site created by sheer force of personal will and longing would be returned to its source, to be preserved as a little pocket of American intellectual industry, a bit of foreign investment, in the busy Apennines. What endurance and genius had kept alive would go along smoothly, buzzing like the lawn mowers in front of the White House, with the efficient routine of public domesticity. Institutionalized, the villa would soon remind one of those inns taken over by a conquering army. Its occupants will have been chosen and assigned. All those hundreds upon hundreds of guests of the past—the surly writers and old ladies from Boston, the dons, the pansies, the actresses, the historians—won't be coming back to gossip, in a whisper in the halls, about how fortunes were made, to sneak into Florence to get drunk at the Excelsior, and to see the unique Berenson, leading his curious life. At the end, the Pope sent his blessing.

1960

MARY McCARTHY

MARY MCCARTHY! "*The Man in the Brooks Brothers Shirt*! That's my Bible!" I once heard a young woman exclaim. No doubt the famous short story is rightly understood as a sort of parable representing many a young girl's transgressions, even if it does not concern itself with the steps in the sinner's rehabilitation. It would be hard to think of any writer in America more interesting and unusual than Mary McCarthy. Obviously she wants to be noticed, indeed to be spectacular; and she works toward that end with what one can only call a sort of trance-like seriousness. There is something puritanical and perplexing in her lack of relaxation, her utter refusal to give an inch of the ground of her own opinion. She *cannot conform*, cannot often like what even her peers like. She is a very odd woman, and perhaps oddest of all in this stirring sense of the importance of her own intellectual formulations. Very few women writers can resist the temptation of feminine sensibility; it is there to be used, as a crutch, and the reliance upon it is expected and generally admired. Mary McCarthy's work, from the first brilliant *The Company She Keeps* down to her latest collection of essays, *On the Contrary: Articles of Belief, 1946–1961*, is not like that of anyone else and certainly not like that of other women. We might naturally wonder from what blending of bravura and commonsense this tart effervescence has come.

In America we have had the quiet, isolated genius of Emily Dickinson, on the one hand, and that of Edith Wharton, dignified, worldly, astute, on the other, each holding a prime spiritual location in the national landscape. In the background we might imagine the highly usual romantic glamor of Edna St. Vincent Millay, the romance of lyrics and lovers and tragic endings. Mary McCarthy, because of the radical turn of her mind, has little connection with any of these figures even if there are occasional correspondences to Edith Wharton and Edna Millay. And yet how difficult it is to define the image of this writer. If it is popular fame to figure somehow in the scheme of persons who have not had the time to examine the actual claims of the famous person, then she has popular fame as well as genuine literary distinction. Perhaps to the world her image is composed of the clear eyes of the Cecil Beaton photographs, the strong profile, the steady gaze; and it is certainly made of the candor about Sex in her novels and stories and the "attacks" on gods like Tennessee Williams. This is all very unexpected. There is charm and vigor and an almost violent holding of special opinions. She is, as someone said of Thackeray, "an uncomfortable writer."

Not so long ago, Brooks Atkinson, the retired dean of American drama critics, had the sobering occasion to report that Mary McCarthy had been very hard, in a review in an English newspaper, on the bright young English drama critic, Kenneth Tynan, whom she found neither very bright nor very young in his literary spirit and style. The event was dismaying. Where are you if Walter Kerr lights into Howard Taubman, an unimaginable act of disloyalty for either of those members of the Establishment?

If there were any real ancestor among American women for Mary McCarthy it might be Margaret Fuller. How easy it is to imagine the living writer as a visitor at Brook Farm, a friend of Mazzini's, a journalist in Rome during the 1840s. Both women have will power, confidence, and a subversive soul sustained by exceptional energy. A career of candor and dissent is not an easy one for a woman; the license is jarring and the dare often forbidding. Such a person needs more than confidence and indignation. A great measure of personal attractiveness and a high degree of romantic singularity are necessary to step free of the mundane, the governessy, the threat of earnestness and dryness. Moderating influences are essential. Madame de Staël, vexing and far-out as she was, needed her rather embarrassing love affairs to smooth over, like a cosmetic cream, the shrewd image. With Mary McCarthy the purity of style and the liniment of her wit, her gay summoning of the funny facts of everyday life, soften the scandal of the action or the courage of the opinion.

In the novels and stories, the "shocking" frankness of the sexual scenes is very different from the hot prose of male writers. These love scenes are profoundly feminine, even though other women writers do not seem to want to take advantage of this same possibility. In her fiction, shame and curiosity are nearly always found together and in the same strange union we find self-condemnation and the determined pursuit of experience; introspective irony and flat, daring action. In the paperback edition of *The Company She Keeps* we see on the cover a pretty girl posed for the seduction scene on the train—bare shoulders, whisky bottle, and a reflecting pout on her lips. But the picture cannot give any idea of the unexpected contents of the mind of the actual fictional heroine. The psychological fastidiousness and above all the belligerent mood of the surrendering girl are the essence of the story. The sexual affair with the second-rate "man in the Brooks Brothers shirt" is for the heroine both humbling and enthralling; and so, also in the same way, is the outrageous coupling on the couch in *A Charmed Life* of the remarried young wife and her former husband. The heroine, in these encounters, feels a sense of piercing degradation, but it does not destroy her mind's freedom to speculate; her rather baffling surrenders do not vanquish her sense of her conqueror's weaknesses and absurdities. Of course, these works are comedies; and it is part of Mary McCarthy's originality to have written, from the woman's point of view, the comedy of Sex. The coarse actions are described with an elaborate *verismo* of detail. (The safety pin holding up the underwear in the train scene; in *A Charmed Life* "A string of beads she was wearing broke and clattered to the floor. 'Sorry,' he muttered as he dove for her left breast." The "left" notation is a curiosity, a kind of stage direction, inviting us to project ourselves dramatically into an actual scene.)

Plot and dramatic sense are weak in Mary McCarthy's fiction. Taste and accuracy are sometimes substitutions. What people eat, wear, and read are of enormous importance. The reader follows the parade of tastes and preferences with a good deal of honest excitement and suspense, wondering if he can guess the morals of the kind of person who would cover a meat loaf with Campbell's tomato soup. He participates in a mysterious drama of consumption, in which goods are the keys to salvation. Taste is also used as the surest indication of character. "There were pieces of sculpture by Archipenko and Harold Cash, and the head of a beautiful Egyptian Queen, Neferteete." Accuracy, unusual situations documented with extreme care, mean for the reader a special sort of recognition. The story "Dottie Makes an Honest Woman of Herself" is about contraception in the way, for instance, Frank Norris's *The Octopus* is about wheat. "Dottie did not mind the pelvic examination or the fitting. Her bad moment came when she was learning how to insert the pessary herself. Though she was usually good with her hands and well-coordinated... As she was trying to fold the pessary, the slippery thing, all covered with jelly, jumped out of her grasp and shot across the room and hit the sterilizer. Dottie could have died." This story, *memorable* to put it mildly, could not have been written by anyone except Mary McCarthy. Reading it over again, the suggestion came involuntarily to mind that perhaps it was meant as a parody of the excesses of naturalistic fiction, a parody, too, of the brute, prosaic sexual details in, for instance, a writer like John O'Hara. There is an air of imparting information—like whaling in Melville or, more accurately, the examination of dope addiction in Gelber's play, *The Connection*. This aspect of *information* brings to memory the later story by Philip Roth in which a college girl suggests she knows all about contraception because she has read Mary McCarthy.

In a writer of this kind there is an urgent sense of the uses to which a vivid personal nature may be put by a writer's literary talent. There is very often an easily recognized element of autobiography and it is in autobiography that Mary McCarthy excels—that is, of course, if one uses the word in its loosest and largest sense. *The Company She Keeps* and *Memories of a Catholic Girlhood* are richer, more beautiful, and aesthetically more satisfying than, say, *A Charmed Life* or *The Groves of Academe*. The condition that made *The Oasis* somewhat stillborn was that it was more biography than autobiography. In autobiography, self-exposure and self-justification are the same thing. It is this contradiction that gives the form its dramatic tension. To take a very extreme case, it is only natural that critics who find importance in the writings of the Marquis de Sade will feel that the man himself is not without certain claims on our sympathy and acceptance. In Mary McCarthy's case, the daring of the self-assertion, the brashness of the correcting tendency (think of the titles *Cast a Cold Eye* and *On the Contrary*) fill us with a nervous admiration and even with the thrill of the exploit. Literature, in her practice, has the elation of an adventure—and of course that elation mitigates and makes aesthetically acceptable to our senses the strictness of her judgments.

She is not moved by reputation. Indeed her congenital skepticism bears down hardest on the most flattered. Only occasionally, as in her essay on the fashion magazines, does she write about what is known as "popular culture." She does not bother to discuss television, but she might discuss the imperfections of, for instance, J. D. Salinger. In her dramatic criticism, collected in *Sights and Spectacles*, there are times— I think of her remarks on Shaw and Ibsen—when she seems in an uneasy relationship with the great men. Shaw's mad reasonableness is put to the test of her own reasonableness; the toils of Ibsen appear to come off less prosperously than her own toils to define them. One sometimes has the feeling of a mistake in tone, rather than a perversity of judgment, as if the meeting of the author and the subject that everyone expected to go so well had unaccountably gotten off to a bad start.

In her new book, *On the Contrary*, she has written her two best essays: "Characters in Fiction" and "Fact in Fiction." In their manner and feeling these essays suggest a new gravity and sympathy, a subtle change in the air, a change already felt in her large books on Florence and Venice. As for the ideas in the two essays: they are the only new things said about the art of the novel in many years. Paraphrase is difficult because the examples are very fresh and the insights rather angular.

On "Fact in Fiction": fact, "this love of truth, ordinary, common truth recognizable to everyone, is the ruling passion of the novel. Putting two and two together, then, it would seem that the novel, with its common sense, is of all forms the least adapted to encompass the modern world, whose leading characteristic is irreality."

As for "Character in Fiction," the decline in the ability to create character comes, in this view, from the modern tendency to try to reach character from the inside. The author has become a sort of ventriloquist; he is not content to describe but must try to impersonate the very soul of someone quite different from himself. The reader is perplexed; he feels the strain, the insecurity. Water has been put into the whisky; the dilution is the poor author himself, struggling to blend in.

1961

LOVELESS LOVE

Graham Greene

"Do you love me, Ticki?"

"What do you think?"

"Say it. One likes to hear it—even if it isn't true."

"I love you, Louise. Of course, it's true."

THIS EXHAUSTED domestic dialogue is used with remarkable power in Graham Greene's novel, *The Heart of the Matter*. Greene has stolen the trivial chatter of marriage from Noel Coward and given it an existential, neo-Catholic varnish, the high polish of fear and trembling and sickness unto death. The petulant archaisms, the white lies, are profanations of the lost ability to love; they bring moral fatigue, not satisfaction ("Say it again, darling!"). The nasty emptiness of the evening compliment ("Dear, how absurd you are. I've never known anyone with so many friends"); the anxiety that one's desperate separateness will be noticed ("He flinched a little away from her, and then hurriedly in case she had noticed, lifted her damp hand and kissed the palm"); the nervous wretchedness of politeness; the anguish edging outrageous promises to provide for another's happiness ("Don't worry. I'll find a way, dear")—in all of this dry, light material Greene finds the terror of, to use Marianne Moore's phrase, that "interesting impossibility," marriage and ideal love.

Scobie, an official in a British-governed town on the west coast of Africa, does not love his wife and so the reckless, embarrassing language of marriage, the optimistic accent, fill him with a dread of such great dimensions that each expected deception appears as a terrible crime. The vocabulary of Scobie's heart is responsibility, self-hatred, anxiety, and guilt. There is a scalding monotony and desperation in his life because of his supererogatory sense of pity. Scobie is mild, dutiful, just, a Catholic who loves God with the bitter passion that has died out in his earthly attachments. All of his secular life is contained in his reluctance to inflict pain. He suffers the agonies of the dinner table and the bedroom as if they were an immense crime against God; his wife's tears are a death sentence; her inevitable moments of ugliness fill him with the "pathos of her unattractiveness"; her absurdity, a malicious remark at her expense arouse in him a bereaved, tragic defense of the right of everyone to live without scorn. With intense seriousness he accepts the burden of her dissatisfaction as his due responsibility. With a kind of fury he compromises his deepest principles to get the money for her voyage to South Africa. After she has gone, he expects to find peace in his loneliness, in the honesty of being accountable only to himself, but, instead, and without wishing it, he becomes involved in a love affair. Again his sharpest emotion is pity; again, to avoid pain, he is brought back to the painful depths of "I love you" and "I'll never leave you." His very act of adultery is a sin which he cannot repent without dishonoring his mistress; he cannot make the required religious effort to abandon the relationship without bringing unhappiness to the woman who depends upon him. His wife returns and to please her he takes Communion, although in a state of mortal sin. His love of God and his duty to life conflict at every point. At last he commits suicide, sacrifices his soul to be relieved of the torture of sacrificing others.

Greene finds in his weary, sad sinner a great religious personality. Scobie is ordinary, inconspicuous, hiding his profound struggle behind his decent, rather colorless appearance. Apparently Greene had a figure in mind like the knight of faith, of whom Kierkegaard said, "Good Lord, is this the man? Is it really he? Why, he looks like a tax-collector!"

"I think he loved God," the priest says, after Scobie's impious death. This mystical resolution, weak and perverse as it is, is the only thing the Catholic novelist can salvage out of the modern, secular ruins in which he feels compelled to place his hero. There is this element of snobbishness in serious Catholic writers. They are bored with the regular devotions, the bland submissiveness—modern man is so much more "interesting." These writers want multiplicity, waywardness, spiritual torment, weakness, and pride; they are in love with sin and intimate with spirituality only as the capacity for suffering from weaknesses. Toward the conventionally pious they are inattentive and Greene is positively churlish. Sebastian in *Brideshead Revisited* is a drunkard, neurotically enslaved to an evil German boy, and yet he is "holy." Waugh says, "He'll develop little eccentricities of devotion, intense personal cults of his own; he'll be found in the chapel at odd times and missed when he's expected. Then one morning, after one of his drinking bouts, he'll be picked up at the gate dying, and show by a mere flicker of the eyelid that he is conscious when they give him the last sacraments. It's not such a bad way of getting through one's life."

Greene, in the dramatic self-slaughter, pushes personal heresy to the limits with a greediness that is convincing neither as fiction nor as religion. His hero must be everything at once. He must not only be a sinner, but must commit the worst sin, and with paradox upon paradox, be nearer to grace than anyone else. Mrs. Scobie, a devoted Catholic, is "furiously" reprimanded by the priest for her impudence in assuming that Scobie will be damned forever. She is guilty of the most sluggish literal-mindedness.

Scobie cannot be understood, cannot be reached or commented upon in terms of psychology or theology. His feeling of responsibility to others approaches arrogance; his death is almost frivolous since it is his last act of pity for a wife whose needs are expressed, "Oh, Ticki, Ticki . . . you won't leave me ever, will you? I haven't got any friends—not since the Tom Barlows went away." As Mary McCarthy wrote about an earlier novel of Greene's, "One cannot imagine a character whose behavior is wholly governed by pity, and one feels that Greene, in pretending that it is possible, is being pious and insincere."

And yet, in spite of Greene's obstinate extension of one emotion, he has done a great deal with Scobie's pity, his loveless love, his anguish over the uncommitted, unmarried part of himself. *The Heart of the Matter* is interesting and serious for its plain, grim understanding of the moral pain of exaggerated sentiment, the tragic heroism of watching over another's life.

1948

"The passenger wondered when it was that he had first begun to detest laughter like a bad smell."

"...I suffer from nothing. I no longer know what suffering is. I have come to the end of all that, too."

"The boat goes no further."

"...I am sorry, I am too far gone, I can't feel at all, I am a leper."

THE PASSENGER, a distinguished church architect named Querry, is the hero of Graham Greene's last novel, *A Burnt-Out Case*. Querry has been loved by many women; he is successful and famous—above all, *famous*. And from it he has ended up tired, morally despairing, filled with self-loathing, insisting upon his loss of feeling, his deadness. Loss of feeling? What does it mean? Fitzgerald's "Crack-up"—what is really meant, what has happened? "And then, ten years this side of forty-nine, I suddenly realized that I had prematurely cracked." The cracked plate, the burnt-out case, the reserved, evasive actually, description of some overwhelming emotional crisis. Fitzgerald: "I saw that even my love for those closest to me was become only an attempt to love..." Querry: "She was once my mistress. I left her three months ago, poor woman—and that's hypocrisy. I feel no pity."

Fame and emptiness. Fame burns out Querry; it surrounds him with horrors who draw near to touch or to fall in love. "Fame is a powerful aphrodisiac." Publicity, the bed sore of the fame-sick, inflicts its pains. Querry has abandoned his career and gone to a leprosy hospital in the Congo. He is at the end of the road; the boat goes no further; his vocation for building and for loving women has given out; he is empty, desperately and courageously "dead." But his fame runs along after him; he is discovered; he is exposed by a journalist; he is pursued by a European manufacturer of margarine, Rycker, who feels for the famous man the mad, easily resentful but somehow grotesquely transfigured, love made of Querry's success and their shared Catholicism. The famous architect and lover is now, in some sense, impotent. ("He told me once that all his life he had only made use of women, but I think he saw himself in the hardest possible light. I even wondered sometimes whether he suffered from a kind of frigidity.") Rycker kills the object of his over-weening curiosity, Querry, because of an imaginary infidelity. "Absurd," Querry said, "this is absurd or else..."

There is an absence of particularity, of the details of experience, in Querry's crack-up, just as there is in Fitzgerald. We reach the end of a great and adored man and accept the despair without any real idea of how it came to be. Curtness, coolness, even carelessness mark the mode of expression. Fitzgerald: "Sometimes, though, the cracked plate has to be retained in the pantry, has to be kept in service as a household necessity. It can never again be warmed on the stove nor shuffled with the other plates in the dishpan; it will not be brought out for company, but it will do to hold crackers late at night or to go into the ice box under left-overs." Querry in disgust: "The darkness was noisy with frogs, and for a long while after his host had said good night and gone, they seemed to croak with Rycker's hollow phrases: grace: sentiment: duty: love, love, love." Self-condemnation, indifferent, impersonal, given out as a Confession, a general statement of sinfulness, without names or places. Art has failed to bring peace; success does not bring happiness to wives, mistresses, or children.

From *Death in Venice*: Art "engraves adventures of the spirit and the mind in the faces of her votaries; let them lead outwardly a life of the most cloistered calm, she will in the end produce in them a fastidiousness, an over-refinement, a nervous fever and exhaustion, such as a career of extravagant passions and pleasures can hardly show." This is a price, perhaps, but a noble, classic fate—far from the sardonic ashheap of Greene. Or compare Mailer's *Advertisements*, a confession in which I, at least, do not find the voice of personal suffering and so assume it was not intended. The alcoholic reserve of Fitzgerald and the manic expressiveness of Mailer show the twenty years or more that separate the personal documents. For Mailer more and more experience, more and more fame—the Congo as an assignment, perhaps, not as a retreat. "Publicity can be an acid test for virtue," Greene says. Poor Hemingway, honorifically carried to his grave by those wooden angels, the restaurant owner Toots Shor and the gossip columnist Leonard Lyons.

In *The Heart of the Matter* the weary hero faced damnation because of his unconquerable pity for the women whom destiny, capriciously, or due to his own wanting, left in his care. Pity is way beyond Querry. He doesn't want to pretend any longer; it is all meaningless. Fornication is a burden and love is impossible. And yet, what is it about? How to account for the flight, the coldness, the refusal? We have Querry's "aridity" seen by the priests at the leper colony, but we do not have the love affairs or the life of the great architect that make the extraordinary final emptiness important. We see the soul at a point of theological instability, and there only.

Greene has a unique gift for plot and a miraculous way of finding a clever objective correlative for his spiritual perplexities. Loss of faith in art and love equals the "cure" of the leper, mutilated, but at last without pain. The humid tropical atmosphere, the tsetse flies, the intense *colons*, with their apologies and their arrogance, the strained, disputatious priests, interestingly pockmarked with weaknesses: this is the properly exotic and threatening setting for the Greene dialogue. *A Burnt-Out Case* seemed a partial failure to V. S. Pritchett in his *New Statesman* review. He felt the influence of the stage had been unfortunate and worked less well than an earlier absorption of film technique. Yet he is not entirely dissatisfied and decides that Querry, the hero, succeeds as a vehicle for certain ideas if not as a "man." Pritchett calls Graham Greene, "the most piercing and important of our novelists now."

Frank Kermode in a brilliant article in *Encounter* is unhappy about *A Burnt-Out Case*. He finds it "so far below one's expectation that the questions arise, was the expectation reasonable and has there been any previous indication that a failure of this kind was a possibility?" In

Kermode's view *The End of the Affair* is Greene's best novel because, to simplify, here the author more openly and with greater seriousness faces his case against God.

Querry, a builder of Catholic churches, is only, the novel tells us, "a legal Catholic." He doesn't pray, he loathes being dragged into other people's lives by the ropes of his religion and his fame; he doesn't want his sins to be made interesting as priests in novels like to do with villains; he resents having his vices stubbornly interpreted as incipient virtues. Father Thomas frantically insists upon accepting Querry's devastated spirit. "Don't you see that you've been given the grace of aridity? Perhaps even now you are walking in the footsteps of St. John of the Cross, the *noche oscura*." In trying to come to some sort of judgment about Greene as a novelist one would have to ask himself whether a significant picture of modern life in the last thirty years could be made from doctrinal puzzles, seminarian wit and paradox, private jokes, Roman Catholic exclusiveness. The characters take their sexual guilt and stand at the edge of damnation discussing possibilities for fresh theological interpretations. They are weary and romantic and fascinated by suffering and they look upon themselves and their feelings in a peculiarly intense Catholic-convert way, a sort of intellectual, clannish, delighted sectarianism. The question is not, in the great Russian manner, how one can live without God, or with God; the question is how one can exist as a moral, or immoral, man without running into vexing complications with the local priest. Marriage, love, sex, pride, art, no matter where you turn things are not quite as the Church would have it and to function at all one has to break rules or offer new versions of the old.

Of course Greene is fascinated by sin and heresy; it could not be otherwise. His terse novels, with their clear, firm themes and symbolic situations, are acted out by men with beautifully apt gifts for language, men raised on Cardinal Newman and Ronald Knox. His world is anti-psychological; the world of psychoanalytical motivation does not exist; its questions are never raised, its interpretations never suggested. Class, childhood, history are irrelevant, too. These are indeed peculiar novels. The omission of so much life and meaning, of the drama of social and psychological existence would seem to be ultimately limiting.

There is a sense of disfiguration, baffling sometimes, and yet always intellectually exciting. Everything is sharper and more brilliant than the effects of other writers. God is a sort of sub-plot and the capricious way He treats Roman Catholics is a suspenseful background to love and boredom and pity. It is most perplexing.

How often Greene sees the living thing as a dead or trivial object, an article of manufacture. "A smile like a licorice stick"; "the pouches under his eyes were like purses that contained the smuggled memories of a disappointing life"; "he was like the kind of plant people put in bathrooms, reared on humidity, shooting too high. He had a small black moustache like a smear of city soot and his face was narrow and flat and endless, like an illustration of the law that two parallel lines never meet."

Licorice sticks, purses filled with snakes, leggy bathroom plants are lined up for the argument, the great debate over a whisky and soda at some peaceful, intellectual Priory. And meanwhile it is really to church that Sarah (*The End of the Affair*) is going and not to meet her lover. God laughs maliciously. On this stage, with its oddly clear and yet humanly peculiar themes, with its weary, engaging purity of design, these brilliant, original works take place, each one as arresting as the other, Catholic-convert dramas of sex and renunciation, belief and defiance.

1961

THE INSULTED AND INJURED

Books About Poverty

> I descend from no name—
> poor from my mother's womb,
> poverty claws me down.
> My father was poor; Horace,
> his father, was the same—
> on my ancestor's tomb,
> God rest their souls! there is
> neither scepter nor crown.
>
> —VILLON

UPPER Broadway, Riverside Drive, the ulcerated side streets hanging on the edge of the academic plateau, shuddering over the abyss of Harlem and the gully of Amsterdam Avenue. In the 1940s, when I was at Columbia, I used to live in the rooming houses around the University. Those bricky towers in the smoky air had huge, dark apartments inside. Some of them, under sly arrangements violating the rent-control laws, were divided into rooms which were rented singly. Downgraded but still rather collegiate and hopeful, the region was preparing itself with great practicality for the dismal future.

Very little adjustment was necessary for the coming residential exploitation of the Puerto Ricans and the restless Negroes in the next decades. The marigold odor of multiple occupancy, the airless arithmetic of "co-operative facilities," the greasy couches and scarred table tops (furnished) were waiting to receive the bodies of the new tenants, ready to pile them on the top of the bones of the old West Side bourgeoisie whose history and stay in the region have been annihilated, as if by a bomb. Blank brick, dirty mirrors, flaking cherubs on forgotten, undusted cornices. These houses stand now in the menacing scene, bursting with the boredom of the exile, the relentlessly exhausting dissipation of the idle. Sordid dawns and bleary mid-nights; Mayakovsky's "men as crumpled as hospital beds, women as battered as proverbs." The cool, drained look of dark-skinned men lounging on the steps of decrepit Windsor Manor, sodden Carleton House, scandalous Excelsior, leprous Queen's Palace.

Julius Horwitz's novel, *The Inhabitants*, is hopeless as a work of fiction and so should be read for what it is, an important document of our people on Welfare assistance, the West Side rooming houses, the illegitimate children, the drug addicts, the tubercular swains, the squalid kitchens, the rats, roaches, and the eternal, vain search by the state and the mother for the vanished fathers of countless children. "I watched the baby hungrily sucking its milk. The baby would never know happier days." Mothers born on relief have their babies on relief. Nothingness, truly, seems to be the condition of these New York people. They are somehow abandoned by life, and exist without skills or meaning. Blankly they watch the drug addicts rip the telephones off the walls in order to get the nickles and dimes. They are nomads going from one rooming house to another, looking for a toilet that functions. There is a loss of domesticity that the crowding together of several generations cannot conceal. They live in a doom for which none of our concepts has prepared us—the queerness, the uselessness. I think I read recently that before many years have passed it is expected that nearly half of the residents of Manhattan will be living on public assistance. Horwitz gives a vivid picture, through the eyes of a social worker, of this perplexing peculiarity. Is this the world of the destitute as we have been accustomed to think of it? I have stood in front of the houses and imagined every sordid corner. I can feel the crowding, the crying, the dirt, the illness, the hopelessness. There is the soiled, careless white man, a sort of guard, looking after the owner's putrefying property. But out of the houses come the beautiful babies in the Welfare layettes, being pushed along in their new Welfare prams. Infancy is indeed the most prosperous moment in these new lives; they come forth into the world, as if for a confirmation, spotlessly, chastely dressed.

The clothes of the urban indigent are often so nice that only the drunks *look* poor; hot dogs, pizzas from the corner shop, and candy bars prevent hunger. There is a strange lack of urgency, as if all these people had been sentenced to an institution of some kind where food and warmth are provided and where one waits, waits for the father of the baby to turn up, for the lover to telephone, the Welfare check to arrive in the mail. Who would ever have thought that urban poverty would become the nervous fatigue and hopelessness of institution life? For these younger people are not exactly unemployed; for one reason or another—illness, pregnancy, psychological disability—they are tragically unequipped. Our ideas are somehow out of date; they do not really tell us what we want to know about all this. New York City, with its Bosch-like horrors, its hideous deformities, has this rotten density everywhere. There is some connection between the New York of the "national-market" offices and the old and new slums. It is of the essence that Manhattan should be the "borough of the very poor and the very rich."

In the Sicily of Danilo Dolci's book, *Outlaws*, poverty, hopelessness, hunger, played-out land—classical economic tragedy and suffering—survive, old relics of injustice and indifference. Dolci, formerly an architect, went to Sicily in 1952 to study Greek temple ruins. The misery of the people led him to the decision to dedicate himself to the relief of their condition. He settled in a poverty-stricken fishing village and married a fisherman's widow with five children. The personal decision, the individual act on behalf of mankind, the belief in possibility, the ultimate responsibility: these are still the only relief from guilt and indifference the human soul can offer.

His first book, *Report from Palermo*, dramatized, by the very successful literary method of direct quotation in the language of the people, the plight of the poor at Trappeto. The Sicilian desperation, the extreme conditions of life there have led Dolci to ask for nothing less than a total moral reorganization of society. In *Outlaws*, an account of the people of Partinico, a center of Sicilian banditry, he writes,

The best concerts, films, and plays in the world should be dedicated to the sick of mind and spirit. The least we can do is to see that the highest recompense goes to those with the most unpleasant jobs, those who clean out drains and toilets.... A less barbarous society than our own would see to it, at least, that the old, the defenseless, the destitute, and the children, the 'last' of today, were the first to occupy the first-class compartments in the trains and boats and to receive the best treatment in hotels and hospitals, on the most favorable terms or entirely free.

There is an account of Dolci's arrest and prison term which grew out of his project whereby unemployed men began working to rebuild an abandoned road rather than remain in demoralizing idleness. Some of the affidavits offered by fellow writers show an interesting insight into Dolci's character. The novelist Vittorini writes, "I have always distrusted the sort of activity which mixes religion with social reform. As soon as I got to know Danilo, however, all my doubts vanished. And as for his ideas, his plans, and his methods...I must admit that I found them eminently suited to conditions in Sicily."

Carlo Levi says of Dolci: "It is this confidence which overflows into the lives of the poor among whom he lives and whose sorrows he has so taken to heart. It is this confidence which has opened their eyes to hope...." As the essence of Dolci's thought Levi chooses the statement: "We are living in a world of men condemned to death by all of us."

The importance of Dolci's literary work comes from his decision to allow the people to speak for themselves, in their own words, without trying to find another form, such as the novel, for their story. When you have actually felt the lives of the bandits of Partinico, at that time Dolci's recommendations have all the urgency of a living need: "If the seven or eight hundred million lire which were found *immediately* for the upkeep of the police force in Partinico alone, had been used *immediately* for building a dam...the winter flood waters could have been utilized for irrigating 8,000 hectares and today there would be no banditry and no unemployment."

We are all inclined to undervalue a great rare effort of the sort made by Dolci, and to feel a certain embarrassment about, for instance, Albert Schweitzer. I heard a woman who had met Schweitzer express her dismay that he was more concerned with his *own salvation* than with a disinterested love for the natives!

The Children of Sánchez: Autobiography of a Mexican Family by Oscar Lewis:

The children of Jesus Sánchez live, along with some seven hundred other souls, in a huge, one-story slum tenement, the Casa Grande, in Mexico City. Not a member of this family has ever known happiness; they cannot succeed or realize their hopes; no matter what drudgery, effort, or inspiration they try to bring to their existence, they will inevitably fail because they were born in poverty. Indeed the four children of Sánchez—Roberto, Manuel, Consuelo, and Marta—are actually sinking into greater deprivation than they were born in. Their efforts are not as effective as those of their father. The children live in a modern state, but they are "marginal," unprotected; they are sophisticated and knowledgeable way beyond their father but it does not yet mean a genuine advantage. The Sánchez children represent in their lives and the drama of their condition something of all the poor young people in all the great cities of the world. In this book about them, the anthropologist, Oscar Lewis, has made something brilliant and of singular significance, a work of such unique concentration and sympathy that one hardly knows how to classify it. It is all, every bit of it except for the introduction, spoken by the members of the Sánchez family. They tell their feelings, their lives, explain their nature, relate their actual existence with all the force and drama and seriousness of a large novel. The stories were taken down by tape-recorder, over a period of years, and under various circumstances. The result is a moving, strange tragedy, not an interview, a questionnaire, or a sociological study.

For a number of years, Dr. Lewis has been making radical literary experiments with his Mexican families, struggling, through them, to tell the story of the poor of the world, to render the actuality beyond statistical truth. And yet he measures his own work by the standard of "scientific" truth, not by the measure of fiction. The huge slum tenement—the neighbors, relatives, lovers, enemies—surrounds the family, enlarging and deepening the personal history so that what one actually has is the story of the condition itself, poverty. Poverty is the fate of this whole world; it is the chief character in this book. The Sánchez family is not of the lowest economic group; the prodigious efforts of the father have given the family a slight, brief lift. The father, a wooden, earnest man, was born in ignorance and destitution in the state of Veracruz. "We always lived in one room, like the one I live in today, just one room." His wife, the mother of the children, dies and Sánchez gradually takes new wives, new mistresses and *their* children, under his harsh but uniquely protective care.

In a world where "marriages" are subject to the most careless cancellation and children regularly abandoned, the sense of personal and family responsibility shown by poor Sánchez has a solemn beauty. By grim labor as a food buyer for La Gloria restaurant and the slow accumulation of further enterprises, he manages to keep an astonishing number of people going. For good reason he is the center of his children's lives, the object of their most intense longings and fears. Roberto says, "Although I haven't been able to show it, I not only love my father, I idolize him. I used to be his pride and joy when I was a kid. . . . He still loves me . . . except that he doesn't show it any more because I don't deserve it." What is so dramatically striking in the story of the Sánchez children is that the same incidents and experiences are described by each one, but with pitifully different interpretations because of pride, natural lack of self-knowledge, and the enormous need of each child to keep the love of his father. The family is hemmed in at every point, confused and desperate, and yet they are powerfully interesting, full of vanity, of piercing if somewhat vague ambitions. They are conscious of hateful disappointments and have to rely, at last, on the mere capacity to endure suffering—a capacity from which little good comes and which cannot give meaning to their lives.

Sexual pride, in both the men and the women, is a strong and often harsh master. The pregnant woman and the illegitimate child; the resentful wife and the unsatisfied husband; the drunken beatings and the bitter mornings; the casual religion and the ultimate hopelessness; the idleness and the dreadful work; the over-crowding and loneliness

—alternatives of equal pain, struggles whose unsatisfactory outcome is inevitable. The lives in the Casa Grande tenement are not torpid, but violent and high-pitched. The economy and the nation have no real use for these people, and yet the useless are persons of strongly marked temperaments who must fully experience, day in and day out, the terrible unfolding of their destiny. The story truly inspires pity and terror; we fear to gaze upon these unjust accidents of birth, of nationality, of time.

A previous book by Oscar Lewis, *Five Families*, is just as remarkable and beautiful as *The Children of Sánchez*. In that book, also taken down by tape-recorder and rearranged, the scheme was a single day in the life of five different families in Mexico City, of which the Sánchez family was one. Both *Five Families* and *The Children of Sánchez* are works of literature, even though they are true stories, told by real people. One would ask, certainly, can a work of literature be written by a tape-recorder? It cannot. Dr. Lewis's books are both literally true and imaginatively presented. In the end it is his rich spirit, his depth of dedication, his sympathy that lie behind the successful re-creation. Dr. Lewis's role is that of the great film director who, out of images and scenes, makes a coherent drama, giving form and meaning to the flow of reality. There is repetition in the monologues, but it is the repetition of life and one would not want it diminished. Dr. Lewis's hope, as an anthropologist, is that his experiments with the tape-recorder will lead other investigators to the means of understanding and presenting the actual life of the unknown urban and peasant masses. This hope has the charm of modesty, but its fulfillment seems unlikely. It is the directing and recording imagination of Dr. Lewis himself that brings to light the dark words of the children of Sánchez, the pitiful summing up of Consuelo. "But though I try to disengage myself, I cannot fail to see what is happening to my family. Oh, God! They are destroying themselves, little by little.... Now my aunt Guadalupe is like a light going out, a wax candle at the foot of the altar; Marta is but twenty-four years old and looks over thirty.... Manuel? yes, he will live, but at whose cost? How many times will he test the love of his children by denying them food? It is horrible to think he will survive his own children!"

1961

GRUB STREET
New York

MAKING a living is nothing; the great difficulty is making a point, making a difference—with words. Here in New York you walk about the shattered, but still unreformed, streets and it seems the city has suffered a scar or wound that has not only changed its appearance but altered its purpose and deepest nature. Outside my house the old Central Park Stables are empty, the windows broken. The warm yellow brick and faded blue trim still glow in the afternoon sun; pigeons tend their nests inside, squatting until the verdict is handed down about this waiting, hurt space. One does not know what to reject, what old alley of desolation to resent, what corner of newness to despise. If one hardly knows what to reject, how much harder it is to be oneself rejected. Is there anyone who hasn't, as we say in our expressive rhetoric, made it?

Yes, some old grubbers, still suffering. The doorbell rings and you are face to face with an outcast who has come on some errand of career that can never be accomplished. He is dark, rather small and thin, hostile and yet briefly hopeful, brightly beaming with suspiciousness. A relief to believe his desperation and obsolescence are somehow closer to literature than to life. He seems to be out of a novel rather than to be writing a novel. Good! True characters, men with a classical twitch, are still alive, old veterans with their frayed flags, creatures such as fiction used to tell of. But the man is not a character in a book; he is himself a writer. His theme is, "If you're not a pederast, a junkie, a Negro—not even a 'white Negro,' ha, ha!—you haven't a dog's chance! Just put your foot in a publisher's office and someone will step on it!" This novelist, in his middle fifties, has known a regular recurrence of literary disaster; and yet he has stayed on the old homestead, planting seeds year after year, like those farmers in drought places who greet each season's dryness with anguished surprise. Even teaching, our first and last refuge, had closed its heart after the poor writer gave out too many failing grades. With his special beam of despairing self-satisfaction, he said, "The students know no more about punctuation than a fly in the air! No, I will not have an illiterate Ph.D. on my conscience." Unpleasant, insignificant, intransigent man—born without an accommodating joint, trying to grasp without thumbs. But, indeed, he makes his point; a certain pleasure, or relief, lies in the assurance that a genuine paranoid solidity cannot be absorbed by American life, that it will not break to the crush of the tooth. And that is a sort of role, perhaps.

Age and outmoded purity and patience may kill sometimes. Old lady writers, without means, without Social Security, reading in bed all day—dear old Sibyls, almost forgotten, hardly called upon except perhaps at midnight by a drunken couple from a pad down the street. Failure is not funny. It is cockroaches on the service elevator, old men in carpet slippers waiting anxiously by the mail slots in the lobby, neighborhood walks where the shops, graphs of consumption, show only a clutter of broken vases, strings of cracked beads, dirty feathers, an old vaudevillian's memorable dinner jacket and decades of cast-off books—the dust of ambition from which the eye turns away in misery.

But the young, the active, rely upon themselves, or perhaps they are desperately thrown back upon themselves, literally. The drama of real life will not let down the prose writer. He can camp for a while in the sedgy valley of autobiography, of current happenings, of the exploration of his own sufferings and sensations, the record of people met, of national figures contemplated. There is beauty to be torn out of the event, the suicide, the murder case, the prize fight. The "I," undisguised, visits new regions for us and pours all his art into them. Life inspires. The confession, the revelation, are not reporting, nor even journalism. Real life is presented as if it were fiction. The concreteness of fact is made suggestive, shadowy, symbolical. The vividly experiencing "I" begins his search for his art in the newspapers.

From the first the reader is captivated by his surprise that this particular writer should be a witness to this particular event. We are immediately engaged by a biographical incongruity: Dwight Macdonald, the famous radical, with his beard, his "ideas" on Doris Day;

Norman Mailer on Sonny Liston; William Styron on a poor convict up for parole; the novelist John Phillips on Teddy Kennedy's campaign. Truman Capote is writing an entire book on an interesting murder case in Kansas and is even said to have provided the police with an important clue. Capote left his villa in Switzerland and went to the bereft, gritty little town in Kansas to study the drama of the trial. An author's unexpected marriage to his subject is in many ways the essence of each new plot.

Real events, one's own vices completely understood, will have a certain, and sometimes, a pure interest. It works, it is convincing. Actuality sustains in a world that does not appear to care very much for fiction writing. In art, the labels from a can of soup, the design of motor cars, the square of the American flag—objects from everyday life put on to canvas—announce themselves as a protest against the idealism and tyranny of abstract expressionism. Imaginary people, fabricated loves and deaths, conclusions not given but to be created in loneliness: are these not also a tyranny from which the writer will some day shrink? Another puzzle: much good writing appears in entertainment magazines other writers seldom read. Circulation without audience. The re-creation of what has truly happened is a self-propelled activity, addressed to no one in particular. Or should we accept the need for money? "What God abandoned, these defended, and saved the sum of things for pay."

Art as a religion—Rilke—seems to be passing; not the work of Rilke, but the style of life, the austere dedication, sustained by the hope that poems and novels would save us. Those holy pages, produced in pain (Flaubert: "You don't know what it is to stay a whole day with your head in your hands trying to squeeze your unfortunate brain so as to find a word")—is there time? From patience, at last, they had perfection. And a security, a fringe benefit, a pension fund such as one can hardly imagine nowadays. Think! Richard Ellmann tells us that Joyce thought the worst thing about World War II was that it distracted the world from reading *Finnegan's Wake*.

Glass is the perfect material of our life. James Baldwin recently had a long, astonishing essay in *The New Yorker*. The work began as an unbearable memoir of Baldwin's youth in Harlem, but it did not remain simply a painful memoir. It became one of those "children in the hands of an angry God" sermons on the Hell of American life for the Negro. Baldwin was determined to make us feel each unutterable day of suffering and humiliation, to make us cringe from the fraud of the democracy and Christianity that had betrayed the Negroes, those most faithful in their devotions. The work was written in a mood of desperation, with full eloquence and intellectual force—and with something more. It was clearly threatening. Baldwin felt the Negro to be approaching a final, revengeful fury.

So there it was. Everyone read it. Everyone talked about it and seemed to feel in some way the better for it. The guerrilla warfare by which the weak become strong, or at least destructive—even the threat of that could be taken, apparently, accepted, turned into glass. Only Russia and Communism arouse—there, writer, watch out.

A peculiar glut, historically interesting. But who wants to be a cook in a household of obese people? The poor, the hungry, fly in by air, brought on official visits, missions of culture. A South American in a brushed, blue serge suit, wearing polished black shoes and large cufflinks of semiprecious stones. His fingernails and his careful, neat dress tell you of all the polish, the care, the melancholy mending done at home by mothers and sisters. This man was one of those whom struggle had drained dry. He had arrived, by hideously hard work, at an overwhelming pedantry, a bachelorish violence of self-control. The pedantry of scarcity. This pale glacier had been produced in the tropics, a poor man in a poor country, trying to lift himself into the professions, to cut through the jungle of deprivation, save a few pennies of ambition from the national bankruptcy. At last with his nervous precision, his aching repression, he declared that the huge, romantic, excessive Thomas Wolfe was the American with whom he felt the closest spiritual and personal connection. He meant to write a book on Wolfe, in Portuguese. He sat looking out of the window, glumly taking in the commercial spires in the distance; his sallow, yearning spirit seemed to have come forth from some mute backland in which his efforts had a bitter, pioneer necessity. Thomas Wolfe! He blinked. "He is my life."

At the entrance to the subway station, there is often an archaic figure giving out a folded sheet of information about the Socialist

Labor Party, or some other small, oddly extant group. In only a few minutes after the distributor takes up his post the streets are littered with his offering. The pages are not thrown away in resentment or disagreement, but cast down as if they were bits of Kleenex: clean white paper with nothing at all written on it, falling into the gutter.

1963

FROST IN HIS LETTERS

SIMPLICITY and vanity, independence and jealousy combined in Robert Frost's character in such unexpected ways that one despairs of sorting them out. He is two picture puzzles perversely dumped into one box and, no matter how much you try, the leg will never go rightly with the arm, nor this brown eye with that green one. Perhaps the worst you could say about Frost was that he could not really like his peers. The second circumstance the observer of "the man" must deal with is that, as an engaging but insistent monologist, he was not especially mindful of the qualities of his auditors and therefore spent a good deal of time in the company of mediocrities. And, further, you could say about Frost, as Dr. Johnson said of Pope, that he had the felicity to take himself at his true value.

If these faults are unfortunate, at least one must say that retribution has not been lenient or slow to come. During Frost's lifetime he was the subject of many astonishingly uneventful books and hopeful was the soul who imagined his death would bring an end to this. His friends were and are dismayingly disposed to sentimental reminiscences. People could not only listen to Frost and read his verse, they could also write about him as if they somehow felt he was not much better than they themselves were. No hesitation intervened and few complications of feeling arose. Frost was his own stereotype. He was already written, so to speak, and one had only to put it all down. He was the *spécialité* of many a comfortable *maison*—a college president here, a governor or two there, and at last even the great Chiefs themselves. Nice, successful people tended to see him as, simply, Robert Frost, a completed image. And as for his work, well, that too was clear. New England human nature he loved and next to nature, art—although as the most tenacious of old, old men he was never, not even at eighty-eight, "ready to depart."

Here are Frost's letters to Louis Untermeyer. They begin in 1915 and they end in 1961. That is a long time and it would take a heart very hard indeed not to agree that Louis Untermeyer, having set upon these eggs for forty-five years, was naturally impatient. His idea had always been to bring the letters to print at the earliest possible moment. Actually, relief had been promised in 1961 and Untermeyer, at that time, prepared the volume for publication. But Frost stalled and stalled. ("When the manuscript was ready for the printer, he made excuses for delaying the publication.") No matter, here they are. They are printed without an index and are very difficult to use for that reason. Still they are certainly quite "interesting." And one must confess, full of vanity, ambition, and ungenerosity.

Frost was a good letter writer, but not a superlatively good one. Indeed, except of course in his poetry, he is untranslatable from the spoken to the written word and that is why those thousands, under the enchantment of what he *said*, will always be perplexed about how cold he appears in his letters and how dull in his biographies. He was malicious and capricious, but there was, hanging about it all, the famous blue-eyed twinkle, the liquid chuckle, the great head, handsome and important at all ages. And when he had said everything his hurt heart had stored up inside him, then he twinkled once more and took it all back, calling it "my fooling."

In 1915, when the letters begin, *North of Boston* had just been enthusiastically received in America (by Louis Untermeyer, among others, and therefore the correspondence) after the very important reception it had received the previous year in England. From that time on, Frost was recognized as a major American poet, even though, of course, he had the usual dismal scratch to make a living and there were many ways in which he endured the intermittent neglect of fashion and the narrow interpretations of some of his more complacent admirers. In 1915, when fame and assurance came, Frost was forty-one years old. That fact is often made to bear the burden for whatever limitations of spirit he may sometimes have shown as a man.

Until the publication of *North of Boston* in England, Frost lived a lonely and more or less isolated life with his wife and children. He had various jobs—always he worked as little as possible because he never had any doubt from the first that his fate would be to devote his whole life to writing poetry. He had started writing in high school and even after he was married he went back to Harvard to study the classics, to prepare himself for his clear destiny. He was never more than an indifferent farmer. He wrote slowly and did not flood the offices of magazines with his verse, only to suffer rejection. He was not immediately recognized and no doubt the tardiness was cruel; yet when fame came it was not dramatically late and it was certainly dramatically brilliant. One cannot altogether credit the indifference he showed to the claims of his fellow poets to an unbearably long wait for public approval. After the success of *North of Boston*, he began the rounds of readings, intervals at various colleges, appearances and so on from which he made a living—this, with his writing, filled up the rest of his life. He was to be the most gregarious of lonely men, the most loquacious of taciturn Vermonters, the most ambitious of honest Yankees.

Frost had a very active and expansive idea of the kind of figure he meant to cut, the kind of role a poet should play in society. His sense of public demand was always acute even though much of his best work, nearly all of it, grew out of his early days of isolation, his experiences with the farm people of New England. That was the treasure upon which he drew. The privacy of his earlier years was as much a reflection of his wife's character as his own. About his wife, Frost writes to Untermeyer:

> Elinor has never been of any earthly use to me. She hasn't cared whether I went to school or worked or earned anything. She has resisted every inch of the way my efforts to get money. She is not too sure that she cares about my reputation. She wouldn't lift a hand to have me lift a hand to increase my reputation or even to save it.... She always knew I was a good poet, but that was between her and me, and there I think she would have liked it if it had remained at least until we were dead....

Frost, even in great poverty and defiance, was as far as anyone could be from the *poète maudit* or the bohemian. In his personality and in his conception of the dramatic possibilities of the literary life, he appears to have united two strains. On the one hand he shows a clear connection with the old New England sages in their role of public instructors. Emerson was a hero of Frost's and Emerson's great career as a lecturer was of course not lost upon his young admirer. The two men were indeed different, but Frost with his poems and his sagacious anecdotes meant, as much as Emerson in his lectures, to save the nation. The writer counted, he was an important public figure and his ideas were urgent. Secondly, Frost seems to have been stirred by the vast audiences, both literary and public, of men like Edgar Lee Masters and Vachel Lindsay. The sales of *Spoon River* were extremely annoying to him. The fantastic popularity of the manic performances of Vachel Lindsay made their point. (So greatly stressful has the life of a writer ever been in America that Lindsay, when his hold upon things began to weaken, drank Lysol, saying as he sank into death, "They tried to get me, I got them first.") E. A. Robinson and Frost gradually took the attention away from Lindsay and Masters. (Masters, in his quite unusually interesting biography of Lindsay, published in 1935, says that the Jews were to blame for the vogue of the New Englanders. To the Jews, "pioneers are objects of aversion...." By "pioneer" he did not signify anything technical or revolutionary, but rather that he and Lindsay were Middle Westerners.) In any case, forensic powers were part of the writer's baggage as Frost saw it.

The relation of Frost to other poets was frankly one of rivalry—indeed one of frank rivalry. He had a certain good-natured, off-hand way of expressing this that saved him from any hint of fanaticism, but it must be said that he was quite anxious about E. A. Robinson's reputation. He made fun of Wallace Stevens's "Peter Quince at the Clavier." He was ungracious about Walter de la Mare ("I have been in no mood to meet Walter de la Mare. He is one of the open questions with me, like what to do with Mexico"), and even had the odd notion that de la Mare was an imitator of Edward Thomas, who in turn was Frost's most important disciple. In late life when Frost, visiting out in Ohio, was taken to see the old reclusive poet, Ralph Hodgson, he reported, "I couldn't see that it gave Ralph Hodgson much pleasure to see me...." Frost was a man of great culture, of naturally good taste, and had the deepest seriousness about poetry—it was vanity and not simplicity of mind that led him to fear his great contemporaries. His praise went to Untermeyer, Raymond Holden, and Dr. Merrill Moore. That the Nobel Prize should have gone to T. S. Eliot and Camus he considered, as Untermeyer tells us, "a personal affront."

Frost's private life was marked by the regular appearance of disaster. Except for his devotion to his wife and—what to call it?—the clamorous serenity of his old age, he was spared little. His sister went insane during the First World War. His letter about her condition is not sacrificial. "As I get older I find it easier to lie awake nights over other people's troubles. But that's as far as I go to date. In good time I will join them in death to show our common humanity." His most talented daughter, Marjorie, died late in her twenties and his wife never fully recovered from her grief. She herself died suddenly, leaving Frost utterly bereft and disorganized. Untermeyer describes this period: "It was hard for Robert to maintain his balance after Elinor's death. He sold the Amherst house where he and Elinor had lived; he resigned from the college; he talked recklessly, and for the first time in his life the man whose favorite tipple was ginger ale accepted any drink that was offered."

After a sad life spent in a futile attempt to become a writer, Frost's son, Carol, committed suicide. Another daughter broke down and had to be put in an institution. There is no doubt that Frost grieved deeply over these tragedies—horrors the audiences coming to see him and to read him knew nothing of. Still he endured and he gradually settled down to his spectacular old age and to those multifarious activities that made his final image.

His reputation as a poet was, one might say, put into order by the brilliant essays of Randall Jarrell. Those essays—so far as I can be sure without an index—are not mentioned in the letters to Untermeyer. They had a stunning effect upon Frost's reputation with the most serious young writers and readers. At the end, Frost was *in* with everyone, with Sherman Adams and W. H. Auden alike. This is a circumstance of great rarity in our literature. Of course, it was the nature of Frost's poetic talent, as well as the prodigality of it, that allowed this ubiquitous prospering of his work. As Yvor Winters puts it: "A popular poet is always a spectacle of some interest, for poetry in general is not popular; and when the popular poet is also within limits a distinguished poet, the spectacle is even more curious. . . . When we encounter such a spectacle, we may be reasonably sure of finding certain social and historical reasons for the popularity." Winters goes on to say that Frost writes of rural subjects and "the American reader of our time has an affection for rural subjects . . ." and so on. In spite of the misinterpretations of some of Frost's readers, he was at least to everyone *readable*. How difficult it is to imagine even so well-liked a poet as T. S. Eliot at the Eisenhower board. Perhaps Eisenhower did not even read Frost, but if he had he could certainly have understood at least some of his work; one cannot be sure of a patience for "Prufrock" or "Journey of the Magi."

One of the most arresting aspects of Frost's character was his genuine interest in power. And for him power did not lie, as it does with most artists, in the comradeship or the approval of the *avant-garde*. Also, he cared nothing for "smart" people, for chicness, for the usual intellectual celebrity world. What he liked was the institutionalized thing. He was perfectly serious in his relationship to power. When he was Consultant in Poetry at the Library of Congress he expected to be "consulted," and not about what went on the poetry shelf, but after important matters of state. So great was his idea of public possibility that he went beyond factionalism, serving Republican and Democrat in turn, in a spirit of poet-laureatism and also in some strangely conceived Public Spokesman mask. His political ideas were usually capricious. A certain coldness entered into his notions. If he had a consistent political theme it was self-reliance. The New Deal with its atmosphere of optimistic enthusiasm was antipathetic to him. But Frost was not in any way a fanatic. He never went very far; somehow inside him there was always the desire to please. Take Untermeyer for instance: layered over his person, like a house with its coat after coat of paint, is nearly every folly and every enthusiasm of liberal belief of the last forty years. Frost teased him; he never became angry with him or broke with him. The independent old Vermonter side of Frost has been exaggerated. He was indeed independent, but he wanted to count, to have importance: this gave him a steady flow of prudence. Frost did not even want disciples. That would be a two-way street and except for those in his family he didn't want to share himself. (Edward Thomas died in the First World War.)

The strain of some unnamed trouble that we feel in Frost is inexplicable. He was brilliant, adored, available, and even his resentments were not the sort that stripped a man of his charm. They did form his ideas to some degree. Somehow he had suffered and come through: there are no Welfare State lessons to be learned from that. There is, instead, only the example of individual initiative. Even his relation to those people who, like Ezra Pound, had the highest regard for his powers was touched by ambivalence. Amy Lowell wrote an early and very impressive essay about him, but he was, if pleased, not *entirely* satisfied. (Didn't like what she said about his wife and was not happy to share the stage with Robinson.) The only mention I can find—in Elizabeth Shepley Sergeant's book—that Frost actually made of Randall Jarrell is not about Jarrell's writing and is a bit querulous: "Randall Jarrell thinks poets aren't helped enough. But I say poetry has always lived on a good deal of neglect." We shall have to wait for other Frost letters to get his full opinion of Untermeyer.

But Frost was not a conservative, either. He was only a writer. He did not care for money, but for position, whatever position he could gain from his work as a poet. Sometimes we feel he bought his claim to the Old American virtues at a considerable price. He was fulfilled, charming, and he lived to a great old age and yet to go back over his life, in these letters, back, back, to the early years of the century, fills us with a sadness too. At the end, sick, tired, too old for the journey, he paid a visit to Khrushchev—interestingly described by his companion, F. D. Reeve, in a recent issue of *The Atlantic Monthly*. What he had come for, we find out, was not for the ceremonial edification of both countries. Frost had, in truth, gone to Russia to tell Khrushchev how to settle the question of Berlin.

1963

RING LARDNER

WHEN RING Lardner died in 1933, Scott Fitzgerald wrote an interesting and somewhat despairing tribute to him. "The point of these paragraphs is that, whatever Ring's achievement was, it fell short of the achievement he was capable of, and this because of a cynical attitude toward his work." Fitzgerald thought Lardner had developed the habit of silence about important things and that he fell back in his writing on the formulas he always had ready at hand. It is easy to imagine how this might have appeared true thirty years ago when the memory of the great short story writer working away at his daily comic strip text was still painfully near to those who cared about him. Lardner was a perplexing man, often careless about his own talents. How to account for the element of self-destroying indifference in the joshing preface to *How to Write Short Stories*, a volume that contained "My Roomy," "Champion," "Some Like Them Cold," and "The Golden Honeymoon." Edmund Wilson's review of this volume in *The Dial* spoke warmly about the stories and mentioned the disturbing unsuitability of the preface, which he found so far below Lardner's usual level that "one suspects him of a guilty conscience at attempting to disguise his talent for social observation and satire." If Lardner knew of this criticism, he was unmoved by it and introduced *The Love Nest* in a similar manner. (That volume contained, among others, "Haircut" and "Zone of Quiet.") The palpable incongruity of the jocular prefaces as an introduction to the superlatively bitter stories serves as a mirror to the strangeness of Lardner's personality and work.

Reading Lardner again now is almost a new experience. Somewhat unexpectedly one finds that he has a dismal cogency to a booming America: his subjects are dishonesty, social climbing, boastfulness, and waste. For that reason, Maxwell Geismar's new collection is valuable as a way of bringing Lardner once more to public notice. This new volume, because of larger print, is easier to read than the Viking *Portable Ring Lardner*, but it is not otherwise an improvement. Indeed the Viking *Portable* has the advantage of the complete text of "You Know Me, Al" and "The Big Town." Geismar's preface does not supply more than the usual demand; nevertheless his selection will not fail anyone who wants the unsettling experience of discovering Ring Lardner or of rediscovering him.

Out of a daily struggle to make a living by literary work of various kinds, Lardner produced many short stories and some longer works of great originality. These stories were also immensely popular and nothing touches us more than this rare happening. In a country like ours where there will necessarily be so much journalism, so much support of the popular, the successful, we are complacently grateful when we find the genuine among the acceptable. And with Lardner there is something more: he made literature out of baseball, the bridge game, and the wisecrack. Of course he was terribly funny, but even in his funniest stories there is a special desolation, a sense of national spaces filled by stupidity and vanity.

Now, in the 1960s, the distance from the twenties reduces some of the journalistic aspects of Lardner's writing. We are struck most of all by his difference from popular writing today. His is a miserable world made tolerable only by a maniacal flow of wisecracks. "That's Marie Antoinette's bed," the four-flusher says as he shows a couple around his Riverside Drive apartment. The wisecracker asks, "What time does she usually get in it?" When the wife says, "Guess who called me today?" the husband answers, "Josephus Daniels or Henry Ford. Or maybe it was the guy with the scar on his lip that you thought was smiling at you the other day." Out of the plain, unabashed gag, and the cruel dialogue of domestic life, Lardner created his odd stories, with their curious speed, rush of situation, explosion of insult, and embarrassment.

Lardner's characters have every mean fault, but they lack the patience to do much with their meanness. The busher is boastful and stingy, and yet quite unable, for all his surface shrewdness, to discover his real place in the scheme of things. He is always being dropped by the women he had boasted about and all his stinginess cannot help to manage his affairs. Lardner's stories are filled with greedy, grasping people who nevertheless go bankrupt. You cannot say they are cheated, since they are themselves such awful cheats. The Gullibles have the fantastic idea of going to Palm Beach to get into "society." Mrs. Gullible does at last meet Mrs. Potter Palmer in the corridor of the hotel and Mrs. Palmer asks her to put more towels in her suite. The squandering of an inheritance by the characters in "The Big Town" shows a riotous lack of elementary common sense. The husbands usually have some idea of the cost of things and of the absurdity of their wives' ambitions. But they cannot act upon their knowledge. It comes out only in the constant static of their wisecracks. Wildly joking, they go along with their wives into debt and humiliation. It is hard to feel much sympathy and yet occasionally one does so: the sympathy comes, when it does, from the fact that the jokes played upon these dreadful people are after all thoroughly real and mean. Even the language they speak with such immense, dismaying humor is a kind of joke on real language, funnier and more cutting than we can bear.

Vanity, greed, and cruel humor are the themes of Lardner's stories. The lack of self-knowledge is made up for by a dizzy readiness with cheap alibis. No group or class seems better than another; there is a democracy of cheapness and shallowness. Lies are at the core of nearly every character he produces for us. The only fear is being caught out, exposed to the truth. Love cannot exist because the moment it runs into trouble the people lie about their former feelings. Because of the habit of lying, it is a world without common sense. The tortured characters are not always victims. They may be ruined and made fun of, but they have the last word. They bite the leg that kicks them.

"Haircut" is one of the cruelest pieces of American fiction. Even Lardner seems to have felt some need for relief from the relentless evil of the smalltown joker and so he has him killed in the end. This cruel story is just about the only one that has the contrast of decent people preyed upon by a maniac. "Champion" is brutal and "The Golden Honeymoon" is a masterpiece of grim realism. Alfred Kazin speaks of the "harsh, glazed coldness" of Lardner's work. He wrapped his dreadful events in a comic language, as you would put an insecticide in a bright can.

Lardner's personality is very difficult to take hold of. In spite of poor health that came, so far as I can discover, from his devastating drinking, he had the continuing productivity of the professional journalist. He went to work every morning. Why he drank, why his views were so bitter are a mystery. He came from a charming, talented family and married a woman he loved. He was kind, reserved, hard-working; his fictional world is loud, cruel, filled with desperate marriages, hideous old age, suburban wretchedness, fraud, drunkenness. Even the sports world is degraded and athletes are likely to be sadists, crooks, or dumbbells. The vision is thoroughly desperate. All the literature of the thirties and forties does not contain such pure subversion, snatched on the run from the common man and his old jokes.

1963

GRUB STREET
Washington

HE IS IMAGINARY, not meant to be a true person. As a young man he showed an interest in public affairs, showed it early, but, of course, he was too bookish, too arrogant, too much disliked to think of real politics, of the state legislature, the Senate. And yet his earliest moral frustration came from his sense of history and biography, his living through today and yet imagining how it would all appear in a book tomorrow. He had only to read the newspapers to be seized by the agony of lost opportunities, the refusal of presidents and leaders to greet the true moment, utter the simple eloquence, jump into the open pit of possibility for memorable behavior, note the instance with a ready witticism. He had always wanted to help them. For he knew that few Americans slice their own bread: much that an American leader does and thinks is done for him. The president is a vessel into which suitable waters are daily poured. But at the same time he is a difficult man and it is only a sort of hollow arm he will allow to be filled up by expert waters. For the rest, he keeps himself dismayingly dry. All of our recent history shows the inability or refusal of our leaders to be other than themselves, as they were born. They will not undergo for us that dramatic metamorphosis the imagination and the spirit long for. Accents from babyhood stutter down through history, forever recorded on a thousand tapes. A president needs only to be, not to become. And our imaginary helper, the writer who would somehow live and write history simultaneously, suffers pitifully. Having success-fully attained an elective office seems to freeze the personality in its winning shape. Only an idiot would tamper with success. An elected official does not fear the knowledge of professors or heed the vexations of aesthetes.

Our writer, our economist, our thinker, this person who would bring to Washington and to national affairs some of the order that goes into the making of books or even into the reading of them did at last enter the city with Kennedy, a few to them entered at least. What he was to do there we do not quite know, since government is not a book. We may think of him as wanting to please and yet himself hardened to criticism. A certain ambitiousness makes one forgiving— the sort of ambition that yearns for effectiveness rather than perfection. But if power and the opportunity to observe power were simply a lofty form of office work, no one would want it. It is also tall women in splendid dresses, black limousines at the door, and the lust for the ultimate historical gossip satisfied at last. To know, truly, what the people in power are like: is that not some of the charm, the interest, as well as legislation passed, policy defined?

Our young man—no, our *youngish* man—a father, long resident of some simpler community than Washington, has a pleasant enough vanity based on his past accomplishments. The little cavities of self-doubt have been filled with the cement of a quick psychoanalysis, the determination of wives, and, with power and fame, women other than wives. Even the poor legislator, and certainly the Washington intellectual *personage*, find that men at the center of things appear to women in the most affirmative light, creating a climate of assent, of romantic and personal prosperity that sweeten the long work day. (All our presidents, according to the press, rise early.) He finds that she who wishes to buy will not be deterred by small defects. The poor bookworm, the faithful teacher, the economist at his desk had not realized that political power, or even the nearness to it, will make of one the hero of a novel, and there will inevitably be subplots.

History starves many, but fattens a few. All the tortured ambivalence Voltaire felt for Frederick (Macaulay says it was "compounded of all sentiments, from enmity to friendship, from scorn to admiration...") might have been in a more usual country felt by our man. But here where the occasion to serve in the capitol is so rare, gratitude and opportunity will naturally incline one to an unduly full acceptance, and even to considerable suppression or denial of the observing faculties. The real person, the elected man, is, so far as we can learn, nearly always a person of the most rigid contrariness. In the present world he is likely to be exactly the opposite of all the public imagines. Behind the ruddy, folksy downrightness insiders know conceit, anger, vindictiveness. Family men, pictured a million times with their first ladies, die in the arms of their second ladies. Every exalted hill is a loathsome valley. Perhaps this, the final falseness or fraud, is the ultimate reward of our greed for publicity. Because we want to know everything we are told nothing but lies. The president appears like one of those television commercials run over and over again. He is always typecast, wearing his make-up. The opposition always chooses the wrong vices to whisper about. If a man is a drunkard they will tell the voters that he has syphilis. The lie is the only thing we can count on in our image of the president.

But all this is merely "social" and trivial. Serious men do important work—they must whether they wish to or not. They must "save the free world," save it again and again. Work, crises, trips; our man floats through space with everything petty done for him by a gigantic bureaucracy; the hard work of government is also impersonal. He is a tenor in a chorale that may or may not receive good reviews, but at least he is not always personally accountable. Few people ever quit the movies or political life. These callings, therefore, must not be as "exhausting" as we are told, since so many notoriously lazy persons refuse to abandon them unless met with irrevocable rejection. Speeches, conferences, and confrontations, the satisfaction of ceremonial interludes: to these the dullest and the cleverest creatures assent, grateful, "prayerful," going forth to them with the help of God. Our writer, our intellectual will be thought by many not to be a "real" writer. It is felt that to the real writer or thinker no harm can come from history; only the private catastrophe, the individual suffering, can give pause to an authentic inspiration. But how are we to judge the melancholy, how to estimate the strain on the heart muscles in the effort to go back once more, to live again with elected American essence, how to know the ulcerative struggle to bring the word to the wordless?

The black limousine draws up in Georgetown, but now it picks up a mortified man with a cramped smile. He who is pursuing his intellectual work in Washington is back again in the little ranch house of political America. All would be disposed to pity. And yet even the true poet, the fiction writer—how will he flee the merciless strength of the American spirit, the cactus that lives without water?

1964

SELMA, ALABAMA
The Charms of Goodness

SELMA, ALABAMA, MARCH 22, 1965

WHAT A sad countryside it is, the home of the pain of the Confederacy, the birthplace of the White Citizens Council. The khaki-colored earth, the tense air, the vanquished feeding on their permanent Civil War—all of it inevitably brings to mind flamboyant adjectives and images from Faulkner. Immemorial, doomed streets, policed by the Snopeses and Peter Grimms, alleys worn thin in the sleepless pursuit of a thousand Joe Christmases, and Miss Coldfield and Quentin behind the dusty lattices, in the "empty hall echoing with sonorous, defeated names." And as you pass Big Swamp Creek, you imagine you hear the yelp of movie bloodhounds. The cabins, pitifully beautiful, set back from the road, with a trail of wood smoke fringing the sky; the melancholy frogs unmindful of the highway and the cars slipping by; the tufts of moss, like piles of housedust, that hang trembling on the bare winter trees; the road that leads at last to just the dead Sunday afternoon Main Streets you knew were there. We've read it all, again and again. We've seen it in the movies, in the Farm Security Administration photographs of almost thirty years ago: the voteless blacks, waiting tentatively on the courthouse steps, the angry jowls of the racists, the washed-out children, the enduring Negroes, the police, the same old sheriff: the entire region is fiction, art, dated, something out of a second-hand bookstore. And this, to be sure, is the "Southern way of life," or part of it—these photographs of a shack standing under a brilliant sky, the blackest of faces, the whitest mansions with front-porch columns, the impacted dirt of the bus station, the little, cottagey, non-denominational churches, standing in the dust, leaning a bit, and the big Methodist and Baptist with yellow brick turrets and fat belfries. If this that meets the eye as an expectation as familiar as the New York City skyline is not the South, what can the word mean? The rest might be anywhere, everywhere—mobile homes, dead cars in the yard, ranch houses shading their eyes with plastic awnings.

Life arranges itself for you here in Selma in the most conventional tableaux. Juxtapositions and paradoxes fit only for the most superficial art present themselves again and again. The "crisis" reduces the landscape to genre. At their best the people who rule over Selma, Alabama, seem to suffer from a preternatural foolishness and at their worst just now from a schizophrenic meanness. Just as they use the Confederate flag, so they use themselves, without embarrassment, in the old pageantry. A tableau which might have been thought up decades ago by one of the Hollywood Ten: the early morning fog is lifting and a band of civil rights demonstrators stands at its post at the end of a dusty street. At just that moment a State Highway truck appears and lets out three desolate Negro convicts wearing black and white striped convict uniforms, uniforms still in use but appearing to the contemporary eye to be a selection from a costume warehouse. The convicts take up their brooms and, heads down, jailhouse and penitentiary hopelessness clinging to them, begin their morose sweeping up. The brooms meet the very shoelaces of the demonstrators, brush against the hem of a nun's black skirts. Soon the soft melodies fall on the heads of the convicts: We will overcome or else go home to our Lord and be free.

Great, great, we say of the arrangement, the curious, fortuitous performance. Then off the convicts shuffle in their black and white trousers, part of Alabama's humble devotion to symbolism.

How do they see themselves, these posse-men, Sheriff Clark's volunteers, nearly always squat, fair-faced, middle-aged, now wearing helmets and carrying guns and sticks? The state troopers seem one ghostly step ahead on the social ladder. The troopers ride around in cars, their coats hanging primly in the back seat. They might be salesmen, covering the territory, on to the evening's motel. The posse-men do not appear contented or prideful so much as merely obsessive and meager, joyless, unconsoled. The ignoble posture one observes so frequently in them is a puzzle. This cramped, hunched distance from bodily, even from masculine, grace makes them indeed among the saddest-looking people in the world. Even the hungry, bone-thin poor of Recife do not present such a picture of deep, almost hereditary, depression.

This group of Southerners has only the nothingness of racist preoccupation, the burning incoherence. Their bereft, static existence seems to go back many generations and has its counterpart in the violent, deranged hopelessness of the deprived youth in the cities. Here in the ameliorating sunlight of the Civil Rights Movement, the volunteer posse-men lead one to thoughts of remedial assistance. Who will open the doors of the University of Alabama or Clemson or Tulane to the children of Klansmen?

A poor young man, a native of Alabama, in a hot, cheap black suit, and the most insistent of false teeth clinging to gums not over twenty-one years old, back-country accent, pale, with that furry whiteness of a caterpillar, rimless glasses, stiff shoes, all misery and weakness and character armor, said to me, "When I saw those white folks mixed in with the colored it made me right sick." And what could one answer: Go to see your social worker, find an agency that can help you, some family counsellor, or perhaps an out-patient clinic? I did say, softly, "Pull yourself together." And he too shuffled off, like the convicts, his head bent down in some deep perturbation of spirit.

What charity can lift up the young man? There are no students welcomed to sleep on the floor of the racist home, no guitars and folk lyrics transposed to the key of the moment. It is true that these outcasts, men who are not in the state legislature and who do not belong to "nice" white Southern society because they are back-country and ignorant of style, make certain claims. They carry guns and whips and vote for the senators and governors. They try to have influence over who buys the books in the window in Montgomery (*Herzog, Les Mots* in translation) and subscribes to *The New Republic*. They keep in line, or try to, those Southern queers who are "mad about Negroes" and who collect jazz records. Their main "influence" is over the black population, an influence their very existence assures. And yet they are a degraded and despised people, even if their ferrety kinsman, Lester Maddox, can get on the ballot in Georgia.

The intellectual life in New York and the radical tone of the thirties are the worst possible preparation for Alabama at this stage of the Civil Rights Movement. In truth it must be said that the demonstrators are an embarrassment of love and brotherhood and hymns offered up in Jesus's name and evening services after that. Intellectual pride is out of place, theory is simple and practical, action is exuberant and communal, the battlefield is out-of-doors and demands of one a certain youthful athleticism that would, in a morning's work, rip the veins of the old Stalinists and Trotskyites.

The political genius of Martin Luther King is, by any theory, quite unexpected. The nature of his protest, the quality and extent of his success sprang from the soil of religion and practicality most liberals had thought to be barren. Looking back, it is curious to remember how small a part the Negro's existence played in the earlier left-wing movements. The concentration on industrial labor, white sharecroppers, the Soviet Union and the Nazis left the Negro as only a footnote. That it should with King have come to this was unthinkable: this cloud of witnesses, this confrontation of hymn singers and local authorities. Martyred clergymen, Negro children killed at their Sunday School prayers, the ideas of Gandhi imposed upon restless blacks and belligerent whites—these appear as some sort of mutation of a national strain. "God will take care of you," they sing, Billy Eckstine style.

In the demonstrations and marches in Alabama you are watching—good people. The foundation is the Civil Rights Movement built by Southern Negroes and into this plot, like so many extras, these fantastic white people have come. On that "hallowed spot," Sylvan Street in Selma, you feel you are witness to a new Appomattox played out with the help of exceedingly refined, somewhat feminine Yankee clerics, upright people, marching in their prudent overshoes, some of them wearing Chesterfield coats with velvet collars.

The deputy sheriff spoke of these "so-called ministers," but that indeed was a joke. Even a deputy can see that these are preacher faces.

On a Sunday after the white churches had turned away the groups of "mixed worshippers" who had knocked at the doors, a Church of Christ found a verse in the Gospel of Matthew that seemed to explain the refusal of the morning. The verse was put up outside in the announcement box and it read: "When you pray, be not as hypocrites are, standing in the street."

But of course hypocrisy is as foreign to these people as vice and that, perhaps, is their story. There is no doubt that they have been, before this opportunity to be a witness, suffering from considerable frustration, aching with the shame of a Christian who is busy most of the time ridding the church of the doctrine of the past as he waits for some meaning in the present. The moral justice of the Civil Rights Movement, the responsible program of the leaders, the murderous rage of the white people: this was the occasion at last. For the late-comers perhaps the immediate instrument had to be the death of a young white idealistic Protestant minister.

So, in Alabama the cause is right, the need is great, but there is more to it than that. There is the positive attraction between the people. The racists, with their fear of touch, their savage superstition, their reading of portents, see before them something more than voting rights. They sense the elation, the unexpected release. Few of us have shared any life as close as those "on location" in the Civil Rights Movement. Shared beds and sofas, hands caressing the shoulders of little children, smiles and a spreading comradeship, absorption: this is, as the pilgrims say again and again, a great experience. The police, protected by their helmets, are frightened and confused by these seizures of happiness. The odd thing is that it should not be beatniks and hipsters and bohemians who are sending out the message, but good, clean, downright folk in glasses and wearing tie clasps.

1965

AFTER WATTS

THE DISASTER and then, after a period of mourning or shock, the Report. Thus we try to exorcise our fears, to put into some sort of neutrality everything that menaces our peace. The Reports look out upon the inexplicable in private action and the unmanageable in community explosion; they investigate, they study, they interview, and at last, they recommend. Society is calmed, and not so much by what is found in the study as by the display of official energy, the activity underwritten. For we well know that little will be done, nothing new uncovered—at least not in this manner; instead a recitation of common assumptions will prevail, as it must, for these works are rituals, communal rites. To expect more, to anticipate anguish or social imagination, leads to disappointment and anger. The Reports now begin to have their formal structure. Always on the sacred agenda is the search for "outside influence," for it appears that our dreams are never free of conspiracies. "We find," one of the Reports goes, "no evidence that the Free Speech Movement was organized by the Communist Party, or the Progressive Labor Movement, or any other outside group." Good, we say, safe once more, protected from the ultimate.

It is also part of the structure of a Report that it should scold us, but scold in an encouraging, constructive way, as a mother is advised to reprimand her child. For, after all, are we to blame? To blame for riots, assassinations, disorderly students? The Reports say, yes, we are to blame, and then again we aren't. Oswald, friendless, and Watts, ignored. Well, we should indeed have done better—and they should have done better, too.

*

Watts—a strip of plastic and clapboard, decorated by skimpy palms. It has about it that depressed feeling of a shimmering, timeless afternoon in the Caribbean: there, just standing about, the melancholy bodies of young black boys—and way off, in the distance, the looming towers of a Hilton. Pale stucco, shacky stores, housing projects, laid out nicely, not tall, like rows of tomato vines. Equable climate, ennui, nothingness. Here? Why here? we demand to know. Are they perhaps, although so recently from little towns and rural counties of the south, somehow longing for the sweet squalor of the Hotel Theresa, the battered seats of the Apollo Theater? This long, sunny nothingness, born yesterday. It turns out to be an exile, a stop-over from which there is no escape. In January there was a strange quiet. You tour the streets as if they were a battlefield, our absolutely contemporary Gettysburg. Here, the hallowed rubble of the Lucky Store, there once stood a clothing shop, and yonder, the ruins of a super market. The standing survivors told the eye what the fallen monuments had looked like, the frame, modest structures of small, small business, itself more or less fallen away from all but the most reduced hopes. In the evening the owners lock and bolt and gate and bar and then drive away to their own neighborhoods, a good many of those also infested with disappointments unmitigated by the year-round cook-out. Everything is small, but with no hint of neighborliness.

The promise of Los Angeles, this beckoning openness, newness, freedom. But what is it? It is neither a great city nor a small town. Sheer impossibility of definition, of knowing what you are experiencing exhausts the mind. The intensity and diversity of small-town Main Streets have been stretched and pulled and thinned out so that not even a Kresge, a redecorated Walgreen's, or the old gray stone of the public library, the spittoons and insolence of the Court House stand to keep the memory intact. The past resides in old cars, five years old, if anywhere. The Watts riots were a way to enter history, to create a past, to give form by destruction. Being shown the debris by serious, intelligent men of the district was like being on one of those cultural tours in an underdeveloped region. Their pride, their memories were of the first importance. It is hard to find another act in American history of such peculiarity—elation in the destruction of the lowly symbols of capitalism.

And now, how long ago it all seems. How odd it is to go back over the old newspapers, the astonishing photographs in *Life* magazine, the flaming buildings, the girls in hair curlers and shorts, the loaded shopping carts, "Get Whitey," and "Burn, baby, burn," and the National Guard, the crisis, the curfew, and Police chief Parker's curtain line, "We're on top and they are on the bottom." In the summer of 1965 "as many as 10,000 Negroes took to the streets in marauding bands." Property damage was forty million; nearly four thousand persons were arrested; thirty-four were killed. A commission headed by John A. McCone produced a report called, "Violence in the City—An End or a Beginning?" (Imagine the conferences about the title!) It is somewhat dramatic, but not unnerving since its cadence whispers immediately in our ear of the second-rate, the Sunday Supplement, the *Reader's Digest*.

The Watts Report is a distressing effort. It is one of those bureaucratic documents, written in an ambivalent bureaucratic prose, and it yields little of interest on the surface and a great deal of hostility below the surface. (Bayard Rustin in *Commentary* shows brilliantly how the defects of Negro life are made to carry the blame for Negro behavior in a way that exonerates the conditions that produced the defects.) In our time, moral torpor and evangelical rhetoric have numbed our senses. The humble meters of the McCone Report are an extreme example of the distance a debased rhetoric puts between word and deed. A certain squeamishness calls the poor Negroes of Watts the "disadvantaged" and designates the police as "Caucasians." "A dull, devastating spiral of failure" is their way of calling to mind the days and nights of the Watts community.

The drama of the disadvantaged and the Caucasians opens on a warm night and a drunken driver. Anyone who has been in Watts will know the beauty and power of the automobile. It is the lifeline, and during the burning and looting, car lots and gasoline stations were exempt from revenge. Watts indeed is an island; even though by car it is not far from downtown Los Angeles, it has been estimated that it costs about $1.50 and one-and-a-half to two hours to get out of Watts to possible employment. One might wonder, as he reads the opening scene, why the police were going to tow the drunken driver's car away, rather than release it to his mother and brother who were trying to claim it? For this is a deprivation and frustration not to be borne in the freeway inferno. Without a car you are not truly alive; every sort of crippling, disabling imprisonment of body and mind attends this lack. The sight of the "Caucasians" and the hot night and the hatred and deprivation burst into a revolutionary ecstasy and before it was over it extended far beyond Watts, which is only the name for a small part of the community, into a much larger area of Negro residence.

And what is to be done, what does it mean? Was it gray, tired meat and shoes with composition soles at prices a little starlet might gasp at? Of course we know what the report will say, what we all say; all that is true and has nevertheless become words, rhetoric. It's jobs and headstarts and housing and the mother at the head of the family and reading levels and drop-outs. The Report mentions some particular aggravations: the incredible bungling of the poverty program in Los Angeles; the insult of the repeal of the Rumford Fair Housing Act; the Civil Rights program of protest. The last cause is a deduction from the Byzantine prose of the report which reads: "Throughout the nation, unpunished violence and disobedience to law were widely reported, and almost daily there were exhortations, here and elsewhere, to take extreme and even illegal remedies to right a wide variety of wrongs, real and supposed." *Real* and *supposed*; in another passage the locution "many Negroes felt and *were encouraged* to feel," occurs. These niceties fascinate the student of language. They tell of unseen enemies, real and supposed, and strange encouragements, of what nature we are not told.

Still, the Watts Report is a mirror: the distance its bureaucratic language puts between us and the Negro is the reflection of reality. The demands of those days and nights on the streets, the smoke and the flames, are simply not to be taken in. The most radical re-organization of our lives could hardly satisfy them, and there seems to be neither the wish nor the will to make the effort. The words swell as purpose shrinks. Alabama and California are separated by more than miles of painted desert. The Civil Rights movement is fellowship and Watts is alienation, separation.

"What can violence bring you when the white people have the police and the power? What can it bring you except death?"

"Well, we are dying a little bit every day."

The final words of the Report seem to struggle for some faint upbeat and resolution but they are bewildered and fatigued. "As we have said earlier in this report, there is no immediate remedy for the problems of the Negro and other disadvantaged in our community. The problems are deep and the remedies are costly and will take time. However, through the implementation of the programs we propose, with the dedication we discuss, and with the leadership we call for from all, our Commission states without dissent, that the tragic violence that occurred during the six days of August will not be repeated."

How hard it is to keep the attention of the American people. Perhaps that is what "communications" are for: to excite and divert with one thing after another. And we are a nation preeminent in communications. The Negro has been pushed out of our thoughts by the Vietnam War. Helicopters in Southeast Asia turned out to be far easier to provide than the respect the Negro asked for.

"The army? What about the army?"

"It's the last chance for a Negro to be a man...and yet it's another prison, too."

The months have gone by. And did the explosion in Watts really do what they thought afterward? Did it give dignity and definition? Did it mean anything in the long run? We know that only the severest concentration will keep the claims of the Negro alive in America, because he represents all the imponderables of life itself. Anxiety and uncertainty push us on to something else—to words which seem to soothe, and to more words. As for Watts itself: the oddity of its simplicity can scarcely be grasped. Its defiant lack of outline haunts the imagination. Lying low under the sun, shadowed by overpasses, it would seem to offer every possibility, every hope. In the newness of the residents, of the buildings, of the TV sets, there is a strange stillness, as of something formless, unaccountable. The gaps in the streets are hardly missed, where there is so much missing. Of course it is jobs and schools and segregation, yes, yes. But beyond that something that has nothing to do with Negroes was trying to be destroyed that summer. Some part of new America itself—that "dull, devastating spiral of failure" the McCone Commission imagines to belong only to the "disadvantaged" standing friendless in their capsule on the outskirts of downtown Los Angeles.

1966

THE APOTHEOSIS OF MARTIN LUTHER KING

MEMPHIS, ATLANTA, 1968

THE DECAYING, downtown shopping section of Memphis—still another Main Street—lay, the weekend before Martin Luther King's funeral, under a siege. The deranging curfew and that state of civic existence called "tension" made the town seem to be sinister, again very much like a film set, perhaps for a television drama, of breakdown, catastrophe. Since films and television have staged everything imaginable before it happens, a true event, taking place in the real world, brings to mind the landscape of films. There is no meaning in this beyond description and real life only looks like a fabrication and does not feel so.

The streets are completely empty of traffic and persons and yet the emptiness is the signal of dire and dramatic possibilities. In the silence, the horn of a tug gliding up the dark Mississippi is background. The hotel, downtown, overlooking the city park, is a tomb and perhaps that is usual since it is downtown where nobody wants to go in middle-sized cities. It is a shabby place, poorly staffed by aged persons, not grown old in their duties, but newly hired, untrained, depressed, worn-out old people.

The march was called for the next day, a march originally called by King as a renewal of his efforts in the Memphis garbage strike, efforts interrupted by a riot in the poor, black sections the week before. Now he was murdered and the march was called to honor him. Fear of riots, rage, had brought the curfew and the National Guard. Perhaps there was fear, but in civic crises there is always something exciting and even a sort of humidity of smugness seemed to hang over the town. Children kept home from school, bank and ten-cent store closed. If one was not in clear danger, there seemed to be a complacent pleasure in thinking, We have been brought to this by Them.

Beyond and beneath the glassy beige curtains of the hotel room, the courthouse square was spread out like a target, the destination of the next day's march and ceremony. All night long little hammer blows, a ghostly percussion, rang out as the structure for the "event" was being put together. The stage, slowly forming, plank by plank, seemed in the deluding curfew emptiness and silence like a scaffolding being prepared for a beheading. These overwrought and exaggerated images came to me from the actual scene and from a crush of childhood memories. Memphis was a Southern town in which a murder had taken place. The killer might be over yonder in that deep blue thicket, or holed up in the woods on the edge of town, ready to come back at night. Of course this was altogether different. The assassin's work was completed. Here in Memphis it was not the killer, whoever he might be, who was feared, but the killed one and what his death might bring.

Not far from the downtown was the leprous little hovel where, from a squalid toilet window, the assassin had been able to look across and target the new and hopeful Lorraine Motel. Now the motel was being visited by mourners. The black people of Memphis, dressed in their best, filed silently up and down the ramp, glancing shyly into the room which King had occupied. At the ramp before the door of the room where he fell there were flowers, glads, and potted azaleas.

All over the Negro section, rickety little stores, emptied in the "consumer rebellion," were boarded up, burned out, or simply empty, with the windows broken. The stores were for the most part of great modesty. Who owned that one? I asked the taxi driver.

"Well, that happened to be Chinee," he said.

Shops are a dwelling and their goods and stuffs, counters and cash registers are a form of interior decoration. Sacked and disordered, these Memphis boxes were amazingly small and only an active sense of possibility could conceive of them as the site of commercial enterprise. It did not seem possible that by stocking a few shelves these squares of rotting timber could merit ownership, license, investment, and produce a profitable exchange. They are lean-tos, chicken coops—measly and optimistic. Looters had sought the consolations of television sets and whiskey. The intrepid dramas of refrigerators and living room suites, deftly transported from store to home, were beyond the range of this poor section of the romantic city on the river.

The day of the march came to the gray, empty streets. The march was solemn and impressive, but on the other hand perhaps somewhat disappointing. A compulsive exaggeration dogs most of the expectations of ideological gatherings and thereby turns success to failure. The forty to sixty thousand predicted belittled the eighteen thousand present. The National Guard, alert with gun and bayonet as if for some important marine landing, made the quiet, orderly march appear a bit of a sell.

The numbers of the National Guard, the body count, spoke almost of a sort of psychotic imagining. They were on every street, blocking every intersection, cutting off each highway. There, in their large brown trucks, crawling out from under the olive-brown canvas, were men in full battle dress, in helmets and chin straps which concealed most of their pale, red-flecked and rather alarmed Southern faces. They guarded the alleys and the horizon, the river and the muddy playground, thoroughfare and esplanade, newspaper store and bank. It was as if by some cancerous multiplication the sensible and necessary had been turned into a monstrous glut.

The march, after all, was mostly made up of Memphis blacks. Was this a victory or a defeat? There were also some local white students from Southwestern, a few young ministers, and from New York members of the teachers' union with a free day off and a lunch box. Mrs. King came from Atlanta for the gathering, a tribute to her husband and also a tribute to the poor sanitation workers for whom it had all begun.

The people gathered early and waited long in the streets. They stood in neat lines to indicate the absence of unruly feelings. Part of the ritual of every public show of opinion and solidarity is the presence of a name or, preferably, the body of a Notable ("Notable" for a routine occasion, and "Dignitary" for a more solemn and affecting event such as the funeral to be held in Atlanta the next day). Notables are often from the entertainment world and the rest are usually to be known for political activities. Like a foundation of stone moved from site to site, only on the Notables can the petition for funds be based, the protest developed, the idea constructed.

The marchers waited without restlessness for the chartered airplane to arrive and to announce that it could then truly begin. A limousine will be waiting to take the noted ones to the front of the line, or to leave them off at the stage door. The motors are kept running. After an appearance, a speech, a mere presence, out they go by the back doors used by the celebrated, out to the waiting limousine, off to the waiting plane, and then off.

These persons are symbols of a larger consensus that can be transferred to the mass of the unknown faithful. They are priests giving sanction to idea, struggle, defiance. It is believed that only the famous, the busy, the talented have the power to solicit funds from the rich, notice from the press, and envy from the opposition. Also they are a sunshine, warming. They have the appeal of the lucky.

The march of Memphis was quiet; it was designed as a silent memorial, like a personal prayer. Hold your head high, the instructions read. No gum chewing. For protection in case of trouble, no smoking, no umbrellas, no earrings in pierced ears, no fountain pens in jacket pockets. One woman said, "If they make me take off my shades, I'm quitting the march." Among those who had come from some distance a decision had been made in favor of the small gathering in Memphis over the "national" funeral in Atlanta the following day. "I feel this is more important," they would say.

In the march and at the funeral of Martin Luther King, the mood of the earlier Civil Rights days in Alabama and Mississippi returned, a reunion at the grave of squabbling, competitive family members. And no one could doubt that there had been a longing for reunion among the white ministers and students and the liberals from the large cities. The "love"—locked arms, hymns, good feeling—all of that was remembered with feeling.

This love, if not always refused, was now seldom forthcoming in relations with new black militants, who were set against dependency upon the checkbooks and cooperation of the guilty, longing, loving whites. Everything separated the old Civil Rights people from the new black militants; it could be said, and for once truly, that they did not speak the same language. A harsh, obscene style, unforgiving stares, posturings, insulting accusations and refusal to make distinctions among those of the white world—this was humbling and perplexing. Many of the white people had created their very self-identity out of issues and distinctions and they felt cast off, ill at ease, with the new street rhetoric of "self-defense" and "self-determination."

Comradeship, yes, and being in the South again gave one a remembrance of the meaning of the merely legislative, the newly visible. Back at the hotel in the late afternoon the marchers were breaking up. The dining room was suddenly filled with not-too-pleasing young black boys—not black notables with cameras and briefcases, or in the company of intimidating, busy-looking persons from afar—no, just poor boys from Memphis. The aged waitresses padded about on aching feet and finally approached with the questions of function. Menu? Yes. Cream in the coffee? A little.

So, at last business was business, not friendship. The old white waitresses themselves were deeply wrinkled by the stains of plebeianism. Manner, accent marked them as "disadvantaged"; they were diffident, ignorant, and poor and would themselves cast a blight on the cheerful claims of many dining places. They seemed to be the enduring remnants of many an old retired trailer camp couple, the men with tattooed arms and the women in bright colored stretch pants; those who wander the warm roads and whose traveling kitchenettes and motorized toilets are a distress to the genteel and tasteful.

In any case, joy and flush-cheeked nuns were past history, a folk epic, full of poetry, simplicity and piety. The pastoral period of the Civil Rights Movement had gone by.

At the funeral in Atlanta, rising above the crowd, the *nez pointu* of Richard Nixon... Lester Maddox, short-toothed little marmoset, peeking from behind the draperies of the Georgia State House... Many Christians have died without the scruples of Christian principles being to the point. The *belief* of Martin Luther King—what an unexpected curiosity it was, the strength of it. His natural mode of address was the sermon. "So I say to you, seek God and discover Him and make Him a power in your life. Without Him all our efforts turn to ashes and our sunrises into darkest nights."

At the end of his life, King seemed in some transfigured state, even though politically he had become more radical and there were traces of disillusionment—with what? messianic hope perhaps. He had observed that America was sicker, more intransigent than he had realized when he began his work. The last, ringing, "I have been to the mountaintop!" gave voice to a transcendent experience. It is this visionary strain that makes him a man elusive in the extreme, difficult to understand as a character.

How was it possible for one so young as King to seem to contain, in himself, so much of the American past? At the very least, the impression he gave was of an experience of life coterminous with the years of his father. The Depression, the dust bowl, the sharecropper, the old back-country churches, and even the militance of the earlier IWW—he suggested all of this. He did not appear to belong to the time of Billy Graham (God bless you real good) but to a previous and more spiritual evangelism, to a time of solitude and refined simplicity. In *Adam Bede*, Dinah preaches that Jesus came down from Heaven to tell the good news about God to the poor. "Why, you and me, dear friends, are poor. We have been brought up in poor cottages, and have been reared on oatcake and lived coarse.... It doesn't cost Him much to give us our little handful of victual and bit of clothing, but how do we know He cares for us any more than we care for the worms ... so long as we rear our carrots and onions?" There remains this old, pure tradition in King. Rare elements of the godly and the political come together, with an affecting naturalness. His political work was indeed a Mission, as well as a political cause.

In spite of the heat of his sermon oratory, King seems lofty and often removed by the singleness of his concentration—an evangelical aristocrat. There is even a coldness in his public character, an impenetrability and solidity often seen in those who have given their entire lives to ideas and causes. The racism in America acts finally as an exhaustion to all except the strongest of black leaders. It leads to the urban, manic frenzy, the sleeplessness, hurry, and edginess that are a contrast to King's steadiness and endurance.

Small-town Christianity, staged in some sense as it was, made King's funeral supremely moving. Its themes were root American, bathed in memory, in forgotten prayers and hymns and dreams. Mule carts, sharecroppers, dusty poverty, sleepy Sunday morning services, and late Wednesday night prayer meetings *after work*. There in the reserved pews it was something else—candidates, former candidates, and hopeful candidates, illuminated, as it were, on prime viewing time, free of charge, you might say, free of past contributions to the collection plate, free of the envelopes of future pledges.

The rare young man was mourned and, without him, the world was fearful indeed. The other side of the funeral, Act Two ready in the wings, was the looting and anger of a black population inconsolable for its many losses.

"Jesus is a trick on niggers," a character in Flannery O'Connor's *Wise Blood* says. The strength of belief revealed in King and in such associates as the Reverend Abernathy was a chastening irregularity, not a regionalism absorbed. It stands apart from our perfunctory addresses to "this nation under God." In a later statement Abernathy has said that God, not Lester Maddox or George Wallace, rules over the South. So, Negro justice is God's work and God's will.

The popular Wesleyan hymns have always urged decent, sober behavior, or that is part of the sense of the urgings. As you sing, "I can hear my Savior calling," you are invited to accept the community of the church and also, quite insistently, to behave yourself, stop drinking, gambling, and running around. Non-violence of a sort, but personal, thinking of the home and the family, and looking back to an agricultural or small-town life, far from the uprooted, inchoate, *communal* explosions in the ghettos of the cities. The political non-violence of Martin Luther King was an act of brilliant intellectual conviction, very sophisticated and yet perfectly consistent with evangelical religion, but not a necessary condition as we know from the white believers.

One of the cruelties of the South and part of the pathos of Martin Luther King's funeral and the sadness that edges his rhetoric is that the same popular religion is shared by many bellicose white communicants. The religion seems to have sent few peaceful messages to them insofar as their brothers in Christ, the Negroes, are concerned. Experience leads one to suppose there was more respect for King among Jews, atheists, and comfortable Episcopalians, more sympathy and astonishment, than among the white congregations who use, with a different cadence, the same religious tone and the same hymns heard in the Ebenezer Church. Under the robes of the Klan there is an evangelical skin; its dogmatism is touched with the Scriptural, however perverse the reading of the text.

At one of the memorial services in Central Park after the murder, a radical speaker shouted, "You have killed the last good nigger!" This posturing exclamation was not meant to dishonor King, but to speak of his kind as something gone by, its season over. And perhaps so. The inclination of white leaders to characterize everything unpleasant to themselves in black response to American conditions as a desecration of King's memory was a sordid footnote to what they had named the "redemptive moment." But it told in a self-serving way of the peculiarity of the man, of the survival in him of habits of mind from an earlier time.

King's language in the pulpit and in his speeches was effective but not remarkably interesting. His style compares well, however, with the speeches of recent presidents and even with those of Adlai Stevenson, most of them bland and flat in print. In many ways, King was not Southern and rural in his address, although he had a melting Georgia accent and his discourse was saturated in the Bible. His was a practical, not a frenzied exhortation, inspiring the Southern Negroes to the sacrifices and dangers of protest and yet reassuring them by its clarity and humanity.

His speech was most beautiful in the less oracular cadences, as when he summed up the meaning of the Poor People's March on Washington with, "We have come for our checks!" The language of the younger generation is another thing altogether. It has the brutality of the city and an assertion of threatening power at hand, not to come. It is military, theatrical, and at its most coherent probably a lasting repudiation of empty courtesy and bureaucratic euphemism.

The murder of Martin Luther King was a "national disgrace." That we said again and again and it would be cynical to hint at fraudulent feelings in the scramble for suitable acts of penance. Levittowns would henceforth not abide by local rulings, but would practice open housing; Walter Reuther offered $50,000 to the beleaguered sanitation workers of Memphis; the Field Foundation gave a million to the Southern Christian Leadership movement; Congress acted on the open housing bill. Nevertheless, the mundane continued to nudge the eternal. In 125 cities there was burning and looting. Smoke rose over Washington, D.C.

The Reverend Abernathy spoke of a plate of salad shared with Dr. King at the Lorraine Motel, creating a grief-laden scenery of the Last Supper. How odd it was after all, this exalted Black Liberation, played out at the holy table and at Gethsemane, "in the Garden," as the hymns have it. A moment in history, each instance filled with symbolism and the aura of Christian memory. Perhaps what was celebrated in Atlanta was an end, not a beginning—the waning of the slow, sweet dream of Salvation, through Christ, for the Negro masses.

1968

CHICAGO

PHARAOHS of a Late Dynasty, Mayor Daley and Governor Connally, behind the podium, rock-strong in their desert, brooding, grunting, and nudging. Sometimes a finger was lifted to direct the hapless felaheen of the Illinois delegation, a band of folk sunk in apathetic unanimity. Or glumly a sign exacted a cheer from the citizen-guests of the Mayor's own Chicago hectares. Their hymns, rising up, spoke not of Right or Necessity, but, simply, of Love. We Love Mayor Daley!

Everyone in Chicago, in the lobbies, in the bars, at the Amphitheater, had his story, bore his witness to horrors in the park, shoving and fraud at the convention, the menace of powers. There was even a certain amount of competition to have large Experiences, since experience could not be avoided altogether. At the beginning of the week, even the squares for Humphrey clung to the Yippies, gulping, "Did you hear they have arrested Pigasus?" Heavy, sheepish smiles. "Platform of garbage, a pig you see ... No pay toilets ..." Ha, ha.

No pleasure or irony or pop humor attended the world debut of Mayor Daley. He was visible and comprehensible instantly and as a whole: a figure to fear. Who would willingly have dealings with him? Affection and good deeds would no doubt be attributed to him, as an explanation, but if he fell it would be like the fall of King Farouk or Nkrumah. Goodbye, goodbye, forever; the same banners would suddenly say on the other side. Even as he began his plans to gather the flocks in Chicago, vanity and folly and cruelty trailed him like glowering bodyguards. Johnson, of course, deferred, as to the military, confident that Himself could handle it. The end was five days of pain and suffering, of lawless squalor and idiocy in the name of the State. Try as you would to remain fixed on the local and to be faithful to the particular, to the American root, images of Stalin and Hitler refused to fade away. The obvious was the most accurate.

Wednesday night, during the siege of the Hilton, when the police mercilessly beat young men before the eyes of everyone, you could hear the timid but determined voices of "concerned" women calling out, "What are the charges against that young man?" Or, "Stop, please, Sir, you are killing him!" The mention of the instruments of law and order sent the police into a wild rage and for a moment they stopped beating demonstrators and turned to threaten the frightened suburbans. During the raid on the McCarthy Headquarters, a girl in tears asked, "What are the grounds?" The police answered, "Coffee grounds." With this lawlessness of the Law, misery fell from the sky. Suppose, you found yourself wondering, *they* should take over! "I have been a lifelong Democrat," people kept whispering in bewilderment. Few had realized until Chicago how great a ruin Johnson and his war in Vietnam had brought down upon our country.

Hysterical supervision and repressiveness edged every important arrangement and decision of the Chicago administration. And even the most trivial details were marked by an intense, mystifying, futile fraudulence. What actually was there behind the ugly fences put up along the route to the Amphitheater? Sometimes a run-down building much more pleasing to one's sense of life than the blind fences stood in hiding there—or we were, in this menacing way, simply being protected from an encounter with a vacant lot. One side of an old brick slum was painted a glaring, fresh, improbable red—a grotesque compliment to the sensibilities and common sense of the visitors. The coarseness of mind that produced these improvements and camouflage blacked out the beauty and fascination of the city. Inevitably with so much care and effort all artfully flowing from the singular inspiration of Mayor Daley, a style came to life. The style was defined by its unmistakable origin in a previous tradition: it was police-state, concentration-camp style, a mode always available to the mood of tyranny. One is almost ashamed to admit how frightening it was.

*

Fear and anger: these had been growing and gnawing in many a Chicago planning session, in all those burly conferences. They feared, dismaying as it is to imagine—at the least a blot on the name of Chicago! At the worst—a disaster, single tragedies, multiple blows, assassinations, fire, poisoned water, Japanese-style suicide planes crashing on the gathered delegates, blackouts. Humphrey spoke with feeling of threats to himself; and indeed who among the crowd of youth honored him, who would save him, when there was not a single vote winging his way from out there, unless it might be those of the five plainclothesmen, shoeless, in hirsute disguises? "It was all programmed!" he exclaimed. They were out to get him, out to get Mayor Daley's city, out to get the Nomination, out to get the Democratic Party. These hordes, born too late to understand those who had made their way, those who, as they kept insisting, "loved and believed in this country." Several times, in the last year, Humphrey had, using a homely verb phrase, found that demonstrators and striking students made him "feel sick to my stomach."

Assassinations: why should we doubt that the threats were made? It is a question simply of who made them. And here, without evidence, what can we call upon except our sense of things? Perhaps there is *some* secrecy in the militant peace groups, but secrecy is hard to credit among those whose strength comes from free and open assault on the sensibilities, the frayed nerves, of those in charge of things.

Answer this: how could youngsters milling and screaming in the streets possibly assassinate in their hotel rooms the heavily guarded candidates who sat, safely working the dials on the TV set. CBS or NBC? Exhausting. Shut out the message from Gulf. And what was threatened except the grass and certain city ordinances by the Yippies in the cold dark park after the curfew? It was anger, surely, and not fear that drove the scourgers against the Yippies. A father, sweating, red-faced, unchallenged, beating up his son, "over-reacting." Bad young people and, particularly, their "bad language"—standing for what buried offenses? It was a misfortune that the curious, jowly, porky figures of many of the policemen and the memorable configuration of Mayor Daley gave a stinging lift to the shout of "Pig!" (Mayor Daley has some difficulty with speech; he grunts out words that are themselves prone to mishap. Thus in his welcoming he said the visitors to Chicago would be "*subjected* to the famous hospitality of the middle West.")

The words of the demonstrators enraged because with a frankness and economy they represented attitudes. They speak of an unwanted future. Clothes, hair: this too is language. A terrifying succession stands impatiently in line. The brutality of the nightstick, the thick skin of the victorious candidates, the meanness, the lies, the unmanly fears: all of this allowed the sordid, parental self-protection to show itself. Insofar as the safety of the community was concerned, the actions of the police were a dangerous and stupid diversion, alas like Vietnam. We see that, deep down, truly, the police and Mayor Daley did not believe in hidden and sinister danger from the demonstrators; otherwise they would not have been out on the street beating them up, making it easy for some clean shaven Nihilist to wander where he would.

When the authorities spoke, in justification, they trembled at the recollection of the revolutionary, guerrilla warfare rhetoric of the "Free Press" and student newspapers. These publications so filled with jokes and gags and dirty cartoons are read with iron literalness by the FBI, the vice president, the leaders of the Democratic Party, and by the police. I am reminded of Disraeli who, although a Jew himself, did not know much about the Jews and found the Jewish power described in the protocols of Zion strangely fascinating. He hadn't until then thought his people controlled so much. "Why they've got maps of the city, of the transportation system!" Mayor Daley said. Surely, he was talking about the newspaper *Rat*, whose Convention Special with its maps and its account of the action to come was an encyclopedia for all who were puzzling over the distance between the Hilton and Grant Park. The "intelligence" gathered from the newspapers around Greenwich Village will apparently be a large part of the case for the defense. There is pathos and humor in all this, like a dinosaur choking on bubble gum. A fearful gap, not only in generations, but in common sense, in ordinary understanding of the world about us, has opened up. And how can we face this, except with dread?

*

In Grant Park, the demonstrators gathered for the Wednesday afternoon march they were not allowed to have, just as they had not been allowed permits for any of their rallies or marches. Here again swollen fear seemed determined to make the "confrontation" uniquely dramatic. In the late afternoon the "non-violent" group began to assemble under the statue. A middle group, apparently made up of those willing if necessary to suffer violence but not to inflict it, gathered elsewhere. And a third group, "those who would take part in the *action*," was directed to its starting place. Tom Hayden—"Mr. Underground" they were calling him now—said, "if they gas us, the gas will go all over the city; if they burn us they will burn." This is militant dialogue and one is never quite sure just what is meant by it, how "self-defense" is to work for the appallingly outnumbered and weak. But in Chicago exaggeration became fact. The police—"over-reacting"—caught everyone up in their violence. Tear gas vexed the eye of candidate, party hack, and demonstrator. What revolutionary could have imagined the useful violence against the press and the television crews?

The youngsters assembled for the "action" were told, "You may be going to your death, but it will be worth it." In those words, there in the bright, crowded, excited afternoon all of the pity and terror of the future lies. Bolivian adventures in unprepared mountains—and death. Wave a Viet Cong flag and drive them out of their minds! Take down the stars and stripes and watch them charge, ready for the kill. The more militant demonstrators, resting later in the week, told newsmen they were going into training for battle, they would learn, among other things, how to trip the horses that carried the policemen when they came charging down on them. In Chicago, neither a shooting, nor a stabbing, nor a burning, nor a sabotage has been reported. Guerrilla rhetoric, determination to cross the line into the street, rocks and bottles provoked outstandingly furious, awful reprisal. And we remember the story of the policeman, true or not, who fainted when a stream of hairspray surprised him. As he went down no doubt he felt on his face the cool touch of a death-dealing Commie ray.... The "confrontation" took place. Many dreams came true. A bunch of ministers and minstrels could not have brought it off by songs and prayers of PEACE NOW. Is it birth or death?

Hubert Humphrey is an altogether embarrassing figure, with his dyed black hair and glowing television make-up. He creates a sense of false energy—like an MC on an afternoon show. The present Democratic leadership appears to be divided between bullies and cowards and Humphrey asks us to take our chances on the coward. You will find me less dangerous, he seems to be trying to assure us.

The vice president has many words and he uses them over and over. "I am the Captain of the team," he says. Many of the choice sentences of his acceptance speech had been the choice remarks of his appearance before the California delegation. (Peace and freedom do not come cheaply, my friends.) He brought forth Winston Churchill and St. Francis of Assisi—one strong and one humble—and topped the embarrassment of the first by the second. He is always frantically smiling; repose is a rapid fade to sentiment. In between, where feeling and person would lodge, there is simply nothing. He does not seem in touch. Empty smiles, a wound-up toy. Nothing in him inspires confidence. He cannot allow himself to be distracted by events. The entire convention appeared to intrude upon his smiles. Nothing has happened since the thirties: that is his message, that is the real Humphrey, now, "Captain of the team."

A poor-boy rise through the graceful apertures of The System; labor support, early Civil Rights legislation. He seems alarmed and confused that this should not be sufficient. I am a good man! the manic manner cries out. The sense of an arrested consciousness makes him appear daily more empty. Now to be Here, at last, and to have nothing to say. Humphrey and Nixon, madly waving from the top of the pole: both of them must realize, with a peculiar helplessness, how oddly alike they are. One, a brash, free-wheeling liberal, the other, cautious, obedient, longing: in the course of their lives they have converged and are fixed, as with wax, in a numbing similarity. They are blind and deaf, but still wholesomely smiling.

It was not hard to tell the Humphrey supporters: they looked like

Republicans, conservatively dressed, provincial, not quite at ease with the psychedelic *Hubie, Baby* button on their lapel. In the elevator at the Hilton, after the beatings in the lobby, several Humphrey supporters gossiped away saying, "Well, they were told not to come here." The party system collapsed in Chicago, leaving instead Candidates. There were only memorials to The Nomination. And how long Humphrey had waited to lie down, naked, at last, with her.

McCarthy: nothing in his campaign became him more than the losing of it. His blossoming eccentricities separated him from the breathless mediocrity and banality of Nixon and Humphrey on the one hand and, on the other, from the more plausible and popular style of the Kennedys. A hatred of cant was not, as some would have liked, replaced in his speeches by an austere eloquence but rather by a flat recital of his position on the "issues." These sensible and deflating addresses to a large, self-congratulatory audience were a perturbation. No, no, it is not a lot of mush and butter we want, they would say, but *something*. Perhaps something very scholarly and boring and thereby satisfying to the ego, or perhaps he might be cryptic, poetic, curious. Anything, anything except the dead fish thrown back into the warm, receptive waters. His wit seemed merely a rumor at Madison Square Garden, at the palpitating turn-out in Boston. Stories of a *really* good speech in Maryland came back to the followers. In the long run, no one turned away from him and perhaps they finally came to know what he would say and what he wouldn't. In an "amateur" campaign—if that is what it was—in the participatory democracy of the kind the McCarthy volunteers practiced, each boy and girl seemed to think of himself as a sort of vice-nominee, ready with ideas, with suggestions for theory and practice. The disciples were tested, once and then once more, by their candidate's surprising indifference to expediency and political maneuvering as we ordinarily understand them.

It is not possible to describe such a large group as the McCarthy workers: they were not as young as the newspapers implied and were closer to graduate school age and temperament than to youngsters. Perhaps some will become "radicalized" by the finale in Chicago. And yet, perhaps what held them besides the peace issue was the whole excitement of politics, this absurd theater of primaries and delegates, voting blocs and challenges, county chairman, caucuses, candidates. The sadness is that they have discovered the fun of something that has, in this presidential election, gone rotten.

In Chicago, the three candidates had an interesting debate before the California delegation. The presence of two genuine persons on either side of him put Humphrey at a disadvantage. He fell back on his empty frenzy, waffling about his opponents. "America is lucky to have these two men!" McCarthy passed up the chance to make a rousing speech by saying, "My position on Vietnam is well known." Senator McGovern took the opportunity and was rapturously received. McGovern was a pleasing mixture of the two other candidates. His position on the issues was solid and courageous and in support of it he brought a character and style far enough from the inane, boyish masochism of Humphrey but still within our weary tradition. He spoke of the "great" state of California and addressed the delegates as "distinguished." In the end he went to the Convention for the nomination and said he would support the Party. He appears to believe we can go on as before.

The most radical thing about McCarthy was his refusal to make the expected gestures. This was an unsettling condition and aroused anger and suspicion everywhere. True, the California delegation knew his position, but why not take the opportunity to score? He seems unwilling to tell people what they already know and feels apparently that a political campaign is the last place to instruct them in what they don't know. He held even the Holy Grail itself—The Hallowed Nomination—at a distance and failed utterly to be grieved when he lost it.

There was a plainness to his views and the plainer they were the more unlikely they sounded amidst the elaborate rigidity of our familiar political discourse. He was asked early in the campaign if he thought he would make a good president and he said he would make an adequate one. God! they gasped. Another boo-boo! He conceded certain defeat at least twenty-four hours before one is allowed to concede certain defeat. His eccentricities were inexplicable; he peeled off a dozen political skins, this one the proper manner, that one the guarded answer, and yet another, the drooling hunger for the office itself. McCarthy missed all those sweet opportunities to "show compassion" but he had no company when he talked with the demonstrators, visited the wounded, stayed away from the Convention, and said he would not support Humphrey. Nevertheless there is something brilliantly troubling about him, in his political role: Perhaps what will last the longest from his campaign is the hint that many of the acts in our political repertoire aren't worth putting on your makeup for.

Out of the meanness and hollowness, the degrading events and the worrying future, one suddenly saw a little Yippie with a sign saying, CHICAGO IS A GAS. That was transcendence, rebirth.

1968

REFLECTIONS ON FICTION

ART, OF course, lives in history. We are obliged to consent that a work is not today what it was yesterday, neither as a whole nor in its details. It is easy enough to agree that time alters the past and all its terms, but the agreement is rather abstract. In taste, as in love, the preferences are violent and few are willing to look ahead, to profit from experience. We have little power over our own sensibilities, even though they appear to us as singular and personal as our bodies. We know our ideas and likes to be formed by the present and yet it is hard to resist a belief that they are somehow in touch with eternity.

The novel: history sends the reader away and brings him back again. We explain the decline in great reputations as the working of a cyclical force, which dips low for a decade or a century only to swing up once again. Fashion corrupts, but, like artificial respiration, it also gives a second life to the fallen. Structure bores in this generation; freedom repels in the next. What is it they have in common, those great novels of the past? We cannot find words, except in tautology, for the power of splendid creations. Merit is an assertion, subject if not to proof at least to *convincingness*. Every work struggles for its rights, and few maintain them without remissions. Certain works, as if they were sovereign states, weaken from time to time and whole generations turn their attentions away.

The once large, well-defended kingdom of Sir Walter Scott comes to mind. Even over one hundred years ago, Bagehot detected an uneasy wandering in Scott's audience. V. S. Pritchett thought the decay of regionalism and the dislike of dialect were at the source of the gradual loss of appeal. Galsworthy is a territory fallen into decay and a novelist like Sinclair Lewis seems used up, absorbed, like a fertilizer. There is much sadness in the history of taste, and joy, too, when he who was lost is returned. Still, it is not the sudden recognition of an over-estimation that puzzles so much as the apparent impossibility of reviving our own and other people's interest in a major novelist like Scott.

It is not quite so easy to think of revived reputations and works in the novel as in poetry. Henry James? It seems now that an ebbing and flowing of popularity will attend his work—and not without a certain rightness. The beauty and grandeur and peculiarity of his novels and stories benefit from the proper setting, the propitious moment, the waiting and receptive sensibility. Melville? A discovery, not a revival, a correction of a mistake, an omission. It is not merely capricious taste that works upon us, but violent changes in the moral, political, and social environment.

The novel has always been resistant to abstract analysis, to structural definition, to purely formal speculation. When the English critic, Percy Lubbock, tried in *The Craft of Fiction* to build, brick by brick, a mild and sensible structural frame for the novel, he found immediately a mournful amount of difficulty with the work of the supreme Tolstoy. Lubbock wrote about *War and Peace*: "Tolstoy's novel is wasteful of its subject: that is the whole objection to its loose, instinctual form. Criticism bases itself upon nothing whatsoever but the injury done to the story, the loss of its full potential value." The critic has worked here according to an interesting and useful principle ("point of view") and yet it hardly seems worthwhile to labor so forcefully on behalf of such wan rewards. Because, of course, few of us feel "the injury done to the story," and are instead powerfully moved by "the loose and instinctual form." You have the feeling, in the case of Lubbock, that a well-built house has collapsed in the first thunderstorm of a summer.

From the very beginning the novel was loose and unmanageable, unpredictable, and inclined to be formless a good deal of the time. Indeed too strict a demand for form will often lead to a loss of the rushing, raging sense of life that is the special mystery of certain novelists such as Dostoevsky and Dickens. The high degree of formal concern in a novelist like Flaubert is not typical of the novel, although many great novelists share it. Flaubert made a heroic and victorious assault upon the form and yet he understood with an ironic anguish his mother's remark that "the mania for phrases has dried up your heart." In the usual practice of fiction, the style of the lines, the symmetry of the paragraphs, the balance of the elements are likely to give way, almost unconsciously, under the stress of incident, plot, and characterization. Thus we cannot often make judgments on the claim of formal purity, or on the accusation of formal corruption.

"Non-fiction novels" and "fictionalized fact" are phrases of the moment, perhaps not always significant, but interesting in a critical sense. They would seem to indicate a high degree of impatience with the very roots of the novel form, to question the value of the designation itself. Sartre, in an essay on Nathalie Sarraute, speaks of the "anti-novel," of works that "make use of the novel in order to challenge the novel, to destroy it before our very eyes while seeming to construct it, to write the novel of a novel unwritten and unwritable . . ." We cannot quite know whether the discontent with the form lies in the inability for cultural reasons to practice it in the old way or whether it points simply to the restlessness of the creative spirit. (Picasso could "draw like Raphael" and Joyce became a parodist out of a fabulous mastery of all the arts of prose.)

Even if the conception of the "novel" does not continue to satisfy we still feel that the word stands for something real and recognizable as an aesthetic entity. We acknowledge the presence of its possibilities when we speak of their absence. For how often we say of a piece of fiction that it is very good and interesting, but not very good "as a novel." Some novels are clearly more novelistic than others. We do not use this distinction as a measuring rod for excellence, and indeed the last stronghold of the calculation and distribution of laughter and tears, plot and counterplot, sex and sentiment, comedy and pathos may be the arithmetical construction of popular fiction, manufactured dutifully for its audience, and a mode no doubt doomed to extinction, like the western story and the love story. To say that something is not pure as a novel is simply a description of its technique, not a judgment. And this becomes more and more true every day as the serious writers discard not only the skin but the bone of fiction.

We might say of a book like *The Way of All Flesh* that it is a fascinating work, but not supreme as a novel. In this case we would mean that Butler's story is somewhat dry and narrow in a peculiar way. It is to the book's credit and part of its satisfaction that it contains "the sum total of the author's ideas on religion, economics and philosophy" and nevertheless we feel the *ideas*, if that is the right word, are bought at the expense of imaginative richness and detail, dramatic inventiveness. On the other hand, *The Way of All Flesh* is entirely genuine and deeply engrossing, and one could hardly wish it to be other than it is. In a sense we are *most* grateful for its "defects," for the odd combination of the discursive and an on-going autobiographical narrative. You might say history, culture, wants it as it is, wants the unconsciously self-loving and distorted author as much as the self-loving fictional father he created for himself. Scope, grandeur, largeness, completeness are the grounds of the highest values—and yet smallness, perfection, inspired narrowness and concentration—in Jane Austen, in Kafka—share in the supremacy. The utterance of the obvious always accompanies the discussion of works of high rank: this is the acknowledgment of our certainty about their value, the hopelessness of trying to rank princes. To assert greatness does not give us the key; it is only the lock.

A novel is a long and complex creation. The parts bear a mysterious and clouded relation to the whole. The pages turn, one after another, and it is a distinguishing aspect of the novel that, around the next corner, almost anything can happen. We hardly know which to treasure most: expectation confounded or satisfied. A new chapter is a psychological shift and the interesting dislocations afforded by a flashback make great demands on the imagination. In the older works we were often grateful for the relief, the relaxation, as if for a short nap, brought to us by a sudden shift to the sub-plot.

In the novel, length is of obvious importance in excluding the merely anecdotal and in making a distinction from the short story. Yet the interesting thing about length is the calculation of its effects upon our mind, the way it dominates the art and defines its relation to the reader. How difficult it is to remember the mere incidents in a long work of fiction. Novelists themselves forget what has gone before. The passage of time need not be long to promote forgetfulness, nor the incident trivial. What indeed was Bulstrode's crime in *Middlemarch*? If sometimes one cannot quite remember the shape of Bulstrode's part in the plot, or even the final resolution of the Rosamund-Lydgate story, what can one mean when he says, with passion and conviction, that *Middlemarch* is a favorite novel? (*Middlemarch* is only an example; many great books are much more dense and clotted in incident than this one.)

The length of a novel, the abundance of detail have a disturbing and exciting effect on the imagination; in a sense one reads on to find out "what happens" and yet what happens is exactly the most quickly forgotten, the most elusive. It is even difficult to know how to state the problem: is it psychological, simply rooted in biology, or, instead, an aesthetic condition, necessary to the special effects of the novel? What seems to remain locked in the memory is a general impression, a selection of detail, a blur of interesting scene, the shape of character, and, above all, a sort of remembrance of how one felt when one was first reading the book. The remembered exhilaration of the mind, pleasure of the senses, hang upon the frailest thread of incident, the dimmest recollection of language. You know you were fascinated, you were convinced—at the time, when you were deeply there, in the story, in the turn of phrase here and the observation there, the surprise, the resolution that pleased. Tracks, not very deep, laid down in the memory prompt us to assert merit and excellence.

So much of a novel, after all, is information, necessary fact that gives a floor of understanding from which the flights of inspiration are launched. Filler, stuffing, dressing: all are dutifully manufactured—or at least they were in the past. But many writers question the production of so much direction and advice, analysis and landscape. The machinery of fiction is simply ignored in Burroughs and Genet. Only the genius of Vladimir Nabokov keeps alive the rather disappointing development of a surrealistic fiction. The destructive power of Joyce had a peculiarly disguised effect upon the history of the novel. The effort to move along the same rubble-filled road did not prove practical and most novelists simply turned back as though nothing had happened, back to more or less regular sentences and to stories, fractured and not very ample, but stories nevertheless. Still, there is always an uneasiness about a retreat, a feeling of anxiety and guilt, and many good novels show a degree of panic about the form. Where to start and how to end, how much must be believed and how much a joke, a puzzle; how to combine the episodic and the carefully designed and consequential.

Time: this is what the novel asks of the writer and the reader. And time is just what our contemporary existence is determined to shorten. So much of our homely, domestic technology is meant to make things go faster, the human effort shorter. And it is curious that saving time at one point does not make one ready to give it at another. Quite the contrary. If the laundry washes and dries quickly, the grateful housewife does not then think that she will give to the dishes the time left over from the quickened wash: no, she demands instantly that the dishes keep pace with the laundry. But it is really a more subtle time the novel depends on. A spiritual and intellectual lengthening, extending like a dream in which much is surrendered and slowly transformed. Perhaps it is the fear that something has happened to time, some change has taken place, which makes us wonder if a new generation will always be there to read the novels, particularly the novels of the past. The terms of the contract between the author and the reader are severe, the demands are serious. Frequently we hear the doleful warning of a retreat on the part of the reader, a withdrawal of attention, an indifference to the august tradition that stands there like so many stone and marble college buildings, ready for parody or destruction.

Tranquility, slow hours and days, the need to discover, through the imagination, what the world about us contained: this was the first condition of the novel. Curiosity was the second—curiosity about the most knotted as well as the simplest of human activities, communal life, of love and marriage and family and work and fulfillment; poverty and riches, town and countryside, accident and consequence. In the minds of many young people, whole stretches of literature seem to be becoming impossible, closed, and the past is a slow, uncomfortable train ride through scenery erased, villages lost to memory.

If it is really true that there may be a psychological hindrance, rooted in the overturned earth of our daily life, new fiction will itself be written by those altered psyches and will be inevitably accommodating. Yet the form seems more threatened than the other arts by the alterations in sensibility, by the unease of the world, the sense of destiny beyond control and comprehension, by the feeling of borrowed, shortened time and relationships subject to cancellation. The very openness of our life, particularly of sexual life, makes the discoveries of fiction far less striking. Much that was veiled in the past came forth in the novel, in complicated family histories, in love stories.

"The principle of procrastinated rape is said to be the ruling one in all the great bestsellers," V. S. Pritchett remarks in a discussion of *Clarissa*. Seduction is now a comedy in which both are laughing. "The tragedy of the bedroom," as Tolstoy called it, can hardly be said to have been wiped out, like smallpox, and yet the sufferings are, as the scientists would say, being "researched," and "treated." Sexual longing, repression are the stuff of irony and comedy. Recently on the stage when Orestes spoke with horror of his obligation to murder his mother the audience helplessly, understandably laughed. The laughter did not have its source in mockery of the anguish of the son or the punishment of the mother. The laughter was a sort of cultural product, compounded of all those explanations, studies of "myth," the rivers of words of interpretation. Primitive urgings, infinitely analyzed, cannot lead to pity and terror, but to the comedy of a rather over-worked recognition. World horrors have stepped into the bloody shoes of domestic cruelty and private revenge. Art has not yet seemed wide enough to stand for these horrors and the horrors are too vast, we have witnessed them too closely and perhaps too indifferently to see them reduced to symbol.

"Wuthering Heights is the name of Mr. Heathcliff's dwelling" or "High above his head swung Mrs. Melrose Ape's travel-worn Packard car, bearing the dust of three continents" or "It is a truth universally acknowledged that a single man in the possession of a good fortune must be in want of a wife": these bells ring out, signaling, like lines of poetry. They promise a certain kind of drama, to be explored and developed in a more or less orderly way. They tell us, each differently, of the tone of the inspiration and they promote readiness to surrender the whole of our interest to the special and unique atmosphere of each book. Or remember the poignant opening scenes of Dreiser's *An American Tragedy*. We see the Griffiths family on a lonely street corner, with their portable organ, singing in the chill night, "How Sweet the Balm of Jesus's Love." We feel immediately the depression glumly hanging over the lives, the instincts denied, the promises of life confused. All of this meager and lowering scene prefigures the sensual, worldly long-ing of the son, Clyde, and seems to prophesy that his hopes will not be fulfilled but doomed.

In most novels of the past, you entered a life, as if you were walking through a door. The ordered and arranged destiny of the characters lay before you, satisfying the desire that life be first of all interesting and then in some way reasonable, shaped. The sense of place, and the per-sonal drama pushing up inside it, became your own birth and death. Those little villages, the cities beyond ready to destroy hopes or to give a complex success: the stories come forth from them naturally and regularly, like the seasons. Jude watching the schoolmaster, Phillotson, set out for Christminster. Lena, in *Light in August*, thinking "I have come from Alabama, a fur piece. All the way from Alabama a-walking. A fur piece." Paul Dombey, born into death. Every novel was different and yet in most of them, except for some strange mutations, the action accompanied life, as it were, gave a feeling of truth to experience. The plots, the descriptions, the artifice were like vines over a stone wall, a natural and pleasing decoration.

So many of the new conditions of life have altered in the most surprising way our sense of the foundations of character, of motivation, of the importance of place and regions. The provinces have, for many reasons, lost much of their character and the cities are too splintered, shifting, and complex to be understood except in fragments. And yet one wants the fiction of his own day to take some notice of the conflicts and feelings of the time, either to be extensively engaged through the grandeur of design or else to discover some appropriate, deeply telling image or situation that will stand for our concerns and passions.

In the novel, the example of the past, of the great and splendid arc of the fiction of realism can no longer stand as the measure of expectation. What was natural and orderly and pleasing in Victorian fiction does not often give the flavor of our own times, and some of the devices that were formerly acceptable, if not pleasing, are not useful for serious authors. We look back to the past as a sort of novelist's paradise. Energy gave forth the large production of Dickens and Thackeray and George Eliot, and later of James and Conrad and Proust; and there was a like energy in the reader that went out to meet the inspiration of the writers. We are sometimes told that the plots, the sheer interest of the narrative, the structure of theme and variation clearly working itself out, held the audience to these books created by a majestic intelligence and moved by the most profound intentions. But the fact is that the Victorian plots are very perplexing and this is particularly true of the very popular Dickens. The plotting is downright bad and the amazing thing is that so much genuine life managed to connect with the awkward stories.

In *Our Mutual Friend* the fascination of Podsnap and the Boffins, of the Veneerings and Twemlow has the stone of the plot about a will tied to its ankles. And yet the will and the lawyers and the reappearance of a drowned man hardly do the kind of damage they would nowadays. The Victorian audience knew as much about human nature as any that came after it, but somehow it was able to go along with contrivances and coincidence, with false identities and sudden rescues. No doubt they were a sort of indulgence and we can never be sure that the novel, in that country and time, could have prospered without the cumbersome plots.

It is interesting to compare the self-conscious contemporary use of Victorian plots on the part of Ivy Compton-Burnett. She has said on this subject: "As regards plot I find real life no help at all. Real life seems to have no plots. And as I think a plot desirable and almost necessary, I have this extra grudge against life. But I think there are signs that strong things happen, though they do not emerge. I believe it would go ill with many of us, if we were faced by a strong temptation, and I suspect that with some of us it does go ill." Ivy Compton-Burnett shocks us with her prim use of old plottings because she reverses our expectations. Brother and sister, separated in infancy, later meet, fall in love and marry—and they live happily. Another novel uses the contrivance of a forged or lost will. The wrong person finds the will, makes himself—or was it herself?—the heir, gets the money, and has a splendid, civilized time spending it, all the while guiltless, even though under the eye of the deprived soul for whom the money was intended. The old plots are turned into a complicated comedy, quite austere and demanding, asking, as the earlier books did, intelligence and strength from the reader.

The Russian novel is almost a critique of the English novel. The Russians kept the exuberance, that sense of a large life at hand, eager for the transformation of fiction, of characters significant in meaning and convincing in action, but the Russians were somehow able to get rid of the heavy, mechanical plots and put in their place a simpler, large and more natural development of incident. Perhaps this tradition provides a useful model for the writers of the present and sets a genuine standard for judgment. And yet there is something dream-like about Moscow and St. Petersburg, life grandly and painfully fixed in its rounds in Tolstoy, nervously elated and magnified in Dostoevsky. The scheme of things still held, even though it was the special grace of the fiction to show how it was bursting apart, falling into ruin and change.

With the Russians there is a grandeur and completeness in single works that the contemporary imagination cannot call upon. Everything seemed to be in waiting, open, wishing to have its story completed, its destiny defined. What seems often to swim up to the surface of our own life, as a paradoxical product of the immensely known, unbearably extended regions of observation, is not largeness and openness, in the fictional sense, but a sense of static mystery, a peculiarly poignant paralysis, a feeling of repetition, and, in the density, of insignificance.

The last great believer in plot was Freud. He knew only one story—the Oedipal one—but he meant this to touch life at every point from birth to death, to take in existence in a wide, brilliant sweep of illumination. For a time it appeared that Freud by restoring coherence to human motivation and explanation to the action and the feeling might act as a reprieve from the overwhelming mass of raw experience, life, too much of it, coming down upon the imagination like a glacier. Of course Freud changed literature when he changed thought and sensibility, but unabashed psychological contrivances and ready solutions fatigued early, surprisingly.

George Eliot said she wrote out of a belief in "the orderly sequence whereby the seed brings forth a crop of its kind." And this is the mood, grand and satisfying, of classical fiction. Through a natural determinism, character and action came together, the intermingling of stories and destinies, of cause and effect, of crime and punishment, gave us most of the great novels of the English and European tradition. Environment, moral choice, defects of character, defaults of luck; these could be depended upon to lead to some plausible resolution. The relativism we now feel undermines the centrality of character. It is difficult to create fictional characters without plots by which the character can reveal itself. What will the seed bring forth? Indeed what does the seed itself contain?

Extraordinary *belief*, mysterious *saturation*, seized the authors of the past like bouts of hallucination. When *The Sound and the Fury* was reissued in the 1940s, Faulkner told us of the continuing history of his imaginary characters: Candace, the heroine of a novel published in 1929, had, we were told, vanished in Paris with the German occupation. She was still beautiful. (The map of Yoknapatawpha County was not a jest.) Thomas Hardy's "philosophy" was almost a part of the vegetation of his English region; it grew along with the fate of his characters, filling the landscape with a piercing melancholy.

In most contemporary fiction, the author would sensibly hesitate to invite such mysteries; and perhaps he could not, even if he wished, will them into being. Instead the mood of the writer is to admit manipulation and design, to exploit the very act of authorship in the midst of the imagined scene. The broken, the episodic, the ironical are whispers from the wings, reminding us not to be swept away, someone is in charge. (Mary McCarthy spoke of this as "ventriloquism.") A suspicious and cautious approach to the imaginary does not strike one as temporary or merely fashionable. Instead it seems to come from the very center of our view of life and art. Certain societies, such as the Soviet, by their very rigidity, their fear of movement within, somehow lend themselves to the old forms in fiction, as if they had been granted a sort of extension. *Dr. Zhivago*, an interesting and largely conceived novel, is old-fashioned and we accept it on those terms, the very fixed form of the novel corresponding to the fixed and immovable structure of the Soviet system. Solzhenitsyn, even in the bitterness of his feelings, can contain his contempt within the traditional form, again because of the tyranny that keeps the orderly expectation, cruel though it be, intact.

The art of the past presents itself to us as a consensus, and although we know that history is not just and many worthy things have disappeared we nevertheless gratefully accept the claims of the tradition. We accept it because there is much joy to be found in those things that have given joy before. The individual greets the consensus each time as a discovery, a surprise that can transform life. But what can we ask of fiction today? Can we ask that it present interesting and significant characters who reveal their natures by means of a plausible and satisfying plot? It does not appear that we can set any such standard. We are left with only one demand: that a work be interesting.

Television and the press, and also the "press" of life and population, of reduced privacy, make every day an enormous number of persons known to everyone else. Whatever the day brings forth is quickly, like the loaves and fishes, multiplied for the thousands and the millions. Each person assigns, to the quick and superficial knowledge he is given, his own idea of motivation, of meaning. He writes the story as it comes to him, turning over the possibilities in his mind about candidate and criminal, the celebrity and the merely accidental personal life cast up before the public. With so much "reality" seen in its dramatic moment, the products of the imagination fail often to measure up in excitement, even in "reality."

It is not surprising that much recent American imaginative writing comes to us as a fact of personal or national history, dressed up and arranged, but still a record of lived experience, taking its origin outside the entirely "made up." (William Styron's *The Confessions of Nat Turner* and the recent works of Norman Mailer come to mind.) The interest rests not only in the creation of the seemingly true, but in the creative rendering of the actual, the re-constructed, the twice-told life. The assurance of reality acts as a release to the creative spirit. It is also a *re-assurance* to the reader, suspending his disbelief. The singular and personal is offered as a substitute for the unlimited perils of the imaginary, that over-crowded continent still without paths or frontiers. Consistency and motivation need not be questioned. The person in this kind of literature is no more required to have the arbitrary order of art than is the person on television or in the news. Existence is not questioned and one asks only that the person be interesting and in that way the actual rendering, the details of the art, assume again a grand importance, something like the language in poetry.

If the stories that are acted out for us every day are more extraordinary than the controlled imagination could permit itself, we could say that it was always thus. The great difference is that the dramas of real life were not known to so many until this age of technology. An existence, teasing and mysterious, lived out under public scrutiny is a sort of novel. The story of the Kennedy family is a novel on the grand scale, so strange and tragic that it is almost "unconvincing." It is difficult for fiction to compete with the aesthetic satisfactions of the actual. Buried in our minds is the demand that fiction give us not the story of life itself, but the key to the mystery. It must tell us what we do not know, find the unexpressed, give us the clue to the meaning of Malcolm X or President Johnson or Aaron Burr—and even the clue to the whole nation itself. This knowledge lies hidden like a nut in its shell. In the past it has revealed itself in myth and symbol, in the image and the fable, in those miraculous constructions of the imagination that burst out of their concreteness to stand for the world itself.

But the truth is that we cannot sensibly make that kind of demand on fiction, on the living imagination. The vastness of sensation and experience, of history and knowledge, limits us, sends us back to the small as a relief from the incomprehensible. Ironic modesty and refusal, the disorganized personal, the colorful actual may at least offer authenticity. If we are not sure about character, suspicious of too clean and plausible structures, uncomfortably aware of the breaks in the chain of cause and effect, fiction, in its classical outlines, will naturally be under painful strain. Great characters and plots are not forthcoming.

Erich Auerbach in *Mimesis* sees the fragmentation of contemporary fiction in dark and despairing terms. Writing about Virginia Woolf and other authors who "dissolve reality into multiple and multivalent reflections of consciousness" Auerbach finds the new technique "a mirror of the decline of our world." Works such as Joyce's *Ulysses* are surrounded by an atmosphere of doom and leave the reader "with an impression of helplessness." Auerbach feels a sense of aching personal bereavement and writes that in the fiction of broken consciousness "there is hatred of culture and civilization brought out by means of the subtlest stylistic devices which culture and civilization have developed, and often a radical and fanatical urge to destroy."

As we from another decade look back to the explosions and destructions of Joyce and others, we think with another sadness, beyond Auerbach's, that so much more was standing for the authors he mentions than for those writing now. In the midst of the mock-heroic, characterization and plot survived, and above all there existed the possibility of a grand conception, a dedication to art, the sacred fount, the willingness literally to give up one's life to creation, as we can perhaps say Joyce and Virginia Woolf gave up their lives. Fiction, the novel, is a fairly recent form. It was born for death because we live in a direct, and yet obscure relation to society. Just now the bourgeois period of the novel would seem to be ending. It is possible that earlier fiction, perhaps something like *Moll Flanders* is nearer to our possibilities than Trollope or Hardy. *Tristram Shandy* may be a more usable model than *The Scarlet Letter*.

For the reader, the novel is the history of his lifetime, marking his existence from youth to old age with a trembling richness. Each work came into being as a mystery of inexplicable strength. We look about us and feel certain humane joys and powers receding, quickly in some cases or slyly, slowly in others, like the bleaching away of the brightness of a shell in the sand and sun. We grieve for the time, the idleness, the longing curiosity, the energy, the need for the great novels of the past. Try to find a young person who has read Thackeray or Cooper or, in America, Balzac or Zola. The end comes painlessly, silently.

1969

DEAD SOULS

Ernest Hemingway

CARLOS Baker's biography of Ernest Hemingway is bad news. The friendliness with which it has been received would seem to give sanction to this unfortunate development in the practice of biography. Baker's work is an enterprise of a special kind, not the first of its sort, and, one supposes, not the last. It is a form of book-making that rests upon only one major claim of the author: his access to the raw materials. The genre rises out of a vast collection of papers, letters, interviews, and junk, and is itself, in the end, still an accumulation, sorted, labeled, and dated, but only an accumulation, a heap. In a hoarding spirit it has an awesome regard for the penny as well as the dollar. (Like poor Silas Marner, who "loved the guineas best, but would not change the silver ... he loved them all.") The original accumulation—the "facts," the private papers, the authorized commission—is thought of as pre-determining not only in content but in form. Condensation would seem to be insulting to the beseechments of the papers, one and all. The book is written by "the material" and nothing is weighed or judged or pondered. A catalog does not gossip about its entries.

Whatever narrative must be constructed as a scaffolding for the events is not distinguished. The infant "cries lustily," early on, and a hat is worn "rakishly." Bad weather is "abhorred." Dawns are bright and nights are dark. When the monotony must sometimes be broken by hints of an inner life, the rhetoric is rather of that inspirational, metaphorical kind journalists write in their sleep. "At the time when he wrote the story of the dying writer on the plains of Africa, he knew very well that he had climbed no further than the lower slopes of his personal Kilimanjaro."

Baker's biography is both official and academic. Neither of these moods is denied by the fact that the Hemingway he presents is quite unattractive. What one finds tiresome and displeasing is just this flesh-ing out of the old Hemingway public persona. After all, so much of this role was determined by the natural inclination of publicity to be repetitious and to see again only what it saw before. In *A Moveable Feast*, Hemingway revealed some of his mean-spirited thoughts about other writers, but he did so with a great deal of beauty and style. And that mattered. Just as most official biographies hesitate to dramatize the discreditable, Baker hesitates to look beyond the coarseness of the "legendary" Hemingway. In this life, the sources of the refinement of the imagination are all that remain hidden. The bland, insistent record-ing of the insignificant, respectful, worshipful as it is, cannot honor a human being and it is particularly useless in the case of a writer—out-standingly inappropriate.

Full-length biographies are a natural occupation for professors, for only they have the inclination to look at a life as a sort of dig. Strange disproportions occur. Matthew Arnold in his essay on Shelley (itself a brilliant, brief, "critical" life) reminds us that Shelley's life was very short, but Professor Dowden's life of Shelley was very long. Professor Frederick Pottle tells us in his introduction to *James Boswell: The Earlier Years* that his book had taken him three times as long in the writing as Boswell took for his life of Johnson—and Pottle has thus far reached only half a life. A rather uninteresting work on Byron presents itself lengthily as a corrective to the briefer pleasures of Sten-dhal and Trelawny. "The concern of memoirists to portray themselves in relation to Byron rather than to portray Byron causes a large amount of literature to yield a very small proportion of reliable information." This, then, is an occupation of a special nature. The temptation to length is irresistible. Little corrections and emendations act upon the biographing mind like revelations and visions utterly absorbing to him who has received them but rather less striking to the rest of us.

Most academic biographies are justified on the grounds of fresh research: that is the claim at least. But fresh research, itself so much rarer than researchers believe, might better present itself in papers and articles. A biography is, after all, an extended form of literary composition and asks first of all for literary and intellectual talent. The "inaccurate and incomplete" memoirs so many scholars spend a lifetime irritably, nervously correcting are among the treasures of our culture, and the spirit of many a great man has been better served by interesting "misconceptions" than by these tedious, researched lives.

And how odd it is that persons, while they are living, so often turn away from the best picture of themselves. Hemingway very sadly rejected Philip Young's interesting, distinguished book on him. Mrs. Thrale, who might be lost in the dust without Boswell, kept writing in the margin when her name appeared, "Spiteful again!" Mary Todd Lincoln thought Herndon made up the story of Ann Rutledge just to spite her. Edgar Lee Masters's biography of Vachel Lindsay is an extraordinary American document even though it is full of the author's rancor and prejudice. Still it has Lindsay, a strangely affecting figure, caught in his success and tragedy.

Is a life truly the same as A Life of. . . .? Upon this question so much of the problem of the biographer seems to turn. This is particularly acute in the case of Hemingway whose life and personality are still close to us. Professor Pottle obviously cannot get Boswell up in the morning or put him to bed at night. The distance in time would not allow a serious scholar to attempt such a feat of impersonation—and Boswell's comings and goings were of such an unbuttoned kind that discretion forbids too great a closeness. (Actually Pottle's biography is a rare one in its intellectual and critical power.) But Professor Baker has written his book under the impression that a life and A Life of may come near to being the same thing. He has, as he tells us, tried to create Hemingway out of a thousand pictures, a thousand scenes, a thousand instances. It is the flow of actual existence he has tried to give us and on that ground he avoids all ideas and judgments, all analysis and opinion.

Baker has put together an extensive, exhausting, repetitive record of the events of Hemingway's life. There is no doubt that this is "the material." But it is not an existence. No book can be that. When Sartre called his autobiography *The Words* he perhaps meant mostly to underline the intensely literary nature of his life. "I began my life as I shall no doubt end it: amidst books." At the same time the title shows us the true nature of an autobiography. In the end it is the writing down of the words. Professor Baker tells us that he spent seven years in preparation of his book on Hemingway and so in the most literal sense his book is Professor Baker's life, seven years of it at least.

The words? Baker has chosen the mode of journalistic informality, exceedingly relaxed and undemanding. This tone is seldom pleasing and never impressive. It has the paradoxical effect of creating by its easy intimacy a spiritual distance. For the intimacy is with "the material"—the mountain of papers under which a life and work are buried. And it is an intimacy, like journalism, that is self-obliterating. By means of this mode the author convinces himself of an illusion: in this case the illusion that Hemingway exists in the book and that Baker does not. "Tom and Lorraine Shevlin arrived early in September to be introduced to the wonders of the region. They made a fishing excursion to Granite Lake and another, after pronghorn antelope, to Nordquist's ranch near Cody. On September 10th, Lawrence Nordquist put out baits for grizzly bear." The names of the guests, the date, the helper who put out the bait: this is research, no doubt about it. But who is served by it, except the facts themselves? They alone live and breathe, aimlessly reproducing, wandering.

We have been told that no man is a hero to his valet. Professor Baker's method makes valets of us all. We keep the calendar of our master's engagements, we lay out his clothes, we order his wine, we pack the bags, we adjust to his new wives, endure his friends, accept his hangovers, his failings. We travel from here to there, serving, now the house in Cuba, then the yacht, *Pilar*. We are often thoroughly sick of it, feel we need time off, a vacation, a raise in pay. We get the dirty work and somebody else, somewhere, gets the real joy of the man, his charm, his uniqueness, his deeply puzzling inner life. Someone else gossips about him, turns over his traits, ponders the mystery of his talent: all we get are signed copies of his books for our grandchildren.

Was this biography necessary? Long as it is, it tells you little for the first time. One does not feel any novelty about it, nor is it even one of those corrective exercises we are accustomed to. A correction is an idea and, while Professor Baker has ideas about Hemingway, he has decided to keep them safe in his checking account. And so the lengthy spinning out is just more of what we have always known from the public picture, the interviews, the popular image. Perhaps it is too early for a book like this on Hemingway. Scribners's eagerness was ill-advised, the widow's cooperation not necessarily in the dead man's ultimate interest. Much of Hemingway's image asks to be forgotten, at least for a while. There has been too much "Papa" and "the Kraut" and "daughter" and Hotchner, too much drinking and hunting and fishing and bull-fighting. If the pastimes could be removed somewhat perhaps we could recover the dedication; if the leisure would stand aside perhaps the work could come forth more clearly.

The truth is that Hemingway's life, lived as the life of an American writer, is deeply interesting as a matter of speculative concern. The good things that have been written about him—Philip Young's critical biography, Edmund Wilson's essay in *The Wound and the Bow*, John Thompson's review of the Hotchner book—are all suffused with sadness. History has brought into question so many of the pleasures and principles he lived by. The great animals he liked to shoot are becoming extinct. The hunter's gun inspires us with fear of the madman, not pride in the ancient rites. We pity him when we read that "he made no attempt to conceal his scorn for those who had not been in uniform," and we wonder if the courage of young soldiers, "grace under pressure," is not more useful to the North Vietnamese than to the hardware-heavy American. The whores of Havana are cutting sugar cane.

What was there in American life that Hemingway needed to get away from? His acceptance of Spanish culture must mean something about him. He said his mother was a bitch who drove his father to suicide. And his own suicide? Would it be facile to connect it with his father's, when it came upon him so much later and accompanied so many other physical torments? Perhaps it came not from his youth but from his skull fractures, those injuries he, or the life he led, was prone to. Why did he drink so much? No one could give an answer to all this. What one wants is to feel the questions somewhere in the shadows.

Hemingway's last year, his terrible suffering, does not bring a pause in the blank recitation, neither in Leicester Hemingway, in Hotchner, nor in Carlos Baker. It appears that if you have forsworn thought about a man's life, you cannot then think about his death, even though it was a pitiful one. In Baker we learn that, the night before, Mary Hemingway sang "Tutti Mi Chiamano Bionda," that the red robe was put on the next morning and "He slipped in two shells, lowered the gun butt carefully to the floor, leaned forward, pressed the twin barrels against his forehead just above the eyebrow, and tripped both triggers." The end. It would not do for us, as valets, to go on too much. In fact, right at the end, we are busy as usual with the facts of life, remembering that "the gun was a double-barreled Boss shotgun with a tight choke."

And so here it is, this long, "successful" biography of Hemingway. It neither says anything new nor questions anything old. It is there like a new unfortunate skyscraper. It takes up the space, and will do so for a long time. No one of talent would wish, because of it, to plough this unhappy ground again soon.

1969

IN MAINE

THE FADING lilacs of June, wild lupine along the road, standing in rows of spiky pinks and jagged blues. Pines and spruces—and then a patch of road with white birch groves dressed in their pale paper sheets of bark. In the evenings the lights of your car startle the blazing eyes of the big, furry Maine cats. They are strangely impressive, especially the bizarre matings of blacks and browns and yellows, the colors smeared in patches or fixed in stripes—ugly, anarchic. These large cats seem well suited to the northern part of the country, but there is a desperation about them too as they slink into the lonely, silent, black canals of wet earth next to the roads. No lights in the distance, no paths cut through the trees, no domestic breaks in the forest of alders.

The steady beat of the local people's days—puttering, dreaming, working. There is something meditative and faraway about the Maine person—in his movements, in the controlled cadence of the jokes, the reserved, cool smiles. From birth the weather has marked him as it has marked everything around him. The clearest of blue skies, the dazzling sun on the bay, the warm grass, the brilliant summery white of the harbor alive with sails: still, even so, there is always behind the brightness the domain of winter—fog, rain, and snow. It never vanishes; it just seems to step back for a little.

When it is dark or rainy or cool the afternoons are endless; they stop—glooming. The light drops, the day waits. Time seems to hang in the air, thick, motionless. The stillness of the old, small village is complete, the rhythmical flow peculiar, as if repeating moments lived before, perhaps long ago, or by someone else. This sensation is touched with melancholy and sometimes one feels a pang of panic. In the drawer there are old photographs of our square, my house on the left, just as it was a hundred years ago. A sense of continuity oppresses just as much as it reassures.

"Many a noble heart mourned the fall of those great oaks."

People speak of worrying about the trees. The great old elms, with their terminal woe, are dying grandly, a real death like that of the old chancellor in Rilke's story. But what about the grand dukes—the cedars, the maples? They wait, reprieved, harboring the winds. On the rooftops, in the gutters, damp, yellowing leaves. From the shore, islands live and die, appear and disappear, depending upon the light, the fog.

A fantastic love of difficult, awkward islands gripped the heart of rich people at the turn of the century. Grandeur and privation, costliness and discomfort. Some years ago we took a friend from South America to an island quite a distance off Machias, Maine. The launch pulled up to a long, wooden pier to which the owner's sloop was moored. The house was a large yellow frame with two graceful wings and inside there were beautiful dishes, old maps on the wall, fine painted chests, and handsome beds. We lived there in silence and candlelight for a few days, stumbling about with our guttering tapers, coming upon steep back stairways where we had been expecting a closet with our nightgowns in it. "This is madness! No, it is not one bit amusing!" the Brazilian lisped in fury.

The house on the island in our bay is notable for its uncompromising, flawless memory of those good-sized dwellings in important towns of the Middle West. Cleveland, St. Louis? Strong and solid structure, placed on a broad avenue, fifty years ago, out of style with too many colored panes and redundant porches. Memory built it brick by brick on a Maine island.

Downstream a little red wooden farmhouse, local, stands on a rise, its field running down to the shore. It is utterly serene, pure, one of those sentimental bits of landscape, existing by accident, perhaps not even treasured. It is dazzling, simple, forlorn and yet free of the psychodrama that mars the paintings of Wyeth when he comes upon similar scenes. The beauty is that nothing is happening in the red wooden house; it does not mean anything or hide anything.

From one spot on high ground, back from the road leading out of town, you can look down on the Bagaduce River and across to the other bank where small villages with white spires seem to stand, trapped and glistening. All of the whiteness is tipped with sunlight, but it is so small and still and fixed that it does not seem quite real. Our own language and our own day unfit us for the Maine landscape and even the Maine "experience." There is a bland vacation quality to most Maine literature and it is all, except for Sarah Orne Jewett, a sort of translation. (From her story "The Town Poor": "My good gracious, ain't this a starved-looking place? It makes me ache to think them nice Bray girls has to brook it here.")

From the window, in front of my desk, an old worn-out apple tree extends a branch with its little, wormy green fruits hanging on it like Christmas ornaments. Swishing through the frayed leaves, a cedar waxwing, two flickers. Here, in Maine, every stone is a skull and you live close to your own death. Where, you ask yourself, where indeed will I be buried? That is the power of those old villages: to remind you of stasis.

There is no place to go! You just stay at home. Then systole (the post office), diastole (the grocery store). Back home again. A trip sometimes to Bucksport, and then to Bangor, to meet the airplane. But nothing to do. Claustrophobia and coming to terms with it, living with it, that is the Maine theme. You are enclosed in your village, in the whole state, its position, its distance, its weathers.

What affects me so deeply about Maine is the sense of loss. Lost people, lost mills, lost fish in the sea, lost berries and livestock, unpredictable potatoes, bereft farms, stony and slighted fields, patchy pastures. Maine lost 25,000 farms between 1880 and 1940. More than half the improved land had reverted to forest over thirty years ago. And yet so romantic and nobly unreal are the residents here that they live with a sort of nightmare peopling their emptiness. They are always predicting hordes of one kind or another, tourists, summer-house buyers, marinas, dense developments from the icy tip to the barely warm south. They are coming, watch out!

We all say that constantly. But nothing comes and nothing lost returns. Shrinkage continues, developments pour the foundation and that is the end of it. "Poor drainage!" the local people say, triumphantly. The movie house went before I came to Maine and the shoemaker has been a memory for longer than I've been alive. Our only lobster restaurant burned to the ground last year. The gap, the leveled ground has melted into the landscape, as though it had been waiting, this emptiness, for its natural turn. They goeth and they do not return, ever. The agitation of July and August always subsides. The roads are soon empty, the hamburger stands close, the postal clerk's load is lifted. The wistful, sweet torpor returns.

I am sure I don't understand Maine. I have been here for three months a year for sixteen years. But is this a long or a short time? I have, however, *worked* on this place, as one speaks of working on some new language. I have studied it a bit, driven about alone, inland, looking, wondering. Is the quiet a true tranquility and peacefulness? I sometimes think it is and then again—perhaps it is something else. There is about the region a curious and fascinating softness that seems to spread like a blanket over the hardness of rock and woods and icy turf. This is a perturbation, this ambiguous softness in the drifting fogs, the thick greens of the trees, the dampness, the swampy meadows. It is in the people too, in the men as well as in the women. Not a tropical softness, of course, but the odd snowy lassitude of isolation. Whole countries and people formed by these long, huddling winters. "Well," he told me, "November is the suicide season. Summer is over, winter's ahead. Long months of closing in." Pregnancies, breakdowns.

"Oh, when I think of winter I just think of poverty spread over everything. The cold makes everything poor. They are always saying they like it, like it the best of all, calling it better than summer. But I don't think they are telling the truth. . . . I think winter does something to your head, your feeling, something not even the summer's heat can undo." And he looked with a soft melancholy toward the waving sea. "Well, anyway, this is a handsome place."

My own town of Castine stands out on a point and thus has something of the feeling of an island. It has attractive houses; boats and docks and shores give it beauty and life; it has gentility and promotes its history. The Main Street slopes down to the harbor, slowly, and houses curve along the waterfront, some ours (summer people), some theirs (town people). There is a turn-of-the-century quality to life here, pre-swimming and sunning and beaching; instead, eager boating, rather pure and difficult and special, again like decades ago. Relations with people are of a gentle and genteel sort; it gives a stinging pleasure, not being what has come to be your true self, putting it aside for three months, like going home and as the C&O pulls into the old station adjusting and rearranging yourself. Or perhaps it is calling upon some self always there, but, like a telephone, in suspended service.

In Maine I have lived with those I loved, my family, and I have also spent several summers more or less alone. The puzzle to me is that both are the same: it is always sweet, strange, protective. That is because the town is small and the colony of summer folk, or those once summer folk, is intelligent without being in any way fanatical. Like the weather, we know we are inclined to be disappointing and yet one must take a sort of positive stand, say that the faulty is not so bad, the winters less severe, the rain beautiful when compared to the devastating heat in the cities. One of the things it takes to make a good Maine summer is an inferno of heat elsewhere: if New York or Long Island or the Cape boils, a steady beauty, warm and sunny, exhilarates us in Castine. And so we profit by the ill luck of those to the south of us, but we are not, reciprocally, able to make them share our desolation.

Like all odd groupings Maine gives love for love. One day recently between about four and six o'clock a fierce wind whipped around the tennis court. There were four of us playing, the rest frightened off by hurricanes at Portland and the sleet-gray sky. The wind at the court became soft as water; it was like swimming to raise your arm to serve— and on and on we played, all of us drowned in the magic of the cool rushing wind and the heat of running. A peculiar happiness sometimes comes upon you in these northern places and you feel—ecstasy.

I have sometimes wondered if spending all my life, through college, in Kentucky has brought me closer to Maine. Streets and towns and familiar persons. But it is vanity to go on too much about these things. I am skeptical of everything in America just now, wary of roots and character. The past is a cliché, just as the future is. Perhaps we were never Puritans and that is the trouble. Everything in our lives seems subject to revision. Surgery cuts away all those appendices and gall bladders of belief and national temperament.

Still, some things must count. How can it be otherwise? To live in an old, sparsely settled, cold region, to endure it, to face it—that matters. Maine seems so much less open to the universalizing of television than, for instance, the South. There is a commercialized aspect to a Southerner's very conception of himself—that I have thought for a long time. Even his bigotry is standardized, packaged, predictable. You do not often find people in the South who think the cause of all the trouble in the world is the use of aluminum cooking pots. That is too individual, too personal—better stick to the same nuttiness everyone else has. Discomfort of body and mind is the condition of the north: solitary lives with solitary ideas. One does not live out a large myth so much as contribute his lonely, authentic bit to the "whole," making the whole hard to express, slippery, peculiar, puzzling. To be poor, isolated, damp is not a character so much as a condition and yet man and nature are one here, or seem to be.

Nature more than man inclines toward the general in Maine. The place always reminds one of some abstract pictorial representation of itself. Rotting boats, apple green. The cold, severe seas, home to old sailors with grizzled, undulating beards, boots, rubber coat, head turned to one side in a rocky smile. Is it Winslow Homer? The face is on the calendars and somehow you run into it at the docks. The piers with the loose boards, the native waterfront houses, tilting, listing. Leaning wharves, splintering lobster boats, abandoned dories, the boat builder's fantastic shed. Tides and fogs and herons, seals, the osprey's nest on the tip of an island, the gulls' breeding ground. It is indeed like a painting and every little inlet, with its empty boat, the mast standing watch, is an illustration from a bad book.

Water: This is everything. These waters are sacred. "Going down to the bay is the closest to heaven I will ever come," an old man said. They are all afraid of the water. It seems absurd to learn to swim and many do not know how. It is too cold for man. You can stand on a corner and hear an argument about whether you die in fifteen minutes or fifteen seconds in the really cold part. They talk about that and what happened to the lobster. Some say it's the Gulf Stream.

"I guess there is a remaining respect for those who have been out in all weathers. At twenty below your clam flats freeze. Still, one man got enough from a night's herring catch to buy an Oldsmobile."

The clam diggers and their families. "I don't know what they are going to do this winter. Eight or nine kids, all living in a tent. Two of the girls sleep in the car."

Inland: Why does the hummingbird return to the north? "They live more intensely than any other being on our globe," an old book says. The hermit thrush—suitably named for the Maine airs and branches. And yet so many of the birds are oddly bright and tropical in coloring.

Near Skowhegan—a long, narrow shed which shelters the little shops from the wind and the rain. The variety store, the grocery, the hamburger and crab roll stand. In the grocery very little sign of the local—browning bananas and hard, grassy tasting tomatoes from the opposite coast of the country. The smell of Wonder Bread somehow pierces through the wrapper, or is it the wrapper itself that is now the characteristic scent of country stores, taking the place of the pickle barrel?

The abundance of flags puzzles. Fine houses, with their flagpoles jutting out from the second story, as if in a permanent, steely salute— these often seem to call attention to the claims of the house, to its white clapboards and black shutters, its fan-shaped glass over the doorway. The place itself is honored as much as the country; sentiment attaches to ownership and upkeep as well as to patriotic and ceremonial occasions.

But it is the flags on the tiniest little shacks, those frail wooden wounds, the barest sort of dwellings, coverings rather than houses. These often have two little flags, cheap ones on sticks, over the gashlike door. In Maine, those who have been born here and who remained, endured, even the poorest and quietest, appear to share a common feeling about themselves. They feel a part of something very old, a sense of living in an ancient land, with ports once so busy you could step from ship to ship for a mile, and they feel the empty forest still there, as it was in the earliest America, the beginning. They seem to have an unconscious image of being original stock, neither good nor bad, just what was always here.

There is a poetic mysteriousness about these forlorn, poor inland people, not at all like the patriotic Americanism of other parts of the country. It is a dreamy thing, not an aggressive challenge. The claim does not seem to be an accusation against others—they are too poor for the fiercer bigotries. It has instead all to do with the recalcitrant landscape, the remoteness, the hardness. And so when you see a flag pinned to an old shack you almost feel the person announcing himself, saying, Look, I am still here.

Things: An abandoned mill at the bottom of the hill, over a stream. A little shack, up an old, empty road, the very earth depressed. On the right, the woods of birch and pines, resting upon a gutter filled with twigs and sticks and leaves, nature's garbage. I have felt frightened on the roads in Maine, as if I had stepped into a sudden darkness. The bleak northern air is unwelcoming, madly inward. Out of the darkness some old, ragged, melancholic Massasoit might now step, prophetic, resigned, subdued, aching.

A streamer of wood smoke. White paint that has rusted to a deep gray—and a disastrous rim of darkening, peeling coral paint around the window panes of the shack, like nail polish, expressing an elation, shortlived, inappropriate. Some of the coral paint clings like specks from birds to the glass of the windows. It is bitterly ugly, wrongheaded, a defeat of misplaced hope.

Deep and lasting deprivation settles and clings, not yesterday's or last year's but poverty with old, sturdy roots. A horrifying clutter screams through the lonely air. It is as if the history of the family were strewn around the yard, a desolating iconography. Everywhere a crowd, a multitude of rust, breakage, iron, steel, and tin. Here, almost blocking the door, is the rusting wheel of an automobile. It has lain there so long it has become something natural, like stone, taking its place in the scheme of things.

Large objects are like piercing, menacing hurdles. A heavy, rain-dulled bit of obsolescent plow, blade upward, glittering brownly in the weak rays of the sun. Three large planks, remnant of some construction dream, nails upright like steeples. A slide upside down, the ladder broken; a huge tin garbage pail, dented everywhere, as if from a thousand blows, its bottom a sieve. A battered baby stroller, clumps of wood, old chair legs, bed springs, a tarpaulin in which an old puddle of water nests. A sled, a barrel, rubber tires. All crowned by the object just to the left, the car itself, leprously scarred, squat on the ground, but permanent like a dependent building, stripped of window glass and cushion, of steel and handle and headlight, a shell, gathering its cellar of worms and wearing its own metallic patina. Grand as some Step Pyramid, meant for the hereafter. A grackle swoops down on the snubbed, black nose of the engine. The bird rests a moment, sleek, shiny, radiantly blue-black against the dead tin.

But what would you have, what setting would be suitable to the unproductive, disdained back road, the barren hill? Sometimes in a dream you imagine the perfect setting for the poor, or the not-poor, for that matter. It is always a beauty based on emptiness and lack dressed and furnished in an inspired sparseness. Think of the old New England clapboard, of some historical meaning, open to the public, with nothing in it except iron pots hanging over the wide hearth, the wooden bed and worn quilt, the scrubbed floorboards, the little homemade chairs for the children primly set about a tea table. Or a Japanese sense of fitness, the perfect, bare utility of mat and pallet and cushion. Or the rooms of young married students, crates and candles, baskets and posters.

But what idle snobbery all of this is. With the poor, and all of us, truth is found in the rusting, immovable car. This is a serious object and it has a life without end. It is its immovability, its heaviness that awe you. A defunct automobile that has come to rest in the front yard, well, it will be there next summer and the one after that and you can only pity the poor householders, singled out for this heavy misfortune.

And all the other parts and bits seem to represent some kind of odd hope that afflicts the poor when they are faced with a damaged but not utterly valueless object. One day the bolt will meet the nut, the broken saw will find a function, the new child will play in the rubber tire, the broken slide will one morning grow upright like a stalk of corn. This is not psychotic hoarding, but normal bewilderment riding on the back of consumption. These broken, damaged, smothering things are reminders of all those miserable down payments and you cannot utterly disown them any more than you can bring yourself to throw away the mistaken coat, the shoe that lightly pinches.

What sadness in the fuchsia plastic flower amid the steely, violent grays of the landscape. One day on display in the warm store it represented eternal possibility. What is an old appliance except a tomb of sorrow, a slab of disappointment, a fraud not really acknowledged but kept around mournfully, a reminder of life's puzzling lack of accommodation? Everyone feels in his bones his own weakness and helplessness. What energy and success and determination are necessary to rid oneself of the heavy, doomed appliance, the inert, out-of-order iron and steel. It is part of life's ill luck that you choke on the mistakes of your hope, and live in a martyrdom to the strength of that which is useless and yet long-lived.

Stepping among these dormant accumulations a child must walk as nimbly as a mountain goat. The clutter is life history, autobiography. It depresses with its bulk, its sharp, tetanus edges; and yet it is homage, belief, loyalty, hope. It is the same everywhere except that in Maine you come upon the heroic trash by surprise, for you hadn't thought there was anything living around the corner. The debris is oddly settled in an emptiness and you see the old plastic as if you were an antiquarian looking for musket balls.

The fine house, the beautiful harbors and islands, yes. But Maine is a museum of another kind, a collection of the deserted and abandoned, a preservation of the feel of long, catatonic winters. Its exhibitions tell of no money and nothing to buy anyway, of nothing to do and no place to go. It preserves the face of lack, of minimum, the bottom—the pure, lost negative. Living in it your heart seems to stop sometimes, gripped by a fearfulness that is not altogether painful. You have seen your great-grandparents, their static, browning profiles; and you have put them back into their still and slow, hard scenery.

1971

MILITANT NUDES

TROUBLING Images: 1.) Professor Theodor W. Adorno, at the University of Frankfurt, was, not long before his death, the audience for—or the object of—a striking bit of symbolic action. Adorno, a distinguished philosopher and the teacher of many leftist students, had come to be worried about student zeal for immediate action, about spontaneity, random rebellion, and, of course, the possibility of repressive actions by the government. And how was the sacred old father rebuked? A girl got up in the classroom and took off her clothes.

A bit of *The Blue Angel* here? No, perhaps the key is found in the famous scene in *Swann's Way*. Mlle. Vinteuil, making love to her girl friend, puts the photograph of her doting, gifted father on the table next to the sofa so that the girl can spit on it. Proust says about the scene: "When we find in real life a desire for melodramatic effect, it is generally the 'sadic' instinct that is responsible for it."

Sexuality—the word has become a sort of unfleshed abstraction as it trails along with liberty, fraternity, and equality in the youth revolution—is suddenly political. The body, the young one at least, is a class moving into the forefront of history.

In *Gimme Shelter*, a brilliant documentary film about the Rolling Stones and their concert outside San Francisco that ended in murder, several accidental deaths, and an outburst of desolation, anger, and danger that is thought to have signaled the end of something in the rock and roll scene—in this film a number of people, mostly girls, take off their clothes. Each has an expression both blank and yet sure that something is being done, accomplished, signified. They stand there in the crowd, enclosed in their sad flesh, as lonely as scarecrows among the angry, milling thousands. The gestures did not cause a head to turn and all one could feel was that the body, the feet, the breasts were foolishly vulnerable, not because of any attractions they might have for the crowd, but merely due to the lack of protecting clothing. The nude bodies were no match in dramatic interest to the fabulously dressed performers, whose tight pants, scarves, snakeskin boots, spangled boleros, red silk ruffled shirts, represented what is meant in the entertainment world by a "personal statement."

2.) Huey Newton in New Haven, visiting Bobby Seale in jail. "If Ericka and Bobby are not set free, if the people can't set them free, then we'll hold back the night, there won't be day—there'll be no light." The eschatological mode has in modern times wearied the Christian world, but it served them well enough for centuries and so perhaps militant leaders naturally feel there is some life left in this style. At the Black Panther convention recently—a small and dispirited gathering, according to journalists—Huey Newton outlined the program: "First, focus on closing down Howard University, second on liberating Washington, and third the seizure of the White House." Liberating Washington. For a little group of the faithful these words perfectly represent the "schizophrenic bind" R. D. Laing writes about. If the words are not genuinely taken seriously and only a pretense about them is kept up, this creates an impossible and corrupting cynicism very difficult for all except leaders to live with; if the commands are treated as genuine their insane and sadistic nature will unhinge all who try to act them out. This is perhaps what is truly meant by the phrase, revolutionary suicide—the killing in oneself of the uses of reality by submitting to "the program."

The film, *Ice*, and the novel, *Dance the Eagle to Sleep*, are both imaginary projections of revolutions and civil wars to come, and there is a coercive and mystical inevitability claimed, not directly but aesthetically, that links them with the program Huey Newton gives to his followers. And the concentration upon revolutionary "balling" in the novel goes back in my mind to the poor professor in his classroom, to the mysteriousness of the girl's answer to the professor's worries.

In *Ice* there is a deliberate lack of art, decoration, plot, characterization. All of these elements are missing and in their place is revolutionary dedication. Dedication to the revolution *is* the plot, *is* the characters.

They have surrendered personality, differences, past and future history, and this mingling of people with their guns, their propaganda, their "actions," and their indistinguishable faces and voices is the substance and the interest of the work. Everything moves by the pulsing of "inevitability" and the pretense of belief in the coming revolution. The belief is not directed at the public but is simply a picture of the mind of the creator, Robert Kramer. *Ice* is filmed as if it were something on the TV evening news, something that has already happened.

In the film, the United States has become involved in a military intervention in Mexico, and proceeds with force against leftists or peasants, whoever is rising up there and threatening "imperialist" interests. In New York, and no doubt in other cities, the young radicals have opened up a second front of guerrilla warfare against their own government. The scene is upper Broadway, the courtyard of the Belnord, the New Yorker Bookstore at 88th Street, and a large apartment house in Greenwich Village. The actors look like Columbia or Hunter students, but not teen-agers by any means. They might well remind you of people about to get their licenses to teach in the New York City public school system since they have about them an oppressive and oppressed look, an air of dissatisfaction coupled with dedication, a feeling for work that is necessary, directed toward the welfare of the person and the community but which is, revolution and school alike, somewhat unappetizing.

Some scenes from *Ice*: The revolutionaries occupy an apartment house in Washington Square. They go up and down the halls with machine guns, blocking elevators and escapes, beating on the doors of the hard-pressed, random tenantry of New York City. They gather together some of the people—middle-aged men in undershirts, women in wrappers—and a revolutionary says to them: "You are closer to the Mexican students than to your own country." This is a reading lesson to a class watching the clock, and a complete falsification of the experience and nature of the tenants, who can't speak Spanish, and who aren't students. What is interesting about it is the lack of questioning on the part of the radicals, the survival in them of the grim sectarianism of the Communist International thirty or forty years ago.

The value of constantly predicting revolutions, civil war, violent accountings is to give a sense of power to the powerless. Sukhanov, thoroughly involved in revolutionary life, was sitting at his desk in February, 1917, sure that the revolution was decades away. And those to be overthrown were not in a state, either, of practical, counterrevolutionary readiness. Trotsky quotes Prince Lvov's account of a visit to the Tsar at a time when everyone could see the monarchy was collapsing: "I expected to see the sovereign stricken with grief, but instead of that there came out to meet me a jolly, sprightly fellow in a raspberry-colored shirt."

The activism in *Ice* and *Dance the Eagle to Sleep* is not a replacement of deadening alienation but simply an addition to it. Even though *Ice* was filmed in the basements and bookstores and streets of New York City, one often feels in it a memory of the suffocating boredom and darkly sexual crowdings of an old army post, the kind of waiting and frustration that made soldiers before Vietnam long for some action. So, after a few years of threats and promise of revolution, rebellion, change, militant encounter, *Ice* and *Dance the Eagle to Sleep* are tours of active duty at last.

Another scene: A young revolutionary is trapped in a basement by the enemy—powerful, short-haired policemen or rightists—and subjected to terrible genital torture. We hear the screams of pain and the horror of the scene makes it difficult to watch. Later another radical is in bed with his girl. He tells her that he is sometimes afraid. Our mind goes back to the torture. "You know what they do to you," he says softly. The girl, rather heavy, depressed, touches the boy's arm and mumbles, "You can't let it get to you."

Ice is as cold as its title, a glassy radical vision, austere, masochistic, longing for the "inevitable." To think of the revolution is to prepare to die. "They kill; we kill." You endure approaching death in a fantasy of activity: "regional offensive," arrival of "the Mexican footage," admitting "We had some bad losses." One of the most interesting things about it is that it is old-fashioned, humorless, like Maoists or the Progressive Labor youths, and we are thus spared endless fornications and commune banalities.

This is not true of *Dance the Eagle to Sleep* by Marge Piercy—a harsh and sentimental "youth" novel, vaguely set in the future but quite openly counting on the reader's acquiescence in the reality of its themes and obsessions. Actually many of the reviews thought the book was needlessly cast into the future and seemed to want to allow the fantasy the status of fact. The novel is about a pathetic group of "acid revolutionaries," all very young, most of them in high school. It is a destructive fantasy, full of suffering, dreary phallic obsessiveness, and it is meaningless in a political sense.

Still, the book's claim to immediacy is insistent and its scenes of brutal police activity, school occupations, drugs, communes are true enough. However, the real source of the action is a sadomasochistic death dream. The people in *Ice* seem to be Marxists, but in *Dance the Eagle to Sleep*, they are "tribes" brought together by the visions of a young Indian boy named Corey. "We belong to a new nation of the young and the free, and we're going to win!" The radicalization of some of the students starts at a police gassing and beating up in Tompkins Square, the others at the occupation of a high school in New York: both of these occasions not only solidify political activism but offer some pretty good "sexuality" as well. The young people set up a commune in New Jersey, and send out others to keep organizing "tribes" all over the country. The principal activity at the commune, or at least the ritualistic experience that shapes the movement, is a tedious and often repeated evening of drug-taking, nude dancing, and sexual excitement.

The language of the book has, in the dialogue, a coarse power, but the exposition, the thought, and the structure are very weak. Almost every idea or opinion in the book is a banality from one side of the gap or the other. Here is the dreaming mind of Corey, the Indian boy, leader of the tribe. "Just stride into school cool and easy some morning with the rifle on his back like a guerrilla fighter. Better a machine gun. Line up the faculty. Torture the principal to learn where they kept the anxiety gasses and the chemicals they put in the soup to make the kids stupid and passive." When you get to "the anxiety gasses," and the chemicals that keep the kids "stupid and passive," you have passed, amateurishly, from the boy's dreams to mere opinions about our schools. It goes on, smothering teen-age life in the spelled-out opinions about that life. "Keep your hands to yourself. Don't look like you're enjoying yourself, ever. Don't laugh out loud over your peanut butter sandwich; don't get into excited conversation about anything you care for."

It is the intellectual assumptions of the book that interest me rather than its literary quality. A reviewer, leaning on the staff of comparison, mentioned *Lord of the Flies*, *Lord of the Rings*, and . . . *Moby-Dick*. The dreary sexual scenes go from, "Her cunt ached," to formal cadences in the late Hemingway manner: "She had prepared herself carefully, and he would wait for her. He would spend the night with her, he decided. She was plump the way he liked and he liked too that she had stopped to make herself ready." Symbolic moments are of a surprisingly handy sort. Corey has attacks of suffocation and panic. "It was an eagle [America?] that stooped on him as he slept and tore into him, that carried him bleeding high up so he could not breathe, and dashed him to the ground." The book ends—after Corey and Billy and others have been killed, Joanna has gone over to "them," and everything is destroyed—with one of those odd but oft-remembered finales of contrived hope, the birth of a baby. "The baby lived and she lived and it was day for Marcus and for him, it was day for all of them."

There is a brutal murder in the book. Joanna, Corey, and Shawn—the principals of the novel—participate in the torture and shooting of one of their members because he has been selling "bread"—the hallucinogenic drug the tribe manufactures—for his own profit. This scene has a moral numbness and indifference to physical pain quite characteristic of all the works I am concerned with. After the comrade has been shot and thrown into a grave, Joanna makes a smooth, "literary" switch to sex and takes that moment to tell her lover, Corey, that she once "made it" with Shawn, the other participant in the crime.

Remember the opening of Malraux's *Man's Fate*, the foot sticking out from under the mosquito netting, its throbbing life stinging the consciousness of the assassin. The foot. . . . What repels in the new works is the loss of pity for the poor body, of respect for its life, its suffering. Perhaps this is the underside, just as it was in Sade, of the worship of the body, of reverence for its sensations.

NOTES ON *TRASH, THE GROUPIES, GIMME SHELTER*

Trash is a homosexual film produced by Andy Warhol and directed by Paul Morrissey. *The Groupies* has to do with deranged, obscene girls who follow rock stars around, hoping to sleep with them, if one may use such a drowsy, untimely phrase for these wandering, never-sleeping hunters. *The Groupies* is a documentary, although there is considerable staginess in it; *Trash* is a concoction that is also a real life thing part of the time.

The nature of sexuality is repetition. Phallic compulsiveness is an exaltation of repetition and yet a reduction to routine of the most drastic kind. Still, novelty and challenge never lose their hold on the imagination and in the phallic hell the center of interest will be reserved for the refusing, even for the impotent. The hero of *Trash* is an impotent junkie. He wanders through the long hours of the film. He is quiet, handsome, mysterious, stoned, but arouses almost insane desire in everyone he meets. In a world of compulsive sex, dramatic interest can only be achieved by complications, particularly since every frontier of practice has been crossed.

In *Trash*, the little drag queen, Holly Woodlawn, pursues, waits on, loves the impotent junkie, Joe Dallesandro, with an air of blind necessity, like that of an animal running on and on in the plains in search of food. Joe's drug addiction has released him from "performance," and although he keeps trying in a nodding fashion it is never because he himself feels the loss but rather that he is a nice, passive boy and the frenzy he arouses in others makes him attempt an accommodation. Joe has the charm of silence—he also talks very little—in a room of screaming deviates.

In *Ice* one of the revolutionaries has a "hang-up" and one of the girls sneers (in the sort of folk poetry that decorates all of these works), "If you're having trouble with your prick, don't take it out on me!" It is almost impossible to keep face, statement, and shadow of personality together in one's mind about *Ice*, but if memory serves, the troubled young man was far from being weak and inadequate and was instead particularly zealous, concentrated, and effective. In *Dance the Eagle to Sleep*, the girls are constantly available and practical—I'm afraid rather like a jar of peanut butter waiting for a thumb. Billy, the most intelligent and the most violently intransigent, is by comparison with the others noticeably reserved sexually, partly out of temperament, and partly because he gives thought to other matters. The revolution, at least in the beginning, is for puritans.... Later....

In *Gimme Shelter*, Mick Jagger, Grace Slick, Tina Turner—the rock stars—are a disturbing contrast to the dull, sullen, angry hundreds of thousands who have come to hear them. For one thing the performers are *working* and even if the pay is outrageous, and the acts somewhat tarnished by time, there is still discipline, energy, travel, planning, and talent. Each one is a presence, unique, competitive, formed by uncommon experiences. The crowd, however, is just a huge clot of dazed swayings, fatuous smilings, empty nightmares, threatening hallucinations, and just plain meanness.

There is death everywhere, and of every sort, in the dead, drugged eyes and in the jostling, nervous kicks and shoves. Everyone is a danger to himself and to others. One could be stabbed by a "mystic" who thought he was God or Satan; or choked by the lowering, alcoholic violence of the Hell's Angels just for brushing against one of their sweating arms. Someone is having a baby—another corny freak-out, you find yourself thinking. The owner of the Altamont Speedway, where the concert took place, wants the birth mentioned in the media as a "first." "Easy, easy," Grace Slick pleads from the stage. "Why are you people fighting?" Mick Jagger wants to know. After the concert, two young boys were killed when a car left the highway and crashed into their campfire. Another young man, drugged, fell into a canal and was drowned.

Thinking about the predatory girls who call themselves "the groupies," remembering their obscene reveries and their moronic self-exploitation, one wants to hold back from description. One of the young men connected with the film said, in a press interview, that he was horrified by the girls and that they were stoned out of their minds all of the time. The girls are hoarse and coarse and not one arouses pity of the kind we feel for the pimply, snaggle-toothed synthetic girl, Holly Woodlawn, in *Trash*. All are despised by everyone, by the cameramen, the producers, the rock stars, just as Holly is despised by Andy Warhol and Paul Morrissey.

The main life of *Trash* comes from the perverse, proletarian vitality of Holly Woodlawn, who comes across to us as rotting skin and bones, kept alive by the blood of mascara and the breath of discarded clothing from the city's trash barrels. Still, the people in charge of the film show their hatred by a long, boring, hideous scene in which Holly buggers herself to some sort of satisfactory exhaustion with a beer bottle.

The "groupies" take plaster casts of the parts of rock stars—or they claim the stars as the origin of their "collection." The idea came to one of them, she says into the waiting microphones, when an art teacher said one could make a plaster cast of "anything hard." "Wow," grunts the groupie. She later describes herself in the more delicate moments of the casting as being "very gingerly."

Certainly these girls are in extremity, pushing out beyond the horizon. Yet they are not much more freakish nor are they more obscene than the teen radicals in *Dance the Eagle to Sleep*. In the novel, Joanna, the girl most admired and desired by the boys, is serenaded with a little song that goes:

> Joanna has a hairy cunt.
> It's the kind of cunt I want.
> I get on my knees and grunt
> For a touch of Jo-Jo's hairy cunt!

The groupies contain in every swagger and delusion genetic reminders of their parents, longing for the kiss of celebrity; aging Stalinists seem to haunt the memories in *Ice*; Holly Woodlawn says in the film she was born on welfare and while that is probably a fiction there is no reason why she might not have been. Hell's Angels and the vaguely disoriented crowds are both caught up in the mindless anarchy. What can one make of these deaths, since death is the feeling most clearly projected by radical and freak, girl and boy: death by drugs, by the misery and dreariness of the commune; death *by* political enemies, death *to* political enemies, death in "regional actions," by helicopters raining destruction on teen tribes, death at the free rock festival, in the eyes of Miss Harlow, the little groupie with frizzy hair.

At his trial, perhaps feeling the sorrow of his complicity in the death of Che Guevara, Régis Debray said: "The tragedy is that we do not kill objects, numbers, abstract or interchangeable instruments, but, precisely, on both sides, irreplaceable individuals, essentially innocent, unique...."

Something pitiless and pathological has seeped into youth's love of itself, its body, its politics. Self-love is an idolatry. Self-hatred is a tragedy. But the life around us is not a pageant of coldness and folly to which we have paid admission and from which we can withdraw as it becomes boring. You feel a transcendental joke links us all together; some sordid synthesis hangs out there in the heavy air. No explanation—the nuclear bomb, the Vietnam War, the paralyzing waste of problems and vices that our lives and even the virtues of our best efforts have led to—explains. Yet it would be dishonorable to try to separate our selves from our deforming history and from the depressing dreams being acted out in its name.

After the squalor of *Trash*, *The Groupies*, and *Dance the Eagle to Sleep*, one comes back to the girl in Professor Adorno's class. What did she think her bare breasts meant? What philosophy and message could this breathing nude embody? In one of his last essays Adorno wrote, "Sanctioned delusions allow a dispensation from comparison with reality...." And he also said, "Of the world as it exists, one cannot be enough afraid." The students may have known all about the second idea, but perhaps they could not forgive him the first.

1971

SUE AND ARABELLA

SUE AND Arabella, in Hardy's *Jude the Obscure*, are like a Pre-Raphaelite painting of Sacred and Profane Love. There they stand—assuming the absent man, the abashed, overwhelmed Jude. Sue is thin, pretty, with a light, abstracted, questioning gaze; Arabella is round, sly-eyed, sleepy, with the dreaming torpor of a destitute girl pondering an exchange of sexual coin. It is scarcely worth noting that they are different, almost opposites. The sources of feeling could not be more reflective than they are in Sue, or more immediate and formless than they are in Arabella. Experience, with them, is not merely the sum of events gone through; it is the response of their differing understanding of love, want, greed, or renunciation.

In the novel, Sue and Arabella are *connected* as women with Jude Frawley. But he does not initiate or control. Instead, he is identified by them and his situation is dominated by what they offer or withhold. In youth he comes under the sexual domination of Arabella, a surrender rather casual that immediately becomes a trap very steely. With Sue, a miserable life is redeemed by the joys of enlightenment and by the special importance that is given to a love or to an attachment by one who cares to think about it in a deep way.

There is every kind of suffering and failure in *Jude the Obscure*. This is its great glory as a novel—the passion, the complexity, the completeness, if you will, of petty, mean, bitter failure. Waste, oppression, injustice, indifference have soaked into the very soil of life, washing away all of the yearnings and rights of those with unlucky natures or unfortunate birth. Social and spiritual deprivation bears down on these modest persons who have asked only the lightest measure of possibility. Every single character fails and falls, in great pain, each one. The children, the lovers, the married, the ignorant, the intellectual. The only moments of happiness are the innocence of early hope and perhaps those instances of love and respect Sue Bridehead, a singular, deep creation, brings to the lives about her. Love and respect—or is it, instead, affection and sympathy, emotions a little more distant.

Sue is an original, mingled being. The outlines of her nature waver and flow. She is as we find it often in our lives one of these striking, haunting persons who endlessly talk, act, and analyze and yet never quite form a whole as a simpler and more rigid character would. Too many parts and each with its quality and interest; the design is there but it fades suddenly. Sue *thinks* and that is her mystery. It is not at all the usual mystery. The most fascinating and startling complications of her character have to do with sex and with the power of abstract ideas upon a truly superior female mind.

Sue Bridehead is frail, delicately balanced. She is a radical skeptic and it is her custom to ponder and question the arrangements and tyrannies of society. She is intense, "all nervous motion," and yet "artless" and "natural." Sue is more or less self-educated and has encountered avant-garde ideas about religion, art, and Biblical interpretation. When we first see her she is reading the chapter in Gibbon on Julian the Apostate. Somehow her involvement with critical, radical thought, the cluster of aesthetic and social attitudes, forms a frame for her disappointments and for the rebukes of society. It is the common thing of an intellectual alienation that gives an assurance to one's character and even a measure of tranquillity and resignation to balance the shatterings and shakings of psychological intensity.

In quite a different way, the pained, stumbling efforts of Jude to gain knowledge have about them a despondent, almost imprisoning aspect. His books, his noble, baffled yearnings create in us a great pity for him, but it is as if a necessary sense had been denied him along with the cruel denials of society. Jude's hopes for education are linked with the natural hopes for a profession, whereas with Sue ideas and learning have a gratuitous, spontaneous, altogether unprofessional character, that of the deepest inclination. When Jude is brutally turned down in his dream to enter Christminster (Oxford):

... and, judging from your description of yourself as a working man, I venture to think that you will have a much better chance of success in life by remaining in your own sphere and sticking to your trade than by adopting any other course....

he adjusts his hopes and plans to study theology, with the idea of making his life in the Church. He is astonished by Sue's lighthearted dismissal of much of religion and by, for instance, her contempt for the Church's efforts to deny the erotic meanings of the Song of Solomon. He cries out several times that she is a "perfect Voltairian."

In the end what is so poignant is that Sue's brightness and will to freedom cannot save her. She goes down into despair with Jude and, finally, under the strain of life, sinks into a punishing denial of her own principles about marriage and religion. She has not, through ideas and strong personal leanings, been able to break out of poverty and defeat and the undermining force of an accumulation of disasters. Life simply will not open itself to her frail, unsupported brightness. In despair she tries to name the mystery of implacable barriers. "There is something exterior to us which says, 'You shan't!' First it said, 'You shan't learn.' Then it said, 'You shan't labour!' Now it says, 'You shan't love!'"

Jude the Obscure is about poverty and the crushing of the spirit that goes along with it like a multiplying tumor. It is also about sex and marriage. Marriage is, as the plot develops, an experience violated by need, by the drastic workings of chance, and by the limitations of choice. It is also seen as an idea, an institution, open to the "higher criticism" in the same manner as religion and scriptural problems. At best it is a thunderclap, the sky lights up, and then a storm of entrapment, manipulation, and bad feeling rains down. Wholeness and freedom are violated and, for Sue at least, these qualities are of the first value. In putting this value upon them she creates a violent uneasiness in what would otherwise have been a more usual plotting of forces and resolutions.

The price of sex is a destruction for every fulfillment, and often a destruction without fulfillment. Love exhausts itself as a spur to action, in any case, and its claim upon the soul is not greater than the claim of pity—even less at times. Part of the peculiar quality of this suffering, tragic novel is that the relationships, worn down as they are by life, have, nevertheless, a kind of loveliness. Perhaps it is the glow spread by Sue's complicated candor and by her patient, analytical effort to understand her feelings and convictions. Only Arabella, limited, greedy, "normal" at least in her lack of the fastidious scrupulosities of Sue—only she is outside a certain grace and sweetness.

Arabella is as much a convention in the history of the novel as Sue is an original. It is the rule of conventions to ask us to accept as given a certain gathering of traits and motives. Arabella represents the classical entrapment by sex: the entrapment of an "innocent" sensual man by a hard, needy, shackling woman. Arabella's coarseness is a mirror of Jude's weakness. Her qualities are a force of a negative kind; their bad effects upon others are far more devastating than any advantages she may reap for herself. Advantage is forever in her mind and in many ways the failure of dishonest sex to bring about anything prosperous is always interesting. The person exploited by dishonest sex is weakened, distracted, and a falling off of personal and worldly fortune is likely to be observed. This is true for both the men and the women and especially striking if both are poor since, in that case, the entrapment has not found its proper object. In Arabella, sexual exploitation is combined with other deceits. Indeed the deceits are inevitable since she has no plan, conviction, or order that could give her relations with men a genuineness. What is absent in Arabella is love. Her compulsions arise from the survival struggle and not from obsessional passion. All of these exigencies are meant to signal that she is "bad" in some intrinsic way.

Arabella begins with the physical charms of youth, a bosomy air of possibility. But this is presented as a fraud. Her tendency is to face life as a desperate improvisation and she will naturally lack the discipline that might protect her small, early capital of beauty. Arabella's driven poverty, the crude urgings of an unenlightened family, the scheming habit of the other poor girls in the village have severely limited her vision. Hardy's presentation of her ignoble struggle scarcely hints at the numbness inside.

And her sullenness: only this has the shape of a deeply personal and meaningful condition of Arabella's feeling. It is a sullenness shrouded in peasant melancholy. The sullenness is her own comment on her deceitfulness and is some always dawning awareness of its futility. Even deceit needs a more nourishing soil than society has allowed Arabella. Her efforts are the traditional ones the novelist will give her: she works as a barmaid and early unsettles Jude with her knowledge of malts and hops. In the course of the novel she will move on to Australia; she will marry for the second time without unmarrying the first. She always ends up without money or help. She has a pitiful child whom she looks upon as one would look upon a mongrel dog loosely and accidentally attached to one's life.

For a poor and lonely young man like Jude, pleasure is not to be taken without cost. He is not hard enough for his encounter with Arabella—that is the way it has been designed. In the same way he is not gifted enough for the life of scholarship and learning his heart is set upon. Jude's longings have falsely come to rest in his dream of Christminster. He is a man who would sacrifice everything for the journey and yet takes the wrong road. Arabella's offering of sex is seen as a menace to learning and ambition and that does not prove to be wrong. There is a heavy consequence, a large bill to be paid for the perfunctory surrender. Latin and Greek are not accommodating. After he has been with Arabella he comes home to the accusing books.

> There lay his book open, just as he had left it, and the capital letters on the title-page regarded him with fixed reproach in the grey starlight, like the unclosed eyes of a dead man.

We are given Jude's collision with Arabella as a weakness, but one of those weaknesses most persons believe make men human, real. Arabella is deeply in tune with the consequential. By asserting cause and effect the weak avenge themselves and, of course, not always upon the strong. They avenge themselves as they must and can. They demand, they imprison. When Jude thinks of ending his affair with Arabella, she deceives him about pregnancy and they marry, in hopelessness, without any joy or understanding of each other. Jude must sell his books "to buy saucepans."

The misery of this marriage is so great that Hardy has dipped the courtship and early days in the slow, filthy waters of the pig sty. Arabella and Jude undertake to kill a pig they have raised. Jude hears the animal scream and wishes to get it over quickly; but Arabella has a country knowledge of pigs and their killing. She cries out in anger against the idea of a quick passage to death. "You must not! The meat must be well bled and to do that he must die slow.... I was brought up to it and I know. Every good butcher keeps un bleeding long. He ought to be up to eight or ten minutes dying, at least." The connection with Jude hastily comes to mind. His life is to be a long-drawn-out suffering and pain. The gentler tones of nature surround the brute factuality of a hard existence only as an accompaniment, an aside. "A robin peered down at the preparations from the nearest tree, and not liking the sinister look of the scene, flew away, though hungry."

"Married is married," Arabella says when the child does not appear in due time. She grows tired of Jude and mercifully moves on, to Australia. It cannot be the end, for there is no end to consequence, connection. "But she's sure to come back—they always do," Jude says. It is hard to tell what has real power over Arabella except the depressed, sullen downhill slide based on flirtations, marriages, alliances made and dropped, hopes grabbed and abandoned, listless enterprises, absence of plans. These liabilities and follies are not in the real sense her own. They are part of the *given* and also of the absences of her life. She is destitute, anxious, brutalized by the blanks in the tradition, the only one she knows, a tradition she has to live out in the lowest, rural, most diminished terms. It is in no way softened as it is in more fortunate women, such as Eustacia Vye, who live also by manipulation and deceit.

Arabella is harshly treated by Hardy because she is so great a part of Jude's paralysis and despondency. In his other novels there is usually a great insistence upon the virtues of the poor folk who are hemmed in by nature and custom. The furze-cutters, the reddlemen, the country mothers are heroic in their simplicity, authenticity, and constancy of feeling. Restlessness—Eustacia Vye, Lucetta, Mrs. Charmond—is inclination to spoil, to appropriate, to introduce a worldliness and standard that corrupt. The waste of talents is condemned by Hardy with a strong class feeling in a doctor like Fitzpiers in *The Woodlanders*, who neglects his work; in an engineer, such as Wildeve in *The*

Return of the Native, who out of sloth and distraction ends up running a tavern. There is a repetitiveness in this rural life that Eustacia Vye is overwhelmed by. It is the same repetitiveness Arabella is doomed to, although, in her, it is stripped of its romantic, dark, and arresting aspects.

Arabella is the bad side of the ignorance and pain of the country, just as Tess is the good aspect of rural courage and beauty and naturalness. The thing that finally seeps through the story is that a "sensual" risk like Arabella is really as abstract about life as Sue, as much a creature of skeptical reaction if not of thought. In her relentless trudging after the relief of love affairs, Arabella looks for the hopeless ideal. The numbing disappointments, the raging need for the means of survival, make the ignorant Arabella finally show the same lack of reverence for conformity, for the legalities of things, the same vaulting of the stony fences of convention that are found in Sue's fascination with ideas. Of course there is nothing critical or reforming in Arabella's delinquencies. She is blackness in action, and yet she is as miserable with Jude as he with her. Her tricking him into marriage, her lies, her abandonment of him on his deathbed are the deepest betrayals that follow on the first betrayal, their lack of real meaning for each other.

Arabella finds Jude's goodness and yearnings boring; it is her habit to consider them as a rebuke to herself. Jude's exacerbated sensitivity, his bouts of drunken frustration, his passion for the refined and the gentle in life—these can scarcely be offered for Arabella's realistic approval. Her sense of things is different. Pigs have to be killed and the robin's dismay is not to the point. Arabella's flaws are traditional; she is harsh, but comprehensible. A contrast indeed to Sue Bridehead.

Bridehead: it is curious that Hardy should have chosen this name for Sue. It is a curiosity and something of an embarrassment because the plot of Sue's life circles around two great reservations—refusal of sex and grave misgivings about marriage. Is "maiden-head" to be thought of? Is the idea of attaching "bride" to the name of a young woman genuinely questioning about marriage meant as a telling incongruity? Yet there is a sound to the name that does not impugn the high tone of Sue's discourse or the ambivalences that are the very skin of her being.

Sex and marriage—of the two, marriage is the easiest surrender and Sue thoughtlessly submits to it with the unsuitable Mr. Phillotson, the schoolmaster. He is confused to learn that the other submission is not forthcoming. Sue asserts her right to chastity as one would, without shame, assert any other inclination. Chastity—how embarrassing it is in a love story. And how odd that it is faced so candidly and childishly rather than as a distortion and disguise, a great, devouring secret, veiled in subterfuge and duplicity. Sue is very unsettling in the prodigal openness with which she greets these dark holes of withdrawal. She tells Jude of the most important experience of her youth, her meeting with a young undergraduate at Christminster.

He asked me to live with him, and I agreed to by letter. But when I joined him in London I found he meant a different thing from what I meant. He wanted to be my lover, in fact, but I wasn't in love with him; and on my saying I should go away if he didn't agree to my plan, he did so. We shared a sitting-room for fifteen months; and he became a leader-writer for one of the great London dailies; till he was taken ill, and had to go abroad. He said I was breaking his heart by holding out against him so long at such close quarters.[...] I might play that game once too often he said. [...] I hope he died of consumption, and not of me entirely. I went down to Sandbourne to his funeral, and was his only mourner. He left me a little money—because I broke his heart, I suppose. That's how men are—so much better than women!

Jude is distressed and cannot understand her "curious unconsciousness of gender." And yet Sue is all charm and sympathy. Jude and Mr. Phillotson are in no way graceful or inspired enough to be her companions but it would never occur to us that some "better" man would alter the curious course of Sue's character. We might say that the brute reduction of her prospects, the bleaching rural impoverishment, the rootless, unprotected strangeness of her life with Jude are a terrible burden upon her great intelligence and upon her wandering, artless courage. Those calamities do indeed push her to the edge, but there is the *essential* Sue, mixed and misty as it is, that is not in any way circumstantial.

Sue's marriage to Mr. Phillotson is the baldest inconsistency. She has a sort of unworldliness and caprice that allows her to undertake this union. The schoolmaster has none of the stirring pathos of Jude. He has early been overwhelmed by the hypocrisy and deadness of the small educational institutions of his time. He sees the lightness of Sue, her indifference to advantage, and he believes that he might appropriate some of her wayward magic to relieve his own heavy spirits. Sue, as it turns out, feels a profound aversion to Mr. Phillotson. She is aware of it—awareness of feeling is, as Irving Howe says in his brilliant portrait of Sue, part of her *modernity*, her fascination—aware not as an idea, but as an emotion completely personal and pressing. She hides in a dismal closet rather than enter the bedroom. Once, dreaming that he was approaching her, she jumped out of the window.

Is this neurasthenia and hysteria? To look at it in that way is to impose a late abstraction of definition upon a soul, one might almost say a new kind of human being, struggling to take form in history. The personal, the analytical, the passion for self-knowledge that raise *authenticity* above everything, and certainly above duty and submission, come so naturally to Sue that she is almost childlike. Hypocrisy, especially in matters of feeling, is to her a sacrilege. At one point, Jude asks her if she would like to join him in evening prayers and she says, "Oh, no, no! . . . I should feel such a hypocrite."

After she has been married to Phillotson for eight weeks, Sue tries to voice her feelings. "Perhaps you have seen what it is I want to say—that though I like Mr. Phillotson as a friend, I don't like him—it is a torture to me to live with him as a husband!" She goes on to say in despair that she has been told women can "shake down to it," and yet "that is much like saying that the amputation of a limb is no affliction, since a person gets comfortably accustomed to the use of a wooden leg or arm in the course of time." In addition to aversion, she laments "the sordid contract" of marriage and "the dreadful contract to feel in a particular way in a matter whose essence is its voluntariness."

Authenticity, chastity, renunciation. Of course, Sue is not able to live out completely the deep stirrings of her nature. She feels a sympathy for Jude that is a transcendent friendship as profound and rare as love. It is sanctified by their sufferings and by the ever-spreading insecurity of their existence, by the unreality of themselves as a plan of life. In the absence of *surroundings*—they are like itinerants with no articles to offer as they wander in a circle from town to town—in the way their need has no more claim upon society than the perching of birds in the evening, they come to fall more and more under the domination of the mere attempt to describe themselves. They live under the protection of *conversation*, as many love affairs without a fixed meaning, without emotional space to occupy, come to rest in words. Their drama is one of trembling inner feeling and of the work to name the feeling.

Sue does have children—an inauthenticity for her. The children come under the doom of thought, of analysis. They die in the nihilistic suicide *decision* of Little Father Time, the watchful, brooding son of Arabella and Jude. Nothing seems more sadly consequent than that the tragedy should finally come to Sue, after the pain of it, as a challenge to principle, a blinding new condition in her struggle to give shape to her sense of things and of herself. She begins to go to church and gradually moves away from her old self to the decision that her original marriage to Phillotson has a remaining churchly validity and therefore the highest claim on her. She returns to him and also at last submits in every sense. An immolation. In this ending Sue is faithful to her passion for an examined life; for indeed religion is at least an idea for her, not a mere drifting. The necessity for this is pitiful and even if it seems to have a psychological truthfulness as the end of the road for one who has been utterly rejected by destiny, religion and the bed of Phillotson are for her a sort of coma that destroys the life of a living mind. The defeat of Sue is total.

1974

SAD BRAZIL

LARGENESS, magnitude, quantity; it is common to speak of Brazil as a "giant," a phenomenon, spectacular, outrageously favored, and yet marked by the sluggishness of the greatly outsized. And if the giant is not quite on his feet, he is nevertheless thought of as rising from the thicket of sleep and the jungle of apathy, coming forth on some dawn to seize the waiting riches of the earth. This signaling, promissory vastness is the curse of the Brazilian imagination. Prophecies are like the rustling of great trees in a distant forest. They tell of a fabulous presence, still invisible, scarcely audible, and surely there, as possibility lying in the singular vastness.

Remember the opening of *Tess of the D'Urbervilles*? The father with his rickety legs, his empty egg basket, his patched hat brim, is addressed on the road as "Sir John" because it has been discovered that he is indeed a lineal representative of the ancient, noble family of the D'Urbervilles and thus he somehow includes what he cannot lay claim to. Brazil is a lineal descendant of Paradise, a remnant of the great garden of natural surfeit—a sweet, bountiful place sometime to be blessed. In Brazil the person lives surrounded by a mysterious, ineffable plenitude. He lives in a grand immensity and partakes of it as one partakes of pure spaciousness, of a magical placement in the scheme of nature. Small he may be, but the immensity is genuine. His own emptiness is close to the bone and yet his world is filled with the precious and semiprecious in prodigious quantity, with unknown glitters and granites, with sleeping minerals—silvery-white, ductile. These confer from their deep and gorgeous burial a special destiny. To say that Brazil is the land of dreams is a truth.

Rio Grande, Mato Grosso, Amazonas. Numbers enhance, although there is a dreamy stupefaction about them also. Brazil is larger than the continental United States, excluding Alaska, and slightly larger than the bulk of Europe lying east of France. Its borders flow and curve and scallop to the Guianas, Uruguay, Argentina, Paraguay, Bolivia, Peru, Colombia, and Venezuela. Out of this encroaching, bordering, nudging sovereignty, life has a peculiar statistical consolation. Where there is isolation, loneliness, and backwardness, where the tangle of existence chokes with the complexity of blood and region, where torpor, negligence, and an old historical lassitude simply and finally confuse—there even the worst may be thought of as an unredeemed promise, not an implacable lack. Delay, not unalterable deprivation, is the worm in the heart of the rose.

Growth, exploitation, coming forth to meet modern possibility—a necessity, impatient, and oh, so maddeningly slow. The military rules partly under the banner of growth-mystical and its battle against the living is often represented in the name of growth-practical. The histrionic jungle, the romantic coffee and sugar plantations, the crazy rubber Babylon at Manaus with its ruins and the marble shards of the opera house, these last representing the old tropical slack, and, of course, misfortune: against the authoritarianism of nature, the police and political oppression takes on a private character of merely human vengeance, feeding upon itself insatiably.

A beggar, bereft, a scabby bundle of ancient Brazilian backwardness, a tatter of the rags, an eruption of the sores of underdevelopment; there he sits against an "old" 1920 wall of São Paulo. Without a doubt, he, shrunken as he is, salutes the punctured skyline, salutes the new buildings that from the air have the usual look of some vibrating necropolis of megalomaniac tombs and memorial shafts—all, like our own, enshrouded in a thick, inhuman vapor, the vapor that sustains the alertness of all the world's cities. Around the somnolent beggar the cars, with their attractive, volatile occupants, whir in a thick, migrating stream. Or come to a halt, the barrier created by themselves in multiplicity.

And there it is, in the explosion of automobiles and their infinite signification, magic visible, quantity realized, things delivered.

Yes, all will be filled, all will be new, tall, thrusting, dominating, rapid, exhausting, outsized like the large, stalky watercress, the plump, round tasteless tomatoes grown by the inward, enduring will of the Japanese farmers. Everything new is an emanation, sacred; and the "growth" is the inevitable mocking paradox, the challenge and puzzle and menace of almost every useful scrap of perpetual inventiveness. Brazil, beggars and all, has in movement something quick and almost preternaturally "modern" about it, something dashing and sleek and ironical. That is in movement; at rest and for the misbegotten it is old, lethargic, indifferent and casually destructive. The centuries seem to inhabit each moment; the diamonds at Minas, the slave ships, Dom Pedro in his summer palace at Petrópolis, the liberal tradition, the terrorists, the police, Vargas, Kubitschek, the Jesuits. All exist in a continuous present—a consciousness overcrowded and given to fatigue.

It is as it must be. There is no other way and the sun is very strong. In Brazil the presence of a great, green density, come upon like yet another gift to the over-laden, makes the soul yearn to create a gray, smooth highway. Thus Le Corbusier in 1929 saw Rio, radiant, and said, "I have a strong desire, a bit mad perhaps, to attempt here a human adventure—the desire to set up a duality, to create 'the affirmation of man' against or with 'the presence of nature.'" The affirmation was to be a vast motor freeway and why not, since space turns the inspiration to engineering. The glory of Brazil is glory elsewhere, a vast junk heap of Volkswagens, their horns stuck for eternity. The imagination does not contain enough motor cars for the creative possibility of Brazilian spaciousness; indeed all contemporary manufacture, foolish or brilliantly unexpected, would find its happy and fitting rest here in the very up-to-date, end-of-the-century backwardness.

The new world rises from a hole in the ground where once stood a mustard-colored, decorated stucco with its small garden. Now, buildings, offices, hotels with their anxious dimensions that give, no matter, a kind of happiness to practicality and newness. In the swimming pools beautiful butterflies float in their blue-tiled graves. Birds, hammers, the high hum of traffic: the mellifluousness of the tropics.

The endless, blue shore lines. Life under the Great Southern Cross, Cruzeiro do Sul: under the blazing sky or the hanging humidity a resurrection of steel and concrete, a transfiguration of metals, of dollars and yen. And this year, death to students, to radicals and guerrillas, and a fear, very modern, up-to-date, of the teacher, the writer, the priest, the reporter, the political past. The pastoral, romantic, and romanticized world of Gilberto Freyre, with the masters and slaves in a humid commingling, the stately old prints of the family and servants in brilliant dresses and hairbands walking to the plantation chapel—where is that? The land and its murky history are buried under "methods," and Nordic interrogations, and fresh words for the spirit of the times, "decompression," and electric, motorized, screaming initials (DOPS, Department of Public Order and Safety). Words and "equipment" fill a vacancy, the hole in the heart of the Brazilian government. In the torrid air how cold is the claim of development.

I had been here in 1962 and now, 1974, I returned. Indeed it is impossible to forget the peculiarity and beauty of this rich and hungry country. Paradox is the soul of it. Droughts and floods, fertility and barrenness seem to reside in each individual citizen, creating an instability of spirit that is an allurement and a frustration, a mixture that was formerly sometimes thought of as feminine. It was the time of the installation of the new president, Geisel, under the military rule. Latin America's wars are, for the most part, of the internal kind, the kind beyond armistice. Heavy police work that gives the generals time to run the country. *General*, the word itself appears to be a sort of validation, a kind of Ph.D. without which General Perón and General Pinochet might have appeared to be mere citizens presuming.

Geisel, the new president of this land of color—olive, black, mixed, European, Indian, reddish-brown like dried flowers—turned out to be a lunar curiosity thrown down from some wintry, arctic, celestial disturbance. He is thin and colorless, as ice is colorless. A fantastical ice, solid in the heat of the country. No claim to please, astonish, nothing of the cockatoo or macaw. Dark glasses shield the glacial face, as if wishing to filter the tropical light and darken the glow of the chaos of bereft persons, the insects, slums, French fashions, old ports at Bahia and Recife—the brilliant, irredeemable landscape.

Is there symbolism in the whiteness of the leader? He is not, as we would view it, the will of the people, but Will itself. Will set against underdevelopment, against the sheer obstruction everywhere, and so much of it one's fellow beings.

A small card sent out by the family of a young student killed by the police:

Consummatus in brevi, explecit tempora multa
Tendo vivido pouco, cumpriu a tarefa de una longa existencia. Profundamente sensibilizada, a familia de jose carlos novais da mata-machado agradece a solidariedade recebida por ocasian da sua morta.

(Having lived little [1946–1973] he accomplished the task of a long existence.)

The pictorial in Brazil consumes the imagination; leaf and scrub, seaside and treacherous inlands long for their apotheosis as word. Otherwise it is as if a great part of the nation lay silent, unrealized. Your own sense of yourself is threatened here and speculative description seizes the mind. A landscape drenched in philosophical questions finds its masterpiece in the great Brazilian prose epic, *Os Sertões*, translated into English by Samuel Putnam as *Rebellion in the Backlands*.

A Brazilian newspaper around the turn of the century noted: "There has appeared in the northern backlands an individual who goes by the name of Antônio Conselheiro, and who exerts a great influence over the minds of the lower orders, making use of his mysterious trappings and ascetic habits to impose upon their ignorance and simplicity. He lets his hair grow long, wears a cotton tunic, and eats sparingly, being almost a mummy in aspect."

The appearance of the deranged evangelist, "a crude gnostic," and his gathering about him a settlement of backlands people in the town of Canudos in the northeast was the occasion for military campaigns sent out from Bahia in 1896 and 1897 in order to subdue the supposed threat of the Conselheiro and his followers to the new Republic. Euclides da Cunha went on the campaigns as a journalist and what he returned with and published in 1902 is still unsurpassed in Latin American literature.

Cunha is a talent as grand, spacious, entangled with knowledge, curiosity, and bafflement as the country itself. The ragged, impenetrable Conselheiro is himself a novel, with his tortured beginnings as Antônio Maciel, his disastrous marriage, and his transformation as a wandering anchorite, solitary and violently ascetic in habit. His distorted Catholicism, his odd prophecies ("In 1898 there will be many hats and few heads"), and prediction of the return of the monarchy "with all his army from the waves of the sea," attracted ragged followers and he made his way north to Canudos.

The campaigns against the Conselheiro are the occasion for the book, the center from which Cunha engages Brazil itself and the nature of its people. Even to his great mind it is a mystery, a *mestizo* mystery of contradictions of blood, of north and south, backland and coast, soil, temperament, climate, destiny.

In the campaign Cunha is struck by the unknown country, his own, by the relentless conundrums of race and space, by the very nature of the forgotten, lost, unnamed—in the sense of undescribed, uncontemplated—population of the northeast. The horsemen and cattlemen have lived in a long isolation from history, lived amid the destroying natural vicissitudes this part of the Edenic promise can provide. The people of the northeast are strong and weak, superstitious and crafty, backward and yet a large, "natural," product of peculiar Brazilian history.

As the author sees it, the backland people are under the misfortune of the country's haunting *mestizo* heritage, a racial mixture of African, Indian, and European, cut off from the "opulent placidity" of the south. They are "atavistic"—and still Brazil itself. He describes the land and the people with a passionate curiosity that is without condescension. Instead there is an obsessive quality to his exploration of psychological and environmental detail. On every page there is a heat of idea, speculation, dramatic observation that tells of a creative mission undertaken, the identity of the nation, and also the creation of a pure and eloquent prose style. Everything interests him, the scrub, the flora and fauna, the temperatures, the posture of the men, the clothes, the way they sit on a horse, the droughts, well-known and always unprepared for, the separation of types within the backlands and their ways.

When the soldiers from Bahia, themselves of the same *mestizo* stock as the backlanders, set out on their campaigns they have no idea where they are going, except that they are to reach a rebellious settlement in a town by the name of Canudos. They have their equipment and no premonition of the guerrilla warfare that will meet them. They go off in their brilliant, somewhat Napoleonic uniforms to encounter the heat of the day and the dampness at night and the horror of the thick scrub. "In the backlands, even prior to the midsummer season, it is impossible for fully equipped men, laden down with their knapsacks and canteens, to do any marching after ten o'clock in the morning."

In the end it took four campaigns and ten months of fighting before the settlement of fifty-two-hundred houses and all of the people, each one, was destroyed. Cunha sees the campaign as "an act of crime and madness," and worse, as the destruction of "the very core of our nationality." It was "the bedrock of our race, which our troops were attacking here, and dynamite was the means precisely suited. It was at once a recognition and a consecration."

The dramatic, unreal, deranged image of the poor Conselheiro prevails over the final charred scene. His corpse, "clothed in his old blue canvas tunic, his face swollen and hideous, the deep-sunken eyes filled with dirt," was "the sole prize, the only spoils the conflict had to offer." At last the corpse was dug up from its shallow trench, decapitated, and "after that they took it to the seaboard, where it was greeted by multitudes with delirious joy."

Euclides da Cunha was a military engineer by profession and by curiosity and learning also a botanist, a geologist, geographer, a social historian, and an inspired, inflamed observer. His mind is a thicket of interests and ideas and if some of them, such as "atavistic traits" as the result of racial mixture, come out of the science of the time, he transcends his own categories by humane, radical, obsessive genius. The extraordinary landscape of northern Brazil, the fantastical environment, and the people of the backlands who live in "unconscious servitude" to nature and isolation seem to appear to him as a demand, an intellectual and emotional challenge he must find his energetic art to give word to and to honor.

His "vaqueiros" and "jagunços" of the north are men of a different breed from the "gauchos" of the south, who live under the "friendly" natural abundance of the pampas. The gaucho "does not know the horrors of the drought and those cruel combats with the dry-parched earth . . . the grievous sight of calcined and absolutely impoverished soil, drained dry by the burning suns of the Equator."

This backland epic with its "philosophy" of environment and biologic predisposition is an unrolling landscape of collective psychology, of Brazilian temperament with its ebb of inertia and flow of primitive guerrilla and politically sanctioned violence and disorderly bravery. The book gives the sense of a summing up, a conclusion of a part of history that nevertheless stands amidst the unpredictability of Brazil, an astonishing country so peculiar that its inclusion in the phrase "Latin-American" never seems entirely appropriate.

Euclides lived to be only forty-three years old. In 1909 he was shot and killed by an army officer. Putnam's introduction says that the assassination is thought to have come about "as the result of a grim domestic tragedy that rendered the victim's life a tormented one." In that he leads back to Antônio Maciel whose wife ran off with a police officer and in so doing created the wandering Conselheiro of the backlands tragedy. Cunha's appearance also, from contemporary accounts, reminds one of the "crude gnostic" on his travels: "An intimate acquaintance tells us of his disdain for clothes, of his face with its prominent cheekbones, his glance now keen and darting and now far away and absorbed, and his hair which fell down over his forehead, all of which made him look altogether like an aborigine, causing him to appear as a stranger in the city, as one who at each moment was conscious of the attraction of the forest."

At the time of his death, Euclides da Cunha was at work on another book about the backlands. Its title was to be "Paradise Lost."

The magnificent Rio landscape of sea and thick, jutting rocks, which Lévi-Strauss thought of as "stumps left at random in the four corners of a toothless mouth." Like *Os Sertões*, *Tristes Tropiques* is a classical journey of discovery, a quest for the past and for the realization of self. It is also in many ways a discovery of Brazil as an idea. Speaking of the towns in the state of Paraná Lévi-Strauss writes:

> And then there was that strange element in the evolution of so many towns: the drive to the west which so often leaves the eastern part of the towns in poverty and dereliction. It may be merely the expression of that cosmic rhythm which has possessed mankind from the earliest times and springs from the unconscious realization that to move with the sun is positive, and to move against it is negative; the one stands for order, the other for disorder.

Lévi-Strauss left France in 1934 and went to teach at the university in São Paulo and from there to travel into the interior of Brazil in order to pursue his anthropological studies of various Indian tribes. He was ambitious, abstract, learned, in exile, and violently open, as one may speak of a violence of inspiration and energy coming when the mind and spirit meet the object of dedication. This French mind met not only the Indians of the interior but the obstinate, dazed fact of Brazil. And immediately Lévi-Strauss conveys to us that sense of things standing in an almost amorous stillness. Standing still—or when moving somehow arduously turning in a circle that sets the foreign mind on edge, agitates the thought of possibility, of loss and renewal.

Tristes Tropiques, written fifteen years after Lévi-Strauss left Brazil for the last time, has the tone of a memorial. It is a work of anthropology, grandly speculative and imaginative in the encounter with the Caduveo, the Bororo, the Nambikwara. And the anthropology lives like a kernel in the shell of Brazil. The search for metaphor, the weight of doleful contradiction; these tell you exactly where you are.

In the town of Nalike, on the grassy plateau of the Mato Grosso, Lévi-Strauss studies the body painting, leather and pottery designs of the Caduveo Indians. The style of representation—hierarchical, still, symbolic in the manner of playing cards—is of a striking sophistication and inevitably calls forth a sense of "kinship" with primitive styles far away in time and place. These remarkable chapters, so intense in their contemplative beauty, are aspects of scientific investigation—and beyond that always is the presence of an absorbed, French genius, living out, in a hut next to a witch doctor, his exemplary personal history and intellectual voyage.

> Great indeed is the fascination of this culture, whose dream-life was pictured on the faces and bodies of its queens, as if, in making themselves up, they figured a Golden Age they would never know in reality. And yet as they stand naked before us, it is as much the mysteries of that Golden Age as their own bodies that are unveiled.

The Mysteries of the Golden Age. When Lévi-Strauss traveled to Brazil in 1934 and later, fleeing the Nazi occupation in 1941, he found, one might say, in Brazil his genuine autobiographical moment, found it as if it were an object hidden there, perhaps a rock with its ornate inscriptions and elaborate declamations waiting to be translated into personal style. The book is a deciphering of many things. One of them is a magical and profound answering of the descriptive and explicatory demand Brazil has at certain times made upon complex talents like Lévi-Strauss and Euclides da Cunha.

What is created in *Tristes Tropiques* is a work of science, history, and a rational prose poetry, springing out of the multifariousness of the landscape, its baffling adaption or maladaption to the human beings crowding along the coast or surviving in clusters elsewhere. Lévi-Strauss was only twenty-six when he first went to Brazil. The conditions are brilliantly right. He is in a new world and it is ready to be his, to be named, described. The newness, freshness, the exhilaration of the blank pages are like the map of Brazil waiting to be filled. When the passage grates and jars, it is still *material*. Two French exiles in their decaying, sloppy *fazenda* on the edge of the Caduveo region; a glass of maté; the old European avenues of Rio; the town of Goiânia: he speculates, observes, re-creates in a waterfall of beautiful images.

It is the brilliance of his writing at this period that is Lévi-Strauss's deepest preparation for his journey through the Amazon basin and the upland jungles. He is pursuing his professional studies, but he is also creating literature. The pause before the actual writing was begun, when he was forty-seven, is a puzzle; somehow he had to become forty-seven before the demand that was the inspiration of his youth presented itself once more. It was stored away, still clear, shining and immediate. Often he quotes from the notes he made on the first trip and they, perfect and intense, seem to have brought back the mood, and the mode also, and to have carried the parts written later along on the same pure, uncluttered flow.

A luminous moment recorded by pocket-lamp as he sat near the fire with the dirty, diseased, miserable men and women of the Nambikwara tribe. He sees these people, lying naked on the bare earth, trying to still their hostility and fearfulness at the end of the day. They are a people "totally unprovided for" and a wave of sympathy flows through him as he sees them cling together, man and woman, in the only support they have against misery and against their "meditative melancholy." The Nambikwara are suddenly transfigured by a pure, benign light:

> In one and all there may be glimpsed a great sweetness of nature, a profound nonchalance, an animal satisfaction as ingenuous as it is charming, and, beneath all this, something that came to be recognized as one of the most moving and authentic manifestations of human tenderness.

Tristes Tropiques is not a record of a life so much as a record of the moment of self-discovery. At times, in a place "few have set eyes on" and among uncharted images and decimated tribes, he will feel the past stab him with thoughts of the French countryside or the music of Chopin. This is the wound of the journey, the cut of one place against another. But there is nothing of love, of family, of his personal history in France. At the same time the work is soaked in passionate remembrance and it does speak of a kind of love—that is, the love that determines the great projects of a great man's youth. It is the classical journey again, and taken at the happy moment. Every step has its drama; all has meaning and the shimmer of creation; the mornings and evenings, the passage from one place to another are fixed in a memorial light.

And it is no wonder that *Tristes Tropiques* begins: "Travels and travelers are two things I loathe..." and ends, "Farewell to savages, then, farewell to journeying!" The mood of the journey had been one of youth and yet, because it is Brazil, the composition is a nostalgic one. At the end there is a great sadness. The tropics are *tristes* in themselves and the traveler is *triste*. "Why did he come to such a place? And to what end? What, in point of fact, *is* an anthropological investigation?"

Lévi-Strauss was in his youth, moving swiftly in his first important exploration; and yet what looms out of the dark savannahs is the knowledge that so much has already been lost. Even among the unrecorded, the irrecoverable and the lost are numbing. The wilderness, the swamps, the little encampments on the borders, the overgrown roads that once led to a mining camp; even this, primitive, still, and static, gives off its air of decline, deterioration, displacement. The traveler seldom gets there on time. The New World is rotting at its birth. In the remotest part, there too, a human bond with the past has been shattered. *Tristes Tropiques* tells of the anguish the breakage may bring to a single heart.

Breakage—you think of it when the plane lets you down into the bitter fantasy called Brasília. This is the saddest city in the world and the main interest of it lies in its being completely unnecessary. It testifies to the Brazilian wish to live without memory and to the fatigue every citizen of Rio and São Paulo must feel at having always to carry with him those alien Brazilian others: the unknowable, accusing kin of the northeast, the backlands, the *favelas*. If you send across miles and miles the stones and steel, carry most of it by airplane, and build a completely new place to stand naked, blind, and blank for your country, you are speaking of the unbearable burden of the past. Brazilians have more than once moved the capitals that stand for collective history; they shifted from Bahia to Rio and now to Brasília. This new passage, the crossing, was a stark and at the same time manic gesture. It is a sloughing off, thinning out, abandoning, moving on like some restless settler in the veld seeking himself. At last, in Brasília there is the void.

It is colder, drearier in 1974 than in 1962. Building, building everywhere so that one feels this prodigal people can produce new structures as simply as the national cuisine. In every direction, on the horizon, in the sky, the buildings stand, high, neat, blank, and below cruder housing, called "superblocks." Everything leads to a highway and there are, strictly speaking, no streets and thus no town or corner life. A soulless place, a prison, a barracks. *There are no streets*, you remind yourself even as you keep looking for them, as if, as a foreigner, you had misunderstood. At every turn there is a roadway, wide, smooth, filled with cars. Nothing to do with the sad tropics, with the heart of history. Still, this city without memory is the dead center. Everything comes from this clean tomb, a city that only can have been conceived in order to be dramatically photographed from an airplane.

So Brasília has its space, its contours, its placement and design at a removal; that is, in the sky. Down below in the red dust, in the sunshine, it is yet another mysterious dark entrance. The purpose of the new capital, away from the coastal cities, was to open up the country, to make a whole of this very large "little Portugal." This city, pure idea, coldly dreamed, a modern folly, seems to represent only itself, another contradiction. It could not perhaps be otherwise, for it is still Brazil about which Cunha wrote, "There is nothing like it, when it comes to the play of antitheses."

1974

SENSE OF THE PRESENT

GUILT

DO YOU know a brooding Bulstrode? Guilt, central to classical fiction, was the secret of dramatic natures who found themselves greedy for something and, when seizing it or annihilating obstruction, were nevertheless conscious of their usurpation and its violation of others. This "type"—greedy, impatient, violent, and as the saying goes, "filled with guilt"—lives in a condition beyond irony, the attitude that sweetens guilt and alters it to absurdity or, most frequently, rotten luck.

The private and serious drama of guilt is not often a useful one for fiction today and its disappearance, following perhaps the disappearance from life, appears as a natural, almost unnoticed relief, like some of the challenging illnesses wiped out by drugs or vaccines. The figures who look out at us on the evening news—embezzlers, crooks, liars, murderers—are indeed furiously inconvenienced by the trap that has sprung on the free expression of will. It seems unfair, their chagrined countenance indicates, that they should be menaced by arithmetical lapses, by their natural, self-protecting gun shots from the window of the getaway car, by insurance policies cashed with impugning haste, by the follies of accomplices. And how rapidly does the startled glance of the accused shift to the suspicious, outraged grimace of the wronged.

The ruin of one's own life as the result of transgression is punishment, but it is not guilt, not even remorse. What sustains the ego in its unhappy meeting with consequence, the meeting that was so felicitous for drama and fiction? The "popular" response to error, crime, bad faith in which our own actions are involved, is paranoia. Bad luck, betrayal, enemies, the shifting sands of the self-interest of accusers, briberies, lies: these indeed enter the mind with blinding rapidity. The culprit is carrying a thousand mitigations in his pocket, whether his delinquency be legal or merely having to do with offenses in personal relations. When he is being judged, he is judging, and not himself, but the tangle of obstructions oppressing him. He rages about in a crowd of others, saying that he is not alone; individuals and abstract society are whoring about, shooting, thieving, and going scot-free. You can't go to heaven on other people's sins, we used to say. Well, why not?

CHARACTER

The literature of paranoia is naturally different from the literature of guilt. A wild state of litigious anxiety slides, as if on ice, into the spot held by the ethical. Free-floating, drifting in his absorption and displacement, the paranoid is not a character at all. Most of all he comes to resemble a person with a cerebral stroke and shows peculiar, one-sided losses, selective blocks and impairments, unpredictable gaps.

Nathalie Sarraute said in a lecture that she could not imagine writing a novel about, for instance, a miser, because there is no such thing as a miser. Human beings with their little bundle of traits and their possession of themselves as a synthesis. Yes, they have vanished because they are not what they seemed to be and least of all to themselves, which confuses and undermines the confidence of the observer.

The coquette, the spendthrift, the seducer, the sensitive were points of being, monarchies of self, ruled over by passions and conditions. How smoothly the traits led those who possessed them, led them trotting along the path of their lives, to the end of cause and effect, to transgressions that did not fade but were still there at the last stop. This was known as plot.

When the young man in *The Mayor of Casterbridge* comes into town and decides in his misery to sell his wife and daughter we *know* what is ahead. He will succeed, he will be mayor, and the wife and daughter will return, borne on the wheels of plot, the engine of destiny, and he will be ruined. As he says, in the midst of gathering consequences, "I am to suffer, I perceive."

For us the family could very well vanish into its fate, which is expressed in the phrase, "making a new life." Still, mayors fall, the past is discovered by the opposition and we have our plots—in the conspiratorial sense. Ruin is another matter. It becomes harder and harder to be ruined; for that one must be a dedicated fool. For the well-placed there are always sympathizers. Through support, flattery, and the wonderful plasticity of self-analysis, paranoia enters the wrongdoer's soul and convinces him of his own innocence as if it had been confirmed by the accounting of St. Peter at the gates of Heaven.

Fiction, taking this in, shrugs, and while a shrug is not as satisfactory as ruin in the aesthetic sense, it will have to do. Aesthetics, Kierkegaard said, "is a courteous and sentimental science, which knows of more expedients than a pawnbroker."

POSSIBILITIES

Contrivance is offensive to the contemporary novelist and it bears the further strain of being impossible to make use of without full awareness. Awareness turns contrivance into a self-conscious jest. But without it the novelist is hard put to produce what everyone insists on—a novel. It is easy to imagine that all possibilities are open, that it is only the medium and not life itself that destroys the branches one by one. Caprice, fashion, exhaustion, indulgence: these are what the novelist who has not produced a circular action of motive and resolution is accused of. Meanwhile he looks about, squinting, and he sees the self-parodying mirror and this is his present, now, in its clothes, make-up, with its dialogue, library of books read, his words, his memories of old spy stories, films, baseball scores, murders, revolutionaries, of *Don Quixote* to be rewritten, Snow White, and "all of this happened, more or less."

The newspapers are alive with inexplicable follies. Men, safe in important positions, earning huge salaries, *forget* to file income tax forms. What a block-headed, unrealistic contrivance, *out of character*. We see, particularly in persons high in public and political life, the recurrent, bold dissolutions of the very core of themselves as it has been supposedly observed in endless printed repetitions, in biography, in assertion of principle. The puritan drinks too much it turns out, the Christian is a heathen. Even if a number of opinions and habits have attached themselves like moles to the skin of personality, it is not unnatural that our favorite word for character is *image*—"a reproduction of appearances." Since the image is impalpable, one is not obliged to keep faith either with the details or with the gross accumulation of what one is supposed to be.

Spiro Agnew, an almost forgotten, verbose vice president, with his long donkey face, his arresting alliterations, his tall, broad-shouldered ease in the pulpit, was, in his reign, old fiction. He might have been Mr. Bounderby. "I was born in a ditch, and my mother ran away from me. Do I excuse her for it? Have I ever excused her for it? Not I." Yet, in collapse, Agnew became an unaccountable post-modernist who ceased suddenly to be a character, his own character, and became a man who roams the world without a memory of alliterative abuse, without a voice, born again in middle age as a baby, alien to the "role" that had brought him to our attention in the first place. So there he is somewhere, freely "mutating" like V.—Veronica, Victoria, Venus, VD, "the incursion of inanimate matter into twentieth century life."

TIME

The three-act play is no longer in fashion, having given way to the long one-act, occasionally punctuated by an intermission, an intermission that is a convenience for the audience rather than the signal of a diversion in the flow. Impatience plays its part as one of the powers of our existence and no doubt it has much to do with dramatic structure. The celestial arithmetic of three acts turned out to be authoritarian and oppressive to the shooting-star conceptions. More importantly—a three-act play implied a three-act life.

Curtain lines ending the first act with a question, a riddle leading to unexpected turns in act two, act three resolving and returning in some way the call of act one. In the realistic American theater it was the habit to have, in the end, flashes of "understanding" which arose like a perfume out of the soil of the past. Yes, these characters would say, I discover that I have been a selfish dolt and just where I had been most convinced of my nobility and rectitude. The curtain fell.

In life, in domestic conflicts, in matters of wounded feelings, it is so often those who have been acted against who are required to uphold a pretense of form. (I don't mind what you do to me, but it is so awful for the children.) The pedantry, the conservatism, the intransigence of the hurt and the inconvenienced are scarcely to be separated, we feel, from bitterness and frustrated will. Suspicion of motive afflicts the decent as well as the dishonorable.

Resolutions, recognitions, the strands at last tied in a knot? Whose experience can that be faithful to? In contemporary theater, it is usually the popular and commercial work, manipulating the assumed moral and aesthetic traditionalism of the audience, that insists the gun hanging on the wall in act one must indeed go off before the final curtain falls.

The tyranny of the nineteenth-century three-volume novel leaves its wreckage in Gissing's *New Grub Street*. A chapter entitled "The Author and his Wife": the wife anxiously inquires about a work in progress, where are you? what have you done?

Reardon, the burdened novelist, cries out, "Two short chapters of a story I can't go on with. The three volumes lie before me like an interminable desert. Impossible to get through them. The idea is stupidly artificial, and I haven't a living character in it."

THE NOVEL

Perhaps we cannot demand a "novel." The most practical solution seems to be an acceptance of whatever designation the publisher has put into his catalog. The object in hand, its length not defining beyond a hundred pages, is not an essay, not a short story, not autobiography since we are told so much of it is "made up" and altered from the truth; it is then a novel of some kind. In the reviews of Renata Adler's *Speedboat*, a work of unusual interest, many critics asked whether they should consider the fiction *truly, really* a novel. The book is, in its parts, fastidiously lucid, neatly and openly composed. Its structure is linear and episodic as opposed to a circular development and while this is more and more the rule in fictional practice, traditional readers sometimes question the nature of what they are reading.

In *Speedboat*, the narrator—a word not entirely apt—is a young woman, a sensibility formed in the 1950s and '60s, a lucky eye gazing out from a center of a complicated privilege, looking about with a coolness that transforms itself into style and also into meaning. Space is biography and conflict finally, and going from one place to another is the thread of experience.

The girl takes flying lessons; she lives in a brownstone in New York among others little connected to her except as voices, scenery; she visits the starving Biafrans as a journalist ("We had been told to bring cans of food, jerry cans of gasoline, and a lot of Scotch"); she examines her generation ("Some of us are gray. We all do situps or something to keep fit"); she teaches at City College and worries about language ("'Literally,' in every single case, meant figuratively; that is, not literally").

For the girl, the past has not set limits and the future is one of wide, restless, interesting "leaps." Not the leaps of lovers (she has lovers, but this is a chaste book), not leaps of divorces, employment liberations, but a sense of the way experience seizes and lets go, leaving incongruities, gaps that remain alive and are valuable as conversation—conversation the end result of experience. She writes that, "the camel, I had noticed, was passing, with great difficulty, through the eye of the needle.... First, the velvety nose, then the rest." And how right she is. If the rich can't get into heaven, who can?

To be *interesting*, each page, each paragraph—that is the burden of fiction composed of random events and happenings in a more or less plotless sequence. *Speedboat* is very clear about the measure of events and anecdotes and indeed it does meet the demand for the interesting in a nervous, rapid, remarkably gifted manner. A precocious alertness to incongruity: this one would have to say is the dominating trait of the character of the narrator, the only *character* in the book. Perception, then, does the work of feeling and is also the main action. It stands there alone, displacing even temperament.

For the reader of *Speedboat*, certain things may be lacking, especially a suggestion of turbulence and of disorder more savage than incongruity can accommodate. But even if feeling is not solicited, randomness itself is a carrier of disturbing emotions. In the end perhaps a flow is more painful than a circle, which at least encloses the self in its resolutions, retributions, and decisions.

AMERICAN PRACTICALITIES

Our novelists, sensing the shape of lives around them that do not conform to the finalities of the novelistic, nevertheless are reluctant to alienate, to leave so much of life morally unaccounted for. Novels that are profoundly about illicit fornication have a way of ending on accidents, illness, or death.

In John Updike's *Rabbit, Run*, the young husband is in a restless mood of flight and infidelity; the wife is confused, sore, exhausted, and not sober. The new baby dies in the bath in a powerful scene very near the end of the novel. This is meant as a judgment on poor Harry and Janice. It says that Harry is not supposed to run around and Janice is not supposed to be sitting, drunk, before the television set in the afternoon. In Joseph Heller's *Something Happened*, the hero pays for his disgruntlement, acrimony, and self-absorption by the death of his damaged son. In Francine Gray's *Lovers and Tyrants*, the heroine has a hysterectomy, in what may be thought of as a rebuke to her promiscuity. In *Speedboat*, the girl, perhaps worried that her autonomy is out of line, like an overdrawn expense account, announces that she is going to bear a child. In this way she chooses the impediments of nature to act as a brake on the rushing, restless ego.

Deaths, accidents, illnesses, and babies are a late resurgence of normality or morality (late in the books, that is). They seem to say that a distraction in the order of things will not go unpunished. It appears that free as we are, determined upon experience as we are, there is a lingering puritanism somewhere, a mechanical accountability that links transgression with loss and grief.

The resolutions are not always convincing, being as they are an afterthought of moral contrivance. The drowning of the baby in *Rabbit, Run* is the most truly prepared for and has the least hinting of an unnecessary, retroactive moral assertion. The unconvincingness of most resolutions is a measure of the practicality, the businesslike accounting at the end of a spree, the drawing back from observed life. The telegram about your mother's death after you have been in bed with your secretary, the automobile accident as you come home from an infidelity: how far all of this is from the indulgent grip on experience that preceded it. The willingness to accept, or to offer for the public, a bleak vision without palliative intrusions is not in the end congenial to the American writer. Perhaps it is that the author steps aside from the scene he has created in such zestful detail to punish not on his own behalf but on behalf of his audience, whom he judges, somewhat patronizingly, as more vindictive than himself.

BANALITIES

A strict and accurate ear for banalities provides much of the subject matter in the work of Barthelme, Vonnegut, Philip Roth, Renata Adler, and many others. Blood, sex, and banality, as Malraux recently described the "terrible world in which we are living."

> Vonnegut:
> Toward the end of maneuvers, Billy was given an emergency furlough home because his father was shot dead by a friend while they were out hunting deer. So it goes.

> *Speedboat*:
> The girl was blond, shy, and laconic. After two hours of silence, in that sun, she spoke. "When you have a tan," she said, "what have you got?"

From a California newspaper:

The pastor of the New Life Center Church in Bakersfield and a woman member of his congregation were arrested on suspicion of plotting to murder the pastor's invalid wife.

Banalities are not meant as a narrowing of intention. They are quite the opposite. Banalities connect the author with the world around him. They connect the extreme and the whimsical with the common life, with America, with the decade, with the type. They serve, in a sense, as a form of history.

BOREDOM

Emma Bovary, struggling along with her last lover, Léon—a man whom even romantic love and adventure cannot sever from the anxious calculations of a bourgeois—finds "in adultery all of the banality of marriage." The most moving instance of such boredom in literature is Vronsky's exhaustion with Anna Karenina's love and with his own. It is not so much that he falls out of love as that the conditions of the great passion are a weariness: isolation, anxiety, idleness, the criticism of society. Boredom with love is as powerful as love itself and, psychologically, much more confusing to the spirit. Anna herself falls into one of the masks of boredom with love, obsessive, random jealousy.

Both of the women, Emma and Anna, try to modernize, to politicize the illicit. Anna and Vronsky live in a corrupt, self-indulgent world that retains its pieties about the details of indulgence. At one point Anna pathetically cries out that in living with Vronsky she is at least being "honest." Emma, a naïve provincial, nevertheless understands that her nature inclines her toward the bohemian, the sophistications of the demimonde. She appears with a cigarette in her mouth and can be seen in town "wearing a masculine-styled, tight-fitting waistcoat." Anna's passion is inseparable from her position in society and Emma's passions soon cannot be severed from her debts. Still, in their different ways, they are "new women," and their husbands represent to them an intolerable boredom they do not see themselves destined to endure.

They are to be trapped in a further boredom, but of course that lies ahead.

Sex, without society as its landscape, has never been of much interest to fiction. The limitations of the human body are nowhere more clear than in the fantasies of Sade. Nearly all of his "imaginative tableaux" involving more than two persons are physically impossible. In current American fiction, the novels that are most concerned with sex are becoming more traditional in form and imagination each year, and especially those that attempt solemn scenes of gasping and thrusting, the hopeless pursuit of the descriptive language of sensation, without the comic spirit of, for instance, Henry Miller. The body is indeed a poor vehicle for novelty. In many women writers on the current scene, the union of license and literary conventionality is quite noticeable. More and more they suffer from what Colette called the great defect in male voluptuaries: a passion for statistics.

CONSERVATIVES

The enclosed, static, oppressive nature of Soviet society makes it possible for Solzhenitsyn to write books that are formally conservative and yet profound and far-reaching in their significance. His fictions concern nothing less than the soul of Soviet Russia itself. The cancer ward is more than itself; it is the diseased state; the prison, the concentration camps are the setting in which history acts upon imagined characters realistically. The resonance of these great works from the cage is greater than we can produce in the openness and freedom of our lives; and altogether different. Totalitarianism is nothing if not a structure.

In *Mr. Sammler's Planet*, a novel that is very American and yet conservative in both form and matter, Bellow needs the voice of one who has not shared the experience of the American last thirty years, one who has not come under the free-wheeling economic conditions here after the War, who in his own life has felt no strain from the sexual revolution, the draft, divorce, television—anything. He has chosen rightly. Mr. Sammler, over seventy, a European, profoundly formed and sure in character and values, another planet. Mr. Sammler is a suitable instrument of refusal: he says, I will not accommodate the New Left students or the nihilism of New York. I will not find the Negro pickpocket in his camel's hair coat, his Dior dark glasses, his French perfume, *merely interesting.*

A novel like Pynchon's *V.* is unthinkable except as the composition of an American saturated in the 1950s and '60s. It is a work that, in its brilliant decomposition, explodes in a time of seemingly endless expanding capitalism. It comes out of our world of glut, reckless consumption, enviable garbage, and disorienting possibility. Life is not a prison. It is an airplane journey and on this journey the self is always disappearing, changing its name, idly landing and departing, spanning the world in hours. Geography is a character and town names have as much meaning as the names on the passenger lists. The novel does not end. It journeys on in a floating coda: "Draw a line from Malta to Lampedusa. Call it a radius...."

In a recent article on the new fiction, Tony Tanner looks upon much of the work as a game, "games trying to break the games which contemporary culture imposes on us at all levels." Entropy, carnival, randomness—the language of the critics of "post-modernist fiction"—seem to bring the novel too close to a poem, to put it under the anxiety of influence and to find it more subject to refinements and tinkerings of craft than a prose work of some length can actually be.

What is honorable in "so it goes" and in the mournful brilliance of Barthelme's stories ("'Sylvia, do you think this is a good life?' The table held apples, books, long-playing records. She looked up. 'No.'"), in *Speedboat*, in the conundrums of *V.* is the intelligence that questions the shape of life at every point. It is important to concede the honor, the nerve, the ambition—important even if it is hard to believe anyone in the world could be happier reading *Gravity's Rainbow* than reading *Dead Souls.*

1976

SIMONE WEIL

SIMONE Weil, one of the most brilliant and original minds of twentieth-century France, died at the age of thirty-four in a nursing home near London. The coroner issued a verdict of suicide, due to voluntary starvation—an action undertaken at least in part out of a wish not to eat more than the rations given her compatriots in France under the German occupation. The year of her death was 1943.

The willed deprivation of her last period was not new; indeed refusal seems to have been a part of her character since infancy. What sets her apart from our current ascetics with their practice of transcendental meditation, diet, vegetarianism, ashram simplicities, yoga, is that with them the deprivations and rigors are undergone for the payoff—for tranquility, for thinness, for the hope of a long life—or frequently, it seems, to fill the hole of emptiness so painful to the narcissist. With Simone Weil it was entirely the opposite.

It was her wish, or her need, to undergo miserly affliction and deprivation because such had been the lot of mankind throughout history. Her wish was not to feel better, but to honor the sufferings of the lowest. Thus around 1935, when she was twenty-five years old, this woman of transcendent intellectual gifts and the widest learning, already very frail and suffering from severe headaches, was determined to undertake a year of work in a factory. The factories, the assembly lines, were then the modern equivalent of "slavery," and she survived in her own words as "forever a slave." What she went through at the factory "marked me in so lasting a manner that still today when any human being, whoever he may be and in whatever circumstances, speaks to me without brutality, I cannot help having the impression that there must be a mistake...."

For those of us here in America who have known Simone Weil from the incomplete translation of her work and from the dramatically reduced and vivid moments of her thought and life, she has taken on the clarity of the very reduction itself. There the life was as if given in panels of stained glass, each frame underlined by a quotation from her writings, quotations unforgettably beautiful and quite unlike any others of our time. It is only in quotation, not in paraphrase, that the extraordinary quality of her concerns shines through. ("The intelligent man who is proud of his intelligence is like the condemned man who is proud of his large cell.")

This "life," written by her friend, Simone Pétrement, is a work of the most serious kind of affection and the most serious dedication. And yet the result of it all is to obscure and blur by detail and by a wish, no doubt unconscious, to retain memories and moments of the normal and natural in a character of spectacular and in many ways exemplary abnormality. Those who live with a breaking intensity and who die young have a peculiar hold upon the world's imagination. The present fashion of biography, with the scrupulous accounting of time, makes a long life of a short one. It is not the careful gathering of facts or the mere length—a year is a long book—but the way the habit and practice work upon the grand design, turning form into bricks. Short lives that sum themselves up in final explosions of work and action are especially vulnerable to amiability, discretion, and accumulation. (Sylvia Plath is another example of reduction by expansion—high school, tennis lessons, dates.)

Simone Weil was born in 1909 into a Jewish family with little interest in Jewish religion or Jewish culture. The parents were unusually attractive because of their elevated traits of mind and patient sympathies. Both Simone and her brother, André, a distinguished mathematician, were clearly gifted from the beginning, having talents that revealed themselves in inspired concentration. The family was a close one and Simone's frail intensity and her ingrained refusals—luxuries of all kinds, personal comfort in the manner of living, indifference to girlish ways—caused the parents anxiety which did not, however, take the form of denunciation. Throughout her life, her parents are to be found urging people to give her decent food without her knowing it, worrying about the unheated rooms she invariably discovered, taking her for vacations, visiting her in factory towns, tracking her down among the dangers of Spain during the Civil War, where she had gone as a volunteer and where she had suffered a terrible burn on her leg which they were anxious to have properly treated. The daughter's letters to her parents are noble, loving, and real. The cover of *Seventy Letters* reproduces an envelope addressed to these now uprooted Europeans, then living at 549 Riverside Drive, coming from the daughter in London and written during her last week of life; it is extraordinarily moving.

Simone Weil was a student of the philosopher Alain (Émile Chartier). Alain was a special figure as a writer and teacher in Paris in the 1920s—one of those arresting French academic stars who throw the light of their ideas and the style of their thinking over young intellectuals and have a dramatic fame quite unusual here. His *Propos*, essays on many aspects of culture, very likely confirmed Simone Weil's own genius as a philosopher working in the form of passionate essays rather than in theoretical explication of positions and arguments.

Alain's attention was given to morality, good deeds, the exercise of will by which one becomes free, to pacifism and to suspicion of the need to exercise power over others. In many ways these thoughts prefigure the great themes of Simone Weil's writings. Her own nature was, of course, much more extreme; that is, she was determined to live out truth, not as an example which would have involved the vanities and impositions of leadership, but as a dedication marked by obsessive discipline.

She appeared odd and, to some, rigid and forbidding, giving "the impression that some element of common humanity was missing in her, the very thickness of nature, so to speak." In her revolutionary youth she was a striking, intransigent, awkward figure. Simone de Beauvoir tells of meeting her when they were preparing for examinations to enter the Normale. "She intrigued me because of her great reputation for intelligence and her bizarre outfits.... A great famine had broken out in China, and I was told that when she heard the news she had wept.... I envied her for having a heart that could beat round the world." When the results of the examination in general philosophy were posted, de Beauvoir says, "Simone Weil headed the list, followed by me."

The "saintly" shape of Simone Weil's life grew amidst the unbelievable density of left-wing politics in the Europe of the 1930s. The various parties, the strikes, the violent factionalism in unions, the eschatological intensity of theoretical disputes, Russia under Stalin, the challenge of Trotsky, the nature of Marxism, the ruthlessness of colonial rule, and the anguished clinging to pacifism with its horror of conscription as a central theme of radical thought—all of this Simone Weil took part in, writing a prodigious number of pamphlets and political letters, giving speeches, organizing meetings.

Trotsky had been allowed asylum in Paris under the Daladier Government, with the condition that he refrain from political activities of all kinds. Nevertheless, Simone Weil convinced her parents to allow a meeting to be held with Trotsky in their apartment house. Trotsky arrived with his family and armed bodyguards, all of them entering "with their hats pulled down over their eyes and their coat collars raised to their noses," looking exactly like what they had wished to disguise, like conspirators. Simone took advantage of the chance to have a discussion with Trotsky. "The discussion quickly turned into a quarrel; in the adjoining room, where they were seated, the Weils heard a series of loud shouts."

This period, with its organizations and counterorganizations, its cells and splits, is almost impossible to return to its genuine context because of the simplifications of thought and possibility finally brought about by Nazism, the war, the atomic bomb, the cold war, and the devastation of serious left-wing hopes in Europe and America under the power realities of postwar existence.

For Simone Weil, peculiar and "eternal" as her profound concerns were, it is impossible to imagine that she would have remained on the outside, quietist, contemplative, unpolitical. Oppression, exploitation, liberty, national prestige, force, dignity, history, faith: in her reflections upon these conditions rest her claims upon our minds and feelings. Without the common political life of her time surrounding her writings with its urgencies, her essays would be different. They would be literature rather than prophecy, a tone they clearly have and by means of which her language achieves its beauty and uniqueness.

Her reading of history and her culture were enormous. But she read history without objectivity, meaning that she read the past in a mood of violent, agitating partisanship, believing that it mattered not in the sense that an educated person must know the past but with the conviction that the legacy of the past was as much a part of life as airplanes, automobiles, or armaments. Thus her dislike of the Romans and the Hebrew tradition of the Old Testament and her love of the Greeks and the Gospels.

"The Great Beast: Some Reflections on the Origins of Hitlerism" maintains that the Roman Empire was the model upon which the iniquitous, militarized, centralized states of Europe developed their totalitarian policies. Louis XIV lacked the true spirit of legitimacy, she thinks.

> The miseries of his childhood, encompassed by the terrors of the Fronde, had induced in him something of the state of mind of those modern dictators, sprung from nothing and humiliated in their youth, who have thought that their peoples must be tamed before they can be led.... The degradation of hearts and minds in the second part of his reign, when Saint-Simon was writing, is as sad a phenomenon as anything of the kind that has been seen since.... Domestic propaganda ... reached an almost unsurpassable degree of perfection.... base flattery ... or cruel persecutions and the silence that surrounded them, foreign policy conducted in the same spirit as Hitler's, with the same ruthless arrogance, the same skill in inflicting humiliation, the same bad faith.... Louis XIV took Strasbourg in exactly the same way as Hitler took Prague, in time of peace, amid the tears of its helpless inhabitants.

About the Romans: the sacking of Epirus, the destruction of Carthage, Caesar's "bad faith" in his negotiations with Ariovistus, Cartagena, Numantia, on and on. The sacrificing of peoples to the concerns of Roman prestige. "They knew how to undermine by terror the very souls of their adversaries, or how to lull them with hopes before enslaving them by force of arms." She connects the uprooting of peasants in her own day with the lines from Virgil's first "Eclogue": "We are leaving our country's bounds and our loved fields....We go to parched Africa." Elsewhere she says, in comparing the *Aeneid* to the *Iliad:* "God would be unjust if the 'Aeneid,' which was composed under these conditions, were worth as much as the 'Iliad.'"

Her attitude about Hebrew history in the Old Testament rested upon the same ferocious objections. Yahweh, "the god of armies"; God's rejection of Saul because he did not exterminate the Amalekites down to the last man; Elisha dismembering forty-two children who had called him "Baldhead"; subjugation of the people of Canaan. In answer to the objections that the Canaanites themselves were immoral, she would have answered that we were not brought up to honor them. Also, in her feeling about "historical perspective" and its tendency to understand cruelties of the past as part of the sanctions of earlier cultures, she seemed to believe that morality did not improve and to hold with Plato that all people, at all times, had knowledge of the ideal "good."

Catholicism was attractive to her spirit, although in her dealings with priests and Catholic friends she was contentious, vehement about certain doctrines such as no salvation outside the Church and, as always, inclined to look upon history as alive. "What frightens me is the Church as a social structure....I am afraid of the Church patriotism that exists in Catholic circles....There are some saints who approved of the Crusades or the Inquisition. I cannot help thinking that they were in the wrong." In any case, she was never baptized.

The 1945 publication of Simone Weil's essay, "The Iliad, or The Poem of Force," in Dwight Macdonald's magazine *Politics*, in a translation by Mary McCarthy, was, it is no exaggeration to say, an event of great importance to those of us who read it. This is one of the most moving and original literary essays ever written. "For those dreamers who considered that force, thanks to progress, would soon be a thing of the past, the 'Iliad' could appear as an historical document; for others, whose powers of recognition are more acute and who perceive force, today as yesterday, at the very center of human history, the 'Iliad' is the purest and loveliest of mirrors."

In the *Iliad* the afflictions of force grow and grow, and each side weaves back and forth under the dominion of suffering.

> At the end of the first day of combat ... the victorious Greeks were in a position to obtain the object of all their efforts, i.e., Helen and her riches ... That evening the Greeks are no longer interested in her or her possessions: (*For the present, let us not accept the riches of Paris; nor Helen*; ... He spoke, and all the Achaeans acclaimed him.) What they (the Greeks) want, is, in fact, everything. For booty, all the riches of Troy; for their bonfires, all the palaces, temples, houses; for slaves, all the women and children; for corpses, all the men.

The losses fall upon everyone, without mitigation and finally without meaning. "The death of Hector would be but a brief joy to Achilles, and the death of Achilles but a brief joy to the Trojans, and the destruction of Troy but a brief joy to the Achaeans."

In 1942, Simone Weil came to New York with her parents. Her whole mind was taken up with returning to Europe, with ideas for getting back into France to participate in the suffering and the resistance of her country. That was her mind at least insofar as action was concerned. Otherwise this was a period of intense religious contemplation. She did succeed in making her way back to London at the end of the year, saying as she left her grieving parents: "If I had several lives, I would have devoted one of them to you, but I have only one life."

Her will to undertake dangerous missions in France was frustrated. Instead she wrote her celebrated *The Need for Roots*, a group of very personal and typical essays that must have bewildered the Free French who had asked for a sort of government report, filled with the usual bureaucratic "recommendations." Instead Simone Weil addresses herself to "the needs of the soul."

In this work and in others, the peculiarity of her vocabulary arises from the fact that she is occupied with the expression of distinctions, with definitions not of much interest to most thinkers. The difference between affliction and misery, for instance. Affliction is the suffering that separates one from others, causes in them dread and repulsion. "It is the mark of slaves." It is "anonymous" and does not arouse the emotion of pity. "The same incapacity for paying attention to affliction that inhibits compassion in someone who sees an afflicted man also inhibits gratitude in an afflicted man who is helped. Gratitude presupposes the ability to get inside oneself and to contemplate one's own affliction, from outside, in all its hideousness. This is too horrible."

In London her health vanished, even though the great amount of writing she did right up to the time she went to the hospital must have come from those energies of the dying we do not understand—the energies of certain chosen dying ones, that is. Her behavior in the hospital, her refusal and by now her inability to eat, annoyed and bewildered the staff. Her sense of personal accountability to the world's suffering had reached farther than sense could follow. She died young, like so many of the wretched in history whose misery had haunted her throughout her rare and noble life.

1977

DOMESTIC MANNERS

HOW ARE we living today? Of course, there is no "we" except for those who address us, advise us, praise us in the round, as "the American people." The phrase is a signal for the wary, doing as it so often does more honor to the exhorter and his plans than to those millions gathered in under the grand title.

Only the forgetful can easily ignore the duplicity practiced upon the defining imagination by the sudden obsolescence of attitudes and styles just past, styles that collapsed or scattered into fragments just as one had felt free to identify them as facts, changes, alterations of consciousness, shiftings of power, or threats to power. These elements, at least at the moment of identification, had the shape of reality, of historical presence, of genuine displacements; and even though they could not be asserted as eternal they still could not be experienced as mere historical moments soon, very soon, to be reversed or simply erased. It is with some perturbation that one has to learn again and again that the power of external forces is greater than style, stronger than fleeting attitude.

"Confidence in the future" is a peculiar phrase, although in frequent use. It is not meant to signify the mere expectation of continuing existence, but rather to signify hope—perhaps for the stock market, for relations with recalcitrant and truculent foreign countries, for our own life as a whole, or for small groups, rich or poor, protected or beleaguered, who are in need of reassurance. It seems to mean that it is reasonable to assume the future will not diminish rewards in some cases or that the future will augment rewards in others. Most seriously it imagines that the future will, with all its attendant inequities and surprises, remain open to the understanding and to the effort of those leaders and advisers we have grown accustomed to and from whom, given the nature of things, we have generously not asked very much. These assumptions about the future are in grave disorder and "confidence" is merely a sentiment.

There is always the question of the will to understand first and then the greater will of society to undertake even the most reasonable alleviations, for alleviations on the one hand are the cue for disgruntlements elsewhere. Lacking the will, society waits for events to which it must respond, often in a final condition of fear and crisis and anger; or, in long, drawn-out, hopelessly tangled injustices and dangerous defaults it simply waits not to respond at all. Things reveal themselves in an atmosphere of grotesque folly. The persons exploiting oil in Arab countries are the same persons theatrically throwing pound notes on the ground in London rather than on the parched land of the poor of their own regions. The waste of Western capitalism is not always different, but America at least is used to the waste and looks upon the reduction of it with alarm.

To speak of persons as the "product" of their decade, or half-decade in some cases, is a severe telescoping of history, and yet it has an obvious descriptive usefulness, a conversational meaning that is measured by the clear recognition others give to the terms, a recognition coming out of the very grossness of the designations.

Certain persons and certain aspects of our society appear to be a product of the 1960s. The legacy of the period is intractable morally and socially in the manner of all history and it bears the peculiar opacity of its closeness to the present—that is, the period is *experience*, and its transformation into history is somewhat a work of the subjective imagination, a work close to autobiography in the way it reenters the memory.

There is sadness and regret in the memory of the sixties. For those who reached the age of eighteen in the last years of the decade the temptations to self-destructions were everywhere, bursting forth from what was called the "counter-culture." The hallucinations of LSD, deformations by drugs that lingered on in apathy, addiction, aborted education, restlessness; the deprivations and fantasies of numerous torpid "communes," the beginnings of hysterical youth cults—this still

lies there behind us, for it seems that historical rubble is no more easily disposed of than the stone and steel and concrete of misbegotten
highways, shopping centers, overweening towers for habitation. For
those who in the sixties were "revolutionaries," it meant hiding, police
records, death, exile, the delusions of youthful power that took little
account of the brutal rebukes the genuine power of society can command. It meant disillusionment with "infantile leftism," with postures
that time and the sluggishness of history outmoded.

For the youth of the sixties who remained outside the general reaches
of a vibrating, rebellious youth culture, the decade meant death in
Vietnam, mutilation, bad dreams, drug addiction, the bad faith of
corrupted authority, and, at the least, a weird and agitating confusion
of values. President Carter's campaign made an effort to give voice to
the youth who accommodated the sixties, those who agreed with the
old values in peace and war, those who suffered; but it was disheartening to realize how little he could find to say, how vague and unreal were
the consolations, the approbations. If sacrifice is not to be praised as a
value based upon its objectives, the gratitude of authority is therefore
bound to be mixed with shame and to come forth merely as rhetoric.

Casualties of every spiritual and personal nature lay about as the
legacy of the sixties. Authorities experienced much of the decade as a
form of insult and fell into a state of paranoia. It was only by accident
that the paranoids were removed from the domination of the state and
from the determination to corrupt many of its institutions.

On the other side, the agitated scrutiny directed in the sixties to
the arrangements of society discovered many pieties and hypocrisies
which had claimed the aspect of eternity but which were, in fact, mere
prejudices and matters of unexamined convenience. Many benign and
practical refusals and reversals marked the period—the questioning
of unnecessary, self-serving authority in the home and in institutions,
the pure hopes of the Civil Rights Movement. Informalities of all sorts,
trivial and important, could, it turned out, be more or less painlessly
accepted and removed from the domain of social oppression. Tolerance
of deviation, acceptance of a pluralism long ago established by ocular
evidence, concern for the integrity and endurance of nature, ridicule
of the endless consumption of redundant goods, personal relations,

masculine presumption, the old and the young—the mere listing of customs and tyrannies challenged in the sixties is, as Chaucer said, like "trying to catch the wind in a net."

The children of the sixties had been brought up in the fifties and no doubt this earlier, seemingly plausible and hopeful, period floated about parent and child like an ectoplasmic memory. The fifties—they seem to have taken place on a sunny afternoon that asked nothing of you except a drifting belief in the moment and its power to satisfy: a handsome young couple, with two or three children, a station wagon, a large dog, a house and a summer house, a great deal of picnicking and camping together.

For the middle class the fifties passed in a dream, a dream in which benevolent wishes for oneself were not thought of as always hostile to the enlarging possibilities of others. The treasured child would do well in school and the psychiatrist could be summoned for the troubled. The suburbs offered the space and grass that would bless family existence. The cars and the second cars were symbols of power over one's life, as anyone can see who looks at the gleaming chariots that decorate the filthy, blasted streets of the ghettos.

The sixties seemed to grow, nationally and personally, upon the beguiling confidence of the decade just past. Wars to establish credibility are for the prosperous. Time was not slow, however, but speeded up, unreal, very much like time in the air; by the late sixties the happy child was scarcely to be distinguished as he went into his teens from the quarrelsome one. Complacent parents had, after all, expected more than they realized, more of their children and more of each other. And so a decade was only ten years. And a new year could be more like a tornado uprooting the grass than another period of growth.

But how *real* the sixties were, how dreadfully memorable the horrors, how haunting the alterations, everywhere, in feeling, in belief. Already the receding years have character, violently ambivalent, and beyond repeal. And how American, one is tempted to insist. In what way? Perhaps in the way destruction was created out of the pleasures of plentitude, assassinations out of the riveting excitements of leadership, diminishment out of a manic sense of expansiveness. What went down were people here, whole countries far away, and a few of the unnecessary follies that had been sitting in our lives like memorial plaques on the mantelpiece.

A strange decade indeed. How is one to set a value upon the sensible pleasures of "informality" and the limited liberation of maligned groups against the slaughter of people? And what is the historical connection, finally? The connection between the rights of personal style in dress and living arrangements, the right to homosexuality, to marihuana, and the present nightmare in Cambodia? It was a terrifying decade, anarchic, brutal—and fortunately for all of us, the saving energy of a profound protest, sustained by youth and a few older allies, a protest against dehumanization, military control, political lying, and power madness.

The 1970s have passed their zenith. Did they take place—this handful of years—somewhere else, in another land, inside the house, the head? Fatigue and recession, cold winters and expensive heat, resignations and disgrace. Quietism, inner peace, having their turn, as if history were a concert program, some long and some short selections, a few modern and the steady traditional. For young people, it is common to say that things have settled down. *Down* is the key: accommodation, docility, depression of spirit.

Many people are going to law school, searching, one supposes, for the little opening, the ray of sun at the mouth of the cave. It does not seem possible that what our world needs is a generation of new young lawyers. In certain respects what is being honored, at least by the approving adults, is not always the actual profession so much as the sign of a willingness to begin and to persevere to the end for a practical purpose, to memorize, to master a process without the demands for the gratifications of supreme interest at each moment along the way. Yet, out there at the end are the litigious anxieties of the corporate world to which whole young lives are to be prosperously dedicated and consumed.

Advanced studies in the humanities are another matter. They are felt to be impractical—and that means that society does not find them necessary. There are not only enough of you scholars, it says, there are too many. To go on in the study of literature, philosophy, or history can be a personal passion, but as a profession it depends upon someone out there to teach and a supply of teachers in a reasonable relation to the waiting learners. At the present time, the Ph.D.s remind one of the feverish, superfluous clerks in Russian literature, anxious persons floating in a menacing void, waving their supererogatory diplomas. It is not quite clear that to come to the end of one's college years is to have arrived anywhere.

The seventies have not been free of definition; even drift has its direction. Intimacy, the validation of the self in a narrow, intense relation with a few others, or one other, is seen by many thinkers as a definition of our period. Very few of those who do the naming are pleased with the turn of the wheel. It is not the activism of the sixties that is mourned by conventional commentators but rather a wish for a more aggressive, outward-looking intrusion of the individual ego into the realities of power, into concern for a material grasp of self-interest rather than the vaporous transcendence of self-absorption.

The past reclaimed as an image, the opacity of life lightened by dichotomies, the fall and the rise. Our own time: "It is the localizing of human experience, so that what is close to the immediate circumstances of life is paramount." The quotation is from Richard Sennett's ambitious book called *The Fall of Public Man*, a fall which led naturally to the elevation of private man, ourselves, and "The Tyrannies of Intimacy."

The public life, as Sennett somewhat vaguely reconstructs its lost shape, was lived out of a rich variety of experiences and acceptances largely impersonal. The life of the city was possible then; intimacy, however, lives out of a fear of the unknown and the different and allows the self to retreat, nervously, into absorption in the private. Finally, one cannot in present history know others unless one knows them in a fearful closeness, accepts them as part of the returning reassurance of looking into a mirror. It is the nature of intimacy to be unattainable, a mood trembling with anxieties and insecurities because the self is insatiable. The city, along with many other things, dies, frozen by the retreat from the public domain.

Sennett's book is an abstruse effort in cultural history, designed to reach its destination—contemporary "narcissism." Narcissism, awareness, intimacy, new consciousness—these terms appear again and again in theoretical and autobiographical descriptions of the seventies. The words are strikingly varied in quality and seriousness—the least "serious" usually being revelations and transcendencies achieved in a few balmy autobiographies, the very process of "success" providing the despairing material of the more distant and critical theoreticians.

The self's unanchored demand for security and relief from psychological unease dominates the inhabitants of Christopher Lasch's brilliant essays on the "narcissist society." (It is part of the puzzle of current writing on the elusive present that Sennett's *reign* of private man is in many respects another way of describing Lasch's "The *Waning* of Private Life." "Private life" in Lasch's work appears to represent roughly what has been called "family life.") About the ubiquitous drift to narcissism, Lasch writes, "Having no hope of improving their lives in any of the ways that matter, people have convinced themselves that what matters is psychic self-improvement: getting in touch with their feelings, eating health food, taking lessons in ballet or belly dancing, immersing themselves in the wisdom of the East, jogging, learning how to 'relate,' overcoming the 'fear of pleasure.'"

The cultural analyst, Philip Rieff, has assumed the present under the notion of the "triumph of the therapeutic"—the hunger for personal satisfaction that imposes upon the will the privilege or the burden of escaping painful feelings. The "therapeutic" (strangely, at times Rieff speaks of it, or to it, as "him"), in the writing of the often-hectoring Rieff, means many things, among them that ideas, emotions, experiences take their moral and social value from how they make you feel. The contemporary soul escapes from anxiety, duty, orderly thought by means of therapy and by therapeutic assaults upon intellectual and social authority. All of these writers, naming the not-quite-measurable sense of the present, are different in tone and in the atmosphere of recommendation, warning, regret that is the surrounding mist of the intellectual, political, and temperamental inclination of the individual writer at his desk. There is not doubt that they all prefigure (in Rieff's case) and describe one phenomenon of the seventies—the demonic acceleration of investments in gurus, encounters, magical healings, diets, transcendencies and transformations that compete, like varieties of aspirin, for the remission of aches of the mind and psyche.

Life at home, domestic drama, sexual warfare are part of history, and the matter of fiction. Divorce statistics are little figures of decline that reveal more than mere legal possibility and fact. The numbers are rich in attitudes, assumptions, hopes and lost hopes. It is not necessary to seek a divorce in order to live out personally the deepest skepticisms about the future of marriage. Irony about romantic love is the inescapable soil of existence upon which both marriage and divorce grow simultaneously, shooting up in the same season like plants in the garden.

Irony represents the recognition of the shortened life of the feelings. It says that the attachment to a particular person, even the legal attachment, defines the moment or the years but is far from being the key to the future. Disruption may represent failure, but it also represents the sweet boundaries of new hopes. If we can trust fiction and film, our period is, like that of Restoration drama, *comic*.

An abundance of cynical wit and coarseness are the necessary conditions for verisimilitude about prevailing manners. In speaking of the cynical and coarse one is not investing the words with moral outrage; they are instead descriptive. With the appearance of a large number of licentious works by women, even the cuckold has returned as a familiar figure in literature. Certain types return and certain are lost forever, figures such as the awkward, trusting ingénue or country girl of the Restoration period. *Don Giovanni*'s *"mille e tre,"* the once singular arithmetic of the frenzied aristocrat, appears as a natural accumulation of the normal sexual exuberance of men and women freed, instructed, and determined.

The comic destinations of romantic love are shown in Saul Bellow's last novel. In *Humboldt's Gift*, the most engaging of the novel's female characters, Renata, leaves the intellectual, Citrine, to marry a mortician. In Joseph Heller's *Something Happened*, the hero sighs and says it sometimes occurs to him that he got married so that he could then be divorced.

Ennui is an attendant of irony. Andy Warhol, the painter, said about his decision to abandon his emotional and sexual life: "I was happy to see it go." Love with its ancient distresses cannot be removed from the landscape by fashion. It cannot be separated from power, for one thing. Nevertheless, the pains of rejection and loss, representing as they do

interferences encountered by the individual will, are not sympatheti-
cally understood as sufferings to be endured. And in no way does
such suffering take on any of the sweetness of fidelity injured, loyalty
degraded.

Improvisation, moving on, substitution, defiance, inner healing—
characteristics of the strategies by which a sexually relaxed society copes
with regret and denial—have a moral dominance in matters of painful
love. A broken heart, caressed too long, is a dishonor often seen as a
weapon of revenge, manipulation. "Anger" is the word psychiatrists
give to assertions of the anguish of love.

Sex, sex—what good does it do anyone to "study" more and better
orgasms, to open forbidden orifices, to experiment, to put himself into
the satisfaction laboratory, the intensive care ward of "fulfillment."
The body is a poor vessel for transcendence. Satiety, in life, is quick
and inevitable. The return of anxiety, debts, bad luck, age, work, thought,
interest in the passing scene, ambition, anger cannot be deferred by
lovemaking. The consolations of sex are fixed and just what they have
always been.

In the seventies sex has become information, about yourself, about
others, about yourself in relation to others. The practices of "polling"—one manner of invading or pretending to invade the public
mind—works here in the interest of sexual technique and attitude,
giving a quasi-consensus, often to nothing more than the mere practice
of polling itself. Questionnaires, reports, new studies, "probing surveys"
(*sic*), the "real" truth about women, homosexuality, premarital and
postmarital intercourse, about changing views and changing positions.
These dubious statistics are an industry, and like the manufacture of
other products there is little worry about repetition, need, accuracy,
or significance. The title of each new book is very much like a new
brand name for an old offering.

The most depressing part of the sexual information business is that,
in the way of commerce, it is offered for our health and reassurance.
Pessimism, naturally, does not sell, nor does skepticism—that, one
assumes, the poor consumer can provide for himself, from his own
experience. In the books and articles conclusions never fail to liberate,
and if there is nothing new, whatever exists takes value from its mere

occurrence, that is, if one believes the surveys give any true picture of contemporary sexual life. Piety, exploitation, complacency, triviality, and spurious objectivity deface these scrofulous enterprises.

Sexual Behavior in the 1970s is a study exposed to the public by Morton Hunt on behalf of the Playboy Foundation. The pastoral note on which the study ends is typical of this kind of work. "The changes that are taking place are none the less important and profound for taking place within the culture rather than breaking away from it; indeed, they may be more valuable than total sexual radicalism would be. For while they are bringing so much that is pleasurable, healthful and enriching into American life, they are doing so without destroying emotional values we have rightly prized, and without demolishing institutions necessary to the stability of society itself." More valuable, pleasurable, healthful, emotional values, stability of society. The sadness, the corruption, the meaninglessness of all this is one aspect of the 1970s.

To think of the family today is bewildering because the classes are so far apart in the scenery in which daily life takes place. For those in the light the uncertainties have to do with hanging on, imagining the future, imagining if possible the meaning of the generations, of youth and old age, money, and the menace of reduction. In the darkness below, within the family there are joblessness, crime, madness, cruelty, and despair. It is not easy to remember that these scenes are part of the same play.

When the politicians, the candidates, speak of the "poor" and the unemployed, of those on welfare, they are being no more empty than the rest of us in being unable to convey any sense of the experience of the condition, the misery and horror. There is still an inclination to see the poor in previous images, perhaps the more consoling ones of the 1930s: a wrinkled face, battered but benign; a worn body in which Christian doctrine still circulates in the veins; young families in decaying bungalows with an unpaid-for car in the drive. The sharecropper, the Okie, the miner, the laid-off factory force, memories from one's own family. Television, magical as it is for certain events in real life, cannot fully picture on its small frame the slums of the city, the menacing breakdown, the insanity, the brutality, the isolation. What has become unimaginable exists in images of fear, hatred, and withdrawal. Fear is sanctioned just now because there is much to be afraid of.

One thing that distorts our comprehension of the life of the poor is that on the street, in the supermarket, the marvelous disguise of the mass-produced American clothes gives a plausible surface, almost a shine, to what is really implausible and dark. On the evening news, the young thief or killer in his sneakers, his jacket, his jeans; his family in turtlenecks, jerseys. Together they appear in a state of health, often beautiful, well provided for, their clear and startling contemporaneity like a miraculous mask.

In the city slums it is the houses, the rooms, the halls, the very walls that define the actual life. It is here that everything necessary and hospitable to a decent life is lacking. This is home and family and re-lationship. It is here, inside, that deformations are so pervasive and inescapable, here that the devastations of character and purpose grow. Society is never asked to experience directly the misery and its attendant, hidden rages and abusive idleness.

In New York City the old, the very old have become victims of the very young. Poor, crippled people, eighty-two years old or even in one case one hundred and three years old, are beaten, killed for two dollars, ninety-five cents, for nothing. The age of the victims, the paltriness of the "take," the youth of the criminals, the bizarre equality of poverty between the robbed and the robber, outrages every sense of reason, even criminal reason, and makes one look beyond the act. Part of the choice of victim is that his weakness is immediately evident and is itself a sort of affront. An old and enfeebled, poverty-worn person is, appar-ently, to the battered children of the slums an object that is contempt-ible and finally not quite real, for to imagine old age one has to imagine life as a long flow, something protected by nature and therefore meaningful in its orderly progress from one stage to another.

Part of the preying upon each other comes from the familiarity of neighborhood, the known turf, known for its vulnerability, its exposure to every injury and insult. Middle-class neighborhoods in the city are places of warm beauty, utterly beguiling behind the curtained, plant-filled windows. The nice streets are a shimmer of light and power, taxis and doormen, smiles and golden belief—an obstacle in their foreignness, their dreamy protection and unassailability. Great sophistication, vigilance, imagination are needed to storm these heights, and the very young, poor criminals do not possess that felonious experience. The clever criminals of the old school are like figures in a film comedy. They drive up to expensive hotels in limousines, dressed in dinner jackets, in order to plunder the safes filled with diamonds; their actions are swift and efficient, and above all, mannerly, out of consideration for the quality of the loot.

Here in the city the worst thing that can happen to a nation has happened: we are a people afraid of its youth. One's own memory—the memory of a girl—was of turning about on a dark street at night, fearful of footsteps coming closer, turning and saying, Oh, it is only a boy. Relief. Now for a young man to be in his twenties or thirties, out of jail, is in some way a guarantee of accommodation to society—at least in the mass, if not of course in particular cases.

For the sick and dangerous young, the idea of "treatment" is a cliché, the joke of a psychiatry which does not know how to treat such devastating deviations, such appalling dislocations, such violence that baffles by its fecklessness. There is no will to undertake reconstruction of society. Not only is the imagination lacking just now, but the very terms of the reconstruction, the extent of it, freeze speculative thought and reasonable recommendation.

Revolutionary societies destroy or brutally "reeducate." Some countries like India have long ago learned to look upward and inward as they step around filth and hunger. The torpor of the Indian millions is a blessing for the prosperous. In America among the poor, there is a political accommodation, or at least no symptom of organized revolt. Instead there is random crime. Random—a felicitous phrase that gives no substance to the devastation.

The wild growth of dangerous criminal insanity in the cities is a comment on the meek young with their ashrams in old brownstones, on Moonies in costly hotels and country estates, on clean-cut groups quietly meditating. Poverty and its abuses to children have their transforming power. Young persons stab and kill, throw each other off the roof, beat each other to death on the playing ground, rape, mutilate, set buildings on fire. To allow the facts to enter the mind is a guilty act, as if one were recording the scene of a porn film with a suspicious degree of imagination. And from the public pathetic screams for protection, when there is no protection. In the cities there has been a profound derangement of whole generations of the urban poor.

We cannot take it in. All we had planned on was Appalachia and the sweet, toothless smiles, the pale, white faces, ragged dresses, bare feet, hungry glances. No matter—a vibrant, ferocious, active, heartbreaking insanity is as much a part of the seventies as intimacy, retreat to the private.

It is always a relief to return to the middle classes, to ponder the way culture, economics, fashions work upon these citizens who are a mirror, returning what society puts before them.

To think of our domestic life is to ask what sort of person is actually needed by society. What parents, what children, young adults, workers. What makes sense—the tough and practical, the unsure and idealistic? The inner-directed and the outer-directed, to use David Riesman's terms, seem merely private, accidentally characterological, as one may be stingy or generous. The work ethic describes one who lives in a society that invests work with great spiritual and historical necessity, seeing in toil, advancement, tenacity, a virtue beyond material reward—the definition of self. All must work, but how hard and at what and with what motivation beyond dollars? In the late sixties many young people answered the question of dollars by casual work quite unrelated to their advancement, their interests, and their future: driving cabs, working as waiters, making jewelry, teaching transcendental meditation, walking dogs, playing the guitar. Marginal occupations are suitable to prosperous times and have little reality in inflationary, unstable periods.

"I love long life better than figs," Charmian, Cleopatra's attendant, says in Shakespeare's play. If things go on as we reasonably expect, young people will experience long life as an unruly challenge to morals, possibilities, fantasies. They will, in huge numbers, live way up into their seventies and that means they will have three lives, with each one perhaps wiping out the one before as though it had never been. Who can easily imagine a young son or daughter marrying and living with the same person for close to fifty years? Or with two for twenty-five

years each? This is not the way of hearts in love with the shifting demands of the ego, with painful pressures for new experience, second
and third chances, lost hopes that are an accusation to self-esteem.

In a long life in which little can be taken for granted, it is not reasonable to project a fearful clinging to the known on the part of the
contemporary sensibility—so far removed from the peasant-like stasis
of times past. Instead, a nomadic search for the new waters and pastures
of each period of life leads one on, running from the dryness of the
past. Hell is no exit—and without social, moral insistence many would
not wish to honor the contract of youth.

It is no wonder that with parents authority seems to have become
a burden. Part of it is the peculiar melding of parents and young adults
in the way they look and dress, in their common reverence for sexual
experience, which they have been told need never end for the good and
the healthy. Custom is shattered by the parents' fear of age and the
children's disaffection about age's wisdom, difference, and virtue, by
the vacation spirit of a people who are not sure that society needs its
work, by the blurred future of the species—on and on. Coolness rather
than domination is the complaint of children against parents, neglectful confusion rather than insistent assertion. Those who imagine that
this can be reversed by the will, by mere opinion, are not credible because
the will to rule has itself collapsed along with the painful recognition
of limits everywhere of every kind.

The women's movement has crystallized in domestic life changes
that have been going on for decades. Historically, the political and
social expression of the themes of women's liberation coincides with
the needs of a world in which there are almost as many divorces as
marriages, with smaller families, longer lives, the economic expansion
desired by the average household for which two incomes are required,
education of women, diminishment of the need for heavy muscular
work, which meant that the lives of men and women—talking on the
phone, sitting at the desk, managing—became more and more alike.

The inner changes within women can scarcely be exaggerated. Ambition is natural to new groups freed, or demanding to be free and
equal. No group demands equality for nothing, as a simple adornment
of status. The arrival of women's ambition, transforming as it does

private life, inner feeling, and public life is not at all simple but instead resembles the subtle shiftings of human thought and life brought about by enormously challenging ideas such as evolution and Freudianism. Many hang back; just as many would stand on the literal truth of Genesis; but no matter what the ideological reluctance may be, every life is an inchoate but genuine reflection of the change. We begin to act upon new assumptions without even being aware of the changes.

Society does not want women to lead a long life in the home. It is not prepared to support them and cannot give the old style true sanction. Children do not want their parents' lives to be given to them forever. Husbands cannot take the responsibilities for wives as an immutable duty, ordained by nature. Women's liberation suits society much more than society itself is prepared to admit. The wife economy is as obsolete as the slave economy.

But more than dollars are at stake. Power, the most insidious of the passions, is also the most cunning. The women's movement is in some respects a group like many others, organized against discrimination, economic and social inequities, legal impediments: against the structural defects of accumulated history. Perhaps it is that part of the movement the times will more or less accommodate in the interest of reality. The other challenges are more devastating to custom, uprooting as they do the large and the small, the evident and the hidden. The women's movement is above all a critique. And almost nothing, it turns out, will remain outside its relevance. It is the disorienting extension of the intrinsic meaning of women's liberation, much of it unexpected, that sets the movement apart. It is a psychic and social migration, leaving behind an altered landscape.

In the 1970s the insecurity of life, the rapid using up of resources, the alienating complexity of every problem from nuclear proliferation to falling reading scores, can scarcely fail to bewilder and lacerate relations between people in the family, in the streets, among the classes. When one tries to think of "domestic manners"—all of the rules and customs and habits which people have assumed as a group—one cannot imagine just who is sure enough of his ground to pass on the beliefs that grow out of reasonable certainty. And to whom are they offered, these beliefs and customs? The life of the young is far more complicated and murky than the life of those older. One thing looms out of the shadows: the reluctance of so many *promising* young people to have children.

1978

WIVES AND MISTRESSES

For who are we, and where from,
If after all these years
Gossip alone still lives on
While we no longer live?
—PASTERNAK, *Zhivago Poems*

I

THE FAMOUS carry about with them a great weight of patriarchal baggage—the footnotes of their lives. Footnotes worry a lot. They, loved or unloved, seem to feel the winds of the future always at their back. The graves of the greatly known ones are a challenge to private history; the silence is filled with riddles and arcane messages.

These "attendants" are real people: mistresses and wives, sometimes but not often husbands; friends and enemies, partners in sudden assignations. Some have been the inspiration for poems or have seen themselves expropriated for the transformations of fiction. They have written and received letters, been lied to, embezzled, abandoned, honored, or slandered. But there they are, entering history with *them*, with the celebrated artists, generals, prime ministers, presidents, tycoons.

The future may be an enemy. Time can turn happy days and nights into nothing. It can uncover secrets that impugn experience. Children in old age struggle to remember games on the lawn, agreeable picnics once shared with the infamous old tyrant whose photograph keeps appearing in the newspapers as yet another drudge of information and interpretation offers the assertive intimacy of long study in a tone that would surpass all life acquaintance.

The maligned see their quarrels with the famed one as a battle which can have no ending, see themselves squirming in an eternity of calumny which they would contest with document, affidavit, witness—right up to their own death. The determination of footnotes cries to Heaven. Lady Byron vindicated!

"On his marriage-night, Byron suddenly started out of his sleep; a paper, which burned in the room, was casting a ruddy glare through the crimson curtains of the bed; and he could not help exclaiming, in a voice so loud it wakened Lady B., 'Good God, I am surely in hell!'"

Where are all my years, my thirteen confinements, my seven copyings of *War and Peace*, Sofia Behrs Tolstoy asked again and again. Forty-eight years and, of course, one quarrel will be the last and all is too late. She is kept away from the bedside in the stationmaster's house. Distraught, accused, excluded beyond endurance, the Countess wanders about begging for reassurance, repeating, explaining her devotion, her understanding, her care. The young Pasternak, rushing with his father to the amazing, outstanding death scene, wrote in *I Remember*: "Good Lord, I thought, to what state can a human being be reduced, and a wife of Tolstoy at that!"

The Tolstoys knew all there was to be known about marriage and therefore all to be known about each other. More indeed than one is put on earth to understand. More than could be endured but certainly not more than could be recorded by one or the other. "Immense happiness... It is impossible that this should end except with life itself."* And soon, quarrels, and he will be found writing: "I arrive in the morning, full of joy and gladness, and I find the Countess in a tantrum.... She will wake up absolutely convinced that I am wrong and she is the most unfortunate woman alive!" She writes: "How can one love a fly that will not stop tormenting one?"

How real the Countess and her inflamed nerves are. There is no question of authenticity and she cannot maneuver with any more design than a trapped bat. With her mangled intelligence, her operatic, intolerable frenzies of distress, she comes forth still with an almost

---

* The quotations from the Tolstoys are from Henri Troyat's biography, *Tolstoy* (New York: Doubleday, 1967).

menacing aliveness, saying it all like a bell always on the alert. Years and years, threats of suicide, collapse, hysterias, and the swiftest remorse as defeat hits her at the most passionate moment of declaration. Weeping reunions: "The bonds uniting me to him are so close! ... He is a weak child, delicate, and so sweet-tempered." Again jealousies and plots. He feels a horrible "disgust and outrage" as he finds her creeping into his room when she imagines him asleep. She is looking for the will, or for the diary; always looking for herself in history, the self the pious, pedantic Tolstoyans would disinherit and deny, looking, too, to find the way to remain the inspiration, the adviser, the considered one whom the hated disciple, Chertkov, would supplant.

Problems of life and often the distorting, defacing mirror of his work, which sent forth its scarred images of home into the public view: when *The Kreutzer Sonata* was published with its murderous rages against carnal passion and marriage—"two convicts serving a life sentence of hard labor welded to the same chain"—the Countess felt herself mocked all over Russia, pitied even by the Emperor, gossiped about in the street.

She recorded her feelings: "I always felt the book was directed against me, mutilated and humiliated me in the eyes of the whole world, and was destroying everything we had preserved of love for one another. And yet never once in my marriage have I made a single gesture or given a single glance for which I need feel guilty toward my husband."

Also after the publication of *The Kreutzer Sonata* there were comic consequences for *him*, who had after all "stigmatized all fornicators." Suppose his wife were to become pregnant again? "How ashamed I would be...." he wrote. "They will compare the date of conception with the date of publication."

It was, of course, impossible for the Countess to bring her will, her great temperament, and her devotion to Tolstoy into a harmony that could survive more than a few sundowns. The overwhelming scene, the tremendous importance of the union and its dismaying, squalid complications of feeling, Yasnaya Polyana, the children, the novels, the opinions. The programs for transcendence and her thought: "This vegetarian diet means that two menus have to be prepared instead of one, which adds to the cost and makes twice as much work."

It is not quite clear how they found the time for the *record*—the fascinating, violently expressive record, like some strange oral history which catches the rises and falls of the voice, the impatience, the motive, the love itself heard in a sigh as sleep comes down—when it mercifully sometimes does. Every quarrel, every remorse, moments of calm and hope and memory. Diaries, rightly called voluminous, letters, great in number, sent back and forth. Longing for peace and the provocation of discord. "Until five in the morning he sighed, wept, and inveighed against his wife, while she, exhausted, momentarily contemplated suicide." *Momentarily.*

The cross the Countess hung upon was not inadequacy or even that crucifixion of mismating, common enough in all conditions of life. It may be said of her that one cannot imagine anyone else as the wife of Tolstoy. Their struggles always have about them the character of fate. He is as vehemently occupied with her as she is with him. The record alone, each in so great a hurry to say what the day had brought, indicates a peculiar obsession, one of those obsessions often punitive and yet inescapable. She had energy and mind of an extraordinary sort and so she moved back and forth one can only say *naturally*, calling upon the word so often used to describe the greatness of Tolstoy's art. She lived out a penalizing contradiction, devoted one minute, embattled the next. An adjutant, wracked by drama, brilliant in her *arias*; and then awakening to uncertainty, shame.

The Countess Tolstoy herself is a character in a great Russian novel, perhaps one by Dostoevsky rather than Tolstoy. Tatyana Tolstoy in her recently translated memoir, *Tolstoy Remembered*, writes about the more or less "serene" survival of her mother for nine years after Tolstoy's death. Serene, perhaps, "but she retained one weakness: she was still afraid of what people would say and write about her when she had gone, she feared for her reputation. As a result she never let slip the slightest opportunity for justifying her words and actions. There was no weapon she would not use in her campaign of self-defense...."

The Countess Tolstoy had no more need for self-defense than a barking dog. But the eminence of Tolstoy brought the very existence of her frazzled nerves into question. The dazzling scrutiny they directed upon their marriage left behind a rich dustheap of experience, but the documentation was not a court of judgment, as she imagined. It was simply their life itself.

In his beautiful reminiscence of Tolstoy, Gorky tells of walking along the beach with the "old magician," watching the tides roll over the stones. "He, too, seemed to me like an old stone come to life, who knows the beginnings and the ends of things.... I felt something fateful, magical, something that went down into the darkness beneath him ... as though it were he, his concentrated will, which was drawing the waves and repelling them." No doubt the Countess felt also that Tolstoy controlled the tides. What she often could not do was to flow and ebb in the certainty of nature, like a wave.

Lady Byron: from her short union with Byron she got her name and a lifetime of poisonous preoccupation. In her bad faith, deceits, and, above all, in her veiled intentions, so veiled indeed that gazing about with her intrepid glance she could not find the purpose of her intense lookings, there is nothing of the tragic exhaustion of the Countess Tolstoy. Lady Byron is unaccountable. She is self-directed, dangerously serious, and became a sort of Tartuffe in petticoats. "Marry Tartuffe and mortify your flesh!"

Lady Byron's industry produced only one genuine product: the *hoard* of dissension, the swollen archives, the blurred messages of the letters, the unbalancing record of meetings, the confidences, the statements drawn up, and always the hints with their cold and glassy fascination. The hinter, Lady Byron, was in a drama upon which the curtain never came down, and never will. An eternity of first acts. Her marriage lasted one year, ending in 1816; Byron, the *perpetrator*, as the police now refer to the accused, died in 1824, a century and a half ago. But the story of the marriage and the separation knows no diminishment. Instead it accelerates, develops, metamorphoses: all of it kept bright by its original opacity, all enduring forever out of the brevity.

No doubt, Byron, hard up, capriciously married Annabella Milbanke for her money and for the weary interest aroused by her first rejection of him. (When she at last accepted his offer, he is supposed to have said: "It never rains but it pours.") She married Byron for the fame of his notoriety and because of its engaging unsuitability to her own nature. But most of all they seemed to have married in order to create the Separation.

The story is well known, but the details, told and retold so many times, are unknowable. "So here we must beware of ignoring the sharp incompatibility of Lady Byron's original attitude and that which so suddenly took its place." Or "Compare that with Lady Byron's statement in 1830: the discrepancy, already observed by Drinkwater (1,54) is highly significant." (These tangles quoted in G. Wilson Knight's *Lord Byron's Marriage* are but a few among hundreds in his book, and cannot indicate the manifold puzzlements in the huge number of important Byron studies, each with its dazed laborings to cope with the hoard.)

As for Byron, "On the sixth Byron cheerfully assured Lady Melbourne that 'Annabella and I go on extremely well.'" However, "His opinion changed completely during the following week as he wrote to Lady Melbourne on the thirteenth: Do you know I have grave doubts if this will be a marriage now; her disposition is the very reverse of *our* imaginings" (*Lord Byron's Wife* by Malcolm Elwin). Marry they did, allowing Hobhouse to make his famous remark, "I felt as if I had buried a friend."

The Separation—often called The Campaign—followed the next year, after the birth of a daughter, Ada. The legal inferiority of women and wives gave a good start to the rise of Lady Byron's litigious temperature and to the onset of symptoms of "proof." She also wanted custody of the child, even though most scholars think she greatly "overused" this point since it was hard to imagine Byron assuming the care. (He had once written his half-sister Augusta Leigh that the sound of her squalling children gave him "a great respect for Herod.")

Byron had been throwing bottles of soda water on the ceiling (stains never found), posing with his pistols and bottle of laudanum by the bedside, and speaking of "crimes unimaginable." Murder, sodomy, incest? None of these? All of these?

So began the vivacity of the separation months, the deliriums of dissimulation, the doctors consulted, the families, the meetings and the refusal of meetings, the solicitors and their huge bills, the advice of friends, the decisions taken and rescinded, the demands counter-manded. All of this gave witness to the resonant incompatibility of the two persons, even though each might sometimes pretend for purposes of the "case" to warmer emotions drifting in and out.

The incongruity of Lady Byron was to have devoted a long life to a short marriage that ended in her youth. She had, at the church, taken an injection of poison into her veins. To Byron's fame and uncertain character, to the charm and scandal of it, she would oppose her recti-tude, her virtue, her injuries. But she did this in the most complicated, insinuating way, finding as she did that the achievement of a virtuous appearance in the midst of her accusations of horrors is to ground oneself on ice. She slipped and slid, tottered and regained her balance with an almost admirable audacity and endurance.

The incest of Byron and his half-sister, Augusta: Lady Byron brought to her suspicious concentration on this an imagination in flame, a motive of the left and right, like the blinders worn by a horse, and behavior so shadowed with contradiction that it is only her pursuit of the theme that can be counted on. She was determined to prove the incest and yet was not quite sure when she preferred it to have taken place—the problem being an uncertainty about the usefulness of its continuing during her marriage.

"Now, she had two objects in view: one, to establish the fact abso-lutely, preferably by getting Augusta to confess, and thus to know for certain whether Byron had ever persuaded her to repeat the crime after his marriage (that was important to her)....The jealousy which her principles would not allow her to acknowledge found sublimation in a truly sadistic zeal to extract the sin from Augusta's life and save her" (*Byron: A Biography* by Leslie A. Marchand). Lady Byron was also sliding about on the wish to discover a secret and to insist she would not divulge what she had discovered. An insane complexity of effort went into divulging while not divulging. Byron thought her purpose was to "sanction the most infamous calumnies by silence."

Lady Byron maintained a careful "friendship" with Augusta, broken only for a period late in life and even then mended. She was driven by a curiosity deeper than she knew and also by fear of losing control over any of the large cast of actors. Augusta experienced for years the most painful dilemmas of confusion. "Lady Byron presumably wants a confession of incest: Augusta, still not seeing the point, assumes she is merely being accused of some kind of disloyalty" (G. Wilson Knight).

Lady Byron had so many confidantes, advisers, doctors, and lawyers that of course the accusation was known to everyone—and, in any case, it had been spread about by Lady Caroline Lamb. Still, Lady Byron, talking and insinuating with a violent energy that left no gap, took moral refuge in the legalistic balm of never having *publicly* stated or "confirmed" what she had spent so much time proving.

Toward the end of her life, she had her operatic encounter with Mrs. Harriet Beecher Stowe. One could play a scene and the other could write it. They sequestered themselves after a luncheon in 1856, now forty years after the Separation. The "silent widow" spoke: "The great fact upon which all turned was stated in words that were unmistakable: 'Mrs. Stowe, he was guilty of incest with his sister!'"

Lady Byron was "deathly pale." H. B. S nodded, saying, yes, she had heard as much. Lady Byron went through her drama once more, starting with her childhood to set the stage. At one point she was asked by her American sympathizer whether Augusta was beautiful. Lady Byron answered, "No, my dear, she was plain."

All of this appeared in Mrs. Stowe's *Lady Byron Vindicated*, published after the death of the subject. There had been a *Lord Byron Vindicated* published the year before.

Lady Byron suffered in her calculations from the promptings of an outlandish pride. Her dilemma was that she took pride in the marriage to Lord Byron and pride in the Separation. In the various positions she assumed, many deforming conditions were working against one another. No sooner was she secure in her virtuous behavior than she was thrown from the ladder by the shakings of Byron's fame, which could turn every scandal into an attraction. She had always to be wary and wariness wore down her command of strategy. "Public outcry against Byron" could be punishing to him but it could not be depended upon. She understood this from the surest knowledge: her own peculiar attraction to and pursuit of him, a man she deeply disapproved of.

Lady Byron, an arrogant, intelligent heiress, appears to have needed a daily, yearly exercise of power and to need it in union with moral superiority. She feared no one, unless it may be said that she feared the shade of Byron. Byron's *Memoirs*, his account of the marriage and separation, was destroyed by a murky alliance of his own friends and Lady Byron's supporters. In life it cannot be said that she feared Byron. When asked if she were not afraid of the madman, she said, "My eyes can stare down his" (G. Wilson Knight).

It was her own life rather than history Lady Byron was most zealous to conceal and color—and a good thing too. She, voluble, alert, devious, has been looked at subsequently with a devastating alertness to motive, wish, contradiction that rather resembles her own deep archival diggings for "proof." In Doris Langley Moore's new biography of the daughter, Ada, Lady Byron is standing naked under an avalanche of falling rock. Her ill-health, her charities, her friendship with Augusta, her resistance to publicity, her jealousy of kind servants, her devotion to her daughter, her truthfulness: every noun except jealousy must from Mrs. Moore's researches be put within impugning quotation marks.

Lady Byron brought up her daughter, in relation to Byron, with a dreary contrariness, always displaying the will to retain and the will to renounce at the same time. Thus, a portrait of Byron hung in the house "perpetually covered by a green cloth." Ada was made to know she was the daughter of a renowned poet, "but all specimens of his handwriting were locked away from her."

Ada, an interesting result of the cynical union, was a good deal like her mother. She inherited from her mother—"the princess of parallelograms" as Byron called her—a genuine gift for mathematics. She had ambitions, too, and studied with the distinguished Professor Babbage, who was working on ideas later developed into computer mathematics. Ada married an agreeable, suitable man, who fell under the insistent domination of her mother.

There was much that was promising in the girl's beginnings, but she began somehow to sink into the mud of maneuver, manipulation, and her own marked self-satisfaction. Her mathematical skill turned toward the race track and she soon lost money, went into lying and debt, and squirmed around miserably in the pit of blackmail. From badly diagnosed illness, and the for-once inattention of her mother, who was intent upon her own notorious hypochondria, Ada went to larger and larger doses of morphine, to glittering eyes and vague drug elations and depressions. She suffered an excruciating death from cancer, dying when she was thirty-six and leaving Lady Byron to carry on for eight more years. To persevere with new problems of denial and blame, new ruptures, as Ada's gambling debts were revealed.

Both Ada and Lady Byron were afflicted with the wrinkles of class arrogance. Ada's belief in her own "phenomenal brain" inhibited the progress of her learning. Mother and daughter loved themselves too ardently. Mrs. Moore writes that Ada had a strong "desire to collaborate with Babbage in developing the intricate machinery to bring the computer to a state of practical usefulness, which would have been an unprecedented triumph for a woman." But Ada was often high-handed with the great Babbage and wrote him letters in "an air of conceit which is not to be found in any claim her father ever made, even in his artless boyhood." Riches, flattery for every cleverness, the oppression of her mother's rule, cut Ada off from serious work while leaving her the comfort of a boastful superiority.

What was Lady Byron's wish? If she was a victim, she was a most active one, responding long to Byron's fame and her short connection with it. Byron, of course, fared better in the time he had to live after the separation. He soon produced an illegitimate child elsewhere, he traveled, wrote poems, occupied himself with ideas and certainly with life. He had other affairs, also "historic," and also remembered and "published." The Countess Guiccioli, "the last alliance" as Iris Origo calls her, wrote her own recollections for the world. After she was widowed, she married the Marquis de Boissy who, the report went, used to introduce her as *"La Marquise de Boissy ma femme, ancienne maîtresse de Byron."*

Katherine Mansfield wrote in a letter to Middleton Murry: "Did you read in *The Times* that Shelley left on his table a bit of paper with a blot on it and a flung down quill? Mary S. *had a glass case* put over same and carried it all the way to London on her knees. Did you ever hear such rubbish!"

Tolstoy, after a miserable time, said about his wife: "She offers a striking example of the grave danger of placing one's life in any service but that of God." True—not that he meant it.

II

The loved ones—what a sinking it is from the high-flying insistence of the miserable to the slow, steady hum of affirmation. Egotists of affirmation have problems of form spared the truculent and the misrepresented, who carry their injuries about on their persons like a glass eye. In the pastoral mode, the drama will often come from without, from the obstructions of others, from the recalcitrance bred into the very nature of things, from bad reviews, the envy of rivals, tyrannies of the social order.

My Years With —— are likely to form a part of the title. Blank must be one whose years with are of interest to others besides oneself. For compositions in the pastoral mode, friends perform more felicitously than family members or lovers: the gloss need not be so radiant. In love memoirs, psychological inquiry is either missing or inadvertent; one does not usually loiter over the question of why he might be loved. It is the loss of love that arouses the speculative faculty and its rich inventions.

Anna Dostoevsky and Nadezhda Mandelstam are in no way similar, except that both by character and intelligence survived marriage and devotion to great writers without loss of common sense. The diary kept by Anna Dostoevsky is a plain reminiscence of a life of singular shape. The gambling in German towns, the epileptic attacks, the composition of the great novels, the bitter contest with debts, greedy relations, thieving publishers, the raising of children: all of this survives in her modest intelligence and truthfulness. One cannot leave a record of another without leaving a record of oneself.

Nadezhda Mandelstam's two large volumes, *Hope Against Hope* and *Hope Abandoned*, are of such brilliance and passion they cannot rightfully be called "memoirs." Her books are a battle against tyranny and death. The poet, Mandelstam, was extinguished in the flesh during the Stalin purges. It was his widow's determination to keep his poetry from extinction, to discover the awful circumstances of his murder in a prison camp, to write the history of the tyranny as she lived it, and still lives it, to analyze the circle in which they lived and Russia itself. In doing this, she has produced her own monument, one of the outstand-ing literary and moral achievements of her time.

Olga Ivinskaya, the mistress of Boris Pasternak, has written her book. It is called *A Captive of Time: My Years with Pasternak*. A florid, obsequious composition, issuing from an uncertain and harsh life. Her love memoir of her fourteen years as the mistress of Pasternak brings to mind that "fat brute of a word"—*poshlust*—as Nabokov examines it in his book on Gogol. "What the Russians call *poshlust* is beautifully timeless and so cleverly painted over with protective tints that its pres-ence (in a book, in a soul, in an institution, in a thousand other places) often escapes detection." Gogol tells the story of a German gallant, trying to conquer the heart of his Gretchen. "Every evening he would take off his clothes, plunge into the lake and, as he swam there, right under the eyes of his beloved, he would keep embracing a couple of swans which had been specially prepared for him for that purpose." Here, as Nabokov has it, "you have *poshlust* in its ideal form and it is clear that the terms trivial, trashy, smug and so on do not cover the aspect it takes in this epic of the blond swimmer and the two swans he fondled."

Pasternak met Olga Ivinskaya in 1946. He was fifty-six and she was thirty-four. The writer who, as Tsvetaeva remarked, "looked like an Arab and his horse," was a revered, romantic figure. His beautiful work attracted to him the positive radiance that shines around the poet in Russian society, an effulgence matched by the negative reverence of the state, which displays itself in constant surveillance and oppression such as other countries would think a waste of time.

All young girls may have been in love with Pasternak, and many not so young. In any case, when Olga first attended a Pasternak read-ing she went home with her book and greeted an interruption by her mother with, "Leave me alone, I've just been talking to God!" They met, they met once more, fell in love, and ushered in, like a reign in history, the fourteen years.

It settled into a triangle, in which all suffered—he the least. Paster-nak had been married to his second wife, Zinaida, for ten years. This second marriage took place from materials near at hand, perhaps one could call them, since Zinaida's first husband was Pasternak's friend, the pianist Neigaus. That indeed was a "move." The first Pasternak wife was a painter and they had one son. So there was his life—choices, consequences, things settled in the past.

Olga herself had a daughter by her first marriage. The husband committed suicide: her second husband died. When Olga and Pasternak met, the marriage with Zinaida was a "mess"—but it had that paradoxical quality of marriages in being a *solid* mess. Ivinskaya's habit is to put memories of conversations uttered long ago into direct quotations and, thus, dialogue of a doleful reduction sounds throughout her account. She quotes Paternak on the state of things: "It was just my fate ... and I realized my mistake during my first year together with Zinaida Nikolayevna. The fact is that it was not her I really liked, but Garrik [Neigaus] because I was so captivated by the way he played the piano. At first he wanted to kill me, the strange fellow, after she left him. But later on he was very grateful to me!" He explains that "in this hell" he had been living for ten years—and so on and so on.

Pasternak did not leave Zinaida and in a deep hidden way that fact is the occasion for this book. Ivinskaya's love-haunted spirit wanders in the shades without rest, needing always proof of love from him and proof offered to the world. This is a curiosity since she is a good deal better known to the world than the wife and even appears in the 1975 *Columbia Encyclopedia* as an "intimate friend and collaborator," in the entry on Pasternak. She was an openly acknowledged, beloved mistress.

Still the memory of his hesitations troubled. From the beginning she reports her mother's nagging: "They were always harping on the need for BL [Pasternak] to make a clean break and leave his family, if he really loved me." Her mother rang up, made scenes, which Pasternak tried to "fend off," assuring everyone that he loved Olga more than life, but that one couldn't change things so quickly. Even when Olga is in the prison camp her mother renews the theme in a letter to her: "He lives in a fantastic world which he says consists entirely of you—yet he imagines this need not mean any upheaval in his family life, or in anything else. Then what does he think it means?" (There may be something Russian in all this. A marvelous scene in Madame Mandelstam's book: Mandelstam for a time also had his Olga. At one point her mother came to the house and in the wife's presence urged Mandelstam to take the daughter off to the Crimea. When Nadia objected, the mother told her to shut up, that "she was here to talk business with her old friend Mandelstam.")

Of the fourteen years with Pasternak, Olga spent four in a prison camp, entering in 1949 and coming out in 1953. The caprice of Stalin's imprisonments and murders leaves each one under a question mark of motivation. To look for provocation, however insignificant, is to imagine a lingering legality, or appearance of legality, even in the heart of the most anarchic criminal whim. The immediate prelude to her arrest had to do with dealings about her desperate need for an apartment where she could meet with Pasternak. The woman involved in this turned out to be engaged in dishonest bribes and was arrested. Ivinskaya's arrest followed immediately. However, in so far as one can tell, the true reason for the arrest was her relation to Pasternak. In a letter written some years later he says: "She was put in jail on my account, as the person considered by the secret police closest to me, and they hoped that by means of grueling interrogation and threat they could extract enough evidence from her to put me on trial. I owe my life and the fact that they did not touch me in these years to her heroism and endurance."

The strangeness of Olga's arrest to inform on Pasternak is equaled by the caprice of Pasternak's escape from arrest during the most brutal years of Stalinism. Everyone who writes about him ponders his lucky fate, just as the ill fate of so many was the subject of tragic speculation. "Do not touch this cloud dweller," Stalin is rumored to have said when Pasternak's name came up for arrest. But that is only a rumor, a suggestion of some benign fascination with Pasternak on the part of Stalin—a peculiar quirk that may have been true in fact.

Ilya Ehrenburg wrote, "I can see no logic in it," and wondered why "Stalin did not touch Pasternak, who maintained his independence, while he destroyed Koltsov, who dutifully did everything he was asked to do." In his introduction to Alexander Gladkov's *Meetings with Pasternak*, Max Hayward recounts various complicated hypotheses for the relative immunity of the free-spirited Pasternak. Perhaps Stalin did not want the squalor of the Mandelstam case repeated; or it has been noted that Pasternak's refusal to sign the abominable hyperbole of the letter sent to Stalin on the death of his wife, whom some think he murdered and others believe committed suicide, while sending instead a courteous, reserved note of his own, may have moved Stalin by its "sincerity." The most appalling theory of all is Gladkov's bitter view that they had decided to "make do with Meyerhold and Babel," both of whom lost their lives.

Pasternak was indeed persecuted in the literary and spiritual sense, and in spending most of the 1930s doing translations experienced an "inner migration"—the refuge of gifted writers. He was expelled from the Writers Union, harassed and denounced over the Nobel Prize, and yet he kept his treasured house in Peredelkino and his work, with the exception of *Doctor Zhivago* and some of the religious poems, is not only published but "canonized."

During Olga's prison years Pasternak supported her family, who otherwise would have starved. In 1950, he had his first heart attack, soon after her arrest; in 1952, he had a second attack, a year before she was released in 1953. At this time he wrote to Olga's mother, saying that his wife had saved him. "I owe my life to her. All this, and everything else as well—everything I have seen and gone through—is so good and simple. How great are life and death and how insignificant the man who does not know it."

Just before Olga's release he seemed to fall into a kind of panic, perhaps a dream of retreat. A message was sent to her daughter, saying that perhaps "change might come about in our relationship," meaning that it would not fall back into the previous fixed and settled intimacy. As always, Olga, writing in retrospect, skates around this rock as if it were a pebble. And indeed she must, having set for herself two mind-numbing conditions: first, an idealized human being, Pasternak, and second, an idealized love, without pause, for herself. His hesitation on the doorstep of reunion is described as "candor, guileless charm and undeniable heartlessness." Olga's words, in moments of distress, always war with each other, although it is a rhetorical slaughter between dummies on horseback. And always the nouns and adjectives of a sunny armistice prevail. They reunite: "In short, our life, after being torn apart by sudden separation, all at once bestowed an unexpected gift on him—so once more nothing mattered except the 'living sorcery of hot embraces,' the triumph of two people alone in the bacchanalia of the world." Bacchanalia?

There is nothing she will not write. "While I was with him it was not given to him to grow old." She presses us to read between the lines to find any of the reality of this now ill man, with the desperate personal and financial conditions of his life, with his devotion above all to finding peace in which to work, with his past, his age, his love for her which like any love, especially an additional one, brings along the moonbeams of guilt and confusion with its happiness. Other tarred statements of his on the subject of his wife offered in direct quotations: "Let us not look ahead, or complicate matters, or hurt other people's feelings.... Would you want to be in the place of that unfortunate woman?" Indeed, yes, she would.

He reassures: "For years now we have been deaf to each other... and of course she is only to be pitied—she has been deaf all her life— the dove tapped at her window in vain ... And now she is angry because something real has come to me—but so late in life!" Olga's own thoughts sum up: "Happy as I felt at being his chosen one, I had to listen to narrow-minded reproaches and expressions of sympathy, and this upset me.... I suppose I longed for recognition and wanted people to envy me."

Ivinskaya speaks of her book as one he wanted her to write. Pasternak, with the miraculous purity and lyricism of his own style in poems and in prose, with his brilliant portrait in *Safe Conduct* of Mayakovsky and the "black velvet" of his talent, and the magical sweep of *Doctor Zhivago* ("her book"), did not catch her ear. As a reminder of his own way with a sliver of imagined speech, his thoughts on the suicide of the gifted, corrupt Fadeyev, head of the Writers Union:

And it seems to me that Fadeyev, with that guilty smile which he managed to preserve through all the cunning intricacies of politics, could bid farewell to himself at the last moment before pulling the trigger with, I should imagine, words like these: "Well, it's all over! Goodbye, Sasha!"

(*I Remember*)

Olga's jealousy of Mrs. Pasternak is not mitigated by her own reports of Pasternak's discreditable animadversions on Zinaida, who died in 1966 and thus was not an impediment to discourteous description. A meeting between the two women is left for "history" by Olga and here she admits that she was ill and perhaps hasn't got it quite straight. "I no longer remember exactly what passed between me and this heavily built, strong-minded woman, who kept repeating how she didn't give a damn for our love and that, although she no longer loved BL herself, she would not allow her family to be broken up." There is no reason this scene should be credited literally, especially since the notion that a rival does not love, but is instead moved only by the slyest attention to self-interest, is a provincial vulgarity.

Zinaida Pasternak does not get a good "press" from any account readily at hand, unless it may be considered that Pasternak's legal, "semi"-fidelity is a sort of remote credit. In *Hope Abandoned*, Madame Mandelstam tells of a visit to Peredelkino: "He told us he thought his wife was baking a cake down in the kitchen. He went to tell of our arrival, but came back looking glum; she clearly wanted to have nothing to do with us." A few years later, during a time of their great suffering, Zinaida said on the telephone to the Mandelstams: "Please don't come out here to Peredelkino." Worst of all, the scandal of the wife of Pasternak saying, "My children love Stalin most of all, and me only second."

A scene for which research turned up two versions: Toward the end of his life, Pasternak went with his wife for a visit to the Caucasus: as Olga puts it, Zinaida "took him off to Tiflis with her." Olga was wounded and angry and Pasternak begs her not to talk like a bad novel. She went off to Leningrad and refused to answer his sad, lonely letters—but of course soon she is remorseful. "To this very day the misery of this last quarrel in our life still gnaws at me."

An account of the visit is given in the introduction Lydia Pasternak wrote for her translation of an English selection of her brother's poems. "This short visit to the Caucasus had a wonderful effect on my brother. The wild majestic scenery, the universal love and admiration for him of the Georgians, the freedom and the recollections of the happy days they had both spent in the same surroundings in the thirties, before their marriage—all of this gave Pasternak new strength and a feeling of peace and fulfillment. He returned to Peredelkino happy and rejuvenated...." Who can say? Sisters often incline toward the status quo.

Lara in *Doctor Zhivago*—when a friend from abroad meets Olga: "She said we were exactly as she had imagined us—BL and me." Pasternak wrote in a letter to a Swedish correspondent: "Lara, the heroine of the novel, is someone in real life. She is a woman very close to me." Zinaida is also, he says, somewhere in the conception of Tonia, Zhivago's wife. In a letter Pasternak wrote of "my wife's passionate love of work, her eager skill in everything—in washing, cooking, cleaning, bringing up the children—has created domestic comfort, a garden, a way of life and daily routine, the calm and quiet needed for work."

In *A Captive of Time*, the dilemmas of Pasternak's career are examined with the fullest compassion: his survival, his leanings toward Christianity, the famous telephone conversation with Stalin when Mandelstam was arrested, his response to the desperation of Tsvetaeva just before her suicide, the cringing letter to Khrushchev renouncing the Nobel Prize, a letter Ivinskaya says she wrote herself and urged upon Pasternak. There is much of interest in all of this even if it comes, also, under the disaster of Ivinskaya's style and the hallucinated folly of the transformation of life and history into questions of their love.

What is the intention of her book and to whom is it addressed? All we know is that it has been sent out to the West, to us, and in some odd fashion sent back to herself, her memories. "My love! I now come to the end of the book you wanted me to write.... The greater part of my conscious life has been devoted to you—and what is left of it will also be devoted to you." What is the meaning of *conscious*?

After Pasternak's death, Ivinskaya and her daughter were arrested on the claim, or pretext, of dealing with rubles smuggled into the country by way of the Feltrinelli firm, Italian publishers of *Doctor Zhivago*. She served another four years. The misery of this life seemed to have no ending. It must be said of Ivinskaya that she can take a cold, icy bullet into her flesh, pull it out with a wince, sugar it and offer it to the world, to herself mostly, as a marshmallow. Out of prison once more, she speaks of the "total lack of sympathy for me in influential Soviet circles." Here she is not speaking only of party hacks, but of the hostility of such persons as the courageous novelist, Lydia Chukovskaya, who even at this moment is being persecuted in the Soviet Union as a defender of human rights. Another puzzle.

Ivinskaya is now old, poor, and bereft. Pasternak's death certainly left her quite undefended, without, as she says somewhere, "the protection of his name." She has occupied herself with this book, a success in the West. There is much awry in her character and understanding, and thus Pasternak, one of the great writers of the century and a man who seemed to have no enemies, is much reduced. But that is the turn of the wheel of history for *him*. Her own apotheosis, so beautifully accomplished in Pasternak's poems to her and in the novel, in the many hundreds of letters in her keeping, might better have been left to stand alone.

At the end of *Hope Abandoned*, Madame Mandelstam prints a letter she wrote to Mandelstam just before she learned of his death. It was never sent, was put away, retrieved thirty years later. She speaks of her love in a way that her quirky, thorny nature might not have allowed years before. It is one of the most beautiful letters we have:

> You came to me every night in my sleep, and I kept asking what had happened, but you did not reply. In my last dream I was buying food for you in a filthy hotel restaurant....When I had bought it, I realized I did not know where to take it, because I do not know where you are. When I woke up, I said to Shura, "Osia is dead."

The letter ends: "It's me, Nadia. Where are you? Farewell."

POSTSCRIPT: HUSBANDS

From *Close to Colette* by Maurice Goudeket:

> There is great temptation to consider that the intimate hours of a person or a couple, whatever their public position may be, belong to themselves alone. But when a wave of fervor such as

has rarely been seen irradiated the last years of Colette . . . would it be fair not to offer in exchange the most precious thing one has kept?

Mmmmm. So, a modest memoir, not very interesting. Houses, gardens, animals, food, journeys in motor cars, holidays on handsome yachts, writing, the German occupation, death. "Suddenly there was silence and Colette's head bent slowly to one side, with a movement of infinite grace."

Katherine Mansfield, Letters and Journals, edited by C. K. Stead. From the introduction by Stead:

Murry's promotion of his wife's literary remains brought him royalties and opprobrium and increased her fame. The good and the bad seem inextricably mixed in his work on her behalf. He transcribed, edited, and wrote commentaries tirelessly but in a way which encouraged a sentimental, and sometimes a falsely mystical interest in her talent. He could not keep himself out of the picture either, seeing the development of her art always in relation to the development of her feeling for him.

1978

UNKNOWN FAULKNER

THIS IS a daunting enterprise: 677 pages of unpublished or previously uncollected works of short fiction by William Faulkner, along with interesting notes that tell of the circuitous, tireless creation of the Faulkner canon. They tell, also, of the need for money along the way, the need that turns visions into "submitted manuscripts," pieces of paper chugging along—to the eyes of George P. Lorimer at *The Saturday Evening Post*, to the desk at *Collier's*, and to the editorial scrutiny of other magazines.

This publication is offered to advance, perhaps to complete, the record. An industrious writer of the first rank leaves his inventory, which breeds a sort of marsupial industry of its own, one often endowed with a larger capitalization than the original source. The multiplication of texts, the expropriation, if that is a suitable word, by Faulkner of previous work to be renewed for later work, the absorption of single stories and episodes into large designs: all of this is happy grounding for books, articles, and advanced degrees. Most of the work offered in the *Uncollected Stories* has long been available to scholars working with the various depositories of Faulkner material. Now, divided into stories revised for later books, uncollected stories, and unpublished manuscripts, the work is offered to the general reader.

It is a question whether Faulkner has ever had a general reader, unless the term may be thought to describe those who give their time throughout life to literature without the spur of the classroom or the project. His original union of high classical style and vocabulary with the most daring and unaccommodating experiments with form, fractured methods of narration, shifting, shadowy centers of memory and documentation makes an art that was very demanding in his lifetime and not less so now. Perhaps it is more difficult now if the reader must also place upon his mind the inhibiting genealogies, the mythical, unpronounceable kingdom that begins with a *Y*—all of the learning and sorting out that, like all learning and sorting, gives knowledge of a kind. Such knowledge is inevitable without being necessary. What are necessary are the magical, unique texts themselves with their passions that ask everything of the receiving mind, ask that the sensibility submit to a profound saturation. These are not stops for the passer-by. Indeed, not one of the novels will reveal even its form, its story, without submersion again and again.

"On November 7, 1930 Faulkner sent a story entitled of 'Lebanon' to *The Saturday Evening Post*, which rejected it." And one week later, another story to the same magazine, "but met with no success." The stories were not written in a week. Sometimes, reading the scholarship, one gets the idea that there is no first version of anything in Faulkner, perhaps because of his hallucinated imagination in which forms flow and alter, replace and displace without end. In the same way, he does not often reject what was once brought into being; it reappears, renamed, defined in some new connection.

The Saturday Evening Post accepted many stories, among them the early version of "The Bear," and *Collier's* printed the first "Go Down, Moses." None was written "for" the *Post*, "for" *Collier's*. For instance, in the *Post*, one sentence of "The Bear" runs to thirteen lines of type and ends: "... not even a Moral animal but an anachronism, indomitable and invincible, out of an old dead time, a phantom, epitome and apotheosis of the old wild life at which the puny humans swarmed and hacked in a fury of abhorrence and fear, like pygmies about the ankles of a drowsing elephant: the old bear solitary, indomitable and alone, widowered, childless, and absolved of mortality—old Priam reft of his old wife and having outlived all his sons." We know that to be Faulkner, unconceding. What may be learned from the quotation is the presence of certain amnesties in the prison code of the *Post*.

Sanctuary was, so far as I know, Faulkner's one effort to make, with deliberation, a sow's ear out of a silk purse. The first version, "a cheap idea deliberately conceived to make money," was rejected as being too violent for the period, or perhaps too violent for itself. When he rewrote it a few years later, he hoped it would not "shame *The Sound and the Fury* and *As I Lay Dying*" and called it a fair job and hoped people would buy it, which they did reasonably and without excess (a pleasant superfluity Faulkner never achieved). Of course, *Sanctuary* is a book unlike any other, one of the author's six or seven masterpieces. André Malraux thought of it as "the intrusion of Greek tragedy into the detective story."

Considering the publication of leftover and subsequently revised work in this new volume, the loss, the absence most to be regretted is the disappearance, apparently, of the first version of *Sanctuary*. Led to reread the final *Sanctuary* by thoughts of the writer and money, thoughts of Faulkner's way of working, of what is now called his process, one finds that the novel with its spectacular vitality does not exploit its genre so much as shatter it. What strikes one now is not the exaggeration of the central character, the criminal Popeye, not the stage effects, but the way Faulkner prefigures the vogue of those real-life Popeyes who make their eternal returns to the front pages and into books.

The forlorn criminal mind, beyond interpretation, this bafflement and destiny, filled with gestures, scraps of eccentricity, outbursts, fornication, drinking bouts, and always, of course, murders—its audience has aggrandized and changed. *True Detective* gave the facts but did not know how to solicit the aura. The criminal does not stimulate the contemporary appetite for scandal, either. Scandal now feeds on happy people, beautiful and rich, with their divorces and drugs, and inclinations to behave in ways that have an arresting inappropriateness. The miserable criminal is not a scandal; he is too lowly for that. Instead, he seems to engage the sophisticated mind by his overwhelming thereness—that alone—a thereness that is itself a sufficiency.

The sheer interest of such a man. This is what Norman Mailer takes to be the beginning and the end when he offers a hugeness of detail about the killer Gary Gilmore, and withdraws himself from it as quite unnecessary to the man's totemic sufficiency. Imagine a being with no good intentions and therefore less cant than most. Enter the criminal mind, all underground passages with the only glimmering of light the interviewer and his tape recorder. By the concentration of his own flaming energies Mailer seems to be saying about Gary Gilmore: Few men can make such great claims on our attention.

Popeye, the creation, is certainly imagined in the fullest degree, but he is not unimaginable as a reality. He is, instead, true to the appetite or knowledge produced by a later speculative journalism. He has the necessary excited flatness of character, a flatness arising from his domination by isolated and singular aspects of the will. This is perhaps what Faulkner partly meant by his innocent use of "cheapness" to describe his original idea; that is, a decision to watch the movements of the uncomplicated will, the movement characteristic of pornography and of much detective and crime fiction.

However, a book is written as well as conceived. In this case, the "selling" idea was the rape of a college girl by a corncob, which serves as what Sade might have called the "instrument" for the impotent Popeye. In the rendering of the idea, intensities of language and oblique modes in the narration transform flatness and shock into a contemplation of the mysteries of action. The writing is also impelled by a curious and powerful disgust, the pessimistic insight aroused in particular by the promiscuous, empty, arrogant young Southerners. "He's as good as you are. He goes to Tulane" and "My father is a judge," they like to say.

The brilliant concentration of images by which Popeye is introduced would be a problem for the writer looking at an actual criminal—going over the record, as it were. The strain of verisimilitude, of accuracy, of conformity to photograph and news story would hinder the flight of independent metaphor: "His face had a queer, bloodless color, as though seen by electric light... he had that vicious depthless quality of stamped tin... his tight suit and stiff hat all angles, like a modernistic lampshade."

These are the striking thoughts that led Malcolm Cowley to see Popeye as one of those "who represent the mechanical civilization that has invaded and partly conquered the South." And further as "the compendium of all the hateful qualities that Faulkner assigns to finance capitalism." This is indeed a heavy historical burden for the reduced, perverse, and changeless psychopath, and Popeye can bear it no better than The Misfit in Flannery O'Connor's "A Good Man Is Hard to

Find" ("You can do one thing or you can do another, kill a man or take a tire off his car. . . ."). Popeye is relevant only to himself, and his human connections are with others of his type, the replications that turn up year after year to work out their unalterable passages, like birds flying south in the autumn.

Vice, coldness, impulse attached to a nature that is flat and toneless, in spite of a certain bravura and little bits of "style." "Fix my hair, Jack," Popeye says as he approaches the scaffold. Gary Gilmore says: "Let's do it."

Faulkner imagines, in an epilogue, an interesting sociology for Popeye, a sort of placing or rooting of the extreme, which also has its beginnings. The sweep of devastation is not unfamiliar. Popeye's mother meets his father, a professional strikebreaker, on a streetcar. When she becomes pregnant and says they must marry, the father replies, "Well, don't get upset. I just as lief. I have to pass here every night anyway." Of course, the father is soon gone, leaving the mother with Popeye, syphilis, and her own breakdown. The boy is left in the care of a pyromaniac grandmother, and nearly perishes when she burns down the house. He is stunted and abnormal physically, but survives to cut up birds and a half-grown kitten and to be taken off to institutions. In the body of the novel he has some success in bootlegging and commits the two murders that form part of the plot. In the end, refusing counsel, indifferent to his own life, he is hung for a murder he didn't commit. So it is "Fix my hair, Jack," and all is over.

In the *Uncollected Stories* there are two versions of a story about bootlegging written in the late 1920s, a few years before *Sanctuary*. No one would make a connection between the two, not even a Faulkner scholar with his special eyeglasses that can see in the dark. The notes of the *Uncollected Stories* do inform us that Faulkner claimed to have worked at bootlegging in New Orleans around 1925. And we believe it.

1979

NABOKOV
Master Class

WHEN VLADIMIR Nabokov died in Switzerland in 1977, a life chronically challenged by history ended in the felicity of a large, intrepid, creative achievement. Nabokov left Russia with his family in 1919, took a degree at Cambridge University and in 1922 settled among the Russian colony in Berlin, where he began his work as a poet and novelist in the Russian language. In 1937, after fifteen or so un-Teutonic years "among strangers, spectral Germans," he pushed on to France for three years, to those "more or less illusory cities" that form the émigré's past. In 1940, with his wife and son, he arrived in the United States, "a new and beloved world," as he calls it in his autobiography *Speak, Memory* where, among other adaptations, he patriotically stopped "barring my sevens."

To America, Nabokov brought his supreme literary gifts and wide learning and a great accumulation of losses: childhood landscape devastated, gravestones blurred, armies in the wrong countries, and his father murdered, hit by a bullet intended for another on the stage of one of those intense political debates among the Russian exiles in Berlin.

From 1940 to 1960, here he is among us, cheerful it seems, and unpredictable in opinion. Not a bohemian, not at all, and not a White Russian dinner partner, but always dramatic and incorruptible. On the present occasion he is standing before his classes at Cornell University in Ithaca, New York, delivering the now published first volume of *Lectures on Literature*. He is forty-nine years old, an outstanding modern novelist in the Russian language, and still in need of money. During the next ten years, the Ithacan afternoons and evenings will be spent writing in English: *Pnin*, the memoir *Speak, Memory*, and his uncompromised masterpiece, *Lolita*, a financial success that released him from one of the cares of the literary life. When he goes back to Europe, to settle with his wife in an old, interesting hotel in Montreux, Switzerland, he will be one of the great twentieth-century novelists in English.

Not much happened during the American years that escaped transformation to the mosaic of the Nabokov page, with its undaunted English words glittering in their classical, rather imperial plentitude, a plentitude that is never a superfluity. Although Nabokov himself was unassimilable, his imagination is astonishingly porous. It is rather in the mood of Marco Polo in China that he meets the (to us) exhausted artifacts of the American scene. Motels, advertisements, chewing-gum smiles, academics with their projects like pillows stuffed under an actor's tunic, turns of speech advancing like a train on his amplifying ear—for Nabokov it is all a dawn, alpine freshness. His is a romantic, prodigal imagination, with inexhaustible ores of memory buried in the ground of an unprovincial history. "And one day we shall recall all this—the lindens, and the shadows on the wall, and a poodle's unclipped claws tapping over the flagstones of the night. And the star, the star."

As a teacher, Nabokov had, before Cornell, spent a good deal of time at Wellesley College, and not much time at Harvard. His misadventures with the Comparative Literature Department at Harvard, told in Andrew Field's biography, *Nabokov: His Life in Part*, have the comic "Russianness" of some old head-scratching tale of serf and master. Nabokov lectured at Harvard in 1952. There the exile's brightly confident dimming of a long list of classic authors and works shed its blackening attention upon Cervantes. Professor Harry Levin, on behalf of the old Spaniard, said: Harvard thinks otherwise. The remark, put into Professor Levin's pocket like a handkerchief, has the scent of Nabokov's own wicked perfume on it . . . but no matter. And all to the good indeed. Cambridge, Massachusetts, was not the proper setting for the touching derangements of Nabokov's created Professor Pnin and Dr. Kinbote—and not the right New England village in which Humbert Humbert would marry Lolita's mother. So, it was to be Cornell.

The published lectures are, apart from everything else, dutiful, even professorial. They are concrete, efficient, not the wanderings of an imported star who takes off early by way of discussion periods. We are told by Andrew Field that Nabokov's scientific work on butterflies was "painstaking" and marked by a "scale by scale meticulousness." There is something of this also in the approach to the performance before as many as 400 students and the acceptance of certain ever-returning weekends with 150 examination papers to read.

The young audience is there to hear him, even if he does not know what they may have brought with them. Nabokov stands aside in the beginning, perturbed, it may be imagined, not only by the rarity of literature, but by the rarity of reading, true reading. He solicits rather poignantly from the students the ineffable "tingling spine" and "shiver" of the aesthetic response, all that cannot be written down in notebooks and which is as hopeless of definition as the act of composition itself.

The first of Nabokov's Cornell lectures, as printed here, was given to Jane Austen's *Mansfield Park*. This author and this particular novel had been urged upon Nabokov by Edmund Wilson. Wilson was dismayed by Nabokov's cast-offs, those universally admired works that seemed to be resting in overflowing boxes in the Nabokov vestibule, as if waiting to be picked up by the Salvation Army. A lot of it appears to be mischievous teasing by Nabokov, good-humored, even *winking*, if such a word may be used. ("Henry James is a pale porpoise.") Satire is one of Nabokov's gifts, and nearly all of his novels are appliquéd with little rosette-asides of impertinent literary opinion.

In any case, *Mansfield Park* finds Nabokov laying out the plot with a draftsman's care, patiently showing that one parson must die so that another can, so to speak, wear the dead man's shoes. And Sir Bertram must be sent off to the West Indies so that his household can relax into the "mild orgy" of the theatrical presentation of a sentimental play called "Lovers' Vows."

Here there is a curious intermission in which Nabokov tells the class about the old play, summarizing it from the original text. And again when Fanny cries out against a plan to cut down an avenue of trees, "What a pity! Does it not make you think of Cowper? 'Ye fallen avenues, once more I mourn your fate unmerited,'" Nabokov takes time out for a reading of the long, dull poem, "The Sofa" by William

Cowper. It is true that Nabokov liked to remember the charm of vanished popular works of the sort that slowly made their way over land and sea to the Russian household of his youth. Still, the diversion to these texts is strikingly unlike the microscopic adhesion to the matters at hand in other lectures. There are brushings of condescension in the Jane Austen chapter, delicate little streakings, like a marbleizing effect. She is "dimpled" and "pert," a master of this dimpled pertness.

"Style is not a tool, it is not a method, it is not a choice of words alone. Being much more than all this, style constitutes an intrinsic component or characteristic of the author's personality." Nabokov's method in these carefully prepared lectures is somewhat less impressionistic and darting than one might have expected from his irreplaceable book on Gogol and the fantastical commentaries to *Eugene Onegin*. Words and phrases, even the words of Joyce, Proust, or Dickens, are not themselves often the direct object of inquiry. Plots, with their subterranean themes, are the objects, plots to be dug up tenderly so as not to injure the intention of the author by too gleeful an excavation.

Nabokov goes along the plot, step by step, telling us where we are now and what is happening there; and the steps are not mere excavations but attended by readings aloud from the texts. About Joyce's *Ulysses*: "Demented Farrell now walks westward on Clare Street, where the blind youth is walking eastward on the same street, still unaware that he has left his tuning fork in the Ormond Hotel. Opposite number 8, the office of the dentist..."

Flaubert's punctuation and syntax most interestingly command Nabokov's attention. "I want to draw attention first of all to Flaubert's use of the word *and* preceded by a semicolon." And the use of the imperfect form of the past tense in *Madame Bovary*. Translators are rebuked for not seeing, in Emma's musings about the dreariness of her life, the difference between "She would find [correct translation] again in the same places the foxgloves and wallflowers," as against the simple "she found." These moments are the grandeur of Nabokov in the act of reading a novel. And when he speaks in the voice we know from his own novels, "Notice the elaboration of the moonlight in Proust, the shadows that come out of the light like the drawers of a chest...."

Madame Bovary, Mansfield Park, Swann's Way, Bleak House, Ulysses, The Metamorphosis—two in French, one from the German, two from English—and to these a third from English, *Dr. Jekyll and Mr. Hyde*, a Nabokov surprise, so as not to confound expectations. The mad pseudo-science of "Dr. Jekyll" appeals to Nabokov, who in his discussion of *Bleak House* lingered lovingly on the "spontaneous combustion" of the gin-soaked Mr. Krook. He likes the "winey taste" of Stevenson's novel, and "the appetizing tang of the chill morning in London." "Appetizing" is the word most often used about the fable. The plan of Dr. Jekyll's house is the back and front of the man himself. Not too little and not too much is made of the work, "a minor masterpiece on its own conventional terms" and far from *The Metamorphosis*, with its "five or six" tragic dimensions.

Kafka is "the greatest German writer of our times." Yes, yes—pause—"such poets as Rilke or such novelists as Thomas Mann are dwarfs and plaster saints in comparison to him." So, proceed. *The Metamorphosis*, an exceedingly painful tale about Gregor Samsa waking up one morning to find that he has turned into an insect, arouses in Nabokov the most passionate and emotional moments in the lecture series. As an entomologist, he pronounces Gregor a large beetle, the lowly cockroach being just that, too lowly, for the largeness of Kafka's descriptive inventions. The doors, the poor beetle's legs or teeth or whatever finally turning the lock, the family theme, the "Greek chorus" of the visit of the clerk from Gregor's office, the "coleopteran's" food slipped under the door, the appalling suffering: all of this is tragically affecting once more as the lecturer puts it before us.

Nabokov judges Gregor's world with great feeling, even with indignation. The Samsa relatives are "parasites" exploiting Gregor, eating him "out from the inside." His beetle carapace is the "pathetic urge to find some protection from betrayal, cruelty." But it is no protection and he remains as a beetle as vulnerable as his "sick human flesh and spirit had been." Gregor's sister, in the beginning the only one to acknowledge the metamorphosis and to act with kindness, becomes his worst enemy at last. Gregor is extinguished so that the family can go out in the sunlight once again. "The parasites have fattened themselves on Gregor," Nabokov wrote in the margins of his copy.

If it were not the trade name of a commercial series, Nabokov's lectures might be called "Monarch Notes," in honor of their stately, unfatigued progress through the crowd of words, styles, and plots. What is most unexpected is the patience. *Bleak House*: "Now let us go back to the very first paragraph in the book." *Madame Bovary*: "Let us go back to the time when Charles was still married to Héloïse Dubuc." *Ulysses*: "Bloom's breakfast that she is to make for him that morning continues to fill her thoughts...."

Following these lectures with their determined clinging to detail, and with the insistent foot on each rung of the scaffolding of the plot, is to be asked to experience the novel itself in a kind of thoughtfully assisted rereading, without interpretation. There is very little ripe, plump appreciative language. "Beautiful" turns are acknowledged by "note" and "mark." In *Madame Bovary* "note the long fine sunrays through the chinks in the closed shutters" and "mark the insidious daylight that made velvet of the soot at the back of the fireplace and touched with livid blue the cold cinders." A novel is a rare object. Look at it with a magnifying glass and the earphones turned off. And curiously each work is alone, not milling about among its siblings, *Emma*, *Our Mutual Friend*, *Portrait of an Artist*, and so on and so on.

Novels are fairy tales; *Madame Bovary* yet another fairy tale. Of course, with Nabokov a thing is asserted to counter a repellent, philistine opposition. A novel becomes a fairy tale so that it will not be thought to be a sociological study or a bit of the author's psycho-history, two ideas he may rightly have believed to be running like a low fever among the student body.

Nabokov's own novels very often end, and no matter what the plot, in a rhapsodic call to literature itself. "I am thinking of aurochs and angels, the secret of durable pigments, prophetic sonnets, the refuge of art. And this is the only immortality you and I may share, my Lolita." Also in his novels there are books within books and literature is almost a character. About *The Gift*, Nabokov said, "Its hero is not Zina, but Russian literature." The brilliant *Pale Fire* is entirely a deranged annotation of a dreadful poem.

Perhaps in the end it is not surprising that this writer who has walked every step of the way in two languages should look upon style as the self in all its being and the novel as a slow, patient construction of a gleaming fairy tale. "Let us look at the web and not the spider," he writes about Dickens. The web, the inimitable web, is what these lectures are about.

1980

ENGLISH VISITORS IN AMERICA

Englishman has hard eyes. He is great by the back of his head.
—EMERSON, *Journals*

O SHENANDOAH, O Niagara. In a text that bristles like the quills on a pestered porcupine, Peter Conrad, a young English critic of music and literature, fellow of Christ Church, Oxford, has written a book called *Imagining America*. It is easy to read, and yet a torture to unravel. This is not due to the absence of footnotes, bibliography, or to the very reduced index—that is the least of it. The most of it is a great fluency of style, a military confidence, an extraordinary range of intimidation that sweeps over the country, America, and a good many English writers, the two in collision being the subject of the book.

Imagining America follows a number of English persons on their journey here: Mrs. Trollope, Dickens, Anthony Trollope, Oscar Wilde, Rupert Brooke, Kipling, H. G. Wells, Stevenson, Lawrence. In the latter part of the book, Conrad "examines," in the surgical sense, the deformities of the three gifted English authors who chose to remain: Auden, Huxley, and Isherwood.

Unusual conjectures, connections that move from the text to interpretation with the speed and force of a bullet in transit, dazzle and brilliance that often exceed the fluency of the authors themselves: these uncommon gifts in alliance with a nervy vehemence of tone make *Imagining America* a daunting addition to "Anglo-American Studies." We, it appears, have much to answer for, and they, especially the English writers in exile, have a great deal more.

The putative thesis of the book is not striking and, since the book is very striking, the thesis is only in part a suitable frame. The brief statement of intention at the beginning and end is rather like a bit of brown-paper wrapping that disguises the volatile materials within.

> Before America could be discovered, it had to be imagined.... Geographically, America was imagined in advance of its discovery as an arboreal paradise, Europe's dream of verdurous luxury. After that discovery, the political founders were its inventors.

The passage of time from the Victorians to the present does not find the country, America, in a condition more gratifying to the senses and the spirit; instead, the visitors themselves "re-imagine" our obscure or glaring deficiencies into amusements, curiosities, or personal escapes. "Americans tolerate and even abet this contradictory European fantasizing about them. Loyal to the ideal pretensions of their society, they're as much prisoners of their millennial self-image as they are of the prejudicial images Europeans continue to inflict upon them." Thus, the scene opens.

The ending, after the clash of text, person, and Conrad's rhetoric, is a forgiving downfall.

> America is ample and generous enough to tolerate all these impositions on it, and various enough to adapt to all these transformations of it. The moral of this book, like that of America, lies not in its unity but in its diversity.

This benign accommodation, so general in its application to history, would scarcely be worth the ticket. The book, freely speculative, does not have a moral, but is nevertheless rich in statements with a moralizing tone. It is not easy to separate tone and statement, paraphrase and text, opinion and illustration.

"At home [England] you are assigned a surrounding world by the circumstances of your birth; you don't invent a reality for yourself but inherit one, and exist in a society which prides itself on having restricted the range of imaginative choices. A civilized society, according to Matthew Arnold, is one in which the center prevails, in which metropolitan standards constrain the regions, and artists club together in a clique at that center." As for America, it is "centerless, not a claustrophobic, centripetal society... but a chaos of disparate realities." The English writers, grinding their heels in the dust of Vermont, New York, New Mexico, California, and so on, are not experiencing a place fixed by history and tradition. They are caught instead in a sort of whirl and flow, which they identify and use as they will. "Lawrence's New Mexico is not the same as Huxley's, nor is Huxley's California the same as Isherwood's."

Conrad's America, as he extracts it from his literary texts, is hospitable to interpretation, exploitation, and finally to therapeutic manipulation, but its spacious indefiniteness is not hospitable to literature, and not to the novel in particular. The problem of the novel appears in the early pages that announce Peter Conrad's themes and the direction of his thoughts. The refractory landscape and the people dwelling in it are not agreeable matter for the *English* novelists in their transformation of experience and idea concerning America—perhaps, perhaps, that is what Conrad meant. In any case:

> The Victorians assume America to be slovenly and backward, unworthy of the novel's social graces and subtleties of observation. Later writers admit the novel's irrelevance to America, but they suggest alternatives. In Kipling's case, the alternative is epic, in Robert Louis Stevenson's it's chivalric romance.... In Wells's case as in Huxley's the alternative is science fiction....

"England *prides* itself on having restricted the range of imaginative choices"*—many impediments to agreement here, intensified by the accent of the self-evident. "Victorians *assume* America to be unworthy of the novel's social graces and subtleties of observation...." Mrs. Trollope and Dickens did not find America of the 1830s and 1840s a commendable accumulation of graces and subtleties, but there is no evidence that they considered the creation of Victorian novels, on the English

---

*All italics in quotations from Conrad are mine.

model, a task for the Republic or that they were mindful of the country's unsuitability for fiction.

Mrs. Trollope's *Domestic Manners* may be said to have squeezed the American lemon very profitably. Her book is a masterpiece of novelistic scenes, dialogues, and dramatic conflict between herself and her subject. She is the only writer in *Imagining America* to have discovered herself here. Mrs. Trollope, with her intrepid talents, her great ambition and need, transformed her chagrin and her frazzled nerves into a classic. She, more than any other of the travelers in Conrad's book, confronted America in a gambler-emigrant frame of mind—that is, in a confused mood of hope and panic. Her failed Emporium in Cincinnati shows that for all her "refined taste," she understood schlock and kitsch and was drawn in her commercial dream toward the outsized. (A premonition of the World's Largest Drugstore in Los Angeles that Aldous Huxley is later scolded for tolerating.) The front of the Emporium, facing Third Street, was "taken in part from the Mosque of St. Athanase, in Egypt," and the front facing south was an Egyptian colonnade formed with columns modeled after those "in the temple of Apollinopolis at Etfou, as exhibited in Devon's *Egypt.*" The large rotunda was to be topped by a huge Turkish crescent.*

It is true that Dickens's caricature of America in *Martin Chuzzlewit* testifies to the author's loathing of the country, but it does not testify to Conrad's idea of the Victorian novel's "social graces." Instead, the intrusion of the American theme indicates Dickens's anarchic, daring, inventive practice of the possibilities of Victorian fiction.

Anthony Trollope's *North America*, more studious and less journalistic than the other two Victorian accounts, is annoyed by much, but Trollope does not seem as a traveler to be in pursuit of an extension of his novelistic world. He had a tangled view of literature in America and knew something, if not much, about it. Both of the Trollopes were political conservatives. "I do not like them. I do not like their principles, I do not like their opinions," Mrs. Trollope writes about Americans at the end. She laid these vivacious negatives at the door of Equality.

*From the introduction by Donald Smalley to *Domestic Manners of the Americans* (Peter Smith, 1949).

"Later writers *admit* the novel's irrelevance to America...." Here the example is Kipling's *Captains Courageous*, which doesn't admit anything since it is not a document by a literary critic but is instead a "worked up" creative act, which grew out of Kipling's cold, litigious years in New England. Conrad's verbs are an elastic—they stretch in order to confine.

Niagara Falls, a phenomenon, is for Conrad an interesting measure of temperament, English, and tourist obligation, American. His chapter on the great resistant cataract is thoroughly original and diverting, but also, as it swims along, *accusing*, not to the waters, but to some of those who made the trip and, worse, to those who did not.

Dickens rendered Niagara in strenuous prose: "What voices spoke from out the thundering water; what faces, faded from the earth, looked out upon me from its gleaming depths; what Heavenly promise glistened in those angel's tears...." Oscar Wilde, observing the honeymooning couples, said: "The sight of the stupendous waterfall must be one of the first if not the keenest disappointments of American married life." H. G. Wells was more interested in the dynamos of the power company than in the Cave of the Winds. Rupert Brooke wearied of the comparative statistics that established the supremacy of the Falls and wrote that the real interest was not to be found there but in "the feeling of colossal power and of unintelligible disaster caused by the plunge of the vast body of water." But this acceptable sentiment, written in 1913, two years before Brooke died in the war, becomes the occasion for Conrad's own leaping: "The eager self-sacrifice of the waters anticipates the reaction of Brooke and his generation to the war, which excited them not because they wanted to defend a cause but because it promised them heroic self-extinction." *Anticipates, excited, promised*—not only the rushed young Brooke sending back his American dispatches, but his entire generation.

Still at Niagara: "Objects in America aren't determined by history or enmeshed by association like those of Europe." For the Victorians Niagara was a "prodigy of nature," but for later writers "imagining the object comes to mean cancelling it out." On it goes:

This is why the neglect of Niagara by the later writers in this book [Auden, Isherwood, and Huxley] is itself significant, because it is a consequence of the imagination's meditative withdrawal from observation. The later subjects of this book don't even bother to practice imaginative distortion of America's physical reality, for they are simply incurious about it.

No matter that Niagara has suffered a drastic falling of its "ratings" and that the incuriosity of sophisticated travelers and American writers is too widespread for "significant" rebuke. In 1914, Bertrand Russell said, "Niagara gave me no emotion"—said "with priggish philosophical rectitude" in Conrad's disposition of the remark.

In the ordering of the chapter there seems to be some sympathy for the sublimity of the accident of nature which America shares with Canada. Conrad seems to prod the visitors to take leave of themselves and offer an appropriate version or vision. Few are sufficient to it: Sarah Bernhardt wants to harness the Falls to her "capricious egotism." No similar unspoiled challenge occurs again, for any of the writers. A "nightmarish" America, of "nonchalant vacancy" and "savagery" and "moral amateurism" lies ahead.

Extraction of Conrad's thought is outstandingly difficult. Nearly every sentence is a thorn of perplexity. First, there is his *saturation* in the texts, an absorbing so thorough that the texts have little life outside his own mind; they are expropriated. Assertions, declarations, an unbalancing use of the present tense: "America . . . promises death and a rending but salutary resurrection." "Huxley lives in hell . . ." and the "awfulness of America is . . ." It is often Conrad's practice to meet a phrase—his quotations are for the most part brief—and to pass swiftly to revisions, rephrasings, bewildering gifts to the originals of his own intensifications. Dickens, arriving in 1842 in Washington, "the headquarters of tobacco-tinctured saliva," observed the unnaturalness of the city, its formality, its insufficiency as a living town, the ornamental thoroughfares and buildings without people to walk on them or to inhabit them. He thought few would wish to live there, who were not obliged to do so. This scene becomes in Conrad's revision, "These vacant, haunted places, from which people have fled *in fear and loathing....*"

Conrad on Anthony Trollope:

Trollope's longing for a smallness of scale which guards privacy explains his furious resentment of a remark made in Dubuque, alleging that England has no vegetables. The aspersion infuriates Trollope, and he is prompted to a eulogy of his own abundant kitchen garden. He is enraged because the domesticity of England, for him its dearest quality, has been impugned.

Furious, infuriates, enraged have taken wing from Trollope's exclamation mark. "No vegetables in England! I could not restrain myself altogether, and replied by a confession 'that we "raised" no squash.'... No vegetables in England!"

On behalf of the Victorian writers Conrad asserts that they found America to be "the vast death-chamber of English individuality," that the country was indifferent to the civilized separation of public and private life and unable to "validate individual existences." During the thirty years that spanned the visits of Mrs. Trollope, Dickens, and the second visit of Anthony Trollope, roughly 1830–1860, *Walden*, *Moby-Dick*, and *Leaves of Grass* had been published. Lincoln was alive and Poe had lived and died.

The "aesthetes," Oscar Wilde and Rupert Brooke, endure in *Imagining America* the bashing and battering endured by the country itself in the writing of the earlier visitors. Brooke's felicitousness and Wilde's epigrammatic genius are cut down by the power-saw of Conrad's moral disapprobation. The curious and singular slide into the defective. Even with Mrs. Trollope and Dickens, little note is taken of the comic expressiveness, the texture of comic aggression, that give light to their dark detestation and make their records alive today.

Wilde's genius, it appears, is a "pederastic precocity" he shares with his kind. No quarter is given to his lasting turns of phrase on America, such as, "The Atlantic is disappointing, the prairie is blotting paper, the Mormon Tabernacle is a soup kettle, and the vastness of America has a fatal influence on adjectives." Conrad finds that Wilde's "wit not only subverts morality, but subjugates America by diminishing it." When Wilde holds forth on American marriage—"the men marry early, the women marry often"—he is "disestablishing marriage." Why should Wilde on his vaudeville tour be guarding American morality and marriage. And what turn of mind insists that we disallow Wilde's "act"? When he arrives, flamboyantly dressed for his part as a vivid and original self-promoter, he is wearing "a bottle green overcoat of otter fur, with a seal skin cap." For this and other requests for his dress-props, he is denounced by Conrad because the fur coat "symbolizes nature sacrificed to art: seals and otters have been flayed merely to adorn his precious body." The truculent language, the supererogatory *precious*, exceed the provocation of Wilde's fur coat.

In St. Joseph, Missouri, Wilde observed souvenir hunters buying up Jesse James's dust-bin, foot-scraper, and door-knocker, "the reserve price being about the income of an English Bishop." He ends the paragraph from a letter: "The Americans are certainly great hero-worshippers, and always take their heroes from the criminal classes." Conrad interprets this as "by implication" an alignment of Wilde himself with the hero as criminal. The innocent observation in the letter becomes "a self-fulfilling prophecy, for his [Wilde's] subsequent career confirmed his heroism by making him officially a member of the criminal classes." The punitive linking of "homosexual misconduct" and murder is one of many gratuitous asides in this work of literary and social criticism, a work of remarkable self-sufficiency, it might be added, since not a single line of other critics is drawn upon or mentioned and the reader, stopped by the many roadblocks of language and thought, is required to search himself for primary and secondary sources if he should wish to make a few before-and-after comparisons.

Rupert Brooke's mild *Letters from America*, written about his journey in 1913, is thrashed by a belligerent exegesis. Certain "pop" aspects of the American scene strike Brooke as suitable moments for a journalistic expenditure of adjective and metaphor. Automobiles, huge neon signs blinking in the sky, baseball and cheerleaders, the old grads lined up for a Harvard commencement. ("I wonder if English nerves could stand it. It seems to bring the passage of time so very presently and vividly to mind.") On a summer day, Brooke sees a young man driving through the streets in a handsome, expensive motor car and it seems to him that the car is richer than the young man, an observation still of visual and social interest here today, if not to be so tomorrow.

Brooke imagines he might be a young mechanic, taking the car for repair—a decision somewhat "foreign" we might say, knowing the murky economics in America of automobile owner and income. The young driver has "an almost Swinburnian mane of red hair, blowing back in the wind, catching the lights of the day." In the summer heat, he is wearing only a suit of yellow overalls, "so that his arms and shoulders and neck were bare." He is "rather insolently conscious of power," and if perhaps ordinary in real life, behind the wheel he "seemed like a Greek god, in a fantastically modern, yet not unworthy way emblemed and incarnate, or like the spirit of Henley's 'Song of Speed.'"

Conrad decides from this and other passages that Brooke wanted to "undress America." He thinks the description of the young man in the car "conveys the concentration of excitement: Brooke has to notice separately each uncovered area. A divinity of physical delight...." *Delight, excitement,* seem to put Brooke on the street, to say nothing of back at the hotel composing, always in a state of incessant homoerotic dreaming. Even in an "unexcited" passage on American faces: "Handsome people of both sexes are very common; beautiful, and pretty, ones very rare...." To the dots which end the paragraph Conrad gives the name "yearning dots."

Brooke's cheerleader "addresses the multitude through a megaphone with a 'One! Two! Three!' hurls it aside and, with a wild flinging and swinging of his body and arms, conducts ten thousand voices in the Harvard yell. That over, the game proceeds, and the cheer-leader sits quietly waiting for the next moment of peril or triumph."

"Hedonistic abandon"—a phrase Conrad uses about Brooke—applies to his own "pale fire" speculation about the cheerleader, up yelling one minute, mutely down the next: "Brooke considers this contradiction to be 'wonderfully American' because Americans are both agitated and idle, and switch from one state to the other automatically, dispensing with intermediaries, rejoicing equally in the body's dynamism and its inertia, its paroxysms and (as if post-coitally) its repose."

Kipling and the "epical America." It would seem foolhardy to try to outpace Kipling in spiteful utterance about America and yet "atavistic rabble" and "savagery" give the clue to Conrad's efforts. "Epical" in this chapter appears to mean a warring struggle for survival against "punitive nature," and "the minimal human character" determined by weather and the search for a survival technology. What it may indicate about literature is extremely shadowy, since the word "epic" is not meant to jar the brain with *The Odyssey* or *Paradise Lost* but rather to send it back to pre-literate dialect and the specialized language of fishermen and woodsmen.

Robert Louis Stevenson also weaves in and out of Kipling's anti-novelistic America, but he is woefully weak in the chest, soul-sick in the pursuit of his married lady, and suffering from the refinement of his prose style. For Conrad this "chivalric quester" posing in the derelict Silverado mine is just that, a poseur, but then, "so is America, since it is a vacuity onto which each emigrant projects his own fantasy."

Ideas, many in a state of alarming freshness. As you go through Conrad's densely written pages, it is a little like wandering about an arboretum with plaques giving the name and the place of origin of the trees and shrubs. Brought here from China, brought here from India. The English writers have all been elsewhere and have many things, other than America, to think about. Most of them were productive without intermission. In *Imagining America*, it is not precisely the authors, and certainly not the complexity of their *oeuvre*, not even America that are being labeled—no, not exactly. But still they are transplants, for a long or a short time, and onto the tree that is themselves there is a showy grafting of the branches of Conrad's ideas, an ingenious hybridization.

The obsessive, incomparable reflections of D. H. Lawrence on America seem with their jerky, private originality to be beyond paraphrase, all gleaming intuition. Yet when Lawrence uses capital letters in *Studies in America* (THOU SHALT NOT) Conrad is alerted to the grating meeting of mind and country. So, "In corrupting his own language Lawrence was supplying America with a style appropriate to its overbearing crassness."

When we come at last to Huxley, Isherwood, and Auden, the English writers who remained in America, Conrad's language rises with a deplorable heat. The scorching is painful indeed and the critic, like an immigration officer catching aliens whose visas have expired, becomes, in Auden's phrase, "a summary tribunal which in perpetual session sits."

It is as if these extraordinary talents had arrived empty of learning, experience, temperament and were blank pages waiting to be scrawled upon by New York tenements, the sun, American boys, drugs, drive-ins, "hymns and movies and Irving Berlin." Huxley and Isherwood landed as unthinking guided missiles, driven by an awful, deserved destiny, in California. (Suffer any wrong that can be done you rather than come down there.) These three Englishmen are not only to be grounded in America, but each is to be defined by the particularity of New York or California. Places have almost a genetic fatality. They guide the helpless writer as if he and the city were identical twins, separated at birth, but doomed to be hit at last with twin cancers and uniformly faltering heart beats. For Auden, the "numbered grids" of New York's streets "encouraged his punctilious ritualism," his attraction to regular meter and a liking for crossword puzzles.

Perhaps no country can deserve the grace that fell upon California with Huxley, Stravinsky, Schoenberg, and Thomas Mann; or the beneficence to the East Coast of Auden, Hannah Arendt, Nabokov, and I. A. Richards. But the subject matter, the landscape, the magical rendering of American follies and symbolic meanings do not make Nabokov's American novels "American." The strength, the majesty of the creation of self, style, idiosyncrasy—the very claim of art and their individual practice of it the exiles brought with them to America. They are not, like the prairies, blotting paper to soak up the inchoate ink stains of Los Angeles and New York.

Aldous Huxley appears from his letters, his books, his exhausting curiosity, his roots in his family, his large and unexpected learning to be a genuine and valuable person of great innocence and gullibility. Above all, he strikes one as incorruptible. Part of the incorruptibility lies in his removal from class snobbery, and in the austerity of his personal life and habit. Asceticism in him unites with a peculiar experimentalism that had in it an eager supply of hopefulness; the hopefulness of the Bates Method as a way of alleviating his tragic near-blindness, or the hope of a relief from "intolerable self-hood" by way of mescaline.

The mechanistic direction of Huxley's urge to transcendence is characteristic. He seems to have been overwhelmed by the mystery of brain, body, and temperament, and he inevitably saw in Sheldon's classification of body types a clue to the individual struggling with his obdurate self under the doom of height and distribution of weight.

When he first sits down to take mescaline, in the company of his English friend, Dr. Humphrey Osmond, he has a tape recorder beside him, *to see what it does.* His early (1954) and dismaying eulogy of mind-altering drugs, *The Doors of Perception*, is a sad book, telling of happy, rather orderly visions. It is completely out of touch with drug culture and the uses to which his friendly Mind at Large might be put. For himself, in the course of ten years, his "sessions" are estimated to be about a dozen. In the last three years of his life he went through, without complaint, a medically sensible struggle with cancer.

Huxley is one of the oddest figures in English literature: brilliant, credulous, something of a wizard. He is not Californian. Both of his wives were European and his true friends were Englishmen like Dr. Osmond and—how to name his opaque qualities—Gerald Heard. Huxley's world is the library, that first of all, and a sort of libertarian hope for the laboratory. Huxley's curiosity was general rather than intimate and as a wanderer he was tolerant of the vulgar and outrageous, of the drugstore, the drive-in marriage bureau, the most hideous cemetery, and always, it appears, abstracted, not measuring his worth or even his convenience.

Conrad is rancorous on Huxley, clobbering him for abiding some time in a rented house with a naked-lady lamp and a full-size Fay Wray in the paws of King Kong; berating him for stoicism when a fire burned down another house containing his library and files; degrading his concern for overpopulation, treating him as a fool, the object of a ludicrous condescension.

"Drugged" appears as a Conrad adjective again and again. "Huxley *prefers* his chemical heaven to the drab world." The last line in the chapter on this unusual man is: "At last, without noticing it, Huxley became a drugged subject of his brave new world."

Christopher Isherwood is "blithely self-indulgent and self-forgetful, and therefore suits hedonistic California, which licenses Isherwood's peculiar manner of self-deprecating narcissism." That these qualities, even if they were an accurate description, would need a state, a climate to "license" them simply cannot be thought about with any reasonableness. Isherwood is said to have only one subject, himself, and then is told that "he doesn't know himself." This arises as a way of discrediting Isherwood's artistic good fortune in discovering the rightness for him of first-person narration, the rightness of *Goodbye to Berlin*, *Mr. Norris*, and *Prater Violet*, works of art able to stand with the best of the last forty years. It appears to Conrad that Isherwood may write novels but he is not a novelist because his own "nonentity obliges him to write novels about a character who is not a character." Many curious prunings of the tree of art are suggested by Conrad, and Huxley, in a California slump, is rebuked for admiration of Joyce and Lawrence, Boulez and Pollock. Isherwood, in his narrations, has "cancelled himself out" by "treating himself as discourteously and dismissively as if he were someone else."

In *A Single Man*, the central character dies at the end, a very common plot device that has more convenience in fiction than in life. The "blacking out" of George is extraordinarily well done, although there is some worry about point of view in a death that is not seen from the bedside but from the dying heart and fading brain itself. To Conrad this fictional death draws its meaning from geography, not from nature. It signifies that "the choice of America is not the choice of life, but the choice of self-extinction."

Sometimes in this critical work, the intimacy of rejection is so warm that we feel that the author must have had private viewings of the persons. Isherwood, present tense, sometimes "looks tired, lined, and shriveled, like an ancient monk, but when he laughs he regains the face of an adolescent, with a shy smile and sparkling eyes." The agreeable concession of smile and eyes is not, however, entirely a compliment since Isherwood is thought to be impossibly working against time and trapped in the belief that "youthful form is recoverable."

No scruple deters Peter Conrad in the swift execution of W. H. Auden. He slices on, in his practiced, glinting way, gathering authority where he finds it, in yesterday's garbage pail, in policemanlike sifting of texts, in the scene of the crime, New York City, in bad associates, cash in the drawers. Poems are evidence and he investigates them in the sense that a handwriting expert investigates a ransom note. The question through-out *Imagining America* is nearly always the question of evidence, the challenging circumstantial kind, inessential, but rich with adversary hintings. The book is about writers but no sentiment clings to the fact of accomplishment. Irascibility, Conrad's, lies on the pages like some hidden code, impossible to decipher. How far will he go? Ah, don't ask, as we say.

Thus: "The United States offers a sleek affluent new life: Auden and Isherwood in 1938 were ravished by the luxury of New York, dizzied by their own celebrity, teased by the availability of athletic sexual partners, and sustained in a state of euphoria by daily doses of Benze-drine and Seconal; no wonder they hastened back in 1939 for more of the same." Auden, on the one hand, is a "shrewd businessman" out for "top fees," and, on the other, a miserable, rootless derelict. The drastic inflation of the riches to be gained from writing poetry, reviews, from giving readings and lectures was shared perhaps by Auden himself and is a testament to the outstanding modesty of his commercial ambitions.

One of the American texts by Auden, examined by Conrad in a sweeping interpretation suggested perhaps by the theme, is *Paul Bun-yan*. This is an unimportant, throw-away libretto for music by Benjamin Britten, written in 1940, soon after Auden's arrival in America. The text was never reprinted by Auden and exists now in a 1975 publication by Faber, offered when the work had its second performance in England that year. This jazzy working of a folk legend is propitious for Conrad because Paul Bunyan cuts down trees, clears the forests of the West to make way for towns and settlements. Moral judgments of the most extreme kind can fall on Auden who is, as if in some kind of retribution, flattened under Bunyan's murdered trees.

> Let the architect with his sober plan
> Build a residence for the average man;
>
> And garden birds bat not an eye
> When locomotives whistle by...

Conrad: "Milton's justification of the fall is a metaphysical leap of faith.... Auden's justification is more complacently economic. The fall is fortunate not because it immortalizes the soul but because it enriches the body."

When Auden says, in his celebrated phrase, that poetry makes nothing happen, we are advised to see this as an admission that "poetry is artificial, formulaic, inconsequential." In *New Year Letter* the circumstantial evidence of the setting is looked upon as impugning. The poet is on Long Island, at the house of a friend who is in exile from Poland; they are listening to Buxtehude. Conrad's interpretation would have it that Auden and his friends are no longer citizens, being exiles, and are outside the moral conditions imposed by nationality and roots. "Having ceased to be subjects of political authority, they now constitute a voluntary group convened in and by art." But in what sense are they not subject to authority, if only the authority of the Long Island police force?

"Lay your sleeping head, my love, human on my faithless arm," a beautiful poem in the classical English lyric mode, is intolerably chastised in a governessy aside of great foolishness. Conrad writes: "Personal ties in America remain breezily casual, never becoming familial as they do in England, where everyone seems to be related if not by birth then by the homogenizing institutions of school, college club, or adultery." *Or adultery*, a happy afterthought for sequestered England, represented in Conrad's comparative clauses as a smug little group of atoms, homogenized and pasteurized like milk in a bottle.

Auden's house in Kirchstetten, Austria ("Thanksgiving for a Habitat"), by dividing up its space for work, guests, cooking, etc., becomes far from home but another New York, "not a public place but a catacomb of separate privacies...an arbitrary selection from a global crowd of displaced persons." This "compartmentalization of his territory," Conrad imagines to derive from the philosophical reflections of Hannah Arendt who had "decamped [*sic*] from Germany during Hitler's persecution of the Jews." By way of *The Human Condition*, which contains a chapter on public and private space, Hannah Arendt is somehow felt to be in connection with Auden's New York and its "grid" and with the arrangement of the house in Austria because of its allocation of space for various uses.

This is a travesty of Hannah Arendt's thought. If there is any value in her analysis of alienation, it is the value of an analysis of modern life and modern man, and would be as true of Conrad himself in England as of Auden in New York and Austria.

About the person, Auden, Conrad sinks into a galling hysteria, abusive and in repetition somehow savoring of its own adjectival inventiveness. Auden's New York apartment was "a cave of defilement." This rootless, friendless caricature delighted in "domestic ordure" and "the squalor of the nursery." He is "pickled and prematurely aged" and "looked forward to senility and did his best to advance it, behaving like an ungovernable, finicky baby, organizing his regime around regular mealtimes and early nights...."

Auden's eccentricities were harmless and he had the good fortune to be predictable, which relieved his conduct of unexpected rushes of paranoia, violence, and pettiness. If he knocked off from a dinner party at nine, his example was not of sufficient tyranny to drag anyone else along with him. His mind, his loneliness, his ability to love, his uncompetitive sweetness of character survived his ragged bedroom slippers and egg-spotted tie. And his genius, the high seriousness of his life, survived his death. He died of a sudden heart attack in a hotel in Vienna, dispatched in Conrad's requiem ending of his chapter with "callous, merciful American efficiency." Why callous, why merciful, why American?

In a memorial volume, edited by Stephen Spender, one of the finest in this not always profitable lapidary form, there are many anecdotes freely appropriated by Conrad, with of course what is called "a different emphasis." However, he does not call upon any of the excellent appreciations of Auden's poetry and feels no inclination to paraphrase the beautiful tribute by Geoffrey Grigson:

> If we follow him [Auden] round, as he celebrates, investigates, discards, adds, re-attempts, we find in him, I declare, explicit recipes for being human. And implicit ones, in poems, stanzas, lines, again and again, which give us in sonority and movement the additional bonus of what language cannot say—the bonus of great poetry.

1980

BARTLEBY IN MANHATTAN

WHILE preparing some lectures on the subject of New York City, that is, the present landscape in which an astonishing number of people still live, sustaining as they do the numerical sensationalism that qualifies New York as *one* of the great cities of the world, if not the *greatest*, the orotund *greatest* being reserved with an almost Biblical authority for our country as a whole; and also on "old New York," with its intimidating claim to vanished manners and social dominion, its hereditary furnishings of aggressive simplicity and shy opulence which would prove an unsteady bulwark against the flooding of the *nouveau riche*— during this reading I thought to look again at Melville's story, "Bartleby, the Scrivener," because it carried the subtitle: "A Story of Wall Street."

There did not appear to be much of Wall Street in this troubling composition of 1853 about a peculiar "copyist" who is hired by a "snug" little legal firm in the Wall Street district. No, nothing of the daunting, hungry "Manhattanism" of Whitman: "O an intense life, full to repletion and varied! / The life of the theatre, bar-room, huge hotel, for me!" Nothing of railroad schemes, cornering the gold market, or of that tense exclusion to be brought about by mistakes and follies in the private life which were to be the drama of "old New York" in Edith Wharton's novels. Bartleby seemed to me to be not its subtitle, but most of all an example of the superior uses of dialogue in fiction, here a strange, bone-thin dialogue that nevertheless serves to reveal a profoundly moving tragedy.

(Melville's brothers were lawyers, with offices at 10 Wall Street; a close friend was employed in a law office and seems to have been worn down by "incessant writing." About the story itself, some critics have thought of "Bartleby" as a masterly presentation of schizophrenic deterioration; others have seen the story as coming out of the rejection of Melville by the reading public and his own inability to be a popular "copyist." Some have found in the story the life of Wall Street, "walling in" the creative American spirit. All of these ideas are convincing and important. "Bartleby" may be one or all of these. My own reading is largely concerned with the nature of Bartleby's short sentences.)

Out of some sixteen thousand words, Bartleby, the cadaverous and yet blazing center of all our attention, speaks only thirty-seven short lines, more than a third of which are a repetition of a single line, the celebrated, the "famous," I think one might call it, retort: *I would prefer not to.* No, "retort" will not do, representing as it does too great a degree of active mutuality for Bartleby—*reply* perhaps.

Bartleby's reduction of language is of an expressiveness literally limitless. Few characters in fiction, if indeed any exist, have been able to say all they wish in so striking, so nearly speechless a manner. The work is, of course, a sort of fable of inanition, and returning to it, as I did, mindful of the old stone historical downtown and the new, insatiable necropolis of steel and glass, lying on the vegetation of the participial *declining* this and that, I found it possible to wish that "Bartleby, the Scrivener" was just itself, a masterpiece without the challenge of its setting, Wall Street. Still, the setting does not flee the mind, even if it does not quite bind itself either, the way unloaded furniture seems immediately bound to its doors and floors.

Melville has written his story in a cheerful, confident, rather optimistic, Dickensian manner. Or at least that is the manner in which it begins. In the law office, for instance, the copyists and errand-boy are introduced with their Dickensian *tics* and their tic-names: Nippers, Turkey, and Ginger Nut. An atmosphere of comedy, of small, amusing, busy particulars, surrounds Bartleby and his large, unofficial (not suited to an office) articulations, which are nevertheless clerkly and even, perhaps, clerical.

The narrator, a mild man of the law with a mild Wall Street business, is a "rather elderly man," as he says of himself at the time of putting down his remembrances of Bartleby. On the edge of retirement, the lawyer begins to think about that "singular set of men," the law-copyists or scriveners he has known in his thirty years of practice. He notes that he has seen nothing of these men in print and, were it not for the dominating memory of Bartleby, he might have told lighthearted professional anecdotes, something perhaps like the anecdotes of servants come and gone, such as we find in the letters of Jane Carlyle, girls from the country who are not always unlike the Turkeys, Nippers, and Ginger Nuts.

The lawyer understands that no biography of Bartleby is possible because "no materials exist," and indeed the work is not a character sketch and not a section of a "life," even though it ends in death. Yet the device of memory is not quite the way it works out, because each of Bartleby's thirty-seven lines, with their riveting variations, so slight as to be almost painful to the mind taking note of them, must be produced at the right pace and accompanied by the requests that occasion them. At a certain point, Bartleby must "gently disappear behind the screen," which, in a way, is a present rather than a past. In the end, Melville's structure is magical because the lawyer creates Bartleby by *allowing* him to be, a decision of nicely unprofessional impracticality. The competent, but scarcely strenuous, office allows Bartleby, although truly the allowance arises out of the fact that the lawyer is a far better man than he knows himself to be. And he is taken by surprise to learn of his tireless curiosity about the incurious ghost, Bartleby.

The lawyer has a "snug business among rich men's bonds and mortgages and title deeds," rather than the more dramatic actions before juries (a choice that would not be defining today). He has his public sinecures and when they are officially abolished he feels a bit of chagrin, but no vehemence. He recognizes the little vanities he has accumulated along the way, one of which is that he has done business with John Jacob Astor. And he likes to utter the name "for it hath a rounded and orbicular sound to it and rings like unto bullion." These are the thoughts of a man touched by the comic spirit, the one who will be touched for the first time in his life, and by way of his dealings with Bartleby, by "overpowering, stinging melancholy ... a fraternal melancholy."

A flurry of copying demand had led the lawyer to run an advertisement which brought to his door a young man, Bartleby, a person sedate, "pallidly neat, pitiably respectable." Bartleby is taken on and placed at a desk which "originally had afforded a lateral view of certain grimy backyards and bricks, but which owing to subsequent erections, commanded at present no view at all." This is a suitable place for Bartleby, who does not require views of the outside world and who has no "views" of the other kind, that is, no opinions beyond his adamantine assertion of his own feelings, if feelings they are; he has, as soon becomes clear, his hard pebbles of response with their sumptuous, taciturn resonance.

Bartleby begins to copy without pause, as if "long famishing for something to copy." This is observed by the lawyer who also observes that he himself feels no pleasure in it since it is done "silently, palely, mechanically." On the third day of employment, Bartleby appears, the genuine Bartleby, the one who gives utterance. His first utterance is like the soul escaping from the body, as in medieval drawings.

The tedious proofreading of the clerk's copy is for accuracy done in collaboration with another person, and it is the lawyer himself who calls out to Bartleby for assistance in the task. The laconic, implacable signature is at hand, the mysterious signature that cannot be interpreted and cannot be misunderstood. Bartley replies, *I would prefer not to.*

The pretense of disbelief provides the occasion for *I would prefer not to* soon to be repeated three times and "with no uneasiness, anger, impatience or impertinence." By the singularity of refusal, the absence of "because" or of the opening up of some possibly alternating circumstance, this negative domination seizes the story like a sudden ambush in the streets.

Bartleby's "I" is of such a completeness that it does not require support. He possesses his "I" as if it were a visible part of the body, the way ordinary men possess a thumb. In his sentence he encloses his past, present, and future, himself, all there is. His statement is positive indeed and the *not* is less important than the "I," because the "not" refers to the presence of others, to the world, inevitably making suggestions the "I" does not encompass.

Bartleby would prefer not to read proof with his employer, a little later he would prefer not to examine his own quadruplicate copyings with the help of the other clerks, he would prefer not to answer or to consider that this communal proofreading is labor-saving and customary. About his "mulish vagary"—no answer.

As we read the story we are certain that, insofar as Bartleby himself is concerned, there is nothing to be thought of as "interesting" in his statement. There is no coquetry; it is merely candid, final, inflexible. Above all it is not "personal"; that is, his objection is not to the collaborators themselves and not to the activity of proofreading, indeed no more repetitive than daylong copying. The reply is not personal and it is not invested with "personality." And this the kind and now violently curious and enduring lawyer cannot believe. He will struggle throughout the tale to fill up the hole, to wonder greatly, to prod as he can, in search of "personality." And the hole, the chasm, or better the "cistern," one of the lawyer's words for the view outside Bartleby's desk, will not be filled.

What began as a comedy, a bit of genre actually, ends as tragedy. But like Bartleby himself it is difficult for the reader to supply adjectives. Is Bartleby mysterious; is his nature dark, angular, subterranean? You are deterred by Bartleby's mastery from competing with him by your command of the adjective. He is overwhelmingly affecting to the emotions of the lawyer and the reader, but there is no hint that he is occupied with lack, disuse, failure, inadequacy. If one tries to imagine Bartleby alone, without the office, what is to be imagined? True, he is always alone, in an utter loneliness that pierces the lawyer's heart when he soon finds that Bartleby has no home at all but is living in the office at night.

(No home, living in the office day and night. Here, having exempted this story from my study of Manhattanism because of its inspired occupation with an ultimate condition and its stepping aside from the garbage and shards of Manhattan history, I was stopped by this turn in the exposition. Yes, the undomesticity of a great city like New York, undomestic in the ways other cities are not—then, and still now. Bartleby, the extreme, the icon of the extreme, is not exactly living in the office. Instead he just does not leave it at the end of the day. But it is very easy to imagine from history where the clerks, Nippers and Turkey, are of an evening. They are living in lodging houses, where half of New York's population lived as late as 1841: newlyweds, families, single persons. Whitman did a lot of "boarding round," as he called it, and observed, without rebuke, or mostly without rebuke, that the boarding house led the unfamilied men to rush out after dinner to the saloon or brothel, away from the unprivate private, to the streets which are the spirit of the city, which are the lively blackmail that makes city citizens abide.

Lodgings then, and later the "divided space" of the apartment house, both expressing Manhattanism as a life lived in transition. And lived in a space that is not biography, but is to be fluent and changeable, an escape from the hometown and the homestead, an escape from the given. The rotting tenements of today are only metaphysical apartments and in deterioration take on the burdensome aspect of "homes" because they remind, in the absence of purchased maintenance, that something "homelike" may be asked of oneself and at the same time denied by the devastations coming from above, below, and next door. Manhattan, the release from the home, which is the leaking roof, the flooded basement, the garbage, and most of all the grounds, that is, surrounding nature. "After I learned about electricity I lost interest in nature. Not up-to-date enough." Mayakovsky, the poet of urbanism.

So Bartleby is found to be living in the office day and night. But Bartleby is not a true creature of Manhattan because he shuns the streets and is unmoved by the moral, religious, acute, obsessive, beautiful ideal of Consumption. Consumption is what one leaves one's "divided space" to honor, as the Muslim stops in his standing and moving to say his prayers five times a day, or is it six? But Bartleby eats only ginger-nuts and is starving himself to death. In that way he passes across one's mind like a feather, calling forth the vague Hinduism of Thoreau and the outer-world meditations of Emerson. (Thoreau, who disliked the city, any city, thought deeply about it, so deeply that in *Walden* he composed the city's most startling consummations, one of which is: "Of a life of luxury, the fruit is luxury.")

To return, what is Bartleby "thinking" about when he is alone? It is part of the perfect completeness of his presentation of himself, although he does not present himself, that one would be foolhardy to give him thoughts. They would dishonor him. So, Bartleby is not "thinking" or experiencing or longing or remembering. All one can say is that he is a master of language, of perfect expressiveness. He is style. This is shown when the lawyer tries to revise him.

On an occasion, the lawyer asks Bartleby to go on an errand to the post office. Bartleby replies that he would prefer not to. The lawyer, seeing a possibility for an entropic, involuntary movement in this mastery of meaning, proposes an italicized emendation. He is answered with an italicized insistence.

"You *will* not?"

"I *prefer* not."

What is the difference between *will not* and *prefer* not? There is no difference insofar as Bartleby's actions will be altered, but he seems to be pointing out by the italics that his preference is not under the rule of the conditional or the future tense. He does not mean to say that he prefers not, but will if he must, or if it is wished. His "I" that prefers not, will not. I do not think he has chosen the verb "prefer" in some emblematic way. That is his language and his language is what he is.

Prefer has its power, however. The nipping clerks who have been muttering that they would like to "black his eyes" or "kick him out of the office" begin, without sarcasm or mimicry, involuntarily, as it were, to say to the lawyer, "If you would prefer, Sir," and so on.

Bartleby's language reveals the all of him, but what is revealed? Character? Bartleby is not a character in the manner of the usual, imaginative, fictional construction. And he is not a character as we know them in life, with their bundling bustle of details, their suits and ties and felt hats, their love affairs surreptitious or binding, family albums, psychological justifications dragging like a little wagon along the highway of experience. We might say he is a destiny, without interruptions, revisions, second chances. But what is a destiny that is not endured by a "character"? Bartleby has no plot in his present existence, and we would not wish to imagine subplots for his already lived years. He is indeed only words, wonderful words, and very few of them. One might for a moment sink into the abyss and imagine that instead of *prefer not* he had said, "I don't want to" or "I don't feel like it." No, it is unthinkable, a vulgarization, adding truculence, idleness, foolishness, adding indeed "character" and altering a sublimity of definition.

Bartleby, the scrivener, "standing at the dead-wall window" announces that he will do no more copying. *No more.* The lawyer, marooned in the law of cause and effect, notices the appearance of eyestrain and that there is a possibility Bartleby is going blind. This is never clearly established—Melville's genius would not want at any part of the story to enter the region of sure reasons and causality.

In the midst of these peculiar colloquies, the lawyer asks Bartleby if he cannot indeed be a little reasonable here and there.

"'At present I would prefer not to be a little reasonable,' was his mildly cadaverous reply."

There is no imagining what the sudden intrusion of "at present" may signify and it seems to be just an appendage to the "I," without calling up the nonpresent, the future. From the moment of first refusal it had passed through the lawyer's mind that he might calmly and without resentment dismiss Bartleby, but he cannot, not even after "no more copying." He thinks: "I should have as soon thought of turning my pale, plaster-of-paris bust of Cicero out of doors." Ah. The "wondrous ascendancy" perhaps begins at that point, with the notion that Bartleby is a representation of life, a visage, but not the life itself.

The lawyer, overcome by pity, by troubling thoughts of human diversity, by self-analysis, goes so far as to take down from the shelf certain theological works which give him the idea that he is predestined to "have Bartleby." But as a cheerful, merely social visitor to Trinity Church, this idea does not last and indeed is too abstract because the lawyer has slowly been moving into a therapeutic role, a role in which he persists in the notion of "personality" that may be modified by patience, by suggestion, by reason.

Still, at last, it is clear that Bartleby must go, must be offered a generous bonus, every sort of accommodation and good wish. This done, the lawyer leaves in a pleasant agitation of mind, thinking of the laws of chance represented by his overhearing some betting going on in the street. Will Bartleby be there in the morning or will he at last be gone? Of course, he has remained and the offered money has not been picked up.

"Will you not quit me?"

"I would prefer *not* to quit you."

The "quitting" is to be accomplished by the lawyer's decision to "quit" himself, that is, to quit his offices for larger quarters. A new tenant is found, the boxes are packed and sent off, and Bartleby is bid good-bye. But no, the new tenants, who are not therapists, rush around to complain that he is still there and that he is not a part of their lease. They turn him out of the offices.

The lawyer goes back to the building and finds Bartleby still present, that is, sitting on the banister of the stairway in the entrance hallway.

"What are you doing here, Bartleby?"

"Sitting upon the banister."

The lawyer had meant to ask what will you do with your life, where will you go, and not, where is your body at this moment. But with Bartleby body and statement are one. Indeed the bewitching qualities, the concentrated seriousness, the genius of Bartleby's "dialogue" had long ago affected the style of the lawyer, but in the opposite direction, that is, to metaphor, arrived at by feeling. His head is full of images about the clerk and he thinks of him as "the last column of some ruined temple" and "a bit of wreck in the mid-Atlantic." And from these metaphors there can be no severance.

There with Bartleby sitting on the banister for life, as it were, the lawyer soars into the kindest of deliriums. The therapeutic wish, the beating of the wings of angels above the heads of the harassed and affectionate, unhinges his sense of the possible, the suitable, the imaginable. He begins to think of new occupations for Bartleby and it is so like the frenzied and loving moments in family life: would the pudgy, homely daughter like to comb her hair, neaten up a bit, and apply for a position as a model?—and why not, others have, and so on and so on.

The angel wings tremble and the lawyer says: "Would you like a clerkship in a dry-goods store?"

Bartleby, the unimaginable promoter of goods for sale, replies with his rapid deliberation. Slow deliberation is not necessary for one who knows the interior of his mind, as if that mind were the interior of a small, square box containing a single pair of cuff links.

To the idea of clerking in a store Bartleby at last appends a reason, one indeed of great opacity.

"There is too much confinement about that. No, I would not like a clerkship; but I am not particular."

Agitated rebuttal of "too much confinement" for one who keeps himself "confined all the time"!

Now, in gentle, coaxing hysteria, the lawyer wonders if the

bartender's business would suit Bartleby and adds that "there is no trying of the eye-sight in that."

No, Bartleby would not like that at all, even though he repeats that he is not particular.

Would Bartleby like to go about collecting bills for merchants? It would take him outdoors and be good for his health. The answer: "No, I would prefer to be doing something else."

Doing something else? That is, sitting on the banister, rather than selling dry goods, bartending, and bill collecting.

Here the lawyer seems to experience a sudden blindness, the blindness of a bright light from an oncoming car on a dark road. The bright light is the terrible clarity of Bartleby.

So, in a blind panic: "How then would be going as a companion to Europe, to entertain some young gentleman with your conversation—how would that suit you?"

"Not at all. It does not strike me that there is anything definite about that. I like to be stationary. But I am not particular."

Definite? Conversation is not definite owing to its details of style, opinion, observation, humor, pause, and resumption; and it would not be at all pleasing to Bartleby's mathematical candor. Bartleby is *definite;* conversation is not. He has said it all.

But I am not particular? This slight addition has entered Bartleby at the moment the lawyer opens his fantastical employment agency. The phrase wishes to extend the lawyer's knowledge of his client, Bartleby, and to keep him from the tedium of error. Bartleby himself is particular, in that he is indeed a thing distinguished from another. But he is not particular in being fastidious, choosey. He would like the lawyer to understand that he is not concerned with the congenial. It is not suitability he pursues; it is essence, essence beyond detail.

The new tenants have Bartleby arrested as a vagrant and sent to the Tombs. The same idea had previously occurred to the lawyer in a moment of despair, but he could not see that the immobile, unbegging Bartleby could logically be declared a vagrant. "What! He a vagrant, a wanderer that refuses to budge?"

No matter, the lawyer cannot surrender this "case," this recalcitrant object of social service, this demand made upon his heart to provide benefit, this being now in an institution, the Tombs, but not yet locked away from the salvaging sentiments of one who remembers. A prison visit is made and in his ineffable therapeutic endurance the lawyer insists there is no reason to despair, the charge is not a disgrace, and even in prison one may sometimes see the sky and a patch of green.

Bartleby, with the final sigh of one who would instruct the unin-structable, says: *I know where I am.*

In a last urging, on his knees as it were, the lawyer desires to purchase extra food to add to the prison fare.

Bartleby: "I would prefer not to dine today. It would disagree with me; I am unused to dinners." And thus he dies.

Not quite the end for the lawyer with his compassion, his need to unearth some scrap of buried "personality," or private history. We have the beautiful coda Melville has written, a marvelous moment of com-position, but perhaps too symbolical, too poetically signifying to be the epitaph of Bartleby. Yet he must be run down, if only to honor the graceful curiosity and the insatiable charity of the lawyer. He reports a rumor:

> The report was this: that Bartleby had been a subordinate clerk in the Dead Letter Office at Washington, from which he had been suddenly removed by a change in administration.... Dead letters! Does it not sound like dead men? Conceive a man by nature and misfortune prone to a pallid hopelessness, can any business seem more fitted to heighten it than that of continually handling these dead letters, and assorting them for the flames?... On errands of life, these letters sped to death.... Ah, Bartleby! Ah, humanity!

Bartleby in a sense is the underside of Billy Budd, but they are not opposites. Billy, the Handsome Sailor, the "Apollo with a portmanteau," the angel, "our beauty," the sunny day, and the unaccountable goodness, which is with him a sort of beautiful "innate disorder," such as the "innate, incurable disorder" represented by Bartleby. Neither of these curious creations knows resentment or grievance; they know nothing of pride, envy, or greed. There is a transcendent harmony in Billy Budd, and a terrifying, pure harmony in the tides of negation that define Bartleby. Billy, the lovely product of nature and, of course, not a perfection of ongoing citizen life, has a "vocal defect," the tendency to stutter at times of stress. By way of this defect, he goes to his death by hanging. Bartleby in no way has a vocal defect; indeed the claim this remarkable creation of American literature makes on our feelings lies entirely in his incomparable self-expression.

So, this bit of old New York, the sepia, horsecar Manhattan, Wall Street. Bartleby and the god-blessed lawyer. They were created by Melville before the Civil War and were coeval with John Jacob Astor's old age and the prime of Cornelius Vanderbilt. And yet here they are, strange apparitions in the metonymic Wall Street district where the exertions, as described by Mark Twain, were, "A year ago I didn't have a penny, and now I owe you a million dollars."

Looking down, or looking up, today at the sulky twin towers of the World Trade Center, "all shaft," the architects say, thinking of those towers as great sightless Brahmins brooding upon the absolute and the all-embracing spirit, it seemed to me that down below there is something of Manhattan in Bartleby and especially in his resistance to amelioration. His being stirs the water of pity, and we can imagine that the little boats that row about him throwing out ropes of personal charity or bureaucratic provision for his "case" may grow weary and move back to the shore in a mood of frustration and, finally, forgetfulness.

There is Manhattanism in the bafflement Bartleby represents to the alive and steady conscience of the lawyer who keeps going on and on in his old democratic, consecrated endurance—going on, even down to the Tombs, and at last to the tomb. If Bartleby is unsaveable, at least the lawyer's soul may be said to have been saved by the freeze of "fraternal melancholy" that swept over him from the fate he had placed at the desk beside him in a little corner of Wall Street. It is not thought that many "downtown" today would wish to profit from, oh, such a chill.

1981

KATHERINE ANNE PORTER

KATHERINE Anne Porter died at the age of ninety. She had one of those very long lives the sickly, with their bronchial troubles and early threats of tuberculosis, achieve as a surprise to us and perhaps to themselves. It was just two years ago, in September 1980, that she died and now we have a biography devoted to this long life.

Biographers, the quick in pursuit of the dead, research, organize, fill in, contradict, and make in this way a sort of completed picture puzzle with all the scramble turned into a blue eye and the parts of the right leg fitted together. They also make a consistent fiction, the fiction being the arrangement, artful or clumsy, of the documents. Biography casts a chill over the late years of some writers and, perhaps from their reading the lives of those they had known in the too solid flesh, has often provoked the insistent wish that no life be written. Among those who wished for no life after life were W. H. Auden, George Orwell, and T. S. Eliot. The result has been two lives already of Auden and Orwell, and Eliot's life is in the making, waiting to be lived again by way of the flowing bloodstream of documentation.

Sometimes very fine writers and scholars undertake biographies, and their productions have at least some claim to equity between the subject and the person putting on the shoes. Others hope to establish credentials previously lacking by hard work on the abounding materials left by a creative life. In any case, a biography appears to be thought of as a good project, one that can at the very least be accomplished by industry. And if there is a lot of busywork in it—many visits to the libraries, a store of taped interviews, and, of course, the "evidence" of the writer's work itself (the last rather a difficulty since it is not precisely to be understood by research)—the book gets written, and the "life of" is, so to speak, born.

In her eighty-sixth year, Katherine Anne Porter appointed Joan Givner to undertake the re-creation of her many decades. The biographer might be thought to be in luck since Miss Porter advised her to "get at the truth," an always murky command when ordered on one's own behalf. The real luck about the truth turned out to be that the distinguished writer was unusually inclined to fabrication about her past. These fabrications, dashing often and scarcely news and only mildly discrediting, seem to be the driving engine behind Joan Givner's accumulation of the facts of life.

How certain human beings are able to create works of art is a mystery, and why they should wish to do so, at a great cost to themselves usually, is another mystery. Works are not created by one's life; every life is rich in *material*. By the nature of the enterprise, the contemporary biographer with his surf of Xerox papers is doing something smaller and yet strikingly more detailed than the great Victorian laborers in the form. Our power of documentation has a monstrous life of its own, a greater vivacity than any lived existence. It makes form out of particles and finds attitude in a remembered drunken remark as easily as in a long contemplation of experience—more easily in fact. It creates out of paper a heavy, obdurate permanency. Threats to its permanency will come only by way of other bits of paper, a footnote coup d'état. No matter—a territory once colonized in this way has had its indigenous landscape and culture put to the heel.

In Joan Givner's book, the root biographical facts have the effect of a crushing army. Everything is underfoot. Each character and each scene of Miss Porter's fiction is looked upon as a factuality honored by its provenance as autobiography. And separate fictions are mashed together as bits of the life recur or are suggested in different works. Miss Porter, in a manner impertinently thought of as dilatory, did not often translate experience in a sequential fashion. So she is writing "Hacienda" while she is "living" "The Leaning Tower." She is boarding the ship of fools before the Mexican stories have been accomplished. It is something of a tangle to get this particular life and its laggard production into time slots, and the result is an incoherence in regard to the work. Information about when each story was actually completed, when published and where, is lost in the anecdote of days and nights. No doubt the information is somewhere among the pages, but it is a slogging task to dig it out.

The life—some scandal and a considerable amount of folly: Katherine Anne Porter was born in a log cabin in Texas and grew up in hardship without a really good education. She knew a genuine struggle to provide for herself and slowly to define herself. Gradually, along the way, after her stories became known, she slipped into being a Southern belle and into being to some extent a Southern writer after "Flowering Judas." The role was there for the choosing since to be a belle and to be a Southern writer is a decision, not a fate. (Poe, for instance, was a Southerner but not a Southern writer.) Perhaps under the influence of the very talented Southern Agrarians—Allen Tate, Caroline Gordon, and others—she began to appropriate a rather frantic genealogy of Daniel Boone and certain Southern statesmen; in addition, she developed some soothing memories of plantation dining rooms, "several Negro servants, among them two aged former slaves," and so on. In this way, she filled in the gap between what she was and what she felt like.

She was handy, too, in disposing of the traces of her various mismatings, the first a marriage at sixteen. "I have no hidden husbands," she once said. "They just slipped my mind." She was beautiful, a spendthrift, an alert coquette, and, since she lived long, a good many of her lovers and three of her husbands were younger than she was. She lopped off a few years here and there. The book goes into a determined sorting out, and the husbands are lined up, the years restored.

Her serious work was slow in coming about because of a scratchy, hard life after she literally ran away from her first husband—just ran off, as they say. She tried acting, did very provincial newspaper work and finally got a job on *The Denver Post*. Everything was hard, poorly paid, hand-to-mouth. During this period, she seems quite Western or Middle Western, like someone in a Willa Cather story trying to find the way out. Her story "Maria Concepción" was published when she was thirty-four, and her first book, *Flowering Judas*, appeared when she was forty. Fortunately for her future work, she went to Mexico as a reporter; she was in and out of Greenwich Village, where she met writers and no doubt increased her sophistication about literature and the act of writing.

At this point, the shape of her life falls into a sort of twenties pattern. She went to France and to Germany with her third husband, Eugene Pressly—her second husband, a person named Ernest Stock, "deadly Ernest," as she called him, having been run away from while he was sleeping. In Mexico, she met the Russian film director Eisenstein; in Germany in 1932 she met Göring; in Paris, she met Hemingway. Eisenstein became Uspensky in "Hacienda," the ship upon which she traveled from Mexico to Germany became the *Vera* in *Ship of Fools*. In Berlin, she stayed on alone, having encouraged Pressly to return to America for a holiday without her. She never liked the constant presence of her husbands or lovers and did not like, she soon found out, to be alone—a dilemma in one shape or another common to most of mankind. The pension where she stayed in Germany went, with little need for renovation, into "The Leaning Tower."

Research finds that in Germany, Katherine Anne Porter did not always conduct herself with generosity or moral refinement. She had a young friend, Herb Klein, a newspaper reporter, who tells years later of her leaving a seamstress without paying for a dress she had ordered—leaving the dress, too—and in this way embarrassing Klein's mother, who had brought the two together. He also discredits her claim to have met Hitler and feels strongly that she did not move widely or knowledgeably about the Germany of the time. So, a little more unstitching of the embroidery here.

Also, and again many decades later, she made in an interview slanderous, nasty remarks about Sigrid Schultz, a reporter in Berlin in the thirties for *The Chicago Tribune*. All of this, no doubt rightly, brings on a fit of temper by the biographer, who finds that the German experience, as the chapter is called, "forms a dismal record of cheating, lying, slander and malice." She sees ruthlessness, alienation (?), and brutality at the "beginning of her fifth decade." Garrulousness and a certain untidiness in 1932 are excavated and rebuked in 1982, showing at least one of the dangers of living. The celebrated do not understand that they are chatting away in a bugged universe.

The few times in the biography that a particular work comes under Joan Givner's critical scrutiny—divorced for the moment from her main concern, which is the presumed umbilical attachment of life and fiction—the same inclination to outrage flares up. She finds Braggioni, the revolutionary in "Flowering Judas," to be a "complete caricature." She adds that he "looms in the story like a grotesque Easter egg in shades of purple and yellow."

Katherine Anne Porter wrote:

> He bulges marvelously in his expensive garments. Over his lavender collar, crushed under a purple necktie, held by a diamond hoop; over his ammunition belt of tooled leather worked in silver, buckled crudely around his gasping middle; over the tops of glossy yellow shoes Braggioni swells with ominous ripeness.

So, the animadversion of the biographer is not quite to the descriptive point. And to be a revolutionary is in some sense to assume a pose. Costume, gesture, personal style, slogan, poster become personification of idea, especially in Latin America.

Perhaps in this remarkable early story, the pure, tasteful, puritan elegance of the American girl, Laura, is somewhat extended beyond credibility. Yet this girl, who has been born a Catholic and is now living among the Mexican revolutionaries, provides an outstanding instance of the magical detail that gives the stories their preeminence.

Laura sometimes slips into church, but no suitable emotions come to her. "It is no good and she ends by examining the altar with its tinsel flowers and ragged brocades, and feels tender about the battered doll-shape of some male saint whose white, lace-trimmed drawers hang limply around his ankles below the hieratic dignity of his velvet robe." It is not always clear that the biographer understands the elegance of the prose. Instead, she knows from her file cabinet that it was Mary Doherty, an interesting radical living in Mexico, who was probably the model for Laura.

On the subject of Adam, the young soldier in *Pale Horse, Pale Rider*, Mrs. Givner is also casually dismissive: "An insubstantial figure, completely lacking in vivid details and turns of phrase that usually animate the characters based on people whom Porter knew." "Completely" implies the self-evident in what is a sketchy opinion. The young soldier who is to die of influenza after looking after and being enchanted by the infected Miranda—who does not die but recovers—is necessary to the structure of the story. He serves it well by the charm of his dialogue; the irony of the romantic, accommodating American gives a tragic force to this thoughtful creation about a moment in history, the devastating influenza epidemic of 1918.

The influenza epidemic, Mexico in the days of the Revolution and after, the feeling of World War I, Berlin in the thirties, the Irish in America: The situations in Katherine Anne Porter's stories show the unexpected felicities of "homelessness." Afterward, she came to disown the log cabin that sent her out to the highway, and she fell back, still with her stylistic gracefulness, on nostalgia and memory, or the aura of it, of a more traditional kind.

In what are called the "Miranda" stories, Miranda seems to stand for the author's sensibility, if not for the actual author. These stories often combine scenes contemporary with Miranda's (Porter's) life mixed with family anecdotes about dead relations—the "old order." The old order is a cavalier landscape of powerful grandmothers; a former slave, Old Nannie; the scandalous, bewitching Aunt Amy; the little girls, Miranda and her sister; their attractive father who reads from Spenser, Shakespeare, and Dante and brightens their childhood with prints from Dürer and Holbein—all the pleasant baggage, supposedly, of the old Southern aristocracy. It does not seem to the point that this was not the author's life, that it is a burial of the detested log cabin in which she was born. The eye that looks across the track might be dangerous to Southern presumption, but what we have so often in the "old order" work is an eye that is too readily assimilating. Miranda's present is nearly always more vivid and original than her past. The present is harder, more shaded with sadness and uneasy defiance, and in the long run more genuinely dramatic. "Old Mortality" is elevated as a conception by the bitter alcoholic collapse of Uncle Gabriel, his decline into a brilliantly observed social seediness by way of his hysterical, misplaced hopes at the racetrack.

"Noon Wine" is a success indeed, a story of plot, a sort of realistic tale, tightly composed in the manner of *Ethan Frome*. In this story, felt to be odd because of the backwoods setting, there is no doubt that Porter knows where she is. She knows in transfiguring detail what a dairy farm is like. "The churn rumbling and swished like a belly of a trotting horse." And hens "dying of croup and wry-neck and getting plagues of chicken lice; laying eggs all over God's creation so that half of them were spoiled before a man could find them, in spite of a rack of nests." If this knowledge came from the time she lived on a relative's farm outside Buda, Texas, and from certain characteristics in the dairy farmer, Mr. Thompson, that can be traced to her own father— "ambivalence" toward whom figures gravely in the biographer's grave quilt of patches—that is only the beginning. The story has its roots in pioneer and rural American fiction and even in Faulkner. The ancestry of literature is, of course, another story of kinfolk.

Katherine Anne Porter, from the first appearance of her stories, made her mark and impressed other writers by the way she wrote. It is not easy to define her purity of style. The writing is not plain, and yet it is not especially decorative either; instead, it is clear, fluent, almost untroubled. Everything necessary seems at hand: language and scenery, psychology and memory, and a bright aesthetic intelligence that shapes the whole. Sometimes she claimed to have written certain stories at one sitting, but it is known that many were started and abandoned, taken up again and made into something new. She was dilatory perhaps, but the completed work as we now have it does not reveal any deformation of character, and indeed is expansive enough in theme and achievement to satisfy the claims of her high reputation. She was very vain as a beauty and just as vain as a writer, and this latter vanity perhaps accounted for a good deal of the waiting and stalling, a stalling filled with romantic diversions.

Joan Givner, throughout, sees what are often creative problems as problems of life, usually linked to an unsteady childhood that weeps its lacks and resentments right up to the age of ninety. In the case of a complicated egoist like Katherine Anne Porter, the biographer is altogether too insistent upon the writer's "longing for love." A typical passage reads: "It should be remembered, however, that Porter's need for love was far beyond the ordinary, a desperate, compulsive need inspired by the nagging, ever present sense of her deficiencies." The biographer's rather smug provincialism distorts the worldly and amusing mishaps of a woman who was not made for marriage and thus married four times. It is agreeable to come upon the writer's sniffs in the midst of the biographer's rampaging "longings" and doubts of "self-worth." When she happened to remember the fiftieth anniversary of her first marriage, Miss Porter observed that the fiftieth was a lot more pleasant than the first.

Ship of Fools was a long novel and long in the making: from 1941 to 1961. The book made over a million dollars and, of course, for poor Miranda that made a difference. Its reception was very favorable at the beginning, but thereafter followed some fierce reservations. The setting of the book is 1931, a ship going from Vera Cruz to Bremen with a passenger list very long and outlandishly challenging. A fixed arena in which persons who would not ordinarily meet can be realistically gathered together would seem to be a gift of structure, in the manner of large hotels or prison camps or hospitals. But the gift of this natural and ordained diversity is claustrophobic, like a sea journey itself. Characters are given their traits, their tics of manner, their past histories. But then they are trapped in them in the dining room, on the deck, in the bar. Diversions of distress or comedy are offered with great skill, but the sea rolls on and the characters roll on, clutching their gestures.

The significant promise of the novel lies in the date and destination: It is 1931, and the boat is on the way to Germany, carrying with it Germans who must somehow prefigure what is to come by way of German arrogance and moral limitation, what is to come for the poorly conceived solitary Jew—an unattractive man who makes his living selling Christian religious objects—and what is to come for the German whose wife is Jewish but scarcely knows it, an assimilated person answering to the name of Mary. The historical promise is too pressing for the imagination in the novel. All is too static, and the implied parable is never quite achieved. There is something a little musty, like old yellowing notes. The flawless execution of the single scenes impresses, and yet the novel remains too snug and shipshape for the waters of history.

With the publication of *Ship of Fools*, Katherine Anne Porter was past seventy, but since she was to live twenty more years, there was time for a daunting accretion of foolishness. She can fight with faithful friends and relatives, she can spend, she can fall in love, she can drink too much, she can buy a large emerald ring, a "longing" from which she did not run away. She also has time for her increasing anti-Semitism: "Everybody except the Jews knows the Jews are not chosen but are a lot of noisy, arrogant, stupid, pretentious people and then what?" She pronounced on desegregation, leading her close friend Glenway Wescott to declare that "her poor brain is just simply one seething smoking mass of molten lava."

Biographies inevitably record the demeaning moments of malice and decline and have the effect of imprinting them upon the ninety years. In the biographies of today, all things are equal except that the ill winds tend in interest to be—well, more interesting.

Katherine Anne Porter did not have a happy life. She was better at sloughing off love than retaining it. She was often lonely in between her rushes to attachments. Her egotism was disabling. Throughout her life, the most useful condition for her work and for her sense of things came from the part of her that was an audacious, immensely gifted, independent Sister Carrie who knew about poverty and rooming houses and bad marriages and standing alone. The folly of the claim to represent somehow an aristocratic example of taste and moral excellence was not wisdom but just the downward path.

The ending of the biography, a flourish, is an unhappy image of the limitations of the method of composition. It reads: "At the very end she lay, like La Condesa on the *Vera*, drugged and demented, bereft of her home and jewels, but defiant until the last moment when on September 18, 1980, the little point of light flickered and failed." The truth is that Katherine Anne Porter was drugged and demented from strokes and the ghastly illnesses of extreme old age. It is not a useful summarizing sentiment to think of her as a fiction, just as it has not been altogether wise to think of her fiction as her life, or for that matter "the life of" as precisely her life.

1982

SONS OF THE CITY'S PAVEMENTS
Delmore Schwartz

THE POET Delmore Schwartz died in 1966, almost twenty years ago. He was fifty-three years old; not a generous life span, but, as he might have said, one year longer than that of Shakespeare. Schwartz has not been forgotten, far from it. Robert Phillips has produced this excellent edition of Schwartz's correspondence. It follows the appearance of the selected essays and the collection of the last poems, and thus it seems we now have the whole of the writings.

His life story and its relation to his work have been told in the careful and fair-minded biography by James Atlas (1977). Schwartz casts a long shadow in *The Truants*, an autobiographical work by the philosopher William Barrett, an early friend and a late, if not quite friend, perplexed connection. William Phillips, editor of *Partisan Review* and a memorialist of the fifty years of the magazine, tells of his personal and professional relation to "Delmore," as it was natural to everyone, acquainted or not, to call him because of his own delight in the pretty challenge of his first name.

Schwartz made a dramatic appearance on the literary scene in 1937, when he was twenty-four years old, by publishing his most striking creative achievement, the fiction "In Dreams Begin Responsibilities." And his end was unfortunately dramatic also. He had a lonely, tragic death by heart attack in the halls of a run-down hotel in Times Square.

Perhaps it is unfairly vivid that the flow of his life took on a kind of iconographic summation in the endurance of his photographic image. As a young poet, he greatly resembled Pasternak, who, as Marina Tsvetaeva said, looked like an Arab and his horse. At the end he is caught by the camera when he is sitting alone on a park bench, his eyes focused sharply aside, as if in a raging suspiciousness, and his body sadly coarsened. The last years were forlorn and forbidding, not very different from the ruin of many another wandering about the streets. More healthful might have been a quiet removal, something like that of the deranged German poet Hölderlin, living in the family of a devoted carpenter and, all the while, majestically bowing to his imaginary subjects. But Schwartz was irredeemably urban and New York City at that; also poor at the end and given by paranoia to the shedding of friends and wives, angrily plucking them off like flies on the worn threads of his jacket.

The letters begin outside the family, since those to mother, father, and brother, Kenneth, have not survived. It is 1931 and Delmore has gone to the University of Wisconsin, his first escape from Brooklyn and the Washington Heights section of Manhattan. He writes to Julian Sawyer, a high school friend. Mr. Atlas describes Sawyer as an esthete, an enraptured, theatrical young man who went to the dock when Gertrude Stein first returned to America, and "fell to his knees." He could quote "the whole of any Garbo script at will," and liked to perform all the parts of *Four Saints in Three Acts* and *The Cocktail Party*. We see in this friend that indispensable other so longed for in youth, and inevitably one less serious, less learned, less gifted than the imperious master, Delmore, who was only eighteen when the letters begin.

The youthful letters are more lyrical and more exposing than the best of the later years. They are rich in exalted ambition, the agitated, opinionated, tireless reading of a mind already concentrated upon the challenge of literature. Also, the spendthrift, self-dramatizing inclination is full-blown, the unsteadiness of a displaced son of the Jewish middle class. Delmore's father was somewhat flashily successful as a business man, but the parents were divorced, the mother hysterical and unforgiving: the promised legacy to come at the father's death did not arrive, but remained, nevertheless, a taunting, maddening birthright denied.

In the valuable letters to Sawyer, Schwartz enters the "whole provincial collegiate world," and because it is Wisconsin it is, to this son of the pavements, the surprising world of nature, "the woods full of fresh-water brooks, springs and creeks, deer, too, and rabbits, squirrels. And the long quiet streets, tree-lined (tall trees!), New England white houses." Such is the backdrop, although not long to be considered. Instead, Delmore is immediately recognized as a formidable intellectual and a group forms around him that looks to him for "authority."

The letters reveal the almost helpless fascination with his own character, and tenacious the absorption was to be. He is confident enough to see himself as the object of love and also confident enough to caution Julian against counting upon him too greatly. "I always cause those who are near to me more suffering than pleasure." He is gossipy about the great, insofar as he knows about them from hearsay and from books. He begins to drink alcohol in the collegiate manner, without ceasing to drink from the spring of Stendhal "whose taste is of a coolness." He is rebuked by the threat of a poor grade (C) for refusing to write a paper on Stephen Vincent Benet's long poem, "John Brown's Body"; but he floors them, so to speak, by the substitution of "an essay on Paul Valéry, making fifteen quotations in French." Feeling his awkwardness and bursts of aggression, he wishes to study gracefulness so that "life may be a poem." He is a success, he is somebody in the classrooms and yet, " 'Tis bitter chill, and I am sick and hurt."

Thus, here is the man, Delmore Schwartz, a troubled prodigy who is to become, in Karl Shapiro's interesting and emotionally charged foreword, "the touchstone of his generation." We do not have any more communications with Julian Sawyer and the scene changes the following year to New York University, then to Harvard as a graduate student in philosophy, back to New York and beginning to publish, marriage, Harvard once more as a teacher, on and on in the literary and academic world.

The cast of the letters becomes then confined to the friendships and occasions of a career among the well known. There is correspondence with his first wife, Gertrude Buckman, and a few letters to his second wife, Elizabeth Pollet, and to four or five scattered others; for the rest, it is fellow-writers, editors, publishers, professors, almost all of them hyphenated beings, writer-editor, poet-professor, like Schwartz himself.

The most impressive of the letters concern poetry and the occasion is often the disputes or rebuttals arising out of Schwartz's brilliant critical essays on the most intimidating masters of his time—Hart Crane, R. P. Blackmur, Eliot, Auden, Allen Tate, Edmund Wilson, Wallace Stevens, Yvor Winters, and the masters of comedy, W. C. Fields and Ring Lardner. To Philip Horton, the author of a popular biography of Hart Crane, he writes about the famous line from "The Bridge," "Oh thou steeled Cognizance whose leap commits..." that a bridge cannot have cognizance or be cognizance and "...you seem to have answered that such attributions were merely symbols—of whose cognizance is the bridge a symbol?" And the thoughts linger over a line in a letter to Allen Tate: "I think I can show clearly that Blackmur misunderstands Santayana exactly when Santayana is himself engaged in misunderstanding something."

Philip Rahv, in a review of Schwartz's critical essays, suggests that their power and genuineness lay in the fact that, in this form, the author was not so nerve-wrung about "greatness" as he was as a poet and short-story writer. Two letters to Ezra Pound bear on this precocious and unpretentious critical discrimination. They also show a valiant and disinterested attention to important texts.

The first letter, from 1938, came about because of an essay on Pound Schwartz published in *Poetry* magazine. He was then only twenty-five. The essay is a tribute to Pound as a tireless salesman and patron of the best writing of his day; it is also a careful tribute to the prodigious talent and originality of Pound's own poetry. "An enormous transformation of sensibility has occurred since the printing of the first volume of 'Personae,' and no man can have had more to do with this transformation than Ezra Pound." Schwartz insists upon the pleasures of *The Cantos* and does not find the quantities of obscure information and quotation to be so great a "handicap and burden as one might suppose." On the other hand, the absence of a narrative structure means that the work is "many surfaces, presented with great exactitude but with nothing behind them." Schwartz will not concede to Pound a greatness equal to Shakespeare, the *Iliad*, and *The Divine Comedy*.

By letter Pound takes up the animadversions in his characteristic jocular diction. "Suppose you Read some of these writers before telling grandpa he ain't been fotographed in his dress suit." Schwartz replies with an intense insistence on the presence of a narrative structure in

The Divine Comedy, which Pound has denied, seeing the progress from hell to paradise as only a "scheme of values / merely a walk upstairs to a balloon landing." And Schwartz insists once more on the contrast between what one gets in Dante, Shakespeare, and Homer and what one gets in *The Cantos*, "the correlative lack." The correspondence on Schwartz's part is altogether respectful, even reverent, but not conceding.

A year later, 1939, Schwartz writes Pound once more. He has just read "Culture." "Here I find numerous remarks about the Semite or Jewish race, all of them damning.... A race cannot commit a moral act. Only an individual can be moral or immoral. No generalization from a sum of particulars is possible, which will render a moral judgment ... I should like you to consider this letter as a resignation: I want to resign as one of your most studious and faithful admirers." It is interesting to note another essay on Pound, written twenty-two years later. Schwartz examines with distaste the improbabilities in the echoing chambers of Pound's mind, but a book is an object in the world and not an exact equivalent of the whole person. The essay ends: "The first and most important thing to say about Pound's *Cantos* is that they ought to be read again and again by anyone interested in any form of literature."

One pauses over the Pound letters because there is in them a narrative of cause and effect, completely literary. And yet there are almost no letters in the volume that do not arise from the liking or not liking a poem by a friend or colleague, or from the murky snubs and rocky alliances of the academy. Most of all, the letters are called upon to display the gifts necessary to an editor; that is, evading, delaying, sliding, balancing friendship, courtesy, and prudence against what are seen to be the immediate needs and possibilities of a periodical. In the case of Schwartz, *Partisan Review* was seen, and especially by poets, as an instrument of power. Mr. Shapiro stresses this in his foreword: "Acceptance in *PR* was acclamation; it conferred a special ideological status on the accepted."

A frenzy about teaching positions goes throughout the life and the letters. From Harvard, to Dwight Macdonald: "Everything is very difficult right now for me. My job hangs in the balance, my mind is empty...." If one follows the years along with the biography by James Atlas, it will be seen that for the most part the universities were tolerant, even sacrificial, especially the University of Syracuse, the last post.

Malice thrives in the academy and in the beehive interstices of the creative life in a metropolis; it is only in large cities that there is something called the "art world" or "the literary world." There is plenty of malice in the letters written by Delmore Schwartz, most of it amusing, except to the object.

Schwartz addresses himself to Tate, Berryman, Mark Van Doren, and many others. The letters are always interesting, but perhaps only a colleague can decode the fever about reviews, what appeared here and what there. They show a powerful soul of a certain shape, but are not at all like the undisciplined, evocative, unexpected letters of, for instance, Hart Crane. For one thing, Delmore never went anywhere; and did not travel much in his Concord, downtown New York.

Amazingly for one of his generation, Schwartz added amphetamines and tranquilizers in great quantity to his lifelong heavy drinking. During his last years he was a heartbreaking puzzle. The physical deterioration might have been endured with pity and respect by his friends, but the development of his paranoid derangements of the most assaultive kind made many friends flee and others despair of offering help. These distresses are only skimpily represented by his surviving letters. No doubt it is just as well since the final two are answers to creditors, one to a landlady and the other to a doctor.

1984

THE MAGICAL PROSE OF POETS
Elizabeth Bishop

OVER THE years, Elizabeth Bishop, the poet, wrote a number of short stories, several portraits (one of Marianne Moore and another of a primitive painter living in Key West), several descriptive pieces set in Brazil, and an introduction to her translation from the Portuguese of *The Diary of "Helena Morley."* All are now in *The Collected Prose*, edited and introduced by her publisher, Robert Giroux. Herein one will find Elizabeth Bishop's mastery of a moderate tone, even in the most searing fictions based upon painful recollections of her early life. One will note the characteristic curiosity, in her case often a curiosity about the curious, and it will be muted, as in her poems, by a respect and tolerance for what the curiosity discovers. There is also, here and there, the unusual visual sharpness that prompts her to challenge, as in a duel, the expected adjectives of description. She finds the words to make her victory convincing.

I remember when "In Prison" appeared in *Partisan Review* in 1938. This story, or prose reflection, was immediately famous, if such a claim is possible for a single short work appearing in a small magazine. But those were smaller times, the skyline was not so tall, and fame did not demand the most intensive exploitation of available space. So you were not likely to forget "In Prison" and the chain-gang men sometimes at home for the weekend and *their striped trousers hanging on the wash line.*

Poets can, of course, write prose. They can write it as well as or ill as they write verse, although I think certain slothful and not very intelligent poets are more daring in mediocrity when they write prose, the prose of a review for instance. Sometimes these items on the passing scene show a distraction about word and idea more suitable to the

THE MAGICAL PROSE OF POETS · 351

shooing away of the family dog than to a compositional task. Still, when the habit of poetry exists, it will usually invade the poet's prose with a natural suffusion of its peculiar ways. Some have the two talents in a sort of separation. D. H. Lawrence and Thomas Hardy write novels, it seems to me, as novelists—that is, not as poets. Their great production, their themes and ideas, their stories chosen to dramatize a particular history and at the same time to speak of the general fate of human beings: All of this attests to a primary gift for fiction, a conquest of the form so abundant as to seem predestined. They could not refuse to be fiction writers any more than they could refuse to be poets. In their novels we will notice that the thorn of a rose will draw blood at the moment of first love, that the howl of a vicious, virile rabbit will ignite the emotions of a man and woman hesitating in the field. The metaphorical concentrations of poetry quietly seep into the rush and flow of the narration. And yet, neither Hardy nor Lawrence lingered long enough to summon the vast "poetic effects" of Joyce and Proust.

Nothing is more striking to me than the casual prose of poets, with its quick and dashing informality, its mastery of the sudden and offhand, the free and thrown away. "The wretched, fishing jealousies of Leontes." *Fishing*? Yes. That is Coleridge. Corbière's "mild waterfront sensuality"—the words are Laforgue's. Thinking about Mayakovsky's working-class dress, Pasternak saw it not as an affront to the respectable but as a warning to the "black velvet" of Mayakovsky's talent. Protesting the Russian Symbolist's use of images and sets of images as if they were so many handy kitchen utensils, Mandelstam cried out (or so it seems on the page) that an image was inappropriate for everyday use, "just as an icon lamp would be inappropriate for lighting a cigarette."

Elizabeth Bishop's prose, as we read it collected and whole, gives me the idea that she set about the writing as an enterprise, something she would do from time to time with the prose part of her mind. It was the same mind that wrote the poems, but that does not alter the fact that certain of her stories were composed in the generally acceptable manner of the time. I think particularly of "The Baptism," "The Farmer's Children," "Gwendolyn," and "The Housekeeper." I notice that each appeared in due course in such places as *Harper's Bazaar* and

The New Yorker, and were reprinted in the "Best" collections of the year.

These stories are a skillful blending of the parts; they know how to give information, how to dramatize a scene, and how to reach the popular drift of "epiphany" at the end. (Perhaps only a poet could have loved Gwendolyn for her beautiful name: "Its dactyl trisyllables could have gone on forever so far as I was concerned.") The stories are genuine. You learn from them, and your emotions are solicited by the fate of the characters and the construction of the scene. They are fine examples of the kind of fiction still offered weekly and monthly by the more thoughtful magazines and indicate to me that Elizabeth Bishop certainly could have been a fiction writer had she wished it.

Little in that to amaze. What is startling, on the other hand, is that her best prose fictions ("The Sea and Its Shore," "In Prison," "In the Village") are aesthetically radical, rich, and new in conception and tone. They are "experimental," as we used to say. In the late 1930s, the fiction in the little magazines often struggled with the challenge of Kafka. It was possible to come up with an abstract and fixed situation of interest, but to uncover the mobility of the abstract is a rare gift. The static must move the mind, the invention, in a swirl of significance both intellectual and emotional. Much must happen from the point of stasis, otherwise there is a nullity, and with so much stripped away there is boredom.

"The Sea and Its Shore" is a magical instance of creative invention. A man, with no biography, is hired to keep the beach free of paper. For this purpose, he is given a stick with a nail set in the end, a wire basket in which to burn the day's trash, and a little house, a primitive beach shelter. Gradually, he begins to read the scraps of paper, to be knowledgeable about what the different kinds look like, the quality of the sheets wet and dry and, of course, the garbled messages on the crumpled sheets. He watches the paper blown about by the wind: "The papers had no discernible goal, no brain, no feeling of race or group. They soared up, fell down, could not decide, hesitated, subsided." As he read the "insect armies of type," everything seemed to become print, the whole world. A sandpiper, rushing here and there, looked like a "point of punctuation." Finally, everything must be burned since "burning

paper was his occupation." This little treatise and speculation on floating print, wind-tossed paper, fragments of literature, printed letters,
nonsense, mysterious truncations, arrives from the wonderfully resonant
center of the given idea. The contemplation of the prodigality and
expendability of print by way of the man on the beach and his stick
with the nail in it is a pure and serene fiction exemplifying what we
mean by inspiration.

Two stories are of great autobiographical interest and one, "In the
Village," is a brilliant modern short story. The first, "The Country
Mouse," was left unpublished, although it is a finished work. It is not
more revealing and heartbreaking than the other; one might wonder
why it was withheld.

Elizabeth Bishop was born in 1911 in Worcester, Massachusetts.
Her father died less than a year after her birth. Her mother, from Nova
Scotia, suffered a mental collapse, which finally became permanent when
the child was only five years old. From the death of her father up until
the age of seven, Elizabeth Bishop lived with her mother's family in
Nova Scotia. At the age of seven, she was suddenly removed to Worcester, to the father's family, taken from a simple farm and small maritime
village to the well-to-do manufacturing Bishops of Massachusetts.

"The Country Mouse" tells of this removal. "I had been brought
back unconsulted and against my wishes to the house my father had
been born in, to be saved from a life of poverty and provincialism, bare
feet, suet puddings, unsanitary school slates." In her new home, she
was miserable and felt much like the nervous, troublesome family dog,
Beppo. The last paragraph of the story underlines the year 1918, the
recognition that she at seven years was doomed to her identity, to her
"I, I, I," as a poem has it. The story ends: "Why was I a human being?"

"In the Village" tells of the mother's return from the mental hospital when the girl is five years old. A seamstress is brought in to make
a new dress that will signify the end of the black-and-white mourning
clothes. In the midst of the fitting, the mother screams, the scream of
a new collapse and the destruction of hope. "A scream, the echo of a
scream, hangs over that Nova Scotian village. No one hears it; it hangs
there forever, a slight stain in those pure blue skies."

The story then becomes something else, a brilliant rendering and ordering of certain fresh fictional possibilities. It becomes a sort of sonata of sounds filled with emotions for the child. The scream is balanced by the sound of Nate, the blacksmith, at his anvil. "*Clang.* The pure note: pure and angelic." Another sound enters like a patch of color on a canvas. *Whack.* The little girl is taking the family cow through the village to a grazing space. *Whack* goes the child's directing stick when the cow meanders about and must be gently brought into line.

The child passes by the village houses, one of them the house of Mr. McLean. (I note that is the name of the Boston hospital where the mother of "the scream" is confined until her death, but no significance attaches since Mr. McLean is a wholesome figure in the village scene.) His old dog, Jock, is, in italics, *deaf as a post.* The sweet sounds of a pastoral life and the sound of lost hope in the scream are elements smoothly woven into an original fictional tapestry. The degree of composition is great—the pauses, the contrasts, the simplicity of it so very complicated. The story is true, but it cannot be accurate because of the artfulness.

"The Country Mouse" is finely written but written in a spirit much closer to the documentary, to the statement. "My mother was not dead. She was in a sanitorium, in another prolonged 'nervous breakdown.'" And "I had been brought back unconsulted." For a sensitive and reserved nature, autobiographical accuracy is a greater deterrence to publication than the deeper and more disturbing transformations of experience by art. So "The Country Mouse" lay in the drawer, and "In the Village" was published.

The portrait of Marianne Moore was also found unpublished and somewhat unsettled among the poet's papers. As we have it now, it is one of the best of its kind in our literature, a literature more barren than most in significant memoirs. It is kindly, even adoring. The Moore household in Brooklyn, the cadence of the speech, the remembered odd scene, the visit to the circus are treasures of eccentricity and authenticity. Above all, the portrait is illuminated by the equity that prevails between the remembered Marianne Moore and the remembering Elizabeth Bishop. Still, I think perhaps it was withheld not from dissatisfaction but because of a squeamishness about the process of documentation, a hesitation about imposition, about *using.*

Reading over the portrait of Marianne Moore, it occurs to me that Elizabeth Bishop appears to us to have been more like the older poet than she was in life. The friendship leaves things somewhat askew. Both were discreet, brilliant, original, unmarried, quirky, and refined in taste and manners. But Elizabeth Bishop's life was far more complicated—or showed more stress and volatility, since we never know about the inner life. She was less spectacular in wholeness of being, more contemporary indeed as a soul living out the years.

Many things—her orphanage only one of them—weighed on her spirit. She knew also the weight of drinking and the weight of the years of not drinking. She had asthma attacks, allergies, and love affairs that did not always end happily, far from it. She was as open to experience in space as Marianne Moore was pleased to be confined. She went far out to sea in both the literal and metaphorical sense. Like some figure in Thomas Mann, the cold north and the treacherous passions of the south met in her nature. She loved houses and objects, and she had an eye for them, for shells and feathered necklaces made by the Indians of Brazil, for treasures carefully chosen and looked after. And for larger acquisitions also: handsome pieces of furniture, chests and bureaus made from Brazilian woods in various shades and decorated with the diamond patterns of Minas. There was the modern house in Petrópolis, in the hills where the emperor used to have his summer palace. The house was thoughtful and careful, set near a waterfall, and everything in it was standing in its place, arranged just so. There was the ancient house in hard-to-get-to, historic, beautiful Ouro Preto, a folly perhaps, but who could travel to Ouro Preto and not put a hand to a fine, falling-down treasure of bygone days in a Brazil nearly out of its mind with love for modernity?

As I remember, there was very little money. What had passed on to Elizabeth came from one of those faded family businesses and from investments that seemed to wither in the box. To go here and there, to have the things and the houses, required an awful prudence and watchfulness, and yet the span was daring and profligate. She *would* go up to the Amazon, even if she was quite uncomfortable doing so. Strange things happened in her presence, emanations, a sudden efflorescence that might have come from the rubbing of a lamp. Once, we were in a museum in Rio where there were many Indian artifacts, when Elizabeth suddenly stopped and said, "Look." We turned around, and there was a group of naked Indians looking at Indian artifacts.

And then she left Brazil after so many years and returned home to take up the life of our kind in order to make a living. That is, she began to teach, even though for such a long time she had been afraid or shy of it, even shy about giving readings. Her last post was at Harvard. There she found an apartment, not in Cambridge or on Beacon Hill but down on the waterfront, as a sort of pioneer in the development of that part of the city, a modern and very handsome development but a bit out of the way.

Many look forward to the publication of Elizabeth Bishop's letters, look forward to knowing in full the incomparable glow, the luster of the thoughts and sights written in her small, curling, rather crooked script. Someone is weeding the garden, another has just come up the road in the inconvenient tropics.

Elizabeth Bishop was indeed a perfectionist. She was also a natural writer with an unusual patience; nothing appears to have been excavated with visible sweat and aching muscle. And yet perhaps it was that the great natural gifts seemed too easy, and she must wait to make everything absolutely right in tone and rhythm, without insistence. She didn't want to leave too much paper on the beach.

1984

THE TELLER AND THE TAPE

Norman Mailer

THE "ORAL tradition," if that is a suitable slot in which to deposit the large number of books arising from the taped interview, is a labor-saving curiosity in which our country leads the world. We have here a "literature" of remarks, a fast-moving confounding of Gertrude Stein's confident assertion that "remarks are not literature." The exuberant exploitation of the possibilities of this "vampire capital" are just beginning and, indeed, the whole enterprise has about it a limitlessness in all its aspects.

"The transcript totaled twenty thousand pages" (*Mailer: His Life and Times* by Peter Manso). "A major biography."

"For the third time, Cathy Zmuda transcribed hundreds of thousands of spoken words—perhaps millions in this instance" (*Working* by Studs Terkel).

"It is safe to say that the collected transcript of every last recorded bit of talk would approach fifteen thousand pages" (*The Executioner's Song* by Norman Mailer, a novel).

Quite a lot taken down, but why not more? What is to deter? The spoken "pages" each of us produces in a lifetime would outpace all the libraries of the ancient and modern world. First-person narration, this stratospheric memory bank floating freely in the universe, idling there, waiting for the button and the circling tape, is of a simplicity quite beautiful in shape. Like a bank account under a prescription, it can be "attached" by the collector, in print known as the author, and drawn upon in circumstances of great variety and for purposes strange or banal or merely useful. To ponder the field, scan the prospect of effortless remembering and remarking, opens up a prodigiousness on the loose, a monumentality of retailed playback.

Give voice to the voiceless, remember the neglected and the isolated.

Sometimes the starting point is an awareness of the impending ending; we are always at a point where time is running out for those who have lived through this or that, significant or insignificant. Slave narratives, old soldiers, superannuated craftsmen, Indians, Appalachian folk, immigrants, blacksmiths—a bond of mutuality arises between the instrument and the voice, the sophisticated person's research plan and the honoring of the survivor by the very gesture of seeking out, taking down. What is said, details, turns of speech, life rhythms, bygone social patterns might be interesting in themselves and useful for the historian down the way. Of course, the historian's scrutiny will have a somewhat diminishing effect upon the unexamined flow because of the limits of spoken memories as documentation and the limits of each of us as a representation of historical events.

The modesty of the philanthropic intention commends it to us. The tapes and transcripts resting in the eternal peace of the libraries are a sort of gravestone for vanished persons who lived their days among a group not fully articulated. If nothing much is done with it, there is a charitable satisfaction in knowing that it exists. Liberalism, egalitarianism, a form of reverence, sent the WPA researchers to the Okies and tenant farmers, to field hands and prisoners with their songs and stories.

As documents, the innocent tapes bear a resemblance to the letters and diaries of obscure persons who happened to live in a time of upheaval or who by mere placement in the scheme of things were led to thoughts beyond the weather and family greetings. But these solitary compositors worked under the conventions of literacy, of writing, and the restraining self-consciousness of their written documents is different from the restraints, selections, and omissions of speech. It is often the task of the historian and the imaginative writer to discover the silences behind speech, the silences that produced the romantic text of James Agee's *Let Us Now Praise Famous Men*.

LISTENING IN

The tape-recorded books of today are not a gift to the cemetery of history. Instead, what we have here is a sort of decomposed creativity, a recycling similar to that of the obsolete ragman who turned old clothes into paper. Propagation is the intention, and storage is failure. Thus, confrontation enters between the asker and the asked, and the relation is more insinuating, less sentimental, more modern, you might say, and certainly more efficient.

The books are various indeed. Appeal is to the point, appeal of the subjects, the root idea. Except in a few cases, appeal can be said to be the only measure of quality. Taped books are roughly to be divided into the active solicitation of the words of the unknown and the active solicitation of the remarks of the known, or remarks about the known, the celebrated—or if not celebrated, notorious.

MONO

The simplest method is to give each person his time and move on to the next. The sequential interviewer is likely to reign over the text in the benevolent and more or less disinterested manner of the anthropologist or social worker. The "composition" is fluid, open, carefree. Exploitation is circumvented by the general air of affirmation. The worth of the recorded person is what is being affirmed rather than the singularity of the voice, the words.

Studs Terkel, for instance, appears in a manner surely much like that of the scouts in the WPA days. He is updated by the large extent of his own packaged and distributed tapes, but still old-fashioned, the sympathetic, thoughtful leftist, true to the proletariat and the dispossessed and ignored. His task is clever and concrete, even if he must travel hither and yon and come back burdened with a trunk full of *oh* and *well, you know* and *I mean* and *let's see here.*

Working: People Talk About What They Do All Day and How They Feel About What They Do is almost six hundred pages of small, crowded type, some 135 occupations, among them doorman, airline stewardess, farmer, miner, model, cabdriver, spot welder, hooker, and a few names such as Pauline Kael, Eddie Arroyo, Bud Freeman—that is, critic, jockey, jazz musician. About all this Terkel briefly sets the scene or briefly interrupts here and there. ("He's the doorman at a huge apartment building on Manhattan's Upper West Side.... The walls could stand a paint job.... He wears his uniform.")

The pages turn, the workers flow by as if coming out of the mill at the end of the day shift. Not one makes an impression, can be remembered—many they are and many another they might be. Just who is the hairstylist or the cabdriver? Or, rather, what are they? They do not have clothes, tics, parents, houses, fantasies. These persons are not metaphors, not a composite, and none has the weight of a line of statistics on position, social status, religion, training, whatever. The most striking thing is that few have vocal particularity. There is seldom an ear in the talking pages, hardly an echo of the fractured expressiveness heard around us.

> Cabdriver: "I hate to admit that driving a cab is no longer the novelty to me that it once was. It has its moments, but it's not the most ideal job in the world as far as determining one's attitude is concerned."

> Sanitation worker: "You get just like the milkman's horse, you get used to it. If you remember the milkman's horse, all he had to do was whistle and whooshhh!"

The sanitized diction brings to mind *60 Minutes*, and this is not necessarily a prudent pruning for publication. The current stranger and his tape recorder, whether wishing it or not, find the subjects living in the atmosphere of television with its neat dispersal of the claims of the individual person, its condensations and programmings, its inattention and formalized forgetting, its dehydrated vocables ready for the freezer.

Tape recording without an interpretive intelligence is a primitive technology for history. It offers a moment of publicity in an undermining void. The protocol of the meeting and the docile instrument steadily transmitting pages are an orthodoxy, promoting a cheerful but rigid disengagement. The spuriousness of the encounter is ordained by the one-sidedness of advantage, all of it accruing to the "author."

To understand the meaning of attention to the unknown and unrecorded, one can go back to the great Victorian masterpiece, Henry

Mayhew's *London Labour and the London Poor*. Or in our own time to Ronald Blythe's *Akenfield: Portrait of an English Village* (1969). Here the old bell ringer talks and is "taken down" by some method. But his presence moves the listener, Blythe, to reflections: "Lost in an art-pastime-worship based on blocks of circulating figures which look like one of those numismatic keys to the Great Pyramid secret, the ringing men are out on their own in a crashing sphere of golden decibels."

POLYPHONIC

Taped books about persons of established interest are now designed to make a more sophisticated use of the gathered material. A person, or rather a personality, is the center, replacing an abstraction of theme or place. Slabs of recollection, one after another, would dilute the attention to the central subject; the "authors" of interview books are now allowed to slice up the interviews and disperse the remarks throughout the pages, to bring them in at appropriate points, to create something like a conversation in a crowded room. There is no intention to reproduce dialogue; each recollector is on his own, but his or her holding forth is subject to judicious interruption in the interest of narrative. The speakers are witnesses, coins in a box, offerings, gratuities. They are the base metals to be transmuted into gold—that is, into pages.

In *Mailer: His Life and Times* by Peter Manso, "more than two hundred people were interviewed over a period of forty months, some interviews filling more than ten hours." Transcript close to 20,000 pages, offered as a "major biography" of Mailer, and itself a "major literary event"; gigantism is something of a phenomenon in written books and on the fairgrounds, but for the taper the world is a hippo-drome of garrulity.

All contemporary biographers rely upon the interview as one of many sources, including the biographer's vision, necessary for the construction of a life. In Manso's biography, the interview is the only source, except for a few snippets from reviews and letters, and thus it seems to offer a fresh aesthetic of sorts: You, and in this case your times, are what people have to say about you. The high interest of the unfolding of this proposition, the assertiveness of the speakers, has to do with the large proportions of Mailer himself, his confidence and intrepidity, his florid pattern of experience, his disasters met with an almost erotic energy of adaptation. This promiscuity, the volume of precipitous encounters from which he has emerged like a knight from the forest, seems to have encouraged an elevation of indiscretion among the contributing friends, a situation much in the interest of the pages. Manso tells us the right of review was sometimes requested but "in most, not."

The drastic distances between gossip, the libertine loquacity of the dinner table, and print dissolves, as we would expect since the enterprise is committed to print only as a vessel of the waters of orality. Wives are snubbed, well-known people are maliciously hooked by a phrase and flounder about like so many fish trapped in a net. Mailer himself enters briefly here and there, but of course his presence, his invulnerable presence, is in every line.

The absence of an author, the lack of a signature of responsibility, the conception of ideas as shadows of comment, vague and undefended, in a like way absorbs the activity of the commentator, the critic. What can be said about more than six hundred pages of anecdote? Description is possible and recapitulation of lively asides, but that involves a measure of culpability, the passing on of gossip. Yet any reader will think some of these books are more appealing than others, and *Mailer: His Life and Times* might be judged to score—to score more or less, since an equation of judgment rests merely on the availability of consenting voices.

Perhaps one can judge Mailer to be a "good" idea. He is a spectacular mound of images and, like such self-creations, mystifying and impersonal, and thereby a structure of anecdote corresponds in some way to his own accumulated articulations. His writings, the frame of the structure, are to be incorporated only glancingly or studied in the anecdotal pile, but then the work, the sharp intrusion, is the knife in the heart of most biographers.

We see that the writer had a youth, a formidable, adoring mother somewhat along the lines Freud thought friendly to a son's success. The family is smart—cousin, sister, and Mailer himself making their way from Brooklyn to Harvard. Constant writing from the beginning, *The Naked and the Dead*, a splendid success, the army, marriage, political complexity increased by friendship and "reality," second wife, "violent and orgiastic period" (his words), self-advertisement, stabbing of wife, antiwar activity, prisoner of sex, children, more marriages, Marilyn Monroe, Jack Abbott, Gary Gilmore, further marriages and children, impressive alimony, and with a new wife and child a mellow middle age. And, of course, books at every point.

Total recall adds much to the outline, even if Mailer's public has its own storehouse of dramatic recollection. Since little has been hidden along the way, Mailer is then a subject to be discussed rather than discovered. Revelation is scarcely to be wished about the living, but this premature interment is something of a finale. What we have here is a tomb of pharaonic memorabilia, brick upon brick in the sand.

The compositional blur of Mailer's *The Executioner's Song* is once more engaged by the frenzied entrance of the promoter Lawrence Schiller into the life and time of N. M. Schiller claimed his space in the "real-life novel" and received the recognition of the results of his relentless encroachments in the formation of that spectacular publication. Schiller's memory is composed of dollars, deals, contracts, and every kind of worry in the motel room and on the telephone. Crisis is his overcoat, and he sweats from one threatened crash to another, crashes such as Gilmore's "cop-out" suicide attempt or, worse, his refusing to, as they say, die with dignity rather than accept, if it came, a reprieve to a life sentence.

Schiller is a most interesting gladiator in combat with reluctant witnesses, negotiations, speed, and deadlines. In the canniness of his inquisitions he often exceeds himself, but he is a professional and brings to mind the shock of method. (Solzhenitsyn experienced the shock of the West in an encounter with two hopeful biographers. Withdrawing, he said, "The collection of 'information' in this way is not different from police spying.")

Preparation for *The Executioner's Song* is detailed once more in Manso's compilation. Schiller: "By then [May 1977] I'd given him about 9,000 pages of what eventually was over 16,000 pages of interview transcript." The interviews are put together and come out quite un-Mailerish, as was noted. We find the author in a bit of staging such as, "In the mountains, the snow was iron gray and purple in the hollows, and glowed like gold on every slope that faced the sun." Just a bit of that here and there, nothing much when compared with Truman Capote's *In Cold Blood*, another killer book of great interest and of another kind.

Capote's research, acquaintance with the cast of characters, the reputed dialogue and landscape are presented in the authorial manner throughout, incorporated into a text. About one of the killers, we read that he had a face "halved like an apple, then put together a fraction off center. . . . The left eye being truly serpentine, with a venomous, sickly-blue squint that although it was involuntarily acquired, seemed nevertheless to warn of bitter sediment at the bottom of his nature." This could not be *said* by anyone.

Mailer had his tapes in abundance; having them, he came forth, to the astonishment of a few, with a text remarkable for its plainness, its anonymity. He *shaped*, as it were, *The Executioner's Song*.

Arthur Kretchmer, editor of *Playboy*: "You've got the fucking plains in your text. It's right there." Earlier Mailer said: "I picked it up from Norris. If the book has any feeling of small-town life, I guess I picked it up from Norris." Norris Church, his wife, grew up in Atkins, Oklahoma, population 1,391.

Schiller, about *The Executioner's Song* and the possibility of its winning the Pulitzer Prize (it did, for fiction): "Because the detailing is there, the flatness, and Mailer doesn't exist in the book. They have to give him the award." This bit of literary criticism is engaging. Schiller seems to fear that *The Executioner's Song* would be written—like Mailer's *Marilyn*, perhaps. At the worst in the thick, resonant diction, the demonic, original clutter of Mailer's high style, which would impugn the gray-hide, elephantine mass of the record and its extraordinary, deathly appeal.

It's true that Mailer "doesn't exist in the book"—or largely true. And has he created the voice, the plains, the flatness, the Westness of it? Aren't the voices and landscape those of Vern and Brenda, Nicole and Garry and Bessie, accurately taped, recounting the scenery of their life with Gilmore, filling in for Schiller or whoever, appearing on every page against the dental drill of the pursuit?

THE INVISIBLE HAND

A bit of neatening, of course, and punctuation, the period, the comma. The taped text is always a great, gluey blob, and what is needed are sentences dry and separate as kernels of corn. A close reading of taped books suggests that the invisible hand is less busy than might be imagined. Punctuation, laying it out, pasting it up. The real labor of the books returns to the source, the wretched bulk of the testimony, the horror of its vast, stuttering scale. The collector is much impressed, and perhaps depressed, by the challenging magnitude. He has lifted it, sorted it, had secretaries hard at work to contain the monstrousness of what his machine has brought into being.

We notice the invariable publicity given to numbers: the thousands of pages, the millions of words, the long, long hours of interviewing, the large cast tracked down. The insistence upon number indicates that it is a validation. But a validation of what, of whom?

Tapes are what they are, no more and no less than themselves. They are the property of the speaker, even if he has freely surrendered his rights; surrendered or not, nothing belongs to the author. Excision, deletion, yes, and placement, the packaging of the property. It is accepted that the gibberish must be shaped up and, thereby, allowed to become itself, the speaker's words made legible.

Additions are a moral problem. The author can receive his book as a liberal, in all senses, gift, but he cannot reciprocate, cannot in good faith add decorative phrasing and color as an advancement of the verbal interest and appeal of his given text. For the imaginative writer, wit and a pleasing intervention of adjective and image might be a natural temptation. But here the prohibition seems clear. The author's own words in the mouth of an interviewed subject are artificial, illicit, a reverse and most peculiar form of plagiarism. There is little evidence that the compiler of talk feels this as a constraint. What is needed from time to time is the practical matter of emphasis, keeping the attention of the reader.

The Executioner's Song is the apotheosis of our flourishing "oral literature" thus far. (To see it as Mailer's best book, as many have done, is much too fast. Mailer is a river of words, ornamental, evocative words, and cascading notions and designs. There is no plainness, flatness in him, but there is, was, a lot, in the tapes.)

He—and Capote also in his different construction—had a plot and, through none of their devising, an adjunct in the death penalty. This publicly ordained ending from which there was no escape might have prompted Mailer to his most genuine contribution to the tale of Gary Gilmore. Mailer's mark on the book is an accentual one. By accent, placement, and distribution, and finally insistence, no matter what a contrary cynicism about reality might have suggested, he created a romance. From Schiller's pit, we can say that Mailer has excavated a *Liebestod*, possibly proposing it as a redemption of the squalor of this long, long death trip so arresting to the voyeur in most of us.

We can imagine a fraudulent tape-recorded production offered by a shy recluse as his own thousand pages of unheard sound. No, that would mean writing—and the tape recorder is first and last a labor-saving instrument.

1985

THE GENIUS OF MARGARET FULLER

So passed away the loftiest, bravest soul that has yet irradiated the form of an American woman: thus wrote the editor Horace Greeley. Yet before this noble soul, Margaret Fuller, passed away, many would have forgone *irradiated* in preference for *irritated*. She was brave and lofty, and she did irradiate and also irritate, irritate herself especially with strained nerves, fantastical exertions, discomforts large and small.

Margaret Fuller, a New England creation, commemorated in Mount Auburn Cemetery in Cambridge in impressive blocks of stone, was born in the wrong place, the place thought to be the only right one for an American intellectual in the nineteenth century. That is, she was born in Cambridgeport, Massachusetts, around Harvard, Boston, Concord, and all the rest. She sprang out of the head of all the Zeuses about: her father Timothy Fuller, Emerson, Goethe. The head being the protesting organ it is, she suffered lifelong from migraine headaches, and even as a young girl left on the scene more than a bit of the fatigue and sense of pounding insistence thought to be the dispensation of a learned woman. There were many enlightened and cultivated women about, but she was the only seriously learned one in her circle, perhaps in the country.

As a life, a biography, hers is the most dramatic, the most adventuring of all the "flowerings." Her life was strikingly split into two parts by experience and ended by tragedy. Staying at home in Concord and Boston, she might have ended as comedy.

She was born into an incestuous air, this world that provided as a wife the sister of one's best friend, as a husband, the son of a family connection. Hawthorne married Sophia Peabody; Emerson married Ellen Tucker; Henry Adams married Marian Hooper, the daughter of Dr. Hooper and a Sturgis on the maternal side. This sexual handiness, as it were, the prudent over-the-fence alliances, narrowed experience in Margaret Fuller's circle but seemed to produce around Boston and Concord a domestic placidity that encouraged the high notes of Transcendentalism, a local philosophical blending, an indefinable idealism of the divinity within humanity, union with nature, the "eternal One." Henry Adams, thinking of Emerson and pondering his own non-Boston experience of the nation as a whole, thought all this *naif.*

(It is almost elevating to learn from a discreet footnote here and there that Clarence King, the distinguished geologist and Adams's great friend in *The Education of Henry Adams*, was the common-law husband of a New York black woman and the father of a son by her. King himself was from Newport, Rhode Island, and a graduate of Yale rather than Harvard; perhaps this climate slightly to the south had an effect upon this far-flinging, if that is what it was. Allowing for the condescension of "common-law," King apparently wished to do right and to honor the union. Upon his death, Mrs. King brought a lawsuit to secure for her son the trust fund assured her in King's letters. She lost, defeated by the WASPs and their mastery of *per stirpes*.)

Margaret Fuller did not attract the passion for neighborly unions. Indeed, one might say her only true American lover was Professor Perry Miller of Harvard, born more than a century later. Margaret Fuller herself was born in 1810 and was thus seven years younger than Emerson. She was the daughter of Timothy Fuller, a scholarly man, graduate of Harvard, representative in Congress from Massachusetts, and later a practicing lawyer. His education of his daughter began early. Like John Stuart Mill, she was put in the stocks, and one of her finest pieces of writing has to do with the memory of her father's wish to make her "heir to all he knew."

> Thus I had tasks given me, as many and various as the hours would allow, and on subjects beyond my age; with the disadvantage of reciting to him in the evening, after he returned from his office.... I was often kept up till very late; and as he was a severe teacher, both from his habits of mind and his ambition for me, my feelings were kept on the stretch till the recitations were over. Thus frequently, I was sent to bed several hours too late, with

nerves unnaturally stimulated. The consequence was a premature development of the brain, that made me a "youthful prodigy" by day, and by night a victim of spectral illusions, nightmare and somnambulism, which at the time prevented the harmonious development of my bodily powers and checked my growth, while, later, they induced continual headaches, weakness, and nervous affections, of all kinds. As these again reacted on the brain, giving undue force to every thought and every feeling, there was finally produced a state of being both too active and too intense, which wasted my constitution, and will bring me—even although I have learned to understand and regulate my now morbid temperament—to a premature grave.

Overwork, as she names it. Hysteria and the nightmares, whatever torments remembered, the result was a storehouse of knowledge and certainly an identity, even a vanity. Long after her father subsided as a tutor, she spent her youth in frantic application, reading, as Emerson wrote, "at a rate like Gibbon's." Thomas Wentworth Higginson's biography has her, at the age of fifteen, up at five, with the hours laid out: one for the piano, one for Sismondi's *European Literature* in French; then Brown's philosophy, then a lesson in Greek; in the evening, two hours reading in Italian, a bit of walking, more piano, and retiring at eleven to write in her diary.

Thus, we have the forced bud continually self-forced, nerve-wrung, eccentric, and, as we might expect, proud of her learning, aggressive in conversation, tremendously eager for friends, given to crushes, and yet with it all a devoted daughter. Timothy Fuller died suddenly, leaving the family in a bad way. At this moment, Margaret had planned to accompany the Farrar family to Europe. But she gave it up and remained at home to help in the support of her brothers and sisters. This meant teaching. First, a spell at the Temple School, Bronson Alcott's leafy squirrel house of learning; and then a real position for two years in Providence, whence in a letter to Emerson she made one of her many confident pronouncements that were to be long remembered and to decorate her memory in the manner of a bit of local scandal: "I see no divine person; I myself am more divine than any I see—I think that is enough to say about them." After two years, she returned to Boston to make her way as a writer, beginning with a translation of Eckermann's *Conversations with Goethe.*

From the first, she was a figure, a star, a somewhat blinding one, constantly talked about as a sight to be taken in, like Bronson Alcott's unworldliness and Thoreau's recalcitrance. Conversation was her love and even if some were fearful in approach because of the intrepid "truthfulness" of her social exchanges ("Stand from under!" Emerson cautioned himself), she had the trait of all conversationalists; an immense availability. She liked to visit and sometimes stayed too long. One of the saddest periods of her youth came after her father's decision to retire from the Boston scene and to take his family to the smaller village of Groton, thus removing his daughter from the company of the young men and professors around Harvard with their spiritual and intellectual interests.*

Her mission was self-culture, as one memorialist phrased it. And always the wish to uplift others, friends, anyone. She practiced a kind of hot Transcendentalism alongside Emerson's cooler sort. She could be found holding an arm, gazing into eyes, insisting upon inspiration, sublimity, and *grow, grow, grow.*

She was very noticeable to the men around Harvard, some of whom she had known earlier at a private academy where she, although a female, was allowed at fifteen to go for special study in Greek recitation. There was her mind to startle and also her appearance, her black cloak, and many odd features of the head, not always easy to describe.

The Transcendentalist Frederic Hedge, her friend from his Harvard days: "No pretension to beauty then or at any time, her face was one that attracted, that awakened a lively interest."

Emerson: "nothing prepossessing. Her extreme plainness—a trick of incessantly opening and shutting her eyelids—the nasal tone of her voice—all repelled; and I said to myself, we shall never get far."

---

*It was from Bell Gale Chevigny's book, *Margaret Fuller: The Woman and the Myth*, with its masterly organization of many then-unpublished letters, along with the comments of contemporaries, that I came first to understand the complexity of Margaret Fuller and her situation.

Poe worried about her upper lip, which, "as if impelled by the action of involuntary muscles, habitually uplifts itself, conveying the impression of a sneer."

William Henry Channing on the matter of her neck found its curve "swan-like when she was sweet and thoughtful, but when she was scornful or indignant it contracted, and made swift turns, like a bird of prey."

J. R. Lowell: "a pythoness."

Oliver Wendell Holmes: "ophidian."

The concentration upon appearance is somewhat overwrought among those who took beauty if it arrived on the doorstep and did without if a fine and useful character prevailed. Emerson's first wife, Ellen Tucker, has been described as a "remarkable beauty"; Ellen Fuller, Margaret's younger sister, was a romantic charmer who married the romantic, quite unsteady, charmer Ellery Channing. Henry Adams, writing about his engagement to "Clover" Hooper, said, "She is certainly not handsome; nor would she be quite called plain, I think."

So, Margaret Fuller was homely, even distracting in mannerisms, but she charmed by an overwhelming responsiveness and curiosity and had many women friends from whom she received confidences and to whom she gladly gave advice. Emerson, in his essay after her death, wrote that she wore her friends "like a necklace of diamonds around her neck" and that "her friendships, as a girl with girls, as a woman with women, were not unmingled with passion, and had passages of romantic sacrifice and ecstatic fusion."

Be that as it may, it was her habit throughout her years in America to presume on male friendships, pushing them to intentions that were not forthcoming, with a result very distressing to her spirits. She is so often not quite in touch, confused perhaps by the dramas of friendship, a sort of insufficiency in nuance, missing signals. Soul mates appeared— or so it seemed—but her "soul" was too soon declarative and consuming.

First, her cousin George Davis is said to have "thwarted her." Then a true falling in love with a member of her circle and a close friend, Samuel Ward: "No, I do not distrust you, so lately have you spoken the words of friendship. You would not be so irreverent as to dare to tamper with a nature like mine, you could not treat so generous a person with levity...if you love me as I deserve to be loved, you cannot dispense with seeing me.....*J'attendrai*." Still, the nest-like scene, and it turned out that Samuel Ward, a close friend, was going to marry another close friend of his and also a close friend of Margaret Fuller's—Anna Barker. Later in New York she was to experience the painful debacle of her "romantic" connection with a man named James Nathan.

Emerson and Margaret Fuller formed a complicated alliance and one of the most interesting friendships between a man and a woman in American literature. Before their meeting and while Emerson was still a clergyman, she was somewhat doubtful of fame in the pulpit. "It is so easy for a cultivated mind to excite itself with that tone." On the other hand, she was eager to show him her translation of Goethe's drama *Tasso*. They met in 1835, and she first visited Emerson in Concord in 1836. "His influence has been more beneficial to me than that of any American, and from him I first learned what is meant by an inward light."

Emerson found her, at the age of twenty-six, well read in French, Italian, and German literature but needy in the matter of English literature. He pressed upon her the works of Chaucer, Ben Jonson, Herbert, Sir Thomas Browne, and others. The absence of English fiction represents Emerson's indifference to the form as perhaps too much shackled to event and casual life. Of Dickens he wrote: "London tracts...local and temporary in his tints and style, and local in his aims."

Margaret Fuller "adored" Mme. de Staël and was often called the "American Corinne" because of her dramatic and romantic presentation of herself. She came to forgive George Sand for the laxness of her life and greatly admired her and her work. But what would she have thought of the refined obscenities of *Clarissa*? Of *Tom Jones* or *Tristram Shandy*? The mixed and complex English fictional tradition cannot be what Emerson meant when, in "The American Scholar," he called for "the meal in the firkin; the milk in the pan; the ballad in the street; the news of the boat; the glance of the eye; the form and gait of the body," but where was one to find the expression of "the common and the low" if not in English fiction? It is the development of Margaret Fuller's style—not to be laid at the door of Emerson—that suffered from an absence of dogs and cats and rude particulars and the humorous. She did not have Emerson's wit, his rapid concentration of an image, a quick short sentence. She told him that he used too many aphorisms, and he said that if he used too many, she used too few.

Her letters are a heat of energy, warmth of friendship, family love, and family duty, a blazing need to communicate, no matter the aching head and midnight coming on. In the New England period, there is also a wrenching struggle with nature, the woods, sunsets, moonlights. "The incommunicable trees begin to persuade us to live with them, and quit our life of solemn trifles." Emerson: "What is a farm but a mute gospel?"

The sweetness of the Massachusetts countryside, the little villages, the fields and woods and streams. This is what they had—literary genius in a sort of retirement; rustication, snowy nights and early flowers. The great writer Thoreau redeemed the nature-writing workshop in Concord with his daunting struggle in letters and notebooks to catch the kiss of a moonbeam and honor the hoot of a barn owl. It was Thoreau's genius to carry landscape and weather as far as they could go.

Hawthorne in his notebooks fought with the whortleberry bush and the gleam from the lighthouse at Marblehead. "And its light looked very singularly, mingling with the growing daylight. It was not light, the moonshine, brightening as the evening twilight deepens; for now it threw its radiance over the landscape, the green and other tints of which were displayed by daylight, whereas at evening all those tints are obscured." And so on, with here and there a hit: the neighbor's ox who looked very much like Daniel Webster.

Margaret Fuller attempted, early, a composition on the passion-flower and would sometimes advise one to see a certain sunset at *exactly a quarter to six*. A great deal of moonlight occupies her pen. Emerson, in his memoir, is rather contemptuous of her naturing, even though he himself may be said to have led the charge for these confrontations.

Margaret's love of beauty made her, of course, a votary of nature, but rather for pleasurable excitement than with a deep poetic feeling. Her imperfect vision and her bad health were serious impediments to intimacy with woods and rivers. She never paid—and it is a little remarkable—any attention to natural sciences. She neither botanized, nor geologized, nor dissected.

What was not known then, and certainly not known to herself, was that her nature was profoundly urban and her talent, in the end, was for sightseeing, meeting people, for issues; her gifts as a writer were for a superior journalism. Everything that happened, in her head, in her reading, in her travels, was there to be used. In 1843, she made a journey to the western part of the country, and the next year her first original book was published, *Summer on the Lakes*. She sees a lot, thinks about the Indians, the settlers, Chicago, immigrants, and forswears a descriptive account of Niagara Falls. "Yet I, like others, have little to say, where the spectacle is for once great enough to fill the whole life and supersede thought, giving us only its presence....We have been here eight days, and I am quite willing to depart. So great a sight soon satisfies, making us content with itself, and with what is less than itself."

In Concord, visiting the Emerson house, the second Mrs. Emerson—not a beauty like Ellen, who died young of tuberculosis—experiences the discomforts arising from the presence of a husband-adorer and disciple in the house, waiting for him to be free to inspire, to read his poems aloud, to take a nature walk. Hurt feelings, tears; Mrs. E. asks Margaret to take a walk with her one evening and M. answers that she cannot because she is going to walk with Mr. E. That sort of thing.

And the inevitable "friendship" discussions with Emerson, heavy with feeling on Margaret Fuller's side. She wants some sort of exclusiveness, recognition: "I am like some poor traveller of the desert, who saw, at early morning, a distant palm, and toiled all day to reach it"—followed by a transparent Persian fable, which Emerson pretends not to understand. And, another letter,

I have felt the impossibility of meeting far more than you; so much, that if you ever know me well, you will feel that the fact of my abiding by you thus far, affords a strong proof that we are to be much to one another.... How often have I left you despairing and forlorn. This light will never understand my fire.

Emerson in his memoir does not avoid analysis of this disconcerting appeal for more, more.

> Our moods were very different; and I remember, that, at the very time when I, slow and cold, had come fully to admire her genius, and was congratulating myself on the solid good understanding that subsisted between us, I was surprised at hearing it taxed by her with superficiality and halfness. She stigmatised our friendship as commercial. It seems her magnanimity was not met.

Together they began *The Dial* in 1840, with Margaret Fuller as the editor for two years. It was a Transcendentalist forum, "to lift men to a higher platform." Criticism, it was felt, would be most useful to the soul of the country, and, not to be forgotten, criticism is what the group was able to compose and thus to celebrate Genius and the Transcendental calling.

Fuller offered an essay on Goethe, the supreme genius, a defense against accusations of immortality and egotism. Her essay is intense and rather more parochial than it need be, except for being addressed to an audience alarmed and distrustful. "Pardon him, World, that he was too worldly. Do not wonder, Heart, that he was so heartless. Believe, Soul, that one so true, as far as he went, must yet be initiated into the deeper mysteries of Soul."

Emerson thought the Goethe essay her best, and Professor Perry Miller views it as a moment in history. Here Margaret brashly defends *Werther* against the prevailing American opinion that it was a foul corrupter of youth; and she praises *The Elective Affinities*, which American men regarded as the nadir of sensual depravity. Viewed in this perspective, Margaret's essay is a basic document in the history of intellectual freedom in the United States.

The work on *The Dial* exhausted her, and Emerson assumed the editing for the next two of the magazine's four years. "I remember, after she had been compelled to relinquish the journal into my hands, my grateful wonder at the facility with which she assumed the preparation of laborious articles that might have daunted the most practised scribe."

CONVERSATIONS

The famous gatherings in Boston in which Margaret Fuller led and instructed a number of well-bred women began in the rooms of Miss Elizabeth Peabody on West Street. The object was "to pass in review the departments of thought and knowledge, and endeavor to place them in due relation to one another in our mind." Since eloquence was the leader's gift, she had to do a good deal of orating to pinch the minds of her fellow explorers into speech. The account of one conversation that survives is a comedy, and perhaps that is why it survives. The topic was "What Is Life?" Pushed and prodded, a Miss C. replied, "It is to laugh, or cry, according to our organization."

"Good," said Fuller, "but not grave enough."

Another reply by Mrs. E., perhaps the second Mrs. Emerson, who was an attendant, "'We live by the will of God, and the object of life is to submit,' and went on into Calvinism."

When pressed to give her own idea of what life is, M. F. began with "God as Spirit, Life, so full as to create and love eternally, and yet capable of pause."

The conversations were said to spread her fame about town. She dressed for them and assumed a sibylline manner quite extraordinary. Some thought she got the idea from Bronson Alcott's everlasting questioning and his Orphic Sayings. But what seems more likely is that the conversations were a sort of reduced, miniature, and homebound wish for a platform, and a platform such as Emerson had in his lectures in this hall and that, in little towns and cities. She, too, could speak on the great subjects, but Miss Peabody's parlor, excitable as it was in the hour before noon, with the wives of the great men, Mrs. Bancroft, Mrs. Child, Mrs. Parker, and various Misses looking on, was the only lyceum available.

The second part of Margaret Fuller's life was to last only six years, from 1844 until her death in 1850. Act 2 was overcrowded with incident after the pastoral, repetitive Act 1, which was book after book, the same friends, much talk, letters, reviews, and the management of *The Dial*. In spirit, it was a sort of treadmill of enthusiasms for Goethe, Beethoven, Michelangelo, Raphael, mythology, the classics, French socialism—all written down, somewhere. "Her pen was a non-conductor" merely signified her flat failure as a poet, which of course she had struggled with also. Emerson continued to think of her as a talker, a parlor orator, or even as a monologist "who seldom admitted others upon an equal ground with herself." She could also gossip, which frightened him. "The crackling of thorns under the pot."

In *The Dial*, she published "The Great Lawsuit—Man versus Men; Woman versus Women." The article was much expanded and elaborated into *Woman in the Nineteenth Century*, published in 1845. And then she left Boston for New York, thought at the time to be an outpost in the intellectual life. "The high priestess of Transcendentalism cut her ties with the provincial homeland," Perry Miller wrote.

"Let them [women] be sea-captains if they like." This offhand swat to seafaring Massachusetts, the China trade, the widow's walk at the top of the house, the codfish cake for breakfast, remains the best-known statement in Margaret Fuller's long, prolix defense of women. The work was completed in less than two months, during a vacation in a Hudson River town, and probably written without a library, except for the one in her head. It is a compendium of custom relating to women, ancient and modern opinion buried in poetry, literary allusion, and common observation. The index lists Elizabeth Barrett Browning, Dante, Desdemona, Petrarch, Plato, Spinoza, Swedenborg, Xenophon, and many others. The author herself appears in the disguise of a certain Miranda, well educated, taught honorable self-reliance from the cradle, privileged in learning and preparation for independence of thought; and not hindered by beauty from the development of talents and sense of self. "She was fortunate in a total absence of those charms which might have drawn to her bewildering flatteries, and in a strong electric nature, which repelled those who did not belong to her, and attracted those who did."

It is a bookish book, a fundamental document in the history of feminist thought. An intense, pleading tone, elevated, careful not to give offense, but determined. The strong and dignified women of literature and history—Iphigenia, Antigone, Britomart, the French Revolution's Madame Roland ("O Liberty, what crimes have been committed in thy name!")—appeal to her more than the powerful, devious Queen Elizabeth, "without magnanimity of any kind."

Margaret Fuller certainly knew Mary Wollstonecraft's *Vindication of the Rights of Woman*. Here, she makes an unaccountable mistake, seeing Mary Wollstonecraft's marriage to the prodigious nitwit William Godwin as her best claim upon our attention: "a woman whose existence better proved the need for some new interpretation of woman's rights, than anything she wrote."

Mary Wollstonecraft's work is much more homely and practical, less rhetorical and less respectful—and more cynical about the world. She despises women brought together in boarding schools; too much giggling and lounging about in dirty undergarments. "Parental affection is, perhaps, the blindest modification of perverse self-love," and she asserts that the habit of overlooking the faults of one's parents inclines the child to overlook his own. "The two sexes mutually corrupt and improve each other."

Mary Wollstonecraft's worldliness may have offended Margaret Fuller. She does not mention the *Vindication*, but points instead to Godwin's book in support of his wife. The omission indicates a distaste, just as distaste, conscious or not, might explain why Emerson in his cramped and complicated essay on Fuller, thought by some to be patronizing but in fact the most alive and brilliant words written about her, never mentions *Woman in the Nineteenth Century*, the work that established her fame in America and abroad.

In Fuller's book, we notice again and again the belief in the "electrical" and "magnetic" element in women's nature. "Women who combine this organization with genius are very commonly unhappy at the present time." What makes *Woman in the Nineteenth Century* affecting beyond its arguments for education, independence, and so on, is the pathos of autobiography lurking in the text. Even the often lamented diversions into higher learning and allusion show the will to transcendence. She herself, in the wide sweep of her being, is the best American woman the nineteenth century had to offer; and she is, for all that, merely a phenomenon, an abandoned orphan. That is part of what the book means to say.

Emerson on Margaret Fuller: "A complacency that seemed the most assured since the days of Scaliger." Also, "the presence of a rather mountainous ME." Who can doubt it? But what the whole span of her life shows is that she got it all from being around Boston at the trans-figuring moment and would have lost it all had she not escaped. She was a sort of stepchild, formed and deformed by Concord, by the universalism and the provincialism. Emerson notes this so-willing adaptation to the best of the intellectual landscape, as well as its grad-ual unsuitability, not only to the fact that she was a woman who had to earn her living, but to her nature. Among other things, she was not a solitary, not a gardener.

> I think most of her friends will remember to have felt, at one time or another, some uneasiness, as if this athletic soul craved a larger atmosphere than it found; as if she were ill-timed and mis-mated, and felt in herself a tide of life, which compared with the slow circulation of others as a torrent with a rill.

She was altogether too familiar in the minds of New Englanders. They loved her—the word is not too strong even for Emerson's feelings. Noble, truthful, faithful, brave, honest: The words appear again and again in what was written and said about her. Yet it is the fate of an eccentric to be repetitive in the hometown. There is no intermission. Each appears in his hat and coat and tics day after day. The first thing to be noticed as she moves to New York and then to Europe is that she is no longer quite so noticeable, so fixed and peculiar, perhaps because being one of many, even if Poe, a New York acquaintance, divided the world into men, women, and Margaret Fuller. Above all, Transcen-dentalism—"going to heaven in a swing" as one mocker put it—nearly turned her into a fool.

She moved to New York in December 1844, invited by Horace Greeley to be a professional book reviewer for *The New York Tribune* and also to contribute general articles; and invited by Mrs. Greeley to stay with them in their house in the Turtle Bay section of the city. For the paper she wrote reviews and "pieces" on just about everything: the theater, concerts, prisons, asylums, poor women, institutions. Her reviews were, for the most part, short and quickly written. She gives too much space to the novels of Charles Brockden Brown and too little to James Fenimore Cooper and the stories of Hawthorne, although she is generally favoring in her glances. She made a striking attack on Longfellow as "artificial and imitative." As a critic, she does not have the mind for the details of a work but rather for its general effect, and so there is a sameness in the language and a tendency, strong, to moral description of literature. "The atmosphere of his verse refreshes," and again, "a lively though almost sensuous delight in the beautiful," "the richness and freshness of his materials," and so on. She has little notion of the power of William Prescott's *Conquest of Mexico*.

The most interesting of the critical pieces in the *Tribune* is a cool and sly rebuke to Emerson's *Essays: Second Series*. A maddening part of the review is taken up with a description of a populace too busy and too shallow to grasp the fineness in its midst. This is followed by an interesting, but again generalized and exhorting, picture of Emerson on the platform. "One who could see man in his original grandeur...raising to the heavens the brow and the eyes of a poet." Yes, Emerson is a father of the country. But then in an indirection, as if some disembodied critic and not herself were speaking: "The essays have also been obnoxious to many charges.... The human heart complains of inadequacy, either in the nature or experience of the writer, to represent its full vocation and its deeper needs.... These essays, it has been justly said, tire like a string of mosaics or a house built of medals." A string of mosaics or a house built of medals—one of her best prose moments. At the expense of the master and still a friend to whom she wrote letters up to the end.

Then the entrance in 1845 of James Nathan, when they were both about thirty-five years old, he being six months or so younger, both unmarried, but he certainly more *experienced*. Nathan was born in Holstein, Germany, came to New York as a young man, worked in the "commission business," but, in common with many another, liked to wonder if he had not sold the soul of a poet for, well, what?—"commissions" perhaps. He had blue eyes, played the guitar, and after a meeting at the Greeleys', took her to see a plaster model of the city of Jerusalem.

Alas, she is quite soon set off, on the road again. A large group of letters begins, because the Greeleys didn't much like Nathan and the two had to meet here and there, missing each other at planned meetings; and as a writer, she has the natural inclination, highly developed, to put every turn of feeling on paper.

When they went to see the model of Jerusalem, she learned that Nathan was a Jew, and although at times Fuller had shown the inclination of the period to Jewish stereotyping, she takes a quick leap. "I have long had a presentiment, that I should meet—nearly—one of your race, who would show me how the sun of today shines on the ancient Temple—but I did not expect so gentle and civilized an apparition and with blue eyes!"

A lot is to be discovered. Nathan was in the process of rehabilitating a "maiden" and when the maiden turns out to be his mistress, so far as we can tell from M. F.'s letters, his explanation, too, has to be taken in. "I only wished to be satisfied, and when you told me how you viewed the incident I really was so. Do not think of it ever again."

Then Nathan makes an "assault upon her person," as it was spoken of at the time. She rebuffs him, but here it is possible to think of more complication of feeling, during and after, than most commentators might find evident. She writes to him, of course, and quickly about this "sadder day than I had in all my life." She had been exposed to "what was to every worthy and womanly feeling so humiliating." And,

> I know you could not help it. But why had fate drawn me so near you?...You have said that there is in yourself both a lower and a higher being than I was aware of. Since you said this, I suppose I have seen the lower!...Will you not come with me before God and promise me severe truth, and patient tenderness, that will never, if it can be avoided, misinterpret the impulses of my soul?

Nathan sends her a little dog, a burdensome gift for one moving here and there in the city and working day and night and writing to him day and night. The letters become quite frenzied with that pitiful wonder of the injured person of what she might have done wrong. Nathan is given to confessions of weakness that interest her, being new, no doubt. "Your hand removes at last the veil from my eyes. It is indeed myself who have caused all ill." What is unbalancing in this episode is that she is still writing in the transcendental mode of friendship and beauty and perfect trust in which the "assault"—unthinkable in Boston among familiars—was confusing but quite a new circumstance to think about.

But the weighty letters, the difficulty of reading them to say nothing of responding, this made its mark, and Nathan took flight to Europe, with the "maiden" along and promising to return. She wrote and received no answer. Did the letter arrive? Had his letter gone astray? When he does write, it is to ask for a favor, and then months pass without a word.

In 1846, she left the *Tribune* and sailed at last for Europe, where she still hoped to unite once more with Nathan. In Edinburgh, he wrote that he was being married, but he refused to return her letters, refused even a second request, saying, "I shall do nothing with them but what is right, manly, and honorable." He promised to destroy the letters but did not do so. His son tried to sell them. In the end, Nathan left a stipulation in his will that they should be published. And published they were, in 1903, a half century after Margaret Fuller's death, as *Love-Letters of Margaret Fuller*, with a fatuous, unnecessary introduction by Julia Ward Howe and a swinish "reminiscence" by Nathan, written in 1873 and apparently left with the letters for posterity.

> I cannot suffer their [the letters'] exquisite naturalness and sweetness to sink into the grave.... I can wreathe no fresher laurels around the cherished memory of Margaret than by showing, through these letters, that great and gifted as she was as a writer, she was no less so in the soft and tender emotions of a true woman's heart.

"Had I only come ten years earlier! Now my life must be a failure, so much strength has been wasted on abstractions, which only came because I grew not in the right soil," Margaret Fuller wrote to Emerson, from Italy. She went first to England and Scotland, with letters from Emerson to Carlyle and others; useful, but she was herself known. *Woman* had been published in England, *The Dial* was admired, and her reviews in the *Tribune*—along with the fact that she was, in the same journal, to support herself abroad by interviews with "personalities" and descriptions of the scene—did not hinder any more then than now.

She met everyone, even the aged Wordsworth at Grasmere and De Quincey, and picked up gossip. "It seems the cause of Coleridge's separation from his family was wholly with himself; because his opium and his indolence prevented his making any exertions to support them."

The most important meetings of her later life were with two vivid, spectacular, radical intellectuals: Giuseppe Mazzini, fabulous throughout Europe, and Adam Mickiewicz, the great Polish poet and patriot. And another meeting with a young Italian, the Marchese Giovanni Angelo Ossoli, by whom she had, at the age of thirty-eight, a son out of wedlock and whom she later married or did not marry.

Most of the admiring commentaries on Margaret Fuller are eager for her to "find herself as a woman" and also to become a radical in social reform. It is not possible to know if she found herself as a woman, but she did love and was loved by Ossoli, although she was careful not to claim apotheosis.

She became a radical by way of her passionate response to the European upheavals of 1848. (Emerson was in Europe in 1848, and she wrote him from Rome: "Why did you not try to be in Paris at the opening of the Assembly? There were elements worth scanning.") There was social reform and then some around Concord, but as an aesthete she was bored by Brook Farm, and the Boston Abolitionists were "so tedious, often so narrow, always so rabid and exaggerated in their tone." Her thoughts about political agitation changed when she began to connect the antislavery movement with the liberation of Italy, for which she hoped in her *Tribune* dispatches to arouse American sympathies.

It was at the Carlyles' that she met Mazzini.* He was in exile, raising money for Italian refugees, planning a campaign of return, writing in all the leading English journals not only on politics but on art and literature, and charming almost everyone in the nation with his great personal beauty and the purity of his idealism and self-sacrifice. "The most beautiful man I ever saw," was the comment of men and women alike. The cause of Italian liberation and the character of Mazzini, and later that of Garibaldi, electrified the English literary imagination and found its way into countless poems, novels, and plays. In 1879, almost thirty years after Margaret Fuller's death, there appeared an imaginary

---

*I am indebted for much about the European period of Margaret Fuller's life to Joseph J. Deiss, *The Roman Years of Margaret Fuller.*

conversation in verse, written by the radical journalist W. J. Linton. The title was "Mazzini and the Countess Ossoli." At the end of this curious bit of versifying, Mazzini has left the stage and "the Countess, alone, prays for him."

The friendship with Mazzini was genuine in England and grew even closer in Rome. They held many important things in common, Mazzini wrote to his mother, whom Margaret Fuller visited when her boat landed in Genoa. Before leaving England for Paris, there had been a plan to smuggle Mazzini into Italy in disguise and with a false American passport. More than one thing went wrong and just as well.

In Paris, Fuller met Mickiewicz at George Sand's apartment. Their encounter, he said, was one which "consoles and fortifies." She was "a true person" and "the only woman to whom it has been given to touch what is decisive in the present world and to have a presentiment of the world of the future."

Mickiewicz was a bohemian, more forthright and intimately observing than the spiritual Mazzini. To Fuller, he suggested, and apparently without any wishes of his own, that the first step in her deliverance "is to know whether you are permitted to remain a virgin."

When Mickiewicz came to Rome to recruit among the Poles living in exile, he stayed in her lodgings, and when she was suffering from illness brought on by her pregnancy, he was the first to be told the secret. "You are frightened at a very natural, very common ailment, and you exaggerate it in an extravagant manner," he told her. Mickiewicz was to be the child's godfather, but he was not about when Ossoli, determined upon the baptism both for his Catholicism and to legitimate the child, proceeded with the certification.

Fuller and Ossoli met in Saint Peter's Church, after an Easter service. Somehow, Fuller became separated from her companions, and while wandering about the church was asked by a young Italian if he could be of help. They walked back across the Tiber to the Corso. So, Mickiewicz said when he was told, it was at last to be, *"un petit Italien, dans l'église."*

Ossoli was twenty-seven, ten years younger. His mother died when he was a boy, and he lived in the family palazzo with his older brothers and sisters and their ailing father, whom he was taking care of. Later, much about Ossoli was obscured or questioned, either by malice, the secrecy of his connection with Margaret Fuller, or by his reserve and scant English. What seems to be true is that he was from an old family long attached to the Papacy, not rich, and certainly conventional in thought. His father and one older brother were high papal functionaries; two other brothers were in the Pope's Guardia Nobile. It seems, although it is disputed, that he had Republican sympathies before meeting Margaret Fuller, rather than that she swayed him in that direction. In any case, he joined the Civil Guard, put himself in much danger, and with the fall of the Republic would have had to flee Rome in any case.

The marriage, or the "underplot," as Henry James called it: soon after their first meeting he proposed marriage, not necessarily legal. Margaret Fuller drew back. "The connection seemed so every way unfit." Instead, she went off to Florence and Venice as planned, but after a few months she changed her mind and returned to Rome, with almost nothing to live on.

Were they ever actually married? There is confusion here and no sure date or place. The impediments to marriage were many, among them the difficulty of getting a dispensation to marry a Protestant and the confusion of bureaucratic documentation in the city's chaos. Also, Ossoli did not wish to be disinherited of the little property that was to come to him on his father's death. (His unfriendly brothers, owing to his Republicanism, managed to disinherit him in any case.) Then there is the question of whether Margaret Fuller cared about marriage vows. William Henry Channing argued that marriage was against her principles. Emerson thought otherwise: "When it came to be a practical question to herself, she would feel that this was a tie that ought to have the solemnist sanction; that against the theorist was a vast public opinion, too vast to brave." Some evidence can be made to support an actual marriage between the two, but uncertainty remains.

During 1849, Margaret witnessed the flight of the Pope, the announcement of the Constituent Assembly, the declaration of the Republic, and Mazzini's triumphant entrance into Rome. The happiness did not last long; French troops intervened, and the slaughter of the siege of Rome set in. She herself nursed the wounded, along with one of Europe's most celebrated beauties, the romantic, radical Princess Belgioiso. Margaret Fuller's conquest of the "radical chic" figures in Italy—and even of her conservative friend, the important, rich Marchesa Arconati Visconti—seemed to have come about in a natural, unexceptional fashion. She was not seen to be too *exalté*, aggressive, and learned—after all, they knew their Tasso, Dante, and the divine Raphael also.

There had been a cooling off, a winding down, we imagine, achieved by the surrounding acceptance of herself, her learning, her rapturous zeal and gift for friendship. She was as she was, interesting, unique in many ways, and companionable. Only her writing still suffered from orphic diffusion, from a sentimental femininity of accent. "Hard was the heart, stony and seared the eye, that had no tear for that moment."

Her dispatches to the *Tribune*, covering all the great events, were written in the first person and were personal in every sense, filled with pleading, and descriptive passages a bit commonplace. There is also concern for the diplomatic and military tangle of alliances and events. Her Republican bias is candid, in a manner that would not be thought suitable today. Indeed, her reports of disillusionment with the waverings of Pope Pius IX outraged the Catholic diocese in New York. Complaints were made, but Greeley published the accounts uncensored.

Toward the end of her stay in Rome, her writing begins to show a greater control and becomes more graceful and useful, with fewer "effects" that stress her own emotions.

> I entered the French ground, all hollowed and mapped like a honeycomb. A pair of skeleton legs protruded from the bank of one barricade; lower, a dog had scratched away its light covering from the body of a man, and discovered it lying face upward all dressed; the dog stood gazing on it with an air of stupid amazement.

By the end of June, the Republic had fallen to the French troops, and the losers were fleeing. The Ossoli family left for Florence and the following summer embarked for America. The last years of Margaret Fuller's life had been horrible: poverty, overwork, illness; her son nearly starved to death in the town of Rieti where she had left him with a wet nurse in order to return to Rome to make her living.

All the while, she had been preserving documents, taking notes, in addition to her dispatches, for a work to be called "History of the Italian Revolution." The loss of the book has been lamented. She had made inquiries about the possibility of publication in England, which were refused. Part of her reason for returning to America was that she thought it would help in making the arrangements for publication.

She asked Emerson's advice, and the answer shows that he was well aware of her "situation" with a husband, perhaps, and a little boy, certainly. Her family and various others had been informed. (Earlier, when she was awaiting the birth of the child, she received a letter from Emerson, in Paris at the time, quite sweetly urging her to come home with him, where he said he would find a pleasant little house for her.) But now the possibility of the return of the irregular family was not so agreeable to imagine. He advised that Italy was an important advantage to her work. "It is certainly an unexpected side for me to support—the advantage of your absenteeism."

However, return she did, even if in a spirit of gloom about her reception, her devastating poverty, Ossoli's poor prospects, her ill health and exhaustion. They could not afford a steamer and took a merchant boat, a voyage of over two months. She packed all her documents, her notes, and the letters between herself and Ossoli, as well as others. The manuscript for the book was stored in another box.

The journey was a disaster from the start. The captain took sick of smallpox and died; the child contracted the disease but lived. The ship went on, reaching New Jersey for a landing in New York the following day. Trunks were brought from the hold, the child dressed in his best, America to be faced. A fierce storm came up in the night and the ship began to go down off Fire Island. It started to sink near enough to the shore for some of the passengers to make land by the use of a plank; some drowned in a like attempt. A steward tried to take the child to shore but was swamped by a wave. Margaret Fuller was last seen in a white nightgown, holding the broken mast. The body of the child was recovered and claimed by the Fuller family. The box of letters and other personal documents survived, but the manuscript box was lost. The bodies of Margaret Fuller and Ossoli were not recovered. Bell Chevigny came upon a note in the Harvard Library that indicated that the bodies were indeed found, put in coffins, and shipped to Greeley, who refused to take any kind of action. The captain of the boat in this account worried about his jurisdiction in the matter and buried the bodies at night on Coney Island.

"I have lost in her my audience," Emerson said. Thoreau, not the dearest of her friends, paid her the finest tribune—a journey to Fire Island to look for the remains. Margaret Fuller was forty years old when she died.

EPILOGUE: PERFIDIOUS HAWTHORNE

The background is rather sketchy, although Hawthorne's dislike is not surprising. An early entry in his journal: "I was invited to dine at Mr. Bancroft's yesterday with Miss Margaret Fuller; but Providence had given me some business to do, for which I was very grateful."

Two years later, a more pastoral entry:

> After leaving the book at Mr. Emerson's I returned through the woods, and, entering Sleepy Hollow, I perceived a lady reclining near the path which bends along its verge. It was Margaret herself. She had been there the whole afternoon, meditating or reading.... She said that nobody had broken her solitude, and was just giving utterance to the theory that no inhabitant of Concord ever visited Sleepy Hollow, when we saw a group of people entering its sacred precincts.

Perhaps a bit of irony in the final clause.

Sophia Peabody Hawthorne, the placid, settled wife of the disturbed, settled Hawthorne, on "The Great Lawsuit":

> What do you think of the speech Queen Margaret Fuller has made from the throne? It seems to me that if she were married

truly, she would no longer be puzzled about the rights of women. This is the revelation of woman's true destiny and place, which can never be *imagined* by those who do not experience the relation.

No doubt Hawthorne would have expressed it differently, as men and women married to those not concerned with the refinements of writing have good reason to know.

Hawthorne's *The Blithedale Romance*, in which the principal character, Zenobia, is often identified with Margaret Fuller, appeared in 1852, two years after her death. The death was a profound shock to the New England countryside, with the grieving family and old friends caught up in the tragedy and faced with the sharp conundrum of the life. While Hawthorne was writing *The Blithedale Romance*, the *Memoirs of Margaret Fuller Ossoli*, with an account of the history of the family and personal essays by Emerson, James Freeman Clarke, and W. H. Channing, was being composed and arranged. Both books appeared in the same year.

The "striking" remarks by Emerson do not altogether reveal his own and the others' great swell of reverence for their departed friend. The memorial volume edited, omitted, and even destroyed with a free hand; it also wished to assure that the object of veneration was safely married at the time of the conception of the child. Later scholars have been quick to point out the moral scrubbing of documents and to see the volume as a reduction of the vitality of the subject. Still, *Memoirs*, containing many letters and reminiscences of encounters among the group, is extraordinarily interesting and moving; it is possible to view it as the true salvaging of Margaret Fuller's life and thought, which otherwise might have been greatly shadowed in American literary history.

The setting of *The Blithedale Romance* is, as Hawthorne said, "based on my experiences and observations at Brook Farm," the hopeful and not quite practical socialist community established in Roxbury, outside Boston. Hawthorne also insists that the characters are fictional. Nevertheless, Zenobia, "the high spirited Woman, bruising herself against the narrow limitations of her sex," was thought by contemporaries to be a reflection of Margaret Fuller.

There are elements that correspond, but Hawthorne knew as a

novelist that he could not have as the central figure a heroine he saw as wholly unappetizing. Had he drawn Margaret Fuller as he saw her, the results are not pleasing to anticipate, but the novel would have been less foolish, as in many ways it is; it might have been a strange modern fiction.

Zenobia is a great and riveting beauty; she is rich, with a mysterious past. She is a performer and a sort of writer with a "magazine signature." She is a feminist who "scorns the petty restraints that take the life and color out of other women's conversations." Zenobia, pretentious, nevertheless has no real culture, "her mind is full of weeds," which Hawthorne may have believed about Margaret Fuller, even though her culture was greater than his and greater than he needed.

In the book, the narrator, close to Hawthorne himself, has a sudden intuition about Zenobia. He divines, by some special mannish knowledge: "Zenobia is a wife! Zenobia has lived and loved!" The revelations about Margaret Fuller were distressing not only to the morals but to the vanity of the Concord circle. She was an "adulteress" and, if married at all, the wife of a titled foreigner, all rather exotic and *superior. The Scarlet Letter* was begun the year of the death off Fire Island. No just connection can be made but in practical reality Margaret Fuller was the big A in the experience of the countryside. In *The Blithedale Romance*, it may be noted that Zenobia, in a gruesome description, drowns herself because of love for an unworthy man.

In 1858, Hawthorne made his own Italian journey, and one of the things he did was to run down, like a detective, the Margaret Fuller and Ossoli affair. Hawthorne left in his notebooks an account of a conversation with Joseph Mozier, an Ohio merchant who had gone to Florence to become a sculptor and who had known Fuller. These strange unearthings, violent and above all relishing in tone, are contradictory to the facts and to the moral and emotional remembrances of Margaret Fuller in Italy and at home.

Hawthorne is concerned to remove the title "Marchese" from Ossoli and, if he cannot quite do that, to reduce him to a boy picked up on the street, an idiot, and to see Margaret Fuller as a sort of desperate procuress. His recording of his conversations with Mozier reflects as much his own feeling as that of one who had known Margaret Fuller in Italy.

Mozier... then passed to Margaret Fuller, whom he knew well. His developments about poor Margaret were very curious. He says that Ossoli's family, though technically noble, is of no rank whatever; his elder brother, with the title of Marquis, being at the time a working bricklayer, and the sisters walking the streets without bonnets—that is, being in the station of peasant girls.... Ossoli, himself, to the best of his [Mozier's] belief, was Margaret's servant, or had something to do with the care of her apartments. He was the handsomest man Mozier ever saw, but entirely igno-rant even of his own language, scarcely able to read at all, desti-tute of manners; in short, half an idiot, and without any pretensions to be a gentleman.... As for her towards him, I do not understand what feeling there could have been, except it was purely sexual; as for him towards her, there could hardly have been even this, for she had not the charm of womanhood.... She had a strong and coarse nature, too, which she had done her utmost to refine with infinite pains, but which of course could only be superficially changed.... Margaret has not left in the minds of those who knew her any deep witness to her integrity and purity. She was a great humbug; of course with much talent, and much moral reality, or else she could not have been such a great humbug.

She had no manuscript, Hawthorne insists; it did not exist. And he concludes:

Thus there appears to have been a total collapse in poor Marga-ret, morally and intellectually, and tragic as her catastrophe was, Providence was, after all, kind in putting her, and her clownish husband, and their child, on board that fated ship... a strange, heavy, unpliable, and in many respects, defective and evil nature ... she proved herself a woman after all and fell like the lowest of her sisters.

1986

GERTRUDE STEIN

In the midst of her unflagging cheerfulness and confidence, Gertrude Stein can be a pitiless companion. Insomniac rhythms and melodious drummings: She likes to tell you what you know and to tell it again and sometimes to let up for a bit only to tell you once more: "To know all the kinds of ways then to make men and women one must know all the ways some are like others of them, are different from others of them, so then there come to be kinds of them."

Her writing, T. S. Eliot once said, "has a kinship with the saxophone." That could be one of her own throwaways, but she would not have used a word like *saxophone*. The saxophone is an object with a history, and she didn't care much for nouns with such unique significance.

What can Eliot mean? The saxophone, invented in 1846 by Adolphe Sax, has little standing in the hereditary precincts of the classical orchestra. So it must be that Gertrude Stein is a barbaric and illicit intrusion. Preceding the curiosity of the saxophone, Eliot said about her work: "It is not improving, it is not amusing, it is not interesting, it is not good for one's mind." No doubt, Eliot wasn't aware of the improvisations of the great American masters of the saxophone.

In any case, Gertrude Stein was born in 1874, nearly thirty years after the birth of the saxophone. Her family and its situation must have been the womb of her outlandish confidence, confidence of a degree amazing. She was, after all, determined to be, even if *in absentia*, or because of that exile, our country's historian. There is nothing hothouse in this peculiar American princess. For one thing, she is as sturdy as a turnip—the last resort of the starving, and native to the Old World, as the dictionary has it. A tough root of some sort; and yet she is mesmerized and isolated, castlebound, too, under the enchantments of her own devising.

Confidence is highly regarded by both citizen and nation; it is altogether warm and loving. Without confidence, fidelity to death, as it were, the work Gertrude Stein actually produced cannot easily be imagined. Other writings, perhaps, since possibility was everywhere in her; but not what we have, not what she did. In her life, confidence and its not-too-gradual ascent into egotism combined with a certain laziness and insolence. It was her genius to make the two work together like a machine, a wondrous contraption, something futuristic and patented for her use.

She wrote her Cambridge lecture at the height of her fame, while waiting for her car to be fixed. She sat down on the fender of another car and, waiting around, wrote "Composition as Explanation." Several hours it took her: "Everything is the same except composition and as the composition is different and always going to be different everything is not the same." So it was. And: "Now if we write, we write; and these things we know flow down our arm and come out on the page." Yes. So she told Thornton Wilder.

Many wires and pieces of string went into the contraption, the tinkering, and the one result was that she wrote at great length and used a vocabulary very, very small. It was her original idea to make this vocabulary sufficient for immensities of conception, America, Americans, being perhaps her favorite challenge. When she is not tinkering, we can see her like a peasant assaulting the chicken for Sunday dinner. She would wring the neck of her words. And wring the neck of sentences, also.

Miss Stein lived until 1946, through two world wars and much else. Perhaps she never seemed young, and everyone would certainly have wished for her to live on and on, since there is a Methuselah prodigiousness about her. Everything we know about her life contributes to her being.

When was she not a prodigy—and even without exerting herself to represent the exceptional in action? She went to Harvard and studied with William James. Anecdotes appeared on her doorstep, anecdotes quite enduring. No, she didn't want to take an examination because the day was too fine. William James understood and gave her the highest mark in the course, if we can trust the *Autobiography of Alice B. Toklas*, which we can and cannot.

Premedical studies at John Hopkins; that is part of her aura. Perhaps she's a scientist, so look, when the pages confuse, for the rigors of the laboratory. She abandoned the medical studies, and we must say that, too, added something to the whole. The willful simplification she practiced can make her, to some, appear to be a philosopher in the most difficult mode of our own period.

It will be said William James taught her that everything must be considered, nothing rejected. Simple enough and not quite a discovery. What you can say is that while she was not learning, actively not learning, other young women were going to finishing schools, primping, dancing, and having babies, and she was becoming Gertrude Stein. Every refusal was *interesting*, a word she liked very much.

Both of her parents were German Jews. Whether she thought of herself as Jewish is hard to say. Perhaps she didn't, or not quite. She didn't like to be defined and that helped her to stay on in Occupied France. Her brother Leo thought of himself as Jewish, even at Harvard—or (why not?) certainly at Harvard.

Her parents were, in terms appropriate for American history, early settlers. That she knew and took in seriously. If, as one can read, the definition of Old New York, of New York aristocracy, is to have made your money before the Civil War, the Steins were aristocrats. The Stein brothers, one of whom was her father, arrived in 1841; her mother's family had settled in Baltimore previously.

A Stein Brothers clothing store was set up in Baltimore with success, but Gertrude's father and the brother moved on to Allegheny, Pennsylvania, where she was born. Then quite soon the characteristic behavior of the family began to assert itself. They showed a desire to take off, for Europe. They are inclined to be Americans abroad.

The family finances are not easy to make out, at the beginning or at the end. But even when the Allegheny store was not quite flourishing, Amelia Stein took herself and the children to Vienna. There they lived with governesses and tutors, the lessons and practices of the upper class. The Steins early on must have realized that one could be almost rich in Europe at that time without being rich enough at home. And they liked to buy things, to go shopping. The mother and children went to Paris to buy clothes and trinkets and to have a good time. In a later period, while Gertrude and Leo remained abroad, the older brother, Michael, and his wife, Sarah, came back to stun California with their collection of modern paintings.

From Pennsylvania, the family settled in Oakland, California, and the father, Daniel Stein, went into the streetcar business—a good career move, it would be called nowadays, even if Daniel was not quite the master of it. He died when Gertrude Stein was seventeen, and she wrote about his disappearance: "Then our life without a father began a very pleasant one." But more of that later, about the pleasantness of not having family members and the strain when you have them.

The older brother, Michael, took over the family business and made good investments for the fine purpose of not having to work. He was able to set Gertrude and Leo up abroad: a princely situation. Michael and his wife, Sarah, were connoisseurs of the new, not of the refectory table from an old monastery or the great decorated urns to put in the hall and fill with dead reeds. For a time, they lived just outside Paris in a house designed by Le Corbusier.

In this family, you are not concerned with provincials—never at any point in their history. Not one of them seemed afflicted with puritanical, thrifty scruples, with denial or failure of nerve. Works of art were, in the end, their most daring and prudent investment. The paintings and the great international celebrity of the creative one, Gertrude, and even the fading claims of Leo make of the Steins one of the truly glittering American families. They stand in history along with the Adams and James families—along with if not quite commensurate with. They were immensely important in the history of American taste, by way of their promotion of modern painting through their collections and in their influence on the many painters, writers, and intellectuals who came to the *salon* on the rue de Fleurus.

The Cone sisters of Baltimore, contemporaries of the Steins, were to merit a kind of immortality when they used their cotton-mill fortune to buy Manets, Renoirs, Cézannes, and Matisses for the later glory of the Baltimore Museum. Acquisition has need of special conviction and taste, but neither of the Cone women could claim for themselves an art to rank with that of Cézanne and Picasso—a claim that Gertrude Stein did not hesitate to make.

Picasso, bewildered by the Stein entourage, coming and going in Paris, said: "They are not women. They are not men. They are Americans."

The Stein family was to be The Making of Americans. "It has always seemed to me a rare privilege, this of being an American, a real American, one whose tradition it has taken scarcely sixty years to create." There is no doubt Gertrude knows how to look at it, this subject of being American—the sixty years names it just right. An amused chauvinism—that is her tone. And elsewhere she notes that America is the oldest country in the world because it's been in the twentieth century the longest, something like that.

Still, it must be said Gertrude Stein feels more sentiment for America than she does for her fellow Steins, except as a subject. The mother, the Baltimore bride, faded into illness and at last died when Gertrude was fourteen: "We had already had the habit of doing without her." Simon, older (Gertrude was the youngest), ate a lot and was slow. Bertha, well, she never cared for Bertha: "It is natural not to care for a sister, certainly not when she is four years older and grinds her teeth at night."

The alliance between Gertrude and Leo ended in bitter contempt on both sides. It was said that Gertrude gave Picasso's portrait of Leo to Etta Cone in order to get it off the wall. When Gertrude died, she and Leo were so greatly estranged he knew of her death only by reading about it in the papers. His comment was: "I can't say it touched me. I had lost not only all regard, but all respect for her." They were an odd lot, except for Michael, but then, as she put it herself: "It takes time to make queer people, and to have others who can know it, time and a certainty of means."

Three Lives was finished in 1906, published in 1909—in every way a work of resonating originality, even if no aspect of its striking manner will persist in the eccentric shape of the works that follow. The stories are composed in the manner of a tale. The characters are sketched by a trait or two, and they pace through their lives, as the pattern has ordained; and then each one dies.

Sometimes there is an echo of realistic fiction, the setting of a scene, the filling in of detail, but we are given almost everything by assertion, and thus there is an archaic quality to the tone. But, of course, the tone is new, partly because of this archaic picturing. No other writer would have composed these moving portraits as Gertrude Stein composed them. One, "Melanctha," is of a higher order than the other two, "The Good Anna" and "The Gentle Lena."

Nothing is sentimental. We are not asked to experience more emotion than the scene can render; the stories do not manipulate in excess of their own terms. A distance is maintained, a distance—perhaps it is objectivity—that provides a fresh, bare surface for the sketching of the lives of the two German women of what used to be called "the serving class" and the extraordinary daring of the picture of Negro life and character as she has imagined it.

"Melanctha" is the most challenging as a composition, and the character is the most challenging because she has an interior life. The presentation is for the most part in dialogue of a radical brilliance that lies on the page with a calm defiance. It is as stunning today as when it was first written.

Whether this dialogue is the natural rhythm of Negro speech is not altogether the point. Such a rhythm if discovered for transcription cannot be copyrighted; no author can own it for a certain number of pages. On the other hand, it is clear that the language of "Melanctha" is some kind of speech rhythm not written down before, some catching of accent and flow the reader recognizes without being able to name. Of course, it is a literary language, constructed of repetition, repeated emphasis, all with great musicality. There is a stilted openness to it; that is, it is both declamatory, unnatural, and yet somehow lifelike. It is a courteous dialogue and not condescending because it does not proceed from models, from a spurious idea, from the shelf of a second-hand store.

Inauthenticity is so often remarked when authors need to find a speech for those not from their own class or experience. Stephen Crane's powerful but badly written *Maggie: A Girl of the Streets* is an example of prefab ethnic or class speech. "Hully gee!" said he, "does mugs can't phase me. Dey knows I kin wipe up d'street wid any tree of dem"—Hell's Kitchen.

Gertrude Stein's way in "Melanctha" is so simple and arresting that her ear, in an offhand passage, does have a ghostly attuning. Note the distribution of the *you*s in a plain bit of dialogue spoken by Melanctha's father: "Why don't you see to that girl better you, you're her mother." Pure ear, quite different from the formal cadences of Dr. Jeff Campbell, the mellifluous suitor with his high-pitched arias to the "wandering" Melanctha: "It certainly does sound a little like I don't know very well what I do mean, when you put it like that to me, Miss Melanctha, but that's just because you don't understand enough about what I meant, by what I was just saying to you."

Hemingway learned from Gertrude Stein how to become Ernest Hemingway. Perhaps one could say that. He decided most of all to strip down his sentences. (It is curious to learn condensation from Stein, who stripped, reduced, and simplified only to add up without mercy, making her prose an intimidating heap of bare bones, among other things.) One can see it in 1921—before they had met, but not before he would have read *Three Lives*. Perhaps he learned more from the *you*s than from the more insistent rhythms in "Melanctha."

From "Up in Michigan":

Liz liked Jim very much. She liked it the way he walked over from the shop and often went to the kitchen door to watch for him to start down the road. She liked it about his mustache....
She liked it very much that he didn't look like a blacksmith. She liked it how much D. J. Smith and Mrs. Smith liked Jim. One day she found that she liked it the way the hair was black on his arms and how white they were above the tanned line when he washed up in the washbasin outside the house.

And then he ends the paragraph: "Liking that made her feel funny." Gertrude Stein would not have written the last line. It is too girlish for her, and is a repudiation of the tone and rhythm that goes before.

Soon after *Three Lives*, *The Making of Americans* was resumed, since it had been started earlier. It was taken up—if that is not a contradiction of what it is, a dive into the deep waters of the Stein Sea. Down into the Stein Sea she went between 1906 and 1908, and the book was not actually published until 1925, for reasons not a mystery. It is very long. It swims about and about and farther and farther out with the murmurous monotony of untroubled waters.

The enormous ambition of the book is shown in the roundness of the title. It may be a sort of chronicle, imaginative history, of the Stein family, but that's the least of it. It is the making of Americans, just as she says. That is the intention.

In his introduction, Bernard Fay writes, not without leaning in the direction of her own style: "She likes too much the present; she is too fond of words; she has too strongly the love of life; she is too far from death, to be satisfied with anything but the whole of America."

Consider her idea of the bottom nature of human beings: "A man in his living has many things inside him, he has in him his way of beginning; this can come too from a mixture in him, from the bottom nature of him." So we live and so we die. "Any one has come to be a dead one. Any one has not come to be such a one to be a dead one. Many who were living have come to be a dead one." The cold, black suet-pudding of her style, said Wyndham Lewis.

The "continuous present" is another of her rhetorical discoveries, and it seems to be just a circling round and round, a not going back or forward. *Four in America*: It is not clear how much she knows about her four Americans, how much she wished to know about Ulysses Grant, Henry James, the Wright Brothers, and George Washington. Her meditations do not run to facts or dates, and her vanity would preclude a quotation or even an appropriation. Instead, she asks herself what the four would have done had they been other than what they were. Suppose Grant to be a saint, Henry James a general, the Wright Brothers painters, George Washington a novelist.

What is the difference between Shakespeare's plays and Shakespeare's sonnets? "Shakespeare's plays were written as they were written. Shakespeare's sonnets as they were going to be written." Sometimes an interesting bit comes upon one suddenly, like a handout on the street: "Henry James had no failure and no success." Everything is process.

There is no need for revision since the work celebrates and represents process itself, like an endless stirring on the stove. One gift never boils away: She is a comedian.

Such was her gift, and she created a style to display the comedy by a deft repetition of word and phrase. To display the comedy of what? Of living, of thinking? The comedy of writing words down on the page, perhaps that most of all. She was not concerned with creating the structure of classical comedy, the examination of folly. What she understands is inadvertence and incongruity. Imperturbability is her mood, and in that she is herself a considerable comic actor, in the line of Buster Keaton.

Remarks are not literature, so she said. But the remark is her triumph. She lives by epigrams and bits of wit cut out of the stretches or repetition, as if by a knife, and mounted in our memory. Her rival in this mastery is Oscar Wilde, with whom she shared many modes of performance: the bold stare that faced down ridicule, a certain ostentation of type, the love of publicity and the iron to endure it.

> I like a view but I like to sit with my back to it.
> What is the point of being a little boy if you are going to grow up to be a man?
> Before the flowers of friendship faded friendship faded.
> I am I because my little dog knows me.
> Ezra Pound is a village explainer, excellent if you were a village, but if not, not.

Oscar Wilde was an aesthete. Gertrude Stein thought up something more stylish and impressive. She came forth as an aesthetician: more severe and riddling, yet dandyish in her handsome wools and velvety in her sentences.

"Continuous present": Her most valuable continuous present or presence was the alliance with Alice B. Toklas. It appeared she could achieve herself, become Gertrude Stein, without Leo, and she found him expendable. He combined her vanity with a down-turning contentiousness and tedious pretension, all bereft of her revolutionary accent and brilliant dogmatism.

But still she ponders ones and twos and twos not being ones and then had the luck to turn a corner and find this small, neat person from California, one with the intelligence, competence, and devotion to complete the drama of the large, indolent, brooding, ambitious sibyl, herself.

They are a diptych: figures gazing straight ahead, with no hint of Cubist distortion. A museum aspect to their image—wooden, fixed, iconographic in the Byzantine style. They are serene and a bit sly in the direct gaze.

Everything works, above all the division of labor. Carl Van Vechten considered that Gertrude couldn't sew on a button, couldn't cook an egg or place a postage stamp of the correct denomination on an envelope. Alice's labors over the manuscripts, the copying and proofreading, with a numbing attention to the mysteries of the commas that are and the commas that are not, make of her a heroine of minute distinctions.

The Autobiography of Alice B. overwhelms by charm and the richness of the cast and the rosy dawn in Paris at the time. The tone and the wit of the composition stand in an almost perfect balance to the historical vividness of the moment. The book is valiant in self-promotion also, boldly forward in conceit, but that is what spurs the recollection. Otherwise it would not have been worth the effort, Gertrude Stein's effort.

She enjoyed the *Autobiography* a good deal more than some of the great personages on the scene. More than one felt himself or herself to be wrongly presented. Matisse was not amused; he charged she knew nothing about painting. Braque was dismayed by her account of the beginnings of Cubism. Tristan Tzara called her "a clinical case of megalomania."

"Testimony Against Gertrude Stein" appeared in *Transition*. Eugene Jolas, who edited the pamphlet, wrote: "There is a unanimity of opinion that she had no understanding of what really was happening about her, that the mutation of ideas beneath the surface of the more obvious contacts and clashes of personality during the period escaped her entirely."

No matter, she was now a bona-fide international celebrity and had an American public. Books, poems, lectures, plays appeared—and she appeared in person. She returned to America in 1934 for a lecture tour, and everyone knew she had said a rose is a rose is a rose. Newspapermen came to the ship, crowds were waiting at the dock. She and Alice were photogenic, and Gertrude was ready with a reply to every question. It is Oscar Wilde landing in America in the 1880s with nothing to declare but his genius.

She returned to Paris, and then there was World War II and the Occupation—tragic, complex events not suitable to her talent and disrupting to her comfort. Her removal from large events, the hypnotic immersion in the centrality of her own being, made it possible for this very noticeable couple to stay on in France, move here and there, get food, in a sense to brazen it out and be there when the Americans arrived. And wasn't she first and last an American, a true example of the invulnerability of the New World? To be imperturbable, root strong, can be a kind of personal V-day.

Wars I Have Seen, published in 1945, covers these ruminating years in the countryside. It reads like a diary, the recording of events of the day. Perhaps it was dictated to Alice in the evenings. The landscape of the Occupation provided splendid vignettes and an awesome and rich cud of complacency. She did not understand the war, and she did not like things to be troublesome, and so she is increasingly conservative. Both Pétain and Franco pleased her—comfort requires order, that she understood.

But, at last, she had to mull over the question of Jewishness:

The Jews have never been an economic power as anybody knows who knows and as everybody knows who knows. But the Europeans particularly the countries who like to delude their people do not want to know it, and the Jews do not want anybody to know it, although they know it perfectly well they must know it because it would make themselves to themselves feel less important and as they always as the chosen people have felt themselves to be important they do not want anybody to know it.

If it were not for the fact that the reader supplies his own vision of Gertrude and Alice hanging on with the fortitude of lambs hunting for the sheepfold, the whimsicality of *Wars* would offend. "Oh dear. It would all be so funny if it were not so terrifying and so sad."

She lived a long time with her wondrous contraption, the Model T of her style, and sometimes she could run on things with a turn of phrase, but sometimes not. So, she opines, "Soviet Russia will end in nothing so will the Roosevelt administration end in nothing because it is not stimulating it will end in nothing." From the sheep-fold, she took up dangerous challenges and offered a work called "Reflections on the Atomic Bomb." She found that the bomb was not interesting.

Anyway, she, the first American, loved the GIs, and they loved her. But she didn't know anything about the young men, and *Brewsie and Willie* (1946) is the aesthetician's defeat. The dialogue is atrocious. She had forgotten that she must fabricate speech, not believe she has captured it at the train station. By now, she is speaking in her own voice, just like any other old person, and confident always, she addresses the nation: "Find out the reason why, look facts in the face, not just what they all say, the leaders, but every darn one of you so that a government by the people for the people shall not perish from the earth, it won't, somebody else will do it if we lie down on the job." And so on.

Finally she emerged as a strange figure, competitive and jealous and also unworldly in her self-isolation. She could not understand why *Ulysses*, radical and difficult—or so she had been told for perhaps she hadn't read it—should have been selling more than *The Making of Americans*. Joyce is difficult because he has more knowledge, more language, more rhythmical musicality than the reader can easily summon. With Gertrude Stein we are frequently urged to forgetfulness, to erasure of tonal memory, so that we may hear the hypnotic murmurings of what is a literature in basic English.

Gertrude Stein, all courage and will, is a soldier of minimalism. Her work, unlike the resonating silences in the art of Samuel Beckett, embodies in its loquacity and verbosity the curious paradox of the minimalist form. This art of the nuance in repetition and placement she shares with the orchestral compositions of Philip Glass.

1987

THE FICTIONS OF AMERICA

Rien ne vous tue un homme comme d'être obligé de représenter un pays.
—JACQUES VACHÉ, in a letter to André Breton, quoted as the frontispiece by Julio Cortázar in *Hopscotch*

IMAGINATIVE literature does not have a long history in the United States. It is not even as old as the country itself—this strange world always ferociously impatient to reach the twentieth century, bored with the notion of a peasantry, ready from Plymouth Rock for the Model T, without an ivied ruin in its landscape. And proud enough to be young—its youth, as Oscar Wilde observed in his velvet wanderings to the mining camps, being its oldest tradition.

It was not until the nineteenth century that our fertile surroundings produced our handful of reassuring genius in the art of literature. Hawthorne, Melville, Emerson, Whitman, Poe, Emily Dickinson, each his own patron you might say, starting anew, giving a special visionary aspect to Ben Franklin's assurance that God helps those who help themselves.

Had we not had the good fortune to bring the English language to the northern woods, there amid the tiresome Wampanoag, and the great American Indian King Philip to be drawn and quartered, dispatched in the diction and rhythms of the King James Bible and Shakespeare, our classics might today be greeted with the glazed condescension so familiar to the recessive languages of the world and to their masterpieces. It is just as well that the feudal-minded Dutch patroons, with their land grants on the Hudson River, for the most part mismanaged, that they did not, in this case, have the "business sense," the aboriginal maize necessary to prevail. On the other hand, the spirit of Erasmus might have thawed the chilblains of Increase Mather. Everything indeed was, as we say, a toss-up.

But here we are, speaking and writing English, feeling both the last born and yet the overburdened, self-appointed patriarch of the world family. To be a young patriarch is troublesome. It is to be a schoolmaster and to face much recalcitrance in the dormitories of an evening. It is ever burdensome and frustrating, also bankrupting, and offers little except the gratifying self-pity of the dutiful.

Here we are under the celestial protection of two oceans. This protection is one of those matter-of-fact realities scarcely worth noting. The oceans might be as pleasing and impractical as the Rocky Mountains after the wagon trains pushed through. But the oceans are deeply rooted in the American unconscious. Only a savage amount of nudging, shouting, and alarming can make the often exhorted American People feel threatened by insidious microbes and ideological poisons winging in from little islands and destitute countries to the south of us, to be carried on the vapors to Florida and on, on to California. No doubt the fear is cant. What we have is better called *annoyance* when the microbes are studied under the microscope of military science or contemplated as a sting and rash we could do without.

We are also to be evermindful of the ocean-spanning detonations crossing each other on the two-way street from here to Eastern Europe. Unless intercepted in the heavens, God's last frontier. The newfound land is not altogether at ease and happy, but other than that . . . fine.

The interesting thing is that we are where we are. We are living in the United States, in our mostly temperate and potentially self-sufficient large land mass. Our placement in the scheme of things is more real, more to the point, than our indefinable national character. America is more concrete than American. In spite of the most insistent drumming, we are not a folk. That lump of a word is an elusive signification, but it does appear to have some meaning when one thinks of, for instance, the peoples of Europe.

Even our early settlers are still to be described and accounted for, filled in like characters in a novel, with their accents from the Thames valley and the Outer Hebrides, their frieze coats, worsted stockings, and faces pitted with smallpox. The Harvard historian Bernard Bailyn has written recently about the "peopling of British North America" in the late eighteenth century, before our revolution, in preindustrial America. At that time the press for immigration from the British Isles became so intense and politically embarrassing that serious thinkers considered it should be put under a government ban—in the manner of one of the great powers of the present day. Some were convicts, but many were dispossessed peasants and unemployed artisans who, needing to pay debts incurred by the often thieving brokers of the sea passage, allowed themselves to become indentured servants, to be sold on arrival, and committed to service for five years. These transatlantic crossings, removal from the pastures and cemeteries of one's ancestors, from the worn cobbles of London, represented the greatest population movement in early modern history. From the very first the American imagination was faced with the promise of the land and the cultural instability of its uprooted people.

Englishmen, involuntary slaves from Africa, families from the whole span of Europe, Asia, and the present, the 1980s, high birthrate of the new Spanish-speaking arrivals, are all somehow to be translated, perhaps transmogrified, into Americanness. We were never quite settled and perhaps are never to be. Migrations continue, surge, in stealth or otherwise, by land and water, ditch, over every porous border:

> The dreadful sundry of this world,
> The Cuban, Polodowsky,
> The Mexican women,
> The Negro undertaker
> Killing the time between corpses
> Fishing for crayfish...
>
> (Wallace Stevens)

"The dreadful sundry" is in reality to be thought of as a group of lottery winners, all of us. To be living here, and not in what we mostly believe is the insupportable there, elsewhere, is to be assimilated into a powerful abstraction, the abstraction of never-ending possibility. The American situation is not so much to overthrow the past as to overthrow the future before it arrives as a stasis; thus in our architecture the destruction of the new in favor of the newer. The country is concrete in its parts: this town, this group, this couple, this family, this western or eastern or southern landscape. But to be an American is to try to make a rock out of a waterfall.

In our fiction it has always been difficult to find the parts that would somehow stand for the whole. Just as our metropolis, Manhattan, for all its dominance as a vision of the twentieth century, does not have the wholeness of London, Paris, or Rome, is not quite the measure of national destiny, so the country is not a whole, despite its being a genuine union and not a spurious union of conquered nationalities.

America does not easily lend itself to metaphorical representation. Perhaps Ahab, in *Moby-Dick,* in malevolent pursuit of the white whale, the source of injury, pursuit unto death, is a symbolic temptation of power and obsession in battle with the vastness. And we might offer *The Golden Bowl, The Scarlet Letter, Huckleberry Finn, The Great Gatsby,* and *Leaves of Grass,* all powerfully resonant, somehow going beyond their creative terms and representing an intuition of national character and fate.

As a large and modern destiny, the country is resistant, forever in transition. When Kafka sat down to write *Amerika*, a place he had never seen, he said he came to the creation by way of Benjamin Franklin, "the first American dummy," as D. H. Lawrence called him. But somehow *Amerika* is the least "modern" of Kafka's works. He, who lived his short life under the shadows of the ancient city of Prague, could not find in his imagination a symbolic center for the wanderings of the cheerful, bewildered Karl Rossmann in the "boundless theatre" of the space, with a sign saying "Everyone Is Welcome."

The episodic *Amerika* bears a resemblance, or a counterresemblance,

to Melville's *The Confidence-Man*, usually considered a failure and
certainly a failure at its birth. This bitter litany of crookedness and
dissemblance is bereft of anything resembling a sympathetic character;
it is a curiosity of moral chagrin, or worse, moral revulsion, first published in 1857. Melville gathers his unseemly crowd on a steamboat
going from St. Louis to New Orleans, down the Mississippi. The crowd
displays the phantom physiognomy of the American:

> Natives of all sorts, and foreigners; men of business and men of
> pleasure; parlor men and backwoodsmen; farm-hunters and
> fame-hunters; heiress-hunters, gold-hunters, buffalo-hunters,
> bee-hunters, happiness-hunters, truth-hunters, and still keener
> hunters after all these hunters.

Hunters, on the trail, wary and seeking whatever may be off guard.
On and on Melville goes with his listing: Quakers, soldiers, slaves,
Creoles, old-fashioned French Jews, Mormons and Papists, Sioux chiefs,
hard-shell Baptists and clay eaters...

In *Amerika* Karl Rossmann's journey, meeting after meeting, incident after incident, that sort of inchoate journey, is held together by
the naïve hope and the bounding, naïve energy of a young immigrant.
A folly of misunderstandings in a world so ready with offerings and
disappearances it defeats the imagination. "I greet you in the name of
the Theatre of Oklahoma." The biggest theater in the world, "almost
no limits to it." All of this at the end of the novel which remained
unfinished. The actual last words Kafka wrote are interesting. Karl is
on the train to Oklahoma, going across America:

> Broad mountain streams appeared, rolling in great waves down
> on to the foothills and drawing with them a thousand foaming
> wavelets, plunging underneath the bridges over which the train
> rushed; and they were so near that the breath of coldness rising
> from them chilled the skin of one's face.

Perhaps in some insomniac revery Kafka imagined himself taking off
for America. It would be strange if it were otherwise for a Jew in Cen-

tral Europe, if the thought did not appear from time to time. But of course the actual transformation was unimaginable, that is if he were to remain himself and not the altogether other, the innocent Karl Rossmann.

In *The Confidence-Man*, the swindler on shipboard takes on every disguise, one after another; he is the solemn, posing widower, "the man with the weed," the black crepe of mourning; he is a beggar posing now as a deaf-mute and then as a Negro cripple. Melville calls his book a masquerade and the mutual corruption of the swindler and the swindled would seem to leave none free from dishonesty, false piety, presumption of charity at the moment of deceit. It's a dark vision, somewhat tedious and overwrought, just as *Amerika*, another vision of the country as ephemeral, is perhaps tedious in its more cheerful tendency to disorient.

The American sections of *Martin Chuzzlewit* open with what is now called the media. "Here's the morning's New York Sewer!" From there it proceeds to boastfulness, hyperbole on behalf of the glories of the nation, chicanery and fraud in the Eden Land Corporation. And much else, streaming to the target with a thud like tobacco in the spittoon. Satiric asperity indeed, not quite on the classical model, here broad and there on the mark. America in comic place, but not humorous, too big and imposing and self-loving for that.

There you are, young, just out of the Harvard Business School, and you enter a Wall Street firm with all the chilly, serpentine slithering of the old commercial barons. As Mark Twain wrote, "Yesterday I didn't have a nickel, and now I owe you a million dollars." And nowadays all accomplished quickly and gracefully by one in fine shape from the squash courts and the jogging track. The leaps, the disgust with sequential development here—just roll, roll, roll with it. What was the use of it when the young man was already making a million a year? Mere legalism, old fictional habits in the question. Straight ahead and why not?

Henry Adams wrote an essay about Jay Gould and Jim Fisk and the Great Gold Conspiracy of 1869, which brought about an investigation of "the causes that led to the unusual and extraordinary fluctuations of gold in the City of New York." The richness of Adams's historical imagination composed a stock-market story, dramatic, and just now with the pertinence of a pistol shot. "One of the earliest acts of the new rulers [Gould and Fisk] was precisely such as Balzac or Dumas might have predicted and delighted in. They established themselves in a palace." Inside they built an opera house and a "suite of apartments was then furnished by themselves, as representing the corporation . . . in a style which, though called vulgar, is certainly not more vulgar than that of the President's official residence." An opera troupe was engaged for the transplanted Vermont Yankee, Mr. Fisk, with a "permanent harem."

Charles Francis Adams in the same historical series described Cornelius Vanderbilt who began as a near illiterate as becoming an American figure on the heroic scale:

> a dictator in modern civilization, moving forward to this end step by step with a sort of pitiless energy which has seemed to have in it an element of fate . . . He has combined the natural power of the individual with the factitious power of the corporation.

An impudent line from Flannery O'Connor's stories: "You can do one thing or you can do another, kill a man or take a tire off his car."

D. H. Lawrence: "Where is this new bird called the true American? . . . Go on, show us him."

Well, where is he in our fiction? We note the intricate, small-muscled talent for self-destruction in our presidents, the almost bejeweled talent, glittering with faceted opportunity. Sometimes it appears that way, so densely structured are the details of folly. And then again it appears to be just the gross stumbling and trampling and lumbering of some inexplicable maladaptation. The extraordinary plasticity of these wonderfully visible public characters; the relentless deformation of the person, or the *personality*, we had been assured to have knowledge of in the long, encyclopedic presentation of the public self. The imperturbable, glassy wonders; the absence of traditional motivation, the violent exhaustion of cause and effect as it used to be assumed in fiction. In New York City the schemes of the well-named Bureau of Parking Violations might have come from the swarm of scams on the boat cruising down the Mississippi in *The Confidence-Man*.

From day to day it is not always easy to tell whether spectacular national happenings are to be thought of as comedy or tragedy. So many are likely to be a marbleized mixture of both. Our lighter, wind-blown disruptions may bring to mind Restoration Comedy, in which we are, symbolically, hiding behind the screen, putting on the servant girl's dress when the cuckolded husband appears. The great Macaulay maintained that these comedies were not a fixed aesthetic formulation but bore a true relation to contemporary experience and character. The fops, the seducers, the Sir this and Sir that were to be seen everywhere in London, bowing with perfect civility, getting out of carriages, carrying on business. It is not a dishonor to a nation to have produced Restoration Comedy. And there is no doubt that, just now, a rich, comic inadvertence attends many of our national pieties.

It is not the possibility or the purpose of fiction to keep up, be on time. Literalism, in any case, would be dangerous since the landscape is under the domination of rapid obsolescence. Cavaliers and Roundheads change position without a bow to the previous state of mind. Still, the substitution of image for self at the top, the idea of creating an impression of control at just the moment one is displaying confusion, bewilderment, and distraction must be a part of all of us. And not in the sense that this is a natural way of getting through life, but rather the continuing and genuine distance between announced and emblematic virtue and the orneriness of last night. The imposture, the masquerade, the banality of the most admired. And the language of spin control, management style, freedom fighters, hostile takeover, Praise The Lord amusement parks.

In much of the American fiction of the last few years there has been a curious backward revolution, to use the contradiction as it reigns in our politics. The number of well-received stories that have a "down-home" landscape, as if all were waiting to be documented in the Dakotas, in New Hampshire, or one of the southern states. Family novels, often with a bit of World War II, rather perfunctory and peripheral, but intended for spaciousness of conception. In the long run these are individual stories of hometown blight and failure well in the line of Sherwood Anderson.

For the telling, the novels will make use of a first-person narrator in no way imaginable as the author of a long fiction; an illusory voice, stretching credulity as it remembers and shapes experience. The result is to narrow the circle of illumination to the possible language and reflection of the presumptive teller. When the substitution of the more or less unlettered voice becomes a harness, as it will, the novelist often just slips the traces without preparation, and dots the manuscript with bits of poetry and jarring sophistications—and no aesthetic embarrassment. Something like the galloping indiscretions of free verse. In any case, this writing is a relief from contemporary America and has in its fervent confidence something akin to the nostalgic, if troubled, chauvinism of popular politics.

And there are city stories too, of course: youth, cocaine, divorce, child custody. One more disappointment in the fictive arrangements set up and one much like another—the fate of the spirit of documentation.

The peculiar instability of the democratic vistas which face the American author and in which his imagination is rooted does not seem to offer a world view or a view of America in the world. America is very much in the world but when we write a love story we are merely in our own bed, or one of us is in the wrong bed, the bed of trouble, which will provide the beloved illicit and the pornographic pages and scenes and the mess to follow thereupon. But it must be said that government, the national destiny, the deficit, Star Wars, a little Gilbert and Sullivan excursion in Grenada, are of less relevance than a cockroach in the sink. This is freedom and the consequent literature.

On the other hand, what is admirable, aesthetically thrilling, significant, and deeply honoring to the profession of literature as it comes to us from dissident authors in overrun countries is the oppressive government in the bedroom. In this fiction, laughter, too much of it, is like the opening of the gates of a prison. The bureaucrat, the interrogation is as homely as cabbage in the soup. By enormous talent, heroic preservation of sanity, the second half of the twentieth century receives its requiem in this fiction.

The spaciousness of Latin America, single sovereign states tottering as if waiting to be born, flamboyant dictators of vast presumption, the sense that a novel may be the history of the country by the patient, imaginative flow of family history—this too extends the beauty and purpose of literature.

Still, stories and poems are written by men and women and not by "conditions" of states, whether open or suffocating in imposed noxious gases. Genius created the great novel by the Cuban Alejo Carpentier, *El Recurso del Método*, in 1974, the work for some reason entitled in English *Reasons of State*, the substitution not more "catching to the eye" than Descartes. This cosmopolitan novel of such sumptuous learning, wit, and such a cascade of brilliant language makes of the plump, old voluptuary, the Head of State, a truly larger-than-life creation:

> When the Head of State appeared on the balcony of honour, he was greeted with acclamations which sent a great cloud of pigeons over the roofs and terraces that chequered the valley with red and white, between thirty-two more or less aspiring belfries. After the cheering had died down, the President . . . began to make a clearly articulated speech . . . though embellished, so thought some, with too many expressions like "nomadic," "myrobalantic," "rocambolesque," "eristic," "apodeictic"; before this he had already elevated the tone by a glittering mobilization of "acting against the grain," "swords of Damocles," "crossing the Rubicon," trumpets of Jericho, Cyranos, Tatarins and Clavilenos, all mixed up together with lofty palm-trees, solitary condors and white pelicans; he then set about reproaching the "janissaries of nepotism," the "imitative demagogues," the "condottieri of fastidiousness."

In our recent American fiction, sensibility, flickering nuance, in the service of accurate recording are most often the destinations of talent.

A large intention, an intellectual structure making its demands upon language, ideas, originality, all the marks of a high vocation, are increasingly rare, as if impractical, which perhaps they are. The inspirations of an almost pietistic waywardness, a singularity of vision and possibility when the vast span of world literature is alive in the mind, the qualities so formidable in such writers as Borges and, in his way, Calvino: who indeed would wish to claim a stubbornness of such peculiar shape, have the confidence, the vanity to persevere and to insist? Both smallness and idiosyncrasy, as well as large ambition, are more or less signals of a threatening futility of effort. Our knights of faith who practice literature rather than mere publication as a goal are something of an embarrassment as they puff along at the tail end of the marathon.

For the most part, the shadowy scenery of domestic drama, interesting and valuable according to the execution, is quite enough of a challenge in itself. Contemporary manners shift and squirm with a careless speed depressing to the artist. Deciding to be a homosexual, a personal and social engagement of some consequence, falls like the last crab apple in autumn on the crowded, yellowing fruits at the base of the tree. Going to the summer house, packing up after the collapse of an affair; tired, exhausted, dead marriage; the daily round is resolutely local in both setting and imagination; parochial, the fiction of what one knows, experience with a turn here and there, if intolerably redundant. Again and again the documentation of one corner much like another, highway literature, and the last can of beer with its trade name, interior "décor" obsessively significant in a "classless" society. There are many pleasures in this writing. The pleasure of recognition, the pleasure to the ear when the spoken speech hits it just right in rhythm, pacing, and in the fluency with which a small vocabulary grows by the twists and turns, the jumble of inventiveness. Playing by ear; such is the mastery, such is the limitation.

By television, film, clothes, stars, *Dallas*, music, military power we circle the earth like PanAm on its daily journey—New York, Frankfurt, Rome, Tokyo, Bahrain. The Vietnam War occasioned fictions inevitably a reflection of the immense cultural, political, and, in this instance, military infiltration of the American presence as fact and idea. Most were moving to the mind and to the emotions; only a few were moving to the spirit as literature.

If commercial life, our fabulous maneuverings with dollars and cents so often ghostlike in their immateriality, do not have much potency in our fiction, the commercial world is vivid indeed in the life of the writer. The literary world appears to be obsolescent, but the publishing world is as plump and colorful as a new hybrid peach from California and no matter the mealiness inside. The news of publishing is more gripping than the news of what is written. The charms of publication, the escalation of the discovery that almost anyone can be a writer, have been accompanied by a devaluation of the product required. In any case, to admit that the book is a commodity like any other is to face reality, above all the reality that there is a general fatigue with "literature" as opposed to the mere book.

For established writers, even writers of great eminence, there is—to use Gertrude Stein's phrase—a way of winning by having been winning. Perhaps there's equity in this: the high career always there to be drawn upon, collateral for the first and second mortgage. For the celebrated there is little possibility of failure, unless it lives on in the soul of the writer or painter like some nagging, lowlying fever. Ready marketability, with a few points up and down, but no matter. The freshest of literary occasions is not an experiment in style or structure, but rather the book auction of first serial rights or paperback with its attendant publicity.

There is a dedication to production, a shadow of the great productivity that marked all except a few of the glorious fiction writers of the past. Yet it seems clear that the high dedication of the artist in the prime of his powers, dedication to art, has become something of an embarrassment as a "posture." The exalted effort is not necessary to preeminence, preeminence continuing as a public perception, and staring it in the face could well become a crisis in productivity.

Lonely aspiration, lifelong labor, Cézanne's doubts, Kafka's withholdings, exile and cunning, consciousness of the race...

Thomas Mann in California, his residence there a tragic jest of history, did not prefigure anything in the Olympian gesture of his great career, up to the last, the final masterpiece, *Doctor Faustus*. And the curiosity of another exile, Vladimir Nabokov. After his masterpiece, *Lolita*, one of the greatest books about America, after the seductiveness of it became a worldwide best seller, lovely American term, despite the complexity of language and conception—"I am thinking of aurochs and angels, the secret of durable pigments, prophetic sonnets, the refuge of art. And this is the only immortality you and I may share, my Lolita"—the last words; after this Nabokov seems not to have understood. We might say, in American idiom, that he made a "bad career move." He wrote the most unseductive of masterpieces, *Pale Fire*, a novel, among other things, about the fate of a long poem in couplets. Few of our esteemed authors would be likely to wander so far from the newly found, rich pasturage, especially had he spent a lifetime of creative grandeur without much more compensation than a bookkeeper.

The reader who is not a mere consumer can scarcely fail to notice the sweat of calculation, market calculation, on the pages of so many of our best fictions; the acceptance of the indulgence the commodity world offers to the famous high and low. Such creative dilemmas that may exist for the author are to be overwhelmed by assertiveness of one kind or another. Assertiveness of reputation, of championship. This has its power over criticism. It bullies into being a timorous, benign, and forgiving accommodation, which cannot be thought of as condescension since it is itself, the criticism, a part of the tradings in pasts and futures.

The literary scene seems to ask quite bluntly: how important is high literature anyway? There's quite enough of it in the library to serve the need. The news that literature used to bring about how people lived in Wessex, in St. Petersburg, lived as a prince of a father foully murdered, married, in a virtuous action, a sterile pedant—it might be wondered, as others have observed, if those of us living in the United States have need of such news. It is not possible to overvalue the aesthetic interest of the surf of information, gossip, tragedy, crime, miscalculation, good nature, good luck and bad, the dramas of real life beating on the shores of our knowledge and imagination every day by way of the press. A tall Dane in Rhode Island, not quite a prince, this one, with his American heiress-princess oversleeping, as it were...

It may be impertinent to question the American scene and to glide on silver skates over a surface that is, in truth, filled with bumps and lumps and sudden, unexpected views from the pond. What is offered here is a personal view of the literary situation in the gross, and the gross will usually be a libel on the particular. Or at least that is the hope.

1987

MRS. WHARTON IN NEW YORK

I.

EDITH Wharton was born in New York City in 1862 as Edith New-bold Jones. Her mother was a Rhinelander, one of the poor ones, or more accurately not quite one of the rich ones. Her paternal grandmother was a Schermerhorn. Thus the "Knickerbocker element" survived in her pedigree. They were the remnants of the old Dutch patroons who were themselves early overwhelmed by immigrants from the British Isles and by British military force. It was early indeed, since Peter Stuyvesant surrendered and New Netherland or New Amsterdam became New York in 1664. From the beginning, the old society was beleaguered; had it not been, there would be no Manhattan, this world city as porous as cheesecloth. Traders from New England came down from Maine through Connecticut and were not at first as roundly welcomed as we might imagine today. And, needless to note, worse was to follow the little band of old New Yorkers; unappetizing hordes of foreigners collecting like flies and gnats around the carriage horses.

Into this enclave, old New York society, Edith Wharton was born. She took her positioning seriously, and the old stock with its thumb in the dike of Manhattan was one of her themes as a novelist. It might be said of this theme what Henry James wrote of Nathaniel Hawthorne: "It is only in a country where newness and change and brevity of ten-ure are the common substance of life, that the fact of one's ancestors having lived for a hundred and seventy years in a single spot would become an element of one's morality."

Being from New York, rather than from Salem, Massachusetts,

Edith Wharton was not a Yankee and not a lingering Puritan conscience inhabited by ghosts and provincial scruples. She grew up a cosmopolitan from the first, early traveling abroad with her parents; she married after the usual biographical unsteadiness in the matter of broken engagements and again traveled abroad, then settled on Park Avenue and in Newport and, much later, built herself a grand house in Lenox, Massachusetts, kept traveling, finally sold the house, divorced her husband, Edward Wharton—"cerebrally compromised Teddy," as Henry James called him, summing up this wild manic-depressive who gave her a lot of trouble. Along the way, she had a three-year affair with the romantically overextended seducer Morton Fullerton. And then in 1913, after the divorce, she settled permanently in France. Yet there was more to it than that.

Edith Wharton was twenty-nine when her first short story was published and thirty-seven when her first collection appeared in 1899. Two years before, *The Decoration of Houses*, written with the architect Ogden Codman, had been published. Even though starting late, Edith Wharton quickly became a professional writer in the best sense of the phrase. She wrote steadily, novel after novel, made money, and spent money with a forthright and standard-bearing loyalty to those twins of domestic economy, taste and comfort.

She liked expensive motorcars and once told Henry James that the last of these had been purchased with the proceeds from *The Valley of Decision*, a two-volume mistake about eighteenth-century Italy with characters named Odo and the Duke of Monte Alloro that showed Italy can be as dangerous for certain English-language novelists as the vapors from the undrained marshes. (To the point: Hawthorne's *The Marble Faun*, a weary and unsuitable surrender to the moist murk a gloomy eye might discover in the beautiful country. Hawthorne himself did not make the common surrender to Italy and complained of "discomfort and miseries," found the Roman winter an unadvertised blast of chills, and could not countenance nudity in sculptures.)

Henry James, looking at Mrs. Wharton's motorcar purchased by the assault on Italy, and referring to *The Wings of the Dove*, is reported to have said, "With the proceeds of my last novel, I purchased a small go-cart, or wheel-barrow, on which my guests' luggage is wheeled from the station to my house. It needs a coat of paint. With the proceeds of my next novel I shall have it painted."

There is a tradesman's shrewdness in Edith Wharton's work. She knows how to order the stock and dispose the goods in the window. She was a popular author, or, to be more just, her books were popular, not always the same thing. (Even in her day there were writers, many of them women susceptible to sentiment, who trafficked in novels in the present-day manner—more soybeans on the commodities market.) Edith Wharton is free of lush sentiments and moralizing tears. In *The House of Mirth*, her triumph, she is not always clear what the moral might be and thereby creates a stunning tragedy in which the best and the richest society of New York reveals an inner coarseness like pimps cruising in Cadillacs.

Nevertheless, she is often caught up in contrivance as a furtherance of product. And she likes the ruffled cuff and transcontinental glamour, interesting enough in itself but speeding to pointlessness. The novel is viewed as a frank transaction between elements, elements to be laid out and pasted down like tiles in a frame. A "situation" is of course the necessity of fiction. Yet what of the cracks, the anxiety we sense in greater novelists about the very intention of the careful arabesques so purposefully designed and all of a sudden baked hard as rock?

In a story by Chekhov called "Terror," a young man has been flirting with the wife of his good friend, and she has been sighing in the Russian manner for him. Somehow, he at last takes her to his room, which the husband enters to get his cap left there earlier, set up, we would say, by the dramatist's art. At the end, the young man wonders: "Why has it turned out like this and not differently? To whom and for what was it necessary that she should love me in earnest and that he should come to my room to fetch his cap? What had the cap to do with it?"

Neatness of plotting; balancing of the elements by a handy coincidence beyond necessity: That is the way it often goes with this prodigious worker, busy at the morning's pages. She tends to lay hold with some of the gregarious insistence she displayed as the sort of hostess who organizes trips after lunch. Too many caps to be retrieved at the bedside of indiscretion, too much of a gloss. It's the last slap of the polishing cloth and then forge ahead in a majorful fashion.

The Reef, for instance: The young man is hoping to marry the recently widowed woman he has long loved. She puts him off with family affairs in her mother-in-law's château in France and with problems relating to her young child and to her stepson. All are Americans, but the château somehow appears as naturally as if it were a deed to a woodlot. In a fit of chagrin, the young man has an affair in a cheap Paris railroad hotel with a penniless American girl trying her hand at this and that abroad. This manifestation of impatience over and done with, the widow and the young man recombine, so to speak. And soon the girl from the railroad hotel turns up and will become engaged to the stepson, heir to the château and all the rest. The plot is suspenseful and executed with considerable gallantry and many Jamesian pauses in articulation—questions that are not quite asked, answers that hang in the air, the cues in the matter of a dialogue to a moral dilemma. The convenience of the young girl's turning up to be promptly fallen in love with by the heir is too brilliant, too tidy.

The Mother's Recompense: A mother has abandoned her husband and daughter, and New York society has erased the blot of her existence as if she were a smudge to be washed off a window. She lives abroad rather shabbily unanchored but has for a time the pleasant anguish of an affair with a younger man, who proves to be the great love of her life. When the old members of the New York family die, the daughter brings her mother back. It's a lottery ticket for the bolter: everything forgiven, luxury, and social reestablishment. Soon, the young man drops down on the scene; the daughter falls in love and means to marry him. You turn a corner, or rather a page, and there he is, or there she is. Moments of social comedy set out as deftly as the knives and forks; dramatic encounters in the splendid old arks of the Hudson Valley or in the mansions moving upward on Fifth Avenue.

Edith Wharton is a challenging figure just now. In her finesse and talent, her glamour and worldliness, she shares in some of the renewed affection for the threatened New York City architecture of the Beaux Arts period. Even her snobbishness and spendthrift ways are not remote from the activities of the haute couture ladies that daily fill the pages of the city's newspapers. With Edith Wharton, it was always an "approach up a red carpet," as the English man of letters Percy Lubbock says in his courteous but sly memoir of their friendship. She was, in most of her writing life, not one to loiter with curiosity about the crude crunch of New York, and she cannot even be claimed as an old-stock patriot since she fled the frontier and the American presence with its "vainglory, crassness and total ignorance."

In line with the contemporary appetite for tawdry revelation, the grande dame received a boost in her literary ratings thanks to R. W. B. Lewis's biography and the publication of a very knowing fragment of pornography found among her papers. She composed, yes, a father-daughter scene, a frankly hot exercise in appreciative specification not unlike Auden's "The Platonic Blow":

> Letting herself downward along the divan till her head was in a line with his middle she flung herself upon the swelling member, and began to caress it insinuatingly with her tongue. It was the first time she had ever seen it actually exposed to her eyes, and her heart swelled excitedly: to have her touch confirmed by sight enriched the sensation that was communicating itself through her ardent twisting tongue. With panting breath she wound her caress deeper and deeper into the thick firm folds, till at length the member, thrusting her lips open, held her gasping, as if at its mercy.

The House of Mirth was written while Edith Wharton was still living in New York in 1905—or partly living in New York on Park Avenue when not at the new house in Lenox or in Newport or abroad. The tragic force of this ambitious early novel—early in her career at least—has to do with the broadness of conception, the immediacy of the strokes and scenes, rather than, as was so often later the case, a concentration upon details of manners, such as divorce for a woman. (It is interesting that in this novel one woman who seems to be invited everywhere has been divorced twice.)

It is a society novel of city mansions and great country houses, expensive bridge games, Paris clothes, and lavish weddings. Into this, the author has placed a perfect center, Lily Bart, a spectacularly resonant creation, trying to keep afloat after a very realistic collapse of the foundation of the part she was designed to play. Lily is spoiled, pleasure-loving, and has one of those society mothers who are as improvident as a tornado. The father comes home one day from "downtown," and while Lily is chattering about the need every day for fresh flowers in the house at twelve dollars a dozen, the weary man replies: "Oh, certainly my dear—give him an order for twelve hundred." There is a sardonic stress to his reply, and the father is asked if he is ill. "Ill—No, I'm ruined," he says.

Quite soon both parents are dead and Lily is sent to live with an aunt, an old goose in good society and well-heeled but dull and stingy in everything except an allowance for clothes. At the opening Lily is twenty-nine, beautiful, clever, an adornment for dinners and weekends that demand expenditures, at the bridge table for one, which she cannot afford and for which she is secretly in debt. It is clearly time for her to marry, after having foolishly turned down respectable offers. Marriage to a rich man is her aim, and early in the book she has her chance with a plodding, timid young heir, but certain acts of impetuosity and the news of her gambling debts frighten him away.

That is the way it goes. Every move Lily makes, whether innocent or calculating, leads to disaster and compromise. Her efforts go on very much in the manner of a continental farce. Although she is chaste, she tends again and again to be discovered in a sort of rumpled state. Men, married and otherwise, pursue her and, when rejected, blackmail her. Each scene is interesting, and if observers are always on hand to find her walking in the park when she'd rather not be seen or coming out of a house at the wrong hour, no unfortunate arrangement of circumstances is altogether without credibility.

The brilliance of the characterization lies in Lily's self-knowledge. She is never unaware of her own motives, and when her manipulations fail she does not impugn the self-interest of others working against her own. As one who has been on the town too long and who is poorer than anyone knows, Lily quite understands self-interest. She loses every gamble, and each opportunity snaps back like a trap. Her acquaintance with luxury is a fatal habituation. "Of luxury, the fruit is luxury," as

Thoreau phrased it. At last, disinherited by her aunt because of "gossip," she sinks into irreversible poverty, an urban slide something like that of a luckless courtesan, although Lily Bart is only a New York society girl without means and without connections except of the kind that issue invitations. In the end, she takes an overdose of sleeping medicine.

Surrounding this personal debacle is a large society, not a representation of the city so much as a society that twists and turns upon itself, within the list, the mostly rich and sometimes dull and overfed. The predatory sexuality, the heartlessness, and the coarseness are quite startling when viewed against the more mildly rebuked, nostalgic renderings of the old guard in the later works.

For instance, Gus Trenor, whose credentials we cannot doubt since "with all his faults, Trenor had the safeguard of his traditions, and was less likely to overstep them because they were so purely instinctive." Of course, the "instinctive" graces are often out to lunch when life, here and elsewhere, scratches with its small and large irritations. Still, the rather glum and fumbling needs of poor Gus bring to mind instincts of the old urgency.

His wife is Lily's best friend, with all the relevant modifications of both words, and gives parties and weekends on Long Island, or is it up the Hudson? Mr. Trenor has appeared harmless enough but is insufficiently attended to. On one of the occasions, social, at Bellomont, his estate, he hears of Lily's desperate situation and offers to invest her last thousand dollars. Not long after, he presents her with ten thousand dollars, supposedly profit from a tip. Having gone to this trouble, Trenor turns as ornery as a ward boss. He gossips about the money and insinuates that there was no market tip; there was only his generosity, for which he wants womanly attentions of the usual concreteness. He sends her a telegram in his wife's name, summoning her late in the evening to his mansion on Fifth Avenue. Of course, the telegram is a trick of the most benighted asininity and Trenor is alone. He makes a clumsy effort to seduce Lily, but clumsy or not the intention is altogether realistic. Edith Wharton is bold about sex, even something of a nudging procuress when the plot allows. "Hang it, the man who pays for the dinner is generally allowed a seat at the table," the overheated man growls when he is rebuffed. (Lily's last act before committing suicide is to return, in the manner of Socrates before the hemlock, the profit from Trenor's "investment" on her behalf.) But where are the gentle manners, the agreeable repressions attendant upon civility learned at the tables set with the "du Lac Sèvres" and the "van der Luyden Lowestoft" and the "Dagonet Crown Derby"?

The House of Mirth in its flashlighting around New York casts its beam upon a Mr. Sim Rosedale. In the practice of the period, Rosedale is referred to as a "little Jew" and weighted down, as if by an overcoat in summer, with a thickness of objectionable moral and physical attributes—each readily at hand for the confident satirist. The fellow has made a lot of money downtown, and thus his path crosses that of the more or less well-bred Wall Street New Yorkers, who find him useful since their own capacities, with the help of spendthrift wives, are thinning like the hair on their heads.

Rosedale is ferociously set upon entering the society described in the novel; he has the money and is determined to have the dance. It must be said he comes upon the scene as free of family, traditions, religious or otherwise, as bereft of community as a scout on the plains. Rosedale is no slithering continental sybarite like August Belmont, but instead a shrewd, if uncouth, trader, and from history it might be doubted that he would be so quick to wish this particular dilution of himself and his fortune. The author understands it is fate and probity that lead the dull, rich Mr. Gryce to pass over Lily Bart and to unite his pile with that of the dull, rich Evie Van Osburgh. Edith Wharton would not, however, have known of Rosedale's possible familiar life, and so his muscular push into smart society must be taken as, well, natural.

In any case, the advancing Sim Rosedale is an important figure in this plot of threatening circumstance. Since Lily is beautiful, unmarried, and as fashionable as satin, Rosedale has settled upon her as the mate to show his accumulations to advantage. She refuses him, with "repugnance." But as her opportunities wither and her desperation augments, she decides to take the florid Rosedale and his millions after all. In a powerfully executed scene, Lily faces up and says, "I am ready to marry you whenever you wish." The crafty usurper turns her down. Her rotten luck, those scandal-mongering observers of her trek here and there on the stairs of a bachelor-filled apartment house and on a yacht in the

Mediterranean and the compromising reportage they have engendered, are a fund of disadvantage. She is no longer a good investment.

Lily Bart is a flawed, self-absorbed, and, oh, yet decent beauty of the kind that tests the novelist's art. Sympathy is aroused by the honesty of her impulses, and she has an emotional clarity that makes even an occasional charity believable. Emotional clarity—honesty, in fact—is less efficient in society than garrulous self-justification. With Lily, this clarity is like a pinch of arthritis in her manipulating hand.

Her helplessness in poverty may be laid to society's withholding from the clotheshorse beauty the proper training for independence as a woman, independence being knowing how to work and forgo the dressmaker. There is a suggestion of the sadness of laboring incapacity in the exposition Edith Wharton has supplied. Certainly, Lily Bart is not a pioneering candidate for Radcliffe College; indeed, she cannot trim a hat, one of the occupations girls fallen from prosperity attempt in this as in other novels. Yet the author knows the lamentable inadequacy of "the modelling of her little ear, the crisp upward wave of her hair" as a preparation for a paycheck. And, above all, what she stresses is the blight of a conditioning for luxury without the means.

Lily Bart knows what she knows, coquetry for the most part, and to have been prepared otherwise would have been another novel. At one point, Lily explains that people think one can live *on* the rich, when the fact is that it takes money to live *with* the rich. To be without sufficient money is like diving into the concrete of a drained swimming pool. This novel is Edith Wharton's finest achievement because money is the subject, of greater significance than the crippling, if amusing and charming details of convention in a small, historically perhaps attractive but insignificant stockade. That at least was true of Manhattan even when it was "old."

2.

New York: No novelist in his or her volumes has set out to be the social historian of the actual city, this restless monster of possibility and liability. It is not easy to imagine a voraciousness to consume the remarkable, shapeless scope or, even in a practical condensation, to imagine a Zola tramping through the warehouses of meat at dawn or trailing the garment workers home to some godforsaken borough in the evening. The city itself has never been a whole as the other great cities were until recently, when New York's peculiar instability and visionary tribalism became a worldwide condition: Turks in Berlin, Arabs in Paris, colonials in London. New York literature is the literature of the precinct, whether it be the Mafia, Hell's Kitchen in Crane's *Maggie*: *A Girl of the Streets*, or Salinger's Glass family on Central Park West. A great claim is usually made for Edith Wharton as a social historian, although how that can be confirmed by so intensely hermetic an imagination is a puzzle.

The gorgeous innuendo of Henry James's New York pages in *The American Scene*, the lilting metaphors of distress and dispossession: It was 1904 when the chagrined pedestrian made his way through the fatally designed "streets intersecting with a pettifogging consistency." He spent some hours on Ellis Island, the utopian gateway, and cautioned the unwary against doing the same. To witness the "inconceivable alien" in their herded numbers was to have "eaten of the tree of knowledge and the taste will be forever in his mouth." But the effulgent language of James's wounded curiosity can be said to redeem the space of his withdrawal, to honor the gross elaboration and "untempered monotony" of the Waldorf Astoria and to fix in a glance the very topography of the city lying in its rivers and "looking at the sky in the manner of some gigantic hair-comb turned upward."

New York, with its statistical sensationalism, is a shallow vessel for memory since it lives in a continuous present, making it difficult to recall the shape of the loss deplored, whether it be the gray tin of the newsstand or the narrow closet for the neighborhood's dry cleaning, there and gone over a vacation. As for people, the rapid obsolescence of deities makes its point each season; or, if surviving the gleeful erasure of fame, the penalties pursuing society's accommodation can be severe, or so it is often asserted by the fatigued famous.

In my time, the preservationists say, men got up when a woman entered the room. When poor Blanche DuBois, passing the louts at the poker table, says, "Don't get up, I'm only passing through," how is that to be understood without "tradition"? There's a bit of that in Edith Wharton.

The Custom of the Country (1913) was for the most part written in France. It is a curiosity of a hybrid kind. Here we have a fierce scold not of the alien from Odessa or Sicily but of the natives undertaking an interior migration from Apex City to Manhattan. Their landing, ready for absorption, is a twofold pain: their pockets are lined with cash, and they don't know when to get up and when to sit down. The mode of the composition is split in the middle: one half a description of the invaders in a satiric accent, the other a whirlwind of folly and destruction on an international scale.

So we open to the Spragg family from Apex. Spragg, wanting to transpose itself to Sprague or something, but efficient, perhaps in suggesting many backcountry impediments and wonders of maladaptation not unlike those of Ring Lardner's hicks in *The Big Town*, or his Mrs. Gullible finally achieving her wish to meet Mrs. Potter Palmer, doing so in a hotel corridor, and being asked to bring more towels.

Mr. and Mrs. Spragg are woebegone pilgrims, and the old father with his "lymphatic patience" brightened only by the Masonic emblem on his waistcoat is as unlikely a trader on Wall Street as the man behind the pickle barrel in the corner grocery. But he has made money in some way and the hajj to Mecca is, you might say, made on the roller skates of his daughter, Undine, who for a good while has been dreaming about Fifth Avenue in her Apex backyard. The choice of this family to bear the history of new money in the metropolis carries more of the tone of parody than of a serious imaginative decision.

William Dean Howells created similar migratory birds in *A Hazard of New Fortunes*. His Dryfoos tribe hits town with a fortune made from natural gas in Northern Ohio and Indiana. Natural gas would seem to be a very happy source for American finance, but the boomtown alteration of fortune does not decorate the newly rich man's psyche. In New York, old Dryfoos wails, "I ain't got any horses, I ain't got any cows. I ain't got any chickens, I ain't got anything to do from sun-up to sun-down." Dryfoos and his strike have, like the Spraggs, been transported by ravening daughters who want to bust into New York society.

It is no doubt prudent to have daughters if one would display in fiction the barbarities of social climbing and portray in all its anxious athleticism a passion for shopping. Of course, consumption and insatiability are the overhanging atmosphere of the city itself, gathering all classes, top to bottom, in its dreamy, poetic smother.

Undine Spragg arrives on the scene with youth, natural, and beauty, extraordinary, and every moral and practical liability a golden girl from the heart of the country can fold in her trunks. She is an infection, a glassy, little, germ-filled protagonist. We meet her set up with her family in the Hotel Stentorian, in rooms that go by the name of the Looey Suite, to be furnished with a good deal of oversized mahogany and gilt and laughable hangings on wall and window. Undine gets "round" right off and meets, without giving him notice, a young man, Ralph Marvell. Soon, she receives from his sister an invitation, which she throws in a basket, but which is rescued by a Mrs. Heeney, masseuse and manicurist, who cries out, Marvell! His mother is a *Dagonet*, and they live with old Urban Dagonet down on Washington Sqaure!

Mrs. Spragg chews on this: "Why do they live with somebody else? Haven't they got the means to have a home of their own?" Undine, perplexed and suspicious, questions why a sister should have written and why the invitation should ask the mother's permission when it is Undine who is asked to dine and why dine instead of have dinner and why write the note on plain white paper when pigeon-blood red is all the rage?—that kind of thing. *Go steady, Undine*, Mrs. Heeney advises.

Not long after, Undine is married to Ralph Marvell, and the plot advances to the lamentable results of this—for him. The Marvells are old New York, impeccable in birth and manners, not rich, living in their comfortably shabby houses on Washington Square, three generations within. Ralph is bookish and perhaps will himself write books; he is quiet, charming, has been to Harvard and Oxford, tried law but didn't have a flair for it, and now does nothing apart from reading and living according to his nature.

The European wedding journey is the first foreign experience for Undine, and it proves to be an experience foreign to Ralph Marvell's previous life. Undine despises Siena, altogether too slow and too hot. When asked if the summer wasn't hot in Apex, she replies that she didn't marry to go back to Apex. In Paris, the Comédie is "stuffy," and the husband attends alone while she is busy and, surreptitiously, having the family rings reset and buying a lot of clothes without the money. In fact, the couple doesn't have money for the passage home, and there are turns of plot attendant upon that. Undine is piling up the wreckage, flooding the banks of the river, and leaving the Marvell heritage and finances tumbled down in the mud.

Ralph Marvell is a creation of the novelist's art, and his attractiveness is evident on the page. His marriage to Undine is, however, a sort of haystack of implausibility stuck in the middle of urban life. She is given only one quality and that is great beauty. Beauty will always be an assertion the reader is compelled to accept but cannot keep his mind fixed upon. The hair—was it red?—and the "glow" when some diversion pleases the beauty are not exactly traits to be probed so much as color floating and drifting without a trace.

Undine, the character, is a witch of ignorance, insensitivity, vanity, and manipulation. She is mean to her parents, indifferent to the child she finally bears, and impossible to imagine as anything other than tedious. Whatever negotiable assets she has are practical only to certain vulgar sensualists, of which there are quite a few on the scene. She divorces Ralph Marvell without asking his permission and imagines after making herself fully available that she will cause Van Degen, a rich and decadent member of the Marvell set, also to get a divorce and to marry her. But the canny Van Degen thinks better of it and does not come forth.

Along the way, a most fantastical marriage for Undine does come about. She unites with the Comte Raymond de Chelles, a handsome young nobleman with ancient credentials, a house in the Faubourg, a château in Burgundy, little money to combine with Undine's less, since old Spragg has not prospered on Wall Street for all the reasons sufficient from the beginning.

Why must Edith Wharton and, in a different manner, Henry James decorate their pages with ancient titles to confound the romantic history of their Americans? Undine inflicts appalling indignities upon the poor Comte, but she is strangely imagined to be fidgeting about in the cold halls of a turreted castle. What is so interesting about

Gilbert Osmond, the fortune hunter in *The Portrait of a Lady*, is that he acts like a prince of the realm but is indeed quite recognizable as an insufferable American expatriate, long resident in Florence. Prince Amerigo, in *The Golden Bowl*, fortunately does not flourish the papal title, and he is mostly seen maneuvering about London offering his fate to Americans, too many of them as it turns out.

But how peculiar it is to have the delightful, candid Christopher Newman in *The American* set off in pursuit of the daughter of the noble De Bellegarde family. The ancient Europeans will be cut from the cloth, stamped out one after another without distinguishing shapes, a bit like the weird American manufactures from which Newman made his finally unsuitable millions. The titled Europeans represent mystery, inflexible pride, hidden motive, inscrutable manners, melodrama, and unreality: trappings, fuss, and feathers that must stand in the place of the author's having real knowledge or observed experience of the character and intimate life of Europeans so high.

Howells in *A Hazard of New Fortunes* has one of the odious Dryfoos shopping, primping daughters make a similar leap into the European bog. Christine Dryfoos meets her fate in the person of a French nobleman "full of present debts and of duels in the past." It is added that the father and his natural-gas dollars can manage the debts, but the duelist had better watch out for Christine, "unless he's practised with a panther."

The international novels are in fact novels of traveling Americans meeting each other abroad with a few natives thrown in. In *The Golden Bowl*, the Ververs cast their immense fortune at the foot of a prince, but the prince is a passenger, and the motors of the action are in the hands of the Ververs and the American, Charlotte Stant. Mme. Merle, so mysterious, is finally just another American, like the radical-chic Princess Casamassima, another visitor like the Touchetts, whose gifts will buy for Isabel Archer a fantasy of native blood, Gilbert Osmond, decorated with impecunious winters abroad, a little collection of things, and the hauteur of his meaningless displacement.

Undine at last finds a perch on Fifth Avenue as the wife of Elmer Moffat of Apex, an old pal to whom she had been briefly married as a girl. The discovery of her concealment of this fact is a contingent reason for Ralph Marvell's suicide. So Undine will travel from the picket fence to Fifth Avenue on the back of Apex Elmer, loud and red-faced as a fire truck. Elmer is now a railroad magnate, like—can it be?—Commodore Vanderbilt. The much-used bride is to be largely rewarded, and when the dispenser is Edith Wharton the loot will be lavish and banal. Undine is to have "a necklace and tiara of pigeon-blood rubies belonging to Queen Marie Antoinette, a million dollar cheque...a new home, 5009 Fifth Avenue, which is an exact copy of the Pitti Palace, Florence."

As a social historian, Edith Wharton does not pause to get it just right, on the dot. She proceeds from a very generalized memory and an often commonplace fund of attitudes. *The Custom of the Country* has placed its points at extremities that undermine the evolutionary rush of the actual city. The invading Visigoths with their rude instruments of fortune, like Spragg's marketing of a hair-waver from which comes Undine's name and his later having a worthless parcel of land upon which Apex was to build its water system, are not the usual transfers to Manhattan. The middle-sized towns of the Middle West would be more likely to claim the powers of Spragg and to contain the gossip-column ambitions of dressing-up Undine. The old Spraggs' rustic souls are fashioned out of impermeable materials, and the city casts its stones of enlightenment their way without making a dent.

New York City is a frame in these novels, not a landscape: 5009 Fifth Avenue? Even less well foretold is the failure to understand the magical progression of taste, so hasty, in the newly rich of the city. For what is easier than the acquisition of acceptable responses? Culture, as society finds it, is not saturation but an acquaintance with the labels of things valued, be it the Parthenon or white walls. The culture of consumption is infinitely accommodating, and the terms of cultural dissemblance are an available cosmetic, another pot of rouge. Very few Undines would scorn Siena or the Comédie Française, scorn out loud. Quickly, the proper patience appears, no matter how deep the stab of boredom in an actual confrontation.

The Marvell house on Washington Square, the seat of the genteel opposition, is one thing, but in New York "divided space" is preeminent, and the hotel and apartment living the hick Spraggs embrace cannot be thought of as retrograde. Was there in old New York an aristocratic style, an intimate weave of obscure inherited practice and value? Perhaps, but the style as it has come down to us was always drowning in the city's hyperbolic congestion of effects, the glare of the futuristic, the fantastical democratizing compulsion of Manhattan's eternal newness.

When Henry James set up his house in *Washington Square*, he did not force the historical inappropriateness of the terms found in the novels of Edith Wharton. He placed in his house, a memory dear to him from his youth, a member of the professional upper classes, with no worrisome tics about who might be a Dagonet, who a Van der Luyden. Dr. Sloper is an intelligent, hard-nosed, serious practitioner in a useful arena of knowledge, a possible New Yorker. True, the doctor is said to have married into one of the "best" families, but this has no dizzying command over the rather surgical common sense with which he approaches family affairs. What has its woeful effect upon him is that his wife has died and left him an improbable daughter. This chagrin is not unreasonable, or unthinkable perhaps, for a metropolitan gentleman. Catherine is dear, awkward, unfashionable, and indeed would seem to have many qualities of a Boston girl transplanted carelessly to New York. In Boston, among the Yankees, Catherine's modesty and the plainness and wish to please would not be impediments in a girl of good family.

In New York, Catherine is a perturbation. When the selfish, false idler, Morris Townsend, begins to court her, the doctor's intervention is cruel and practical. He is shrewd about Townsend and with his oily, ironic efficiency is not mindful of the fruits of his shrewdness in the broken heart of his daughter. The novel is a perfectly faceted diamond, clear in its icy progression. The drama sits on its corner downtown as confidently as the house Dr. Sloper built for himself. Social habits, conventions, prohibitions of the group have no part in the dilemma. Dr. Sloper knows his objections to Townsend as frankly as if the young man had come begging with a tin cup. Townsend does not care for Catherine, wishes only to marry her money, and while the sophisticated doctor can no doubt understand both, he sees that the conditions promise to be baneful down the road.

Wharton's *Age of Innocence* has great appeal because of the charm of the two figures, Ellen Olenska and Newland Archer. If it has a definition, an engine, it is divorce as a social stigma, a disability not to be incurred by a woman. She must, no matter what provocation, hang on legally, even if at a distance. She must not for a mere wish to be free of it all act on her own behalf. Ellen Olenska, a Mingott connection, has married a titled swine of a Pole. She has left him and returned to New York; he will take her back, but there is no thought of his swaying from whatever disgusts have been his pleasure. If she divorces, there will be scandal, and she will lose her money brought to the marriage and what is spoken of as "everything else."

The scandal of the intriguing Countess, with her irregular escape from her husband, combined with the powerful Mingott clan's displaying her in the family opera box, bring forth the beginning gasps of curiosity and social dismay. It is not a very weighty casualty, and yet Edith Wharton must find something to give reality to the deputed social standards. Good manners and the family plate are not sufficient for drama. Hindrance and exclusion are needed to give the old dominion coherence, to act as a sort of velvet rope in a museum protecting the plunder. Of course, there is great provincialism afoot here, since we know from Proust that a great French aristocrat can drop his Croix de Guerre on the floor of a male brothel without diminishing his prestige.

A good deal of the plot is concerned with who will come to a dinner in honor of the Countess, who will visit her, and so on. The loyalties of the old families are tested, and the best, the oldest, the most valued come forth bravely to smile over the canvasback ducks and to shame the timid, the complacent, and the insecure.

Ellen Olenska is glamorous and in tribute to her cosmopolitan life a bit exotic, a bit of a bohemian in her "little house" on an unfashionable New York street. She reads Paul Bourget, Huysmans, and the Goncourt Brothers. Newland Archer, conventionally reared by doting, placid women, a cousin to everyone who is anyone, has just married an unimaginative, nice young woman of his own set. Archer and Ellen Olenska fall in love, and it is a flaming passion that almost sends the lovers to a hotel room. The consummation is withheld, the Countess Olenska, divorced, returns to Europe, and Archer grows into a husband and father with bittersweet memories, recorded in one of those codas that span the years and might well have been forgone.

Edith Wharton suffered throughout her marriage to the Boston bon vivant, Teddy, as he was called. Teddy was worldly, liked the pleasures of dog and stream and wine cellar. He had no interest in scholarship, high or low, but took over a good deal of the management of houses and practical affairs and that went well, until it didn't. The two seem to have been a poor sexual match. Edith had her three-year affair with Fullerton, her strong affections for Henry James and others, especially for Walter Berry—a New York Van Rensselaer, an expert in international law and widely considered a snob, in her own vein. She was buried by his side, in Versailles.

Morton Fullerton, Harvard, son of a minister in Waltham, Massachusetts, became a political and cultural journalist, at one time the correspondent from France for the London *Times*. Fullerton seems to have been an attractive, perhaps we could say a lovable, young man. In his love life, he is something like a telephone, always engaged, and even then with several on hold. Whether he wished so many rings on his line is hard to tell; perhaps he was one of those who would always, always answer. In any case, among his callers were, in youth, Ronald Gower, a homosexual and friend of Oscar Wilde; Margaret Brooke, the Ranee of Sarawak; his cousin, Katherine Fullerton Gerould; Victoria Chambert, whom he married and with whom he had a child while living with a Mme. Mirecourt—and Edith Wharton.

When you have decided that Fuller likes older women—the Ranee and Mme. Mirecourt—he takes up with those younger, his cousin and Victoria Chambert. At the time of his affair with Mrs. Wharton there was a balance with no special signification: she was forty-five and he was forty-two. The Fullerton women tracked down thus far by academic prurience seem to have been of a forgiving nature and remained friendly to him throughout the years. Mme. Mirecourt clung like a burr and, as an expression of her enduring affection, was quite troublesome.

Teddy Wharton fell into the care of psychiatrists and into mood-swing follies, even going so far as to set himself up with a girl in a Boston apartment. He ran through his wife's money, and his increasing instability led to divorce. Twenty-eight years they had together, and, insofar as one can know, most of them were useful if not "satisfying" in the current sense. But then how satisfying could the dear love of the ambivalent Walter Berry have been? Edith Wharton appears to have been a type found in abundance on the contemporary scene: surprisingly sexy when the availabilities allowed, but owing to a dominant attraction to stylish amusements, happily surrounded by homosexuals, always, of course, of the right sort.

Once the deed was done, the divorce signed, she seemed to settle with a forward-looking fortitude. Even in her day, divorce was common in the best society, and it might be thought she held on to the prohibition mostly as a literary device to serve as a dramatic expression of the old manners—a necessary addition to the appointments of the house and the seating at the table. She used divorce again and again in her fiction, even sometimes seeming to entertain a certain moral nostalgia for its rigors. There is no doubt it was a handy circumstance for exile and for "cutting." The bald fact was that there were not many other stands to be taken in her created world, where the virtues were birth, the grand style, if suitable, with the rich Van der Luydens; good taste and modesty of pretension, the old bourgeois style, with the Marvells.

Edith Wharton had never been "modern" as a writer and had few theoretical questionings about the shape of the novel. "I certainly don't think Edith often read," Percy Lubbock wrote. Visiting her, he sometimes felt "a book had a scared look as she carried it off, as though it knew what it was in for." Yet she was a celebrated novelist, bore many honors, and experienced the threat of displacement in the clamorous, avant-garde elation of the 1920s. *The Waste Land* did not receive her favor, and *Ulysses* was to be named "school boy drivel." Living in upholstered exile, in the manner of Mrs. Wharton and Bernard Berenson, may have the gloomy effect of attaching one to intransigence in the arts, against the uprooted impertinence of modernism.

Mrs. Wharton had her turf, that almost forgotten sepia New York, to be turned over and over again, like setting the plow to the family farm every spring. A group of four short novels, under the title *Old New York* and boxed together, appeared in 1924. At the time of writing them, she was living in her final grand house, Pavillon Colombe, in Saint Brice, France, not far from Paris.

False Dawn, subtitled *The 'Forties*, proposes the adventures of a young man sent out on the civilizing Grand Tour and deputed to bring back works of art for his father's collection: Guido Reni, Carlo Dolci, and the like. Instead, spurred on by the development of a friendship with a young Englishman, who, we are asked to believe, is John Ruskin, he purchases Carpaccio, Fra Angelico, Giotto, and Piero della Francesca. The choices lead to his being disinherited by his father and scorned by old New York. Complacency and backward taste appear to be the indictment. "Carpatcher, you say this fellow's called.... Something to do with those new European steam-cars, I suppose, eh?" the outraged father cries out. Satiric dialogue, engaging enough in conversation, is a crash of dissonance on the Wharton page. And she likes to preen a little, to glide up on Ruskin and sneak up on the unlikely Piero purchase as if they were two cups of tea at Doney's.

In *The Spark*, a crusty old New Yorker claims to have learned human wisdom from a talkative fellow while being nursed in a Washington hospital after Bull Run. It is the dear bard Whitman himself. *The Old Maid*, another of the novellas, is a skillful melodrama set in the 1850s and telling of the sadness of an unwed mother's having to pretend to be a devoted aunt as she watches her child grow up, a condition as common in the villages as in the city.

The *Old New York* volumes are anecdotal fictions. There is not much air in them. Throughout Edith Wharton's work the society is small and its themes repetitive. The reader will become a sort of cousin of the blood as the defining names appear again and again. Memory has been emptied out by the long years abroad, and a certain perfunctoriness and staleness hang over the scene. Christine Nilsson will be singing *Faust* at the Academy of Music; the carriage will give way to the coupé. Characters go to balls and dinners and stop by to drink tea. They scarcely set foot on more than a few predictable blocks and on the way do not pass restaurants or saloons or thieves or workmen going home. Manhattan is a "set" but with no sense of crowds.

An early story, "Bunner Sisters," was rejected by an editor and put aside for many years before being offered in a collection. It is one of the author's most interesting works and an extraordinary wandering from the enclave. The sisters make trimmings and sew on ribbons in their dismal tenement; they meet a dreary opium addict, a wreck of a German who fixes clocks and who devastates their miserable struggle.

The details of existence are vivid; the author knew at one time that people took streetcars, bought a few pennies worth of food with fierce concentration upon the cost, made pitiful journeys to the wastes of New Jersey. Gradually, the feel and the spell of the city were lost and only interiors remained, the stuffs of definition.

Ethan Frome is a village tragedy, and the tale is cut to the measure of rural New England as a strong popular image. The village is named Starkfield; Ethan is a melancholy, silent, and longing country man, ruined by the slow agony of life with his complaining, "sickly" wife, the kind whose neurosis is colored by a run on patent medicines. His hope for redemptive love by way of the young servant girl, Mattie, is thwarted, and their attempt to commit suicide by sledding down a dangerous hill on a splendid snowy night produces not death but a crippled, altered Mattie to be taken in by the now triumphant wife, and the three to be left to their eternal rural isolation and misery. There is less experience of life in this story than in "Bunner Sisters." Short as *Ethan Frome* is, it is heavily designed and shows the difficulties encountered in the telling, the structure. It is operatic, *opera verismo*, with the power to retain its grip on the memory, as the long popularity of the work indicates.

Dreiser's *Sister Carrie* was written in 1900, five years before *The House of Mirth* and twenty years before *The Age of Innocence*. Dreiser, from the Middle West, went over the city on foot, as it were, striking out from the first ring of the city's chimes, the trainman's call of "Grand Central Station!" The first flat is on Seventy-eighth and Amsterdam, and soon Nassau Street is mentioned. The horns of the ferryboats sound in the fog; there is Broadway to give its lessons, and the glaring celebrity of Delmonico's, and Sherry's, too; serge skirts at Lord and Taylor, lights on Plaza Square, and dinner for $1.50, rooms set apart for poker, casinos, barbershops, advertisement billboards, Wooster Street, a half pound of liver and bacon for fifteen cents, chorus girls, soldiers on the street, a strike, significant in the plot. And, of course, the Bowery and Potter's Field for Hurstwood. Carrie at the end will rock in her chair in the Waldorf, the golden monument of the period, and try to read *Père Goriot*, urged upon her by an ever-upward Ralph Marvell sort.

The plebeian "tinsel and shine" of Carrie's destiny and the bankrupt disaster of Hurstwood are not Edith Wharton's world, nor must it have been so. Still, she works with her own tinsel and is a recorder of dreams much less true to the city, as history, than those of Sister Carrie. Density of experience is lacking and not, we gather, lamented. In her novels, Manhattan is nameless, bare as a field, stripped of its byways, its fanciful, fabricated, overwhelming reality, its hugely imposing and unalterable alienation from the rest of the country—the glitter of its beginning and enduring modernity as a world city.

1988

ON WASHINGTON SQUARE

THE JAMES family came from New York State, the father having been born in Albany. Whether they are New Yorkers in the sense of the city is not altogether certain since they fled it early and did not like it much when they came back from time to time. Still the city, its streets, its fluid, inconstant, nerve-wrung landscape, had a claim upon Henry's imagination, even if the neglectful civic powers did not properly return the claim.

In any case, Henry James was born in New York City in 1843, in a house on 21 Washington Place, a street adjacent to Washington Square, itself a small park announcing the end of lower Fifth Avenue and adorned by an ambitious bit of architecture that James would describe as "the lamentable little Arch of Triumph which bestrides these beginnings of Washington Square—lamentable because of its poor and lonely and unsupported and unaffiliated state." That was in 1904, when the sixty-one-year-old author returned from abroad to write *The American Scene*, his prodigious impressions of his homeland from New England to Palm Beach, impressions fresh, he hoped, as those of a curious stranger but still "as acute as an initiated native."

He would, of course, return to Fifth Avenue and to Washington Place. There, he found what he called a "snub." The birthplace of 21 Washington Place had been "ruthlessly suppressed" in one of those early convulsive seizures of destruction New York City to this day does not see as a defect in the municipal nervous system so much as an explosive, rather pagan, celebration of the gods of engineering and speculation. James, viewing the "amputation" of the birthplace, is led to confess that he had somehow imagined on Washington Place "a commemorative mural tablet—one of those frontal records of birth, sojourn, or death, under a celebrated name." This is an affecting aside of family and personal pride, a controlled twitch of chagrin, from which he retreats by observing the supreme invisibility of a plaque, acknowledging some long-gone worthy, placed on an apartment door in a fifty-story building, one of the "divided spaces" that were to be the principal habitations in the city.

The novel *Washington Square*, published in 1880, when James was thirty-seven years old, is an early work, at least early in style and in the untroubled presentation of its strong and thoroughly lucid plot. The novel is not strikingly under the domination of its place name, but we note that the author allows himself a moment of autobiographical diversion, an insertion more or less of his private relation to the title:

> I know not whether it is owing to the tenderness of early association, but this portion of New York appears to many persons the most delectable. It has a kind of established repose which is not of frequent occurrence in other quarters of the long, shrill city; it has a riper, richer, more honorable look . . . the look of having had something of a social history. . . . It was here that your grandmother lived, in venerable solitude. . . . It was here that you took your first walks abroad, following the nursery-maid with unequal step and sniffing up the strange odour of the ailantus-trees which at that time formed the principal umbrage of the square.

In the opening pages of the novel, Dr. Sloper has set himself up in a new house on Washington Square. The doctor is a credible, highly interesting man of the professional class who has achieved the status accruing to the serious practice of medicine. He is busy, successful, intelligent, witty—an engaging figure on the city scene, and while learned in the medical arts he is not "uncomfortable," by which it is meant that Dr. Sloper is one of those popular physicians whose personal attractiveness will somehow soothe the tortures of treatment. He has a well-to-do clientele and is passed by referral from one "good family" to another in the way that was usual before the age of intense special-ization.

The doctor has moved to Washington Square from a house near City Hall, a part of the city being turned into offices and other struc-tures of business. In moving uptown, he is following the direction of residential preference in the early 1880s—one of the details of metro-politan dynamics that interested "old New Yorkers" such as James and Edith Wharton. With a rather vagrant historicism, these authors like to follow, in a mood of amusement, the displacements of fashion as they try to place their characters on the city map. Thus, we are told that the doctor's dead wife had been "one of the pretty girls of the small but promising capital which clustered around the Battery and overlooked the Bay, and of which the uppermost boundary was indicated by the grassy waysides of Canal Street." The doctor has now made his own move uptown, but his drama is not residential; it is familial, an intense battle, almost military, of strategy, retreat, and attack, fought with his daughter, Catherine Sloper.

The doctor is in his fifties, and, while not a man to offer futile protests against the devastations of fate, he has endured two painful wounds, or perhaps we should say three. He lost a treasured son at the age of three and then lost a much-loved wife—a beautiful woman with a fortune, social standing, and every domestic charm—lost her at the birth of a second child, "an infant of a sex which rendered the poor child, to the doctor's sense, an inadequate substitute for his lamented first-born, of whom he had promised himself to make an admirable man."

His was a genuine grief, with the added gall of a professional frustra-tion in having been unable to ensure the survival of his family. But there is the surviving daughter, Catherine, now grown into a robust, rosily—rather too rosily—healthy young woman. Facing this last, lone Sloper, the doctor can assure himself that "such as she was, he at least need have no fear of losing her." The "such as she was" is the plot of *Washington Square:* the destiny of the daughter and the father's tone in his relations with her.

The beginning pages are written in a comedy-of-manners style, and each turn is amusing, calmly and confidently expert. Such a style will command, with its measured cadences and fine tuning, a bit of benign condescension toward the cast and toward the friendly modesty of the New York social landscape in the first half of the nineteenth century. Thus, it is said of the doctor, "He was what you call a scholarly doctor, and yet there was nothing abstract in his remedies—he always ordered you to take something."

Washington Square was written after James made his literary and social "Conquest of London," as Leon Edel phrases it in the title of the second volume of his James biography. The author had breakfasted with Turgenev, met Tennyson, Browning, and Gladstone, visited the great country houses, and indeed, as a cosmopolitan, wrote most of *Washington Square* in Paris. It is a perfect novel of immense refinement and interest, and one feels the execution gave James little trouble—that is, if one keeps in mind the breathless deliberations of the fictions that were to follow. Of course, the moral and psychological insinuations of this early work are not finally so self-evident as they appear to be on the lucid pages.

At the time James was devoting himself to the portrait of Catherine Sloper leading her life in her father's "modern, wide-fronted" house on lower Fifth Avenue, he was already thinking of the more challenging American girl, Isabel Archer, and the complex duplicities of *The Portrait of a Lady*, published soon after. In any case, when he was gathering the New York edition of his novels, which began to appear in 1907, he unaccountably excluded *Washington Square*. Perhaps it seemed to him a small, provincial tale after he had sent heiresses to Europe to test themselves and their American dollars on the ferocious competitions of the international scene. The American girls in the "large" novels are weighted with nuance and with the fictional responsibility to live up to their rather inchoate but grand attributions. Catherine, housebound in New York and incurious about the great world beyond, may have appeared a sort of vacation, one that allowed James a wonderfully re-laxed compositional tone when compared with that of *The Wings of the Dove* or *The Golden Bowl*.

Catherine Sloper is an heiress but not a beguiling "heiress of the ages"; she is heir only to money. Indeed, the early descriptions of Cath-erine are composed with such a boldly discounting eye, such intrepid divestment, that the reader feels a wince of discomfort. Catherine is large and homely, but, at the beginning, a contented, virtuous girl of her class. She is guileless, affectionate, docile, and obedient. She has a "plain, dull, gentle countenance," and, although drastically without coquetry, she wishes to please, most of all to please her father. "She was not quick with her book, nor, indeed, with anything else." Along the way of depiction, James himself seems to draw back from the distance imposed by the manner of composition. If he does not quite retreat, we can say he takes a short little step to the side before persevering to write, "though it is an awkward confession to make about one's heroine, I must add that she was something of a glutton."

And there are woeful brush strokes ahead: Catherine's clothes, her "lively taste for dress." This "taste" causes her father to "fairly grimace, in private, to think that a child of his should be both ugly and over-dressed." There is to be the merciless comedy of the "red satin gown trimmed with gold fringe" into which Catherine will more or less pour herself for an evening party at which her cousin's engagement is to be announced. There, in the awful red dress she will meet her fate, the fortune hunter Morris Townsend, meet that fate in the company of her other fate, her adored, "ironical" father.

So Catherine will meet Morris Townsend—extraordinarily handsome, "beautiful," she calls him—a New Yorker who has been knocking about the world rather than staying at home to sell bonds or to enter the law. In his knocking, he has spent his small inheritance and seems to have spent his friends and made himself unwelcome. Back in his native city, he claims to be looking about for something to do; meanwhile, he is staying with his sister—in fact living on his sister, who is in very reduced circumstances as a widow with five children. A sordid record with a few travel stickers from European hotels. Townsend is a distant connection of the young man Catherine's cousin is to marry. At the party, he goes for Catherine's attention with the watchful concentration of a sportsman waiting for the game to fly in the range of the gun.

Catherine, surprised by joy, as it were, is overwhelmed, hard hit with the rustic fluster of her inexperience. She will be joined by the tirelessly articulating duenna, Mrs. Penniman, Dr. Sloper's widowed sister, who lives in the motherless house and acts as a sort of chaperone and companion for the girl. Mrs. Penniman completes the quartet of the action, her addition to the stage being a fluff-filled swoon of sentimentality and a very intrusive meddling. In the support of Townsend's dubious campaign, Aunt Penniman will show herself as insistent, canny, and devious, as if she were awaiting a broker's fee.

With the unexpected courtship of Catherine, the tone changes; we are not, after all, to witness a deft seduction in the Restoration mode but a tangle of coldness, calculation, and conflicting motive, all at Catherine's expense. If the result is not quite a tragedy, it is a conclusion of most serious and lasting heartbreak. Perhaps in terms of fictional art, James was wise to give Catherine the works: her dismaying vital statistics, her dumpiness, and her baffled maneuvering will set her up like one of those dolls at the country fair, ready to be idly knocked down for a prize. Still, she, all unstylish blushes and innocent gratitude, will profoundly solicit the sympathy of the reader as a heroine from real life, one not so remote from readers of both sexes, each of whom will have some defects in the lottery of romance. (I would not go as far as Leon Edel and claim that Catherine is "the image of himself [James] as victim of his brother's—and America's—failure to understand his feelings." The sibling rivalry Edel greatly favors as the psychological burden and ultimate creative spur of Henry's triumphant life—the wound and the bow—will even find William James lurking in the shadow of Dr. Sloper.)

Dr. Sloper, the most interesting and complicated character in the novel, is perhaps villainous in his genial, confident presence in the family and his also genial, confident intrusions into the love affair. He is a father who will ask when Catherine appears in the disastrous red satin dress, "Is it possible that this magnificent person is my child?" Told of Townsend's pursuit, he will puff on a cigar and reply, "He is in love with this regal creature, then?" Because the doctor is smart and observant himself, we are not surprised to learn that he thinks Catherine "as intelligent as a bundle of shawls." The "ironical" accent in the doctor's intercourse with his daughter is flamboyant, if lightly tossed about. One feels he enjoys the exercise of this established mode of communication; by it, he has turned a flaw of character, the absence of paternal propriety, into a manner, or a mannerism.

The plot of *Washington Square* is simple in its framing. Time is running out for Morris Townsend, and he must find someplace to land. Before meeting Catherine, he has obviously known of her inheritance from her mother, some ten thousand a year, and can figure out for himself her expectations upon the death of her father. So he makes his way to the side of the pleasant, wallflowerish Catherine. And, doing so, he picks up the admiration, if merely as an exciting diversion, of Aunt Penniman. The widowed chaperone's conspiracy on his behalf is immediate, like the burglar charming the housemaid over the fence and coming away with the key to the kitchen door. Visits to the house on Washington Square take place, and Catherine quickly falls into a kind of alarmed love.

Townsend means to marry Catherine, but he is quick to sense the impediment of Dr. Sloper, whom he is not foolish enough to imagine an easy conquest. And Sloper is, as feared, not in the least attracted to Townsend. The doctor says, "He is not what I call a gentleman. He has not the soul of one. He is extremely insinuating; but it's a vulgar nature. I saw through it in a minute. He is altogether too familiar—I hate familiarity."

Townsend will naturally decide that the doctor finds him unsuitable only on the ground of his poverty. He understands the doctor's power but not the fact that this particular father is the last person to imagine an adventurer like Townsend captivated by the unqualified Catherine. Shallowness, idleness, and insincerity, not poverty, are the grounds of Dr. Sloper's contempt:

> The fact that Morris Townsend was poor—was not of necessity against him; the doctor had never made up his mind that his daughter should marry a rich man. The fortune she would inherit struck him as a very sufficient provision for two reasonable persons, and if a penniless swain who could give a good account of himself should enter the lists, he should be judged quite upon his personal merits.

The doctor wishes Catherine to be loved for her moral worth—he gives her that virtue, if not much else.

Dr. Sloper's caustic, teasing banter with his daughter offends but does not amount to inattention; after Catherine has announced her engagement, he can be said to be very much on the case. He will make his way over to Second Avenue to call upon Mrs. Montgomery, the sister with whom the suitor is living. This, the most brilliant scene in the novel, provides a formal advancement of the plot and an advancement of the subtleties in the disposition of James's New York City physician. He has married a rich woman, and we gather he himself is of a respectable if not glittering family, but he is self-created and not a snob.

He goes downtown on Second Avenue, a swerve to the east, an unpromising direction at that time. Basil Ransom in *The Bostonians* lived as an impecunious young lawyer from the defeated South on that outré avenue, lived in close acquaintance with the "fantastic skeleton of the Elevated Railway, overhanging the transverse longitudinal street, which it darkened and smothered with the immeasurable spinal column and myriad clutching paws of an antediluvian monster." Excursions into the slushy, unreclaimed portions of Manhattan had for James the fearful, if beckoning, aspect of an assignation. In the New York City sections of *The American Scene*, we experience alarm for his palpitating heart as he goes—portly, sensitive, alert gentleman with a walking stick—into the immigrant's New Jerusalem, into Little Italy, and visits the portentous hordes with their bundles pouring forth from Ellis Island. In *Washington Square*, Mrs. Penniman, heavily veiled, embarks upon a perilous journey to an "oyster saloon in the Seventh Avenue, kept by a negro," in order to consummate another of her fatuous, capriciously encouraging interviews with Morris Townsend. But then that lady has had some experience of the outside of things, since we have been told that she accepted her brother's invitation to live in Washington Square with "the alacrity of a woman who had spent ten years of her married life in the town of Poughkeepsie."

So the doctor will venture downtown to Second Avenue, where he will observe with approval Mrs. Montgomery's neat little house of red brick and, inside, the tidy, if pitiable, efforts at decoration—"desultory foliage of tissue paper, with clusters of glass drops," and so on. He notes the cast-iron stove "smelling strongly of varnish" and finds the widowed lady to be "a brave little person," to whom he gave "his esteem as soon as he had looked at her."

The visit is crucial in every sense. The doctor states, without quali-
fication, that Catherine will have her ten thousand a year, but if she
marries Townsend, "I shall leave every penny of my own fortune, earned
in the laborious exercise of my profession, to public institutions." The
visit, in a guarded way, also reveals that Mrs. Montgomery has been
giving money, of which she has little, to her brother, who takes it since
he has none. In the end, the poor sister, having in the conversation
formed an idea of the good nature and vulnerability of Catherine says,
"Don't let her marry him!"

Catherine, incurably smitten, would marry without her father's
consent, painful as the possibility might be. This immovable passion
and defiance are most interesting to the doctor. "'By Jove,' he said to
himself, 'I believe she will stick—I believe she will stick!'" And so she
does, even after a year abroad, the old family deprogramming hope, a
year of misery and intellectual waste since she "failed to gather animation from the mountains of Switzerland or the mountains of Italy."
She does not relent, and Townsend is waiting, having, with the hospitality of Mrs. Penniman, made himself at home in the house on Washington Square, smoking the doctor's cigars, sitting by the fire, and
listening to the aunt's prediction that Catherine will in the end get her
father's fortune.

When she returns, Townsend is still idly trying to discount the
possibility of disinheritance; thus, a remarkable dialogue between the
two young people takes place, beginning with Catherine:

> "We must ask no favours of him—we must ask nothing more.
> He won't relent, and nothing good will come of it. I know it
> now—I have a very good reason."
>
> "And pray what is your reason?" She hesitated to bring it out,
> but at last it came.
>
> "He is not very fond of me!"
>
> "Oh, bother!" cried Morris, angrily.

Townsend ungraciously, surreptitiously, takes his leave, and that is
the story.

The plot, among the novels of James, is an open one of a simple heart ruthlessly manipulated, of trust and goodwill dishonored. The central drama is between Catherine and her father, a drama of serious moral questions beyond the struggle of their opposing wills. There is not much questioning to be done on behalf of Morris Townsend, a young man of every conceivable vanity, a natural squanderer of money, friendships, family, anything at hand.

One of the footnotes James has placed in the seduction of Catherine's money is that Townsend, although destitute, puts a remarkably high value upon himself. When Catherine announces she will defy her father and is ready to flee the house with her "lover," she can rightly wonder why her ten thousand should not be sufficient. The repudiation of this income because it will not be augmented at her father's death is an insult of the most severe kind—and another folly committed by the conceited squanderer who imagines he can do better, whether by some vague plans for business or by way of a woman with a greater fortune.

Money in exchange for love is the dilemma of many of the heroines in James's novels. And a most curious way he has with it. Isabel Archer in *The Portrait of a Lady* is, by a tangled and not altogether credible route, willed seventy thousand pounds. She is given the money so that she can be free, so that she can achieve her best self, which, as it turns out, is to make her the object of fortune hunters, just as the rich Milly Theale in *The Wings of the Dove* will be. Love, or the appearance of it, is to be paid for by American money, paid in cash in a transcontinental intrigue that is dark and vastly complicated.

Catherine has been denied beauty, gaiety, all the romantic mystery and glamour of the heiresses abroad. James took the dare of the negative. Catherine is as alone as an animal in a field. No Lord Warburton is seeking her hand as she decides to choose another; no lively young female friend attends her wandering; and if her response is reckless, as it is, the recklessness comes not from her own gift for desperate decision but from credulity and isolation.

The troubling aspect of the doctor's destruction of Catherine's romance lies in the fact that he intrigues with more brio than we can countenance. On the other hand, does the reader wish Catherine to succeed in marrying Townsend? The best that can be said for the match is that the contract of life should guarantee the right to make one's own mistakes. James had thought deeply about the need to "experience," to take the dare, to live, and to him, sedentary as a monument, to live meant personal experience, to risk love. Catherine does "stick," as her father discovers with astonishment.

She meets "The Beast in the Jungle":

> To have to meet, to face, to see suddenly break out in my life; possibly destroying all further consciousness, possibly annihilating me ... striking at the root of all my world and leaving me to the consequences, however they shape themselves.

We are not sure how greatly Catherine understands consequence at the time of her defiance, but she comes to understand humiliation and heartbreak. When a shabby, shopworn Townsend returns years later to ask for friendship, her answer is no. "You treated me too badly. I felt it very much; I felt it for years."

Washington Square is a perfectly balanced novel, narrow in its focus, rather claustrophobic, yet moving along with a speed suitable to the importunate demands of Morris Townsend in the matter of "settling" himself. In *The Notebooks*, James records the novel's origin in a story he heard from his friend the actress Mrs. Fanny Kemble. She told of her own handsome, penniless, selfish brother's pursuit of a "dull, plain, common-place girl, only daughter of the Master of King's Coll., Cambridge, who had a handsome private fortune (£4000 a year)." She was of that "slow, sober, dutiful nature that an impression once made upon her, was made for life." Her father disapproved of the engagement and vowed she would not get a penny of his money if she married. The young man, like Townsend, for a time thought the father could be brought around, but when it was clear there was to be no remission of the disinheritance, the suitor made a rapid retreat, leaving the girl desolated and never to marry. We note that here, too, there is a Mrs. Montgomery in the wings and that, when asked for advice by the unfortunately enamored young woman, she "advised the young girl by *no means* to marry her brother."

It was all there, the structure, the actors to be set down in New York on Washington Square. But James, assembling the bricks and mortar of the action, gradually found Catherine Sloper deeply entrenched on the inside, rather than the witty outside, of his imagination. Magically, he paces through each pause in her articulation, each artless question, each accumulation of baffled emotion, and thus Catherine comes to attract, profoundly. Her painful yet original dimensions come through to us slowly, as if in a haze, in contrast, for instance, to Isabel Archer's claims, rich and brilliant as they are, which begin by assertion: "You wished a while ago to see my idea of an interesting woman. There it is!"

Catherine is just raw feeling itself and literalness. Humbly, she tries to make her way through a crushing thicket of casual remarks, hoping to discover a literalness equal to her own and important to her understanding of her situation. "Did *he* say that?" she will ask Mrs. Penniman, who is busily reporting some putative exchange with Townsend. And, "Did *he* tell you to say these things to me?" By the force of her singular concentration in the midst of the off-hand and careless, she achieves a sort of personal, moral independence and certainly the dignity of the stubbornness and fidelity of her feelings.

And James was to take the father, merely a presence, an instrument, in the anecdote from which the plot derived, and create Dr. Sloper, a grand perplexity, a puzzle of disappointment and self-assurance. He is accustomed to control and boldly exercises it, but he dashes against a daunting sheet of rock: Catherine's feelings. The doctor is perhaps finally to be seen as Catherine's personal protector against certain disaster, but he is a protector of such provoking lapses and gaps that we cannot wish him victory. In the end, his victory, if that is what it is, does not rescue Catherine. Only Morris Townsend's abandonment can accomplish her salvation, if that is what is accomplished.

In any case, Catherine has lived, has known the assault of love. And when she says of her father, "He is not very fond of me," she has bitten of the fruit of knowledge, experienced the classical recognition moment and the power of enlightenment. Perhaps we can say that Catherine will become as clever as her father and can inflict upon him the fiercest vexation, which will amount to his genuine and lasting distress. Long after the romance with Townsend has been devastated beyond renewal, her father will still wish her to promise that she will not, at his death, marry the young man. Her answer: "I cannot promise that, Father."

The matter of the promise beyond the grave reveals Dr. Sloper's utter failure to understand where his daughter has been and where she is. As a final stroke of perverse underestimation, he reduces her portion in his will and writes: "She is amply provided for from her mother's side.... her fortune is already more than sufficient to attract those unscrupulous adventurers whom she has given me reason to believe that she persists in regarding as an interesting class." Catherine's comment about the punitive last testament is: "I like it very much. Only I wish it had been expressed a little differently." A proper burial for the interesting, ironical New York City physician.

1990

WIND FROM THE PRAIRIE

> Roll along, Prairie Moon,
> Roll along, while I croon.

A ROUND World War I, writers from the American Middle Western states began to appear on the literary scene. In fiction, there were Theodore Dreiser, Sinclair Lewis, and Sherwood Anderson, and also the three known as the Prairie Poets, Carl Sandburg, Vachel Lindsay, and Edgar Lee Masters.

Looking into the new biography of Carl Sandburg, a work of exhaustive, definitive coziness in the current American mode of entranced biographical research, I was reminded of having some years ago taken from the library stacks a curiosity, a biography of Lindsay written by Edgar Lee Masters. If Carl Sandburg can be said to have managed shrewdly the transactions of his declamatory, bardic career as a national treasure, born in Illinois on a corn-husk mattress, the other two rose and fell disastrously and literally. Vachel Lindsay committed suicide, and Masters died in want, having been found broke and sick in the Chelsea Hotel in New York and rescued to die in a nursing home.

The two men, Lindsay and Masters, are not quite soul mates. Their union is geographical, a territorial, circumstantial linkage to a mythographic Middle West, the putative spiritual grasslands of the vast native country. Lindsay was a naïve, manic evangelist, preaching the Gospel of Beauty, and carrying with him on his incredible cross-country hikes the Christian fundamentalism and Anti-Saloon teachings of his youth— along with, of course, the prairie, the conviction of being the voice of some real America, *in situ*, that must be honored, as if under threat of extinction by a flood. As a versifier he had no more caution than a hobo hitching a ride, but somehow his voice prevailed for a time, even with some of the respected critics of the day. He appeared and appeared, willing to recite at a high-school reunion as well as in London, where, according to a later biographer, Eleanor Ruggles, "he and his mother met Robert Bridges, venerable laureate and defender of the tongue [*sic*], and John Masefield, always Vachel's admirer, came in from Boars Hill to pay his respects." Feverish days, but, toward the end, in Washington, D.C., an audience of two hundred walked out, puzzling the performer and Edgar Lee Masters but attributed in the Ruggles biography to a microphone failure of which the poet was unaware.

Edgar Lee Masters, for a good part of his life a successful lawyer in Chicago, was a lot smarter than Vachel Lindsay and certainly more worldly—but then everyone was more worldly than Lindsay. Masters was in religion a freethinker, set against the "hypocrisy" of the preachers, even more exasperated by the temperance movement, and along the way set against puritanical sexual inhibitions. He was a handsome man who, step by hesitating step, nevertheless made a rashly uncomfortable marriage to a fundamentalist, teetotaler young woman. He had children, stayed on, was unfaithful (listing in his autobiography nearly as many female loves as Goethe), finally divorced, and remarried a young woman—indeed, thirty years younger than he. Lindsay was one of those too friendly boosters with their often strange imperviousness and faltering sense of the appropriate. Masters was splenetic, the cemetery headstone his natural memorial, cranky in opinion, and, although very productive and for a time immensely successful, there was in his life a feeling of being undervalued, and even of seeing the whole country in an enormous displacement from virtue, pioneer and otherwise.

Of Lindsay, Masters said he was "impelled to write something about the poet who was native to Illinois, as I am in reality, and who knew the same people and the same culture that I do, and who practiced the art of poetry, as I have, in the same part of America, and under the same social and political conditions." In the end, as he reaches Lindsay's declining audience and death, he begins to see the life as a social rather than a personal tragedy, to view the native "singer" as a victim of the East, the money-grubbing, alienated world that preferred the poems of Robert Frost and E. A. Robinson, poets Masters finds essentially "English" in tone and landscape rather than American.

There's more to it than that from this strange man about his stranger fellow bard:

> The motley stocks and alien breeds which have taken America cannot be American until there is an America to mold them into Americans.... Lindsay might sing himself hoarse of the old courthouse America, the old horse and buggy America, the America of the Santa Fé Trail, of Johnny Appleseed.... Did the East, did these alien stocks want to be American? This is what Lindsay was up against. In this connection mention must be made of the Jews who are enormously numerous, powerful and influential. Jews are not Americans in the sense that the Jews are English or French, according to habitat.

Ezra Pound described Vachel Lindsay as a "plain man in gum overshoes with a touching belief in W. J. Bryan." Yes, there was "Bryan, Bryan, Bryan, Bryan," the poem celebrating the Free Silver populist, fundamentalist, and prohibitionist in his losing campaign against McKinley. Almost three hundred lines in which Bryan is seen as "the prairie avenger ... smashing Plymouth Rock with his boulders from the West." His defeat was the "victory of Plymouth Rock and all those inbred landlord stocks" (perhaps it was) and also, in a wild extension, somehow the defeat of the "blue bells of the Rockies and the blue bonnets of old Texas."

Lindsay's life was one of intense, sentimental aggressiveness; and yet there is something unprotected about him. His unanchored enthusiasm has the dismaying aspect of being genuine and unforced, a sort of hysterical innocence, or so it seems. The cheerful, round-faced, fair-haired country boy was in fact town bred, born in Springfield, Illinois. Fate put his birthplace next to the house in which Lincoln had lived, and this—the nearness of the great, solemn son of the prairie, the hallowed walker of the streets of Springfield—had the effect of igniting the boy like a firecracker. Lincoln in Illinois had quite a contrary effect on Edgar Lee Masters, who wrote a long, scathing biography of the fallen president, composed with the racing eloquence of contempt for the man and for the "tyrannous plutocracy" that followed the Civil War.

Both Lindsay and Masters come from professional families. Masters's father was a self-made lawyer, a conscientious man of some influence in Illinois and given, at least in part, to liberal causes and worthy cases. The Lindsay family was an older combination of beliefs and habits. The father, as a young man in impecunious circumstances, worked his way through an Ohio medical school, set up practice in Illinois, and, after the death of his first wife, somehow saved enough for further study in Vienna. On the boat going to Europe, he met his future wife, a teacher of art and other subjects in Kentucky. Throughout their lives, with or without their children, the couple traveled quite a lot, going several times to Europe and even as far as Japan and China, but there were less cosmopolitan strains in the mother. She passed on to her son the ornamental, provincial "art-loving" claim of certain small-town American wives and also a good measure of the missionary qualities he displayed. Mrs. Lindsay was the organizer of church spectacles, liked to officiate in group meetings, attend conferences, and so on.

Her family was attached to the Campbellite Church, also known as the Christian Church. The church had been founded by Alexander Campbell and his son Thomas, originally Presbyterians and then, coming to believe in baptism by immersion, united with the Baptists, before finally breaking away—in one of those organizational disputes so peculiar to the Protestant denominations—to found their own Campbellite sect. From these roots, Vachel Lindsay got his fundamentalism and prohibitionism, the Gospel of Beauty, and a flair for expounding preacher-style. He was sent to the Art Institute of Chicago and later, in New York in 1905, studied with William Merritt Chase and Robert Henri but did not make notable progress as a painter or as a cartoonist.

All the time, Lindsay had been writing verses in his hymn-tune rhythms, reciting at the YMCA, and turning himself into a peddler. With his verses and drawings, the plain, open-faced, clean young man wandered the streets of New York, knocking on the doors of fish markets, Chinese laundries, and bakeries, stopping people to listen to his wares, canvassing, as it were, Hell's Kitchen. A curious, impervious nuisance, bringing to mind the intrepid appeals of the Jehovah's Witness bell ringers. And then he began his years of quite literally tramping across the country, pamphlets and verses for sale, doing missionary work for the Gospel of Beauty. He carried with him a character reference from the YMCA.

It was in California that Lindsay learned of the death of General William Booth, founder of the Salvation Army. And thus he came to write one of his first bizarre incantations, an unaccountable success for which the mind glancing back on our literary history is, well, dumbstruck.

> General William Booth Enters into Heaven
> (To be sung to the tune of "The Blood of the Lamb" with
>   indicated instrument)

The work opens with bass-drum beats and:

> Booth led boldly with his big bass drum—
> (Are you washed in the blood of the Lamb?)
> The Saints smiled bravely and they said: "He's come."
> (Are you washed in the blood of the Lamb?)

The thing flows on apace and concludes:

> He saw King Jesus. They were face to face,
> And he knelt a-weeping in that holy place.
> Are you washed in the blood of the Lamb?

The submission appeared in an early issue of *Poetry* and Harriet Monroe in the annual prizegiving of 1913 awarded it $100. A prize for $250 went to William Butler Yeats, the latter having been pushed for by Ezra Pound. Sometime later, when Yeats was in Chicago, Miss Monroe invited Lindsay to a dinner at which the various important writers on hand were invited. That evening Vachel Lindsay recited the whole of "The Congo" and was apparently "well-received" in spite of its being over two hundred fiercely resounding lines. This most extraordinary embarrassment in our cultural history achieved a personally orated dissemination scarcely to be credited. Anywhere and everywhere he went with it—the Chamber of Commerce, high schools, ladies' clubs, the Lincoln Day banquet in Springfield, the Players Club in New York, where Masters tells that its noise greatly irritated certain members.

"The Congo" is the supreme folly of Lindsay's foolhardy career. There is a sad, no doubt unconscious, complacency in its concussive hilarity, the compositional shove coming from

> an allusion in a sermon by my pastor, F. W. Burnham, to the heroic life and death of Ray Eldred. Eldred was a missionary of the Disciples of Christ who perished while swimming a treacherous branch of the Congo.

The work is subtitled "A Study of the Negro Race," and part one lies under the heading "Their Basic Savagery." The imagery, if such it can be called, is blackface American minstrel, except for a strophe about Leopold of Belgium in hell with his hands cut off.

With a "deep rolling bass," the prairie evangelist sets out on his crusade:

> Fat black bucks in a wine-barrel room,
> Barrel-house kings, with feet unstable...
> Beat an empty barrel with the handle of a broom...
> Boomlay, boomlay, boomlay, BOOM...
> THEN I SAW THE CONGO, CREEPING THROUGH THE BLACK,
> CUTTING THROUGH THE FOREST WITH A GOLDEN TRACK...
> Tattooed cannibals danced in files;
> Then I heard the boom of the blood-lust song....
> Boom, kill the Arabs,
> Boom, kill the white men,
> Hoo, Hoo, Hoo....
> Mumbo-Jumbo will hoo-doo you.

The second section has the title "Their Irrepressible High Spirits." Here, on the Congo River, we run into a round of crap-shooting, whoops and yells, witch-men dressed to kill, "cake-walk princes" in tall silk hats, coal-black maidens with pearls in their hair, and more Boom, Boom, Boom. In the third section, "The Hope of Their Religion," the Apostles appear in coats of mail and, to the tune of "Hark, ten thousand harps and voices," ordain that "Mumbo-Jumbo will die in the jungle." The forests, the beasts, and the "savages" fade away, whispering, in a *pianissimo*, the dying strains of "Mumbo-Jumbo will hoo-doo you." The "bucks" are thus converted, all now down-home Campbellites.

What the far-flung audiences made of this infernal indiscretion is hard to imagine. There is always a market for "carrying on" in public, as we can confirm today. No doubt there was more condescension in the air than the reports would suggest. A performance organized in 1920 at Oxford University by Robert Graves can be read as an elaborate prank on the pretensions of the dons rather than as a tribute to the prairie poet—indeed, the sweating reiterations of the amateur elocutionist might recall Tom Thumb at Queen Victoria's court.

In any case, scholars can excavate in the old magazines many alarming commendations of this native genius, fresh voice, America's Homer, and so on. Harriet Monroe, a promoter of poetry and of the Middle West in tandem, wrote the introduction to the book publication of *The Congo and Other Poems*. The praise is short but unfortunately ranging in reference, like a kangaroo leaping over rich and spacious plains. Whistler and Whitman are called forth before a landing by Miss Monroe on the "old Greek precedent of the half-chanted lyric." The "Greek precedent" is one of those critical jokes like "the Jane Austen of the Upper West Side," but the claims of the Prairie Poets and subsequent idolators to the example of Whitman is an unending irritation.

"The Sànta-Fé Trail" is another noisy work, the theme seeming to be that the sound of the automobile—Crack, Crack, Crack—is trying without success to overwhelm the song "sweet, sweet, sweet" of a local Southwest bird known as Rachel-Jane. Then there is a salute to the firemen, "Clang, Clang, Clang," and an evocation of Jesus in "I Heard Immanuel Singing."

He was ruddy like a shepherd.
His bold young face how fair.
Apollo of the silver bow
Had not such flowing hair.

Tramping and reciting, forever in manic locomotion with notebook in hand to scribble whatever came into his head, head to be laid down at night on a YMCA pillow, leaving little time for romantic life. Actually, Lindsay comes across as more than a little girl-shy in spite of crushes here and there, one falling on the poet Sara Teasdale. But she married a rich shoe manufacturer and for a time was set up grandly in New York, until she too was mowed down by the drastic scythe of taste and died divorced, no longer rich, reclusive and embittered. At last, Lindsay married a young woman from Spokane, a high-school teacher of English and Latin. She was twenty-three, and he was forty-six. They had two daughters and were always in financial distress, since his income came largely from recitations and a good portion went to agents and expenses. On the road, the listeners forever calling for "Congo" and "General Booth," Lindsay was to experience the pathos of repetition: exhaustion and insolvency.

Along the way, uphill and downhill, Lindsay wrote a most interesting book, fortunately in prose: *The Art of the Moving Picture*, first issued in 1915, revised in 1922, and later reprinted with an excellent appreciation of its worth in an introduction by Stanley Kauffmann. After the rant and carelessness of the verses, Lindsay concentrated his mind on the movies. Here it is, he must have decided as he rested his vocal cords in the darkness of the old cinemas—American, popular, infinite in variety, flung out to the folk with a prodigality very similar to his own production methods. He tries to organize what the films can do, sort out the types, explain the power of directors such as D. W. Griffith.

For instance, "The Action Picture":

In the action picture there is no adequate means for the development of full-grown personal passion. The Action Pictures are falsely advertised as having heart-interest, or abounding in tragedy, but though the actors glower and wrestle and even if they are the most skillful lambasters in the profession, the audience gossips, and chews gum.

There are the Intimate Photoplays, the Splendor Pictures, which divide into Crowd Splendor, Patriotic Splendor, Religious Splendor, and so on. Concerning the intimate photoplay, he writes:

> Though the intimate and friendly photoplay may be carried out of doors to a row of loafers in front of the country store, or the gossiping streets of the village, it takes its origin and theory from the snugness of the interior. The restless reader replies that he has seen photoplays that showed ballrooms that were grandiose, not the least cozy. These are to be classed as out-of-door scenery so far as theory goes, and are discussed under the head of Splendor Pictures. The intimate Motion Picture . . . is gossip *in extremis*.

The movies and their vagrant images for him, the lonely traveling man, had the seductive power of the saloon for others of his kind. He was seduced into a contemplation and wish for coherence absent from his verse making. Thus, he finds "noble views of the sea," common to early camera effects, allied to "the sea of humanity spectacles":

> the whirling of dancers in ballrooms, handkerchief-waving masses of people on balconies, the hat-waving political ratification meetings, ragged, glowering strikers, and gossiping, dickering people in the market-place. Only Griffith and his disciples can do these as well as almost any manager can reproduce the ocean. Yet the sea of humanity is dramatically blood-brother to the Pacific, the Atlantic, or Mediterranean. . . . So, in *The Birth of a Nation*, the Ku Klux Klan dashes down the road as powerfully as Niagara pours over the cliff.

A film version of Ibsen's *Ghosts* came to town, and Lindsay reports that it was not Ibsen and should have been advertised under the title "The Iniquities of the Fathers. An American Drama of Eugenics, in a Palatial Setting." The style of these reflections, offhand and colloquial, is usefully attuned to the subject and to his casual but transfixed attentions. Returning from the showing of Larry Trimble's *The Battle Hymn of the Republic*, he recorded that the girl at the piano played "Under the Shade of the Apple Tree" throughout. Among the virtues of the films are their usefulness, nonalcoholic, to the working classes, who, in the heat of summer, "under the wind of an electric fan, can witness everything from a burial at Westminster to the birthday parade of the ruler of the land of Swat."

Los Angeles is the Boston, the Florence of this great flowering, and the stars are national monuments. He pens a tribute to Mary Pickford, "doll divine," which will proceed to rhyme with "valentine." And Blanche Sweet: "Stately are her wiles / filling oafs with wisdom, / Saving souls with smiles." *The Art of the Moving Picture* is the prairie singer's finest, most lasting tribute to the American West, to Hollywood.

He was fifty-two years old when he committed suicide. It is not easy to be certain what was going on in his mind, but there seem to have been frightening mood swings, ups and downs, suspicions followed by remorse, in every way a sad collapse. Doctors were called in, but before a decision could be made for treatment, Lindsay drank Lysol, saying, "I got them before they got me—they can just try to explain this if they can."

Edgar Lee Masters was asked by Lindsay's wife to write a biography and given access to the papers—a very large fund of jottings, since Lindsay showed a self-preoccupation quite precocious, if that is the way to look at his keeping a daily diary almost from the time he first learned to write. Masters's work is rich in thorny attitudes, and that gives it a certain cross-grained interest, especially when compared to the ruthless coverage of the pertinent and impertinent, the sense of being on a long trip with the subject in the family car, that defines the research of Lindsay's other biographer, Eleanor Ruggles, as it does so many other conventional and academic biographies.

Lindsay's limitations are, if not stressed, at least acknowledged when Masters writes:

Lindsay dwelt forever in cuckoo cloudland.... He never grew up. The curled darling became a man of great emotional strength;

but the memory of himself as the apple of his mother's eye, as the child wonder of grammar school. . . . a sort of Santa Claus grown up and made suitable for adult wonder and devotion.

On the other hand, we are asked to view the fantastical footnote, Lindsay, in conspiratorial terms:

> Not being Eastern American he made only a slight impact upon it; and after the first excitement about his poetry subsided he was treated with supercilious indifference, and the field he had broken and harrowed and sowed was taken and reaped by pro-English artists. . . . They preferred the Arthurian legends to Johnny Appleseed and Andrew Jackson.

The accent of grievance, neatly correspondent to Masters's cast of mind, is not to the point in the matter of Vachel Lindsay, and in any case the shape of an individual career is mixed with so many contingencies it cannot easily support a translation to the general. But all that is nothing beside the fact that if Lindsay had some sort of talents, they were not for poetry. He did not write poetry, he wrote jingles and hymns and scenarios for his public appearances. The true melancholy of the life lies in the broad encouragement of his naïveté, the span of his performances, which would inevitably weary. His books were published, he was "famous," and yet somehow he remained a door-to-door peddler.

Edgar Lee Masters was born in 1869, and his major work, *Spoon River Anthology*, did not appear until 1915, although a few of the portraits in it had been published earlier under a pseudonym. He entered his father's profession of law and practiced in Chicago for almost thirty years. He was unhappily married and wrote in his autobiography: "Somehow little by little I got the feeling that my wife in spite of her almost meek compliance was enervating me and cutting off my hair and putting out my eyes." A bitter divorce finally came about, and Masters moved to New York with a new young bride and settled into the Chelsea Hotel, his wife going back and forth to teach in Pennsylvania.

In many ways a companionable man, friend of Mencken, Dreiser, and others who liked their cigars and schnapps, member of the Players Club, somehow Masters seemed to drift into reclusion. We may notice that although he was in partnership for almost eight years with Clarence Darrow in Chicago, the well-known lawyer does not appear in Masters's autobiography. Masters's son, by the first wife, in a memoir attributes this gap to the scandal of the divorce and the appearance on the scene of her replacement, some thirty years younger. Perhaps, he suggests, Darrow took at best a neutral attitude, and the estrangement followed. Also the son tells of visiting his father at the Chelsea. Ellen Masters, now his stepmother, did not seem to be on hand. Present, however, was another young woman, Alice Davis, who lived in the hotel and helped with manuscripts and whatever else she helped with.

In 1944, *The New York Times* printed a story telling that Masters had been taken to Bellevue Hospital suffering from pneumonia and malnutrition. The Authors League and the American Academy came to his rescue, the wife packed him off to a Pennsylvania nursing home, near to where she was teaching, and there he died six years later at the age of eighty-one. Not a happy roundup, even if there is a hint of self-willed recoil and collapse when one remembers the great industry Masters showed throughout his life in the production of works in many forms—verse, plays, novels, biography, and autobiography.

Spoon River Anthology (1915)—a book could scarcely be more of a success. Said to have sold more copies than any other previous work of American poetry, it was translated into all the European languages as well as into Arabic, Korean, and Chinese; it was also transformed for the stage and used as the libretto for an opera, performed at La Scala. The book is an "anthology" of the gravestones around Spoon River, an area near to Lewistown, Illinois, where Masters grew up. The dead come forth to speak the epitaphs of their lives, each one a short free-verse recollection, a sort of *conte*, very often remembering injuries or spoken with a surly ruefulness. The unquiet graves, some 214 of them—"all, all, are sleeping on the hill"—were thought to be somewhat cynical and degrading to the quality of life lived in the Illinois villages of Masters's youth and from which he drew his ruminating characters.

The first one is "Hod Putt," who died by hanging for a robbery in his days of poverty after a life of toil. Seeing an opportunity for the last word, he notes with satisfaction that he lies next to a crook who prospered from clever uses of the possibilities of bankruptcy. "Now we who took the bankrupt law in our respective ways, / Sleep peacefully side by side." The verses today strike one not as acerbic so much as generally soulful, "filled with longing" poems; good, simple people seeking transcendence. "Of what use is it / To rid one's self of the world, / When no soul may ever escape the eternal destiny of life?"

The public appeal of the work must have been in the framing: first, the lachrymal country churchyard with the darkening granite of the tombstones lying in random placement as in village life; then, the brief, anecdotal summations, many of them reading like those civil-court cases that scrape the skins of the litigants into eternity. To this must be added the candid moral framing of the little stories, the accent on the scorned, the unlucky, the eccentric from whom the smothering "hypocrisy" of the village would exact its punishments.

The "valiant" departed one, "Jefferson Howard," is "Foe of the church with its charnel darkness, / Friend of the human torch of the tavern" and hounded by the "dominating forces"—Republicans, Calvinists, merchants, bankers. In *Spoon River*, fate deals out repetitive cards, like the equalizing aspect of death itself. The aesthetic default of the work, pressing upon the mind as one name after another approaches its declaration, is that it could go on forever, the flat proseness of the language contributing, as the rocks in the sod are turned over again and again. There was indeed a second collection of Spoon River tales, a replication and consequent deflation of the original invention. (Another monologue-portrait was published during these years, "The Love Song of J. Alfred Prufrock.")

A biography, *Lincoln: The Man*, appeared in 1931. Hara-kiri, blood on the floor, Masters's as well as Lincoln's, an insult to the prairie, to Illinois, and perhaps to Carl Sandburg, or so Vachel Lindsay thought. The first part of Sandburg's Lincoln book, *The Prairie Years*, had been out for five years, and if its success embittered Masters, the emotion had its source in the picture of Lincoln rather than in the author's success in the market.

Masters's character is a puzzle, and it is hard to understand why this attractive and intelligent man, successful as a lawyer and a writer, should be such a sorehead. He is the village iconoclast, atheist, free lover, and more than a bit paranoid in the matter of local and national forces. He has *ideas* as some have freckles, and the book on Lincoln puts many of them on display with a good deal of eloquence, however alienating. The notion of the book is that the Civil War should not have been fought and that the aftermath—the domination of plutocrats, merchants, bankers, and the later imperial adventurism—was a disastrous drift. "Hebraic-Puritanism" is Masters's phrase for the moral insufficiency of the country. By this he does not appear to indicate anti-Semitism; instead, he felt a corrosive resentment of the Bible, Old Testament and New, and its power to shape the ethical climate of the nation. After the Civil War,

> as if in sublime malice, the choking weeds of Hebraic-Puritanism were sown; and thus the evils of empire and ancient privileges began to thrive, scarcely before the new wheat was started. Ages may be required for creative vision to stand externally in this field and its epos.

The overwhelming offense of the biographer was its picture of the character of Lincoln, who is seen as a creature of swamp-bred shrewdness, a sort of wary, calculating Snopes, retaining in the midst of certain superficial refinements the qualities of his father, Thomas Lincoln, who out of shiftlessness had sunk into the fetid habits of the "poor white" class. Masters stresses the fact that Nancy Hanks, Lincoln's mother, was illegitimate and in the enveloping mist of parental uncertainty had discovered or imagined her supposed father to be a well-bred Virginia planter. Lincoln claimed the presence of his more promising qualities to have come from the absent grandfather. "Lincoln was profoundly ashamed of the poverty of his youth, and of the sordid surroundings in which he grew up." Thus, his life was ruled by the determination to rise above his beginnings, "unlike the more honest Andrew Jackson and Walt Whitman."

The distinction and beauty of Lincoln's prose and of his platform style must be conceded—and also reduced. For Masters, this accomplishment and talent are suffused and diseased with the poison of the Bible:

"Lincoln, whose only literacy was out of the Bible, and who developed an oratory from it, inspired by its artifice of emotional reiteration, and equipped with its sacred curses and its dreadful prophecies, its appeal to moralities where there was no thought, no real integrity." The Gettysburg Address is unfavorably compared to Pericles' funeral oration and subjected to a textual analysis on the matter of truth: "It was not true that our fathers in 1776 had brought forth a new nation; for in that year our fathers brought forth thirteen new nations, each of which was a sovereign state." Lincoln as a statesman and a thinker is accused of the "Hebraic-Puritan principle of assuming to act as one's brother's keeper, when the real motive was to become one's brother's jailer."

Out of indignation and obsession, Masters dug his own grave and sadly inscribed his own tombstone with the acid of the Spoon River meters. The resentment of the Civil War soldier, "Knowlt Hoheimer," killed in battle and lying up on the hill, might be his own epitaph:

> Rather a thousand times
> the county jail
> Than to lie under this marble
> figure with wings,
> And this granite pedestal
> Bearing the words, "Pro Patria."
> What do they mean, anyway?

Carl Sandburg lived to be eighty-nine years old, and he spent those years going here and yon, a hardy tumbleweed of a populist, blown by the wind across the plains. More than forty books to his credit and what for some would have been a burdensome accretion of honors, each one to be accepted and attended like the duties on the court calendar. Of course, he was sustained by the old pioneer energy, and as an early pop-art king his act—writing free-verse poems, collecting and performing *The American Songbag*—was inexhaustible. The six volumes on the life of Lincoln, "a folk biography" some critic was happy to describe it, spread over more than ten years, but of course he was on the hoof a good deal of that time.

These reflections come about from the strenuous busyness of

Penelope Niven's new biography of Sandburg: over seven hundred pages, followed by another hundred of notes. This effort is a sort of rival to Sandburg's *Lincoln: Prairie Years, Chicago Years, National Hero Years*. Professor Niven says in her preface that her previous scholarship was of the sort to exclude the claims of this bygone figure, fallen from eminence, but "a decade after his death, I went to his Carolina mountain home," and then it appears that she fell into the corncrib, so to speak. That is, the vast Sandburg papers in libraries, in possession of the family, lying about in cartons. After this great haystack, the fodder of the book, was pulled apart, she began the Carl Sandburg Oral History Project of more than 150 interviews.

Having gone through the heap, settled into the poet and each member of the family, reliving their nights and days with an intrusive intimacy, the biographer wants to record each scrap. The index cards or data sheets come to have a claim of their own, and the affirmation, the yes, yes, of Sandburg's scurry through life is her own affirming journey. The book is tedious and sentimental and long, long, long. She likes participial descriptions such as "hearty and vigorous," or "erect and vigorous"—and who can doubt that's exactly what the wily old campaigner was, even though the biographer had never encountered him in life. The scholar of the papers, of *the life of*, knows, like some celestial Xerox machine, details that consciousness erases overnight.

One of the amusements of this biography is that it is a kind of informal history of the radio and television shows of the period, not unlike listening to the "golden oldies." Sandburg hit them all: the *George Jessel Show*, the *Milton Berle Show*, the *Dave Garroway Show*, the *Bell Telephone Hour*. Ed Murrow comes in more than once, and with Norman Corwin, the prince of radio Americana, Sandburg had a "fruitful" relationship. At the Philharmonic Auditorium in Los Angeles, he was introduced by Edgar Bergen (sold out, standing ovation); the publication of the *New American Songbag* had an introduction by Bing Crosby. Penelope Niven again and again calls Sandburg the "eternal hobo," but as his fame grows he is usually on his way to the studio or the auditorium.

For a number of years, or for a good part of them, the prairie poet was in Hollywood under contract. Two producers from MGM sought his services for an "epic film about the USA," an undertaking not designed to be a mere motion picture but a "great, ringing message to the people." Sandburg was to write a novel, following in shape a scenario written by Sidney Franklin. The novel would be published, then made into a film. For this he was given $100,000, and the project was a "challenge Sandburg could not resist." The end of it all, after story conferences, residence in the film colony, after years and years, was that the novel appeared under the name of *Remembrance Rock*, 1,067 pages of the American Dream, never made into a film, a critical failure, but in no way a money loss for the author. The second Hollywood adventure was a year and a half of work with George Stevens on *The Greatest Story Ever Told*. "He was not only a pioneer, but an adventurer and an explorer, in his own words a Seeker," Sandburg's biographer writes, her words ever echoing those of her subject.

Sandburg made a bold identification between his own career and the history of the great country itself. Roosevelt wanted him to run for Congress, we are told. He collected Harvard and Yale honorary degrees, among many others, Pulitzer Prizes for history and poetry, invitations to address a session of Congress—a lot of this adulation arising from assuming the mantle of Lincoln as a friend of the Family of Man, and so on. He missed out on a few things such as the Nobel Prize and felt a certain annoyance when President Kennedy, whom he had supported, invited Robert Frost to read a poem at his inaugural rather than himself.

Oscar Wilde called the prairies "blotting paper," and if they are so looked at Carl Sandburg can be said to have sucked up all the nutrients in the soil. His beginning voice in *Chicago Poems* (1916), celebrating the "City of the Big Shoulders," and lamenting the lot of the dispossessed, sustained him, it seems, into the Depression period and the years of the New Deal. As a child of Swedish immigrants, Sandburg was part of the Social Democratic movement in the Middle Western states, and that marked the rhythm of his life: the man, the striker, the dreamer, the immigrant toiler, friend of all mankind. His particular politics were New Deal and the Democratic Party. On and on he goes, each of his affirmations self-affirming.

The People, Yes is 179 pages long, with 107 sections—a statistical plenitude as typical of the Prairie Poets as of the wheat acreage of the region. In his notes, Sandburg writes of the work as coming out of *"Piers Plowman*, seven hundred years ago, a far better handbook and manual of democracy than either Dante or Donne"—a statement of such historical incongruity it raises questions of familiarity with the last two and maybe also the first of the antecedents named. No matter, the sprawl of the work is a "modern epic" and an "odyssey deep into the American Experience," in the reading by the biographer. In some ways, her spacious accommodations arouse sympathy since an attempt to analyze Sandburg's lines flowing down the pages would be profitless. His people, yes or no, are actually just indentured servants, and they did his work, sunup to sundown. The poet's acres and the house in the Carolinas are "open to the public as a National Park and National Historic Site." And that's it.

Spending time with the metered, or unmetered, minstrels of the Middle West is to invite a special melancholy, one not only aesthetic, although that defect predominates since they come into history as poets, not as preachers, philosophers, politicians, or entertainers. Birth or youth in Illinois marked them, a tattoo appropriate enough as experience, the turf of the imagination. Still, they were not ordinary citizens, state proud, but ones making a claim for what were, for the most part, hasty, repetitive, and formless verses, unlike, for instance, the inspirations of Hart Crane of Ohio.

Elitism, belief in the existence of exceptional talents, will here be scorned as a threat to the demotic voices of the prairie. Of course they, too, by publication, must make their entrance into the long tradition, an inescapable transition in the arts. As outlandishly successful as these poets were, the happy circumstance was, as usual, not sufficient, because of the wish for a higher validation that haunts the dreams of the popular.

All three had a proprietary feeling about the country, a longing to transform its restless genetic material into a *folk*, to fashion the inchoate strains into a hardy stock with the name "American" on it, like a packet of sunflower seeds. A futile parochialism for a nation that has ever been, to expropriate a phrase from Kafka, "a cage seeking a bird."

1991

MARY McCARTHY IN NEW YORK

INTELLECTUAL Memoirs: New York 1936–1938. I look at the title of these vivid pages and calculate that Mary McCarthy was only twenty-four years old when the events of this period began. The pages are a continuation of the first volume, to which she gave the title *How I Grew*. Sometimes with a sigh she would refer to the years ahead in her autobiography as "I seem to be embarked on how I grew and grew and grew." I am not certain how many volumes she planned, but I had the idea she meant to go right down the line, inspecting the troops you might say, noting the slouches and the good soldiers, and, of course, inspecting herself living in her time.

Here she is at the age of twenty-four, visiting the memory of it, but she was in her seventies when the actual writing was accomplished. The arithmetic at both ends is astonishing. First, her electrifying ("to excite intensely or suddenly as if by shock") descent upon New York City just after her graduation from Vassar College; and then after more than twenty works of fiction, essays, cultural and political commentary, the defiant perseverance at the end when she was struck by an unfair series of illnesses, one after another. She bore these afflictions with a gallantry that was almost a disbelief, her disbelief, bore them with a high measure of hopefulness, that sometime companion in adversity that came not only from the treasure of consciousness, but also from an acute love of being there to witness the bizarre motions of history and the also, often, bizarre intellectual responses to them.

Intellectual responses are known as opinions, and Mary had them and had them. Still, she was so little of an ideologue as to be sometimes unsettling in her refusal of tribal reaction—left or right, male or female, that sort of thing. She was doggedly personal, and often this meant being so aslant that there was, in this determined rationalist, an endearing crankiness, very American and homespun somehow. This was true especially in domestic matters, which held a high place in her life. There she is grinding the coffee beans of a morning in a wonderful wooden-and-iron contraption that seemed to me designed for muscle building—a workout it was. In her acceptance speech upon receiving the MacDowell Colony Medal for Literature, she said that she did not believe in labor-saving devices. And thus she kept on year after year, up to her last days, clacking away on her old green Hermes nonelectric typewriter, with a feeling that this effort and the others were akin to the genuine in the arts—to the handmade.

I did not meet Mary McCarthy until a decade or so after the years she writes about in this part of her autobiographical calendar. But I did come to know her well and to know most of the "characters," if that is the right word for the friends, lovers, husbands, and colleagues who made up her cast after divorce from her first husband and the diversion of the second, John, last name Porter, whom she did not marry. I also lived through much of the cultural and political background of the time, although I can understand the question asked, shyly, by a younger woman writing a biography of Mary: "Just what is a Trotskyite?" *Trotskyite* and *Stalinist*—part of one's descriptive vocabulary, like *blue-eyed*. Trotsky, exiled by Stalin and assassinated in Mexico in 1940, attracted leftists, many of them with socialist leanings, in opposition to the Stalin of the Moscow Trials, beginning in 1936, which ended in the execution of most of the original Bolsheviks and the terror that followed.

The preoccupation with the Soviet Union, which lasted, with violent mutations of emphasis, until just about yesterday, was a cultural and philosophical battleground in the years of Mary McCarthy's "debut" and in the founding, or refounding, of the *Partisan Review*. In that circle, the Soviet Union, the Civil War in Spain, Hitler, and Mussolini were what you might call real life, but not in the magazine's pages more real, more apposite, than T. S. Eliot, Henry James, Kafka, and Dostoevsky.

Her memoir is partly "ideas" and very much an account of those institutional rites that used to be recorded in the family Bible: marriage, children, divorce, and so on. Mary had only one child, her son Reuel Wilson, but she had quite a lot of the other rites: four marriages, interspersed with love affairs of some seriousness and others of none. Far from taking the autobiographer's right to be selective about waking up in this bed or that, she tempts one to say that she remembers more than scrupulosity demands—demands on the rest of us at least as we look back on the insupportable surrenders and dim our recollection with the aid of the merciful censor.

On the other hand, what often seems to be at stake in Mary's writing and in her way of looking at things is a somewhat obsessional concern for the integrity of sheer fact in matters both trivial and striking. "The world of fact, of figures even, of statistics . . . the empirical element in life . . . the fetishism of fact" are phrases taken from her essay "The Fact in Fiction" (1960). The facts of the matter are the truth, as in a court case that tries to circumvent vague feelings and intuitions. If one would sometimes take the liberty of suggesting caution to her, advising prudence or mere practicality, she would look puzzled and answer: But it's the truth. I do not think she would have agreed it was only her truth—instead she often said she looked upon her writing as a mirror.

And thus, she will write about her life under the command to put it all down. Even the name of the real Man in the Brooks Brothers Shirt in the fiction of the same name, but scarcely thought by anyone to be a fiction. So at last, and for the first time, she says, he becomes a fact named George Black, who lived in a suburb of Pittsburgh and belonged to the Duquesne Club. As in the story, he appeared again and wanted to rescue her from New York bohemian life, but inevitably he was an embarrassment. As such recapitulations are likely to be: Dickens with horror meeting the model for Dora of *David Copperfield*: "What a form she had, what a face she had, what a graceful, variable, enchanting manner!" Of course, the man in the Brooks Brothers shirt did not occasion such affirmative adjectives but was examined throughout with a skeptical and subversive eye. About the young woman, the author herself more or less, more rather than less, she would write among many other thoughts: "It was not difficult, after all, to be the prettiest girl at a party for the sharecroppers."

The early stories in *The Company She Keeps* could rightly be called a sensation: They were indeed a sensation for candor, for the brilliant, lightning flashes of wit, for the bravado, the confidence, and the splendor of the prose style. They are often about the clash of theory and practice, taste and ideology. Rich as they are in period details, they transcend the issues, the brand names, the intellectual fads. In "The Portrait of the Intellectual as a Yale Man," we have the conflict between abstract ideas and self-advancement, between probity and the wish to embrace the new and fashionable. About a young couple, she writes: "Every social assertion Nancy and Jim made carried its own negation with it, like an Hegelian thesis. Thus it was always being said by Nancy that someone was a Communist but a terribly nice man, while Jim was remarking that someone else worked for Young and Rubicam but was astonishingly liberal."

In the memoir, we learn that we can thank Edmund Wilson for turning the young Mary away from writing reviews to undertaking fiction and thereby producing these dazzling stories. We also learn that she thanks him for little else. A good deal of the pages left at her death tell about her affair with Philip Rahv and *analyze* the break, in fact a desertion, from him and her marriage to Wilson. I must say that much of this drama was new to me. I was not in New York at the time. I met Mary for the first time in the middle 1940s when I was invited to Philip Rahv's apartment. She was with a young man who was to be her next husband after the "escape" from Wilson—that is, she was with Bowden Broadwater. Philip was married to Nathalie Swan, Mary's good friend from Vassar.... A lot of water had flowed by.

The picture of Mary and Philip Rahv living in a borrowed apartment on East End Avenue, a fashionable street over by the wrong river, since Philip was very much a downtown figure, rambling round the streets of Greenwich Village with a proprietary glance here and there for the tousled heads of Sidney Hook or Meyer Schapiro and a few others whom he called *Luftmenschen*. The memory, no matter the inevitable strains of difference between them, has an idyllic accent, and she appears to have discovered in the writing, decades later, that she loved Rahv—a discovery I will call amusing for want of a better word. There was to be an expulsion from the garden when Edmund Wilson meets

Mary, pursues her, and finally, a not very long "finally," gets her to marry him.

The account of her moral struggles is a most curious and interesting one, an entangled conflict between inclination and obligation; the inclination to stay with Rahv and the obligation to herself, her principles, incurred when she got drunk and slept with Wilson and therefore had to marry him. The most engaging part of this struggle is not its credibility or inner consistency but the fact that Mary believed it to be the truth. There was a scent of the seminarian in Mary's moral life, which for me was part of her originality and also one of the baffling charms of her presence. Very little was offhand: Habits, prejudices, moments, even fleeting ones, had to be accounted for, looked at, and written in the ledger. I sometimes thought she felt the command to prepare and serve a first course at dinner ought to be put in the Bill of Rights.

I remember telling her about some offensive behavior to me on the part of people who were not her friends, but mere acquaintances, if that. When she saw them on the street up in Maine she would faithfully "cut them"—a phrase she sometimes used—while I, when her back was turned, would be waving from the car. Yet it must be said that Mary was usually concerned to make up with those she had offended in fiction, where they were amusingly trapped in their peculiarities, recognizable, in their little ways, not to mention their large ways. Among these were Philip and Nathalie Rahv, whom she had wounded, painfully for them, in a novella, *The Oasis*. They, too, made up, after a time, after a time.

Details, details: Consider the concreteness of the apartments, the clothes, the inquisitive, entranced observing that had something in it of the Goncourt Brothers putting it all down in the Paris of the second half of the nineteenth century. They will write: "On today's bill of fare in the restaurants we have authentic buffalo, antelope, and kangaroo." There it is, if not quite so arresting as Flaubert making love in a brothel with his hat on. Mary remembers from the long-flown years that they on a certain occasion drank "Singapore Slingers." And the minutiae of her first apartment in New York: "We had bought ourselves a 'modernistic' Russel Wright cocktail shaker made of aluminum with a wood top, a chromium hors d'oeuvres tray with glass dishes (using industrial materials was the idea), and six old-fashioned spoons with a simulated cherry on one end and the bottom of the spoon flat for crushing sugar and Angostura." The cocktail age, how menacing and beguiling to the sweet tooth, a sort of liquid mugger.

Unlike the Goncourts' rather mad nocturnal stenography to fill their incomparable pages, I don't think Mary kept a diary. At least, I never heard mention of one or felt the chill on rash spontaneity that such an activity from this shrewdly observing friend would cast upon an evening. From these pages and from the previous volume, it appears that she must have kept clippings, letters certainly, playbills, school albums, and made use of minor research to get it right—to be sure the young man in Seattle played on the football team. In these years of her life, she treasured who was in such and such a play seen in an exact theater. On the whole, though, I believe the scene setting, the action, the dialogue came from memory. These memories, pleasing and interesting to me at every turn, are a bit of history of the times—going to *Pins and Needles*, the Federal Theatre's tribute to the Ladies' Garment Workers' Union, a plain little musical with fewer of the contemporary theater's special effects than a performance of the church choir.

The pages of this memoir represent the beginning of Mary McCarthy's literary life. She was a prodigy from the first. I remember coming across an early review when I was doing some work in the New York Public Library. It was dazzling, a wonderfully accomplished composition, written soon after she left college. As she began, so she continued, and in the years ahead I don't think she changed very much. There was a large circle of friends in France, England, and Italy, as well as here at home, but Mary was too eccentric in her tastes to be called snobbish, and I did not find her an especially worldly person. She was not fashionable so much as discriminating: but beyond it all there was the sentimental and romantic streak in her nature that cast a sort of girlish glow over private and public arrangements.

Year in and year out, she made fantastical demands on her time and her budget for birthdays, Christmas, presents, banquets, bouquets, surprises, a whole salmon for the Fourth of July, traditional offering. I remember Natasha Nabokov, the mother of Ivan Nabokov, a publisher in Paris, telling me of a Thanksgiving in Paris where Mary found an approximation of the American turkey and brought forth "two dressings, one chestnut and one oyster." Keeping the faith it was. I often thought the holiday calendar was a command like the liturgical season with its dates and observances. Perhaps it was being an orphan, both of her parents having died in the flu epidemic of 1918, that led her to put such unusual stress on the reproduction of "family" gatherings.

Here she speaks of her "patrician" background, a word I never heard her use about herself. It was true that she came from the upper-middle class, lawyers and so on, but all of it had been lived so far away in Minnesota and the state of Washington that one never thought of her as Middle Western or Western but instead as American as one can be without any particularity of region or class. In any case, she created, even in small, unpromising apartments, a sort of miniature *haut bourgeois* scenery, without being imitative. And she would arrive in New York with Mark Cross leather luggage, a burdensome weight even when empty, pairs of white leather gloves, a rolled umbrella, all of it reminding of ladies of a previous generation, and no thought of convenience. Of course, she didn't believe in convenience.

Wide friendships and hospitality, yes, but there were, in my view, only two persons, outside the family circle, for whom she felt a kind of reverence: The two were Hannah Arendt and Nicola Chiaromonte, both Europeans. Chiaromonte, a beautiful man with dark curls and brown, I think, eyes, was a curiosity in the *Partisan* circle because of his great modesty and the moderation of his voice in discussion, a gentle word for what was usually a cacophony of argument. An evening at the Rahvs' was to enter a ring of bullies, each one bullying the other. In that way it was different from the boarding school accounts of the type, since no one was in ascendance. Instead there was an equality of vehemence that exhausted itself and the wicked bottles of Four Roses whiskey around midnight—until the next time. Chiaromonte, with his peaceable, anarchist inclinations, was outclassed here.

I suppose he could be called a refugee, this Italian cultural and social critic and antifascist. Here, he published essays but did not create a literary presence equal to his important career when he returned to Italy in the late 1940s. After his death, Mary wrote a long, interesting essay in order to introduce an American edition of his writings on the theater. I remember an anecdote she told me about Chiaromonte, and it alone is sufficient to show why she so greatly admired him. The story went as follows: stopped at border, trying to escape the Nazi drive across Europe, Nicola was asked for his passport, and he replied, Do you want the real one or the false one?

Hannah Arendt, of course, was or became an international figure with *The Origins of Totalitarianism*, *Eichmann in Jerusalem*, and other works. I can remember Mary at Hannah's apartment on Riverside Drive, a setting that was candidly practical, a neat place, tending toward a mute shade of beige in appointments. For an occasional gathering, there would be drinks and coffee and, German-style it seemed to us, cakes and chocolates and nuts bought in abundance at the bakeries on Broadway. Mary was, quite literally, enchanted by Hannah's mind, her scholarship, her industry, and the complexities of her views. As for Hannah, I think perhaps she saw Mary as a golden American friend, perhaps the best the country could produce, with a bit of our western states in her, a bit of the Roman Catholic, a Latin student, a sort of New World, bluestocking *salonière* like Rahel Varnhagen, about whom Hannah had, in her early years, written a stunning, unexpected book. The friendship of these two women was very moving to observe in its purity of respect and affection. After Hannah's death, Mary's extraordinary efforts to see her friend's unfinished work on questions of traditional philosophy brought to publication, the added labor of estate executor, could only be called sacrificial.

I gave the address at the MacDowell Colony when Mary received the medal, and there I said that if she was, in her writing, sometimes a scourge, a Savonarola, she was a very cheerful one, lighthearted and even optimistic. I could not find in her work a trace of despair or alienation; instead, she had a dreamy expectation that persons and nations should do their best. Perhaps it would be unlikely that a nature of such exceptional energy could act out alienation, with its temptation to sloth. Indeed, it seemed to me that Mary did not understand even the practical usefulness of an occasional resort to the devious. Her indiscretions were always open and forthright, and in many ways one could say she was like an open book. Of course, everything interesting depends upon which book is open.

Among the many charms and interests of her unfinished memoir are the accounts of the volatility of her relations with the men in her life. She will say that she doesn't know why she left her first husband, backed out on John Porter, and deserted Philip Rahv. That is, she doesn't know *exactly* but can only speculate. What, perhaps, might be asked nowadays is why the gifted and beautiful young woman was so greatly attracted to marriage in the first place, why she married at twenty-one. She seemed swiftly to overlook the considerable difficulties of unmarried couples "living together" at the time: the subterfuge about staying overnight, facing the elevator man, hiding the impugning clothes when certain people appeared, keeping the mate off the phone lest there be a call from home—unimaginable strategies in present-day cities. There were many things Mary didn't believe in, but she certainly believed in marriage, or rather in being married. She had no talent at all for the single life, or even for waiting after a divorce, a break. However, once married, she made a strikingly independent wife, an abbess within the cloister, so to speak.

In her foreword to the paperback edition of *Memories of a Catholic Girlhood*, she speaks of the treasures gained from her education in Catholic convent and boarding schools, even finding a benefit in the bias of Catholic history as taught.

> To care for the quarrels of the past, to identify oneself with a cause that became, politically speaking, a losing cause with the birth of the modern world, is to experience a kind of straining against reality, a rebellious non-conformity that, again, is rare in America, where children are instructed in the virtues of the system they live under, as though history had achieved a happy ending in American civics.

Nonconformity can be a tiresome eccentricity or arise from genuine skepticism about the arrangements of society. Think of the headache of rejecting charge cards, the universal plastic that created a commercial world in which trying to use a personal check would bring one under suspicion. Going along with fidelity to old-fangledness, Mary and her husband declined the cards and had to carry about large sums of money, rolls of bills that reminded me of nothing so much as men in fedoras in gangster movies. Still they did it and I think with some amusement in a trendy restaurant or Madison Avenue shop.

So, we meet her here, in 1936, marching in a Communist May Day parade, marching along with John Porter, a new man who looked like Fred MacMurray. The conjunction of romance and the events of the day is characteristic of Mary at all points in her life. At the end of her memoir, two years have passed, and she has covered a lot of ground: divorce, a new marriage, unhappy, one that lasted seven years, "though it never recovered." Never recovered from Wilson's mistakes and short-comings as she saw them.

I would have liked Mary to live on and on, irreplaceable spirit and friend that she was, even though I must express some relief that her memoirs did not proceed to me and my life to be looked at with her smiling precision and daunting determination on accuracy. She had her say, but I never knew anyone who gave so much pleasure to those around her. Her wit, great learning, her gardening, her blueberry pancakes, beautiful houses—none of that would be of more than passing interest if it were not that she worked as a master of the art of writing every day of her life. How it was done, I do not know.

1992

EDMUND WILSON

EDMUND Wilson, one of our country's supreme men of letters, is sometimes remembered as being autocratic and intimidating. My own memory, not the most intimate, is of a cheerful, corpulent, chuckling gentleman, well-dressed in brown suits and double martinis. As a literary and cultural critic, Wilson produced many volumes on an astonishing range of subjects. And beyond that, every scrap of his diaries, his letters, and his autobiographical writings appears to have been collected and published. He liked to write about himself, his friends, his wives, his love affairs, his days and nights, sometimes formally composed in an essay, sometimes transformed, more or less, into fiction or preserved in his voluminous daily jottings. With the author having left so few gaps, it is not surprising that the present biography by Jeffrey Meyers can be said to be the first devoted to Wilson.

A "first" is something of a rarity for the very productive Meyers, who has practiced his craft in the prevailing scene of biography, in which the lives of writers and the remains of certain flamboyant artists and musicians are examined in one large volume after another. A new letter here or there, an untapped acquaintance, a passing stranger remembering a misdemeanor, might offer what is called in court "a window of opportunity." In any case, Jeffrey Meyers has produced biographies of Fitzgerald, Hemingway, Robert Lowell, Joseph Conrad, and others. In this field study, each new digger will need to explore the previously looted pharaonic tombs in search of an overlooked jewel in the stone eyes prepared for eternity.

If Jeffrey Meyers has broken the tape in the matter of Wilson's biography, he might not hold the title for long. The scholar Lewis Dabney has been "working on Wilson" for some years, and his labor is known as "authorized." What that distinction means is not always clear. Is it to be thought of as similar to the Queen of England's stamp on Pear's Soap? For a biographer, authorization seems to indicate the choice and support of family or heirs by providing access to papers, letters, drafts, mementos, photographs not available to all and sundry. In fact, almost everything or its equivalent—another photograph, for instance—is available to all and sundry, leaving the family members or others interested in restriction with not much beyond the power of refusing a personal interview.

Papers are sold, deposited, given as gifts or charitable deductions to libraries and other institutions suitable for preservation, cataloging, and reproduction, and they are for the most part open to academics and others with useful credentials. Collections are not meant usually as an honor to the collector but as a source of cultural history. If a biographer sets about his task, writes letters and receives replies about the subject, goes here and there for interviews, visits birth and burial sites perhaps, reads the work and the critical response to it, offers or stresses a few preferences, then with reasonable experience in doctoral programs or independent critical work, a biography can be produced. They are far from being, in most cases, a rich source of income; a lot of time is consumed, and if one is led to wonder just to whom the works are addressed, there is always one answer—the subsequent biographer.

Auden, George Orwell, and T. S. Eliot come to mind as distinguished writers who pleaded that there be no biography. They were like old wanderers on the road in Russian fiction, crying, "Have mercy on me, good folk!" The prayer seemed to have been heard as an impertinence and certainly an alert. Each got his biography and not one but several, the "interpretation" of Eliot's life flowing down to *Tom and Viv* on the stage. Scandal, or merely selfish and imprudent behavior, can be found in most lives as surely as the dates and ancestral records. It happened, didn't it? The unguarded moment or lifelong indiscretions, yes, or most likely, and so the biographer proceeds, as if under oath "to the best of my knowledge."

In the Victorian period, great figures often shared some of the majesty of the monarch, but even there the authorized memorialist could turn out to be somewhat less awed by the connection than the great one had imagined. Carlyle asked his friend and more or less disciple, the historian James A. Froude, to edit his memorial to Jane and to tell the tale, as it were. Froude wrote: "Carlyle never should have married." A curious emendation or explosion about the celebrated couple who lived together for forty years and famously reigned at 5 Cheyne Row. This assertion later led the unreliable Frank Harris to report that a doctor had examined Jane in her forties and found her to be "virgo intacta."

The poet Philip Larkin may have believed he was out of the literary scene by spending a good part of his life acting as a librarian in the provincial city of Hull. But he spoke and complained and wrote letters that achieved his own damnation by way of deeply unpleasant opinions promiscuously expressed. These utterances of ideas and prejudices appear in the recent biography by his sincere admirer, Andrew Motion. Larkin's contemptuous disapproval of blacks, wogs, foreigners, and so on bleakly enshroud the dour melancholy of his witty, beautiful poems—for the moment.

There have been outstanding biographies in our time, works of unremitting scholarly labor that add to our knowledge, elucidate the texts, and are composed with a refinement of style and judgment that honor the subject and give pleasure to the reader. Although these large undertakings are admirable in documentation and many other qualities, English literature is also enriched by odd, personal, less than definitive, glories—De Quincey's exhilarating memories of the Lake Poets, Henry James on Hawthorne, and a forgotten book, a quirky biography of Stephen Crane by the poet John Berryman.

"But they are wrong!" biographers in the stacks complain about so many irreplaceable documents of the past. Even Wilson is condescending to the miracle of Boswell's life of Johnson. Wilson promotes, with reservations, a newer work by Joseph Wood Krutch, itself, of course, superseded. To speak of Dr. Johnson: the heart-rending, brilliant *Life of Mr. Richard Savage* is etched in falsehoods offered by Savage himself. Johnson's "life" is a sort of unwitting forgery written with genius, alive after the original, the true Richard Savage, has fallen into dust.

Edmund Wilson, were he living now, would be over one hundred years old. Jeffrey Meyers begins his biography with the chapter heading:

"Red Bank, 1895–1907." Red Bank, New Jersey, was the scene of Wilson's birth, and for those of a literary inclination he may be said to have put the town on the map. His great-great-grandfather Kimball, on the mother's side, had married a Mather of New England. Meyers's first paragraph opens with this fact or stress:

> Edmund Wilson's ancestors served the altars of learning and committed murders in the name of God. He was descended from Cotton Mather, seventeenth-century puritan divine and zealous witch hunter during the Salem trials, and shared many characteristics—intellect, bookishness, linguistic ability, temperament, energy, productivity and multiple marriages—with his eminent forefather. The prodigiously learned Mather, more widely read than any other American of his time, had entered Harvard at the age of twelve and spoke seven languages. Known for his arrogant manner and aggressiveness in controversy, he overtaxed his nerves by indefatigable industry, poured out more than 450 works on an enormous range of subjects and still managed to acquire three wives.

Except for the demonism that captured the extraordinary mind of Cotton Mather with abominable results, Wilson does share the learning and immense productivity of his ancestor and managed to exceed him in the matter of wives by having four. Perhaps the opening of Meyers's book is not so much to indicate the intellectual brilliance of the two as to alert the reader to a consanguineous "arrogant manner and aggressiveness in controversy."

> During his formative years Wilson grew up with a secure place in upper-middle-class society (a position he was unable to maintain for most of his writing career) and became attached to his ancestral home. He was shy and sensitive, interested in flowers and in drama, fantasy and magic, and always absorbed in books. He felt alienated from his parents, developed a difficult, demanding character, and inherited from his father an irritable disposition and a peremptory mode of discourse.

Wilson was not a New Englander of the seventeenth century in temperament or attraction to religion. When the poet Allen Tate became a Roman Catholic, or a sort of Catholic since he subsequently took advantage of the civil law and obtained two divorces, Wilson wrote him in a letter: "I hope that becoming a Catholic will give you peace of mind; though swallowing the New Testament as factual and moral truth seems to me an awful price to pay for it. You are wrong, and have always been wrong, in thinking I am in any sense a Christian. Christianity seems to me the worst imposture of any of the religions I know of. Even aside from the question of faith, the morality of the Gospel seems to me absurd."

Jeffrey Meyers's *Edmund Wilson* is organized in the conventional chronological manner, which serves well here and follows more or less the organization Wilson employs in his autobiographical volume, *A Prelude*, which takes him up to 1919, the date of his release from service in World War I. Wilson was not much like other young men. He was clumsy and bulky, short, five feet six inches, immune to the attraction of competitive sports. And yet, at the Hill School in Pottstown, Pennsylvania, he made interesting friendships, learned to admire certain of his teachers, studied among other subjects Latin, Greek, and French without, as Meyers tells us, making especially good grades but nevertheless building the foundation of his interest in languages. He went on to Princeton, an important part of his life, and there wrote and studied, made friends, notably Scott Fitzgerald and the scholar Christian Gauss.

Princeton social life lay in the eating clubs: "These clubs are remarkably uninteresting," he wrote, and added: "Since I did not play billiards or bridge, there was nothing to occupy me except to sit, as I sometimes did in winter, in front of our big open fireplace and read the papers and magazines." Odd as Wilson might have been, it does not appear that he felt himself so or in any way suffered from shame or anxiety about his nature or how he might appear to others.

Wilson grew up an only child, but he had a very well-populated family of connections. On his first trip to Europe when he was thirteen years old, the party was large: his parents, uncles, aunts, and cousins, each of whose character and fate he describes. The diary of this thirteen-year-old is printed in *A Prelude*. "I do not recommend for its interest the 1908 diary of my first trip to Europe, but I am printing it for the sake of completeness, and because it provides me with a pretext for explaining certain family matters."

The existence of the diary is the interesting consideration here. The keeping of diaries and, in Wilson's case a lifelong journal, are marks of confidence and self-esteem, an early sense of vocation. What one experiences is important to record, even when events are trivial, because the diarist is present. Still, the confidence, the being comfortable with his body and mind, are perhaps clues to the daunting and, in a way, unexpected inclusion in later years of precise, he believed, details of sexual adventures. Wilson's diaries were not published until after his death, and then they were edited and arranged by decades such as *The Twenties, The Thirties*, and so on up to *The Sixties*. They are a remarkable exercise of creative, intellectual, and physical energy produced as if under some self-appointed duty by one who was forever publishing reviews, extended essays, complex books, and undertaking exhausting journeys all over the world. The diaries are casual, perhaps, but they show a workman's sense of care, craft, and also thrift. Some of the recordings therein, such as those on Scott Fitzgerald and Edna Millay appear intact or, expanded, in book collections.

Throughout his life, here and abroad, Wilson was acquainted with a great number of distinguished and interesting people, and many became attached to him for his charm, his knowledge, his vivid conversation—indeed, the specially high quality of his work and of himself. But there is a latitudinarianism in Wilson, an open spirit, not disclaimed by a certain gruffness at times. As he writes about his daily life, he will give many pages to, for instance, an old farming family, the Munns, to their daily affairs, the various members of the family. The diaries, as we have them, are not different in style from his professional work. The collections of literary articles, written for *The New Yorker* and other magazines, found in *Classics and Commercials* and in *The Shores of Light* and *The Bit Between My Teeth*, are not diminished by thinking of them as the diaries of a professional man at his desk, with the texts to be examined, the author's life to be wondered about, in much the same way as he approaches the vast army of real persons who have passed his way.

In Meyers's biography of Wilson, wives and other ladies, "mistresses" and fumbles, have their place and their more than considerable number of pages. The publications of books are mingled with the calendar of life events and critical judgment is supplied by the reviews lying about in the attic of magazines and newspapers. The "fight" with the IRS over unpaid taxes owes its details to Wilson's book on the subject. More interesting for literary history and personal display is the "quarrel" with Vladimir Nabokov. The combats with the IRS and Nabokov were comedies, however painful each might have been for the participants.

About the IRS: There was Wilson, a gentleman always broke and with expenses not unwarranted, if often uncovered. He worked more diligently and with more conspicuous concentration than a president in the Oval Office. Wilson must have felt that as an independent, self-employed producer of strange small-business goods he was somehow not a wage earner required to give his deputed allotment with a burdensome regularity. The use of the nation's taxes for the Cold War and other misappropriations, as he viewed them, probably entered his mind later, although his distaste for militarism, weapons, and so on was sincere and marked by vehemence. The fact probably was that he simply didn't want to pay his taxes and this led to a pleasing amnesia as the time rolled around and led in the end to grimly calculated penalties and much harassment. Still, the affair was a comedy in the operatic sense, with the distracted, tousled hero and the rogues looking for gold under the bed.

Nabokov's translation with commentaries of Pushkin's *Eugene Onegin* was a folly of such earnest magnitude that it might have been conceived in *Bouvard and Pécuchet*. It was attacked by Slavicists for its wild, peculiar vocabulary in English and for its "original" dissertations on matters of prosody. Wilson was critically dismayed and moved without hesitation to say as much. He felt himself competent in the Russian language and certainly knowledgeable about Pushkin, to whom he had devoted an essay in *The Triple Thinkers*. Indeed, in that volume he translated "The Bronze Horseman" into "prose with an iambic base." The translation is a gift to those who wish to receive it. It is instructive and agreeable to read, much in the helpful spirit of the prose translations at the bottom of the page in the Penguin series of poetry in German, Spanish, and other languages. Wilson had embarked on a formidable accomplishment in his study of Russian, which he followed with his astounding assault on Hebrew. In his mid-sixties, we find him in a state of excitation about Hungarian. About this late effort, he was heard to say that he felt like "an old character in Balzac, huffing and puffing to his last liaison."

Wilson did not show any special modesty or hesitation in his contentious review of Nabokov's *Eugene Onegin;* however, the scholar Clarence Brown found Wilson guilty of the "unbelievable *hubris* of reading Nabokov's petulant little lessons about Russian grammar and vocabulary, himself blundering all the while." The pages of literary magazines were stuffed to grogginess with Wilson and Nabokov eloquently engaged about the properties of Russian and English pronunciation, metrical traditions in both languages, personal and literary qualities. John Updike's review of *The Nabokov-Wilson Letters* takes its title, "The Cuckoo and the Rooster," from an Ivan Krylov fable. In the midst of the battle, Nabokov wrote with his characteristic lefthandedness, "I have always been grateful to him [Wilson] for the tact he has showed in not reviewing any of my novels while constantly saying flattering things about me in the so-called literary circles where I seldom revolve."

Wilson reviewed Nabokov's book on Gogol with a generous degree of plus and a scattering of minus. His reservations are the clue to an irreconcilable difference in the practice of the two writers: the style of composition. Nabokov's Gogol book is one of the most exhilarating, engaging, and original works ever written by one writer about another. Wilson acknowledges its uniqueness, but he finds himself annoyed by Nabokov's "poses, perversities and vanities." These "perversities" are the glory of Nabokov's writing, and they are the grandiloquent, imaginative cascade of images and diversions Wilson could not normally accept. He dismissed *Lolita*: "I like it less than anything of yours I have read." After *The Real Life of Sebastian Knight*, Nabokov's first novel in English, Wilson was more or less "disappointed."

In *Patriotic Gore*, a dazzling monument in the national literature, Wilson has a chapter on "American Prose." It is his idea that American writing abandoned the cultivated standards of the eighteenth century and in the first half of the nineteenth century fell into deplorable exaggeration, rhetorical display, fanciful diversions more or less arising out of the models of the sermon and public addresses. Therein, he writes a shocking appraisal that suggests the impossibility of his finding pleasure and beauty in Nabokov:

> There is nothing in the fiction of Hawthorne to carry the reader along: in the narrative proper of *The Scarlet Letter*, the paragraphs and the sentences, so deliberately and fastidiously written, are as sluggish as the introduction with its description of the old custom house. The voyage of the *Pequod* in *Moby-Dick*, for all its variety of incident and its progression to a dramatic end, is a construction of close-knit blocks which have to be surmounted one by one; the huge units of *Billy Budd*, even more clottedly dense, make it one of the most inappropriate works for reading in bed at night, since it is easy to lose consciousness in the middle of one.

The chapter on Charles Dickens in *The Wound and the Bow* is one of Wilson's glowing achievements. It is rich in complexity, original in ideas, moves around the challenge of the novels and of the life of Dickens with a speculative and interrogating ease that is altogether remarkable. The essay is also a perfect example of Wilson's method as a critic. The title of the collection is suggested by Sophocles' play *Philoctetes*, and the theme is that the sufferings and traumas in the lives of artists have a deep connection with the release of creativity.

In the case of Dickens, the "wound" is well known: The family fell on hard times, and the boy was taken out of school and sent to work in a blacking factory, a cruel, degrading, and forever damaging fate. At the end of the day, the boy would visit his family, now residing in Marshalsea Prison due to the father's debts. Even when the elder Dickens received a legacy, the family did not immediately take the boy out of the factory and return him to school, a lapse he could never forgive. This wound in his youth has naturally been seen as the base for Dickens's hatred of cruelty to children, his exposure of hypocrisy throughout society, his contempt for knavery, social and intellectual pretense, money grubbing, lying—all embodied in a host of characters, an army invading London. These smarmy characters have their opposites in good, long-suffering, generous little people and sometimes good big people.

It is Wilson's idea that the bad people/good people duality arose from Dickens's inability to create characters of mixed motives and believably warring inclinations. He feels the author was approaching this in the unfinished novel, *Edwin Drood*, which is examined in great detail. Scholarship, recounted by Wilson, has shown that there were other humiliations in Dickens's past: His grandparents had worked as domestic servants in the household of Lord Crewe; the father of Dickens's mother was found guilty of embezzlement and fled. The facts about Dickens's past were hidden by Dickens himself. One of the most interesting stories is told by his son; not long before the author's death, the family was playing a word game and Dickens came up with: Warren's Blacking, 30 Strand. No one present understood what he was talking about. So there is a feeling, as the essay maintains, in Dickens himself of a kind of inauthenticity. By an argument too dense and detailed to examine here, the number of murders in the novels, the obsession with the murders indicate in the end that Dickens had murdered himself, a psychological element in Wilson's study.

So there is the "wound," but what about the "bow"—Dickens's style? The breathless flow of adjectives, metaphors, and similes, the description of clothes, houses, streets, alleys, and occupations, the skewered visual genius of one who describes the knobs on an impostor's head as "looking like the crust of a plum pie." The perpetual motion of Dickens's outrageous imagination seems wearisome for Wilson.

Nabokov's lectures at Cornell on *Bleak House* seize the novel when it is flying off the page, seize it with delight. The listeners are invited to note the lamplighter as he goes about his rounds, "like an executioner to a despotic king, strikes off the little heads of fire" or the Jellyby children "tumbled about, and notched memoranda of their accidents on their legs, which were perfect little calendars of distress." On and on the lecturer goes, remarking on names, alliteration, and assonance.

In his essay on American prose, Wilson explains his own preference in literary style. He sees the tragedy of the Civil War as breaking the fabric of romantic exaggeration, embroidery, false eloquence. His models are the stories of Ambrose Bierce and Lincoln's Gettysburg Address, among other examples. Sobriety, terseness, lucidity, and precision—and, indeed, his own compositions are wonderful in clarity, balance, movement, language, always at hand to express the large capacity of his mind and experience, whether current fiction, the Russian Revolution, or the Dead Sea Scrolls.

And yet Wilson, for all the practicality of his method, could be unpredictable and never more so than in his embrace of Joyce's *Finnegans Wake*, another language to learn, as it were. "In conception as well as in execution, one of the boldest books ever written," he remarks in the essay devoted to the novel in *The Wound and the Bow*. The essay is somewhat parental in approach as he guides the reader through whatever factual information might be useful, such as the age, occupation, marriage, and children of Earwicker. There are some rebukes, typical of Wilson's household rules: "And the more daring Joyce's subjects become, the more he tends to swathe them about with the fancywork of his literary virtuosity." Still, he brings to *Finnegans Wake* a beaming affection and solicitude.

Sex, Mary McCarthy, *Memoirs of Hecate County*, and so on. Mary McCarthy has written in her memoirs of her detestation of Wilson's body and soul, information provided by her decision to become his wife. She has disguised him in satirical portraits in her fiction, a disguise on the order of sunglasses. They were divorced after a span of seven years during which she bore a son by Wilson and after which she lived, wrote, and added two more husbands. A marriage, however successfully escaped, rankles more in the memory than an old, ferocious bout of the flu, but no matter, her preoccupation is extreme. She had much in common with Wilson, especially in the need to instruct. Some persons are not content to have a deep aversion to another but feel the command to have others share the documented distaste. This is different from jealousy of, for instance, Wilson's subsequent marriage to the attractive, cosmopolitan, domestically gifted, and loyal Elena Mumm Thornton. It would appear that McCarthy wanted to instruct Elena in the true nature of her husband, instruct Elena and everyone else. Otherwise consider the oddity of the amount of repetitive energy put into denunciation of the past by one so pleasantly situated in life, so rich in experience, friendships, new loves, handsome surroundings—all of that.

What was Wilson thinking of in descriptions in his diaries of his swaying home after an "encounter," only to awaken the next day and put it all down? He was, of course, thinking of himself, the principal actor in the drama, the "I." The "I" in a partnership on the bed or couch, or whatever, will, if he is in a mood to leave a record, need to move into the sensations of the "she." About Marie, a pickup, "Her cunt, however, seemed small. She would not, the first time, respond very heartily, but, the second, would wet herself and bite my tongue, and when I had finished, I could feel her vagina throbbing powerfully."

Memoirs of Hecate County, a fiction, more or less, with the real-life persons serving in the short and the longer story run down by the biographer, like a policeman tracking suspects. The book was banned, but it has survived and is probably still read because of its interesting reputation for salaciousness and the genuine interest of the book. It was a bizarre composition to add to the stately list of literary and cultural studies already long and commanding when it was published in 1946. "The Princess with the Golden Hair," the principal, most arresting tale, became the occasion for a good number of amusing, unfavorable reviews. The "princess," a remote and withholding beauty of the pre-Raphaelite sort for whom the narrator longs, did not arouse a like yearning in many readers. Interest, if not quite yearning, arrives when the princess-frustrated, first-person narrator, an art critic, takes a diversionary spin down to Fourteenth Street and a dance hall called the Tango Casino. There he meets Anna, a "hostess." She is poor, has spent time in an orphanage, has a brutal husband and a little girl and much misery and deprivation in her life. This background is finely done by Wilson as it flows in and out of the "couplings." Anna is a "relief"— not much more, if a lot of relief. Her lower-class "hard protruding little thigh bones" seem inadequate when at last the "luxurious" princess is brought to bed. "Her little bud was so deeply imbedded that it was hardly involved in the play, and she made me arrest my movement while she did something special and gentle that did not, however, press on this point, rubbing herself somehow against me—and then came, with a self-excited tremor."

"Clinical" was applied to the sex writing in the diaries and in the fiction. Cyril Connolly thought the fornications had "a kind of monotony," and John Updike found the writing "leaden and saturnine"; Raymond Chandler said Wilson managed to make "fornication as dull as a railroad timetable."

Jeffrey Meyers has produced a long book, 483 pages. There is a lot of Wilson to be sifted, and so there is a lot of Meyers. We might think the biographer has brought together the immense flow of Wilson's life and work, both of which are scattered in the many publications and collections. Meyers has certainly not made of the object of his labors the worst one could imagine—drinking, vanity, and so on—nor has he been able to create the brilliant, irreplaceable mind and spirit. Too many facts, of whatever laudatory or dismissive nature, destroy the shape of all lives as they are experienced by even the most unreflective in a flashing, quick, and unstable form. But that cannot be the way of biographers. And so we bid farewell to the unlikely presence in our literature of a great thinker, writer, and unusual being. Farewell, until the next time, the Wilson biography Professor Dabney has been working on for lo, these many years.

1997

PARADISE LOST
Philip Roth

AMERICAN Pastoral is Philip Roth's twentieth work of fiction—an accretion of creative energy, a yearly, or almost, place at the starting line of a marathon. But his is a one-man sprint with the signatures, the gestures, the deep breathing, and the repetitiveness, sometimes, of an obsessive talent. Roth has his themes, spurs to his virtuoso variations and star turns in triple time. His themes are Jews in the world, especially in Israel, Jews in the family, Jews in Newark, New Jersey; fame, vivid enough to occasion impostors (*Operation Shylock*); literature, since his narrators or performers are writers, actually one writer, Philip Roth. And sex, anywhere in every manner, a penitential workout on the page with no thought of backaches, chafings, or phallic fatigue. Indeed the novels are prickled like a sea urchin with the spines and fuzz of many indecencies.

In *American Pastoral*, we are, on the first page, once more in Newark; and on page sixteen we are told "I'm Zuckerman the author." Nathan Zuckerman is the author of *Carnovsky* (*Zuckerman Unbound*), an alternative title like those sometimes used in foreign translations. In English, the novel is, of course, *Portnoy's Complaint*, which provoked among many other responses an eruption of scandal. The author of the book that brought about a fame and a "recognition factor" equal to that of Mick Jagger is Philip Roth. Or so it is in *Zuckerman Unbound*, where even a young funeral director, attending the remains of a Prince Seratelli, pauses to ask for the author's autograph—all part of this wild, very engaging minstrel show in which the writing of a book, not just *any* book, may serve as the lively plot for a subsequent book. Of course, we cannot attach Zuckerman or David Kepesh or Peter Tarnopol or Alexander Portnoy to Philip Roth like a fingernail. Not always.

However, if he follows Zuckerman to *The Anatomy Lesson*, the reader will gain or lose a shiver of interest if he knows that the late critic Irving Howe published in *Commentary* some forthright reservations about Roth's work and that Howe is the "source" of the character Milton Appel. Howe had written—among other thoughts, some favorable—that "what seems really to be bothering Portnoy is a wish to sever his sexuality from his moral sensibilities, to cut it away from his self as a historical creature. It's as if he really supposed the super-ego, or *post coitum triste*, were a Jewish invention."

Zuckerman or Roth cries out some years later in *The Anatomy Lesson*: "Milton Appel had unleashed an attack upon Zuckerman's career that made Macduff's assault on Macbeth look almost lackadaisical. Zuckerman should have been so lucky as to come away with decapitation. A head wasn't enough for Appel; he tore you limb from limb." If he is indeed torn limb from limb, this ferocious paraplegic author pursues Appel/Howe in a motorized wheelchair for almost forty pages.

The structure of Roth's fiction is based often upon identifying tirades rather than actions and counteractions, tirades of perfervid brilliance, and this is what he can do standing on his head or hanging out the window if need be. The tirades are not to be thought of as mere angry outbursts in the kitchen after a beer or two, although they are usually angry enough since most of the characters are soreheads of outstanding volubility. The monologues are a presentation of self, often as if on the stage of some grungy Comédie-Française, if such an illicit stretch may be allowed. Here is Monkey, the trailer-park Phèdre of *Portnoy's Complaint*, in a cameo appearance:

Picking on me all the time—in just the way you *look* at me you pick on me, Alex! I open the door at night, I'm so *dying* to see you, thinking all day long about nothing but you, and there are those fucking orbs already picking out every single thing that's *wrong* with me! As if I'm not insecure enough, as if insecurity isn't my whole hang-up, you get that expression all over your face the minute I open my mouth. . . . oh, shit, here comes another dumb and stupid remark out of that brainless twat. . . . Well, I'm not brainless, and I'm not a twat either, just because I didn't go to fucking Harvard! And don't give me any more of your shit about behaving in front of *The Lindsays*. Just who the fuck are *The Lindsays*? A God damn mayor, and his wife! A fucking *mayor*! In case you forget, I was married to one of the richest men in France *when I was still eighteen years old*—I was a guest at Aly Khan's for dinner, when you were still back in Newark, New Jersey, finger-fucking your little Jewish girl friends!

There you have Monkey and her expressive grievance.

For tirades and diatribes of a more demanding content, nothing Roth has written equals the bizarre explosions of *Operation Shylock*, a rich, original work composed with an unforgiving complexity if one is trying to unravel the design. It is about the double, the impersonator, the true self, one's own estimation, and the false self known to the public, the latter brilliantly examined in an account of the trial in Jerusalem of Ivan the Terrible, the allegedly murderous Ukrainian at Treblinka, who is also John Demjanjuk, "good old Johnny, the gardener from Cleveland, Ohio." And standing at not too great a distance from the actual ground of the novel we are reminded of the bad Philip Roth, creator for laughs of American Jewish life in its underwear; and, on the other hand, Philip Roth, artist, observer, inspired comedian, "the litanist of the fleas, the knave, the thane, the ribboned stick, the bellowing breeches"—comedian of the folkloric Portnoys and others of their kind.

In *Operation Shylock*, Philip Roth is in New York, recovering from depression and suicidal impulses brought on by the drug Halcion. (The doubling mystery of pharmaceutical messages—may cause insomnia or drowsiness. Remember President George Bush, reportedly on Halcion, ever windblown and smiling as he relentlessly raced up and down in his "cigarette" boat on the waters outside the summer White House in Kennebunkport, Maine.) Roth, from Halcion, down as a bottom-dwelling flatfish, is planning to go to Israel to interview the novelist Aharon Appelfeld. He learns, as if he had already departed and landed, that someone is giving interviews and lectures under his name, speaking on the radio and announcing an appearance in the King David Hotel on the subject of "Diasporism: The Only Solution to the Jewish

Problem. A lecture by Philip Roth." The double, the imposter, given the fairy-tale name of Pipik, is one of the disputatious inhabitants of the mind of the actual Roth, who creates at interesting length the faux, but not altogether faux, debate on the present position of Israel in the world.

Diasporism: "The time has come to return to the Europe that was for centuries, and remains to this day, the most authentic Jewish homeland there has ever been, the birthplace of rabbinic Judaism, Hasidic Judaism, Jewish secularism, socialism—on and on. The time has come to renew in the European Diaspora our preeminent spiritual and cultural role." In questions and counterarguments between the true and false Philip Roth, the horror of the Holocaust is remembered but is now claimed to be a "bulwark against European anti-Semitism." The mad Pipik is arguing in effect: Europe's had that, it's over. "No such bulwark exists in Islam. Exterminating a Jewish nation would cause Islam to lose not a single night's sleep, except for the great night of celebration. I think you would agree that a Jew is safer today walking aimlessly around Berlin than going unarmed into the streets of Ramallah."

Pipik has in the name of Roth not only proposed his program of diasporism, he has also organized ASA, Anti-Semites Anonymous, which leads to the appearance in the plot of a nurse who is valiantly and with commendable self-discipline in "recovery," *she* having taken the twelve steps. In this Israel, "the pasturalization of the ghetto," prophets and pundits roam the streets, all the while giving off the noise and fumes of opinion. Here, Philip Roth encounters an acquaintance from the past, a Harvard-educated Egyptian enrolled at Roth's time as a graduate student at the University of Chicago and now a famous professor. His name is George Ziad (*sic*). Zee, as he is called, is also a diasporist but for his own reason. His program is to get the Jews out of Israel and thereby return the land to his ancestors, the Palestinians.

Believing that the old Philip Roth of his acquaintance has been transmogrified into the passionate diasporist of Pipik's caper, Zee holds forth with feeling about the sufferings of the Palestinians and the inferiority and provincialism of Israeli culture by comparison with that of the Jews in their true homeland, Manhattan. "There is more

Jewish spirit and Jewish laughter and Jewish intelligence on the Upper West Side of Manhattan than in this entire country. . . . There's more Jewish heart at the knish counter at Zabar's than in the whole of the Knesset!"

Then the true Philip Roth, taking on the garments of the imposter Pipik, performs in his fluent rhythms about the greatest diasporist of all, Irving Berlin.

> The radio was playing "Easter Parade" and I thought, But this is Jewish genius on a par with the Ten Commandments. God gave Moses the Ten Commandments and then He gave to Irving Berlin "Easter Parade" and "White Christmas." . . . Easter he turns into a fashion show and Christmas into a holiday about snow. Gone is the gore and the murder of Christ—down with the crucifix and up with the bonnet! . . . If supplanting Jesus Christ with snow can enable my people to cozy up to Christmas, then let it snow, let it snow, let it snow!

So goes this curious, hilarious work of a profligate imagination unbound.

Along the way, it dashes into subplots of many befuddlements and allocations of adventures offered with the pedantic assurance of a mock court indictment. It is suggested, or more or less sworn to, that Philip Roth, the living author, acted as an agent for the Mossad, the CIA of Israel, by spying upon "Jewish anti-Zionist elements threatening the security of Israel." Serving counterintelligence by impersonating the impersonator? The novel is subtitled: *A Confession*. The preface claims that "the book is as accurate an account as I am able to give of actual occurrences that I lived through during my middle fifties and that culminated, early in 1988, in my agreeing to undertake an intelligence-gathering operation for Israel's foreign intelligence service, the Mossad." A solemn affidavit? Not quite. A note to the reader at the end of the book reads, "This confession is false." An operatic divertissement? Aida, the Ethiopian princess stealing war plans from her Egyptian lover for the benefit of her country. Or the false Dimitri and at last old Boris Godunov, Philip Roth, saving the state from the diasporists and in a cloud of redemption expiring.

The talent of Philip Roth floats freely in this rampaging novel with a plot thick as starlings winging to a tree and then flying off again. It is meant perhaps as a sort of restitution offered in payment of the claim that if the author has not betrayed the Jews, he has too often found them to be whacking clowns or whacking-off clowns. He bleeds like the old progenitor he has named in the title. Since he is, as a contemporary writer, always quick to insert the latest item of the news into his running comments, perhaps we can imagine him today as poor Richard Jewell, falsely accused in the 1996 Olympic bombing in Atlanta because, in police language, he fit the profile but was at last found to be just himself: a nice fellow good to his mother.

And yet, the impostor, the devil's advocate for the diaspora, has, with dazzling invention, composed not an ode for the hardy settlers of Israel but an ode to the Wandering Jew as a beggar and prince in Western culture, speaking and writing in all its languages.

After fame and mischief on the streets of Jerusalem, Roth in a sort of recidivism returns to the passions of his youth with a "hero," Mickey Sabbath, certainly not in his first youth, but shall we say, still trying. *Sabbath's Theater*, a much admired book, is seriously filthy. *Portnoy's Complaint*, by comparison and to put the best face on it, is lads and lassies a-Maying. *Sabbath's Theater* is mud, a slough of obscenity with some lustrous pearls of antic writing embedded in it. The first line: "Either forswear fucking others or the affair is over." That is Drenka, a fifty-two-year-old Croatian voluptuary with ovarian cancer of which she dies, but not before thirteen years of insatiable carnality with Sabbath and more years than that with others.

Sabbath, now sixty-four, refuses to forswear, saying it would be repugnant to him to break the "sacrament of infidelity." And that is, perhaps, why he is given the name Sabbath, the day of worship, to suggest a sort of Black Mass of fucking. The world is out to crucify the master puppeteer of his Indecent Theater, but the aging, arthritic, disheveled puppeteer is irresistible to all except his wife Roseanna, who spends her days in an alcoholic stupor and when at last belligerently sober, by way of AA, takes off with a lesbian and often turns her thoughts to the penis clipper, the well-named Lorena Bobbitt.

Among the breathlessly accommodating are a Barnard girl; Christa, a runaway German au pair; and Rosa, a Spanish-speaking maid, "four childs," another in her belly; and a student at a liberal-arts college from which Sabbath is fired as an adjunct professor of puppet theater, owing to the discovery of a taped telephone conversation of outstanding lasciviousness, published in full at the bottom of the pages, a priapic academic footnote. This leads to an apologia, attributed to Sabbath, which can be attributed to the author, Philip Roth.

> Not even Sabbath understood how he could lose his job at a liberal arts college for teaching a twenty-year-old to talk dirty twenty-five years after Pauline Réage, fifty-five years after Henry Miller, sixty years after D. H. Lawrence, eighty years after James Joyce, two hundred years after John Cleland, three hundred years after John Wilmot, a second earl of Rochester—not to mention four hundred after Rabelais, two thousand after Ovid, and twenty-two hundred after Aristophanes.

To the challenge of white satin, spring flower epithalamia, the "realist" offers the rude, raging insistence of Nature. In Roth's novels, the erotic pushes and thrusts where it will, even in imagination to the iconic Anne Frank and Franz Kafka. In *The Ghost Writer*, a young female student, a refugee from Europe at the time of the Holocaust, turns up as an assistant to the esteemed writer Lonoff, living in Massachusetts, the snowscape Yankeeland. Zuckerman, young and only on the first arc of the happy curve of his talent, enters the shrine of literature as a guest in Lonoff's house. He soon imagines the attractive assistant to be a living Anne Frank, rescued from death only to be sent in the still of the night to the bed of Lonoff, or he to her bed.

In *The Professor of Desire*, David Kepesh this time, rather than Nathan Zuckerman, goes on a journey to Prague, the holy city of the painfully reserved, tubercular genius, Franz Kafka. In a dream, a jeu d'esprit, Kepesh is taken to see "Kafka's whore," a hideous old fraudulent tourist attraction, and a foul scene follows.

Sabbath's journey into the underworld is sex and death, the classical Manichaean union. He is haunted by his mother, who was haunted by the death of his brother, Morty, shot down in the Philippines during World War II. Sabbath, at the end of his tether, or so you might put it, masturbates and pisses on the grave of the exuberant Drenka of the "uberous breasts." He is found there by her son, a cop, whose outrage is so great he will not arrest or shoot him to death, as Sabbath wishes. Let him lie in the muck. "You desecrate my mother's grave. You desecrate the American flag. You desecrate your own people. With your stupid fucking prick out, wearing the skullcap of your own religion!" So Sabbath is doomed to life. "He could not fucking die. How could he leave? How could he go? Everything he hated was here." Here is Drenka's cemetery, in America, in the spurious romanticism of lovemaking, marriage, fidelity? Sabbath and his theater of indecent puppets like Drenka, Christa, and so on are not a happy band of buskers. There is illness, prostate affliction, ovarian cancer, madness, drunkenness, the scars of his brother's death and his mother's annihilating grief. Perhaps he is saying he cannot bring himself to suicide because of the life-giving force of hatred—an idea indeed. But it is not always useful to seek abstractions in fiction. When you turn to the last pages of *Sabbath's Theater* not much is clear beyond the anarchic brilliance of the swarm of characters, the rush of language, the willful chaos of the inspiration.

American Pastoral: Paradise remembered; The Fall; Paradise Lost in New Jersey, Philip Roth's singular turf, Newark "before the negroes," its raucous, fetid airs memorialized by his art as if they were the zephyrs in a sportsman's sketches. Zuckerman is called to tell the story of the fate of Seymour Levov, a supreme high-school athlete, called "the Swede." His is a life that began in gladness and came to an end in a conflagration of appalling desolation. The Levov family, the marriages, the children, the business, the houses are the landscape of toil and success, an ever-upward curve horribly deflected by the America of the 1960s. The elder Levov has through his unceasing labor and shrewdness, his toughness, built a business in the manufacture of ladies' gloves, the firm going by the name of Newark Maid Leatherwear.

Newark Maid at the time of the novel's action has moved to Puerto Rico, but the roots of the family go back to the old Levov grandfather, who arrived in America in the 1890s and "found work fleshing sheepskins fresh from the lime vat." The slow, punishing development of

Newark Maid by Lou Levov, the father of Swede and his brother Jerry, is the ancestral cord of blood and sweat that will be broken in subtle ways by the agreeable Swede and in violent ways by the bomb-throwing murders committed by Swede's daughter, Merry, a child of the 1960s.

The elder Levov was "one of those slum-reared Jewish fathers whose roughhewn, undereducated perspective goaded a whole generation of striving, college-educated Jewish sons." Lou Levov went to work at the tannery at fourteen: "the tannery that stank of both the slaughterhouse and the chemical plant from the soaking of flesh and the cooking of flesh and the dehairing and pickling and degreasing of hides." At the workhouse, "the temperature [rises] to a hundred and twenty degrees.... with hunks of skin all over the floor, everywhere pits of grease, hills of salt, barrels of solvent—this was Lou Levov's high school and college." The labor, powerfully imagined and researched here, brings to mind the Lower East Side tenements and the brutal hours at the sewing machines that led in time to the garment district on Seventh Avenue.

On the domestic scene, the increasing prosperity of Newark Maid gloves sends the Levov family from the streets of the lower- and middle-class Jews to "Keer Avenue...where the rich Jews lived." They become Keer Avenue Jews, "with their finished basements, their screened-in porches, their flagstone front steps,...laying claim like audacious pioneers to the normalizing American amenities." Swede, the athletic, tall, blond Levov, "as close to a goy as we were going to get," survives the Marine Corps, plays baseball at Upsala College in East Orange, New Jersey, turns down a club contract offer, and joins his father's business. And in a sort of sleep-walking way, out of natural inclination, he crossed a line—or what would seem to be a line to the old inbred Levovs: he married Miss New Jersey. "Before competing at Atlantic City for the 1949 Miss America title, she had been Miss Union County, and before that Spring Queen at Upsala.... A shiksa. Dawn Dwyer. He'd done it."

As the novel opens, the Swede is almost seventy, and he has sent a letter to the author, Zuckerman, asking for a dinner meeting. The old Levov had died at age ninety-six, and the son is struggling to write a memoir about him to be distributed to family and friends. He wants to discuss his father with Zuckerman, who is a friend from high-school days. In the note, he says about his father that he suffered "because of the shocks that befell his loved ones." Indeed, the shock that caused the old man to keel over dead was the discovery that Seymour's daughter, Merry, had, after a somewhat fortuitous connection with young radicals in New York City, fallen under the spell of violent resistance to society, the Vietnam War, rejection of family, the whole package. One early morning, she planted a bomb at the post office of her town and blew up the popular town doctor who was picking up his mail. She went into hiding at the home of her speech therapist, for little Merry suffered from a stutter; in time, she "connected" again and after robbery and rape and gross ill treatment took part in an "action" that killed three people in Oregon.

This is the fall, paradise lost, the dramatic center of the novel. Yes, it could have happened; young men and women better educated than Merry Levov blew up a house in Greenwich Village, killing some of their own, went underground, and later some of them, low on funds, held up a Brinks money truck, killed the black driver, and subsequently went off to jail. There are other bombings and deaths listed in the book. So poor Seymour, the Swede, still well meaning and now a suburbanite, must wake up one morning like the Mayor of Casterbridge and say: I am to suffer, I perceive.

The bomb-throwing plot is not altogether convincing on this particular stage. Merry must make a passage from her Audrey Hepburn scrapbook days to a loquacious, sneering radical life that has to be accepted as given. The most provocative shift in the portrait of Merry as a death-dealing 1960s revolutionary is that she later passes from radicalism to the old Indian religion of Jain, which sought to release the spirit from the bonds of the flesh. Merry adds her own self-destructive interpretations of Jain, with its passivity and pacifism. She eats almost nothing out of regard for the integrity of animals and also that of plants. When found by her father, she is shrunken, living in filth, wandering alone in dangerous spots of Newark with the serenity of the abandonment of selfhood. This reminds us of the cultist aspect of the American revolutionaries of the sixties, sometimes a small band bound together by their rants, paranoia, and above all the exaggeration of their power and the foolish underestimation of the power of society.

Even the militia groups of the nineties with their guns and explosives are swollen with a cultish sense of empowerment, a poisonous edema of stockpiling, camaraderie on the rifle range—until the transition of indictment for murder turns them into whimpering, plea-bargaining, helpless victims of consequence. Little Merry Levov takes instead the spiritual life in a drastic extension, but Roth, if he must have her as a bomber, has shown imagination about the loss of revolutionary enthusiasm when the aftermath must be faced alone.

That the Levov family is to suffer, by way of Merry, a catastrophe remote in a statistical sense, undermines the interesting close calls on the road of the Swede's American journey. The Swede has made a right turn into the highway of assimilation and this, it appears, is the true direction of the novel's intellectual and fictional energy. First, the Swede has married the beauty queen, Dawn Dwyer, a Roman Catholic. Even though Dawn surreptitiously had Merry baptized in the faith, they are, in the words of Seymour's brother Jerry, a bullying, big-time coronary surgeon in Florida, a "knockout couple. The two of them all smiles in their outward trip into the USA. She's post-Catholic, he's post-Jewish, together they're going to go out there to Old Rimrock to raise little post-toasties."

Old Rimrock is a posh bit of the New Jersey countryside to which Seymour takes himself and Dawn in a sort of paroxysm of enthusiasm for open fields and great old trees. Old Rimrock in WASP, Republican Morris County. His father had wanted him to settle in a modern house in the "rock-ribbed, Democrat" Newstead Development, where he could live with his family among young Jewish couples. No, for the Swede it is to be a hundred acres of land, "a barn, a millpond, a mill-stream, the foundation remains of a gristmill that had supplied grain for Washington's troops." And an old stone house and a fireplace "large enough for roasting an ox, fitted out with an oven door and a crane to swing an iron kettle around over the fire." Why shouldn't it be his? Why shouldn't he own it? "Out in Old Rimrock, all of America lay at their door. That was an idea he loved. Jewish resentment, Irish resentment—the hell with it." Dawn is somewhat concerned with Protestant ill feeling about Catholics, but for the Swede, "the Protestants are just another denomination. Maybe they were rare where she grew up—they were rare where he grew up too—but they happen not to be rare in America. Let's face it, they *are* America."

In the 1940s, Jews might have felt some anxiety about their reception in a rich enclave of old-family inhabitants viewing them with condescension if not rudeness. Such would not be true today, when a Jewish media billionaire would, if such an opportunity arose in a period of regal retrenchment, be urged to buy an ancient bit of land in the woods of Windsor, where he could, on an occasional weekend, tramp about over the bones of Queen Victoria. In Old Rimrock, the Levovs make the acquaintance of an architect, Bill Orcutt, from a Morris County family that has filled the local cemetery with worthies for two hundred years.

The Swede, by the time he meets Zuckerman in a New York restaurant, has been divorced from Dawn and has a new wife and children; and Dawn, brought near to suicide by the cruel biography of her daughter, has returned to life with a Swiss face-lift and, in a thunderous rush of plot, made an alliance with the tombstone genealogist, Orcutt. It didn't work out, as the saying goes, the idyll of the young couple. Jerry, the angry sawbones brother, turns Merry in to the FBI, and along the way, driven by his fraternal jealousy of his paragon brother, denounces the life Swede and Dawn shaped for Merry. "Out there with Miss America, dumbing down and dulling out. Out there playing at being Wasps, a little Mick girl from the Elizabeth docks and a Jewboy from Weequahic High. The cows. Cow Society. Colonial old America. And you thought all that façade was going to come without a cost. Genteel and innocent. *But that costs, too, Seymour.* I would have thrown a bomb. I would become a Jain and live in Newark. That Wasp bullshit!" But Seymour in his love and grief for his daughter knows better. "It is chaos. It is chaos from start to finish." America gone berserk.

Among the ruins of time is the city of Newark, where Roth reared the author, Zuckerman, with his elegiac memories of interiors, "the microscopic surface of things close at hand . . . the minutest gradations of social position conveyed by linoleum and oilcloth, by yahrzeit candles and cooking smells, by Ronson table lighters and venetian blinds." And outside, autumn afternoons on the football field; down the main drag to movies on a Saturday afternoon; record shops offering Glenn

Miller; and at the high-school reunion, damaged faces that still carry the trace of teenage beauty.

When the Swede and Zuckerman meet so many years later, Newark has been the scene of devastating riots in 1967. It is now the "car theft capital of the world"; shops are boarded up; houses, once the shrines of relentless homemakers, are now smashed and splintered orphans; gunshots split the air, causing no more wonder than the screech of big trucks backing into parking spaces: Newark, long ago the little Jewish Eden of Roth's youth.

American Pastoral is a sort of Dreiserian chronicle of the Levov family. Their painfully built fortune, even without the disgrace, might have declined owing to obsolescence. Maids have not for some decades been in need of the finely stitched, soft leather gloves in matching colors. Gloves, except on the coldest winter days, have gone the way of the ribbon shops in the West Thirties of Manhattan, ribbons for hats that were to go on the heads of proper women whenever they left the house.

Still, the saga of the Levov family is a touching creative act and in the long line of Philip Roth fiction can be rated PG, suitable for family viewing—more or less.

1997

IN THE WASTELAND
Joan Didion

JOAN DIDION'S novels are a carefully designed frieze of the fracture and splinter in her characters' comprehension of the world. To design a structure for the fadings and erasures of experience is an aesthetic challenge she tries to meet in a striking manner: the placement of sentences on the page, abrupt closures rather like hanging up the phone without notice, and an ear for the rhythms and tags of current speech that is altogether remarkable. Perhaps it is prudent that the central characters, women, are not seeking clarity since the world described herein, the America of the last thirty years or so, is blurred by a creeping inexactitude about many things, among them bureaucratic and official language, the jargon of the press, the incoherence of politics, the disastrous surprises in the mother-father-child tableau.

The method of narration, always conscious and sometimes discussed in an aside, will express a peculiar restlessness and unease in order to accommodate the extreme fluidity of the fictional landscape. You read that something did or did not happen; something was or was not thought; this indicates the ambiguity of the flow, but there is also in "did or did not" the author's strong sense of willful obfuscation, a purposeful blackout of what was promised or not promised—a blackout in the interest of personal comfort and also in the interest of greed, deals, political disguises of intention.

Joan Didion's novels are not consoling, nor are they notably attuned to the reader's expectations, even though they are fast paced, witty, inventive, and interesting in plot. Still, they twist and turn, shift focus and point of view, deviations that are perhaps the price or the reward that comes from an obsessive attraction to the disjunctive and paradoxical in American national policy and to the somnolent, careless decisions made in private life.

> I have the dream, recurrent, in which my entire field of vision fills with rainbow, in which I open a door onto a growth of tropical green (I believe this to be a banana grove, the big glossy fronds heavy with rain, but since no bananas are seen on the palms symbolists may relax) and watch the spectrum separate into pure color. Consider any of these things long enough and you will see that they tend to deny the relevance not only of personality but of narrative, which makes them less than ideal images with which to begin a novel, but we go with what we have.
> Cards on the table.

This writer is the poet, if you like, of the airplane and the airport. Offhand journeys to Malaysia or to troubled spots in Central America are undertaken as if one were boarding the New York–Washington shuttle. For the busy men, we learn somewhere in the pages that any flight under eight hours is called a "hop." So, we head out for the blue yonder by air as earlier novelists wrote of signing up for a term on ship. "Sailors are the only class of men who now-a-days see anything like stirring adventures; and many things which to the fire-side people appear strange and romantic, to them seem as common-place as a jacket out at elbows" (Melville, preface to *Typee*). Flying round the world every day is for her characters just a "jacket out at elbows." Nothing unusual. Trying to keep pace with an ethereal mobility now become as mundane as a dog trot is a mark of this writer's original sensibility: "She had been going from one airport to another for some months; one could see it, looking at the visas on her passport.... People who go to the airport first invent some business to conduct there.... Then they convince themselves that the airport is cooler than the hotel, or has superior chicken salad."

And from the current novel, *The Last Thing He Wanted*:

> I see her standing in the wet grass off the runway, her arms bare, her sunglasses pushed up into her loose hair, her black silk shift

wrinkled from the flight, and wonder what made her think a black silk shift bought off a sale rack at Bergdorf Goodman during the New York primary was the appropriate thing to wear on an unscheduled flight at one-thirty in the morning out of Fort Lauderdale–Hollywood International Airport, destination San José, Costa Rica but not quite.

Her first novel, *Run River*, appeared in 1963. It is rich in talent and also rich in the virtues of traditional fiction: families, generations, births and deaths, changes of fortune, betrayals. Set in the Sacramento Valley between 1938 and 1959, it begins with a gunshot: "Lily heard the shot at seventeen minutes to one." ("Seventeen minutes to one" brings to mind the surgical precision of the information that will be offered in the later fiction.) The intervening pages and chapters explain what went before the opening shot. In the final pages of the last chapter, we read, "She sat on the needlepoint chair until she heard it, the second shot." The first shot was the husband killing the wife's lover, and the second shot was the husband killing himself. Some families in *Run River* are descendants of the pioneers who made the trip of hardship and promise across the Great Plains. There are hardship passages in the subsequent fictions, although not in a covered wagon but in an airplane carrying your uncertain identity in a six-hundred-dollar handbag.

Her nerves are bad tonight in the wasteland of Haight-Ashbury; she has migraines, generalized and particular afflictions that bring on tears in "elevators and in taxis and in Chinese laundries." Joan Didion's revelation of incapacity, doubt, irresolution, and inattention is brought into question by the extraordinary energy and perseverance found in *Slouching Towards Bethlehem*, *The White Album*, and the later collection, *After Henry*. If she has "nerves," she also has "nerve" in the sense of boldness and fortitude. She will do the lowest work of a reporter; make the call, try again when the promised callback is not forthcoming. She scouts the neighborhood, finds the houses, and once inside notes the condition of the sink, the baby lying on a pallet and sucking its thumb, and the five-year-old on acid—"High Kindergarten." She spends time with Otto and Dead-eye, among other stoned hippies;

visits that need the self-denial of a Sister of Charity, although what she brings is a presence, free of strategies of redemption.

> At three-thirty that afternoon Max, Tom and Sharon placed tabs under their tongue and sat down together in the living room to wait for the flash. Barbara stayed in the bedroom, smoking hash. During the next four hours a window banged once in Barbara's room.... A curtain billowed in the afternoon wind. Except for the sitar music on the stereo there was no other sound or movement until seven-thirty, when Max said, "Wow!"

Moving down the coast from the numb deprivation of Haight-Ashbury to the alert consumerism of Ronald and Nancy Reagan in the governor's mansion in Sacramento and then in the White House, Didion finds them apart from the usual politicians who cherish, or so pretend, their early beginnings in Hyde Park, Kansas, or Plains, Georgia. The Reagans' habits, or perhaps their modes of operation, do not spring from marks left by their placement on the national map. The Reagans come from the welfare state of Dreamland; their roots are Hollywood.

> This expectation on the part of the Reagans that other people would take care of their needs struck many people, right away, as remarkable and was usually characterized as a habit of the rich.... The Reagans were not rich; they and this expectation were the product of studio Hollywood, a system in which performers performed, and in return were cared for.... She [Nancy Reagan] was surprised to learn ("Nobody had told us") that she and her husband were expected to pay for their own food, dry cleaning, and toothpaste while in the White House. She seemed never to understand why it was imprudent of her to have accepted clothes from their makers when so many of them had encouraged her to do so.... The clothes were, as Mrs. Reagan seemed to construe it, "wardrobe"—a production expense, like the housing and catering and first-class travel and the furniture and paintings and cars that get taken home after the set is struck—and should rightly have gone to the studio budget.

Play It as It Lays (1970) is the first of the digressive, elusive novels, typical in style and organization of the challenging signature of a Joan Didion work. Shadowy motivation, disruptive or absent context in a paragraph or pages here and there are not properly to be read as indecision or compositional falterings. They display instead a sort of muscular assurance and confidence, or so one is led to believe in the face of a dominant, idiosyncratic style that if nothing else scorns the vexation of indolent or even sophisticated readers who prefer matters and manners otherwise expressed. But, as she says, we go with what we have. The author is in control of the invention, and if the machine is a little like an electric automobile or one running on pressed grapes instead of gasoline in a field of Chevrolets, the autonomy—it does run—puts the critic in an uneasy situation.

The opening sentence of *Play It as It Lays* is: "What makes Iago evil? Some people ask. I never ask."

"I never ask" is a useful introduction to Maria Wyeth: the sound of the extreme negativism, withdrawal, depression, or terminal disgust of this still young woman, a marginal figure in the movie business, brought up in Silver Wells, Nevada, by her drifting parents, divorced, finally in the book from her husband, a director. One might, however, question that the unanswerable evil of Iago would be on her mind, an evil that led even the great Coleridge to fall back upon "motiveless malignity." But who's to say she has not at a bar heard a discussion of the ecstatic treachery of Iago that makes its tragic progress to the suffering and death of Desdemona and Othello? It's just that the inclination to pedantry in instances of piddling, measly inconsequence are sometimes the only protection one has against the witchery of this uncompromising imagination, the settings so various and the sometimes sleepwalking players who blindly walk through windows and fall into traps of great consequence such as the Vietnam War or the world of the Contras.

The women in the novels suffer losses, serious blows from fate that enshroud them like the black dress European peasant women wear lifelong for bereavement; but they are not wearing a black dress except for stylish definition, like the black dress of Anna Karenina in her first appearance at the ball. Maria Wyeth in *Play It as It Lays* has a damaged daughter off somewhere in a hospital; she loves the girl obsessively, but there is no reciprocation from the screaming, indifferent child. Maria has had a cruel abortion. At the end of the book, a lover or sometime lover dies in her bed from an overdose of Valium, saying "because we've been out there where nothing is."

In *A Book of Common Prayer*, the daughter of Charlotte Douglas has disappeared and is wanted by the police for a political bombing. In *Democracy* (1984), Inez Victor's daughter is a heroin addict and Inez's father, in an onset of lunacy, has killed her sister and another person. Inez has also had cancer. In *The Last Thing He Wanted*, Elena McMahon has lost her mother and in walking out on her rich husband has lost the affection of her daughter. The interior in which the women live is a sort of cocoon of melancholy, but their restlessness is modern and cannot be expressed like that of a country wife sighing at the moonlight as it hits the silence on the front porch. Maria Wyeth sleeps by her pool when she is not driving the L.A. freeways all night, stopping only for a Coke at a filling station. But she is driving a Corvette. The women have credit cards, bank drafts, an Hermès handbag, or a large emerald ring. In the heart of darkness, men fall in love with them, bereft and downhearted as they are. The sheen of glamour is useful to give entrance to the melancholy adulteries and to the plot of costly wild travels and also, in some cases, to politics that come out of the Oval Office or some room in the White House basement and turn up on the runway in Saigon or Costa Rica.

A Book of Common Prayer is a daring title, a risk, even, some would name a presumption. Perhaps the title is meant to bring to mind: "Have mercy on us in the hour of our death... *Prega per noi*." Charlotte Douglas is wandering the earth by air, aimlessly hoping to run into her daughter, Marin, "who at eighteen had been observed with her four best friends detonating a crude pipe bomb in the lobby of the Transamerica Building at 6:30 am, highjacking a P.S.A.L. 1011 at the San Francisco Airport and landing in Wendover, Utah, where they burned it in time for the story to interrupt the network news and disappeared." Charlotte Douglas goes to a miserable, corrupt little place called Boca Grande, an ungoverned and ungovernable country near Caracas. Her plane took her there with the blinkered idea that her daughter must be somewhere—and why not Boca Grande? Charlotte is killed by some machine-gun-toting activist in the almost weekly coups and countercoups. And meanwhile, Marin, the Berkeley Tupamaro, is actually in Buffalo. *A Book of Common Prayer* is an odd and most unusual study of secular violence and, in the case of the wandering mother, a sort of heathen inanition. Unable to think on the appalling plight of her daughter, Charlotte fills her mind with memories of her happy at the Tivoli Gardens in Copenhagen, devouring coconut ice under "the thousand trunks of Great Banyan at the Calcutta Botanical Garden."

Democracy: Washington, Honolulu, Hong Kong, Kuala Lumpur, Saigon, and Jakarta appear along the road in this novel of outlandish ambition, justified and honored by the scope, the subtlety, the agenda, as they call it. The time is 1975, the aftermath of Vietnam still in the air, and we go back to the way of setting the scene, a sort of computer lyricism:

> I would skim the stories on policy and fix instead on details: the cost of a visa to leave Cambodia in the weeks before Phnom Penh closed was five hundred dollars American. The colors of the landing lights for the helicopters on the roof of the American embassy in Saigon were red, white, and blue. The code names for the American evacuations of Cambodia and Vietnam respectively were EAGLE PULL and FREQUENT WIND. The amount of cash burned in the courtyard of the DAO in Saigon before the last helicopter left was three-and-a-half million dollars American and eighty-five million piastres. The code name for this operation was MONEY BURN. The number of Vietnamese soldiers who managed to get aboard the last American 727 to leave Da Nang was three hundred and thirty. The number of Vietnamese soldiers to drop from the wheel wells of the 727 was one. The 727 was operated by World Airways. The name of the pilot was Ken Healy.

One of the leading characters in the novel, Jack Lovett, is in love with Inez Victor, who is married to Harry Victor, a member of the

United States Senate and a onetime candidate for president, easy to believe since it is the dream of everyone who has ever had a term in the state legislature of whatever state. Lovett is perhaps CIA but not a villain, instead a realist who can say, "A Laotian village indicated on one map and omitted on another suggested not a reconnaissance oversight but a population annihilated. Asia was ten thousand tanks here, three hundred Phantoms there. The heart of Africa was an enrichment facility." In these novels, you do not just take an airplane from Florida to Costa Rica, you board a Lockheed L-100; and in another aside, if such it is, you learn how to lay down the AM-2 aluminum matting for a runway and whether "an eight-thousand foot runway requires sixty thousand square yards of operational apron or only forty thousand."

This author is a martyr of facticity, and indeed such has its place in the fearless architecture of her fictions. You have a dogged concreteness of detail in an often capricious mode of presentation. The detail works upon the mind of the reader, gives an assurance, or at least a feeling, that somewhere, somehow all of this is true, fictional truth, or possibility. It could have happened, and Inez Victor did in fact go off to Kuala Lumpur to work in the refugee camps. And that is where we leave her after her love for Jack Lovett and after her escape from a somnambulistic time as a politician's wife who must say over and over, "Marvelous to be here," and be "smiling at a lunch counter in Manchester, New Hampshire, her fork poised over a plate of scrambled eggs and toast." That is, you may accept or allow for the aesthetically doubtful because of the interesting force of the factual in which it is dressed.

In any case, every page of the books is hers in its peculiarities and particulars: All is handmade, or should we say, hand cut, as by the knife of a lathe. Some unfriendly reviewers, knowing Didion has written screenplays, will call the frame or action cinematic. But the fictions, as she has composed them, are the opposite of the communal cathedrals, or little brown churches in the vale, built by so many willing slaves in Hollywood. The first cry of exasperation from the producers, script doctors, watchful money crunchers with memories of hits and flops would be, What's going on here? What's it about?

If you can believe that Robert "Bud" McFarlane, Reagan's national-security adviser, could fly off to Iran, carrying with him a cake and a Bible in order to make a deal for the shipment of arms to the Contras, you can believe the less bizarre happenings in *The Last Thing He Wanted*. In this novel, Joan Didion has placed a woman, Elena McMahon, on a plane filled with illegal arms bound for Costa Rica, or the off-the-map border installations set up by the Americans, the Freedom Fighters. At the end of the flight, she is to collect the million dollars owed her dying father, a man who does "deals." Collect the money and fly back, or so she has been led to imagine. In the usual percussive Didion dialogue, Elena says, "Actually I'm going right back. . . . I left my car at the airport." The pilot says, "Long time parking I hope." She doesn't return and at the end of an elaborate plot is assassinated by "the man on the bluff with the pony tail"—the same sinister man who had met her at the landing strip in Costa Rica.

And there is Treat Morrison, the romantic lead you might say, who first sees Elena McMahon in the coffee shop of the Intercontinental Hotel, where she was "eating, very slowly and methodically, first a bite of one then a bite of the other, a chocolate parfait and bacon." The odd menu is mentioned several times but does not give up its meaning beyond the fact that the parfait and bacon had bothered him, Treat Morrison. Morrison is an "ambassador at large" for the Department of State, a troubleshooter, a fixer. Like Jack Lovett in *Democracy*, this is another love-at-first-sight matter, and, odd as it might be, not necessarily as hard to imagine as some of the more portentous occasions. The attractions are ballads: I saw her standing there and my heart stood still—something like that. Treat Morrison and Jack Lovett are attractive men of the world, at work, as the collision of romance leads them to the forlorn, needy women standing there, waiting.

In *The Last Thing He Wanted*, Joan Didion appears on the page directing, filling in, being, often, a friend from the past or a journalist on the case. "For the record this is me talking. You know me, or think you do." Here she is a moralist, a student of the Contra hearings. "There are documents, more than you might think. Depositions, testimony, cable traffic, some of it not yet declassified, but much in the public record." Of course, Elena McMahon is a fiction, but we are to remember the actual people "all swimming together in the glare off the C-123 that fell from the sky into Nicaragua." Among those caught in the glare was "the blond, the shredder, the one who transposed the numbers of the account at the Credit Suisse (the account at the Credit Suisse into which the Sultan of Brunei was to transfer the ten million dollars, in case you have forgotten the minor plays)."

The Last Thing He Wanted is a creation of high seriousness, a thriller composed with all the resources of a unique gift for imaginative literature, American literature. There remains in Didion's far-flung landscapes a mind still rooted in the American West from which she comes. When in *Slouching Towards Bethlehem* she visits the venerable piles in Newport, Rhode Island, she remembers the men who built the railroad, dug the Comstock Lode for gold and silver in Virginia City, Nevada, and made a fortune in copper.

> More than anyone else in the society, these men had apparently dreamed the dream and made it work. And what they did then was to build a place which . . . led step by step to unhappiness, to restrictiveness, to entrapment in the mechanics of living. In that way the lesson of Bellevue Avenue is more seriously radical than the idea of Brook Farm. . . . Who could think that the building of a railroad could guarantee salvation, when there on the lawns of the men who built the railroad nothing is left but the shadow of the migrainous women, and the pony carts waiting for the long-dead children?

She is saying that Bellevue Avenue in Newport is not what the West was won for.

1997

TRU CONFESSIONS
Truman Capote

CHATTY, gossipy remembrances of the deplorable history of Truman Capote's last years may be read, in some instances, as revenge or payment-due for the dead author's assaultive portraits of friends and enemies, although few of the interlocutors can command Capote's talent for the vicious, villainous, vituperative adjective. George Plimpton has spent some years tracking down and taking down the remarks of those who crossed Truman's journey to literary fame and to his unique crocodilian celebrity. The remarks are deftly arranged to avoid lumps of monologue piling up one after another like wood stacked for the winter. Instead the voices having their say about the charms and deficits of the absent one find Plimpton at the console professionally mixing the sound, as it were. His phrase for the effect is the unrehearsed, companionable exchange at a cocktail party. This is a large accommodation to raw opinion, to mincing literary judgments of hapless inappropriateness, to character analysis sweet as peaches or impugning as a jail-house witness for the prosecution. It must be said that method and result have a suitability to the subject, since Capote himself, when not writing, was party-going, forever receiving and producing banter about feckless stumblings and torrid indiscretions.

He was born in 1924 in New Orleans and spent his early years in Monroeville, Alabama. His mother, Lillie Mae Faulk, married at seventeen a man named Arch Persons by whom she had the child, Truman. He was left in the care of relatives, maiden ladies of an eccentric turn useful to the Southern literature of Capote's period. After a time his mother divorced and the son was brought to New York and to Connecticut, where Lillie Mae, name now changed to Nina, married

Joseph Capote, who adopted the child under the name of Truman Garcia Capote. *Other Voices, Other Rooms* was published when Truman was twenty-four years old, and this happy beginning of his creative life was in pitiable contrast to his family life. His mother committed suicide five years later, and two years after that Mr. Capote was sent to Sing Sing prison for forgery and grand larceny.

So Truman was on his own and on his way. He was an early master of camp flamboyance and defiance. He was short, effeminate, with a very noticeable, high-pitched, whining voice. And pretty enough, if never quite as fetching as the photograph that enhanced the cover of *Other Voices, Other Rooms*. It appears that with his curious voice, his ways, he decided to brazen it out, to be himself with an ornamental courage and an impressive conceit. He was a figure, what old ladies used to call a "sketch," and smart and amusing, ambitious as a writer and as a society darling, a coquette of wit at the great tables, on the yachts, in the splendid houses in Italy, France, and Mexico. Southern accent, cascades of anecdote, boy genius, as all including himself conceded, and productive in the hours of the afternoon when the hostess was napping.

Other Voices, Other Rooms: the best of his down-home fictions, confidently written, picturing a small-town world in the South. Moth-eaten grandeur, garrulous ne'er-do-wells, colored-folk exchanges in the kitchen with the only souls who lift a hand and here named Missouri, called Zoo, and her Papadaddy, Jesus Fever, and others who enter the action with drag-queen names like Miss Wisteria and the hermit, Little Sunshine. It is a coming-of-age story for young Joel Knox, as the fictions of his closest Southern contemporaries are likely to be: Carson McCullers's *The Heart Is a Lonely Hunter* and *The Member of the Wedding*; Harper Lee's *To Kill a Mockingbird*. We might note that in these books the girls are as tomboyish as Capote's Joel is girlish. Reading over these writers brings to mind the triumph of their contemporary Flannery O'Connor, painting a similar landscape and filling it not with cute hunchbacks and dwarfs but with predatory swamp rats, literally God-forsaken Bible salesmen intoning their handy lies in magical speech rhythms, all transcending the fictional clichés in the dramaturgy of the generation after Faulkner.

In Capote's novel, Joel Knox, age twelve, has been left in the care of his relations after the death of his mother and the flight of his father. At last he is summoned by the father, now married to Miss Amy, to join him at Skully's Landing, a run-down estate that will have no modern plumbing facilities or electricity, but the boy will discover that once in the parlor there were gold draperies, a gilded sofa of lilac velvet, and so on—all now covered with dust. Both the present decay and the parlor trumpery of a more glamorous past are not unexpected when the domestic scenery is to be assembled for a place called Skully's Landing and in a Southern state.

The father does not appear, nor is information given about him until later in the novel, and then we learn that he is upstairs, paralyzed, and communicating his needs by throwing tennis balls down the stairs. The plot is complicated by ghostly appearances, crazy down-South ways of passing the time, but we can find it held together by the sweetness of the boy's nature and a lyrical generosity about the follies of grown-ups. And by the kindness of the black cook, Zoo, a sort of kissing cousin to Ethel Waters in the staging of *The Member of the Wedding*.

The most interesting of the "characters" living in Skully's Landing is Cousin Randolph, a connection of the stepmother, Miss Amy. Randolph, a painter and sherry-drinking idler, has a history; he's been around, studied abroad, and while in Madrid copying the old masters in the Prado he meets Dolores, a cold but somehow overwhelming beauty, and they become lovers. The two of them abandon Europe and land in Florida, where Dolores takes up with Pepe, an impressively muscled boxer, mean, handsome, potent and violent. Randolph, in a ferocious epiphany, discovers himself in love with Pepe and filled with a devastating longing.

> I could not endure to see him suffer; it was agony to watch him fight.... I gave him money, brought him cream-colored hats, gold bracelets (which he adored, and wore like a woman), shoes in bright Negro colors, candy silk shirts....

The end of it was Pepe, drunk, destroying Randolph's paintings, calling him "terrible names" and breaking his nose. And then Pepe is off with Dolores, off no one knows where, but Randolph sends letters to random post offices here and there. "Oh, I know that I shall never have an answer. But it gives me something to believe in. And that is peace."

Randolph is a nice, rather lachrymose fellow, a well-born "queer" of some cultivation and too many afternoon sips from the bottle, altogether a configuration at home in the little towns, and no doubt still there. Joel, the boy, is moved by Randolph's confession and also moved to an awakening of his own nature. In a final scene they go to an old abandoned hotel, once a brothel, and in a somewhat murky rendering spend the night together.

Plimpton has printed a review of *Other Voices, Other Rooms* by the majorful Diana Trilling, which was published in *The Nation*, January 31, 1948. Despite the "claptrap" she praises the compositional virtuosity of the novel and finds that such skill in one so young "represents a kind of genius." However, she is morally distressed about Cousin Randolph, "a middle-aged degenerate aesthete," and more dismayed by what she reads as the *lesson* of the plot.

At the end of the book the young Joel turns to homosexual love offered him by Randolph, and we realize that in his slow piling up of nightmare details Mr. Capote has been attempting to recreate the emotional background to sexual inversion. What his book is saying is that a boy becomes a homosexual when the circumstances of his life deny him the other, more normal gratifications of his need for affection.

The devil made me do it. A shirking of moral responsibility, as she sees it, and in no way faithful to the text and to Joel's relation with Randolph. One thing you can say about Capote is that the "closet" was never, never anything to him except a place to find bits of silver cloth, old faded snapshots, love letters, and trinkets.

The Grass Harp is blown about by the winds of whimsy, here, rocking the cradle in the treetop. The narrator, again a young boy once more sent to live with relations, two unmarried ladies who are sisters. They and others spend a good deal of time picnicking and chatting in a house high up in a chinaberry tree. The tree house was fifteen or twenty years old, "spacious, sturdy, a model of a tree house, it was like a raft floating in a sea of leaves . . . to sail along the cloudy coastline of every dream." Up in the tree you can hear the grass harp "always telling a story—it knows the stories of all the people on the hill, of all the people who have ever lived, and when we are dead it will tell ours, too." The novel was composed while Capote was living in an "absolutely marvelous" villa in Sicily, named La Fontana Vecchia. It was, astonishingly, turned into a grandiose Broadway production, music by Virgil Thomson and sets by Cecil Beaton. Thomson describes the debacle:

> The set which Cecil designed, particularly the one with the big tree, was so large and heavy that nobody ever saw it until the opening in Boston. There was no point in setting it up in New York for rehearsals. . . . On the Sunday afternoon before we left for Boston, there was a professional matinee. . . . Everybody wept buckets. Then we moved up to Boston, and once we got into the set, nobody out there in the seats ever wept anymore. The set was too large and complicated—very grand, something for the Metropolitan Opera.

Well, no matter. Such was Capote's celebrity that "House of Flowers," a scrawny short story set in Haiti, was mounted as a Broadway musical with music by Harold Arlen, set by Oliver Messel, choreography by George Balanchine and direction by Peter Brook. The A list for little Tru.

The South, the days of youth gone by, the downtown with its shops and taverns and their funny names, the collection of harmlessly deranged kinfolk, were there to be called on by the writer as a sort of *spécialité*, like Key lime pie and conch fritters, to be exploited again and again in holiday postcards such as "A Christmas Memory," "One Christmas," and "The Thanksgiving Visitor."

Cousin Randolph, the tree house, and the rest of it will serve the muse for a time, and then Capote will bring his fiction to New York City, that place Marianne Moore, in a poem, found "starred with tepees of ermine and peopled with foxes." In his portmanteau, Capote will be carrying, like some revivifying patent medicine, a very useful stimulant in the composition of the successful *Breakfast at Tiffany's*, that is, Christopher Isherwood's *Goodbye to Berlin*.

Into Plimpton's time capsule we have the wish of several young, or once young, ladies to be the inspiration for the beguiling Holly Golightly, the center of *Breakfast at Tiffany's*. Doris Lilly, identified as a gossip columnist and author, is as insistent as if she were the claimant in an inheritance battle.

> There is an awful lot of me in Holly Golightly. There's much more of me than there is of Carol Marcus (who is now Carol Marcus Matthau) and a girl called Bee Dabney, a painter. More of me than either of these two ladies. I know.

Primogeniture does not adhere to any of the pals circling around the house in New York. Fortunately for the attractiveness of *Breakfast at Tiffany's* (1958), the model is the "Sally Bowles" section in Isherwood's book of 1938. In both novellas, the first-person narrator is a young writer who finds himself living next door to an interesting young woman, Sally Bowles in a Berlin pension and Holly Golightly in a shabby New York town house broken up into small apartments.

Both girls are beautiful, each afloat and searching for a place to land with a man if not rich at least giving evidence of being in touch with money. They attach themselves to one after another, only to find themselves abruptly dropped, an annoyance from which they bounce back in a way that reminds one of professional boxers, on the mat one minute and up the next, a little unsteady, but with fist in a salute. Among the many correspondences between Isherwood and Capote we have the fleeing man's tendency to leave a letter.

Klaus to Sally Bowles:

> My dear little girl, you have adored me too much.... You must be brave, Sally, my poor darling child.... I was invited a few nights ago to a party at the house of Lady Klein, a leader of the

British aristocracy. I met there a beautiful and intelligent young English girl named Miss Gore-Eckersley....

And so it goes.

José, a Brazilian diplomat making his escape from Holly Golightly's radar:

> My dearest little girl, I have loved you knowing that you were not as others. But conceive of my despair upon discovering...how very different you are from the manner of woman a man of my faith and career could hope to make his wife....I am gone home.

Sally Bowles gives herself a *faux* "country" background in a very amusing imitation:

> Daddy's a terrible snob, although he pretends not to be....He's the most marvellous business man. And about once a month he gets absolutely dead tight and horrifies all Mummy's smart friends.

Holly Golightly, from Tulip, Texas, real name Lulamae Barnes, was a runaway starving orphan picked up by a country horse doctor whom she married at age fourteen, and ran away from to New York. The horse doctor turns up in New York hoping to reclaim his wife and providing one of Capote's most inventive comic interludes. However, Tulip, Texas, does not always inhabit Holly Golightly's conversational style—the rhythms of Sally Bowles perhaps overwhelming national boundaries. (There is a mention of French lessons given to smother Holly's Texas defect in preparation for a film career.) Nevertheless here she is in a typical locution: "But, after all, he *knows* I'm preggers. Well, I am, darling. Six weeks gone. I don't see why that should surprise you. It didn't me. Not *un peu* bit." At times her diction crosses to the Rhine. "I suppose I'll sleep until Saturday, really get a good *schluffen*."

The two stories come to an end on a postcard. Sally Bowles, off on her amorous journey, sends a card from Paris, another from Rome with no address.

That was six years ago. So now I am writing her. When you read this, Sally, if you ever do—please accept it as a tribute, the sincerest I can pay, to yourself, and to our friendship. And send me another postcard.

Holly in a postcard goodbye from South America: "Brazil was beastly but Buenos Aires the best. Not Tiffany's, but almost...Will let you know address when I know it myself." And the narrator reflects: "But the address, if it ever existed, never was sent, which made me sad, there was so much I wanted to write her."

Breakfast at Tiffany's has its own charms, and if the astute Capote has done a transatlantic rearrangement perhaps we can think of it in musical terms: Variations on a Theme by Haydn. Something like that.

Christopher Isherwood, resident of Los Angeles, was present at Capote's funeral, and Plimpton publishes what the novelist John Gregory Dunne remembered about the moment. "And Chris did the most graceful thing of all. He said, 'There was one wonderful thing about Truman. He always made me laugh.' He started to laugh, turned around, and sat down. Perfectly graceful and gracious." And then Carol Marcus Matthau, who in Doris Lilly's deposition is definitely *not* the model for Holly Golightly, has some unpleasant things to say about Isherwood. (Unpleasantness about persons not the object of the enterprise in "oral biography" is a treacherous fallout of the indiscriminate form.) Truman Capote in his fiction never achieved anything as rich and beautiful as the stories in *Goodbye to Berlin*, of which "Sally Bowles" is only one, or as brilliant as *Mr. Norris Changes Trains* and *Prater Violet*. Not to the point here, since with a few exceptions, it appears that the only "brilliant writer" and "genius" the assembly is aware of is Truman Capote. No, mournful as it is to remember, there is another writer mentioned again and again in Plimpton's pages, a writer who, like Capote, knew a lot of rich people and who wrote something herein called "Proustian."

In November 1966 Capote gave in the Plaza Hotel in New York what you might call his "in-cold-blood party" for five hundred guests. As a sort of provenance for the fête, the calendar moves backward. The murder of the Clutter family, husband and wife and two teenage children, occurred in November 1959, in the town of Holcomb, Kansas. After reading an account in the press, Capote soon took off for the site of the crime. Two young men were arrested a month later and in March 1960 convicted of the crime and sentenced to death. On April 14, 1965, Perry Smith and Dick Hickock, the convicted murderers of the Clutter family, were hanged in the Kansas State Penitentiary for Men in Lansing, Kansas. Six years had passed after the conviction, by way of legal appeals and stays of execution, before the author, Truman Capote, could write *finis* to *In Cold Blood*, his account of the killers, the detectives, the town, the trial. Six months after the hanging, the serialization in *The New Yorker* began, and publication in book form soon followed.

At last it was Carnival time, with beads, masks, spikes of feathers in voodoo headdresses, bunny fur, witch wigs, and a band playing show tunes. The party at the Plaza acquired the fame of a coronation for the very successful book, still a work of riveting interest for its portrait of the misshapen bodies, language, highway felonies, and idiotic plans and dreams of two savage, talkative, rawhide murderers, Perry Smith and Dick Hickock.

After the publication of the book, Capote spends a good deal of his time and thought on nomenclature, that is, his naming of the work a "nonfiction novel" and claiming to be the only begetter of the form. Sometimes in the discussion one might be reading about an eagle-eyed blind man, but that would have a greater philosophical interest. In most works of any length about crimes there is much that is not mere documentation; there is the setting of the scene: the neat little trailer before the blood-splattered walls, the dog at the garbage can with an arm in it, the handsome house, usually called a mansion, where the deceased was just putting night cream on her face when... There are scenes in Capote that appear to be "fiction"; one early chapter has Nancy Clutter, the daughter, at home on the day of her death, chatting on the phone about a lesson in pie-baking or about her boyfriend, Bobby. This is followed by Mrs. Clutter in a conversation with Jolene, the thirteen-year-old for whom Nancy was to give the lesson in pie-baking. The Clutters are dead, and the reader supposes the quite banal chapter to be what the author would imagine to be the actions of a "normal" family living out their last hours in Kansas farm country. Not easy to enliven since the family is denied the bizarrerie of Alabama homesteads. However, in an interview, Capote seems to disclaim imagination and to place the origin of everything in the testimony of the living who overheard or took part in the conversations.

Perry Smith, thirty-one years old, and Dick Hickock, twenty-eight years old, are on parole from prison and, at the beginning of the composition, are making their journey to commit a robbery and kill whoever will frustrate their plan. They made their way to the house in Kansas and in the interest of "leaving no witnesses" slaughtered the four family members. The case was solved when the police were told by a cellmate who had once worked for Mr. Clutter that he had given information about a safe in the house containing ten thousand dollars—given the information to Smith and Hickock as they gathered their meager belongings and abilities and were set free. There was no safe in the house, and the cons came away with forty dollars, a radio, and a pair of binoculars.

On the way from birth to death, as it were, there is an appallingly rich lode of archival gold for Capote to shape and polish and send to market, all of which he does with a skillful hand. The detectives on their way to pawnshops and motels and the very striking confession of the killers about their wanderings before and after, their description of their gruesome destruction of each single Clutter; accounts of the early life of the killers by their relatives and their own summations given at the request of a court psychiatrist; Capote's interviews, his visit to the holding cells where the two awaited execution, his claim of having corresponded with each twice a week for the five years between conviction and execution.

While both the condemned and the author were waiting out the stays, Capote made no secret of his *qué sera, sera* impatience to get it over with. Quite a few remembered this curious bit of literary oral history. When the book was published, it did occasion jokes and some serious memories which the pugnacious and vindictive Capote did not find amusing. On a TV show, William Buckley, Jr., said, "Well, we've only had a certain number of executions in the last few years—whatever it was—and two of them were for the personal convenience of Truman

Capote." The composer Ned Rorem at a party heard Truman say about his book, "But it can't be published until they're executed, so I can hardly wait." Rorem, when the book came out, sent a letter to be published in a magazine, which said, among other things: "Capote got two million and his heroes got the rope." (Needless to say, Rorem got *his* in Capote's later book *Answered Prayers*.)

Party-going with its temptation to social misdemeanors was also the ground of a confrontation between Capote and the English critic Kenneth Tynan. After hearing that the execution date had been irrevocably set, Capote, according to Tynan's wife's interview with Plimpton, said: "I'm beside myself! Beside myself! Beside myself with joy!" Tynan reviewed *In Cold Blood* for *The Observer* in London:

> For the first time, an influential writer of the front rank has been placed in a position of privileged intimacy with criminals about to die and, in my view, done less than he might have to save them.... No piece of prose, however deathless, is worth a human life.

Truman, in his reply to the paper, wrote that Tynan had "the morals of a baboon and the guts of a butterfly."

Capote never showed an interest in political or moral debate, and perhaps that was prudent since ideas, to some degree, may define one's social life and could just be excess baggage he didn't need to bring aboard; and, worse, boring, like the ruins and works of art he declined to get off the yacht to see. In any case, he could not have "saved" Smith and Hickock, who had confessed; the appeals rested upon legal matters such as the competence of the state-appointed defense attorneys, whose summation took only ninety minutes—the jury before returning the death sentence "deliberated" only forty minutes.

Still, one might reflect about the book and wonder what a sentence of life without possibility of parole might have been for the execution of the nonfiction novel. Two alive central characters with plenty of time to become jailhouse lawyers would not have been useful to the author, publisher, or movie-maker. These are troublesome men. And then there is the actual hanging in the dreadful Kansas shed, "a cavernous storage room, where on the warmest day the air is moist and chilly"; and: "The hangman coughed—impatiently lifted his cowboy hat and settled it again, a gesture somehow reminiscent of a turkey buzzard huffing, then smoothing its neck feathers—and Hickock, nudged by an attendant, mounted the scaffold steps." Wouldn't that have been missed?

There is a moment in *In Cold Blood* when Perry Smith says to his partner in the murders: "I just don't believe anyone could get away with a thing like that." In *Answered Prayers*, the unfinished nonfiction novel, using the actual names of a transcontinental cast of mostly well-known persons or, if disguised by a fictitious name, carefully designed to be identifiable, Capote made his own shackled step to the social gallows. The first of the scatalogical offenses to be published was "La Côte Basque," a story or something, taking place in the fashionable restaurant of the same name. It is lunchtime and the proprietor is seating or not seating according to the heraldic rankings of the metropolitan scene. Capote, under his *nom de plume* of P. B. Jones, or "Jonesy," is lunching with "Lady Coolbirth" in the absence of the Duchess of Windsor, she having canceled because of a bout of hives.

Champagne is ordered, which somehow promotes a scurrilous bit of anecdote about the composer Cole Porter. On and on to the supposedly overheard conversation of two identified nymphs about town. Across the way in the restaurant, dining with a priest, is the wife who in a *famous* court case was acquitted of having shot her well-born, rich husband. But she is not to escape the dossier proposed by Jonesy and Lady Coolbirth detailing her rise from a "country-slum" in West Virginia, real trash with a pretty face, who went on to a whirl on the continental carousel where she was known as "Madame Marmalade— her favorite *petit déjeuner* being hot cock butter with Dundee's best." The woman in fact committed suicide a few days before "La Côte" appeared in *Esquire* magazine. Whether she knew the unveiling in store for her is not certain, but at least she was out of the way.

Others were still around to meet themselves in degrading tableaux, sometimes performing under an alias which was a pasted-on Woolworth's mustache that failed to fool any tots in the playground. The chitchat proceeds: "Why would an educated, dynamic, very rich and well-hung Jew go bonkers for a cretinous Protestant size forty who wears low-heeled shoes and lavender water?" It seems the "porcine sow" was the governor's wife, and in a grotesque seduction on the Pierre Hotel sheets the gentleman was proving something, avenging the old days when even the most established Jews weren't welcome in WASP country clubs, boarding schools, and so on. The gentleman in this unaccountably destructive and self-destructive portrait was everywhere quickly identified as the husband of the most elegant woman in the city. From what we read she had been for some years a true friend, the most valuable and perhaps most surprising trophy, solid silver, Truman had won, scored in the field.

Capote had, like a leper with a bell announcing his presence, horrified those he most treasured, and with many he was marked with the leper's visible deformities, a creature arousing fear of infection. There is much ado about this in Plimpton: calls unanswered, intervention by friends unavailing. "Unspoiled Monsters," another section of *Answered Prayers*, concerns itself with the chic homosexual world and what used to be called the stars of stage, screen, and radio. P. B. Jones is again the narrator, about thirty-five, a writer, sponger, and wit: "Starting at an early age, seven or eight or thereabouts, I'd run the gamut with many an older boy and several priests and also a handsome Negro gardener. In fact, I was a kind of Hershey Bar whore—"

Jonesy gets around, to a room in the YMCA, "work" as a prostitute masseur, and off to every grand spot in Europe. It's not quite clear just how a back rub could get the little charmer from the Y to the Ritz in Paris, Harry's Bar in Venice, everywhere. But he must move about in order to reveal all the habits, hang-ups, perversions, fears, unpaid bills of the slit-savoring bitches, muff-divers, whining masochists, drug addicts, patrons of Father Flanagan's Nigger Queen Kosher Café. Woe to all who passed his way, with Capote toting their names, occupations, contorted faces, the passports of their public identities, material that makes *Answered Prayers* resemble the files of J. Edgar Hoover.

What was Capote thinking of? At times one is led to imagine him afflicted with Tourette's syndrome, a disease described in recent years with much sympathy by Oliver Sacks. It brings on facial tics, not unusual in other physical misfortunes; the true peculiarity of the symptoms is echolalia, endless talking characterized by an uncontrollable flow of obscenities. Still, Capote knew all there was to know about gossip and understood that in a gifted form it will not be about imagined persons but about real people, not about John Doe but about Cecil Beaton, to name one of his many punitive divertissements.

In his own love life, about which he never wrote, the record seems to ally Truman with Cousin Randolph and his sudden devasting passion for the boxer Pepe. First, the man who came to fix the air conditioner and was snatched away from his wife and children, spiffed up with new clothes, dental rehabilitation, and taken along to the great palazzos in Venice, to the yachts sailing in blue summer waters. The poor fellow gets very bad reviews at every port and perhaps to his credit returned them by taking off, leaving Truman "devastated," in a "big collapse."

And there was John O'Shea, a sort of financial adviser, with wife and four children, and ready to abandon all for a luxe life with Truman. Vodka, gunplay, theft, and disappearance of O'Shea; heartbreak and atonement by Truman, who helped the O'Shea family and brought the attractive, honest daughter to stay in the flat in New York.

Capote himself wasn't a pleasant vision in his last years of drugs and drink, but he collected new friends who cared for him up until his death in Los Angeles, out West where new life, if you can hang on, begins. An unexpected fact from his last will and testament: In honor of Newton Arvin, a critic and professor of literature and an early friend of Truman and his writing, Capote endowed two handsome yearly prizes, one for fifty thousand dollars and the other for one hundred thousand dollars. They were to be given to writers of imaginative criticism.

1998

LOCATIONS
The Landscapes of Fiction

THE LANDSCAPES of fiction: houses and the things therein, nation-states and States of the Union, oceans, backland; winter nights and the old horse pulling the sledge through a driving snow, summer heat and the arrival of smothering love affairs. For the human drama, the surrounding landscape is not only field and sky but inhabits character and hangs its shadows over destiny. "Wuthering Heights is the name of Mr. Heathcliff's dwelling": one of the most striking placements in fiction. The foretelling resonance of Wuthering and Heathcliff, the solemn musicality of the word *dwelling* could hardly be surpassed as mere sound. Neither name of place nor family name is consoling: a hard, dull wind, a wasteland, a slope of rock. The dramatically opposed names, Thrushcross Grange and Mr. Linton, are useful designations of a more pleasing pastoral world and might belong to anyone in the countryside.

In most fictions, the interiors of a household are the defining land-scape of pride, lack, hope, negligence, pretension—to leave aside the powerful moral and personal shape of rural life with horses, cows, and the drama of the seasons setting the scene.

"A rusty wooden house, with seven acutely peaked gables, facing towards various points of the compass, and a huge, clustered chimney in the midst." Hawthorne built his house and furnished it with all the things of the past and of the present, the time of the fiction. It is a crowded jumble of artifacts and ancestral treasures under a layer of dust: *The House of the Seven Gables.* The house begins and ends the novel and dominates the scene with historical curses of such malignant power that the original builder, Colonel Pyncheon, lies dead in an upstairs bed even as the town arrives for the housewarming celebration.

It's a feudal castle placed on Main Street, where such important statements of display like to be. Inside, old mirrors, maps, a dark antique canopy bed with "ponderous festoons of a stuff which had been rich, and even magnificent, in its time."; a harpsichord which "looked more like a coffin than anything else." Infinite solicitude by the author for every nook and cranny and, as fortunes decline over the years, a notions shop, socially regressive, faces the street at the front. A feeble commerce it is to be, but everything on the shelves is noted: buttons, a pickle jar "filled with fragments of Gibraltar Rock"; a gingerbread concoction that is a little black boy going by the name of Jim Crow, a handful of marbles; on and on it goes. A curious accounting of domestic detail, rather wifely, to furnish the fictional world of old Salem. *The House* is a popular story, not quite one of Hawthorne's finest inspirations, but there he is in the midst of it. In the economy of an artist's life, furniture, spools of thread, barrels of flour, gingersnaps may not serve as moral or social clues but as—just stuff, the bits and pieces of imagined life.

Poverty and riches, good taste and the tinsel ornamentation of bad taste are contraries that battle on the page, stamping their marks in an indelible coloration. In the sentimental fiction of bygone days there is often a union of poverty with moral purity. You enter a modest cottage and if on a plain pine table there has been placed a snow-white cloth, the whiteness is not accidental. Someone is making a statement of value or of respectable habit in dismaying circumstances. The snow-white cloth tells of washtubs, the scrub board, a sunny clothesline, and labor with a flat iron: the spare household of the neat and worth poor. The simple evening meal, potatoes on the coals, a loaf of bread or something bought with the last pennies anxiously laid out on the grocer's counter. In the lamplight or the firelight when darkness falls a good wife or the faithful young daughter or granddaughter is mending or knitting.

I confess to an affection for these pictorial effects of which Dickens is a master, the poet of the starving child—"more porridge!"—and since there is to be a plot, he is also the great portraitist of the hideous villains, overfed always, maniacally stingy horrors who prey with a preternatural cunning on the bereft and needy. The vicious dwarf Mr. Quilp and little Nell, the hardworking Cratchits and Mr. Scrooge before his holiday reformation, and dozens more.

In our own literature, *Uncle Tom's Cabin* is a fiction of the good and the evil. Tom's cabin in Kentucky is only one of the plantation landscapes he will be transported to, in chains, after the practical negotiations of landowners, some of whom must sell slaves to pay debts incurred in high-living or respectable household accommodations. The cabin graces the title perhaps because it is in the past and is thus a memory, the homestead of youth that plays its role in fictions of all sorts. The cabin, showing the moral worth of the slave inhabitants, Uncle Tom, and his wife, Aunt Chloe:

> In front it had a neat garden-patch, where, every summer, strawberries, raspberries, and a variety of fruits and vegetables, flourished under careful tending. The whole front of it was covered by a large scarlet bignonia and a native multiflora rose.... Here, also, in summer, various brilliant annuals, such as marigolds, petunias, four-o'clocks, found an indulgent corner.

In the kitchen, Aunt Chloe, Tom's wife, is preparing her incomparable batter-cakes and her "whole plump countenance beams with satisfaction and contentment from under her well-starched checked turban." Busy, clean, and well starched: emblems of virtue. Uncle Tom is deeply pious, strong in the faith with Mrs. Stowe. Her last words to him and to the world are: "Think of your freedom, every time you see Uncle Tom's Cabin; and let it be a memorial to put you all in mind to follow in his steps, and be as honest and faithful and Christian as he was." (We may note that Mrs. Stowe in her union of domestic virtue and moral life will make the evil Simon Legree's plantation a dismal contrast to the glowing garden of Uncle Tom. Legree's place is mildewed Jessamine, raggedy honeysuckle, and weeds.)

The good poor do not have a noticeable position in contemporary fiction; perhaps the poor of Victorian times are as hard to come upon as the good seen without the qualifying eye that finds motive in the saint as easily as in the crook. Many contemporary characters seem identified by "relative deprivation" rather than outright poverty. They are eating too many fried foods in packages; they have old cars sitting on the lawn with the flat tire sinking into the grass; the television set is on day and night even if still in the woeful black-and-white. Their children are somehow dressed in the same manner as the car dealer's sons, and if there may have been some sleight of hand necessary to acquire the sneakers, that is not exactly criminal.

The bad rich remain in good literary standing, especially the *nouveau riche*, who are in command of funds that put old money, trust fund fortunes, into a sort of withering shade. Edith Wharton in *The Custom of the Country* and William Dean Howells in *The Hazard of New Fortunes* shaped bitter comedies about the pretension, the riveting, loud, almost revolutionary arrival in New York of money made in natural gas and hair-waiving lotions and spending itself in grotesque acquisitions of showy household appointments. All those dollars of such curious provenance appear to be a historical threat to the nation, something like the contamination of the ozone by motor cars. The wonderful squandering hicks in Ring Lardner's stories of the "big town" have, on the other hand, a genuine, foolish pathos. Mrs. Gullible longing to meet the famous social queen Mrs. Potter Palmer, and when the collision is accomplished in the halls of a hotel, Mrs. Palmer asks her to bring the towels.

New York City, urbanism, is often spoken of as "electric." The Russian poet Mayakovsky: "After I learned about electricity, I lost interest in nature. Not up-to-date enough." Manhattan is not altogether felicitous for fiction. It is not a city of memory, not a family city, not the capital of America so much as the iconic capital of the century. It is grand and grandiose with its two rivers acting as a border to contain the restless. Its skyscrapers and bleak, rotting tenements are a gift for photographic consumption, but for the fictional imagination the city's inchoate density is a special challenge. Those who engage this "culture of congestion" today need a sort of athletic suppleness, such as we find in Tom Wolfe's *The Bonfire of the Vanities* and E. L. Doctorow's *Ragtime*.

Among the best of the older New York novels are two melancholy landscapes of defeat. Edith Wharton in *The House of Mirth* was free of superiority to the invading hordes from dumbbell towns in the hinterland and thus wrote a stinging portrait of "society" at the turn of the century. The mood is not elegiac or protective and is instead a picture of the remorseless struggle of a handsome, well-connected young woman to keep up in the rich world she was born to. It is a fiction about money, a genuine creation dramatically staged in Manhattan.

F. Scott Fitzgerald's *The Great Gatsby* is a supreme work of the imagination. It has a tonal purity of style, an unwavering accent of lamentation for those caught in a plot of tragic finality. In Jay Gatsby, Fitzgerald has created an American as unforgettable as Captain Ahab. A good deal of the action takes place on Long Island, but it is a New York City novel, Long Island being a weekend road out of and back to Manhattan. At Gatsby's house, "a factual imitation of some Hôtel de Ville in Normandy," every Friday "five crates of oranges and lemons arrived from a fruiterer in New York."

Jay Gatsby is an impostor, a man deeply interesting as a complex model of the imitative as a force in the creation of character, or if not character at least personality as a series of gestures. Gatsby has devised a name for himself, imagined an eloquent background of situations and accomplishments. The money he has made is also unreal and subject to disappearance, like a ghost vanishing at dawn. And yet he has his "greatness" as a dreamer who created his imaginary self in pursuit of an overwhelming love. So real is this unreal man, Gatsby, that you feel he might still be somewhere in New York today, perhaps on Park Avenue, a signifying address, or like Dreiser's Hurstwood fallen into hell, dying on the Bowery, yet another indicative address in the city.

Hurstwood in *Sister Carrie* is a provincial form of Gatsby, a doomed man of a lower order of desire who manages a New York saloon. His need for Carrie, an old love risen as a sort of star on the stage, leads him to the theft of the night's receipts he was to have deposited in a vault. Both of these men in pursuit of the loved one, the green light as Fitzgerald calls it, know only one kind of ambition. It is money, money in a hurry, not the weekly paycheck of a patient, plodding clerk, clocking in of a morning and out at dusk. They come to utter ruin, to death for Gatsby, but of the two only one, Gatsby, could truly be called great, in the author's conception. Hurstwood, in the majestic *Sister Carrie*, was imagined in the complex spirit of American realism.

Interiors: purchases that represent a hope for expression of private style even if dominated by the most autocratic arbiter of taste, the amount of money at hand, oddly known as disposable income. The spare and elegant, each selection *just so* and fitting together; modern wares if sought with scholarly precision can make claim to being the most expensive, outpacing the search for the cherry hutch or the Victorian claw-foot chair. Instead for knowing characters, citified couples, it will be bits and pieces such as a leather chair, an Eames copy in molded plywood, an architect's name on a coffeepot or a cocktail shaker. Mary McCarthy in her memoir celebrates a 1940s cocktail shaker by Russel Wright.

In most fictions, a change of interior is a move upward to a better house, a better address. In Philip Roth's *American Pastoral*, acute attention is given to the alterations of prosperity. The old family, father a dealer in hides, makes its way up to "finished basements, their screened-in porches, their flagstone front steps." Their children are in a more drastic, dreaming mode: "a barn, a millpond, a millstream ... a fireplace large enough for roasting an ox, fitted with an oven door and a crane to swing an iron kettle on." Up and back to a colonial farmer's domestic landscape, all peacefully lying in history, with two cars in the garage.

In Richard Ford's *Independence Day*, the narrator is a real estate broker, an occupation that will be a gladiatorial combat with buyers in a blinding, paralyzing calculation of cost, street, neighborhood. Images of themselves encased in the mausoleum of their choice, fittings of small and large preference, turn out to be disorienting rather than defining. One troublesome couple wants to forsake its once-loved place in Vermont with "its cantilevered cathedral ceilings and a hand-laid hearth and chimney using stones off the place" for something else in New Jersey. But what?

Aesthetic models torment the greatly, famously rich in a violently expansive way. Bellevue Avenue in Newport, Rhode Island, which Henry James remembered as a pleasant summer escape to long walks, sea breezes, and the town library, had when he visited it in 1904 become the nation's most notable exercise in monumentality. He found castles of Rhenish and French inspiration. White elephants, he calls them, "peculiarly awkward vengeances of affronted proportion and discretion."

The sad, history-heavy countryside, the pain of the Confederacy, the khaki-colored earth, the dusty, immemorial, drowsy streets, the cunning, secretive faces of the Snopes family, the fatal running of Joe Christmas and Miss Rosa Coldfield and Quentin Compson in the "empty hall echoing with sonorous, defeated names." William Faulkner, the grandest fictional talent our country has produced, land-obsessed and with an imagination of staggering fertility and scope, found in Mississippi an epic vision. Shrewd swamp-bred families, disinherited gentlefolk, immense plots that go back and forth in time and yet seem immovably still there, alive.

The landscapes of fiction, the houses and things, are a shell for the creation of human dramas, the place for the seven deadly sins to do battle with probity and reality or outrageous demand and vanity. The shells, the habitations of America are volatile, inventive, unexpected, imponderable, but there they are, everywhere. In recent American fictions, short stories and novels, you will find people cooking dinner inside or shaking the mop outside a trailer. This humble abode that does not weather but shows its age in a bit of rust or chipped paint is becoming more and more the primary "affordable housing" for citizens who cannot qualify for the expense of conventional home ownership and may not even prefer it.

People, large numbers of them, settle in their "park" on the outskirts of town, hook up the gas, electric, and sewer lines, root utilities. Inside all is likely to be a place of old-time memory: rag rugs, a patchwork quilt, a ship's clock, hand-knit nylon pan-grippers providing a sort of Americana coziness. Trailer park, on the page or in speech, will mean hard up, and sometimes on the evening news it projects a sort of un-steadiness as when a relative, friend, or ex-husband invades the hospi-tality to hide out until the police car, top light whirling and flashing, catches up.

In this world too there are wide separations of type and possibility to be found, degrees of identity. The very large, expensive homes rest down in Florida for the winter but take to the road for a summer change in Maine. These deluxe motor palaces may travel in groups for social-izing. Up goes the plastic awning over the door; if the weather is agree-able, out comes a folding table and place mats, and on the lawn, as it were, the flat parking spaces for the spacious machines, there will be arrangements for tea or cocktails. In a photograph of an interesting early motor home, all was plain, handsomely utilitarian. Custom-made for Anne and Charles Lindbergh: puritans.

There's a leveling homogeneity in America today created by television. Each day it passes over the vast land mass, over the states nudging each other like the sovereignties of the Balkans, creating a unifying cloud of aesthetic properties and experience. East and West, North and South are wrapped in a sort of over-soul of images, facts, happenings, celebrities. This debris is as sacred to our current fiction as gossip about the new vicar was to Trollope. And there it is on the page, informing the domestically restless households, father off somewhere, mother chagrined. Sons and daughters writing the books.

1999

MELVILLE IN LOVE

I.

HERMAN Melville died in 1891 at the age of seventy-two. He was buried next to his son Malcolm in a cemetery in the Bronx. His death was marked negatively, as it were, by an absence of public ceremony; just another burial of an obscure New Yorker. This obscurity, or neglect, was to become part of the dramaturgy of Melville's image, even for those who hadn't read him in the past, as well as for those, more than a few, who haven't read him in the present. The man and his work—nine novels, brilliant shorter fictions, poems, and his departing gift to American literature, the beautiful *Billy Budd*, published after his death—were unearthed in the 1920s and the whole skeleton given a voluptuous rebirth.

Melville was not a gifted angel winging up from the streets, the slums of the great metropolis, Manhattan. His father, Allan, came from a good merchant family of Boston who could claim the sort of heraldic honor that to this day, two centuries later, keeps the prideful busy with the genealogists; that is, service in the American Revolution. Allan's father, Thomas Melville, was among the young men who, in 1773, boarded the ships of the East India Company and dumped their tea in the water. A felicitous bit of patriotic vandalism which the family could claim like a coat-of-arms to hang with noble diggings in their Scottish ancestry. Melville's mother was Maria Gansevoort of Albany, prominent Dutch early settlers. Her father was also a hero of the Revolution, fighting at Fort Stanwix against Indian and Tory troops.

When Melville was twelve years old, his father, Allan, died of what seems to have been a virulent pneumonia. He died as he had lived, in debt, a condition for which the Melvilles may be said to have had an almost genetic liability. (Dollars damn me! the author, Herman, could honestly announce. His life after the financially advantageous marriage to the daughter of Judge Lemuel Shaw of Boston was ever to be punctuated by "on loan from Judge Shaw" and "paid for by Judge Shaw.") The father's business in imported luxury goods had led him to move the family from Boston to New York, where the son, Herman, was born in 1819 on Pearl Street. Matters did not go as profitably as the beleaguered entrepreneur had hoped and so it was to be a move to Albany, the principality of the much more prudent Gansevoorts. However, the radiance of these solid patroons did not cast its beams of solvency and, with the death of the father, creditors were in scowling pursuit.

In Albany, unremitting black weather for the Melville household. The widow and her children were forced to sell much of their furniture and other effects and to escape in ignominy to a cheaper town, Lansingburgh, nearby. Herman for a period taught school, took an engineering diploma at Lansingburgh Academy, failed to get a position, wrote some youthful sketches which were published in the local paper—and then, and then perhaps we can say his true life began. However, the life he left behind, the losses, the grief, the instability, the helpless love of a helpless young man in a damaged family marked his sensibility quite as much as the wanderlust, the strong grip of the sea, so often claimed as the defining aspect of his nature. In 1839, he signed on as a common seaman on the *St. Lawrence*, a merchant ship bound for a four-month trip to Liverpool. He was soon to be twenty years old.

Melville's state of mind is revealed some years later with a purity of expressiveness in the novel *Redburn*, one of his most appealing and certainly the most personal of his works. He is said to have more or less disowned the book, more rather than less, since he claimed it was only written for tobacco. Whether this is a serious misjudgment of his own work or a withdrawal, after the fact, from having shown his early experience of life without his notable reserve and distance is, of course, not clear. For a contemporary reader, Redburn, the grief-stricken youth, cast among the vicious, ruined men on the ship, walking the streets of Liverpool in the late 1830s, even meeting with the homosexual hustler Harry Bolton might have more interest than *Typee*'s breadfruit and coconut island and the nymph, Fayaway. But it is only pertinent to think of *Redburn* on its own: a novel written after *Typee*, *Omoo*, and *Mardi* in the year 1849, ten years after he left Lansingburgh to go on his first voyage.

"Cold, bitter cold as December, and bleak as its blasts, seemed the world then to me; there is no misanthrope like a boy disappointed; and such was I, with the warm soul of me flogged out by adversity." Melville was not a boy when he joined the *St. Lawrence*, but the remembrance of his father and the lost years seem in detail to represent his actual thoughts at the time. Despair, rooted in experience, in love of family, and a young son's defenseless anxiety amidst the tides of misfortune leave their mark on his character and on his view of life. The opening pages are a profoundly moving poem to his dead father, to the memory of evenings in New York, talk around the fireside of the cities and sights of Europe, the treasures Allan brought home from his business travels to Paris. There was a large bookcase filled with books, many in French, paintings and prints, furniture, pictures from natural history, including a whale "big as a ship, stuck full of harpoons, and three boats sailing after it as fast as they could fly."

The sea, the traveler's passionate curiosity and longing, "foreign associations, bred in me a vague prophetic thought, that I was fated, one day or other, to be a great voyager; and that just as my father used to entertain strange gentlemen over their wine after dinner, I would hereafter be telling my own adventures to an eager auditory." Most vivid in his memory was an intricately made glass ship brought home from Hamburg. The figurehead of the magical ship "fell from his perch the very day I left home to go to sea on this *my first voyage*." Things are fragile and subject to spots and stains, the rude damages of family life, but the shattering of the familiar glass beauty, named *La Reine*, adds another mournful accent, symbolic if you like, to the breakage in

Melville's early life, if we consider these pages to be a recapitulation of the past feeling as they appear to be.

Nothing in Melville is more beautifully expressed than the mood of early sorrow in the forlorn passage at the opening of *Redburn*. It brings to mind the extraordinarily affecting last word in *Moby-Dick*. The word is *orphan*.

> I had learned to think much and bitterly before my time .... Talk not of the bitterness of middle-age and after life; a boy can feel all that, and much more, when upon his young soul the mildew has fallen; and the fruit, which with others is only blasted after ripeness, with him is nipped in the first blossom and bud. And never again can such blights be made good; they strike in too deep, and leave such a scar that the air of Paradise might not erase it.

"Such blights that can never be made good," the chastening of experience, the deathbed struggle of his father, his mother an improvident widow, his own straggling lack of a future occupation; all of these burdens formed Melville's early sense of the ambiguity, the chaos of life quite as much as the Dutch Reform Calvinism of his mother and underlined his surpassing sympathy for the pagan, the ignorant, even the evil. The black-comedy subtitle of *Redburn* is "Son-of-a-Gentleman, in the Merchant Service." A friend, seeing off the young recruit, tells the captain to take good care of him since his uncle is a senator and the boy's father had crossed the ocean many times on important business. On shore the captain appeared to take this information in an agreeable manner, but once at sea he violently spurns the boy's misbegotten idea of paying a friendly visit to his cabin. In the midst of young Redburn's good manners and proper upbringing, his being the son of a Melville and a Gansevoort is a grotesque irrelevance; the truth of his life as others see it is his abject pennilessness, his humbling ragged clothes.

He will be homesick and yet the anonymity, the nakedness of background are not unwelcome. The ocean is an escape and not a practical decision, not a job from which a young man could send money home to honor a struggling family. It is common in Melville's seagoing stories to find that once back in port the crew will be robbed of its miserable wages by the inspired accounting chicanery of the captain and the owners. Melville's first voyage did nothing to deflect the furtive position of his family when the importunate grocer, landlord, or dress-maker knocked on the door.

Going to sea gave Melville his art, but it also set him apart by dras-tic experience from most of those who surrounded him. He sat at his desk dressed in a shirt and tie and went about as a gentleman, if a somewhat shabby one in the matter of clean linen as Hawthorne noted some years later. Of his seventy-two years, Melville was an active sea-man for only about three and a half, but he returned from those years with an imagination peopled with the ferociously unstable, the demonic, the miserable, the flogged and the floggers, the bestiality in the crowded befouled quarters on a US Navy ship as well as on the whalers. Haw-thorne, whom he met in the Berkshires, had spent his youth at Bowdoin College where his friends were Longfellow and Franklin Pierce, later to be president. Melville's years at sea, along with perhaps troubling sexual yearnings, left him a man shaded, at heart a stranger hiking about country trails, bearing children, drinking brandy and smoking cigars with those who knew the outcast as only a phantom on the streets or locked up in asylums.

The first voyage: In *Redburn*, on board the *Highlander*, as the fictional ship is named, there is a man named Jackson, one of the most loath-some portraits in Melville's fiction. About him, a descriptive vocabulary of depravity is summoned with a special intensity. Yellow as gamboge, bald except for hair behind his ears that looked like a worn-out shoe-brush, nose broken down the middle, a squinting eye, the foul lees and dregs of a man. Jackson is wasting away from his "infamous vices," venereal disease, and yet he is or was the best seaman on board, a bully feared by all the men, this "wolf, or starved tiger," with his "deep, subtle, infernal looking eye." He had been at sea since the age of eight and "had passed through every kind of dissipation and abandonment in the worst parts of the world." He told "with relish" of having crewed on a slave ship where the slaves were "stowed, hue and point, like logs, and the suffocated and dead were unmanacled" and thrown overboard.

Jackson's end comes on the return voyage when the ship is off Cape Cod. He orders "haul out to windward" and with a torrent of blood gushing from his lungs falls into the sea. Melville has imagined this ruined man with a visual and moral brilliance, shown his repellent body with an awful precision, and yet consider his concluding feelings about the miserable Jackson:

> He was a Cain afloat, branded on his yellow brow with some inscrutable curse, and going about corrupting and searing every heart that beat near him. But there seemed even more woe than wickedness about the man; and his wickedness seemed to spring from his woe; and for all his hideousness, there was that in his eye at times, that was ineffably pitiable and touching; and though there were moments when I almost hated this Jackson, yet I have pitied no man as I pitied him.

Jackson's woe, Ahab's "close-coiled woe," and Melville's woe in his youth. *Redburn* was written ten years after the first journey, after the publication of the three previous books. It is a return to his voyage on the *St. Lawrence*, but he has made Redburn a boy, a lad, a shabby waif even though when he himself set sail he was nineteen years old and there is no reason to believe he came on in tatters like the men prowling the waterfront, homeless, illiterate, and wasted. Still when Melville looked back he did so as a writer and magically created Redburn for the purposes of a kind of fiction and for his memories of Liverpool, his first foreign city. The personal accent of the opening pages of grief and forlornness are so striking that they may be read as a memory of the twelve-year-old Melville, the time of his father's death. Redburn carries his father's out-of-date guide to Liverpool and walks the streets in a mood of filial homage. "How differently my father must have appeared; perhaps in a blue coat, buff vest, and Hessian boots. And little did he think, that a son of his would ever visit Liverpool as a poor friendless sailor-boy." What Melville's eye perceives and how his intelligence judges it were quite apart from the conventional sightseeing of the charming dandy, his father. Instead, on a Liverpool street called Launcelott's-Hey, among the dreary, dingy warehouses, Redburn hears a feeble wail that leads to a searing dirge.

In a cellar beneath the old warehouse, he sees a figure who "had been a woman." On her livid breast there are "two shrunken things like children." They have crawled into the space to die. The sailor inquires about the terrible sight, questions ragged, desperate old women in the alleys. The old beggarly people, destitute themselves, are contemptuous of the ghastly family group who have had nothing to eat for three days. A policeman shrugs; the lady at Redburn's rooming house refuses help; the cook, when asked for food, "broke out in a storm of swearing." Redburn snatches some bread and cheese and drops it down the vault. Frail hands grasped at the food but were too weak to catch hold. There is a murmuring sound asking "faintly [for] something like 'water'" and Redburn runs to a tavern for a pitcher, refused unless he pays for it as he cannot. In his tarpaulin hat he draws water from Boodle Hydrants and returns to the vault.

> The two girls drank out of the hat together; looking up at me with an unalterable, idiotic expression, that almost made me faint. The woman spoke not a word, and did not stir.... I tried to lift the woman's head; but, feeble as she was, she seemed bent upon holding it down. Observing her arms still clasped upon her bosom, and that something seemed hidden under the rags there, a thought crossed my mind, which impelled me forcibly to withdraw her hands for a moment; when I caught a glimpse of a meager little babe, the lower part of its body thrust into an old bonnet. Its face was dazzlingly white, even in its squalor, but the closed eyes looked like balls of indigo. It must have been dead some hours....
>
> When I went to dinner, I hurried into Launcelott's-Hey, where I found that the vault was empty. In place of the woman and children, a heap of quick-lime was glistening.

The scene of tragic extremity is composed with a rhetorical brilliance: the dying children with "eyes, and lips, and ears *like any queen*," with hearts which, "though they did not bound with blood, yet beat with a dull, dead ache that was their life"; and the dramatic insertion of pushing the mother's arm aside to reveal yet another being, a dead baby; and the return the next day to find the hole filled with *glistening* quicklime. Here we have the last rites, a gravestone offered for a street burial, a requiem for a hole in Launcelott's-Hey—the majestic reverence of Herman Melville.

Redburn visits the noted sights of Liverpool, hears the Chartist soap-box orators, street singers, men selling verses on current murders and other happenings; pawn shops, the impoverished dredging the river for bits of rope, the rush of life that brings to mind Dickens and also Mayhew's study of the obscure populace in *London Labour and the London Poor.* Throughout Melville's writings there is a liberality of mind, a freedom from vulgar superstition, occasions again and again for an oratorical insertion of enlightened opinion. Note a side glance in Liverpool, written in the year 1849:

> Three or four times, I encountered our black steward, dressed very handsomely, and walking arm in arm with a good-looking English woman. In New York, such a couple would have been mobbed in three minutes; and the steward would have been lucky to have escaped with whole limbs. Owing to the friendly reception extended to them, and the unwonted immunities they enjoy in Liverpool, the black cooks and stewards on American ships are very much attached to the place and like to make voyages to it . . . at first I was surprised that a colored man should be treated as he is in this town; but a little reflection showed that, after all, it was but recognizing his claims to humanity and normal equality; so that, in some things we Americans leave to other countries the carrying out of the principle that stands at the head of our Declaration of Independence.

Sentiment and agitation for the emancipation of the slaves was common enough in the Northeast at the time, but Melville's "reflection" was a stretch of opinion to include the right of a black man and a white woman to mingle as they wished socially and, he seems to be saying, sexually. When the Civil War arrived, Melville followed it with some distress of spirit about the slaughter. Around the conflict he wrote, in *Battle-Pieces*, the finest of his poems.

In the docks Redburn observes the emigrants crowding into the ships to make their way to America. Again Melville speaks:

> There was hardly any thing I witnessed in the docks that interested me more than the German emigrants who come on board the large New York ships several days before their sailing, to make everything comfortable ere starting.... And among these sober Germans, my country counts the most orderly and valuable of her foreign population.... There is something in the contemplation of the mode in which America has been settled, that, in a noble breast, should forever extinguish the prejudices of national dislikes.... You can not spill a drop of American blood without spilling the blood of the whole world.... Our blood is as the flood of the Amazon, made up of a thousand currents all pouring into one. We are not a nation, so much as a world; ... we are without father or mother.*

2.

The last pages of *Redburn* introduce the ineffable Harry Bolton, a young Englishman met on the Liverpool docks. Bolton is perfectly formed, "with curling hair, and silken muscles.... His complexion was a mantling brunette, feminine as a girl's; his feet were small; his hands were white; and his eyes were large, black, and womanly; and, poetry

---

*Philip Rahv, in a collection of essays, *Discovery of Europe* (Houghton Mifflin, 1947), reprints passages from *Redburn* and comments about the description of the German emigrants: "An extraordinarily moving celebration of the hopes lodged in the New World and one of the noblest pleas in our literature for the extinction of national hatreds and racial prejudice."

aside, his voice was as the sound of a harp." A warm friendship develops and in the fiction Redburn and Bolton go from Liverpool to London for a curious bit of private tourism. In London there is a remarkable visit to a male brothel—a strange, fastidiously observed, rococo urban landscape unlike any other dramatic intrusion in Melville's writings or in American literature at the time.

Some commentators speculate that Melville's dislike of *Redburn* was owing to his subsequent realization that he had exposed his own homoerotic longings. Whatever his unconscious or privately acknowledged feelings may have been, Melville was innocent of the instinct for self-protection on the page. The readers of his own time, the publishers and booksellers do not seem to have paused before the enthusiastic and relishing adjectives surrounding male beauty. Hershel Parker's monumental biography has gathered the reviews, and the complaint about the Harry Bolton pages is that they are an unsuitable "intrusion," largely for reasons of fictional crafting. Parker quotes an odd mention of the alliance between Redburn and Harry Bolton: "A dash of romance thrown in amongst a cluster of familiar and homely incidents" is the quotation; impossible to parse except as an instance of the relaxed language and hasty reading of reviewers for the press.

In *Redburn*, the boat is in the Liverpool harbor and the crew is free to roam the city, and Melville is free to have his young hero meet the intriguing person named Harry Bolton. Bolton is lifelike as a certain type of frenzied, melodramatic young homosexual down on his luck and as such he is as embarrassing and interesting as life itself. Redburn, that is, Melville at his desk, is both accepting and suspicious of Harry, but there is everything about the encounter as told that seems to reveal either a striking innocence of heart and mind or a defiance in offering the scenes to the public. Nothing in the early parts of the novel would lead us to anticipate the extravagant, interesting, sudden dive into a richly decorated underworld.

The two meet on the streets of Liverpool and Redburn is immediately attracted. Harry is not a dumb, deadened fish in the human pool of the seamen; he is a friendly stranger, an English youth, fluent in self-creation. It is difficult to imagine how this handsome youth with the perfectly formed legs and so on, this "delicate exotic from the conservatories of some Regent-street," came to the "potato-patches of Liverpool." In a bar, Harry will be chatting about the possibility of going to America and thus the friendship with this "incontrovertible son of a gentleman" begins. Harry will tell his story: born in the old city of Bury St. Edmunds, orphaned, but heir to a fortune of five thousand pounds. Off to the city, where with gambling sportsmen and dandies his fortune is lost to the last sovereign.

More elaboration from the new friend: embarked for Bombay as a midshipman in the East India service, claimed to have handled the masts, and was taken on board Redburn's ship which was not due to leave for a few days. Together in the roadside inns, every fascination— more news about the companion and his friendship with the Marquis of Waterford and Lady Georgiana Theresa, "the noble daughter of an anonymous earl."

Harry is stone-broke one moment, but darts away and will return with money which will provide for an astonishing trip to London. (There is no record of a trip from Liverpool to London during this early journey in 1839 nor by the time the book was published in 1849 when Melville sailed to London for the first time almost two weeks after the publication of *Redburn*.) When they alight in the city, Harry puts on a mustache and whiskers as a "precaution against being recognized by his own particular friends in London." A feverish atmosphere of hysteria and panic falls upon poor Harry and is part of the chiaroscuro mastery with which his character and the club scene that follows are so brilliantly rendered. And fearlessly rendered in sexual images of decadence and privilege in an astonishing embrace.

The club is a "semi-public place of opulent entertainment" described in a mixture of subterranean images—Paris catacombs—and *faux* Farnese Palace decorations. In the first room entered, there is a fresco ceiling of elaborate detail. Under the gas lights it seems to the bewildered gaze of Redburn to have the glow of the "moon-lit garden of Portia at Belmont; and the gentle lovers, Lorenzo and Jessica, lurked somewhere among the vines." There are obsequious waiters dashing about, under the direction of an old man "with snow-white hair and whiskers, and in a snow-white jacket—he looked like an almond tree in blossom...." In a conventional club manner, there are knots of gentlemen "with cut decanters and taper-waisted glasses, journals and cigars, before them."

Redburn, throughout the scene, is curious and alarmed by Harry's way of leaving him standing alone in this unaccountable atmosphere. They proceed to a more private room; so thick are the Persian carpets he feels he is sinking into "some reluctant, sedgy sea." Oriental ottomans "wrought into plaited serpents" and pornographic pictures "Martial and Suetonius mention as being found in the private cabinet of the Emperor Tiberius." A bust of an old man with a "mysteriously-wicked expression, and imposing silence by one thin finger over his lips. His marble mouth seemed tremulous with secrets."

Harry in a frantic return to private business suddenly puts a letter into Redburn's hand, which he is to post if Harry does not return by morning. And off he goes, but not before introducing Redburn to the attendant as young Lord Stormont. For the now terrified American, penniless son of a senator and so on, the place seemed "infected" as if "some eastern plague had been imported." The door will partly open and there will be a "tall, frantic man, with clenched hands, wildly darting through the passage, toward the stairs." On Redburn goes in images of fear and revulsion. "All the mirrors and marbles around me seemed crawling over with lizards; and I thought to myself, that though gilded and golden, the serpent of vice is a serpent still." The macabre excursion with its slithering images passes as in a tormented dream and Harry returns to say, "I am off for America; the game is up."

The relation between the two resumes its boyish pleasantries. Back on ship, Harry, in full *maquillage*, comes on deck in a "brocaded dressing-gown, embroidered slippers, and tasseled smoking-cap to stand his morning watch." When ordered to climb the rigging, he falls into a faint and it becomes clear that his account of shipping to Bombay was another handy fabrication. Nevertheless, Redburn remains faithful in friendship, and they land in New York. The chapter heading is: "Redburn and Harry, Arm and Arm, in Harbor." Redburn shows him around, introduces him to a friend in the hope of finding work, and then leaves him as he must, since he could hardly take the swain back to Lansingburgh. Years later he will learn that Harry Bolton had signed on another ship and fallen or jumped overboard.

In the novel there is another encounter, this of lyrical enthusiasm untainted by the infested London underworld. It is Carlo, "with thick clusters of tendril curls, half overhanging the brows and delicate ears." His "naked leg was beautiful to behold as any lady's arm, so soft and rounded, with infantile ease and grace." He goes through life playing his hand organ in the streets for coins. Now, on the deck, Redburn sinks into a paroxysm of joy at the sound of the "humble" music:

> Play on, play on, Italian boy! . . . Turn hither your pensive, morning eyes . . . let me gaze fathoms down into thy fathomless eye. . . . All this could Carlo do—make, unmake me; . . . and join me limb to limb. . . . And Carlo! ill betide the voice that ever greets thee, my Italian boy, with aught but kindness; cursed the slave who ever drives thy wondrous box of sights and sounds forth from a lordling's door!

The scenes with Harry Bolton were not much admired; as an "intrusion," contemporary critics seemed to rebuke them for structural defects rather than for the efflorescent adjectives, the swooning intimacy of feeling for male beauty of a classical androgynous perfection that will reach its transcendence in the innocent loveliness of Billy Budd, his heartbreaking death-bed vision.

Hershel Parker, the encyclopedic biographer and tireless Melville scholar, finds no charm in the "flaccid" Harry Bolton and has interesting thoughts on why Melville was so clearly dismissive of Redburn, a work of enduring interest. "What he thought he was doing in it, as a young married man and a new father, is an unanswered question." And: ". . . Only a young and still naïve man could have thought that he could write a kind of psychological autobiography . . . without suffering any consequences." Parker suggests that Melville came to understand the folly of what he had written, came to acknowledge that he had revealed homosexual longings or even homosexual experience.

Parker provides another item in the atmosphere that surrounded the days and nights of the writer. At the time, there sprang up in America a group called the Come-Outers, a sect wishing to follow Paul's exhortation in II Corinthians 6:17: "Wherefore come out from them, and be ye separate." It was the object of the group to reveal information ordinarily held private. Parker's research seems to indicate that Melville knew about the sect, but did not notice that he had "unwittingly joined the psychological equivalent of this new American religious sect; in mythological terms, he had opened Pandora's box when he thought he was merely describing the lid."

It is not clear whether the Come-Outers were, as in the present use of the term, to announce themselves as homosexual when such revelations were relevant. In the biblical text, Paul seems to be referring to Corinthians who were worshiping idols or pretending to virtues they did not practice, such as sorrow while rejoicing, pretending poverty while piling up riches.

However, if Melville rejected *Redburn* because he came to see it as an embarrassing and unworthy self-revelation, why did he open the pages of the subsequent *Moby-Dick* with the tender, loving union of Queequeg and Ishmael, a charming, unprecedented *Mann und Weib*? Another wonder about life and art: Where did Melville come upon the ornate and lascivious men's club he described with feral acuteness in *Redburn*? There is no record found in the cinder and ashes of Melville's jottings to bring the night journey into history. But does the blank forever erase the possibility that the extraordinary diversion actually took place? Harder to credit that Melville, in his imagination or from what is sometimes called his use and abuse of sources, was altogether free of the lush, disorienting opening of the door.

The presence of delicate, hardly seaworthy men, some in officer positions on the rigorously hierarchical sailing vessels, is an occupational puzzle that has the accent of reportage, or at least, of plausibility. In *Omoo*, Captain Guy, the commander of the ship, is not one of the usual, pipe-smoking tyrants, but an original being. He is "no more suited to sea-going than a hair-dresser." In one astonishing scene, we find the captain coming from his quarters to investigate the noise of a fight. In perfect "camp" rhythm, Melville's companion, called Doctor Long Ghost, cries out, "Ah! Miss Guy, is that you? Now, my dear, go right home, or you'll get hurt." Selvagee, in *White-Jacket*, with his cologne-baths, lace-bordered handkerchiefs, cravats, and curling irons, although an inept sailor, is a lieutenant on a US naval ship.

Jack Chase, the educated, manly friend in *White-Jacket*, was an actual shipmate never to be forgotten. A man of the world, a brave, respected seaman of the foretop who recites to the winds verses from Camoëns. Yet he is something of a misfit like most sailors; he drinks and wanders the world as he will. Chase stayed in the heart, forever cherished, the only unwavering, beyond the family, friendship of Melville's life. In *White-Jacket* he is addressed: "Wherever you may now be rolling over the blue billows, dear Jack! take my best love along with you, and God bless you, wherever you go!" The same sense of the beloved lost wanderer will forty years later illuminate the dedication to *Billy Budd*: "To Jack Chase, Englishman / Wherever that great heart may now be / Here on Earth or harbored in Paradise."

The beautiful Billy Budd is a foretopman, ready to climb up the rigging. He is far from the pretty street hustler Harry Bolton, for whom work under sail is a mysterious and burdensome affliction. Billy is strong, free, and innocent; an illiterate, an orphan, reminding one of a freshly hatched, brilliantly colored bird. He has the body of a Greek Hercules, with a "lingering adolescent expression in the as yet smooth face all but feminine in purity of natural complexion . . . the ear, small and shapely." In the story, Claggart, the master-at-arms, takes a violent dislike, a raging enmity, to the popular young seaman. He will accuse Billy of wanting to bring the crew to mutiny and, in a confrontation in the captain's cabin, an outraged Billy strikes a blow which kills Claggart. According to marine law, Billy must be hanged and his body cast into the sea.

Melville, in the careful examination of Claggart's soul, inserts a very modern reflection that looks beneath an unnatural enmity and finds there a twisted, jealous, thwarted love.

When Claggart's unobserved glance happened to light on belted Billy rolling along the upper gun deck in the leisure of the second dogwatch . . . that glance would follow the cheerful sea Hyperion with a settled meditative and melancholy expression, his eyes strangely suffused with incipient feverish tears. Then would Claggart look like the man of sorrows. Yes, and sometimes the melancholy expression would have in it a touch of soft yearning, as if Claggart could even have loved Billy but for fate and ban.

Thinking about the sharp stabs in the thicket of Claggart's character, the critic F. O. Matthiessen writes: ". . . A writer today would be fully aware of what may have been only latent for Melville, the sexual element in Claggart's ambivalence. Even if Melville did not have this consciously in mind, it emerges for the reader now with intense psychological accuracy."

Melville married Elizabeth Shaw, the daughter of Judge Lemuel Shaw of the Massachusetts Supreme Court. They had four children, one of whom, the son Malcolm, put a gun to his head. The marriage was deeply troubled during the time Melville, in another riveting, iconographic biographical fact, was chained to his desk in the New York Custom House for nineteen years. A separation was considered but the couple persevered for forty-four years. Whether the fated meeting with Harry Bolton in *Redburn* opened a seam of private apostasy in Melville's life is not known. There are no love letters, no uncovered affairs with male or female "arm-in-arm, in harbor." The fair young men have a dreamlike quality that fades with the break of day and there we leave them.

2000

THE TORRENTS OF WOLFE
Thomas Wolfe

ON THE matter of a manuscript written by Thomas Wolfe, we find his *agent* busy at work.

I've been cutting like mad since it came and have got it down to ten thousand and a half by cutting *very* stringently.

I.

Thomas Wolfe, were he living today, would be a hundred years old. Thus the year marks his centennial, along with that of a few others, including Louis Armstrong. The moment is honored by an exhibition at the New York Public Library, a celebration at the University of North Carolina, and by the publication of the original typescript of *O Lost*, the title that became *Look Homeward, Angel*, Thomas Wolfe's first book. There is disagreement about the number of words eliminated by Maxwell Perkins, an editor at Scribner's—was it 90,000 words or a mere 66,000? The editors of *O Lost* have toiled over word counts, common typographical errors, spacings, and so on, and have come up with some interesting numbers. "With the same typography and design as the 626-page *Look Homeward, Angel*, it [the original manuscript] would have made a book of about 825 pages—not impossible to publish in one volume, as this edition demonstrates. *Gone with the Wind* (1936) had 1,037 pages."

Sometimes Thomas Wolfe seems to belong to editorial history rather than to the annals of American literature. Maxwell Perkins, "Editor of Genius," as his biographer names him with some unintended obscurity: is the editor a genius or are we alerted to Ernest Hemingway,

F. Scott Fitzgerald, and Thomas Wolfe, among others who came under his care? Maxwell Perkins was modest about the professional duty or privilege to draw a pencil through one line or thousands. Thomas Wolfe was anxious but not modest about the gift to write the lines that made up his mountains of pages. We can read that to accommodate the excisions he would often write transitional passages of greater length than the matter deleted.

Thomas Wolfe died at the age of thirty-eight. While traveling out west he was taken very ill with pneumonia and, symptoms unabating, was transferred to Johns Hopkins Hospital in Baltimore, where he died of a tubercular lesion to the brain. He was outsize in every respect; hugeness is his dominating iconography. Six feet four-and-a-half inches tall; awkward, handsome, impressive, and intimidating. A prodigious drinker and brawler, sleepless to produce the pages that arrived at the publisher in a crate, or so it was said. As a writer, he became a statistic of extremity. He was vain in the belief in his talents, and insecure, unsteady in the manner of a refugee who has traveled far from the home that formed his being. *Lost, o lost*, he cries out again and again. *Hunger*, another word that dots the pages. Hunger for experience, for escape, for fame. Himself, every step of his journey, his family, that turbulent crowd of folks from which he came, each passage on a train, each face met on the way, landscape, voices, a thousand vignettes, history, memory uncanny, language at hand like water flowing down a stream. And with all this, a Southerner—there was that clinging to him also.

Thomas Wolfe was born in Asheville, North Carolina, a pleasant small city in the Great Smokies. The mountain air attracted tourists, among them George Vanderbilt, who built there one of those monuments to the imagination or lack of it, a "château" of 125 rooms which he named Biltmore. There were also rather grand hotels with suitable accommodations for well-to-do travelers. To these useful items of commerce, Thomas Wolfe's mother added a shabby rooming house that went by the name of "The Old Kentucky Home," translated to "Dixieland" in *Look Homeward, Angel*. In Asheville there were also "lungers," since the mountain air was felt to be helpful for the victims of tuberculosis.

Thomas Wolfe, the last child, had seven siblings, one of whom, his brother Grover, would die at the age of ten. The father, W. O. Wolfe, born in Pennsylvania to hard-luck farmers, early orphaned, with little education, was apprenticed to a stonecutter and showed talent for simple tombstones, as well as for decorative carvings of lambs and angels. Wolfe drifted to Raleigh, North Carolina, was something of a rake as the proceedings for his divorce indicated; second marriage forced by pregnancy of the wife, who was tubercular, and thus they trailed on to Asheville where she died. For her he had built a house and into it Thomas Wolfe's mother would move on their marriage. The father worked at his craft, but he was an alcoholic of serious, scandalous proportions; after a spree of days, picked up on the streets, carried home to bang on the door where his wife, inside, was screaming, Don't let him in here! and so on. The marriage was a raucous union of mutual distaste.

As the father wanders through the books of his son, he is a dramatic whiner, given to ornate accusations of abandonment and ill-treatment. His death is a misery, but his life on the page has a certain magnitude born of monstrous frustrations and ruined hopes. He is often a frightening father himself frightened by fate. At his deathbed:

> Nothing was left, now, to suggest his life of fury, strength and passion except his hands. And the hands were still the great hands of the stonecutter, powerful, sinewy, and hairy as they had always been, attached now with a shocking incongruity to the wasted figure of a scarecrow.

In the South, and perhaps elsewhere, when the father's origins are dim and better left in the shade, the mother is likely to bear the ancestral burden with some background flourish. So it was with Eliza Gant, true name Westall, known as the Pentland family in the novels. Her father was Major Pentland, "military title ... honestly if inconspicuously earned." The Pentland family was "as old as any in the community, but it had always been poor, and had made few pretenses to gentility. By marriage, and by intermarriage among its own kinsmen, it could boast of some connection with the great, or some insanity, and a modicum of idiocy."

Eliza Gant in fiction and apparently in life is a personal and historical phenomenon. Born before the Civil War, she is a born business woman, seeming to come by her bent as naturally as some girls are born flirts. Property, real estate was her calling. She could not take a walk without saying, "Do you see this corner here—the one you're on? It'll double in value in the next few years.... They're going to run a street through there some day as sure as you live. And when they do ... that property is going to be worth money." About her husband's trade she was skeptical: there's no money in death, people died too slowly in her calculation.

She took herself and most of her children off to Saint Louis at the time of the 1904 World's Fair and tried a business venture that did not work, and once back in Asheville, Altamont in the fictions, she bought Dixieland, a blight on her children's lives, but not on her life, as the owner and manager:

> Dixieland was a big cheaply constructed frame house of eighteen or twenty drafty high-ceilinged rooms; it had a rambling, un-planned, gabular appearance, and was painted a dirty yellow.... In winter, the wind blew howling blasts under the skirts of Dixieland.... Its big rooms were heated by a small furnace which sent up, when charged with fire, a hot dry enervation to the rooms on the first floor, and a gaseous but chill radiation to those upstairs.

Here in the disheveled, "murderous and bloody Barn," as the father called it, Eliza reigned with parsimony and grueling labor. She had the suspicious nature of a miser and could not keep help, colored, "never having been used to service," as her son wrote. The better lodgings had signs reading No Invalids, but Dixieland took anyone that knocked on the door. About a miserably coughing client, the mistress would say that the fellow had only a little bronchial trouble; girls of question-able occupation were agreeable young women who liked to have a good time. The children ate pick-up meals next to the stove and, until they could get away, were shifted from one attic room to another. The father stayed on in the previous house, ill, complaining with considerable rhetorical force to his nursemaid daughters. The church was a definition in small towns at the time; by birth the family was Presbyterian, a middling group in local faiths. The Presbyterians bowed to the richer Episcopalians, condescended to the Methodists, and snubbed the Baptists, but the Wolfes were not church-goers. In *Look Homeward, Angel* the Gants are tribal, occupying a bit of forest in the middle of downtown Asheville, North Carolina.

Thomas Wolfe, renaming himself Eugene Gant, made his way through the thicket into situations of surprising privilege. A good scholar, a reader, he would in the manner of small-town history come to the notice of an English teacher in the public schools. The English teacher: in American literary striving she will again and again appear as a creature of fable, or as Daddy Warbucks to a ragtag orphan. A private school was opened in the town and Wolfe was encouraged to enroll. The cost, the cost—at home a squall of thunder and lightning—but the change was accomplished. At the new school he studied Latin, Shakespeare, the classics, and graduated with honors. Since there is never an end to onward and upward, the next hotly disputed step was college, with the scholar dreaming of Princeton or the University of Virginia. It was to be the University of North Carolina at Chapel Hill. "Now, I've given my word; you'll go where I send you or you'll go no-where at all." And there he is at the end of *Look Homeward, Angel* before moving on to Harvard in *Of Time and the River*.

Look Homeward, Angel was published when Wolfe was twenty-nine years old. At Harvard he had the fantastic notion that his literary destiny was to be playwriting, a mode crippling to his marathon incli-nations. Plays went off to the Theatre Guild, but were not met with approval. *Look Homeward, Angel* was rejected by three publishers and finally turned up at Scribner's where it aroused interest and dismay over length and "other problems." The dismay, already mentioned, the editing, extensive, took on a life of its own, and the book brought Maxwell Perkins into the light with the result that more has been written about his struggle and friendship with Wolfe than about his professional work with Fitzgerald and Hemingway. The reviews of the book were favorable, but they do not bring to memory the affection remembered by those who first came upon it in their youth.

The phrase "O, Lost" might refer to the intense life in the street, the neighbors, the downtown stores, the undertaker, the lawyer, the fallen girl, the drunken pharmacist, the lewd old man who ran the grocery store—all lost in the present homogenization of the village by way of the malls, the motorcars in every yard, national brand-name establishments to take the place of the local enterprises long in one family. Reading *Look Homeward, Angel* is today a recovery of time or a visit to the bygone in the manner of nineteenth-century fiction with its blacksmiths, ragmen, people on foot for seven miles after returning from the sea. Even though it is only the 1920s and 1930s, the reading of Thomas Wolfe seems to need a shifting of mood on the part of the reader to accept the extravagant yearnings of Eugene Gant, the obsessive detail of train journeys, and the swarming challenges to the awkward young man from the mountains:

> He wanted opulent solitude. His dark vision burned on kingdoms under the sea, on windy castle crags, and on the deep elf kingdoms at the earth's core.... He saw for himself great mansions in the ground, grottoes buried in the deep heart of a hill.... Cool hidden cisterns would bring him air; from a peephole in the hillside he could look down on a winding road and see armed men seeking for him.... He would pull fat fish from subterranean pools, his great earth cellars would be stocked with old wine, he could loot the world of its treasures, including the handsomest women, and never be caught.

Thomas Wolfe is a knight on the road, threatened, but rich in armorial splendor. He will reclaim every step of the journey in book after book, an assertion of primordial selfhood. Yet, along the way, there are others who inflame his imagination as his fictional lust embraces the new private school, the owners, the mathematics teacher, the history teacher, preparation for dead-drunk frat nights at Chapel Hill. And then floating in a balloon of descriptive helium it is always back to Dixieland, "all the comforts of the Modern Jail," and the roomers with their "blue phthistic hands"; his brothers and sisters, their mates, their misbegotten efforts, illness and deathbeds. And that fellow in the streets, the great lung specialist:

> Dr. Fairfax Grinder, scion of one of the oldest and proudest families in Virginia, drove in viciously from Church Street, with his sinewy length of six feet and eight inches coiled tensely in the deep pit of his big Buick roadster. Cursing generally the whole crawling itch of Confederate and Yankee postwar rabbledom, with a few special parentheses for Jews and niggers, he drove full tilt at the short plump figure of Joe Zamschnick, men's furnishings ("Just a Whisper Off The Square").

The minuteness of the life around him, the voracious particulars, will battle on the pages with a gigantic abstraction, Eugene Gant:

> He felt that, no matter what leper's taint he might carry upon his flesh, there was in him a health that was greater than they could ever know—something fierce and cruelly wounded, but alive, that did not shrink away from the terrible sunken river of life; something desperate and merciless that looked steadily on the hidden and unspeakable passions that unify the tragic family of this earth.

Look Homeward, Angel was not written until Wolfe had taken a master's degree at Harvard, where he studied playwriting with George Pierce Baker, the Romantic poets with John Livingstone Lowes, and other classes with other professors. With recommendations from Baker and Lowes, he was given a position teaching English composition at the Washington Square College of New York University. When the first term ended, yet another journey for a "poor mountain boy": his mother was somehow persuaded to cough up the money for a trip abroad. England, Paris, Italy, Switzerland for nearly a year: the span to become *Of Time and the River*. On the boat coming home, he met Aline Bernstein, a successful stage and costume designer in New York who will read her story in *The Web and the Rock*. With her help, Wolfe was still trying to place his plays; another term of teaching, another trip abroad, paid for by Aline, and at last *Look Homeward, Angel* was begun. Hope, hysteria; book accepted by Scribner's, revision, excision, grateful compliance on the author's part punctuated by savage resistance, a bloody chapter in the history of publishing. John Hall Wheelock, poet and editor at Scribner's: "I am not aware of any book that has ever been edited so extensively up to that point."

The spindly bones of biography cannot explain why Thomas Wolfe with mad conceit and energy began to compose a voluptuous memorial to his own life, beginning with himself as an infant. In London, in New York, in Brooklyn, wherever he may be, he goes ever back to excavate the cemetery of his remains. *Look Homeward, Angel*, pure in ambition, dressed in the ornaments of his vast reading, rich, almost burdened with a grand style of adjective and metaphor, and homely enough in catching the diction, the pauses, the pretensions and evasions of the strangers and family that explode in the pages. *Look Homeward, Angel* is a pastoral of memory, a graveyard of youth and not a recording but a strange magnification shaped by an untamed imagination.

Of Time and the River, almost nine hundred pages, a farewell to home, a brother dead, a father dying, the train chugging north through Confederate states: "nothing by night but darkness and a space we call Viriginia through which the huge projectile of the train is hurtling onward in the dark." Wolfe sees himself always in a humbling shape: awkward, provincial, haunted, too large and cumbersome for his fragile, trembling inner life. Now he is stumbling through the magical doors of the Widener Library at Harvard: "He pictured himself as tearing the entrails from a book as from a fowl," and claims that "within a period of ten years he read at least 20,000 volumes—deliberately the number is set low—and opened the pages and looked through many times that number." It is no wonder he piled up manuscript with the same gluttony for numbers. At night through a "hundred streets," looking into the faces of a "million people"; "rivers, plains, and mountains and 10,000 sleeping towns; it seemed to him that he saw everything at once." Such is his plot in the novels, himself a numerical grandiosity, at the same time also grossly unhappy, ravenously uncertain and suffering.

The books are rescued by other people, a great talent for vignette, the novellas within the novel. In Boston Uncle Bascom Pentland-Hawke, a curiosity, a local eccentric in the Dickens mode. Once a minister with a Harvard theology degree, he is now in a grimy antique of a building as Conveyancer and Title Expert for the Brill Realty Company. A scarecrow, a miser, in old clothes turned green from wear, a food nut eating only chopped-up carrots, onions, turnips, and raw potatoes, daily in an office of colleagues fashioned in a similar peculiarity. At home with Uncle Bascom in a mock rant against women:

> O, I feel *so* sick! O, dreary *me*, now! I think my *time* is coming on again! O, you don't *love* me any mo-o-ore! ... O, I wish you'd bring me something *nice* from *ta-own*! O, if you loved me you'd buy me a *new* hat!

"A Portrait of Bascom Hawke" was published in *Scribner's Magazine* and tied for first place in the $5,000 Short Novel Prize. However, in *Of Time and the River* Perkins and Wheelock thought it a digression and sliced it into sections interspersed here and there.

Professor Baker-Hatcher's playwriting class and student dialogue: "...The play is nothing.... It's the *sets*—the *sets* are really quite remarkable." Wolfe's portrait of the celebrated professor is impudent and never more so than when he is being respectful to a figure he was aching to impress. "All the professors thought he looked like an actor and all the actors thought he looked like a professor." He would advise the students to brush up on their French and look in on De Musset's "charming trifle." Very *casually* and without *pretense*, his lectures were enlivened by "The last time I was in London, Pinero and I were having lunch together one day at the Savoy" and "I have a letter here from 'Gene O'Neill which bears on that very point. Perhaps you'd be interested in knowing what he has to say about it."

Again, he once came back from New York with an amusing story of a visit he had paid to the famous producer, David Belasco. And he described drolly how he had followed a barefoot, snaky-looking female ... through seven gothic chambers mystical with chimes and incense. And finally he told how he had been ushered into the presence of the great ecclesiastic who sat at the end of a cathedral-like room beneath windows of church glass.

Scattered throughout the pages, more novellas trapped between the impassioned trips back to North Carolina for his father's death and his own drunken nights in Boston. Francis Starwick, an assistant to Professor Baker, invites the bumbling titan Eugene Gant to dinner at the Cock Horse Tavern on Brattle Street. Starwick has the appearance of "those young Englishmen painted by Hoppner and Raeburn": his speaking voice is refined, free from identifying regionalism. He is a dandy, clever in finding the right place to live: fluent, sophisticated in a way that causes Eugene to see him as a rich boy pampered from birth. It will turn out that Starwick is a self-creation of the accumulated flair that took him away from an ordinary family in Illinois, from humiliation as the teacher's pet, a local affected "aesthete."

Starwick has his secret Italian restaurant, Pothillipo's, far from Harvard Square, where he negotiates the dinner in restaurant French and Italian with the bowing waiter Nino:

> When this great ceremony was over, Frank Starwick had done nothing more nor less than order the one-dollar table d'hôte dinner which Signor "Pothillippo" provided for all the patrons of his establishment and whose order—soup, fish, spaghetti, roasted chicken, salad, ice-cream, cheese, nuts and bitter coffee—was unchangeable as destiny, and not to be altered by the whims of common men, whether they would or no.

Years later, after Harvard, the narrator will meet Starwick in the Louvre in Paris and join him and the two attractive Boston women with whom he is traveling for over one hundred pages of youth abroad; their trips, quarrels, sightseeing, money problems, jealousies, and at last a fierce finale. Along the way, Starwick picks up a young Frenchman, Alec, with whom he disappears for days, and also along the way Eugene is seized with recognition of his friend's nature and falls into an almost biblical rage against the infidel, the faithless enemy. The word, the "foul word was out at last"—"you dirty little fairy." He catches Starwick by the throat and slams him against "the facade of a building with such brutal violence that Starwick's head bounced and rattled on the stone":

> And at that moment, Eugene felt an instant, overwhelming revulsion of shame, despair, and sick horror.... He thought he had killed Starwick.... Starwick's frail body retained its langorous dignity and grace ... the buckling weight of the unconscious figure slumped in a movement of terrible and beautiful repose— the same movement that one sees in a great painting of Christ lowered from the cross.... There are some people who possess such a natural dignity of person—such a strange and rare inviolability of flesh and spirit.... If such an insult be intended, if such violence be done, the act returns a thousandfold upon the one who does it ... he will relive his crime a thousand times in all the shame and terror of inexpiable memory.

Wolfe always remains a yokel despite his travels, his learning; and he will struggle with the common heritage of response, seeming so clear and ordained, the many notions brought from home that will be blurred and challenged by the world his shaky fame will leave on his doorstep.

2.

The spectacular, torrential talent races on in *Of Time and the River*; it is a contest with the impossible flood of experience, the maelstrom years of youth, the overwrought competition to outpace the threatening limits of language. The homeward-bound ship itself, a construction of 60,000 tons, is a dreamlike apparition to be given shape by words: "sucking continents towards her, devouring sea and land; she was made to enter European skies like some stranger from another world... to pulse and glow under the soft, wet European sky."

Of Time and the River received many favorable notices and many snarls of fatigue, as if reading the crowded, everlasting pages were an overtime, unpaid chore. More travels abroad, lawsuits, the affair with Aline Bernstein, and a break with Scribner's. *Of Time and the River* was the last of the long books published in Wolfe's lifetime. *The Web and the Rock* and *You Can't Go Home Again* were published from manuscript by Harper's and edited or pieced together by the editor Edward Aswell. The break with Scribner's and Maxwell Perkins is a tangle of murky emotions and conditions: no contract for subsequent books, challenged financial terms, and most of all perhaps Wolfe's chagrin over the gossip that claimed Perkins as the coauthor or at least the instrument by which chaotic, unpublishable pages were shaped into a book. The publication just now of *O Lost*, the original typescript of *Look Homeward, Angel*, shows that the editor has not been born who could write a book of this kind; what he could do was to cut it like a tailor.

The Web and the Rock and *You Can't Go Home Again*, each near to seven hundred pages when published, were left in the hands of Edward Aswell at Harper's. David Herbert Donald's 1987 biography of Thomas Wolfe gives an accounting of Mr. Aswell's exuberant combat with the manuscripts. Aswell's wife noted, "Theirs was to be the Great Collaboration—Tom's genius combined with Ed's power of organization." The howlings by agents, editors, and reviewers that the books were "too autobiographical" had led Wolfe to transform Eugene Gant into George Webber, as the narrator. A horrible mistake, as Maxwell Perkins noted later.

Name changes out of fear of libel, constructing "a pastiche out of several drafts, rearranging the episodes in the love story"; transitional passages written by Aswell himself; the inclusion of an introduction to *The Web and the Rock* taken from a letter written by Wolfe but unfinished and never mailed. In *You Can't Go Home Again*, the creation of a character named Randy Shepperton entirely from the brain of Mr. Aswell.

The biographer's conclusion: "Aswell moved on to modifying the rhythms of his [Wolfe's] prose, altering his characterizations, and to cutting and shaping his chapters . . . and his interference seriously eroded the integrity of Wolfe's text. Far from deserving commendation, Aswell's editorial interference was, both from the standpoint of literature and of ethics, unacceptable."

As a composition, *The Web and the Rock* is an effort to outwit editorial and critical objections. Halfhearted narrative disguises; George Webber, called Monk in youth and persisting; a new family, the Joyners, to replace that of Eliza Gant in the previous books and to avoid the anger of the family and that of certain Asheville citizens. "About 1885, John Webber met a young woman of Libya Hill named Amelia Joyner. . . . In the next fifteen years they had no children, until, in 1900, their son George was born." So, Eugene Gant has now become an only child. His mother dies and he goes to live with Joyner relatives, to be raised by Aunt Maw, a spinster, "a rusty crone of fate." Along the many pages, he will attend not Chapel Hill but an "old, impoverished backwoods college" called Pine Rock and mostly interested in the football team. Much was invented, but again living persons saw themselves caricatured in the Eugene Gant-George Webber overwhelming passion to leave a record of the flow of his actual days and nights.

Before death overtakes, he will have his one love affair to scorch the pages of *The Web and the Rock* and *You Can't Go Home Again*. Aline Bernstein met Wolfe on the boat coming home from Europe, parted with him at the dock; they united when Wolfe wrote a letter asking to see her again. Aline Bernstein was the daughter of a well-known actor, Joseph Frankau, and had spent her childhood in a theatrical boarding house on West 44th Street. When the meeting took place she was an established costume and set designer, married to a successful stockbroker, the mother of two children, eighteen years older than Thomas Wolfe, and Jewish. She will be Esther Jack in the novels:

She became the most beautiful woman that ever lived—and not in any symbolic or idealistic sense—but with all the blazing, literal, and mad concreteness of his imagination. She became the creature of incomparable loveliness, the creature with whose image he would for years walk the city's swarming streets.

They go to a theatrical performance down on the East Side in Manhattan and Thomas Wolfe, still a hopeful dramatist, is immediately overcome with a contempt for the audience, for sophisticated people who are suddenly his enemies and "who would really undermine and wreck his work if he allowed them to." Twitches of paranoia are a natural companion to the self-aggrandizing soul of Thomas Wolfe in New York, where everyone caught alone is a mouse. As for the loved one, Mrs. Jack, "this flushed, rosy, and excited little person... she seemed almost to belong to another world, a world of simple joy... of sweetness and of naturalness, of innocence and morning."

Esther Jack is cheerful, energetic, and a convicted "prisoner of love." The place in which George Webber is living is a squalid dump and she will find a large floor in an old house on Waverly Place, "send a man in tomorrow to wash the windows and to scrub the floors" and furnish the place with things from her own house. She knows the best butchers and greengrocers and cooks huge meals like a farm wife, while working and coming back with stories of famous people and grand parties, which will cause her lover to think of half the population living "in filth and squalor." "How *could* she be a part of it?... It whipped his spirit to a frenzy, it made him turn on her at times and rend her, bitterly accuse her with unjust and cruel words."

George Webber describes his destruction of love with chilling credibility; jealousy, accusation, maniacal demands, monstrous envy, pages and pages of domestic argument blasting through the walls:

He: Do anything you damn please—just leave me alone, that's all!

She: He got what he wanted from her... used her for what she was worth to him.... Now she's no use to him anymore!

He: Used you! Why, you—you—you hussy, you—what do you
   mean by used *you*! Used *me*, you mean!

He rages against "the whole damned crowd of million-dollar Jew and
Gentile aesthetes" who despise him. She: "They neither love nor hate
you. Most of them have never heard of you." The affair is broken and
he is off again for the seventh trip abroad, where in a drunken brawl
at the Oktoberfest in Munich he gets badly beaten up.

You Can't Go Home Again returns to Esther Jack and the long, crowded
pages of imagined and lived scenes are as brilliant as any to be found
in Wolfe's writings. It begins with a curious evocation of Mr. Jack, the
husband, waking up in their apartment on Park Avenue a few days
before the 1929 stock market crash. The bedroom "was one of modest
and almost austere simplicity, subtly combined with a sense of spaciousness, wealth, and power." The bathroom where we will find Mr. Jack
shaving has creamy porcelain and polished silver fixtures. "He liked
the tidy, crowded array of lotions, creams, unguents, bottles, tubs, jars,
brushes"; he mixes the hot and cold water, does a few exercises—all a
wild presumption about the husband of the loved one.

   Mr. Jack in the portrait is a solid, comfortable man of Wall Street,
neither "cruel nor…immoderate," who likes the social swim, is kind
and generous to a friend in need. He is driven to his office by his chauffeur, who is reckless and a swindler in the matter of bills for gasoline,
oil, and tires, which Mr. Jack can accept as the way of the world. He
will help people down on their luck, friends, relatives, and superannuated domestics, but in the false world of speculation such men did not
see themselves as gamblers, but as "brilliant executives of great affairs."
Thus a double edge, not quite so pleasing to the piercing sense of exclusion George Webber is born with as Mr. Jack is born with his distance
from George's furious, "envenomed passages of night." The moral superiority of his own distress, madness, and longing is a dogma, a sacred
oil or unguent in all of Wolfe's encounters with riches or power.

   Esther Jack wakes up in the Park Avenue apartment where she is planning a great party that evening which George will attend. She is usually glowing, jolly, filled with "immortal confidence"; and then again somber and brooding:

> She was three parts a Jewess, and in her contemplative moods the ancient, dark, and sorrowful quality of her race seemed to take complete possession of her....This look...had always troubled George Webber when he saw it because it suggested some secret knowledge buried deep within the woman whom he loved and whom he believed he had come to know.

However, this morning she is struggling with her drunken Irish maid, Nora, in scenes of bright household comedy. In a section called "Service Entrance" the doorman, the man on the front elevator, and the one on the service elevator are introduced with their squabbles, complaints, and doorman obsequiousness, each to play his part in the disaster of the coming evening party. A face, a brief encounter or thicker association with the hundreds that appear in the fictions are magically enlivened by individual patterns of speech, psychological quirks, private history the writer could not have known. "Autobiography" is merely the outer skin, tags of character, not what is accomplished by the imagination in the unaccountable, unrelenting scribbled flood.

At the party, "The hour has now arrived for Mr. Piggy Logan and his celebrated circus of wired dolls." The puppet show, a fleeting rage in the city, appears to be an inspiration created by Alexander "Sandy" Calder:

> There were miniature circus rings made of rounded strips of tin or copper which fitted neatly together. There were ... an astonishing variety of figures made of wire to represent all the animals and performers. There were clowns and trapeze artists, acrobats and tumblers, horses and bareback lady riders.

The trapeze act was the first failure when the two flying dolls failed to catch hands. The sword-swallowing act, a hatpin to go down the mouth of a rag doll, only succeeded in tearing the stuffing out, but the cheerful Mr. Piggy went on. Friends of his, which included some young women that had the "unmistakeable look of having gone to Miss Spence's school" crowded the devastated living room and turned the lavish evening party into a New York item of gossip. And then outside the roar of a fire truck.

Smoke is filling the halls and the guests rush out, but downstairs the elevator men are struggling to get up to an old lady on a high floor. She has made her way out, but the two elevator men on their mission of rescue are stuck when the power goes out and will die of smoke inhalation. For George: "He has sensed how the hollow pyramid of a false social structure had been erected and sustained upon a base of common mankind's blood and sweat and agony." It is the signal for a break with Esther Jack:

> And to make it easier, for her as well as for himself, there was one thing he would not tell her. It would be surer, swifter, kinder not to tell her that he loved her still, that he would always love her, that no one else could ever take her place.

The virtues of Aline Bernstein come to be seen as a smothering shroud from which the genius is determined to free himself: she clings, threatens suicide, imagines Maxwell Perkins has aided the collapse of the stormy love. In fact and in written elaboration, Thomas Wolfe brings wretchedness to Esther Jack, but she at least triumphs in being the single moment of happiness, romantic love, surrender of his own shroud of self-love:

> After all the blind, tormented wanderings of youth, that woman would become his heart's centre and the target of his life, the image of immortal one-ness that again collected him to one, and hurled the whole collected passion, power, and might of his one life into the blazing certitude, the immortal governance and unity, of love. (*Of Time and the River*)

Anti-Semitism: he longs, in his notebooks, for letters from his "little Jew" and in the same notebook, before they had met and when Wolfe dreamed of success as a dramatist:

> Artistically, at any rate, the Jew is a menace. He controls the theatre in New York.... The character of New York audiences is itself determined, in large measure, by the members of his race.... In our small towns, we see our small tradesmen steadily driven to the wall, outwitted and out-reached on every side by their Jewish competitor.... His botanical selection is ever the sunflower, never the violet. Indeed, I am becoming convinced that he gained his title of "chosen of God" because of the many good things he had to say of himself, oft-repeated before the Lord.

Wolfe, ever to remain in many ways a bumpkin from the South, grew up at a time when the local Jews ran clothing and jewelry stores on Main Street and were respected but apart, with little social mingling until the later years when they became lawyers, judges, doctors, and professors if there was a local college. In New York City it will be otherwise indeed; perhaps they are the "web" on the rock in that title.

And yet, a diversion in *Of Time and the River*. While teaching at New York University, Abraham Jones, an A student, arrogant, begins to haunt Eugene Gant as an enemy, a critic never satisfied with the chosen texts, a smirking judge, a nightmare of unendurable superiority. The combative, outraged teacher throws him out of the class, only to have the young man burst into tears and say, "Why, that's the best class that I've got." Jones will become the "first man-swarm atom he had come to know in all the desolation of the million-footed city," a loyal friend.

Wolfe takes on the whole family, hears the story of the name "Jones" from the old Polish, Yiddish-speaking father, the story of sister Sylvia and her illegitimate child raised by the student, Abraham; another sister, Rose, "a dark, tortured and sensitive Jewess with a big nose and one blind eye." Abe himself transformed from "an obscure and dreary chrysalis, and yet a dogged, loyal, and faithful friend, the salt of the earth, a wonderfully good, rare, and high person."

You can find what you will in Thomas Wolfe, every dated cliché and skinhead notion and folly and "niggertown"; and then turn the page for a contemplation that might be in the words of a Boston abolitionist:

> *The South* . . . the whole fantastic distortion of that period where people were said to live in "mansions," and slavery was a benevolent institution, conducted as a constant banjo-strumming, the strewn largesses of the colonel and the shuffle-dance of his happy dependents . . . and the Rebel horde a company of swagger, death-mocking cavaliers. Years later . . . when their cheap mythology, their legend of the charm of their manner, the aristocratic culture of their lives, the quaint sweetness of their drawl, made him writhe—when he could think of no return to their life and its swarming superstition without weariness and horror . . . he still pretended the most fanatic devotion to them, excusing his Northern residence on grounds of necessity rather than desire. (*Look Homeward, Angel*)

Thomas Wolfe, a maw, gulping his family, the streets, the citizens, the Civil War, World War I, the Dempsey-Firpo fight, the Sacco and Vanzetti case, Europe, America. He is too much, too many rhapsodies, an inundation. Not a man you'd want to deal with. Drunken pages and drunken he often was as he prowled the midnight city. And yet the mystery of the books is that they are *written* with a rich, fertile vocabulary, sudden, blooming images, a murderous concentration that will turn everyone he meets into words. The books are all in print; fresh, beckoning paperbacks, American literature. Whether the new millennium with its gifts will include the time to read them is another question.

2000

THE FOSTER FATHER

Henry James

CATHERINE Sloper, in the clear, chilly masterpiece *Washington Square*, must explain to the handsome, corrupt fortune-hunter, Morris Townsend, that if she marries without her father's consent, as she is willing to do, her own adequate fortune will not be augmented at the time of her father's death. Dr. Sloper has correctly diagnosed, as it were, the insidious moral infection of the suitor, a wastrel who could not possibly be in love with his plain, awkward, naïvely trusting daughter. Townsend, however, is desperately in need; he is bent upon *real money* rather than Catherine's sufficient income. He believes that if she pressed her case with more astute insistence she could bring her father around from the threat of disinheritance. The poor daughter knows better. Her reason comes forth at last in a painful recognition: "He is not very fond of me."

Catherine is abandoned to enduring misery and pain. Although still chaste, she brings to mind a poem by Robert Burns about a rustic, betrayed girl. "And my fause luver staw my rose/ But ah! he left the thorns wi me." Henry James's fiction is rich in dramatic arrangements between parents and children. The childless bachelor was alert to the fierce conflictions in the will or doom of parents to be themselves, to live out a daily expression of their nature as singular beings for whom being a parent is only one of a stinging swarm of obligations, desires, follies, willed or accidentally improper involvements. The parents in their history and destiny have been shaped by years of experience, accumulated scars, agreeable turns, and disappointing outcomes. To these, small children look on as a sort of invited guest until they grow up so strangely themselves as to be not a reproduction but often a counterreaction. In the stories of James it is not always the young ones whose fate is at stake, but the grown offspring entering the world with the troublesome baggage of their parents' journey through life.

The fictions do not have the atmosphere of autobiography, do not hint at the author's life as the son of the learned, distinguished, loving and lovable, if somewhat balmy and improvident, Henry James Sr. and the steady, affectionate Mary Walsh James. The biographers, Leon Edel and the more recent Fred Kaplan, would have it otherwise; they find a stressful relation with his brother William hidden in the pages as well as homoerotic threads in the careful weavings.

In the teasing, flirtatious, elaborately composed prefaces for the New York Edition of his work, published between 1907 and 1909, James likes to tell of the "germ" or "seed" of an anecdote heard at the dinner table, a little acorn from which a "great oak" might grow. Like a waiter receiving a tip, modest enough, James puts the gratuity into an investment fund of striking possibilities for growth. Even *Washington Square*, his own fireside tale of lower Manhattan, improbably came to him from an anecdote related by the actress Fanny Kemble.

"The Pupil" begins: "The young man hesitated and procrastinated: it cost him such an effort to broach the subject of terms, to speak of money to a person who spoke only of feelings and, as it were, of the aristocracy." The speaker, or not speaker, is a young graduate of Yale and Oxford, Pemberton, who has taken a position as tutor to Morgan Moreen, the sickly son of an American family traveling about Europe. Wages, which the elder Moreens cannot pay, are somehow to be made up for by the special charm and precocity of their little boy. "He's a genius—you'll love him," the mother says, and to a degree that is true.

The pupil, Morgan Moreen with his damaged heart, is indeed a precocity of candor about the disreputable family. For himself, the tutor feels it would be improper to speak about the invisible wages; for that bit of *politesse* the boy calls him a "humbug." Instead, young Morgan remembers the fate of a treasured nurse who finally left unrewarded for her services, only to have the parents insist they had paid every penny owed to the poor woman. In the pain of so much knowledge left like dust in the household, the child denounces the lying and cheating: "I don't know what they live on, or how they live, or *why* they live!" Their snobbery, immunity to insult in the pursuit of fashionable connections, the way they move from city to city, from hotel to hotel, leaving a stack of unpaid chits—all of this is the ancestral heritage of the child, along with the genuine love the family feels for the boy, their free treasure.

The tutor, Pemberton, is also down on his luck after a mediocre career at Oxford and a time spent seeing the world. He is alive to the charm and oddity of his pupil and it is with regret that, by way of an offer to tutor a rich boy, he is forced to take off. The rich boy is a dolt and when Mrs. Moreen sends a scribbled note saying, "Implore you to come back instantly—Morgan dreadfully ill," he returns. The end of the tale is somewhat in the shade, as fictions by James are likely to be. However, without seriousness of intention, Morgan and Pemberton have chatted about going away together, settling somewhere. Suddenly the mother, claiming the tutor has stolen the boy's affection for the family, insists that he take him in fact. Morgan: "Do you mean he may take me to live with him ... ? Away, away, anywhere he likes?" The boy's joy, the impractical obligation, leads the tutor to hesitate for a moment and, in the moment, Morgan is suddenly stricken and dies. Like Miles in *The Turn of the Screw*, "his little heart, dispossessed, had stopped."

In the unforgettable story, little Morgan Moreen is a neglected child, suffering not from absence or indifference, but from moral neglect. He is like a child visiting a parent imprisoned for fraud, receiving the hugs and kisses and yet always coming away with the terms of the indictment. Good society shuns the Moreen parents, his brothers and sisters are energetically engaged in shady maneuverings, and the tutor will soon learn of the family's bold effrontery. Morgan is a genetic anomaly. His quick and candid revelations to the tutor may be thought almost unnatural, but they serve as an original and tragic moral awareness that literally breaks the child's heart.

In the preface to the story, a "thumping windfall" related by a medical friend during a train journey, the "dear" Moreens are viewed in an unexpected light. The Moreens and I, James writes, go back to the "classic years of the great Americano-European legend; the years of limited communication, of monstrous and unattenuated contrast, of prodigious and unrecorded adventure." Now, he laments the despoiling of the sacred cobbles of the great, old cities "through which the unconscious Barbarians troop with the regularity and passivity of 'supplies,' or other promiscuous goods, prepaid and forwarded."

The wandering tribe in their assault on Rome, Nice, and Venice can speak a number of languages, but only the sick boy has an aspiration to culture. No matter. It would appear that the family's feckless snobbery, their immunity to insult, the sad, rejecting emotions of their son, do not overwhelm the author's back-looking affection for one condition—their impecuniousness. James came to prefer bohemian ne'er-do-wells to the loaded Americans he had seen on the continent in the subsequent years.

The Turn of the Screw, a "ghost story" of such dense complication it might be a strange craft washed up on a beach with a tattered black flag and crew missing. Critics have dived into the watery grave and surfaced to denounce each other, offer this piece of debris and that, and at last haul the mysterious vessel into a maritime museum. There the piratical thing can be viewed as you will. The story is land-locked for the most part, but skull and crossbones fly in the meadows.

James said the tale was a shameless bit of hackwork, "a piece of ingenuity pure and simple, of cold artistic calculation." That may be, but it is a brilliant composition, as humanly deep and convincing in psychological interplay as anything in his vast repertoire. The story is told in the first person by way of a manuscript left at her death by the unnamed governess, the star of her plot. In fact the manuscript was dictated by James to his dour typist, and the governess would not have been pleased. She is a young woman, inexperienced, daughter of a poor country parson. She answers an advertisement, journeys to a fine house on Harley Street in London for an interview. The employer is a handsome man, rich, busy, a lively bachelor about town. He is the uncle of two young children who have been left in his care when their parents, one his younger brother, died. The orphans are settled in a grand old house in the country, under the care, in the absence of the previous governess, of a good-natured, loyal housekeeper and "plenty of people to help." Once the young woman is engaged as governess he makes a rather heartless demand, "his main condition," which had led previous applicants to turn the post down. The condition: "That she should never trouble him—but never, never; neither appeal nor complain nor write about anything; only meet all questions herself, receive all moneys from his solicitor, take the whole thing over and let him alone." Gratefully unburdened of his charges, the attractive uncle "held her hand" and thereby entered the dreams of the poor daughter on her first escape from the prosaic vicarage.

At the estate, the housekeeper, Mrs. Grose, is welcoming and the little girl, Flora, is astonishingly beautiful; the boy, Miles, is to return from school the following day. In the interval, the majestically raddled plot begins. The guardian has forwarded an *unopened* letter which says, *without giving particulars*, that the child has been expelled from school and is never to return. The kindly housekeeper, deeply fond of the boy, is offered the letter which she, illiterate, cannot read. But what has he done, the little thing not yet ten years old? The governess then offers a "mere aid" of her own. "That he's an injury to others." They discuss the nature of boys and agree that a certain amount of mischief is suitable and even agreeable, but then the governess oddly adds that one wouldn't want a boy to contaminate and corrupt. *Injury to others, contaminate and corrupt*: dire intrusions from the brisk vocabulary of the new inhabitant settled in a large bedroom, the best in the house, in a landscape "a different affair from my own scant home."

The inquisitive governess wants information about her predecessor and with her acute grasping of nuance senses that the housekeeper did not approve of the departed one. She learns that the lady, Miss Jessel, went off and did not return from her holiday and it was later told by the master that she had died. Died of what? Mrs. Grose does not know the answer and uncomfortable with the inquisition abruptly excuses herself. Young Miles returns and is beautiful and lovable "with something divine" in his being—for the governess.

The governess, an inspired narrator of past events and the conflicting emotions that enshroud them, has the glorifying position of being in charge and for this elevation she freely expresses vanity and determination. But being in charge calls for the underside of command, watchfulness and suspicion. "I now saw that I had been asked for a service admirable and difficult; and there would be a greatness in letting it be seen—oh in the right quarter!—that I could succeed where many another girl might have failed."

The "ghost" must appear and it will not be in the attic but on a late afternoon walk. It is a man, staring hard at the governess, a stranger and fearful, but she forbears the opportunity to mention the terrifying appearance until on a Sunday morning there he is again, at the window, staring. In the midst of this threatening visitation, the governess has one of her gifted, sudden intuitions: ". . . It was not for me he had come. He had come for someone else." Mrs. Grose enters the room and the exquisitely ordered interrogatory matter proceeds:

"An extraordinary man. Looking in."
  "What extraordinary man?"
  "I haven't the least idea."
  "Have you seen him before?"
  "Yes—once. On the old tower."
  "Was he a gentleman?"
  "No."

At this point, James confounds the reader by a reversal of the manner in which the governess has received information about the past: Mrs. Grose had given the hints for the flights of fancy of the new member of the household. However, as they go on about the face in the window it is the governess who describes him: red hair, queer red whiskers, handsome, wearing good clothes somehow not his own, looking like an actor. "Peter Quint!" the housekeeper cries out. He is now dead, having fallen while coming home "in drink" from a local pub.

Quint came to the estate as valet to the guardian on a previous visit and being in poor health was left to recover in the country air. Miss Jessel will arrive and the lonely house will be aflame with activity distressing to Mrs. Grose. Serious lovemaking between the two shatters the peace of the housekeeper, especially since Miss Jessel was a lady and Peter Quint a "base menial." The two were impudent, reckless, and with the boy, Miles, Quint was "too free," a troubling matter left hanging in the air. The new governess, unnamed as she is, has had her apparition given the name of Peter Quint and in a rush of perception decides he has come for the boy. As the tale unravels, Miss Jessel will float in the infernal mist. She is a frightful figure in suitable black, appearing while the governess and little Flora are outside in the pleasant grounds. The child takes no notice, a signal of her alliance, her corrupted state of collusion with the fascinating, malignant past.

At the beginning of the story, the governess insists that the children loved her, but her dissolute curiosity, her protective, oppressive intrusion will alienate them. Their harmless escapades to annoy her will only serve as interesting proof of their possession by evil spirits forever immune to the offered exorcism. "They're lost" is the pronouncement.

Mrs. Grose says that Miss Jessel, although a lady, was *infamous* and Peter Quint a horror. Nevertheless, Peter Quint had his qualities; the guardian liked his company and for little Miles he could have been an interesting diversion; a rascal, free in his language, a handsome, careless young man of the people. In any case he was a man, flinging about the place, and in his concentration upon seducing the respectable Miss Jessel there is no reason to believe, as some critics do, that he sexually seduced Miles. But Peter Quint, with his red hair, easily seduced the imagination of the governess.

A devastating scene with Flora, Mrs. Grose, the governess, and the evil, "pale and ravenous demon," Miss Jessel. Flora has slipped away and when she is at last spotted, the ghost of Miss Jessel arrives like a cloud. But Mrs. Grose does not see her, nor does Flora. To the girl, the governess insists, "She's there, you little unhappy thing—there, there, *there*, and you know it as well as you know me!" Thus the resolution of the tale begins as Flora attacks the menace of the governess:

> "I don't know what you mean. I see nobody. I see nothing. I never have. I think you're cruel. I don't like you!" Then, after this deliverance, which might have been that of a vulgarly pert little girl in the street, she hugged Mrs. Grose more closely and buried in her skirts the dreadful little face. In this position she launched an almost furious wail, "Take me away, take me away—oh take me away from her!"
>
> "From *me*?" I panted.
>
> "From you—from you!" she cried.

Flora and the housekeeper depart for London, leaving the governess alone with Miles and with the opportunity to assault him about the misbehavior at school. Miles offers that he "said things." To whom had he said things? To only a few, "those I liked." And they must have repeated the remarks to those *they liked*. There is a penetrating knowledge here of the gloomy sludge of youthful experience. Those I liked betraying one to those they liked; *I* and *they*, an acute and pitiful perception of the trench warfare of schoolchildren.

In the prodigious fearfulness of the last few pages, the importunate mistress of inquisition will ask, "What were those things?" Miles averts his face and she falls upon him as if to force a humbling concreteness for her enlightenment. Then yet another visitation from the unquiet graves—"the white face of damnation"—and Miles, having perhaps been told about the previous emanations, in terror asks, "Is she *here*?? ... Miss Jessel, Miss Jessel!" No, it's not Miss Jessel, "But it's at the window—straight before us. It's *there*, the coward horror, there for the last time!" Peter Quint—you devil! Miles looks around the room again, Where?

The governess has her supreme moment. It's all over because "I have you." The child utters a cry of "a creature hurled over an abyss" and

> I caught him, yes, I held him—it may be imagined with what a passion; but at the end of a minute I began to feel what it truly was that I held. We were alone with the quiet day, and his little heart, dispossessed, had stopped.

Miles, left alone with the triumphant, unearthly governess, dies in her ghostly arms.

James included the story in the prefaces for the New York Edition written some ten years later; an edition in which he excluded the perfect *Washington Square*, perhaps finding it too local for the fervent illumination of Americans abroad. *The Bostonians* was put aside, denying the imperious Olive Chancellor, Verena the forlorn elocutionist, the dashing Southerner Basil Ransom—not one agreeable to living Bostonians. About *The Turn of the Screw*, James may have been surprised by the enthusiastic reception here and there of his "bit of hackwork." For aesthetic reasons he declined to offer details of the two wicked goblins and asked the reader to consult his own knowledge of evil. Reading today, one might ask just what the evil of the "ghosts" was, beyond the adjectives and shudders of Mrs. Grose.

The children when first introduced to the governess are surpassingly beautiful and serene, showing no mark of the beast, or beasts. Even Miles, expelled from school, is charming, pleasant, giving no sign of the humiliating scene he has endured. It is the governess who poisons their days and nights with the heavy oppression of her assumed protection, her cunning questions and rampaging suspicions. Flora flees her presence in horror and Miles, despite his previous failure, pleads to be sent away to another school. When he learns that the ferocious governess has banished the ghost and now all is well because Miles is hers, she *has* him; he dies of the fear of *her*. Throughout the governess is before us in action; her perverse miasma of family blight is more evil than the infamy of Miss Jessel and the freedom of Peter Quint.

What Maisie Knew is an elegant novel of wild imagination. Today it might be found among anecdotal, fitfully researched books that appear under the foreboding title *Children and Divorce*. That marketplace, if it knew of *Maisie*, would declare it a singular illustration of a couple's legal breaking apart not useful as a statistical entry. On the other hand, it could not meet two more original parents who have in the mysterious ways of nature given birth to a child.

The story begins, as such will, in the courts. The father, by his wife "bespattered from head to foot," has been appointed to keep the child, but to refund a sum of twenty-six hundred pounds the wife put down for the child's maintenance. That money the father has squandered, but in the battle a compromise has been reached. Also the child, Maisie, has been broken in two and is to spend six months with each.

The parents, mother Ida and father Beale Farange, are pugilists, facing each other with growls and grunts, left and right hooks in the marriage ring. Their personal equipment is very striking. "They made up together... some twelve feet three of stature." The mother, Ida, had "a length and reach of arm conducive perhaps to her so often having beaten her ex-husband at billiards, a game in which she showed a superiority largely accountable, as she maintained, for the resentment finding expression in his physical violence."

The father, Beale Farange, "had natural decorations, a kind of costume in his vast fair beard, . . . and the eternal glitter of the teeth that his long mustache had been trained not to hide. . . ." He had been trained in his youth for diplomacy and momentarily attached, without a salary, to a legation which often enabled him to say, "In *my* time in the East." Indeed the parents are comic figures—comedians who will trip you if you cross their path. Little Maisie first court-ordered to stay with her father finds him showing her letters from her mother, but instead of giving them to her, throwing them in the fire. She is dangled on the knees of his cigar-smoking friends, pinched and tossed about. At last her term with her mother arrives and when the bejeweled, crimson-painted face appears the first words are: "And did your beastly papa, my precious angel, send any message to your own loving mamma?" Maisie answers as if she has been asked for the correct time of day. "'He said I was to tell you, from him,' she faithfully reported, 'that you're a nasty horrid pig!'"

In the care of children, James shows a marked preference for women of the lower classes, ill-educated, homely, familiar with the rebuffs from their "betters." Thus Maisie will have Mrs. Wix, who has lost her own daughter on a crossing on Harrow Road, crushed by a hansom. Her governess, Miss Overmore, if not as malign as the spectral hireling in *The Turn of the Screw*, is an ambitious visitation of a more practical nature, an easy-enough alliance with the divorced father. While the mother, Ida, has foregone her months with Maisie in favor of a time abroad with a gentleman, Miss Overmore and Mr. Farange find the child's extended presence quite heavy and go off together to Brighton to find a school to place her in.

The mother Farange could not abide the pretty Miss Overmore and employs Mrs. Wix for the child's companion when she must suffer her court-ordained rights. Mrs. Wix arrives with a message to Maisie: "You must take your mamma's message, Maisie, and you must feel that her wishing me to come to you with it this way is a great proof of interest and affection. She sends you her particular love and announces to you that she's engaged to be married to Sir Claude." A discussion of this matter with Miss Overmore about the idea that her mother's marriage would establish a special hold on the child is countered by a sly retort about what that would mean if the father were to marry:

> [Maisie:] "Do you mean papa's hold on me—do you mean *he's* about to marry?"
>
> [Miss Overmore:] "Papa's not about to marry—Papa *is* married, my dear. Papa was married the day before yesterday at Brighton.... He's my husband, if you please, and I'm his little wife. So *now* we'll see who's your little mother!"

Maisie, blinking, absorbing her world of ravaged sophistication, is thought to be dumb and indeed in the torrent of wanton insinuations she assumes an air of "harmless vacancy." She is told by one side of the embattled forces that her mother "loathes you" and by the presiding officer of the other side that "your father wishes you were dead." Her mother is not only engaged to Sir Claude, they are married, and Maisie accepts that she now has four parents, even if in her now precocious experience "they struck her as after all rather deficient in that air of the honeymoon of which she had so often heard...."

Sir Claude, like a handsome knight on a white steed, gallops to the rescue of the pummeled offspring of his wife because, in his way, he genuinely likes children and in this instance could not like any child less than he likes his long-armed wife, her mother. He appears at the door of her new little mama, the former Miss Overmore, to take the child for her ordained spell of residence with her first mother. Sir Claude is younger than his wife and Miss Overmore is younger than the toothy Beale Farange; on the doorstep there is, naturally it must be named, a flirtation between the two.

Sir Claude, always spoken of as beautiful, is one of the author's most appealing and credible male creations. He's a blade, not a saint, and from the doorstep meeting with Maisie's stepmother, plotting, with the lady's voracious assistance, to see her again. With Maisie, he's comradely, honest insofar as the circumstances permit, humorous. When Maisie asks him if he is afraid of his wife, his answer is "Rather, old man!" The two go about town, buy sweets as they please, share a complicated interlude on the coast of France, and talk about the conditions of their curious lives. The married couples it soon appears are not together. The mother, when not supposedly off for a billiards competition in Brussels, is seen in the park on the arm of a peculiar alliance. The stepmother has moved to her own place and divorced a not unwilling Mr. Farange; Maisie's mother has divorced Sir Claude and that leaves the two free for an alliance that breaks Maisie's heart. James shapes his young charges with touching affection and sympathy and yet their endings are doleful; the beautiful Flora in *The Turn of the Screw* flees disaster with the loyal, illiterate, uninspiring Mrs. Grose and Maisie ends in the arms of the pessimistic, needy Mrs. Wix. The grown-ups in this superb novel will do as they will or as they must. The licentious *ronde* is composed with vivacity and speed, free of the scrupulous painter's usual second and third coats.

The Awkward Age is written for the most part in dialogue or conversation. The oddity of this glittering novel is that conversation, the plot, is seen as a sort of airborne disease, disabling the heroine, making her unfit for marriage in the manner of a deflowering. Nanda Brookenham is eighteen, the year of her coming-out, as we would have it; here in London it is spoken of as a coming-down to mingle freely in her parents' drawing room, to hear the badinage of her mother's set.

At the time of composition, only three or four months it took, James was still smarting from the disaster of his drama *Guy Domville*, and perhaps wished to illustrate his command of action through dialogue. Indeed he had always mutely spoken his prose, which accounts for the large number of italicized words, even words such as *the* and *that* to give the vocal stress. As the preface to *The Awkward Age* indicates, he is contemptuous of the theater of his time, the "strait-jacket" which renounces the finer thing for "the coarser, the thick, in short for the thin and the curious for the self-evident."

Bewailing the lack of intellectual distinction, here are his thoughts on Ibsen:

> What virtues of the same order would have attached to *The Pillars of Society*, to *An Enemy of the People*, to *Ghosts*, to *Rosmersholm* (or taking also Ibsen's "subtle period") to *John Gabriel Borkman*,

to *The Master Builder*? Ibsen is in fact wonderfully a case in point, since from the moment he's clear, from the moment he's "amusing," it's on the footing of a thesis as simple and superficial as that of *A Doll's House*—while from the moment he's by intention comprehensive and searching it's on the footing of an effect as confused and obscure as *The Wild Duck*.

It must be said that James in reviews written later was more "measured" about Ibsen, but the outburst in the preface to *The Awkward Age* is of interest because it indicates the suffering he endured throughout his life about the public's rejection of his manner, his style, his evasiveness so intensely and vigorously elaborated. The prefaces also give a poignant clue that James was aware of the fragility of some of his "seeds" as they try to hold ground in the downpour of fiction.

At the turn of the century, it was felt by many that England was afflicted by a drastic change in social life. The class system was so greatly weakened one couldn't tell a lord from a manufacturer of leather goods; the latter, if very rich, might soon be a lord. Civilities, deportment, standards were uncertain and a man of the world needn't know which fork to use. Mothers with a daughter in the marriage market became as beady-eyed and calculating as a speculator in the stock exchange. James seemed to feel the decadence of the atmosphere to be lamentable and such is the challenge of his novel *The Awkward Age*.

It is a drawing-room novel, a meeting of the up-to-date and the out-of-date. Mrs. Brookenham, forty-one, has a daughter, Nanda, eighteen, and a very special friend, Mr. Vanderbank, or Van, thirty-four. They are in the England of 1899, the year of publication, to be judged by a man, Mr. Longdon, fifty-five years old. He is unmarried, lives in the country on his comfortable income, is making his first visit to London in thirty years. At the opening of the novel, Mr. Longdon emerges from one of the teatime gatherings at the Buckingham Crescent establishment of Mrs. Brook, as she is called. The older gentleman had been in love with Lady Julia, Mrs. Brook's mother, and he has come to town to see what has happened to the daughter of the lady, long dead, who rejected his suit, a rejection he has never recovered from since he is, and rather proudly, the sort who does not recover from the days of dazzling hope. What Mr. Longdon learns of the daughter, Mrs. Brook, does not please him; in fact, "I think I was rather frightened."

In the rain, he shares a "four-wheeler" with Van and they end up at Van's place and talk until midnight, setting the tone, as it were. Van is charming, light-hearted, well born, not rich, indeed the only member of the set who has a job. Mr. Longdon sees a portrait of Nanda which she has given to Van and, while he questions the propriety of such an exchange, he is struck by the fact that Nanda is the very image of the lost Lady Julia and it will be his mission to save her.

In Mrs. Brook's set there is a duchess, widow of a Neapolitan grandee whose niece, little Aggie, she is keeping in a kind of purdah to assure a proper marriage, but says she would offer her to "the son of a chimney-sweep if the proper guarantees were there." There is Mr. Mitchett, the son of a bootmaker but very rich and very badly dressed in garments that have nothing in common save "the violence and independence of their pattern." Mitchett, genial and unassuming, will marry the violently protected little Aggie who, once released, is soon on the town. There is Lord Petherton, of a "certain pleasant brutality," who lives off Mitchett. And Mr. Cashmore, "who would have been very red-haired if he had not been very bald"; and whose straying wife, Fanny, is much discussed. Mrs. Brook's husband, Edward, according to the crunching images of the duchess, figures in the drawing room "only as one of those queer extinguishers of fire in the corridors of hotels. He's a bucket on a peg."

Van is the prize of the circle; he is handsome, agreeable, available but not dependent. He might be elsewhere if he chose, but here he is, amused, aware of the great charm and wit of Mrs. Brook and of her splendid effort to keep her boat afloat. Mr. Longdon is much taken with him; indeed he had known Van's mother, who was a special comfort to him in the loss of Lady Julia before going off herself to marry another. Mrs. Brook is in love with Van and a competition, hidden and astute, comes about when she learns that Nanda is also in love with him. "He'll never come to the scratch," the mother says.

Nanda, once *down*, is a serious, intelligent girl, strong in the defense of certain friends who are not quite respectable for an unmarried girl—that vulnerable condition. She is polite about the curiosity the men in the set are free to have about her; and penetrating about her pretty mother's gallantry in hanging on with very little money and a worthless son who borrows from everyone with the deftness of Fagin's crew lifting pocket handkerchiefs.

The conversation to which Nanda has been exposed is entirely personal, more than a little cynical; it is gossip of an eloquent and relentless sophistication, rich in discoveries about the wives of the husbands and the husbands of the wives in the group. The many matters the gossip ignores are as interesting as what it squeezes from the lemons at hand. London itself does not often appear with its place names and diversions; the city is atmosphere. There is no mention of politics, nothing of the religious and intellectual turmoil of the period. At the time of writing, Queen Victoria is having her second Jubilee and will live a few more years; Gladstone has recently died and the superb object of gossip, Disraeli, although dead for some years, was a dramatic figure in the youth of Mrs. Brook and her set. Here, the conversation is about whether Lady Fanny will bolt and like Anna Karenina go off with her lover to some little Italian town. It must be said that the talk, if somewhat wrapped in too many shawls of intimacy, is brilliant.

Mrs. Brook and Van are the spectacular accomplishment of the novel; their provocative interchanges are candid on the surface and yet swirling about in undercurrents of emotion, motive, self-awareness, and self-protection. Since Nanda, approaching nineteen, must be married sooner rather than later, Mr. Longdon advances the plot and the conversation by an offer to Van: if he consents to marry the young girl she will have a considerable settlement, money, made over to her. His reason: "I want her got out.... Out of her mother's house." Van, taken aback, says he cannot commit himself without time to consider it. Mr. Longdon proposes, as an inducement, to name the sum, a sum Van refuses to hear. Nanda is not to know, but Van delivers the news to Mrs. Brook and to Mr. Mitchett, honorably telling Mr. Longdon later that he has done so:

[Van:] "We had things out very much and his kindness was extraordinary—he's the most beautiful old boy that ever lived . . . but I feel I can't arrive at any respectable sort of attitude in the matter without taking you into my confidence...though till this moment I've funked it."

[Mrs. Brook:] "Do you mean you've declined the arrangement?"...Her lovely gaze widened out...."You have declined her?...Do you imagine I want you to myself?"

[Van:] "...When he mentioned it to me I was quite surprised.... He's ready to settle if I'm ready to do the rest."

[Mrs. Brook:] "Of course you know... that she'd jump at you....What is it he settled?"

[Van:] "I can't tell you.... On the contrary I stopped him off."

[Mrs. Brook:] "Oh then...that's what I call declining....You won't do it....You won't do it."

Mr. Mitchett enters and they discuss, chat, about the matter and whether Nanda might get more money if Van refuses. Of one thing, Mrs. Brook is still certain: "He won't go in." The banter back and forth seems to distress Vanderbank, as if perhaps it is an indictment of "the liberal fireside" to which Nanda has long been exposed, thereby creating some oblique disadvantage to herself, her life. On the other hand, he has no wish to marry her or her mother. Nanda, ultimately aware that Van is just a friend and nothing more, will tell Mr. Longdon that he did his best: "Oh, he's more old-fashioned than you." And that in the eerie resolution would seem to be the exact truth of the tale.

Little Flora was to have the middle-aged Mrs. Grose and little Maisie to have as her companion the bereaved Mrs. Wix. For Nanda, kind, intelligent about the way things are and forgiving of them, it is to be Mr. Longdon. He has his country place, lovely gardens, and indeed quiet. With some jealousy of the withholding Van, he puts it to the young girl: "You understand clearly, I take it, that this time it's never again to leave me—or to *be* left." So it is yes, tomorrow. For Nanda, never to leave.

In 1915, in the midst of World War I, James gave up his American passport and became a British citizen. It was a year before his death and having spent most of his adult life in Britain, he did not want to be booked as an alien while he was reporting for work with refugees and the wounded; and no doubt it seemed the proper thing to do.

However, in his fictions the new citizen was not pleased by the rapid changes in British life starting at the end of the nineteenth century. He struggled to find a useful spot of environmental contamination from which to dramatize the inchoate mudslides. Thirty years earlier, Anthony Trollope, in his large novel, *The Way We Live Now* (1869), proposed as the landscape of decline and social corruption the history of a great capitalist speculator, Melmotte, and his illusory shares that sent an idle Lord this and Lord that into bankruptcy.

For James, in *The Awkward Age* (1899), the tea-table of Mrs. Brook is the instrument of a vanished propriety and the dilution of suitable ways to raise a young daughter. But just what is the substance of the inflammable conversation in Mrs. Brook's house? For the most part it is clever talk about money, the marriage market, and certain indiscreet follies. In the preface, James analyzes favorably the practical French manner of keeping the "hovering female young" out of the drawing room altogether until they are married. In America, he writes, the young female may be present, but the talk on such occasions is properly trimmed to the innocuous; perhaps a retreat to the weather or the day's passage at school until, mercifully for the adults, the young one curtsies and departs.

Mr. Longdon, with his scrupulous fidelity to the social censorship of the past, is offered as a moral hero; but the true prince is Van, who refuses Mr. Longdon's bribe in exchange for the rescue by marriage of the threatened Nanda. In support of his theme of untethered conversation, James shows a reluctance or an incapacity to compose scurrilous dialogue; such is the charm of the conversation he actually produces, even though it may not serve as sufficient motivation for Mr. Longdon's "I want her out of the house."

In these stories, James creates a span of mistreatment that is death, a drastic removal, for the young boys, Morgan Moreen in "The Pupil" and Miles in *The Turn of the Screw*. Morgan's parents demonstrated neglect by moral or immoral frivolity; the indifference of the guardian in the "ghost" story, his giving the children over to the care of a young woman he spoke with for scarcely more than five minutes is a casual risking of their lives. The young girls, Maisie and Nanda, are stronger, able to survive the instability of their parents and the loss of the "beautiful" young men with whom they have innocently fallen in love. Survival is to be a sort of dimness as they pass into the charge of the caring ones, a twilight escape. The fictions show an acute disillusionment with family life, perhaps a bachelor's cool eye on the common sentiments.

On the other hand, such fondness for children has a dreamlike quality to it, an enchanted protectiveness. Although we cannot quite imagine James comfortably in the presence of a baby, his affection has in it some of the sweetness of the charming Sir Claude who, when asked why he had taken up with Maisie, says: "I'm not an angel—I'm an old grandmother.... I like babies—I always did. If we go to smash I shall look for a place as responsible nurse."

2001

FUNNY AS A CRUTCH
Nathanael West

I.

NATHANAEL West (1903–1940) published four novels, wrote many screenplays, and left strewn about among his papers "Unpublished Writings and Fragments." West had the masochist's subtle attachment to his failures, a recognition which is, in its fashion, somehow self-affirming. He reports that the income from his first three novels was $780: if one keeps accounts, woefully true, but, in a stretch, like Byron hobbling about on his lame foot and swimming the Hellespont. In a letter to Edmund Wilson:

> I forget the broad sweep, the big canvas, the shot-gun adjectives, the important people, the significant ideas, the lessons to be taught, the epic Thomas Wolfe, the realistic James Farrell.... The proof of all this is that I've never had the same publisher twice—once bitten, etc.—because there is nothing to root for in my books and what is even worse, no rooters. Maybe they're right. My stuff goes from the presses to the drug stores.

Biographical and critical studies appear, important reviews, if not in a flood, an impressive stream of recognition. And yet, it is the practice of critics to lament the neglect of Nathanael West, despite the daunting accumulation. West, sly hypochondriac that he was, puts the critics in the position of a crusading doctor reviving the moribund. It may be that West is not so much neglected as unread while more or less well known, a condition obscure and not subject to arithmetic. High reputation and, as the decades pass, the name honored, but the interest, the readers, the glare fading except for graduate students ever in the stacks seeking a "fresh" topic.

Remember Edward Dahlberg, author of *Bottom Dogs*, with an introduction by D. H. Lawrence, many other books and in particular *Because I Was Flesh*, a dazzling autobiography, starring, so to speak, his mother, a lady barber with her chair, her clippers and talc. Perhaps it was Dahlberg's misfortune to have Faulkner, Fitzgerald, and Hemingway as contemporaries.

And there is the case of Willa Cather of Nebraska and Ellen Glasgow of Richmond, Virginia. Willa Cather is still a bright, commanding figure; Ellen Glasgow, honored and read in her time, is but dimly flickering now. True, breaking the sod and hustling cattle out west is more riveting than the manners of Richmond with echoes of Henry James, an old pioneer only in matters of nuance. Nathanael West's "neglect" is not so striking. He is like the boy in the orphanage who, when the lads pass by, will be adopted by the town mayor but, after a time, not quite what was wanted and so returned to the line with his curls and snappy come-backs, there to be "placed" once again.

A letter to Fitzgerald:

> My dear Mr. Fitzgerald, You have been kind enough to say that you liked my novel, *Miss Lonelyhearts*. I am applying for a Guggenheim Fellowship and I need references for it. I wonder if you would be willing to let me use your name as a reference? It would be enormously valuable to me.... I know very few people, almost none whose names would mean anything to the committee.... If you can see your way to do this, it would make me very happy.

Fitzgerald responded, naming West as a "potential leader in the field of prose fiction." Other supporting letters were written by Malcolm Cowley and Edmund Wilson. The application was rejected. West's biographer, Robert Emmet Long, tells of him at a boys' camp in the Adirondacks: "He tried out for baseball, but was the sort of boy who, in fielding a fly, would be struck by the ball on the forehead and fall to the ground, which did, in fact, once happen to him." There you have it.

His first novel, *The Dream Life of Balso Snell*, is not designed to please, beginning perhaps with the choice of the peculiar name "Snell" for the central character. Snell somehow finds himself in the ancient city of Troy, where he comes upon the famous wooden horse of the Greeks. The only way to enter the horse for his journey is by way of the alimentary canal. "O Anus Mirabilis!" A work of only some fifty pages, it is a dazzling parade of literary and cultural references written when the author was only twenty-six years old, years spent apparently reading everything in the public library. Balso's guide in the classical journey through the intestine argues with him about Daudet, Picasso, and Cézanne, "the sage of Aix." Fleeing the contentious guide, Balso comes upon a man, naked except for a derby with thorns sticking out, who is "attempting to crucify himself with thumb tacks."

The man is Maloney the Areopagite, who is writing a biography of Saint Puce, a flea who was "born, lived, and died, beneath the arm of our Lord." Then he meets a young man named John Gilson who calls himself John Raskolnikov Gilson, has a Crime Journal in which he tells of murdering an idiot, a dishwasher at the Hotel Astor, the incident a sort of camp, homely version of *Crime and Punishment*, since this Raskolnikov is Class 8B, Public School 186. The book ends with the thoughts of a young man imagining the suicide of his girlfriend, Janey, who is pregnant. Her young man says, "Suicide is a charming affectation on the part of a young Russian, but in you, dear Janey, it is absurd." Janey's mother, seeing her daughter threatening to jump from a window, says: "Go away from that window—fool! You'll catch your death-cold or fall out—clumsy!"

The Dream Life of Balso Snell was published by Contact Press, a small, avant-garde group based in Paris. It had been recommended by William Carlos Williams, then an editor at the press. The book is generally thought to be a failure and on first reading one is inclined to agree. However, on a second reading, the book gains in vitality, originality, and perhaps bravado. West's novels are offered as satires, asking the reader to have knowledge about what is being satirized: here, it is literary criticism, popular culture and its clichés, popular Christianity, and other matters. Along the way, there is a satirical aside about biography. A schoolteacher, Miss McGeeney, is writing a biography of Samuel Perkins, the biographer of E. F. Fitzgerald. Miss McGeeney explains:

> And who is Fitzgerald? You are of course familiar with D. B. Hobson's life of Boswell. Well, E. F. Fitzgerald is the author of a life of Hobson. The subject of my biography, Samuel Perkins, wrote a life of Fitzgerald.... Perkins' face was dominated by his nose. This fact I have ascertained from a collection of early photographs lent me by a profound admirer of Perkins and a fellow practitioner of his art. I refer to Robert Jones, author of a book called *Nosolgie*.

She continues: "It seems to me that someone must surely take the hint and write the life of Miss McGeeney, the woman who wrote the biography of the man who wrote the biography of the man who wrote the biography of Boswell." This is lighthearted enough, but Balso's passage through the landscape is a malodorous journey peopled with the misshapen and deformed, described with what might be called inspired relish. The suicidal Janey begins as a pregnant hunchback, carrying her baby in the sack. The novel is a masturbatory dream, written with the cleverness that is sometimes spoken of as too-clever-by-half.

Nathanael West had some difficulty deciding just who he was in the literal sense. He was born Nathan Weinstein, which didn't quite suit his idea of himself. His first improvement was to change Nathan, not to Nathaniel, as in Hawthorne, but to the curious Nathan*a*el, the alteration giving the common name a mysterious and somehow glamorous ring. When he was asked by Edmund Wilson how Weinstein became West—the answer: "Horace Greeley said, 'Go west, young man. So I did.'" In any case, he became Nathanael West legally in 1926 when he was twenty-three years old. His maternal family was named Wallenstein and came from what is now Lithuania. His father, Max

Weinstein, was also Russian and both families migrated to the United States in the 1880s. The father became a successful New York builder, first of tenements on the Lower East Side and later of more advanced and spacious buildings in upper Manhattan. Their son, the author, was born at 151 East 81st Street.

In a way that was typical of refined and ambitious families, young Nathan was sent to a progressive school, P.S. 81, that stressed "creativity." He didn't do well there and transferred to another, later entering the competitive DeWitt Clinton High School, from which he failed to graduate. As a natural con man, he added six credits to his transcript and thus was accepted at Tufts University. There he joined a fraternity and had a good time but failed in all his subjects. Then he happened upon the transcript of another Nathan Weinstein with better marks, which allowed him to transfer to Brown University as a sophomore. There he sometimes went by the name of Nathanael von Wallenstein Weinstein. At Brown, his friendship with S. J. Perelman began. He wrote for the college paper, made drawings, and even seemed somewhat preppy in his Brooks Brothers suits. He also managed to contract gonorrhea.

West, a sort of genteel con man in his youth, will in his fiction create characters inclined to sly improvements on the limitations of the given. In the memories of his friends, he appears rather shy and reserved and quietly likable. Edmund Wilson, Lillian Hellman, Scott Fitzgerald were lifelong friends. S. J. Perelman married his sister. True, his sense of the main chance was always there to be exploited; when he was manager of the Sutton Club Hotel with its empty rooms, we find Edmund Wilson, Lillian Hellman, Dashiell Hammett, James T. Farrell, and others happily in line for free lodgings. Before that, Uncle Saul and Uncle Charles had somehow been prevailed upon to fund a trip to Paris. After his second novel, *Miss Lonelyhearts*, he was employed in Hollywood at a respectable salary. His early love affairs had a way of collapsing from inanition on his part. Supposed to meet Beatrice Mathieu, a fashion writer for *The New Yorker*, in Paris for a confirmation of their engagement, he failed "to show." Another backed out when she learned he had slept with Lillian Hellman. At last he married Eileen

McKenney, the subject of a popular book by her sister, Ruth McKenney. Both were killed when West ran through a stop sign outside El Centro, California. He was thirty-seven years old.

2.

Miss Lonelyhearts, a masterwork, came about when he met a woman who wrote a lovelorn column for the *Brooklyn Eagle*. She read out some of the letters she had received and West was inspired to create a man, using the name "Miss Lonelyhearts," for a New York paper. The letters at the beginning of the novel are "stamped from the dough of suffering with a heart-shaped cookie knife."

> ... I think I will kill myself my kidneys hurt so much. My husband thinks no woman can be a good catholic and not have children irregardless of the pain.... I have 7 children in 12 yrs and ever since the last 2 I have been so sick. I was operated on twice and my husband promised no more children on the doctors advice.... I am going to have a baby.... I am so sick and scared.... I cant have an abortion on account of being a catholic....

Another letter:

> I am writing to you for my little sister Gracie because something awfull hapened to her.... Gracie is deaf and dumb and biger than me but not very smart on account of being deaf and dumb.... Mother makes her play on the roof because we dont want her to get run over as she aint very smart. Last week a man came on the roof and did something dirty to her.... I am afraid to tell mother on account of her being lible to beat Gracie up. I am afraid that Gracie is going to have a baby.... If I tell mother she will beat Gracie up awfull ... when she tore her dress they locked her in the closet for 2 days.... So please what would you do if the same happened in your family.

Miss Lonelyhearts, he is given no other name, looks like the son of a Baptist minister although he is a "New England puritan" and something of a Christer. Shrike, an editor at the paper, is a voluble, cynical, barroom orator at the speakeasy, Delehanty's, where the newsmen gather. As Miss Lonelyhearts begins to find the letters neither funny nor stupid, he thinks he should tell the forlorn and miserable to find comfort in Christ. Shrike thinks otherwise:

> Miss Lonelyhearts, my friend, I advise you to give your readers stones. When they ask for bread don't give them crackers as does the Church, and don't, like the State, tell them to eat cake. Explain that man cannot live by bread alone and give them stones. Teach them to pray each morning: "Give us this day our daily stone."

Miss Lonelyhearts is not so much complex as complicated. As an educated young man from New England, successful in New York, he is nevertheless carrying a lot of baggage from home: his Christian roots, a certain provincial suspiciousness. In search of experience, he visits Betty, a cheerful, willing girl. Instead of seducing her, he rants about Christ and suffering humanity. As he goes on, Betty will say: "What's the matter? . . . Are you sick?" Her final words are: "I felt swell before you came, and now I feel lousy. Go away. Please go away."

Next, he visits Shrike and his wife, Mary. She wants to go out and Miss Lonelyhearts takes her to a place called El Gaucho. Mary's theme song, as it were, is: My mother died of breast cancer. She died leaning over a table. Back at the front door of her apartment, he tears at her clothes until she is naked under her fur coat. Unfortunately, the door opens and Shrike is in the corridor. "He had on only the top of his pajamas."

Miss Lonelyhearts is hopeless as a lover, and the scenes of seduction are always unappetizing, comic perhaps, but withering. West's talent speeds everything along with a felicitous assurance that is devastating to romance. The hope of appropriate feeling is as futile as the hope for a pot of gold at the end of the rainbow. His ear for the language, his gift for the landscape of foolishness and deceit are so offhand and accurate they do not alienate. In life, there was that vexatious, crummy family next door and yet you would be alarmed if they weren't all there on the front porch the next day. West is spoken of as "pessimistic" and perhaps he is. On the other hand, he doesn't bring to mind attitudes or preconceptions about life. He is wild, imaginative, and for all the mishaps in his pages and the comic drive, he is a reporter covering a fire and then going out for a beer.

At Delehanty's, Miss Lonelyhearts will meet his final correspondent—Peter Doyle, a cripple whose job is reading meters for the gas company. It turns out Doyle has written Miss Lonelyhearts a letter, unmailed, but now taken out of his pocket. The letter wants to know *what it's all about*. Going up and down stairs for $2.50 per. Doctors have told him to rest his leg. He's always in pain. "It aint the job that I am complaining about but what I want to no is what is the whole stinking business for."

Miss Lonelyhearts is a novel of defiant originality. West introduces suffering characters and scarcely a one arouses sympathy. They are liars, clumsily crafty, their pose of weakness self-serving. Miss Lonelyhearts goes about his sexual seductions in a cold, unfeeling manner; and, with it all, he is obsessed with Christ. W. H. Auden, in an essay entitled "West's Disease," reprinted in *Nathanael West: A Collection of Critical Essays*, is deeply offended by the novel, experiencing a sort of pedantic frisson. First: self-help newspaper columns are written by people who "give the best advice they can." Miss Lonelyhearts, with the ivory Christ hanging in his room, is not the sort to apply for a gossip column and if he did, no "editor would hire him." Shrike is a

> Mephisto who spends all his time exposing to his employees the meaninglessness of journalism. . . . Such a man, surely, would not be a Feature Editor long. . . . A high percentage of the inhabitants are cripples, and the only kind of personal relation is the sado-masochistic.

And: West is not a satirist.

> Satire presupposes conscience and reason as the judges between the true and the false, the moral and immoral, to which it appeals,

but for West these faculties are themselves the creators of unreality.... West's descriptions of Inferno have the authenticity of firsthand experience: he has certainly been there, and the reader has the uncomfortable feeling that his was not a short visit.

Auden, who cannot have read many advice columns, was publicly known as a communicant of the Episcopal Church, a return in his celebrated genius to the church of his English boyhood. The "religiosity" of *Miss Lonelyhearts* appears to have been an annoyance to him. West, an American Jew, was amused by the Methodists and Baptists who may have been liars and cheats while rooted in their down-home Christianity. He is amazed, amused, and thoughtful about them in a way that was too atheistic, skeptical, and "modern" for Auden. The novel is a triumph of local observation by a keen eye and ear and a rhythmical style. There is nothing quite like it in our literature.

3.

"John D. Rockefeller would give a cool million to have a stomach like yours."

—Old Saying

Thus the heading of West's third novel, *A Cool Million*. It is often read as a satire on the popular Horatio Alger books. Horatio, on his way to make his fortune in the world and save the old homestead, is cheated, mocked, preyed upon, but rises in his youthful American rectitude and perseverance to outwit his persecutors, good boy that he is. West's hero is persecuted, robbed, lied to, and hideously mutilated from head to foot. His passage through life is indeed painful to read. Scarcely a comedy, if that was the intent, in scene after scene of "dismantmantling." The novel begins with a masterly tonal memory of the sentimental fiction of the period:

The home of Mrs. Sarah Pitkin, a widow well on in years, was situated on an eminence overlooking the Rat River, near the town of Ottsville in the state of Vermont. It was a humble dwelling much the worse for wear, yet exceedingly dear to her and to her only child, Lemuel. While the house had not been painted for some time … it still had a great deal of charm. An antique collector, had one chanced to pass by, would have been greatly interested in its architecture.

The tale goes along in the rocky way of West's imagination: Mrs. Pitkin, behind in her mortgage payments of 12 percent interest, is threatened with foreclosure. This came about by way of Asa Goldstein, proprietor of Colonial Exteriors and Interiors, "who planned to take the house apart and set it up again in the window of his Fifth Avenue shop." Lem goes to see "Shagpoke" Whipple, once president of the United States and now president of the Rat River National Bank. Lem is advised to go out in the world and make money. On the train he is robbed by well-dressed gentlemen, one of whom will accidentally drop a diamond ring in his pocket, causing the bumpkin to be arrested and sent to prison. Once he is free again, Chicago, socialist, anarchist, and fascist groups of the period appear as part of the crowded background. Along the way, if so it is to be expressed, Lem will lose his left hand, a leg is cut off at the knee, an eye removed in prison for fear it might become infected.

Betty, wandering in from the previous novel, is kidnapped by Italians and sold to a Chinaman who runs a whorehouse with girls of all nations, each set up in suites suitable for their native countries. Betty's rooms are American colonial with ships in bottles, carved whalebone, and hooked rugs. Betty's first client is a "pockmarked Armenian rug merchant from Malta." And Lem, bereft of teeth, thumb, leg, scalp, and one eye, is shot through the heart. But in the spirit of Horatio Alger, the final line is: "All hail, the American Boy!"

A wasteful brilliance perhaps, a treacherous revision of classical comedies in which the clown is knocked about, stamped on, but gets up, tips his hat, and walks off the stage, *A Cool Million* was written in 1933 and published in 1934. It can be read as a Depression novel, set in the time when men on the bread lines were "stripped" of their worldly goods. West took "stripping" with a devastating literalness. The novel did not do well—too many chopped-off body parts for bedside reading. Yet it is an achievement, written in a prose of glittering, unexpected adjectives before the required noun.

Hollywood: *The Day of the Locust*. In West's fiction there is landscape, but not of trees, grassy plains, sunsets on the horizon. His landscape is houses, rooms, bars, and their contents. West is like a decorator with a pad—chintz here, solid color there; no, perhaps a bit of tweed. His narrator, Tod Hackett, graduate of the Yale School of Fine Arts, is brought to Hollywood to learn set and costume designing. His story begins with the streets of the peculiar city:

> An army of cavalry and foot was passing. It moved like a mob; its lines broken, as though fleeing from some terrible defeat.... Tod recognized the scarlet infantry of England with their white shoulder pads, the black infantry of the Duke of Brunswick, the French grenadiers with their enormous white gaiters, the Scotch with bare knees under plaid skirts.... But not even the soft wash of dusk could help the houses ... Mexican ranch houses, Samoan huts, Mediterranean villas, Egyptian and Japanese temples, Swiss chalets, Tudor cottages.... On the corner of La Huerta Road was a miniature Rhine castle with tarpaper turrets pierced for archers. Next to it was a little highly colored shack with domes and minarets out of the *Arabian Nights*.... Few things are sadder than the truly monstrous.

There are no screen stars in this Hollywood novel, but the city and the movies inhabit these settlers, as if they were left from the wagon trains that pulled Americans west. The characters are the story just by being who they are, most of them living in the shabby apartment house with Tod—the San Bernardino Arms, known as the San Berdoo.

Faye Greener, the heroine of the novel, when the term means the center of attention. Faye is a bad girl in the sense of small-town gossips;

that is, one who "puts out." She is beautiful, "shiny as a new spoon," only seventeen, but as experienced as Moll Flanders. In movietown her credits are meager: an extra in a two-reel farce, but she's hoping for a break. She sings in her pretty voice, "Jeepers Creepers! Where'd you get those peepers?" When drunk, "Dreamed about a reefer five feet long." Tod pursues her, but when he tries to seduce her, she says she doesn't want to be messed up. In addition, she can't see that Tod could further her career.

Faye is, somewhat unaccountably, hooked up with a fellow named Homer Simpson, suggesting "simpleton," perhaps. Homer, hotel booking clerk, now retired and living in a house across the street from the Berdoo. He is from the Middle West, from a little town near Des Moines, Iowa: a hick, in Faye's accurate naming, but one who buys her things, takes her to the movies, and is incapable of sex, a convenience, along with his nerdy love of her. "But whether he was happy or not is hard to say. Probably he was neither, just as a plant is neither." Homer, after an illness, is told to get some sunshine and so it's off to California and Hollywood. Homer doesn't belong in Hollywood. Old as he is, he's like a child left in a gas station toilet while the parents, thinking him in the back seat, drive away. He's a stumbling, vivid creation, genuine as a nickel.

Harry Greener, Faye's father, once in vaudeville, now selling door-to-door Miracle solvent, a furniture polish of his own devising. But Harry is now sick, dying, his death you might call an opportunity for a funeral scene. In his "box," he's "wearing a Tuxedo . . . his eyebrows shaped and plucked and his lips and cheeks rouged. He looked like the interlocutor in a minstrel show." Faye, looking beautiful in her black dress, "platinum" hair under a black straw sailor. "Every so often, she carried a tiny lace handkerchief to her eyes and made it flutter there for a moment." Residents of the Berdoo are in attendance and the Gingo family (too?), Eskimos brought to Hollywood for a picture about polar exploration. Unfortunately, an electric organ plays a record of Bach's chorale, "Come Redeemer, Our Saviour." That doesn't go down well with the assembled mourners. There is an invitation to review the remains, not very beckoning except to the Gingos.

Earle Shoop: cowboy from Arizona, occasionally worked in horse operas. Six feet tall, Stetson hat, boots with three-inch heels, always broke, he stages an appalling, murderous cock fight. In the end, Earle and Faye go off to the sunset or to the trailer park.

The final chapter of *The Day of the Locust* is a painful, dazzling scene of the mob outside a theater, waiting for the celebrities to arrive for the première of an important film. West steps aside for an intrusion of his general thoughts about Americans, some of them, at least:

> They were savage and bitter, especially the middle-aged and the old, and had been made so by boredom and disappointment. All their lives they had slaved at some kind of dull, heavy labor, behind desks and counters, in the fields and at tedious machines of all sorts, saving their pennies and dreaming of the leisure that would be theirs....Where else should they go but California, the land of sunshine and oranges?...They get tired of oranges.... They watch the waves come in at Venice. There wasn't any ocean where most of them came from, but after you've seen one wave, you've seen them all.... [Newspapers and movies] fed them on lynchings, murder, sex crimes, explosions, wrecks, love nests, fires, miracles, revolutions, wars....The sun is a joke. Oranges can't titillate their jaded palates.... They have been cheated and betrayed. They have slaved and saved for nothing.

Tod Hackett, the Yale man, is caught in the mob, his leg painfully injured. He, foolish aesthete from New England, is standing on a rail, trying to sketch the scene for a painting to be called "The Burning of Los Angeles." What is burning is "a corinthian column that held up a palmleaf roof of a nutburger stand." *The Day of the Locust* was published in an edition of 3,000 copies. 1,464 copies sold. That's the story for a masterpiece.

Nathanael West's stunning four novels are American tales, rooted in our transmogrifying soil. Morality plays they are, classified as comedies. They are indeed often funny. Funny as a crutch.

2003

SOURCES

"Memoirs, Conversations, and Diaries" first appeared in *Partisan Review*.

"Anderson, Millay, and Crane in Their Letters" first appeared in *Partisan Review*.

"The Subjection of Women" first appeared in *Partisan Review* as a review of *The Second Sex* by Simone de Beauvoir.

"George Eliot's Husband" first appeared in *Partisan Review*.

"The Neglected Novels of Christina Stead" first appeared in *The New Republic*.

"America and Dylan Thomas" first appeared in *Partisan Review*.

"The Decline of Book Reviewing" first appeared in *Harper's Magazine*.

"Boston" first appeared under the title "Boston: The Lost Ideal" in *Harper's Magazine* and also in *Encounter*.

"William James" was first published as an introduction to *The Selected Letters of William James*, ed. Elizabeth Hardwick.

"Living in Italy" first appeared in *Partisan Review*.

"Mary McCarthy" first appeared in *Harper's Magazine*.

"Loveless Love" first appeared in *Partisan Review* as two separate reviews of Graham Greene's *The Heart of the Matter* and *A Burnt-Out Case*.

"The Insulted and Injured" first appeared in *Harper's Magazine*, and the review of *The Children of Sánchez: Autobiography of a Mexican Family* by Oscar Lewis first appeared separately in *The New York Times Book Review*.

"Grub Street: New York" first appeared in *The New York Review of Books*.

"Frost in His Letters" first appeared in *The New York Review of Books* as a review of *The Letters of Robert Frost to Louis Untermeyer.*

"Ring Lardner" first appeared in *The New York Review of Books.*

"Grub Street: Washington" first appeared in *The New York Review of Books.*

"Selma, Alabama" first appeared in *The New York Review of Books.*

"After Watts" first appeared in *The New York Review of Books* as a review of *Violence in the City: An End or a Beginning?* A Report by the Governor's Commission on the Los Angeles Riots.

"The Apotheosis of Martin Luther King" first appeared in *The New York Review of Books.*

"Chicago" first appeared in *The New York Review of Books.*

"Reflections on Fiction" first appeared in *The New York Review of Books.*

"Dead Souls" first appeared in *The New York Review of Books* as a review of *Ernest Hemingway: A Life Story* by Carlos Baker.

"In Maine" first appeared in *The New York Review of Books.*

"Militant Nudes" first appeared in *The New York Review of Books.*

"Sue and Arabella" first appeared in *The New York Review of Books.*

"Sad Brazil" is an expanded version of an essay first published in *The New York Review of Books.*

"Sense of the Present" first appeared in *The New York Review of Books* as a review of *Speedboat* by Renata Adler.

"Simone Weil" first appeared in *The New York Times Book Review* as a review of *Simone Weil* by Simone Pétrement, trans. Raymond Rosenthal.

"Domestic Manners" first appeared in *Daedalus.*

"Wives and Mistresses" first appeared in *The New York Review of Books.*

"Unknown Faulkner" first appeared in *The New York Times Book Review* as a review of *Uncollected Stories of William Faulkner*, ed. Joseph Blotner.

"Nabokov: Master Class" first appeared in *The New York Times Book Review* as a review of *Lectures on Literature* by Vladimir Nabokov, ed. Fredson Bowers.

"English Visitors in America" first appeared under the title "Love It or Leave It!" in *The New York Review of Books* as a review of *Imagining America* by Peter Conrad.

"Bartleby in Manhattan" first appeared under the title "Bartleby and Manhattan" in *The New York Review of Books*.

"Katherine Anne Porter" first appeared under the title "What She Was and What She Felt Like" in *The New York Times Book Review* as a review of *Katherine Anne Porter: A Life* by Joan Givner.

"Sons of the City's Pavements" first appeared in *The New York Times Book Review* as a review of *Letters of Delmore Schwartz*, ed. Robert Phillips.

"The Magical Prose of Poets" first appeared under the title "The Perfectionist" in *The New Republic* as a review of *The Collected Prose* by Elizabeth Bishop, ed. Robert Giroux.

"The Teller and the Tape: Norman Mailer" first appeared in *The New York Review of Books* as a review of *Mailer: His Life and Times* by Peter Manso.

"The Genius of Margaret Fuller" first appeared in *The New York Review of Books*.

"Gertrude Stein" first appeared in *The Threepenny Review*.

"The Fictions of America" was a paper presented at the Wheatland Conference on Literature in Washington, D.C., April 1987.

"Mrs. Wharton in New York" first appeared in *The New York Review of Books*.

"On Washington Square" first appeared in *The New York Review of Books*.

"Wind from the Prairie" first appeared in *The New York Review of Books*.

"Mary McCarthy in New York" was published as the introduction to *Intellectual Memoirs: New York 1936–1938* by Mary McCarthy.

"Edmund Wilson" is an expanded version of an essay first published in *The New Yorker*.

"Paradise Lost" first appeared in *The New York Review of Books* as a review of *American Pastoral* by Philip Roth.

"In the Wasteland" first appeared in *The New York Review of Books* as a review of *The Last Thing He Wanted* by Joan Didion.

"Tru Confessions" first appeared in *The New York Review of Books* as a review of *Truman Capote: In Which Various Friends, Enemies, Acquaintances, and Detractors Recall His Turbulent Career* by George Plimpton.

"Locations" was first published as the introduction to *American Fictions* by Elizabeth Hardwick.

"Melville in Love" first appeared in *The New York Review of Books*.

"The Torrents of Wolfe" first appeared in *The New York Review of Books*.

"The Foster Father" first appeared in *The New York Review of Books*.

"Funny as a Crutch" first appeared in *The New York Review of Books*.

TITLES IN SERIES

For a complete list of titles, visit www.nyrb.com or write to:
Catalog Requests, NYRB, 435 Hudson Street, New York, NY 10014

J.R. ACKERLEY Hindoo Holiday*
J.R. ACKERLEY My Dog Tulip*
J.R. ACKERLEY My Father and Myself*
J.R. ACKERLEY We Think the World of You*
HENRY ADAMS The Jeffersonian Transformation
RENATA ADLER Pitch Dark*
RENATA ADLER Speedboat*
AESCHYLUS Prometheus Bound; translated by Joel Agee*
LEOPOLDO ALAS His Only Son *with* Doña Berta*
CÉLESTE ALBARET Monsieur Proust
DANTE ALIGHIERI The Inferno
KINGSLEY AMIS The Alteration*
KINGSLEY AMIS Dear Illusion: Collected Stories*
KINGSLEY AMIS Ending Up*
KINGSLEY AMIS Girl, 20*
KINGSLEY AMIS The Green Man*
KINGSLEY AMIS Lucky Jim*
KINGSLEY AMIS The Old Devils*
KINGSLEY AMIS One Fat Englishman*
KINGSLEY AMIS Take a Girl Like You*
ROBERTO ARLT The Seven Madmen*
U.R. ANANTHAMURTHY Samskara: A Rite for a Dead Man*
WILLIAM ATTAWAY Blood on the Forge
W.H. AUDEN (EDITOR) The Living Thoughts of Kierkegaard
W.H. AUDEN W.H. Auden's Book of Light Verse
ERICH AUERBACH Dante: Poet of the Secular World
EVE BABITZ Eve's Hollywood*
EVE BABITZ Slow Days, Fast Company: The World, the Flesh, and L.A.*
DOROTHY BAKER Cassandra at the Wedding*
DOROTHY BAKER Young Man with a Horn*
J.A. BAKER The Peregrine
S. JOSEPHINE BAKER Fighting for Life*
HONORÉ DE BALZAC The Human Comedy: Selected Stories*
HONORÉ DE BALZAC The Unknown Masterpiece *and* Gambara*
VICKI BAUM Grand Hotel*
SYBILLE BEDFORD A Favorite of the Gods *and* A Compass Error*
SYBILLE BEDFORD A Legacy*
SYBILLE BEDFORD A Visit to Don Otavio: A Mexican Journey*
MAX BEERBOHM The Prince of Minor Writers: The Selected Essays of Max Beerbohm*
MAX BEERBOHM Seven Men
STEPHEN BENATAR Wish Her Safe at Home*
FRANS G. BENGTSSON The Long Ships*
ALEXANDER BERKMAN Prison Memoirs of an Anarchist
GEORGES BERNANOS Mouchette
MIRON BIAŁOSZEWSKI A Memoir of the Warsaw Uprising*
ADOLFO BIOY CASARES Asleep in the Sun
ADOLFO BIOY CASARES The Invention of Morel
PAUL BLACKBURN (TRANSLATOR) Proensa*

* *Also available as an electronic book.*

CAROLINE BLACKWOOD Corrigan*

CAROLINE BLACKWOOD Great Granny Webster*

RONALD BLYTHE Akenfield: Portrait of an English Village*

NICOLAS BOUVIER The Way of the World

EMMANUEL BOVE Henri Duchemin and His Shadows*

MALCOLM BRALY On the Yard*

MILLEN BRAND The Outward Room*

ROBERT BRESSON Notes on the Cinematograph*

SIR THOMAS BROWNE Religio Medici and Urne-Buriall*

JOHN HORNE BURNS The Gallery

ROBERT BURTON The Anatomy of Melancholy

CAMARA LAYE The Radiance of the King

GIROLAMO CARDANO The Book of My Life

DON CARPENTER Hard Rain Falling*

J.L. CARR A Month in the Country*

LEONORA CARRINGTON Down Below*

BLAISE CENDRARS Moravagine

EILEEN CHANG Love in a Fallen City

EILEEN CHANG Naked Earth*

JOAN CHASE During the Reign of the Queen of Persia*

ELLIOTT CHAZE Black Wings Has My Angel*

UPAMANYU CHATTERJEE English, August: An Indian Story

NIRAD C. CHAUDHURI The Autobiography of an Unknown Indian

ANTON CHEKHOV Peasants and Other Stories

ANTON CHEKHOV The Prank: The Best of Young Chekhov*

GABRIEL CHEVALLIER Fear: A Novel of World War I*

JEAN-PAUL CLÉBERT Paris Vagabond*

RICHARD COBB Paris and Elsewhere

COLETTE The Pure and the Impure

JOHN COLLIER Fancies and Goodnights

CARLO COLLODI The Adventures of Pinocchio*

D.G. COMPTON The Continuous Katherine Mortenhoe

IVY COMPTON-BURNETT A House and Its Head

IVY COMPTON-BURNETT Manservant and Maidservant

BARBARA COMYNS The Vet's Daughter

BARBARA COMYNS Our Spoons Came from Woolworths*

ALBERT COSSERY The Jokers*

ALBERT COSSERY Proud Beggars*

HAROLD CRUSE The Crisis of the Negro Intellectual

ASTOLPHE DE CUSTINE Letters from Russia*

LORENZO DA PONTE Memoirs

ELIZABETH DAVID A Book of Mediterranean Food

ELIZABETH DAVID Summer Cooking

L.J. DAVIS A Meaningful Life*

AGNES DE MILLE Dance to the Piper*

VIVANT DENON No Tomorrow/Point de lendemain

MARIA DERMOÛT The Ten Thousand Things

DER NISTER The Family Mashber

TIBOR DÉRY Niki: The Story of a Dog

ANTONIO DI BENEDETTO Zama*

ALFRED DÖBLIN Bright Magic: Stories*

JEAN D'ORMESSON The Glory of the Empire: A Novel, A History*

ARTHUR CONAN DOYLE The Exploits and Adventures of Brigadier Gerard

CHARLES DUFF A Handbook on Hanging

BRUCE DUFFY The World As I Found It*

DAPHNE DU MAURIER Don't Look Now: Stories

ELAINE DUNDY The Dud Avocado*

ELAINE DUNDY The Old Man and Me*

G.B. EDWARDS The Book of Ebenezer Le Page*

JOHN EHLE The Land Breakers*

MARCELLUS EMANTS A Posthumous Confession

EURIPIDES Grief Lessons: Four Plays; translated by Anne Carson

J.G. FARRELL Troubles*

J.G. FARRELL The Siege of Krishnapur*

J.G. FARRELL The Singapore Grip*

ELIZA FAY Original Letters from India

KENNETH FEARING The Big Clock

KENNETH FEARING Clark Gifford's Body

FÉLIX FÉNÉON Novels in Three Lines*

M.I. FINLEY The World of Odysseus

THOMAS FLANAGAN The Year of the French*

BENJAMIN FONDANE Existential Monday: Philosophical Essays*

SANFORD FRIEDMAN Conversations with Beethoven*

SANFORD FRIEDMAN Totempole*

MARC FUMAROLI When the World Spoke French

CARLO EMILIO GADDA That Awful Mess on the Via Merulana

BENITO PÉREZ GÁLDOS Tristana*

MAVIS GALLANT The Cost of Living: Early and Uncollected Stories*

MAVIS GALLANT Paris Stories*

MAVIS GALLANT A Fairly Good Time *with* Green Water, Green Sky*

MAVIS GALLANT Varieties of Exile*

GABRIEL GARCÍA MÁRQUEZ Clandestine in Chile: The Adventures of Miguel Littín

LEONARD GARDNER Fat City*

WILLIAM H. GASS In the Heart of the Heart of the Country: And Other Stories*

WILLIAM H. GASS On Being Blue: A Philosophical Inquiry*

THÉOPHILE GAUTIER My Fantoms

GE FEI The Invisibility Cloak

JEAN GENET Prisoner of Love

ÉLISABETH GILLE The Mirador: Dreamed Memories of Irène Némirovsky by Her Daughter*

NATALIA GINZBURG Family Lexicon*

JEAN GIONO Hill*

JEAN GIONO Melville: A Novel*

JOHN GLASSCO Memoirs of Montparnasse*

P.V. GLOB The Bog People: Iron-Age Man Preserved

NIKOLAI GOGOL Dead Souls*

EDMOND AND JULES DE GONCOURT Pages from the Goncourt Journals

ALICE GOODMAN History Is Our Mother: Three Libretti*

PAUL GOODMAN Growing Up Absurd: Problems of Youth in the Organized Society*

EDWARD GOREY (EDITOR) The Haunted Looking Glass

JEREMIAS GOTTHELF The Black Spider*

A.C. GRAHAM Poems of the Late T'ang

HENRY GREEN Back*

HENRY GREEN Blindness*

HENRY GREEN Caught*

HENRY GREEN Living*

HENRY GREEN Loving*

HENRY GREEN Party Going*

WILLIAM LINDSAY GRESHAM Nightmare Alley*

HANS HERBERT GRIMM Schlump*

EMMETT GROGAN Ringolevio: A Life Played for Keeps

VASILY GROSSMAN An Armenian Sketchbook*

VASILY GROSSMAN Everything Flows*

VASILY GROSSMAN Life and Fate*

VASILY GROSSMAN The Road*

OAKLEY HALL Warlock

PATRICK HAMILTON The Slaves of Solitude*

PATRICK HAMILTON Twenty Thousand Streets Under the Sky*

PETER HANDKE Short Letter, Long Farewell

PETER HANDKE Slow Homecoming

THORKILD HANSEN Arabia Felix: The Danish Expedition of 1761–1767*

ELIZABETH HARDWICK The Collected Essays of Elizabeth Hardwick*

ELIZABETH HARDWICK The New York Stories of Elizabeth Hardwick*

ELIZABETH HARDWICK Seduction and Betrayal*

ELIZABETH HARDWICK Sleepless Nights*

L.P. HARTLEY Eustace and Hilda: A Trilogy*

L.P. HARTLEY The Go-Between*

NATHANIEL HAWTHORNE Twenty Days with Julian & Little Bunny by Papa

ALFRED HAYES In Love*

ALFRED HAYES My Face for the World to See*

PAUL HAZARD The Crisis of the European Mind: 1680–1715*

ALICE HERDAN-ZUCKMAYER The Farm in the Green Mountains*

GILBERT HIGHET Poets in a Landscape

RUSSELL HOBAN Turtle Diary*

JANET HOBHOUSE The Furies

YOEL HOFFMANN The Sound of the One Hand: 281 Zen Koans with Answers*

HUGO VON HOFMANNSTHAL The Lord Chandos Letter*

JAMES HOGG The Private Memoirs and Confessions of a Justified Sinner

RICHARD HOLMES Shelley: The Pursuit*

ALISTAIR HORNE A Savage War of Peace: Algeria 1954–1962*

GEOFFREY HOUSEHOLD Rogue Male*

WILLIAM DEAN HOWELLS Indian Summer

BOHUMIL HRABAL Dancing Lessons for the Advanced in Age*

BOHUMIL HRABAL The Little Town Where Time Stood Still*

DOROTHY B. HUGHES The Expendable Man*

DOROTHY B. HUGHES In a Lonely Place*

RICHARD HUGHES A High Wind in Jamaica*

RICHARD HUGHES In Hazard*

RICHARD HUGHES The Fox in the Attic (The Human Predicament, Vol. 1)*

RICHARD HUGHES The Wooden Shepherdess (The Human Predicament, Vol. 2)*

INTIZAR HUSAIN Basti*

MAUDE HUTCHINS Victorine

YASUSHI INOUE Tun-huang*

HENRY JAMES The Ivory Tower

HENRY JAMES The New York Stories of Henry James*

HENRY JAMES The Other House

HENRY JAMES The Outcry

TOVE JANSSON Fair Play *

TOVE JANSSON The Summer Book*

TOVE JANSSON The True Deceiver*

TOVE JANSSON The Woman Who Borrowed Memories: Selected Stories*

RANDALL JARRELL (EDITOR) Randall Jarrell's Book of Stories

DAVID JONES In Parenthesis

JOSEPH JOUBERT The Notebooks of Joseph Joubert; translated by Paul Auster

KABIR Songs of Kabir; translated by Arvind Krishna Mehrotra*

FRIGYES KARINTHY A Journey Round My Skull

ERICH KÄSTNER Going to the Dogs: The Story of a Moralist*

HELEN KELLER The World I Live In

YASHAR KEMAL Memed, My Hawk

YASHAR KEMAL They Burn the Thistles

MURRAY KEMPTON Part of Our Time: Some Ruins and Monuments of the Thirties*

RAYMOND KENNEDY Ride a Cockhorse*

DAVID KIDD Peking Story*

ROBERT KIRK The Secret Commonwealth of Elves, Fauns, and Fairies

ARUN KOLATKAR Jejuri

DEZSŐ KOSZTOLÁNYI Skylark*

TÉTÉ-MICHEL KPOMASSIE An African in Greenland

GYULA KRÚDY The Adventures of Sindbad*

GYULA KRÚDY Sunflower*

SIGIZMUND KRZHIZHANOVSKY Autobiography of a Corpse*

SIGIZMUND KRZHIZHANOVSKY The Letter Killers Club*

SIGIZMUND KRZHIZHANOVSKY Memories of the Future

SIGIZMUND KRZHIZHANOVSKY The Return of Munchausen

K'UNG SHANG-JEN The Peach Blossom Fan*

GIUSEPPE TOMASI DI LAMPEDUSA The Professor and the Siren

GERT LEDIG The Stalin Front*

MARGARET LEECH Reveille in Washington: 1860–1865*

PATRICK LEIGH FERMOR Between the Woods and the Water*

PATRICK LEIGH FERMOR The Broken Road*

PATRICK LEIGH FERMOR Mani: Travels in the Southern Peloponnese*

PATRICK LEIGH FERMOR Roumeli: Travels in Northern Greece*

PATRICK LEIGH FERMOR A Time of Gifts*

PATRICK LEIGH FERMOR A Time to Keep Silence*

PATRICK LEIGH FERMOR The Traveller's Tree*

PATRICK LEIGH FERMOR The Violins of Saint-Jacques*

D.B. WYNDHAM LEWIS AND CHARLES LEE (EDITORS) The Stuffed Owl

SIMON LEYS The Death of Napoleon*

SIMON LEYS The Hall of Uselessness: Collected Essays*

GEORG CHRISTOPH LICHTENBERG The Waste Books

JAKOV LIND Soul of Wood and Other Stories

H.P. LOVECRAFT AND OTHERS Shadows of Carcosa: Tales of Cosmic Horror*

DWIGHT MACDONALD Masscult and Midcult: Essays Against the American Grain*

CURZIO MALAPARTE Kaputt

CURZIO MALAPARTE The Skin

JANET MALCOLM In the Freud Archives

JEAN-PATRICK MANCHETTE Fatale*

JEAN-PATRICK MANCHETTE The Mad and the Bad*

OSIP MANDELSTAM The Selected Poems of Osip Mandelstam

OLIVIA MANNING Fortunes of War: The Balkan Trilogy*

OLIVIA MANNING Fortunes of War: The Levant Trilogy*

OLIVIA MANNING School for Love*

JAMES VANCE MARSHALL Walkabout*

GUY DE MAUPASSANT Afloat

GUY DE MAUPASSANT Alien Hearts*
GUY DE MAUPASSANT Like Death*
JAMES McCOURT Mawrdew Czgowchwz*
WILLIAM McPHERSON Testing the Current*
MEZZ MEZZROW AND BERNARD WOLFE Really the Blues*
HENRI MICHAUX Miserable Miracle
JESSICA MITFORD Hons and Rebels
JESSICA MITFORD Poison Penmanship*
NANCY MITFORD Frederick the Great*
NANCY MITFORD Madame de Pompadour*
NANCY MITFORD The Sun King*
NANCY MITFORD Voltaire in Love*
PATRICK MODIANO In the Café of Lost Youth*
PATRICK MODIANO Young Once*
MICHEL DE MONTAIGNE Shakespeare's Montaigne; translated by John Florio*
HENRY DE MONTHERLANT Chaos and Night
BRIAN MOORE The Lonely Passion of Judith Hearne*
BRIAN MOORE The Mangan Inheritance*
ALBERTO MORAVIA Agostino*
ALBERTO MORAVIA Boredom*
ALBERTO MORAVIA Contempt*
JAN MORRIS Conundrum*
JAN MORRIS Hav*
PENELOPE MORTIMER The Pumpkin Eater*
GUIDO MORSELLI The Communist*
ÁLVARO MUTIS The Adventures and Misadventures of Maqroll
L.H. MYERS The Root and the Flower*
NESCIO Amsterdam Stories*
DARCY O'BRIEN A Way of Life, Like Any Other
SILVINA OCAMPO Thus Were Their Faces*
YURI OLESHA Envy*
IONA AND PETER OPIE The Lore and Language of Schoolchildren
IRIS OWENS After Claude*
RUSSELL PAGE The Education of a Gardener
ALEXANDROS PAPADIAMANTIS The Murderess
BORIS PASTERNAK, MARINA TSVETAYEVA, AND RAINER MARIA RILKE Letters, Summer 1926
CESARE PAVESE The Moon and the Bonfires
CESARE PAVESE The Selected Works of Cesare Pavese
BORISLAV PEKIĆ Houses*
ELEANOR PERÉNYI More Was Lost: A Memoir*
LUIGI PIRANDELLO The Late Mattia Pascal
JOSEP PLA The Gray Notebook
DAVID PLANTE Difficult Women: A Memoir of Three*
ANDREY PLATONOV The Foundation Pit
ANDREY PLATONOV Happy Moscow
ANDREY PLATONOV Soul and Other Stories
NORMAN PODHORETZ Making It*
J.F. POWERS Morte d'Urban*
J.F. POWERS The Stories of J.F. Powers*
J.F. POWERS Wheat That Springeth Green*
CHRISTOPHER PRIEST Inverted World*
BOLESŁAW PRUS The Doll*
GEORGE PSYCHOUNDAKIS The Cretan Runner: His Story of the German Occupation*

ALEXANDER PUSHKIN The Captain's Daughter*

QIU MIAOJIN Last Words from Montmartre*

QIU MIAOJIN Notes of a Crocodile*

RAYMOND QUENEAU We Always Treat Women Too Well

RAYMOND QUENEAU Witch Grass

RAYMOND RADIGUET Count d'Orgel's Ball

PAUL RADIN Primitive Man as Philosopher*

FRIEDRICH RECK Diary of a Man in Despair*

JULES RENARD Nature Stories*

JEAN RENOIR Renoir, My Father

GREGOR VON REZZORI An Ermine in Czernopol*

GREGOR VON REZZORI Memoirs of an Anti-Semite*

GREGOR VON REZZORI The Snows of Yesteryear: Portraits for an Autobiography*

TIM ROBINSON Stones of Aran: Labyrinth

TIM ROBINSON Stones of Aran: Pilgrimage

MILTON ROKEACH The Three Christs of Ypsilanti*

FR. ROLFE Hadrian the Seventh

GILLIAN ROSE Love's Work

LINDA ROSENKRANTZ Talk*

WILLIAM ROUGHEAD Classic Crimes

CONSTANCE ROURKE American Humor: A Study of the National Character

SAKI The Unrest-Cure and Other Stories; illustrated by Edward Gorey

UMBERTO SABA Ernesto*

TAYEB SALIH Season of Migration to the North

TAYEB SALIH The Wedding of Zein*

JEAN-PAUL SARTRE We Have Only This Life to Live: Selected Essays. 1939–1975

ARTHUR SCHNITZLER Late Fame*

GERSHOM SCHOLEM Walter Benjamin: The Story of a Friendship*

DANIEL PAUL SCHREBER Memoirs of My Nervous Illness

JAMES SCHUYLER Alfred and Guinevere

JAMES SCHUYLER What's for Dinner?*

SIMONE SCHWARZ-BART The Bridge of Beyond*

LEONARDO SCIASCIA The Day of the Owl

LEONARDO SCIASCIA Equal Danger

LEONARDO SCIASCIA The Moro Affair

LEONARDO SCIASCIA To Each His Own

LEONARDO SCIASCIA The Wine-Dark Sea

VICTOR SEGALEN René Leys*

ANNA SEGHERS Transit*

PHILIPE-PAUL DE SÉGUR Defeat: Napoleon's Russian Campaign

GILBERT SELDES The Stammering Century*

VICTOR SERGE The Case of Comrade Tulayev*

VICTOR SERGE Conquered City*

VICTOR SERGE Memoirs of a Revolutionary

VICTOR SERGE Midnight in the Century*

VICTOR SERGE Unforgiving Years

SHCHEDRIN The Golovlyov Family

ROBERT SHECKLEY The Store of the Worlds: The Stories of Robert Sheckley*

GEORGES SIMENON Act of Passion*

GEORGES SIMENON Monsieur Monde Vanishes*

GEORGES SIMENON Pedigree*

GEORGES SIMENON Three Bedrooms in Manhattan*

GEORGES SIMENON Tropic Moon*

GEORGES SIMENON The Widow*
CHARLES SIMIC Dime-Store Alchemy: The Art of Joseph Cornell
MAY SINCLAIR Mary Olivier: A Life*
WILLIAM SLOANE The Rim of Morning: Two Tales of Cosmic Horror*
SASHA SOKOLOV A School for Fools*
VLADIMIR SOROKIN Ice Trilogy*
VLADIMIR SOROKIN The Queue
NATSUME SŌSEKI The Gate*
DAVID STACTON The Judges of the Secret Court*
JEAN STAFFORD The Mountain Lion
CHRISTINA STEAD Letty Fox: Her Luck
RICHARD STERN Other Men's Daughters
GEORGE R. STEWART Names on the Land
STENDHAL The Life of Henry Brulard
ADALBERT STIFTER Rock Crystal*
THEODOR STORM The Rider on the White Horse
JEAN STROUSE Alice James: A Biography*
HOWARD STURGIS Belchamber
ITALO SVEVO As a Man Grows Older
HARVEY SWADOS Nights in the Gardens of Brooklyn
A.J.A. SYMONS The Quest for Corvo
MAGDA SZABÓ The Door*
MAGDA SZABÓ Iza's Ballad*
MAGDA SZABÓ Katalin Street*
ANTAL SZERB Journey by Moonlight*
ELIZABETH TAYLOR Angel*
ELIZABETH TAYLOR A Game of Hide and Seek*
ELIZABETH TAYLOR A View of the Harbour*
ELIZABETH TAYLOR You'll Enjoy It When You Get There: The Stories of Elizabeth Taylor*
TEFFI Memories: From Moscow to the Black Sea*
TEFFI Tolstoy, Rasputin, Others, and Me: The Best of Teffi*
HENRY DAVID THOREAU The Journal: 1837–1861*
ALEKSANDAR TIŠMA The Book of Blam*
ALEKSANDAR TIŠMA The Use of Man*
TATYANA TOLSTAYA The Slynx
TATYANA TOLSTAYA White Walls: Collected Stories
EDWARD JOHN TRELAWNY Records of Shelley, Byron, and the Author
LIONEL TRILLING The Liberal Imagination*
LIONEL TRILLING The Middle of the Journey*
THOMAS TRYON The Other*
IVAN TURGENEV Virgin Soil
JULES VALLÈS The Child
RAMÓN DEL VALLE-INCLÁN Tyrant Banderas*
MARK VAN DOREN Shakespeare
CARL VAN VECHTEN The Tiger in the House
ELIZABETH VON ARNIM The Enchanted April*
EDWARD LEWIS WALLANT The Tenants of Moonbloom
ROBERT WALSER Berlin Stories*
ROBERT WALSER Girlfriends, Ghosts, and Other Stories*
ROBERT WALSER Jakob von Gunten
ROBERT WALSER A Schoolboy's Diary and Other Stories*
REX WARNER Men and Gods

SYLVIA TOWNSEND WARNER Lolly Willowes*
SYLVIA TOWNSEND WARNER Mr. Fortune*
SYLVIA TOWNSEND WARNER Summer Will Show*
JAKOB WASSERMANN My Marriage*
ALEKSANDER WAT My Century*
C.V. WEDGWOOD The Thirty Years War
SIMONE WEIL On the Abolition of All Political Parties*
SIMONE WEIL AND RACHEL BESPALOFF War and the Iliad
GLENWAY WESCOTT Apartment in Athens*
GLENWAY WESCOTT The Pilgrim Hawk*
REBECCA WEST The Fountain Overflows
EDITH WHARTON The New York Stories of Edith Wharton*
KATHARINE S. WHITE Onward and Upward in the Garden*
PATRICK WHITE Riders in the Chariot
T.H. WHITE The Goshawk*
JOHN WILLIAMS Augustus*
JOHN WILLIAMS Butcher's Crossing*
JOHN WILLIAMS (EDITOR) English Renaissance Poetry: A Collection of Shorter Poems*
JOHN WILLIAMS Stoner*
ANGUS WILSON Anglo-Saxon Attitudes
EDMUND WILSON Memoirs of Hecate County
RUDOLF AND MARGARET WITTKOWER Born Under Saturn
GEOFFREY WOLFF Black Sun*
FRANCIS WYNDHAM The Complete Fiction
JOHN WYNDHAM Chocky
JOHN WYNDHAM The Chrysalids
BÉLA ZOMBORY-MOLDOVÁN The Burning of the World: A Memoir of 1914*
STEFAN ZWEIG Beware of Pity*
STEFAN ZWEIG Chess Story*
STEFAN ZWEIG Confusion*
STEFAN ZWEIG Journey Into the Past*
STEFAN ZWEIG The Post-Office Girl*